The Essential History of Mexico

MW00824517

The full text of *The History of Mexico: From Pre-Conquest to Present* traces Mexican history from the indigenous empires devastated by the Spanish conquest into the twenty-first century. Written in a clear and accessible manner, the book offers a straightforward chronological survey of Mexican history from pre-colonial times to the present, and includes a glossary as well as numerous images and tables for comprehensive study.

This version, *The Essential History of Mexico*, streamlines and updates the text of the full first edition to make it easier for classroom use. Helpful pedagogy has been added for contextualization and support, including:

- side-by-side world and Mexican timelines at the beginning of each chapter that place the national events from each chapter in broader global context;
- bolded keywords that draw attention to important terms;
- cultural and biography boxes in each chapter that help highlight aspects of social history;
- primary documents in each chapter that allow historical actors to speak directly to students;
- annotated suggestions for further reading.

In addition, the companion website provides many valuable tools for students and instructors, including links to online resources and videos, discussion questions, and images and figures from the book.

Philip L. Russell is an independent author who has written six books on Latin America. His writings on Mexico have appeared in publications ranging from the *New York Times* to *La Jornada*.

The Essential History of Mexico

From Pre-Conquest to Present

Philip L. Russell

Routledge
Taylor & Francis Group

NEW YORK AND LONDON

First published 2016
by Routledge
711 Third Avenue, New York, NY 10017

and by Routledge
2 Park Square, Milton Park, Abingdon, Oxon, OX14 4RN

Routledge is an imprint of the Taylor & Francis Group, an informa business

© 2016 Taylor & Francis

The right of Philip L. Russell to be identified as author of this work
has been asserted by him in accordance with sections 77 and 78 of
the Copyright, Designs and Patents Act 1988.

All rights reserved. No part of this book may be reprinted or reproduced
or utilised in any form or by any electronic, mechanical, or other means,
now known or hereafter invented, including photocopying and recording,
or in any information storage or retrieval system, without permission in
writing from the publishers.

Trademark notice: Product or corporate names may be trademarks or
registered trademarks, and are used only for identification and explanation
without intent to infringe.

Library of Congress Cataloging-in-Publication Data
Russell, Philip L., author.
   The essential history of Mexico: from pre-conquest to present/
By Philip Russell.
   pages: illustrations; cm
   Includes index.
   1. Mexico—History. 2. Mexico—Politics and government. I. Title.
F1226.R93 2015
972—dc23
2015007083

ISBN: 978-0-415-84277-8 (hbk)
ISBN: 978-0-415-84278-5 (pbk)
ISBN: 978-0-203-75842-7 (ebk)

Typeset in Perpetua and Bell Gothic
by Florence Production Ltd, Stoodleigh, Devon, UK

Printed and bound in the United States of America by
Edwards Brothers Malloy on sustainably sourced paper

Contents

Figures

FIGURES

Tables

ROUTLEDGE

Now available...

Visit the companion website for *The Essential History of Mexico: From Pre-Conquest to Present* for resources that complement the book

This website offers instructors and students helpful resources that build upon and are integrated with the material in the book:

For Students

- Links to Further Resources

- Links to Video Clips

- Glossary/Pronunciation Guide

- Primary Sources from the text

- Full Bibliography for the text

For Instructors

- Discussion Questions

- Figures and tables used in the text

Visit: www.routledge.com/cw/Russell

Preface

My book *The History of Mexico: From Pre-Conquest to Present* was published in 2010. Based on feedback from that book, *The Essential History of Mexico*—the book you are holding in your hands (or have on your laptop)—emerged. The text of the original book was shortened as well as updated to reflect recent scholarship and events, such as the 2012 presidential elections.

Chapter 1 covers the longest chronological period—from 12,000 BC to AD 1519. It traces social development from hunter-gatherer to village agriculture to sophisticated empires covering thousands of square miles. The next chapter, which considers the Spanish conquest, covers the shortest chronological period—from 1519 to 1521. It describes how a handful of Spaniards were able to conquer the seeming invincible Aztec Empire. The next three chapters describe the society that emerged as a result of the fusion of Spanish and indigenous. Chapter 3 focuses on the administrative tools that allowed the Spanish to maintain hegemony and on the role of the Catholic Church. Chapter 4 describes Mexican society which throughout the colonial period remained divided in multiple ways including race, ethnicity, wealth, and geography. Chapter 5 then considers the colonial economy that supplied food and basic goods as well as silver, which became the financial lynchpin of the Spanish empire. The sixth chapter recounts how Mexico, which lacked the foreign allies that America enjoyed during its struggle for independence, fought a bitter, decade-long struggle to cast off Spanish control.

The next three chapters describe how a modern nation emerged from the destruction of the independence war. Chapter 7 discusses the generally unsuccessful attempts from 1821 to 1855 to restart the post-independence economy and create governing institutions that enjoyed the respect of the population. Chapter 8 then describes how Mexico lost roughly half its territory—first to Anglo settlers in Texas and then to the invading U.S. army. Chapter 9 relates how, after Mexico was wracked by civil war and foreign invasion, the Porfirio Díaz administration re-started economic growth and created a stable political system.

The following three chapters consider how the contradictions built up during the Díaz government led to revolution and destruction, forcing the nation once again to devise a new political system and restart the economy. Chapter 10 recounts the social upheaval known as the Mexican Revolution. Chapter 11 then describes the halting progress made after 1917 in constructing a new political system and in resuming economic growth. Chapter 12 describes how after World War II Mexico once again found the key to rapid economic growth and political stability.

The next two chapters describe how the post-World War II political system and economic model became increasingly dysfunctional. Chapter 13 charts the slow decline of one-party rule and its replacement with multi-party elections. Chapter 14 then considers how economic planners, faced with mounting problems, decided to adopt a new set of policies generally referred to as neoliberal. The final chapter considers the twenty-first century and describes how multi-party democracy has functioned and how the new economic model has yet to produce rapid growth.

Hopefully after finishing this book, readers will gain insight into the long, complex path Mexico has traveled from hunter-gatherer societies to becoming an export powerhouse. That in turn should give insight into why Mexicans sometimes interpret events, such as the 2003 U.S. invasion of Iraq, in a different manner than do U.S. presidents and the American people. Without offering solutions, the book should at least provide a background for understanding chronic problems such as immigration and drug trafficking. Finally, the book will have been a success if it allows the reader to better understand news articles concerning Mexico, or better yet, to understand what they are seeing once they have arrived in Mexico.

Philip L. Russell

The First Three Millennia

Chapter 1

Mesoamerica

TIMELINE—WORLD

8000 BC Crop cultivation begins in Mesopotamia	6000 BC Beginning of settled agriculture in the Nile River Valley	3000–2000 BC Period of pyramid building in Egypt	1000 BC Urban societies beginning in China	850 BC *Iliad* and *Odyssey* composed
AD 1099 Crusaders take Jerusalem	AD 1130–1180 50-year drought in the American Southwest leads to abandonment of settlements	AD 1347–1351 Black Death kills around a third of the population of Europe	AD 1368–1644 Ming dynasty rules China	AD 1403 The settlement of the Canary Islands signals the beginning of the Spanish Empire

TIMELINE—MEXICO

ca. 10,000 BC Naia born	8000–2000 BC Agriculture developed	2000 BC–AD 250 Pre-Classic period	1500–400 BC Olmec culture flourishes	AD 250–900 Classic period
AD 1465 Aztecs consolidate control over Valley of Mexico				

753 BC	215 BC	AD 410	AD 711	AD 1066
Rome founded	Great Wall of China built	Sack of Rome by Visigoths	Muslims invade Iberian Peninsula	England conquered by William, Duke of Normandy

AD 1453	AD 1492	AD 1492	AD 1497–1499	
Ottoman Turks take Byzantine Constantinople, which is renamed Istambul	The surrender of Granada marks the end of the Spanish Reconquest	Jews expelled from Spain	Portuguese sailor Vasco da Gama sails to India and back	

AD 250–900	AD 250–900	AD 850–1000	AD 950–1000	AD 1325
Teotihuacan flourishes	Maya culture flourishes	Chichen Itza flourishes	Tula flourishes	Aztecs found Tenochtitlan

THIS CHAPTER BEGINS WITH A CONSIDERATION OF MEXICO'S GEOGRAPHY—
a key factor determining where people lived, what they ate, how they made their living, and how they moved their goods. Next are descriptions of the first known Mexicans and the hunter-gatherer societies in which they lived. The chapter then considers the beginning of agriculture and how cultivating plants allowed people to live in villages. Indigenous people eventually improved their agricultural practices, which permitted larger political entities. Finally, the chapter considers how intensive agriculture and the collection of tribute permitted sophisticated civilizations. Today the best remembered of these civilizations are the Maya and the Aztec.

GEOGRAPHY

Mexico's central volcanic belt stretches from the Volcán de Colima in the west to the Pico de Orizaba in the east. The Pico's 18,855-foot elevation exceeds that of any peak in the lower forty-eight U.S. states. The permanently snow-capped volcanoes Iztaccíhuatl and Popocatépetl overlook 7,280-foot high Mexico City. These volcanoes produce earthquakes and an extremely fertile volcanic soil. One of the conquistadors (conquerors) who accompanied Hernán Cortés commented on conditions in the volcanic belt, "There are in this province of New Spain [Mexico] great rivers and springs of very good sweet water, extensive woods on the hills and plains of very high pines, cedars, oaks, and cypresses, besides live oaks and a great variety of mountain trees." Abundant rains falling on the volcanic belt, located between 18 and 20 degrees north latitude, produced an agricultural surplus which supported advanced, urban societies well before the arrival of Spanish colonizers in the sixteenth century.

As was the case in the volcanic belt, the abundant rainfall of southern Mexico allowed indigenous residents to produce an agricultural surplus which supported complex civilizations. Southeast of Mexico City the Sierra Madre del Sur fractures the land into many isolated mountain valleys. The relative isolation of people living in these valleys led to great ethnic diversity. Further east on the Yucatán Peninsula flat lands facilitated contact and led to greater cultural uniformity.

North of Mexico City, two mountain ranges, the Sierra Madre Oriental and the Sierra Madre Occidental, extend in the direction of Texas and Arizona, respectively. A high, dry central plateau lies inside the inverted triangle formed by these two ranges. Before 1519, several different indigenous groups lived between these two mountain ranges. Given the aridity of the land, the people living in this area did not produce an agricultural surplus large enough to support major urban centers.

THE FIRST MEXICANS

Humans have lived in the New World for as many as 40,000 years. The classic theory is that people simply walked from Asia to North America during the last ice age, which ended roughly 12,000 years ago. Then seas were lower and what is now the Bering Strait formed a land bridge between the two continents. There is lively, ongoing debate concerning how and when humans first arrived in the New World. There is no consensus on whether there was a single migration route or multiple routes or if there was a single migration or multiple migrations from the Old World.

In 2007, the remains of a teenage girl were found in a cave named Hoyo Negro (Black Hole) close to Tulum, Quintana Roo. Archeologists named the girl Naia for a nymph of Greek mythology.

She had fallen more than 100 feet to her death, likely while seeking water in the cave. Along with her skeleton were the skeletons of at least twenty-six large extinct mammals. Sophisticated dating technology determined Naia's remains to be between 12,000 and 13,000 years old. Her skeleton is the most complete of such antiquity ever found in the Americas.

The remains of another individual, known as Tepexpan Man, were found in the 1940s on the northeast edge of Lake Texcoco not far from modern Mexico City. The age of the skeleton was never established since it is unclear exactly what soil stratum it came from. These remains were actually those of a woman about 5 feet 3 inches tall.

Just to the southeast of Tepexpan Man, the bones of an imperial mammoth were discovered. It was butchered *in situ*, and flint projectile points were found associated with it. Knife marks scar the bone where meat was cut off. We know little of the culture of Naia, Tepexpan Man and of those who killed the mammoth since no artifacts other than the projectile points were encountered. Presumably these individuals had a widely varied diet in addition to the now-extinct mammoth, as is typical of **hunter-gatherers** who hunt big game.

For millennia the descendants of the first arrivals in Mexico survived as hunter-gatherers. They formed loose, egalitarian groups, each one probably numbering fewer than one hundred members who were united by bonds of kinship. Such groups lived in caves and temporary campsites. These highly mobile groups possessed few material goods. They were constantly migrating, skirmishing, and intermarrying with other groups. The imposition of centralized control was impossible since disaffected people could easily vote with their feet.

From what we know of hunter-gatherer peoples, they enjoyed a comfortable margin of existence and did not have to toil endlessly to survive. A key to their survival was low population density. They also developed superior weaponry. These early hunter-gatherers used the spear thrower, or atlatl, which could launch a projectile at fifteen times the speed of a hand-held spear, giving it more than 200 times the kinetic energy.

Between 8000 and 2000 BC, early Mexicans began planting, rather than merely gathering seeds. Various plants, including squash, corn, beans, and chili peppers were domesticated. The development of agriculture allowed the formation of permanent villages by the third millennium BC. These villages were quite small, having perhaps twelve households or sixty individuals. Residence in villages allowed the development of such crafts as pottery making and loom weaving. Since they were no longer constantly on the move, village dwellers could accumulate a much wider range of goods. These included milling stones (*metates*) to grind corn, baskets, nets, cordage, mats, and wattle-and-daub huts. This early material culture is remarkably similar to the material culture still found in many homes of those living in isolated rural areas of Mexico.

The shift to agriculture occurred over a wide area and was a very slow evolutionary process happening over millennia. Just as with their hunter-gatherer forebears, these early villagers remained egalitarian. Since farmers produced more food per square mile than did hunter-gatherers, greater population density was possible.

PRE-CLASSIC MESOAMERICA

Gradually these agricultural villages grew larger and developed a more sophisticated material culture. By roughly 1500 BC, a cultural area known as **Mesoamerica** had emerged. The climate within this 392,000-square-mile area permitted reliance on rainfed-corn cultivation. Mesoamerica extended as far south as present-day Nicaragua. It included highland Guatemala, the limestone plains of Yucatán, and the snow-capped volcanoes of central Mexico. Its northern boundary was just north of present-day Mexico City.

Mesoamerican cultures shared a religious tradition and had complex social, economic, and political organization. A 365-day solar calendar scheduled events of the agrarian cycle. Religious ceremonies, divination, and astrology relied on a distinct 260-day ritual calendar. Urban centers

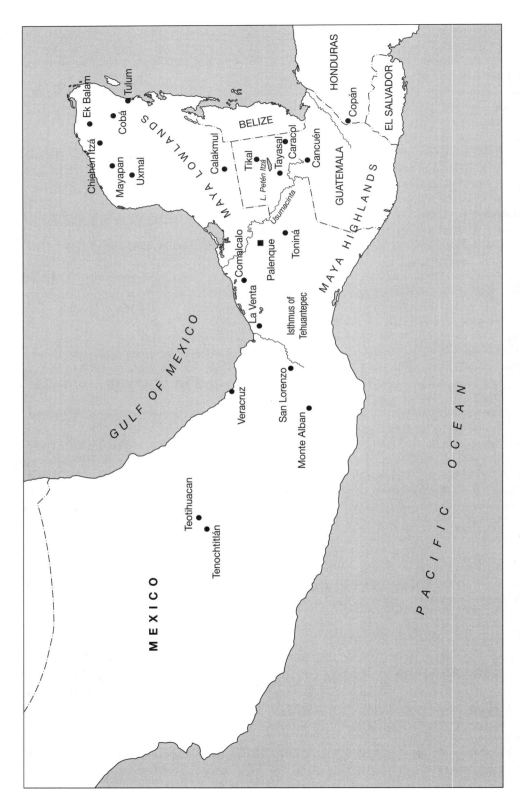

Figure 1.1 *Mesoamerica, the cultural area that gave rise to Mexico's best-known pre-conquest groups, such as the Maya and the Aztec.*

Source: Drawn by Philip Winton. From David Stuart and George Stuart, *Palenque: Eternal City of the Maya* (London and New York: Thames & Hudson, 2008).

typically contained monumental public buildings arranged around a formal open plaza adjacent to pyramidal temples.

All of the Mesoamerican cultures relied on an agricultural surplus generated by cultivating beans, squash, and especially corn. In Mesoamerican cultures, men would typically cultivate corn using a digging stick known as a *coa*. Women would grind the kernels and prepare tortillas—a division of labor that has persisted to the present. Corn was an ideal crop since it has a high yield per unit of land, is easily stored, and is high in proteins.

There are two theories concerning the origin of corn. One holds that early agriculturists bred a weed, teosinte, for a sufficiently long period to convert it into a greatly improved food source. Others think that the teosinte was crossbred with another plant to produce corn. In any case, in 7000 BC, an ear of corn only measured an inch long. After six millennia of cultivation, the ear attained a length of four inches. As a result of this transformation, the corn plant could no longer propagate itself without human intervention.

Complex Mesoamerican cultures flourished between 2000 BC and AD 1519. Archeologists have divided this 3,500-year span into three time periods. The earliest period, known as the Pre-Classic, lasted from roughly 2000 BC to AD 250. The Pre-Classic is distinguished from earlier village cultures by the emergence of large political entities that demanded that its inhabitants contribute material goods and labor. Entrance into and emergence from the Pre-Classic was a gradual evolutionary process that occurred at varying times in varying locations.

The outstanding culture of the Pre-Classic period is known as the Olmec, a name given to its inhabitants by archeologists, since no one knows what they called themselves. The term means "dweller in the land of rubber," since rubber is a major export of the 125-by-50-mile area they inhabited in the steamy swamplands of coastal Tabasco. Between 1500 BC and 400 BC, the Olmec created one of the six pristine civilizations in human history. A pristine civilization is the earliest civilization in its respective region. The other pristine civilizations were the Chavin culture in Peru, China's Shang culture, the Indus civilization in modern Indian and Pakistan, and the Egyptian and Sumerian cultures in the Near East.

Between 1500 BC and 1200 BC, the Olmec settled San Lorenzo, which was perhaps the first urban center in the Americas. San Lorenzo was a hilltop ceremonial center overlooking the Coatzacoalcos River. The site was several times larger than any other Mesoamerican urban center existing at the time. It covered roughly two square miles and had several thousand permanent residents. At San Lorenzo, highly skilled craftspeople produced planned public architecture and a variety of artistic works. Extensive interregional trade networks supplied these craftspeople with materials. Around 900 BC, San Lorenzo declined for reasons unknown.

Radiocarbon dates indicate that a subsequent Olmec urban center, La Venta, flourished between 1200 BC and 400 BC. At its apogee, around 500 BC, its population was perhaps 2,000. It contained several plazas and the largest Mesoamerican structure yet built, whose original shape is still a matter of controversy. There the Olmec created awe-inspiring sculptures, finished without the benefit of metal tools. Much of the basalt they carved was quarried fifty miles away and presumably floated to La Venta on rafts. Today the most recognizable Olmec works are the magnificent stone heads representing their rulers. These sculptures measure as much as nine feet high and weigh as much as 40 tons.

Most of the Olmec lived in small villages linked by an elite that oversaw large-scale projects such as monument construction. These villagers raised corn, beans, squash, cotton, sweet potatoes, and various tree crops. Given the Olmecs' proximity to both rivers and the sea, fish such as the sea bass (*robalo*) were also an important dietary source.

Between 1300 BC and 500 BC, the Olmec culture influenced others throughout and beyond Mesoamerica. Trade routes, which connected areas of different resource endowments, were one of the main channels through which this influence spread. Recent archeological investigation has indicated that the Olmec influence in Mesoamerica was by no means unidirectional. Various other centers were developing and innovating at the same time and passing their knowledge to the Olmec. Major centers of this cultural network include the Valley of Mexico, the Valley of Oaxaca, and the area to the east of the Olmec where the classic Maya civilization would emerge.

For reasons that are poorly understood, the Olmec centers collapsed. At La Venta, the altars and stone heads were systematically defaced and ceremoniously interred. Artisans ceased producing distinctive Olmec artistic works, and the extensive trade networks uniting the Olmec with surrounding regions no longer functioned. The causes for this decline have yet to be determined. Various explanations have been offered for this decline, including peasant revolt, disease, invasion, and agricultural exhaustion.

As was the case with all of the other pristine cultures, Mesoamerica passed through the following stages: 1) a hunter-gatherer population; 2) gradual domestication of plants and animals; 3) agricultural intensification in an area with highly productive land; 4) population growth; and 5) larger settlements which permit a division of labor and a complex social and political hierarchy.

THE CLASSIC PERIOD

Following the Pre-Classic period was the Classic period which extended from roughly AD 250 to AD 900. It saw two of the marvels of the pre-Conquest New World—the city Teotihuacan on the central Mexican plateau and the Mayan cities of southeastern Mexico. The AD 250 date corresponds to the earliest date in the Maya calendar appearing on a carved monument, or *stela*, in the area. Classic cultures differed from their forebears in having more complex political organization, larger populations, full-time craft specialization, increased social stratification, and more centralized political authority.

By the fourth century of the Christian era, a new civilization had emerged in central Mexico. When the Aztecs later encountered the remains of its capital, located thirty miles northeast of the present site of Mexico City, they named it Teotihuacan (the Place of the Gods). The ethnic identity of the city's builders remains unclear. This city, with a population of 100,000 or more, covered eight square miles, an area larger than Rome, which flourished at the same time. Between AD 250 and AD 700, Teotihuacan's trading and tribute empire dominated central Mexico, and its influence was felt from present-day Honduras to the dry non-agricultural areas far north of the city. The city relied on the highly fertile lands of the Valley of Mexico and a special resource— obsidian—for tool making. Some 500 workshops in the city shaped this obsidian—a form of volcanic glass. This material is so far superior to other available stones for producing cutting tools that archeologist Robert Cobean noted that obsidian to ancient Mesoamerica was what steel is to modern civilization. More than 10 percent of the city's labor force appear to have been obsidian workers.

The city's planners laid out more than 2,000 rectangular city blocks arranged in quadrants separated by north–south and east–west dividing lines. Teotihuacan's Pyramid of the Sun, whose construction required an estimated 10,000 laborers working for twenty years, still inspires visitors. Its base covers an area equal to that of Cheops' pyramid in Egypt. Archeological evidence indicates that the notion of **Quetzalcoatl**, a deity depicted as a plumed serpent, originated in the city. Along with the Virgin of Guadalupe, Quetzalcoatl is a quintessential symbol of Mexico.

The city met its end in the seventh century through deliberate burning by the hand of unknown invaders. By AD 750, its population had fallen below 10,000. A likely culprit for the city's decline is deforestation. Trees were felled to supply fuel to burn the lime used in constructing the city. The loss of forests may have led to erosion and desiccation, thus undermining Teotihuacan's agricultural base.

At the same time as the Olmec culture was flourishing, a distinctive Maya culture was emerging to its east. This culture developed over a 39,000-square-mile area extending from the Isthmus of Tehuantepec to modern Honduras. By 1000 BC the inhabitants of this region had settled in villages and were making pottery, and by 800 BC they were erecting small temples. Later, the population

Figure 1.2 *Teotihuacan, in its heyday, the largest city in central Mexico.*
Source: Copyright Michael E. Calderwood.

of this area soared, and a stratified social system emerged. Polities with centralized political power dominated the area.

For a 650-year period, the area reached intellectual and artistic heights no other New World culture, and few in the Old World, could match. When Maya civilization was in full flower, it featured enormous ceremonial centers crowded with masonry temples and palaces facing spacious plazas covered with white stucco. These ceremonial centers, even though they shared a common culture, were never united into a single state. Rather they formed numerous small city-states, as was the case with classical Greece and Renaissance Italy. In the eighth century, these city-states numbered at least twenty-five.

Maya urban centers, some of which may have exceeded 75,000 in population, had administrative, manufacturing, commercial, and religious roles. In each city-state there was a marked division of labor. Nearby peasants produced an agricultural surplus large enough to support an intelligentsia, craftsmen, traders, and corvée laborers who erected massive public structures such as temples. Maya potters achieved chromatic effects of great brilliance by firing their vessels at low temperatures. Traders distributed manufactured goods, including pottery, cotton cloth, and obsidian tools, over a wide area, using both overland trails and seafaring canoes. The urban intelligentsia used a numerical system employing the zero and was so sophisticated astronomically that its members could predict eclipses.

These city-states were ruled over by individuals who formed a hereditary nobility. On occasion women were selected as rulers, especially at times of dynastic turbulence. Rulers emphasized their connection to the supernatural world and controlled rituals that their subjects believed would ensure water, food, and protection.

For the classic Maya, "religion" could not be compartmentalized from other activities and institutions. Their physical world did not consist simply of inanimate, static matter. The Maya recognized a pantheon of gods and spirits dwelling in forests, mountain tops, the sky, bodies of waters, buildings, and caves. The Maya pantheon included a sun god, an hermaphroditic corn god, and gods which defy conventional categorization such as Ixchel, goddess of creation, midwifery, and destruction. The Maya believed one's ancestors affected events among the living and could be communicated with.

Warfare was a staple feature of classic Maya society. Unlike the Inca to the south, the Maya did not use war to expand territorially. Extinguishing a vanquished kingdom and its dynasty was perceived as a threat to the world order. Rather, **tribute** obligations and vassalage were imposed on defeated neighbors. War allowed individual Maya rulers to display their prowess by sacrificing prisoners they had captured on the battlefield. The blood and gore of this constant warfare was frequently depicted on *stelae*, which were erected to glorify rulers and their ancestors.

THE MAYAN WRITING SYSTEM

Up until the middle of the twentieth century, a number of factors prevented the decipherment of Maya hieroglyphics:

- There was a prevailing racist assumption that the Maya were intellectually incapable of developing a complex writing system on a par with Egyptian hieroglyphics.
- Most of the scholars studying the Maya were unfamiliar with the early Old World writing systems, which would have given insight into how the Maya system functioned.
- It was assumed that if the Maya had phonetic writing, it would be alphabetic as is the case with European languages.
- Finally, Cold War rivalries delayed acceptance of a Russian's correct assertion that Maya writing combined symbols with phonetic value and those that conveyed ideas (logographs).

Progress on deciphering Mayan writing began in earnest with a 1952 publication by Yuri Knorosov, a Russian linguist who was familiar with early scripts such as the Egyptian, Mesopotamian, and Chinese, all of which combined phonetic symbols and logographs. He suggested that it was quite likely the Maya followed the same pattern. Once Knorosov's view became accepted, rapid progress at deciphering the hieroglyphs commenced. Anthropologist Michael Coe referred to the decipherment of Maya hieroglyphs as "one of the most exciting intellectual adventures of our age, on a par with the exploration of space and the discovery of the genetic code." Coe also commented on the vast collaborative effort that finally led to an almost complete understanding of the Maya hieroglyphs: "Hardly a day or week seemed to pass without some amazing new fact coming to light, or a new reading being made for a glyph, or someone coming forth with a revolutionary new interpretation of older data."

Eventually it became clear that the Mayan hieroglyphs, which took the form of squares with rounded corners (see Figure 1.3), combined logographs with phonetic symbols that represented the classic Mayan language that was spoken at the time the writing system was codified. The logographs convey an idea, much as the "2" does in modern writing systems. The phonetic component is not alphabetic, with symbols corresponding to a given sound, as our letter "T" does. Rather, each phonetic symbol corresponds to a consonant and to the vowel that follows, just as occurs in the modern Japanese writing system. The Maya had a distinct symbol for each consonant + vowel combination occurring in their language. As a result of deciphering the Maya hieroglyphs, the written history of the New World now extends back nearly 2,000 years.

At its peak in roughly AD 700, the Maya population numbered perhaps 10 million. Slash-and-burn agriculture produced much of the food they consumed. However, as population densities rose, more intensive practices were adopted to increase yields. These included terracing, household gardens, irrigation, raised-bed agriculture, and tree crops such as cacao, allspice, avocado, and papaya. The chief ground crops were corn, beans, squash, chili, and tomatoes.

Perhaps the greatest cultural achievement of the Maya was the development of a hieroglyphic writing system (see the box on the Mayan writing system). Once modern scholars learned how to read the hieroglyphs in the late twentieth century, they gained insight into a dazzling panorama of Maya history, beliefs, and experiences. Hieroglyphs recorded information on Maya kings and queens, their claims to power, supernatural patrons, alliances, wars, triumphs, and defeats.

One of the outstanding Maya city-states was Palenque, set in the lower foothills of the Sierra de Chiapas. The city occupied a commanding position overlooking the Gulf Coastal Plain. Maya architects working there in the seventh century AD had learned to construct lightly built vaults and mansard roofs, so the city has a spacious appearance lacking in earlier Maya sites. Carved *stelae* reveal the dynastic history of the city. Palenque expanded rapidly after AD 615 when K'inich Janab

Figure 1.3 *Drawing from lintel 1, Yaxchilan temple 33, showing accession of Ruler Bird Jaguar IV, holding scepter, with his wife Lady Great skull at right. Mayan writing appears in corners and to left of the illustration.*

Source: Drawings by Ian Graham, Corpus of Maya Hieroglyphic Inscriptions, vol. 3, pt. 1, Yaxchilan, reproduced courtesy of the President and fellows of Harvard College.

Pakal assumed the throne. During his reign, the city became the dominant political, religious, and cultural center of the area. The Maya erected at least thirty-five major building complexes at Palenque, and they walled stream banks and built aqueducts to manage the 120 inches of rain that fall on the city annually. The city's existence was long lost to Europeans. One of the early visitors to the rediscovered Palenque was American diplomat and lawyer John Lloyd Stevens, who visited the area between 1839 and 1842. He observed:

> Here were the remains of a cultivated, polished, and peculiar people who had passed through all the stages incident to the rise and fall of nations; reached their golden age, and perished, entirely unknown . . . We lived in the ruined palace of their kings; we went up to their desolate temples and fallen altars; and wherever we moved we saw the evidence of their taste, their skill in arts, their wealth and power.[1]

A later Maya city-state, Chichen Itza, dominated the Yucatán peninsula between AD 850 and AD 1000. At its peak it was the most powerful and successful of the Maya city-states. It was more commercially oriented than earlier Maya city-states and traded with various regions within and beyond the Maya area. Much of its power was derived from its dominance of newly developed coastal trade networks using seafaring canoes.

An enduring mystery is why the Maya city-states, which flourished for centuries, went into irreversible decline. This decline can be accurately dated since the production of monumental

Figure 1.4 Palenque, a Maya city-state. The photo shows the Palace, center right, with the Temple of the Inscriptions in the background.

Source: Copyright Michael E. Calderwood.

Figure 1.5 *A variety of architectural styles can be found at Chichen Itza, one of the most visited archeological sites in Mexico. Pictured here is a structure known as El Castillo.*

Source: Reproduced courtesy of the Benson Latin American Collection, the University of Texas at Austin.

structures and *stelae* bearing dates ceased. The last date in the Maya calendar carved in *stelae* for Peten corresponds to January 15, AD 910. This decline did not follow a uniform trajectory and played out differently in different polities. However the result was always the same—within 100 or 200 years of reaching their peak population levels, most of the central and southern Maya lowlands lost about 90 percent of their population.

Apparently this decline in part resulted from overpopulation, which led to environmental degradation, whose impact was vastly amplified by climate change. As the Maya population expanded, formerly forested hillsides were cultivated. This resulted in erosion that exceeded the rate of soil formation. Rather than husbanding resources, Maya kings further depleted them by attempting to erect more grandiose monuments than their rivals did. Maya warfare, already endemic, peaked just before the collapse of the Classic Maya civilization. Greatly compounding the Maya's problems of overpopulation and resource scarcity was the worst drought in the last 7,000 years, which began in AD 760.

At the same time as the Maya and Teotihuacan were flourishing, the Zapotecs developed Monte Alban in the Valley of Oaxaca. This city-state, whose population peaked at about 25,000, served as a political and religious center from which the Zapotecs dominated more than 1,000 smaller towns in the valley. Zapotec craftsmen constructed a very long, large plaza there as well as magnificent tombs with lovely murals on the walls. The Zapotecs also developed a writing system, but unlike that of the Maya, it has yet to be deciphered. While there is no sign that Monte Alban suffered a violent demise such as that suffered by Teotihuacan, by AD 900 most of the city was in ruins and the Valley of Oaxaca was divided into dozens of petty city-states.

THE POST-CLASSIC PERIOD

Following the Classic period is a period known as the Post-Classic, which extended from AD 900 to the Spanish arrival in 1519. The Post-Classic period was characterized by renewed population growth, extensive commercial development, and the rise of the most powerful city-states yet seen in Mesoamerica. During this period, two city-states, Tula and later Tenochtitlan, the capital of the Aztec empire, dominated central Mexico. As was the case with the earlier periods, the onset of the Post-Classic occurred gradually and varied by location.

For an extended period after the fall of Teotihuacan there was a power vacuum in central Mexico. During this turbulent period, no dominant power emerged, despite widespread warfare. Several small city-states, such as Xochicalco in the modern state of Morelos and El Tajín in Veracruz, did arise during this period.

After AD 900, the Toltec rose to dominance in central Mexico. The Toltec looked back to their first great ruler, Topiltzin, who was born in the first half of the tenth century. He was responsible for moving the Toltec capital to Tula, located fifty miles northwest of where Mexico City stands today. At its peak between AD 950 and 1150, the city had a population of 30,000–40,000 and covered 5.4 square miles. There the Toltec constructed an impressive formal plaza flanked by ball courts, altars, and pyramids topped by temples. From Tula, the Toltecs dominated central Mexico for two centuries. Toltec influence extended as far north as present-day Arizona and New Mexico and as far south as Yucatán.

In Tula, military artistic motifs outnumbered religious ones. There were abundant images of both the ubiquitous Quetzalcoatl and of his enemy Tezcatlipoca (the Smoking Mirror). Toltec astronomers developed a superb calendar. Within the city there was a sizable community of artisans specializing in the production of pottery vessels, figurines, and obsidian blades. Their skill was reflected by the Nahuatl language—the language of the Aztecs— using the word "Toltec" to refer to artists. Farmers working irrigated, terraced fields supported these workers.

Around AD 1175, a combination of drought, famine, and war led to the fall of Tula. All the evidence points to a sudden, overwhelming cataclysm. Ceremonial walls were burned to the ground. Soon the city was deserted.

Filling the void left by the Toltecs were the Aztecs. According to legend, they came from a place to the northwest of the Valley of Mexico known as Aztlan (Place of the Herons). Upon their arrival in the valley early in the twelfth century, this band of hunter-gatherers was scorned by more sophisticated agriculturists, such as the Colhuacan. For a short period, the Aztecs cultivated the lands of the Colhuacan as serfs. In 1323, the Aztecs' overlords provided one of their princesses to an Aztec chief as a bride. The Aztecs, rather than performing the anticipated marriage ceremony, sacrificed her in hopes she would become a war goddess. The enraged Colhuacan then expelled the Aztecs from their land. The Aztecs withdrew to an isolated, marshy area. There, according to their lore, in the year 1325, they founded the city of Tenochtitlan (Place of the Cactus Fruit) on the present site of Mexico City.

An Aztec legend recounts that an eagle perched on a prickly-pear cactus, eating a snake, indicated the place where the Aztecs were to found Tenochtitlan. Today the Mexican flag and coat of arms depict this eagle.

The Aztecs constructed Tenochtitlan on roughly five square miles of land reclaimed from Lake Texcoco, which surrounded their capital. As was the case with Teotihuacan, major avenues extended out from a sacred precinct along the cardinal directions. Its population reached as many as 250,000, making it larger than any city in Europe, except perhaps Naples and Constantinople, and four times the size of Seville. Only the cities of China, unknown to Spaniards and Aztecs alike, exceeded its population. Sophisticated systems provided food, trade goods, and potable water to the city's population.

The difficulty of hauling grain in societies lacking wheeled vehicles and draught animals imposed size limits on Mesoamerican cities. Tenochtitlan could escape these limits since large cargo canoes, which came from distant waterfronts in the Valley of Mexico, provisioned the city with grain and other produce.

In 1519, Tenochtitlan was the largest city that had ever existed in the New World. Its size and grandeur reflected its status as an imperial capital. Its monumental buildings made a statement about the might and control of its rulers, thus legitimizing and contributing to their power. The city's location allowed nearby food production, easy transport of goods by canoe, and protection against attack. In laying out the city, planners consciously adopted the model of Tula, since Tula and the Toltec practices served as the source of Aztec political and social legitimacy.

With the exception of Tenochtitlan, most Aztec cities were not large. The second largest, Texcoco, had a population of 25,000. Secondary cities served as ceremonial centers of the Aztec territorial division known as the *altepetl*. Temples soared high above the plazas of these cities. The *altepetl* was the political unit responsible for collecting tribute from the villages and rural people within its boundaries. This tribute would then be distributed to the local elite and to Tenochtitlan. The *altepetl* also organized manpower in time of war and for construction projects. A hereditary leader known as a tlatoani, or speaker, headed each *altepetl*. Residents of each *altepetl* considered themselves a separate people from those elsewhere, even though all were Aztecs.

By 1465, the Aztecs had the entire Valley of Mexico under their control. During the next half-century, the Aztecs extended their domain across 140,000 square miles stretching from modern Querétaro and Guanajuato in the north to the Isthmus of Tehuantepec in the south. Economic interests motivated this imperial expansion. The Aztec elite wanted access to a regular supply of riches from foreign lands—riches that included luxury imports which maintained nobles' status. Divine sanction and generations of military triumphs bolstered Aztec confidence.

Generally the Aztecs did not establish permanent garrisons in conquered territory. Merchants, known as *pochteca*, and tribute collectors, known as *calpixtli*, were usually the only Aztec presence among the conquered. Recurrent bloody, punitive expeditions prevented disaffected subjects from challenging Aztec suzerainty or failing to supply demanded tribute. Marriage alliances also formed a link between the Aztec elite and subjugated groups. On the eve of the Spanish conquest, the Aztec empire incorporated some 450 city-states.

The Aztecs instituted a form of tributary despotism. They would rule conquered lands indirectly, leaving indigenous leaders and nobles in place, but subordinating them to the Aztec hierarchy. Given the lack of beasts of burden, Aztecs demanded easily transportable goods in tribute. Textiles were the principle tribute goods. In addition, Aztec subjects supplied corn, beans, amaranth, and *chia* seed. The Aztecs also received as tribute shields, feather headdress, and high value products such as amber, cacao, and jade that were unavailable in the central highlands. As a result of this tribute, as well as the Aztecs' well-developed trading networks, the main Aztec market at Tlatelolco offered consumers pottery, chocolate, vanilla, copper, all sorts of clothing, cooked and unprepared food, gold, silver, jade, turquoise, feather products, and even slaves.

As was the case with other Mesoamerican civilizations, there was a rigid system of social classes, and individuals rarely crossed class barriers. The nobility formed the top social strata. Aztec rulers traced their genealogy, whether actual or invented, back to the Toltec kings. This semi-mythical dynastic origin was a major source of political legitimacy. Rather than having a rigid rule of male primogeniture, as European monarchies of the time did, upon the death of their ruler, adult male members of the ruling lineage selected one of their number to become the next emperor. The nobility, which constituted roughly 5 percent of the population, owned land, commanded armies, and managed government affairs. Under nobles' direction, the Aztec state organized the redistribution of goods and labor on a massive scale, thus maintaining the elite's position.

Priests also belonged to the elite. They performed rituals, managed temples and schools, and were the repositories of Aztec learning concerning gods, ritual, and astronomy. They prophesized and interpreted visions, some of which were induced by psychotropic plants. Priests coordinated and choreographed the numerous public rites and performances.

Some urban commoners, especially the pochteca, enjoyed status well above rural farmers. The pochteca were members of a hereditary merchant guild which traveled long distances within and outside the empire, where they often doubled as spies. They, or more accurately their bearers, brought back luxury goods or the raw material needed to make luxury goods. Feathers, cacao, gold, valuable stones, and animal skins were among the items they acquired. Gold workers and feather workers, who formed tight, endogamous communities, were other groups which, though below the nobility, enjoyed elevated status.

Slaves formed the bottom tier of Aztec society. In contrast to the European tradition, slavery was not hereditary. Most commonly slavery was a matter of contract—the sale of one's labor for an agreed period in return for physical maintenance. In time of hardship a family might contract to supply the labor of a young lad. Children of the socially vulnerable, such as those of concubines, might also become slaves. Secondary wives might sell themselves into slavery to ensure survival upon the death of their protector. Slavery could be imposed as a penalty, to render compensation for some offense, or to expunge a debt. Some slaves were sold at market to be later sacrificed.

Most Aztecs were farmers who cultivated land controlled by the nobility. During the agricultural season, men typically spent the day in their fields. The home was the domain of women who cooked, weaved, kept house, and reared children. Goods that families did not produce for themselves could be acquired through an extensive market system where goods were bartered or exchanged for cacao beans and textiles, which served as a form of proto-money. Commoners paid tribute to the state in labor services. In addition, since there was no standing army, males were called up for military duty when the empire waged war.

Human sacrifice formed a salient characteristic of Aztec society. The Aztecs claimed that human sacrifices propitiated the god Huitzilopochtli (Hummingbird of the South) and thus prevented the destruction of the earth and the sun for a fifth time. Aztec belief held that humans had existed in four previous worlds and that all had perished when these worlds were destroyed. To reintroduce humans to the fifth world, Quetzalcoatl made a perilous journey to steal human bones from Mictlantecuhtli, the lord of the underworld. The gods then gave life to the bones by shedding blood on them.

There have been many attempts to explain why sacrifice played such an important role in Aztec society. Likely the threat of being sacrificed intimidated conquered subjects. Scholars once suggested that the frequency of human sacrifice resulted from the need for animal protein in a society lacking cattle. (Victims were eaten after sacrifice.) Others maintain that sacrifice served to reduce the population. Spaniards used Aztec sacrificial practices to justify the Conquest. However, as archeologist Robert J. Sharer commented, "Before we decry practices such as human sacrifice, we should remember that Europeans of 500 years ago burned people alive in the name of religion and submitted 'heretics' to an array of tortures and protracted executions."

The Aztecs perfected one of the most productive agricultural systems ever devised—the *chinampa*. *Chinampas* were artificial islands, located near lakeshores, which measured from fifteen to thirty feet in width and up to 300 feet in length. Aztecs grew crops such as amaranth, beans, corn, vegetables, fruit, and flowers on these islands. Lake water penetrated the entire *chinampa*, moistening roots. Mud scooped up from the lake bottom and night soil brought from Tenochtitlan by canoe maintained fertility. Eventually *chinampas* covered 25,000 acres in the Valley of Mexico. *Chinampa*-produced food facilitated the rapid expansion of the Aztec empire.

Chinampas formed part of the rich lacustrine culture that developed in the Valley of Mexico. Lakefront villages relied heavily on the abundant fish, crustaceans, mollusks, and 109 aquatic bird species that inhabited the 252 square miles of lakes in the Valley of Mexico. Canoes facilitated communication between villages and with Tenochtitlan. These canoes could transport a ton of grain, roughly ten times what the Spanish-introduced mule could carry.

The charismatic megacivilizations, such as the Maya and the Aztec, only covered limited areas of present-day Mexico and only flourished for relatively short periods. In addition, there were innumerable other ethnic groups. They adapted to the widely varying environments in which they found themselves. Most lacked the attributes of civilization—social classes, states, and hieratic religion. They accumulated knowledge concerning a variety of terrestrial and aquatic species that furnished them with food, fibers, raw materials, and medicines. Many such people lived in the deserts of northern Mexico. Even though they did not have an abundant material culture, what they did have—projectile points, scrapers, milling stones, baskets, and mats—has often been well preserved in desert caves.

Even though the Aztec empire was truncated by the Conquest, Mesoamerica's ethnic diversity continued under Spanish rule, providing continuity to the area. This diversity is indicated by more than 100 distinct indigenous languages surviving until at least the end of the nineteenth century. Of these surviving languages, Nahuatl, the language of the Aztecs, presently has the largest number of speakers. Due to Aztec influence over Mesoamerica, Nahuatl loan words are found in many of Mexico's indigenous languages, and many Nahuatl place names are still used. Nahuatl loan words that have made their way into English include ocelot, coyote, tomato, chocolate, tamale, avocado, chili, and guacamole.

DOCUMENT 1.1: MAYA CREATION BELIEFS

[The creation beliefs of the Quiché Maya indicate the intimate relationship between corn and the Mesoamerican societies that bred it. The *Popol Vuh*, the sacred book of the Quiché, describes how Xmucane, one of the divine grandparents, ground yellow corn and white corn nine times and then fashioned the flesh of the first human from the mixture:]

The yellow corn and the white corn were ground, and Xmucane did the grinding nine times. Corn was used, along with the water she rinsed her hands with, for the creation of grease; it became human fat when it was worked by the Bearer, Begetter, Sovereign Plumed Serpent, as they are called.

After that, they put it into words:

> the making, the modeling of our first mother-father,
> with yellow corn, white corn alone for the flesh,
> food alone for the human legs and arms,
> for our first fathers, the four human works.

Source: Dennis Tedlock (trans.) (1985) *Popol Vuh*. New York: Simon & Schuster, pp. 163–64.

DOCUMENT 1.2: AZTEC CREATION BELIEFS

[The Aztecs believed that the earth had been created and destroyed four times. They thought the earth they inhabited was the result of a fifth creation. Pre-Columbian expert Richard F. Townsend described the five creations, which were sometimes referred to as suns:]

Among the Aztecs the first earth was called "four jaguar." At that time, giants walked the earth but did not till the soil or sow maize, only living by gleaning wild fruits and roots. This imperfect era ended when a jaguar devoured the giants. The hieroglyphic sign for the era was therefore a jaguar head. The second era, "four wind," was also flawed, and was destroyed by hurricanes that magically turned the imperfect existing men into monkeys—human-like, but not fully human creatures. The sign of this earth was the mask of Quetzalcoatl, lord of the winds. The third imperfect earth ended in rain and fire, and its people either perished or were changed into birds. This happened on the day "four rain," therefore the sign of this sun was the mask of Tlaloc, lord of rain. The fourth era was one of rains so abundant and frequent that the earth was deluged and people were changed into fish. For this reason its sign was the head of Chalchiuhtlicue, "Jade Skirt," the deity of lakes, rivers, springs and seas. The fifth, or present earth, was prophesied to end in earthquakes, and its sign was the hieroglyph *ollin*, "movement" (of the earth). It was at the beginning of this earth that the actual sun, moon, and human beings were finally created.

Source: Richard F. Townsend (2009) *The Aztecs* (3rd ed.). New York: Thames & Hudson, p. 123.

DOCUMENT 1.3: MIXTEC CREATION BELIEFS

In the beginning, the gods inhabited a high crag which overlooked the beautiful Apoala Valley in the Mixtec homeland. One day they decided to create the Yutatnoho, or River of the Lineages, which emerged from the bowels of the earth. Its flow nourished the leafy trees which the gods themselves had planted along its bank. From those majestic, sacred trees emerged the first caciques, a man and a woman, from whom the noble Mixtec nation is descended.

Source: Juan Arturo López Ramos (1987) *Esplendor de la Antigua Mixteca*. Mexico City: Trillas, p. 31.

DOCUMENT 1.4: BERNAL DÍAZ DEL CASTILLO'S DESCRIPTION OF THE PRINCIPAL AZTEC MARKET

When we arrived at the great marketplace, called Tlatelolco, we were astounded at the number of people and the quantity of merchandise that it contained, and at the good order and control that was maintained, for we had never seen such a thing before. The chieftains who accompanied us acted as guides. Each kind of merchandise was kept by itself and had its fixed place marked out. Let us begin with the dealers in gold, silver, and precious stones, feathers, mantles and embroidered goods. Then there were other wares consisting of Indian slaves both man and women; and I say that they bring as many of them to that great market for sale as the Portuguese bring negroes from Guinea; and they brought them along tied to long poles, with collars round their necks so they could not escape, and others they left free. Next there were other traders who sold great pieces of cloth and cotton, and articles of twisted thread, and there were *cacahuateros* who sold cacao. In this way one could see every sort of merchandise that is to be found in the whole of New Spain, placed in arrangement in the same manner as they do in my own country . . .

There were those who sold clothes of henequen and ropes and the sandals with which they are shod, which are made from the same plant, and sweet cooked roots, and other tubers which they get from this plant, all were kept in one part of the market in the place assigned to them. In another part there were skins of tigers and lions, of otters and jackals, deer and other animals and badgers and mountain cats, some tanned, and others untanned, and other classes of merchandise.

Let us go on and speak of those who sold beans and sage and other vegetables and herbs in another part, and to those who sold fowls, cocks with wattles, rabbits, hares, deer mallards, young dogs and other things of that sort in their part of the market, and let us mention the fruiterers, and the women who sold cooked food, dough and tripe in their own part of the market; then every sort of pottery made in a thousand different forms from great water jugs to little jugs, these also had a place to themselves; then those who sold honey and honey paste and other dainties like nut paste, and those who sold lumber, boards, cradles, beams, blocks and benches, each article by itself, and the vendors of *ocote* [pitch pine for torches] firewood, and other things of a similar nature . . . Paper, which in this country is called amal, and reeds scented with liquidambar, and full of tobacco, and yellow ointments and things of that sort are sold by themselves, and much cochineal is sold under arcades which are in that great marketplace, and there are many vendors of herbs and other sorts of trades. There are also buildings where three magistrates sit in judgment, and there are executive offices like *Aguacils* who inspect the merchandise. I am forgetting those who sell salt, and those who make stone knives, and how they split them off the stone itself, and the fisherwomen and others who sell some small cakes made from a sort of ooze which they get out the great lake, which curdles, and from this they make a bread having a flavor like that of cheese. There are for sale axes of brass and copper and tin, and gourds and gaily-pained jars made of wood. I could wish that I had finished telling of all the things which are sold there, but they are so numerous and of such different quality and the great marketplace with its surrounding arcades was so crowded with people, that one would not have been able to see and inquire about it all in two days.

Source: Bernal Díaz del Castillo (2008) *The History of the Conquest of New Spain*, ed. Davíd Carrasco. Albuquerque: University of New Mexico Press, pp. 173–75.

NOTE

1   Quoted in David Stuart and George Stuart, *Palenque: The Eternal City of the Maya* (London: Thames & Hudson, 2008), p. 11.

FURTHER READING

Arellano, Alfonso (2008) "Tula: Myth and History," *Voices of Mexico*, May–August, pp. 73–79.
    A beautifully illustrated discussion of Tula and contrasting interpretations of its history.

Carrasco, Davíd (2008) "The Exaggerations of Human Sacrifice," in *The History of the Conquest of New Spain*, ed. Davíd Carrasco, pp. 439–47 (see also pp. 458–65). Albuquerque: University of New Mexico Press.
    Carrasco discusses Aztec human sacrifice, a practice which has tended to obscure many positive aspects of Aztec culture.

Coe, Michael D. (2011) *The Maya* (8th ed.). New York: Thames & Hudson.
    A profusely illustrated description of how Maya civilization and architecture developed.

Coe, Michael D. (2012) *Breaking the Maya Code* (3rd ed.). New York: Thames & Hudson.
    A description of the collective effort to decipher Mayan writing.

Coe, Michael D. and Rex Koontz (2013) *Mexico: from the Olmecs to the Aztecs* (7th ed.). New York: Thames & Hudson.
A survey of Mesoamerican cultures.

Dillehay, Tom D. (2008) "Early Population Flows in the Western Hemisphere," in *A Companion to Latin American History*, ed. Thomas H. Holloway, pp. 10–27. Malden MA: Wiley-Blackwell.
A discussion of various theories concerning the arrival of humans in the Western Hemisphere.

Hodges, Glenn (2014) "Most Complete Ice Age Skeleton Helps Solve Mystery of First Americans," *National Geographic On-Line*, May.
Hodges describes the oldest known Mexican, whose remains were discovered on the Yucatán Peninsula. For a more technical description of this discovery see: *Science*, May 16, 2014, pp. 750–54.

Knight, Alan (2002) *Mexico: From the Beginning to the Spanish Conquest*. New York: Cambridge University Press.
Knight considers how hunter-gatherer societies morphed into the civilizations of Mesoamerica.

Smith, Michael E. (2012) *The Aztecs* (3rd ed.). Chichester, West Sussex and Malden, MA: Wiley-Blackwell.
A description of many aspects of Aztec life before and after the conquest, including art, sciences, and how common people lived.

GLOSSARY TERMS

altepetl	hunter-gatherer	*stela* (pl. *stelae*)
chia	Mesoamerica	tribute
chinampa	Quetzalcoatl	

Chapter 2

The Conquest of Mexico, 1519–1521

TIMELINE—MEXICO

1492 Columbus arrives in the New World	1493 Pope Alexander VI issues bull dividing New World between Portugal and Spain	1502 Montezuma begins reign as Aztec emperor	1504 Cortés arrives in Caribbean	1511 Spanish conquer Cuba
June 1519 Cortés formally founds Villa Rica de la Vera Cruz	August 1519 Spaniards march inland	September 1519 Spanish enter Tlaxcala	October 1519 Cholula massacre	November 1519 Spaniards arrive in Tenochtitlan
April 1521 Spanish launch sailboats (brigantines) in valley lakes	May 1521 Spanish capture the cities at end of the three causeways leading to Tenochtitlan and begin their assault on the Aztec capital	August 1521 Aztec resistance in Tenochtitlan ceases		

The recent history of Mexico, that of the last five hundred years, is the story of a permanent confrontation between those attempting to direct the country toward the path of Western civilization and those, rooted in Mesoamerican ways of life, who resist.

(Guillermo Bonfil Batalla, 1996)

1517 First expedition, led by Francisco Hernández de Córdoba, from Cuba to present-day Mexico	1518 Second expedition, led by Juan de Grijalva, from Cuba to present-day Mexico	1519–56 Carlos I reigns as king of Spain and as Carlos V, Holy Roman Emperor, 1519–56	February 1519 Cortés leaves Cuba	March 1519 Malinche given to Cortés
April 1520 Narváez arrives on coast	June 1520 Spaniards flee Tenochtitlan (Night of Sorrows)	September 1520 Cuitlahuac begins seventy-nine-day reign	December 1520 Cortés's force returns to Valley of Mexico	February 1521 Cuauhtémoc becomes Aztec emperor

CHAPTER 2 CONSIDERS THE SINGLE GREATEST EVENT in Mexican history—the conquest of Mexico by a small number of Spaniards. The chapter first describes the Spanish fleets which left Cuba in 1517 and 1518 to reconnoiter the coast of Mexico. Then it tells of Hernán Cortés assembling a much larger expedition in Cuba and landing on Mexican soil. The narrative then follows Cortés's group as it marches inland after having formed alliances with various indigenous groups. Following that is a description of his reception by the Aztecs in Tenochtitlan (today's Mexico City), his subsequent combat with them, and his final victory. The chapter concludes with a discussion of why Cortés's small expedition and its indigenous allies triumphed over the numerically superior Aztecs.

THE SPANIARDS ARRIVE

In 1517, the Aztecs received reports that strange men had landed in Yucatán. These "strange men" formed an expedition, led by Francisco Hernández de Córdoba, which had sailed from the Spanish colony of Cuba. This expedition, composed of three ships and 110 men, set in motion the conquest of Mexico. While on shore, twenty-five Spanish were killed in a clash with the Maya. Hernández de Córdoba himself was wounded and died of his wounds after returning to Cuba. Quite possibly the clash was touched off by Spanish attempts to capture Maya to take back to Cuba for sale as slaves. Ship-borne Spanish slave raids were common throughout the Caribbean at the time.

When the Spanish arrived in Yucatán, the Maya population was divided into sixteen city-states—each striving to expand its boundaries at the expense of its neighbors. Their society functioned at a lower cultural level than their ancestors had reached five centuries before.

In 1518, news came of a second expedition that had sailed from Cuba to Yucatán. This 240-man expedition, commanded by Juan de Grijalva, followed the Mexican coast north to Cape Rojo, between the present cities of Tuxpan and Tampico. The expedition's four ships then returned to Cuba and whetted Spanish appetites with reports of gold and large Indian populations.

In 1519, the Aztecs learned of the arrival of Hernán Cortés's fateful expedition in what an Indian observer described as "towers or small mountains floating on the waves of the sea."

Cortés, who would forever change Mexican history, was born in the western Spanish region of Extremadura in about 1484. Along with thousands of others, he came to the New World in search of gold and glory, joining a westward migration set in motion by Christopher Columbus. Such a search became especially attractive after 1492 when the last **Moorish** position on the Iberian Peninsula was captured. This marked the culmination of the **Reconquest**—a centuries long process of wresting Spain from Moslem control. After 1492 combating the infidel no longer offered a path to status and wealth in Spain. However, during the centuries-long Reconquest, militarism, religious crusading, and obtaining wealth by plunder had become deeply ingrained in the Spanish psyche.

In 1504, Cortés booked passage on a ship to the Caribbean island of Hispaniola. After spending seven years there, he joined the Spanish force which conquered, or more accurately, occupied Cuba. The Indians there offered little resistance. Cortés was placed in charge of many indigenous people, whom he forced to mine gold. Cuba's indigenous population plummeted as a result of overwork and cultural shock. However Indian-produced gold made Cortés wealthy. His serving from 1516 to 1518 as one of the magistrates of Santiago de Cuba reflected his newly elevated status.

In late 1518, Diego de Veláquez, the governor of Cuba, selected Cortés to lead a third expedition to Mexico. He felt that Cortés possessed the strong leadership that such an expedition would require. He also knew that Cortés had enough wealth to underwrite much of the cost of the expedition.

By the early sixteenth century, the Crown had privatized territorial expansion since the cost of maintaining a standing army and conquering the enormous territory of the Americas exceeded its very limited financial means. In exchange for its granting a private individual a royal license, or contract, to conquer and settle a given area, the Crown was legally entitled to a fifth of the booty obtained. The remaining four-fifths were divided between financiers of the conquest and the conquistadors, who also received the right to control the indigenous population they encountered. Such an arrangement served the Crown since, in addition to a fifth of the booty, it would receive taxes from subsequent economic activity in the conquered area.

Velázquez issued Cortés very detailed instructions which were a model of jurisprudence. If they had been obeyed, Cortés would not have been the conqueror of Mexico. The instructions stated that the principal purpose of the expedition was to serve God, and thus blasphemy and sleeping with native women would not be allowed. If landing parties were needed to secure wood and water, on no account was anyone ever to sleep on shore. The instructions foresaw reconnaissance, gathering information on missing Spaniards, limited trade, and a return to Cuba. Velázquez felt information obtained from the voyage would facilitate his establishing a settlement on the mainland once formal authorization arrived from Spain.

To raise capital for the expedition, Cortés mortgaged his estate, borrowed from wealthy merchants, bought what he could on credit, and begged from friends. He also showed his willingness to ignore the law when it served his interest. To obtain needed supplies, he simply appropriated a shipload of provisions.

Shortly before his scheduled departure, Velázquez decided that Cortés would probably betray him and revoked his command. Cortés remained undaunted. He convinced officials to assist him in assembling the expedition, even though they had orders to stop him. Cortés even recruited for his expedition one of the messengers who had delivered the order revoking his command. No one in Cuba could mount a force to stop him.

On February 18, 1519, Cortés left Cuba with 530 European men. Rather than being career soldiers, most of these men had worked at occupations such as tailoring, shop-keeping, and carpentry—a craft that later proved invaluable. Accompanying them were several hundred Cuban Indians and a few black freemen and African slaves, as well as several women who served as housekeepers. The expedition's twelve ships carried sixteen horses and fourteen cannons. Those who willingly sailed with Cortés had mixed goals. Expedition member Bernal Díaz del Castillo wrote that the Spanish came "to bring light to those in darkness, and also to get rich, which is what all of us men commonly seek."

Upon arriving in Yucatán, Cortés found two Spaniards whose boat had been shipwrecked there in 1511. Cortés picked up one of the survivors, Jerónimo de Aguilar, who had learned the Mayan language spoken in Yucatán. The other Spaniard, Gonzalo Guerrero, who had married a Maya woman and fathered children, said he preferred the life of an Indian and remained behind.

Cortés's fleet arrived near the present site of Veracruz on April 21, 1519. Soon after arriving, some members of the expedition felt they should forgo further exploration and sail back to Cuba, just as Veláquez had ordered. Cortés persuaded them to remain in Mexico using his strong personality and payments of gold, which, as one conquistador noted, served as "such a pacifier!" No one knows when Cortés decided to act independently of Velázquez. His going into debt to finance an expedition four times as large as Grijalva's suggests that he had planned to reject Velázquez's authority even before leaving Cuba.

Upon hearing of Cortés's arrival, Montezuma, the Aztec emperor, sent emissaries with a rich assortment of gifts, including food, large silver- and gold-covered wooden disks, gold nuggets, and ornate headdresses of green parrot feathers. The emissaries, in addition to providing gifts, attempted to glean as much information as possible about the newcomers.

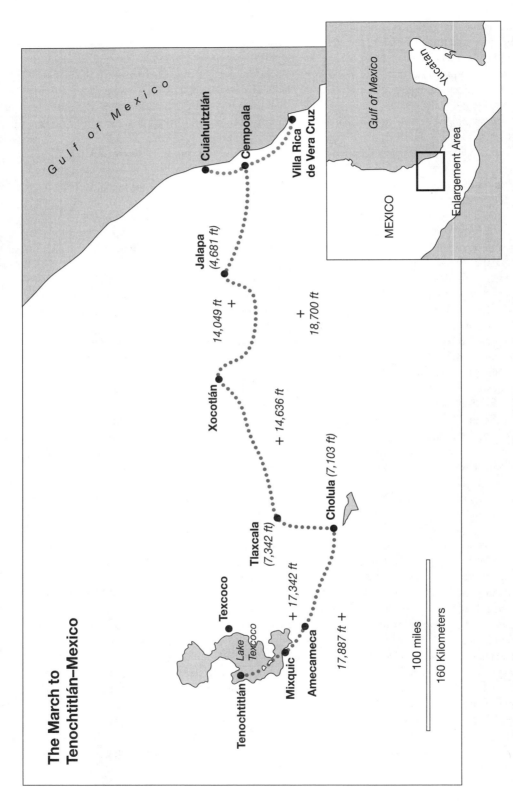

Figure 2.1 *Map of Cortés's march. Subsequent U.S. and French invaders followed an almost identical route.*

Source: From Barbara A. Tenenbaum, *Encyclopedia of Latin American History and Culture*, vol. 2 (New York: C. Scribner's Sons, 1996), 1E. Copyright: Gale, a part of Cengage Learning, Inc. Reproduced by permission. www.cengage.com/permissions

AMARANTH

The term amaranth refers to a plant family with more than sixty species growing on five of the seven continents. In Eurasia amaranth is mainly cultivated as a leafy green vegetable and as an ornamental. In South America one of the amaranth species produces a natural red dye. In broad areas of pre-Columbian North and South America it was also cultivated as a grain. Its small ivory colored seeds are among the smallest of the grain seeds.

When Cortés and his forces arrived in Mexico, they observed that the Aztecs fashioned figures, which represented their idols, out of amaranth seeds. The red juice of the prickly pear cactus was used to bind the small seeds together so that they could be shaped. The Spanish (and some today still) believed that the red came from human blood. In any case, the use of amaranth was closely linked to human sacrifice and religious rites. Every year during the month dedicated to Huitzilopochtli, the Aztec god of war, statues of the god were made with amaranth seeds and then eaten at the end of the month.

Archeological evidence indicates amaranth, a domesticated weed, was cultivated in Mexico as early as 5000 BC. It was one of the most widely cultivated grains in pre-Conquest times and was used in making tortillas, tamales, and a beverage known as atole. Amaranth grain was one of the many items demanded as tribute by Tenochtitlan.

The Spanish were quick to brand as Satanic much that they found in the New World. Unfortunately for the nutrition of those they conquered, due to its association with non-Christian religious rites and human sacrifice, they banned amaranth. Fortunately, despite the ban, the cultivation of amaranth persisted, albeit generally in small isolated pockets.

The removal of amaranth from Mesoamericans' diet was unfortunate since it is a magnificent grain, nutritionally speaking. The seeds supply a good mix of the amino acids that the human body cannot synthesize. This makes it a valuable source of protein. In addition the seeds contain carbohydrates and calcium. Furthermore its green leaves are high in vitamins. Its food value is enhanced by its ability to grow in a wide variety of topographical and climatic conditions.

Today amaranth seeds have a wide variety of culinary uses since their neutral taste allows them to be used in a variety of dishes. The most readily available amaranth product is known as *alegría* (Spanish for "joy"). This confection is a mixture of honey and amaranth seeds. The seeds are toasted on a griddle (*comal*) and then mixed with honey or other sweetener. The resulting material is forced into a mold (*tarima*) so that it forms a large rectangle. The rectangular mass is then removed and cut up into small cakes for sale.

One small town Tulyechualco, now located on the southeast edge of Mexico City, has clung to its pre-Conquest tradition of amaranth cultivation. Each October it has a fair to celebrate the plant. Just as most Mexicans prepare a variety of corn dishes, Tulyechualco residents proudly produce a variety of dishes containing amaranth. At fair time, they set up stalls to sell not only alegría, but cookies, cakes, beverages, and other hors d'oeuvres containing amaranth. The fair attracts visitors who purchase amaranth dishes and gives residents a chance to reinforce their indigenous roots.

Amaranth is now staging a comeback in Mexico. Two women from the United States are furthering this comeback. They created a non-profit organization called Puente a la Salud (Bridge to Health) to promote the cultivation of amaranth. They saw this as a way to reduce malnutrition among the rural poor in Oaxaca where many cannot afford to include meat in their diet. When combined with corn and beans, the resulting food is as good a protein source as meat. To spread this message, they organized workshops explaining the nutritional value of amaranth and passed out free amaranth seeds. Along with the nutritional advantages, presenters stressed that rather than being a foreign plant, it was part of their indigenous past.

Acceptance of amaranth, despite nutritional and cultural appeals, was slow. It was only when the Kellogg Company introduced an amaranth cereal, which came to be viewed as a luxury food, that amaranth cultivation began its rapid spread. In two years, the price of a kilo of amaranth seed tripled. Farmers, in response to the price rise, began to plant it and presumably incorporate it into the family diet.[1]

FROM VERACRUZ TO THE AZTEC CAPITAL

After making it clear that he did not plan to return to Cuba, Cortés established a town named Villa Rica de la Vera Cruz (Rich Town of the True Cross), complete with a municipal government. The Spanish then elected a town council composed of Cortés's friends. The new municipal government appointed him commander-in-chief. The Spaniards' new commander then declared Velázquez's authority to be superseded by that of the Spanish emperor. Cortés then sent a ship back to Spain to notify Emperor Carlos V that he would serve the emperor directly "until such time as His Majesty provided anyone else." Given the slow communications of the time, Cortés knew that no royal response would come before he had had the opportunity to conquer the Aztecs and ingratiate himself to the emperor.

The Spaniards soon contacted the Totonacs, one of the many indigenous groups dominated by the Aztecs. Through them, they discovered that the Aztecs had created an empire that exacted tribute from non-Aztecs. The Spaniards saw how this imperial domination could be turned to their advantage and promised the Totonacs protection in exchange for their allegiance.

Cortés treated the Totonacs as he would later treat other indigenous groups he encountered. He offered them the opportunity to accept Christianity and Spanish political control. If the offer was rejected, the Spanish attacked. If the offer was accepted, Cortés's men would destroy indigenous idols, which they declared to be the work of Satan. However Cortés would prevent looting and physical abuse of Indians by the men under his command. Many villages, when faced with Spanish military might, decided Spanish control constituted a lesser evil than Spanish attack.

To prevent any faint-hearted Spaniards from returning to Cuba, Cortés scuttled his ships. Then on August 8, 1519, Cortés's force began to march inland, accompanied by roughly 250 Totonacs who served as porters, guides, and combatants. Even at this early date, the indigenous-versus-European dichotomy was an oversimplification.

As the expedition wended its way inland, the Spaniards marveled at the strange peoples and magnificent scenery. When they encountered Indians, the Spaniards would try to win their loyalty and Christianize them. They were quite successful at this since, as Cortés noted in a letter to Carlos V, the Indians "would rather be Your Highness' vassals than see their houses destroyed and their women and children killed."

After a month of marching, the Spaniards reached Tlaxcala, a small resource-poor nation east of Tenochtitlan that the Aztecs had never conquered. The Tlaxcalans maintained their independence through tenacious defense of their homeland and the political convenience an "enemy" provided to the Aztecs.

Cortés realized he could benefit from the hostility between the Tlaxcalans and the Aztecs and commented:

> When I saw the discord and animosity between these two peoples I was not a little pleased, for it seemed to further my purpose considerably; consequently I might have the opportunity of subduing them more quickly, for, as the saying goes, "divided they fall."[2]

The Tlaxcalans were unsure how they should receive the Spanish. Some felt they should be welcomed. Others argued that their coming from an Aztec tributary town indicated that they were secretly allied with the Aztecs. Upon deciding the Spanish had allied with the Aztecs, the Tlaxcalans mobilized to defend themselves.

As the Spanish approached, they read the *requerimiento*, a charge in Spanish directing Indians to lay down their arms and accept the Spanish emperor and Christianity or suffer the consequences. It notified the indigenous people of a chain of command from God to the pope to the emperor to the conquistadors. The latter, it noted, were merely implementing the divinely sanctioned donation of American lands and peoples by the pope to the Spanish emperor.

It was immaterial that distance prevented the Indians from hearing the *requerimiento* and that they could not understand Spanish. Merely reading the charge fulfilled the Spanish requirement that infidels be given fair warning before being attacked. In conclusion, the *requerimiento* noted that if the Indians did not follow the order to accept Spanish rule and Christianity, the resulting havoc that would be wreaked on them would be their own fault, not the fault of the Spanish emperor, the reader of the *requerimiento*, or the Spanish soldiers.

The right to conquest proclaimed by the *requerimiento* reflected legal doctrine in European international law that had been developing since the thirteenth century. Europeans claimed that Christians had the right to occupy the territory of the heathen if they assumed the responsibility for evangelizing those living there. This right was further elaborated with the notion of "just war," which could be waged against those who refused to accept Christianity or who later rebelled against Christian authority. Those captured in a "just war" could legally be executed for treason or sold into slavery.

After the reading of the *requerimiento*, a series of battles ensued between the Tlaxcalans and the Spanish. Tlaxcalans provided stiff resistance to the conquistadores. In between battles with the Tlaxcalans, the Spanish would pillage the countryside, sowing fear by burning towns and mutilating civilians. Such tactics had proved to be especially effective on Hispaniola and Cuba.

As a result of Spanish marauding and mounting battle casualties, the Tlaxcalans finally surrendered. The Spanish then entered Tlaxcala unmolested. Its citizens immediately accepted the Spanish offer to form an alliance against their perennial enemies—the Aztecs. Cortés showed his political skills by winning not only the Tlaxcalans' submission but their loyalty. This loyalty later saved the Spaniards' lives.

Cortés next marched to Cholula, an Aztec tributary town that had long served as a destination for religious pilgrimages. Further blurring the European versus Indian dichotomy, some 6,000 Tlaxcalans accompanied the Spanish. After Cortés's force arrived in Cholula, an informer told them that the Cholulans were preparing to attack them. Using this report as an excuse, the Spanish and the Tlaxcalans attacked the Cholulans.

The Spanish priest, historian, and defender of Indian rights Bartolomé de las Casas later commented on the Spanish attack:

> Among other massacres was one which took place in Cholula, a great city of some thirty thousand inhabitants. When all the dignitaries of the city and the region came out to welcome the Spaniards with all due pomp and ceremony . . . the Spaniards decided that the moment had come to organize a massacre (or "punishment" as they themselves express such things) in order to inspire fear and terror in all the people of the territory.[3]

Even if a plot against the Spanish actually existed (evidence is mixed), the punishment inflicted by the Spanish was clearly excessive. Rather than targeting leaders believed to be involved in the plot, the Spanish slaughtered thousands of unarmed Cholulans.

As the news spread that Spanish power rivaled that of the Aztecs, lords from several nearby cities approached Cortés and offered to reject Aztec sovereignty and fight with the Spanish. Cortés accepted such assistance, which later proved to be invaluable.

From Cholula, the Spanish departed for the nearby Aztec capital, which they entered by crossing a long causeway across Lake Texcoco. Causeways to the north, south, and west provided access to Tenochtitlan. A ten-mile-long dike divided the lake into fresh-water and salt-water sections. Streams flowed into the fresh-water section, enabling the Aztecs to fish and irrigate *chinampas*. Water then passed into the salty section, where it evaporated (as does water flowing into the Great Salt Lake in Utah), leaving salt to be collected.

Figure 2.2 *The valley of Mexico in Aztec times. Thanks to its temperate climate and fertile soil, several important Mesoamerican societies flourished in its confines.*

Source: Reproduced courtesy of Michael D. Coe; map drawn by Patrick Gallagher.

FROM ROYAL WELCOME TO SPANISH DEFEAT

Montezuma greeted the Spanish as they entered the city by causeway and invited them to be guests in a palace that had belonged to his father. To add to the impact of his arrival, Cortés had his cannons fired. One of the Aztecs, who had never heard cannon fire, said the sound had the same effect as psychedelic mushrooms.

As the Spanish settled in as royal guests, they realized that they were not only failing to conquer the Aztecs but that they were in a precarious military position, surrounded by hundreds of thousands of warriors. Thus they decided to kidnap Montezuma and use him to gain control of the empire. A group of armed Spaniards went to Montezuma's palace and forced him to return to the palace where the Spaniards were lodged, threatening him with death if he resisted. Rather than risking his life at the hands of the Spaniards, Montezuma permitted them to take him prisoner, claiming he was their "guest."

Montezuma continued to rule the Aztec empire, even though Cortés controlled his actions. He announced that he was ruling in the name of the Spanish emperor and even turned the royal treasure over to the Spaniards. From November 1519 to May 1520, both the Spaniards and the Aztec elite shared a courtly life of leisure.

Just as Cortés was seeing his ambitions fulfilled, he received word that a 900-man force sent by Cuban governor Velázquez had arrived on the Gulf Coast. Velázquez had instructed this force to arrest Cortés for not having returned to Cuba. Cortés placed the Aztec capital under the command of one of his officers, Pedro de Alvarado, and made a forced march to his rival's camp in Veracruz. Before he arrived in Veracruz, Cortés sent runners ahead to contact the men of the other force. Then through a combination of bribes, tales of riches forthcoming, and playing officers off against Pánfilo de Narváez, their unpopular commander, Cortés undermined the will of the opposing force. When Cortés finally attacked under the cover of a storm, resistance was minimal. Narváez later commented that he had been beaten by his own troops, not those of his rival.

The newly arrived Spaniards, eager to share in the anticipated Aztec riches, joined Cortés, more than doubling his force. In addition he acquired many horses and weapons that Narváez had brought.

Soon after this victory, Cortés received word that Aztecs in Tenochtitlan had revolted. After receiving permission from the Spaniards remaining there, the Aztecs had staged a religious festival. During the festival, Alvarado had ordered his men to fire into the crowd in what modern strategists would term a preemptive strike. He claimed that the Aztecs had planned the festival as the prelude to an uprising. After this attack, the Aztec nation rose in arms and besieged the Spaniards' palace. Montezuma, still a captive, ordered the attacks to cease. The attacks then ended, leaving the Spaniards surrounded by the Aztecs.

Cortés marched back to Tenochtitlan. The Aztecs allowed the returning force to cross their siege lines and join Alvarado in the palace, where they felt the Spaniards would be hopelessly trapped.

From the roof of the palace, Montezuma again tried to quiet the Aztecs, but was met by jeers and rocks from the enraged attackers below. One of the rocks struck him, and he died shortly afterward, still a captive. The cause of Montezuma's death remains a mystery. Some claim the rock wound was fatal; others claim the Spaniards murdered him. In any case, Montezuma's death only heightened the fury of the besiegers.

After enduring a month of siege, the Spaniards broke through the Aztec lines on the night of June 30, 1520. Cortés's troops had to swim the gaps their besiegers had dug in the causeway to prevent their flight. Aztec attacks forced the escaping Spaniards to fight their way to the mainland. Many Spaniards were so laden with stolen treasure that they could not defend themselves. Cortés's chaplain estimated that 450 Spanish died that night. In addition, several thousand Tlaxcalans probably died while fleeing the city. Mexicans refer to this Spanish defeat as la Noche Triste (the Night of Sorrows).

Rather than engaging in hot pursuit, the Aztecs permitted the Spanish to regroup. The delay might be attributable to Alvarado's having killed so many nobles that the Aztecs lacked a leader or to warriors being away tending their fields during the rainy season. The Aztecs might also have been observing a mourning period for their own warriors killed on la Noche Triste. Finally the Aztecs may have simply assumed the Spanish to be vanquished and unworthy of pursuit.

Seven days later, as the battered Spanish forces headed for the protection of Tlaxcala, the Aztecs attacked them near the town of Otumba. After they surrounded the beleaguered Spaniards, Cortés and five other horsemen charged into the Aztec ranks, killed their commander, and triumphantly raised the captured Aztec imperial battle standard. At this point, Aztec battlefield organization

LA MALINCHE

While Cortés's expedition was sailing up the Mexican coast, a Maya chief presented the Spaniards with twenty women as a gift. One of these women, Malinche, formed a translation team with Aguilar, the Spaniard who had been shipwrecked in Yucatán. She translated from Nahuatl, the Aztec language, to Yucatecan Mayan. Aguilar then translated the Mayan into Spanish. Malinche soon learned enough Spanish to dispense with Aguilar. Later she became Cortés's lover.

Malinche was born to high status within the Aztec empire. However, while still a youth she became a slave of the Maya. According to one version, after her father died, her mother remarried and bore her new husband a son. To avoid Malinche's claiming high status based on her deceased father, her mother and stepfather decided to remove her from the family, transferring her to the Maya on the Gulf Coast. There she learned the Mayan language, a second language in addition to her native Nahuatl. Upon Cortés's arrival, she was simply given to him as one might give an honored guest a parrot or a dog. Her knowledge of Nahuatl and Aztec life in general proved to be so valuable that Bernal Díaz del Castillo commented, "As Doña Marina [another form of her name] proved herself such an excellent woman and good interpreter throughout the wars in New Spain, Tlaxcala and Mexico . . . Cortés always took her with him . . ."

Her role in facilitating the Conquest has earned her the opprobrium of the Mexican people since. Her name even gave rise to the Spanish adjective *malinchista*, which the dictionary of the Royal Academy of the Spanish Language defines as one who prefers the foreign to one's own. Nobel Prize-winning Mexican author Octavio Paz expressed the general Mexican opinion of her:

> Doña Marina becomes a figure representing the Indian women who were fascinated, violated or seduced by the Spaniards. And as a small boy will not forgive his mother if she abandons him in search for his father, the Mexican people have not forgiven La Malinche for her betrayal.

Until the late twentieth century, she was almost unanimously considered as a traitor to Mesoamericans and as a whore (she bore Cortés a son).

However, in the latter part of the twentieth century, feminists reconsidered Malinche's place in history. The question was raised as to just what she owed the Aztecs who had cast her aside or the Maya who had given her away. Certainly she did not owe "Mexico" anything, since the concept did not yet exist. Similarly, it was only the Spanish who divided humanity into races. To the indigenous, one was Aztec or Mayan or Zapotec. In the indigenous word view of the time any obligation to race per se did not exist any more than Europeans or Africans owed loyalty to others from their respective continents.

As a result a revisionist view of her emerged as a resilient woman who overcame adversity early in life and employed her talents as translator and diplomat to rise to high position in the milieu into which she was thrust. This radical reinterpretation of Malinche, while not completely reversing old notions of her, at least provides an alternate view.

dissolved. The Spanish were saved by Cortés's audacious action and by the open space at Otumba that permitted the effective use of horses. After that battle, the Spanish marched on to Tlaxcala without further combat.

THE FINAL SPANISH VICTORY

Once they arrived safely in Tlaxcala, the Spanish began preparations for the conquest of the Aztecs. Cortés ordered a fleet of sailboats built for use on the 238-square-mile Lake Texcoco. New arrivals from Spain and Cuba reinforced the Spaniards. Cuban governor Velázquez, unaware of Narváez's defeat by Cortés, sent additional men. At the same time, Cortés's indigenous allies, especially the Tlaxcalans, assembled large armies. Once Cortés showed he was able and willing to protect his allies from Aztec retribution, additional Aztec tributaries joined his cause.

The Aztecs attempted to form an alliance with the Tlaxcalans against the Spanish. They noted that the two groups shared a common language, gods, and ancestry. The Aztecs also reminded the Tlaxcalans that the Spanish, even after having been warmly received by Montezuma, had repaid his kindness by imprisoning him. The Tlaxcalans, remembering past Aztec cruelty and arrogance, rejected such an alliance.

While the Spaniards gathered strength, an insidious contribution inadvertently brought by the Spanish—smallpox—weakened the Aztecs. As the indigenous population had no natural immunity to the disease, epidemics swept the country, killing much of the population and demoralizing those who survived.

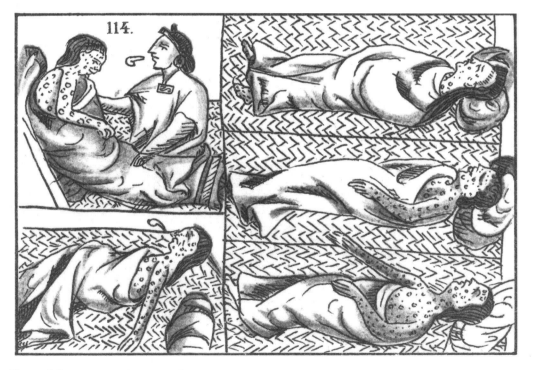

Figure 2.3 *Survivors' depiction of smallpox victims. Small pox was a scourge that swept throughout the Americas, greatly reducing population and forever changing indigenous societies.*

Source: Reproduced courtesy of the Benson Latin American Collection, the University of Texas at Austin.

An Aztec account of the smallpox epidemic reported:

It began to spread, striking everywhere in the city and killing many of the people. Sores erupted on their faces, breasts, bellies. They had so many painful sores over their bodies that they could not move, not even turn over in their litters, and if someone tried to move them, they screamed in agony. This pestilence killed untold numbers of people, many of them dying because there was nobody to feed them, so they starved. Those who survived had holes in their faces, or were left blinded.[4]

The fatalities from the epidemic included Montezuma's brother, Cuitláhuac, who had succeeded him as Aztec emperor. The Aztec elite then chose Montezuma's nephew, Cuauhtémoc, to be the last emperor of the Aztecs.

After months of preparation, the Spaniards began their assault. Eight thousand porters, in a line more than six miles long, carried already formed sailboat parts to Lake Texcoco, where they were assembled. Then the Spanish marched around the lake, subduing villages along the shore and cutting off aqueducts and food supplies to Tenochtitlan. Next they launched offensives down the causeways with the support of the boats, which had been armed with cannons. An estimated 200,000 Tlaxcalans and former Aztec subjects joined the offensive.

The Aztecs stubbornly resisted the eighty-five-day siege, forcing the attackers to fight for every inch of ground. To deny cover to the Aztecs, as well as to provide for the effective use of horses and cannons, the Spanish and their Indian allies filled all the canals and destroyed all the buildings they captured. The Aztecs chose to defend a fixed location, highly vulnerable to Spanish cannons and cavalry. Even if they had conceived of a guerrilla strategy, the Aztecs would likely have found little support among those they had previously tyrannized.

During the siege, the Aztecs refused surrender offers, despite their high casualty rate, disease, and near starvation. To the horror of the Spanish, the Aztecs would sacrifice captured Spaniards, as well as their horses, in full view of the besieging force.

Finally, on August 13, 1521, Cuauhtémoc saw that the Spanish were closing in on the last Aztec-held section of the city. He tried to flee by canoe, but was captured and brought to Cortés as a prisoner.

After Cuauhtémoc's capture, Aztec resistance ceased. By one estimate, more than 240,000 Aztecs died during the siege. Of these, Cortés estimated that 100,000 died in combat. The rest succumbed to disease and starvation. Only 60,000 residents of Tenochtitlan survived. Between 500 and 1,000 of the Spaniards engaged in the conquest died.

The Spanish allowed the Aztec survivors to leave their once beautiful city, which had been reduced to rubble. Cuauhtémoc was not as fortunate as his former subjects. The conquerors imprisoned and tortured him in an unsuccessful attempt to make him reveal the location of additional Aztec treasure.

THE REASONS (VALID AND INVALID) FOR THE SPANISH VICTORY

Ever since Cortés's victory, people have speculated about just how Cortés's force triumphed. The reasons why a handful of Spaniards were able to conquer millions of Aztecs include the following:

- The Spanish incited the Aztecs' subjects to rebel against their imperial masters. Rather than speaking of a Spanish victory, it would be more accurate to state that the Spanish led a successful rebellion. As noted above, 200,000 indigenous allies supported the Spanish in the siege of Tenochtitlan. Other Indians fought with the Spanish elsewhere.
- The smallpox epidemic decimated the Aztecs and left them leaderless. Both Aztec defenders of Tenochtitlan and the Spaniards' indigenous allies fell victim to the disease. However, the

Spanish were largely immune, and their command structure remained intact. In contrast, Montezuma's successor, Cuitláhuac, died of the disease, thus plunging the Aztecs into a succession crisis during the siege.

- The Spanish used a variety of weapons unavailable to the Aztecs, including the crossbow, the notoriously inaccurate matchlock guns known as harquebuses, thundering cannons, and, especially, the long, sharp Castilian sword. After fighting in Tlaxcala, Díaz del Castillo commented, "It was only by a miracle of sword play that we could make them give way so that our ranks could be reformed." Aztec swords, which were made of sharp stones slotted into wooden shafts, were intended to wound, but not to kill, thus providing victims for sacrifice. Mesoamericans made little use of metal aside from bells and ornaments.

- Spanish battle tactics, based on experience in European wars, allowed the Spaniards to integrate infantry, artillery, and cavalry. Spanish soldiers protected their neighbors and attempted to kill the enemy. In contrast, the Aztecs placed a high value on individual duels and heroism rather than on close teamwork. They prioritized capturing an enemy alive for later sacrifice.

- Two animals contributed to the Spanish victory. The horse intimidated, provided a platform to impale and hack at natives, and allowed swift transportation. In addition, war dogs, probably mastiffs or Irish wolfhounds, felled many an Indian.

- Cortés's talent for flattery, courtesy, eloquence, swift decision, improvisation, deviousness, and sudden changes of plan, as well as his will and courage in adversity, determined that he should lead the conquest.

- Cortés could draw on a variety of tactics that had been perfected during the Spanish Reconquest and the colonization of the Caribbean. These tactics included: 1) the wanton use of violence, as at Cholula; 2) kidnapping native rulers, a tactic that was also used in the Caribbean; and 3) allying with one non-Spanish group to conquer another, as was done both in the Caribbean and during the Reconquest. This tactic was especially effective since Native American identity was highly localized. Native peoples saw themselves as members of a particular community or city-state and very seldom as members of a larger ethnic group. They certainly did not feel themselves to be anything even approaching the category of "Indians" or "natives."

- Empires such as the Aztec empire are inherently fragile. The component parts do not need the empire to survive. Having an overlord is unacceptable if independence is feasible. Dominated people constantly seek ways to shed their obligation to supply labor and goods as tribute.

- Sixteenth-century European culture facilitated the conquest. Writing allowed leaders of various Spanish forces to effectively communicate and for Cortés to request help from the rest of the Spanish realm. The wheel allowed the transport of the cannons used in the conquest. Improvements in the safety, price, and capacity of sea travel enabled the Spanish in Mexico to remain in communication with Europe and receive reinforcements. As a result of their relative modernity, more than a year before the conquest was complete, the Spanish were already exhibiting booty from Mexico and spreading information about Mexico through Europe.

- Traditional accounts of the conquest, such as William Prescott's classic *History of the Conquest of Mexico*, stressed that Montezuma was under the influence of strange portents that supposedly appeared during the last years of his reign. Rather than responding to portents, there are several reasons Montezuma may have failed to aggressively confront the Spanish: 1) he accepted Cortés as an ambassador from a distant and unknown ruler, which is what Cortés claimed to be; 2) Montezuma felt the Aztecs were so strong that the Spanish did not pose a threat; 3) unlike invading Mesoamerican armies, the Spanish never clearly announced hostilities; and 4) defeated kings who did not offer resistance were left in power and assessed less tribute than kings who resisted an invader.

After the conquest, the Spanish had a vested interest in claiming portents influenced the Aztecs, since that would establish their opponents as primitives in need of enlightenment by the Spanish.

Indigenous informants who later spoke to the Spanish may have used portents to explain their humiliating defeat. Another possible explanation for Montezuma's call for the Aztecs to lay down their arms was that he recognized that resistance against Spanish technology was hopeless.

THE CONQUEST IN RETROSPECT

The Spanish victory occurred with pontifical blessing. Pope Leo X sent bulls offering indulgences for those who engaged in war against the infidel. The conquistadors themselves fought with a clear conscience, certain that they were bringing civilization and Christianity. They believed their efforts would allow these newly discovered people to leave behind their backward conditions.

However the history that Bartolomé de las Casas published in 1552 did not share the view that the Conquest was religiously motivated. His history stated:

> The reason the Christians have murdered on such a vast scale and killed anyone and everyone in their way is purely and simply greed. They have set out to line their pockets with gold and to amass private fortunes as quickly as possible so that they can then assume a status quite at odds with that into which they were born.[5]

In Mexico, Cortés is now regarded as a ruthless invader. The conspicuous lack of his name on Mexican streets and monuments and Diego Rivera's portrayal of him as a cross-eyed, syphilitic hunchback in a mural in the National Palace indicate these feelings. On the other hand, Montezuma and Cuauhtémoc are national heroes, and innumerable streets and monuments bear their names.

The five-hundredth anniversary of Columbus's arrival in the New World showed that the conquest still arouses strong feelings. Heated debate occurred between those wanting a gala celebration of the anniversary and those wanting somber reflection. Mexicans did not even agree on whether Columbus's arrival should be referred to as a discovery, an encounter, or an invasion.

DOCUMENT 2.1: CORTÉS'S ORDERS

[Cortés received very detailed orders from Cuban governor Diego Velázquez concerning the force he was to lead to Mexico. The orders, dated October 23, 1518, contained thirty provisions:]

ONE: First of all, your principal motive and that of all your force is and must be to serve and praise our Lord and to spread our Holy Catholic faith. Thus you should not allow anyone, regardless of his position or rank, to speak ill of our Lord or of his mother Saint Mary or of the saints or to blaspheme the Lord in any matter. You should emphasize to your group that this is paramount. Those who commit any such offenses should be punished with the utmost rigor.

TWO: To ensure that your expedition can more fully serve Our Lord, you will not permit any sinning, such as public concubinage, or permit any of those under your command to have illegal carnal knowledge of any woman, because that is a sin which God detests and because both divine and human laws prohibit it. You should punish with the utmost rigor any such offense. The law in such cases is clear.

THREE: In undertakings such as yours, group harmony is quite advantageous. Likewise dissension and discord are harmful. Since dice and playing cards cause conflict and lead to the blaspheming of God and the saints, you will ensure that no expedition member brings dice or playing cards. Those who violate this rule should be severely punished. You will also ensure that no one joins your expedition who is not a zealous servant of our Lord and of their Highnesses.[6] Similarly you should not include anyone who is known for belligerence or making trouble.

FOUR: After your fleet leaves the port of Santiago de Cuba, you should ensure that when you dock in other Cuban ports no member of your expedition in any way offends anyone and that they do not forcibly take anything from port residents or the nearby Indians. You should make this known in each port you visit and also let it be known that those who violate this rule will be punished according to the law.

FIVE: After, thanks to God our Lord, you have received the supplies and other items that you need, on each ship, you should inspect the men and their arms. Be sure that no one lends their arms to someone else for the review. Once the ships and the people are in order, you should, God willing, continue with your voyage as rapidly as possible.

SIX: Before setting sail, you will carefully inspect all your ships to determine if there are any Cuban native men or women on board. If you find any, you should deliver them to the authorities in the name of their Highnesses. Under no circumstances should any of your ships have any natives on board.

SEVEN: Once you have set sail, visit each of the ships. You will take with you a scribe who will list the individuals who are on each of the ships accompanying you. The captain of each ship should be supplied with a copy of the list. Also missing individuals should be noted. Those who have provided you with money, but who did not accompany you, should also be listed. You will send me a copy of the lists so we will know who went with you.

[Instructions Eight, Nine, and Ten provide navigation instructions to pilots and ship captains.]

ELEVEN: When, thanks to our Lord, you arrive at the island of Cozumel and at the other islands and lands you encounter, you will speak with the caciques [chiefs] and Indians you encounter and tell them our King has sent you to explore and visit. You should let them know that he is a very powerful king whose vassals we and they are. Let them know that for many generations he has been obeyed and that he has subjugated and continues to subjugate many lands. Inform them of the names of the lands and islands he dominates, including Hispaniola, Puerto Rico, Jamaica, and Cuba. Also let them know that he has granted land to the natives and that in each grant he has appointed captains. Let them know that I have information about the island where they live and that I sent you to subject them to his Highness and his service. Let them know that those who serve his Highness will be well rewarded by him. In his name, I will also favor them. Assure them that they will be protected against their enemies. Tell all the natives that as a sign of serving his Highness they should provide you with gold, precious stones, pearls, and other things they have. Let them know that his Highness will treat them favorably. Inform them they should provide goods so that his Highness can know they are willing to serve him and so he can reward them. You will also tell them how sorry I was to learn of the battle involving Capt. Francisco Hernández de Córdoba. His Highness does not want his vassals to be mistreated due to him. Let them know that in the name of his Highness I have sent you to speak with them, to pacify them, and to let them know of the great power of our Lord. In the future those who want to peacefully serve the Spanish will be well received, and peace will reign. The Spanish will help them against their enemies. Also tell them whatever else you think will further your goals.

TWELVE: In many places on the island of Cozumel crosses have been encountered on burials. These crosses are widely venerated. You will attempt by all possible means and with great diligence to learn the meaning the crosses have for those who erected them. Also inquire if they erected them because they have received the teaching of God Our Lord. You will be very heedful of this matter. All such information you gather should be recorded by your scribe. This should occur in Cozumel as well as in any other places crosses are found.

THIRTEEN: You should determine, whenever possible, if the natives of the islands have sects, religions, rituals, or ceremonies and if they have mosques,[7] other houses of worship, idols, or similar things. Find out if they have people who officiate at their ceremonies, as the Muslim scholars and other ministers do. You will have your scribe record this information in detail and certify what you find.

FOURTEEN: You are aware that the principal reason that our Highnesses permit exploration of new lands is because so many souls, just like the souls here, have been and are outside our Holy Faith for lack of someone who can tell them the true teachings. You will use all means possible to effect the conversion of the natives of the islands and lands where you travel. You should make them understand that there is only One God creator of heaven and earth and of all the other things in heaven and on earth. Explain this as fully as you can and as time allows. Do as much and as well as you can in the service of God Our Lord and of His Highnesses.

[Instructions Fifteen, Sixteen, Seventeen, and Eighteen ordered Cortés to inquire about the Grijalva expedition.[8]]

NINETEEN: You will be very careful to ensure the Indians you encounter, on land as well as at sea, are treated well. You will show them friendship and love. Do what you can, depending on who you encounter and where you are, to make the Indians you encounter happy. You will not allow anyone to harm them in any way. You will do everything you can to ensure that when they leave you they will be pleased to have met you and your men. To do otherwise would be a disservice to God Our Lord and their Highnesses and contrary to your mission.

[Instruction Twenty deals with bartering with Indians for items that belonged to the Grijalva expedition.]

TWENTY-ONE: If you need to land to take on fresh water, firewood, or other supplies, only do so if there is no danger to your men. Send only the people in whom you have the utmost confidence. You will instruct them to be as peaceful and cordial as possible, but at the same time ensure they are well armed. You will instruct them not to cause conflict with the native people. Your men should only go ashore if there is no sign of danger. In no case should they sleep on shore. They should not venture so far from the shore that they cannot quickly return to their ships in case of Indian attack and be supported by those remaining on the ships.

TWENTY-TWO: If you encounter a town close to the coast and if it appears that its residents will allow you to enter without conflict or danger, you may visit it and reconnoiter. You will take with you your most pacific, prudent men and ensure they are as well armed as possible. You will instruct them in front of a scribe who will record your orders. Tell them that they should not take any object from the Indians, even if it is of little value. They should not enter homes nor should they abuse their women, or even touch, speak with, or approach them, or say anything that would lead to immorality. Nor should any of your men separate themselves from the group regardless of what invitations the Indians make.

TWENTY-THREE: Since the Indians, to deceive you or kill you, may feign good will and invite you to their towns, you will be vigilant and keep your arms at the ready. You will not permit the Indians to mingle with your men. You will explain that this is to prevent any Spaniard from doing or saying anything that would cause offense. If they mingle with you, they might grab some of you and drag them off. You will instruct those remaining on the ships to be on the look out, so that they might come to your aid in case of attack.

TWENTY-FOUR: After determining if there are any Spanish captives on Santa María de los Remedios, you will continue your voyage toward Punta Llama, which is the beginning of the land whose coast you will explore. Inspect all rivers and ports until you reach the Bay of San Juan and Chalchicueyecan.[9] That is the point from which Grijalva sent me his wounded and sick and wrote me about what had happened to his expedition. If you encounter him you will work with him because your group and his group have the same interests. You will work together in order to best serve God Our Lord and their Highnesses, bearing in mind the instructions each of you received. You will do this in the name of our Highnesses and in order to please God. If you barter or trade for anything, you will do so in the presence of Francisco de Peñaloza, the inspector.

TWENTY-FIVE: You will work diligently to learn about these islands and lands and about the other regions that in the service of God Our Lord have been discovered or will be discovered. You will note what the people of each place talk about and their abilities, as well as the trees, fruits, herbs, birds, animals, gold, precious stones, pearls, metals, spices, and whatever else you learn about. You will have this all recorded by scribes. It is known that in these islands and lands there is gold. You will learn where and when it was obtained and if there are mines. If so, find out where the mines are. You will attempt to inspect them in order to make as accurate a description as possible. Chalchicueyecan is a likely gold source. From there, Grijalva sent me some grains of gold to be melted down. You will also learn if the people you speak with make their own gold ornaments or if the ornaments are from elsewhere.

TWENTY-SIX: At each place you visit, before your scribe and many witnesses, and in the name of their Highnesses, you will take possession of the land with the greatest possible solemnity. You will perform all the judicial acts and formalities that usually accompany such ceremonies. In each location you will strive by all means possible and in an orderly fashion to gain information about other islands and lands and to learn of the capabilities and weaknesses of such people. It is said that there are people with huge, wide ears and others who have faces like dogs, and that there are amazons.

TWENTY-SEVEN: Many situations may arise that are not considered in my instructions. In such situations I am sure that you will act in the way that best serves Our Lord and their Highnesses. In all such cases, you will act as much as possible in conformity with the instructions provided above. You should make prudent decisions and rely on the wise, trustworthy members of your expedition and on those who are most disposed to serve Our Lord and their Highnesses.

[Instruction Twenty-eight ordered Cortés not to allow those who owed money to the King and Queen to join his expedition.]

TWENTY-NINE: After you have arrived at Chalchicueyecan, you will send the boat that you have least need of back to Cuba. On it you will send me all the gold, pearls, and precious stones you have encountered, as well as spices, small animals, fruits, birds, and all the other things you have found. That will permit me to send an accurate report to the King, who will thus know what is to be found in these lands.

[Instruction Thirty confers on Cortés authority to enforce both civil and criminal law on the expedition.]

Source: Author's translation of Cortés's orders, which appeared in José Luis Martínez (ed.) (1990)
Documentos cortesianos, Vol. I. Mexico City: Fondo de Cultura Económica, pp. 45–57.

DOCUMENT 2.2: THE *REQUERIMIENTO*

[Each time the *requerimiento* was read the names of the ruling monarch and the speaker were inserted. The translated version below was delivered by Pedrarias Dávila, who served as governor of Panama from 1514 to 1526.]

On behalf of Fernando V,[10] King of Spain, Defender of the Catholic Church, subduer of barbarians, and on behalf of Queen Juana,[11] his beloved daughter, I, Pedrarias Dávila, their servant, messenger, and captain, bring you word of God Our Lord, one and eternal. He is creator of earth, of heaven, and of the man and woman from whom all of us are descended and from whom all future humans will descend. A large number of humans have been born during the more than five thousand years since the earth was created. Since no one area could sustain so many people, humans were forced to scatter widely and divide themselves into many kingdoms and provinces.

Our Lord selected one of these people, Saint Peter, to lead the humans on earth. All people, regardless of where they were or what their nationality or religion was, were placed under his jurisdiction. The Lord instructed Peter to govern from Rome, which was the best place from which to administer the earth. He also exercised power in other parts of the world so he could judge and govern Christians, Moors, Jews, gentiles, and those of other faiths. Peter was referred to as the Pope, which meant admirable, elder, father, and guardian. He was father and governor of all mankind. They regarded Peter as master, king, and ruler of the world that they inhabited. The popes who have been elected since then have been regarded similarly. Future popes will also be treated in this way.

One of the pontiffs, who succeeded Peter, granted these islands and the mainland to our King and Queen and to their successors. You can inspect the documents that recorded this grant.[12] As a result of this property transfer, their Highnesses exercise sovereignty over these islands and over the mainland. Almost everyone who has been informed of this grant has received their Highnesses and has willingly obeyed and served them as subjects and has not offered resistance. As soon as they received this information, they welcomed and obeyed the priests that our Highnesses sent to teach our Holy Faith. All of them freely, joyfully, and without reservation became Christians and remain faithful. Their Highnesses received them with great joy and ordered that they be treated as other subjects and vassals. You are obligated to act in a similar manner.

Finally I implore you to fully consider what I have told you. You may take the necessary time to discuss this information and to recognize the Church as owner and administrator of the entire world. You must also recognize our Holy Father, the pope, and the King and Queen, our masters, as rulers of these islands and of the mainland. By virtue of the pope's grant, their Highnesses have dispatched priests to teach you our faith.

If you behave properly and perform your obligations to their Highnesses, I, in their name, will receive you with all love and kindness and will protect your wives, children, and land, and will not impose servitude upon you. Rather than having Christianity forced on you, you are free to do what you wish. After having learned of our Holy Catholic Faith, you may accept Christianity, as almost all the residents of the other islands and of more distant lands have done. If you do so, His Highness will bestow many privileges on you and will shower you with favors.

However if you do not do this, or if you maliciously delay your response, you are hereby notified that, with God's support, I will launch an all-out attack to force you to submit and obey the Church and their Highnesses. Furthermore I will enslave you and your women and children and dispose of them as our majesty may command. Also I will seize your goods and inflict harm on you. You will be treated as disobedient vassals. You will be to blame for the resulting injury and death. The blame will not lie with me, their Highnesses, or the soldiers who accompany me. You have been warned. I request that the scribe who is present with me record this warning. May all who are present serve as witnesses.

Source: Author's translation of the Spanish original contained in José Miguel Martínez Torrejón (ed.) (2006) *Brevísima relación de la destrucción de las Indias*. Alicante: Universidad de Alicante, "Notas complementarias," pp. 258–60.

DOCUMENT 2.3: THE SPANIARDS BEHOLD TENOCHTITLAN

[Díaz del Castillo commented on the Spaniards' reaction upon viewing Tenochtitlan:]

When we saw so many cities and villages built in the water and other great towns on dry land and that straight and level Causeway going towards Mexico, we were amazed and said that it was like the enchantments they tell of in the legend of Amadis, on account of the great towers . . . and buildings rising from the water, and all built of masonry. And some of our soldiers even asked whether the things we saw were not a dream. It is not to be wondered at that I here write it down in this manner, for there is so much to think over that I do not know how to describe it, seeing things as we did that had never been heard of or seen before, not even dreamed about.

Thus, we arrived near Iztapalapa to behold the splendor of the other Caciques who came out to meet us, who were the Lord of the town named Cuitlahuac, and the lord of Culuacan, both of them near relations of Montezuma. And then when we entered the city of Iztapalapa, the appearance of the palaces in which they lodges us! How spacious and well built they were, of beautiful stonework and cedar wood, and the wood of other sweet-scented trees, with great rooms and courts, wonderful to behold, covered with awnings of cotton cloth.

When we had looked well at all of this, we went to the orchard and garden, which was such a wonderful thing to see and walk in, that I was never tired of looking at the diversity of the trees, and noting the scent which each one had, and the paths full of roses and flowers, and the many fruit trees and native roses, and the pond of freshwater. There was another thing to observe, that great canoes were able to pass into the garden from the lake through an opening that had been made so that there was no need for their occupants to land. And all was cemented and very splendid with many kinds of stone [monuments] with pictures on them, which gave much to think about. Then the birds of many kinds and breeds which came into the pond. I say again that I stood looking at it and thought that never in the world would there be discovered other lands such as these, for at that time there was no Peru, nor any thought of it. Of all these wonders that I then beheld today all is overthrown and lost, nothing left standing.

Source: David Carrasco (ed.) (2008) *The History of the Conquest of New Spain*. Albuquerque: University of New Mexico Press, pp. 156–57.

DOCUMENT 2.4: VERSION OF THE CONQUERED

[An Aztec poet of the period recorded his feelings after the conquest:]

> Broken spears lie in the roads;
> We have torn our hair in our grief.
> The houses are roofless now; and their walls are red with blood.
> Worms are swarming in the streets and plazas,
> And the walls are spattered with gore.
> The water has turned red, as if it were died.
> And when we drank it,
> It has the taste of brine.
> We have pounded our hands in despair
> Against the adobe walls.
> For our inheritance, our city, is lost and dead.
> The shields of our warriors were its defense,
> But they could not save it.
> We have chewed dry twigs and salt grasses,
> We have filled our mouths with dust and bits of adobe,
> We have eaten lizards, rats and worms

Source: Miguel León-Portilla (1962), *The Broken Spears*. Boston: Beacon, pp. 137–38.

NOTES

1   See Saul Elbein, "The Seeds that Time Forgot," *Texas Observer* 105 (April 2013): 26–29; Isabel Morales Quezada, "Amaranth: From the Sacred to the Everyday," *Voices of Mexico* 86 (Sept.–Dec. 2009): 71–75.

2   Hernán Cortés, *Letters from Mexico* (New York: Grossman, 1971), p. 66.

3   Bartolomé de las Casas, *A Short Account of the Destruction of the Indies* (London: Penguin, 1992), p. 45.

4   Jonathan Kandell, *La Capital* (New York: Random House, 1988), p. 120.

5   Casas, *A Short Account of the Destruction of the Indies*, p. 13.

6   "Their Highnesses" refers to Fernando V, King of Castile and Aragón, and to Juana, Queen of Castile and León. At this time no one person served as monarch of all of Spain. Velázquez did not know Carlos V had assumed the throne.

7   Early Spanish arrivals in the New World used the term mosque to refer to structures built for religious purposes since the non-Christian religious structures they were familiar with were mosques.

8   Grijalva returned to the Cuban port of Matanzas on October 4, 1518. However since this port was 450 miles west of Santiago, when Velázquez wrote the instructions he was unaware Grijalva had returned.

9   Chalchicueyecan was an indigenous town near the modern port of Veracruz. Santa María de las Nieves is a no-longer-used name for Veracruz.

10 Fernando V was King of Castile and Aragón.

11 Juana was Queen of Castille and León.

12 The documents referred to are Pope Alexander VI's bull that awarded Spain and Portugal sovereignty over the Americas.

FURTHER READING

Casas, Bartolomé de las (1992) *A Short Account of the Destruction of the Indies*. London: Penguin.
    A highly critical account of the conquest written by a sixteenth-century priest and defender of Indian rights.

Cortés, Hernán (1971) *Letters from Mexico*. New York: Grossman.
    A detailed description of Cortés's actions, written during the conquest, designed to ingratiate himself with the Spanish emperor.

Díaz del Castillo, Bernal (2008) *The History of the Conquest of New Spain*, ed. Davíd Carrasco (ed.). Albuquerque, N.M.: University of New Mexico Press.
A classic account of the conquest written by one if its participants.

León-Portillo, Miguel (1992) *The Broken Spears*. Boston: Beacon.
Accounts of the conquest provided by those on the losing side.

Thomas, Hugh (1993) *Conquest: Montezuma, Cortés, and the Fall of Old Mexico*. New York: Simon & Schuster.
The most complete modern description of the conquest.

Townsend, Camilla (2006) *Malintzin's Choices*. Albuquerque, N.M.: University of New Mexico Press.
A consideration of the most important female participant in the conquest.

GLOSSARY TERMS

Moors
Reconquest
requerimiento

Chapter 3

Three Centuries of Colonial Rule, 1521–1810

TIMELINE—WORLD

1530–33 Spaniard Francisco Pizarro conquers Peru	**1588** English fleet destroys Spanish Armada	**1607** Jamestown colony founded	**1620** *Mayflower* reaches America	**1626** Dutch buy Manhattan Island from Indians with fishhooks and trinkets
1756–63 Seven Years War pits France and Spain against England	**1759–88** Reign of Carlos III of Spain	**1763** Treaty of Paris ends Seven Years War, France loses North American colonies	**1776** The 13 British North American colonies declare independence	**1783** Peace of Paris ends American War of Independence
1806 British occupy Cape of Good Hope	**1814** Chinese population estimated to be 375 million	**1814–15** Napoleon's defeat at Waterloo is followed by the Congress of Vienna	**1819** British found Singapore	

TIMELINE—MEXICO

1523 First Franciscans arrive in Veracruz	**1524** Council of Indies established.	**1535** Antonio de Mendoza, the first viceroy, arrives	**1540** Coronado expedition travels through what is today the U.S. Southwest and reaches Kansas	**1542** Guadalajara founded
1700 Bourbon rule begins	**1718** San Antonio, Texas, founded	**1742** Census places population at 3,865,529	**1767** Jesuits expelled	**1769** San Diego, California founded

Among the events that have done violence to Mexican history, none shook the foundations on which the indigenous peoples were based with as much force or was as decisive in the formation of a new society and a new historical project as the Spanish Conquest and colonization.

(Enrique Florescano, 1976)

1644–1912 Manchu dynasty in China	**1652** Dutch found Cape Town	**1655** English capture Jamaica from Spain	**1664** English seize Manhattan Island from Dutch and name the city located there New York	**1684** Frenchman René Robert, Sieur de La Salle founds Fort St. Louis on Texas coast
1789 French Revolution	**1800** Louisiana ceded to France by Spain	**1803** Louisiana sold to the United States by France	**1804–1806** Lewis and Clark Expedition	**1805** British defeat Spanish and French fleets in Battle of Trafalgar

1573 Construction begins on Mexico City Cathedral	**1596** Monterrey, Nuevo León, founded	**1598** Juan de Oñate colonizes New Mexico	**ca. 1620** Indian population hits low point	**1639** Chihuahua City founded as San Felipe de Chihuahua
1786 New Spain divided into intendancies	**1808** Mexico's population estimated to be	6.5 million		

THIS CHAPTER BEGINS WITH A DESCRIPTION OF HOW SPANIARDS EXTENDED their realm beyond the former Aztec capital. It then considers the special institutions established to administer a colony an ocean away from the seat of imperial power in Madrid. Next is a description of how a thin overlay of Spanish culture and control in the sixteenth century evolved to yield a new Mexican culture while at the same time preserving indigenous cultures. Concluding the chapter is a discussion of the Catholic Church, which rather than being separate from the state was inextricably bound to it.

FROM CONQUISTADOR TO ADMINISTRATOR

The fall of Tenochtitlan marked the end of the Aztec empire. However outside the Valley of Mexico, the Spanish presence in the former empire was minimal. In even more distant parts of what is today's Mexico, this presence was virtually non-existent. Centuries would pass before effective Spanish control was established over many outlying areas.

During Cortés's ill-advised 1524 absence from Mexico to subdue an insubordinate lieutenant in Honduras, his enemies irreparably undermined his power, accusing him of keeping booty that legally belonged to the Crown and embezzling other funds. After his return the Crown dismissed the charges filed in his absence. Also forgiven was his own insubordination, which had involved only Governor Velázquez, not the monarch. However, Cortés still presented the emperor with a dilemma. Carlos V wished to reward the conquistador for his services. Yet he wanted to keep Cortés's power in check so that he would not threaten the Crown. He resolved this dilemma by appointing a viceroy (administrator) for Mexico and then removing Cortés from formal administration. At the same time, he amply rewarded Cortés, granting him access to many thousands of acres of grazing land and more extensive *encomienda* (tribute and labor) rights than those of any other conquistador.

To consolidate their control, the Spanish organized various expeditions to extend their domain. In 1523 Pedro de Alvarado led 300 Spaniards and nearly 20,000 Indians south from Mexico City. Alvarado's force passed through Oaxaca and established Spanish rule in territory now forming Chiapas, Guatemala, and El Salvador.

In 1529 Nuño de Guzmán marched west through Michoacán. His foray, brutal even by the standards of the times, reached southern Sonora, burning villages, enslaving Indians, and executing Indian leaders, including Cazonci, the Tarascan king, who was accused of fomenting succession. Guzmán's expedition neatly illustrated the Crown's values. No one raised an objection to his having enslaved Indians to be sold in Spain's Caribbean possessions. The Crown simply levied taxes on their sale. However, royal authorities would not tolerate regicide and in 1537 imprisoned Guzmán for his atrocities.

These expeditions laid the basis for Spanish colonization, which was more pervasive than that of the Aztecs. Unlike the Aztecs, the Spanish imposed their culture and language on others. Spaniards also progressively deprived conquered Indians of direct control of their land. As Mexican historian Enrique Florescano noted:

Pre-Hispanic man was totally integrated with the earth, his land, his community, nature, and the cosmos. This deep, inextricable integration began to disappear with increasing rapidity when the Spanish appeared and appropriated land. Upon losing their land, and as the nature of its use changed radically, the Indians also lost their place in the world and their relationship with other men, nature, and the cosmos.[1]

COLONIAL ADMINISTRATION

> The New World fell before a small group of enterprising conquistadores, yet force alone could not construct an empire. In the end, ideas relegated the conquerors to subordinate positions, and organized a vast and varied aboriginal population of different historical, cultural, and political traditions under royal control.
>
> (Colin MacLachlan, 1988)

While the Spanish were extending their control out from the former Aztec capital, they were laying the foundation for the administration of the newly conquered territory. At the top of this administrative apparatus was the Spanish monarch who presented his kingdom as a political and territorial division within the universal church founded by Christ himself. However, one individual, with or without divine sanction, could not administer an empire. The king readily acknowledged interest groups such as merchant guilds and often granted them self-policing powers and responsibilities now associated with a modern state. Various advisors, councils, and corporate groups surrounded the king. Petitioners, who inflated their own importance in an attempt to gain a hearing, constantly besieged him.

To cope with the increasingly complex demands of administering the New World lands claimed by Spain, Carlos V established the Council of the Indies in 1524. The Council consisted of a president and eight councilors who oversaw the political, ecclesiastical, and judicial affairs of Spain's New World colonies. These nine men answered only to the king.

Since a round-trip voyage between Spain and Veracruz required six months, day-to-day administration obviously had to be vested in officials residing in the New World. Thus the Crown divided the Spanish empire into large administrative units called viceroyalties, each headed by a **viceroy**. The viceroyalty of New Spain, with its seat in Mexico City, included territory stretching from Costa Rica to California, and, in addition, Florida, the Philippine Islands, Spain's Caribbean colonies, and part of Venezuela. Throughout the colonial period, as a result of its being the seat of viceregal administration, Mexico City exercised a greater influence on Mexico than had Tenochtitlan before the Conquest.

Given the influence of local economic interests, as well as isolation from Spain, the viceroy could carry out policy markedly at odds with royal decrees. The phrase "*Obedezco pero no cumplo*" ("I obey but I do not comply") summarized this attitude. To stall on implementing a matter at odds with local interests, the viceroy could simply request clarification and postpone action for a year or more. Viceroys also engaged in semantic evasion. For example in 1585 a royal decree unequivocally prohibited the collection of tribute from Tlaxcala. Authorities in New Spain simply reclassified the tribute as a "*reconocimiento*" ("recognition") and continued to collect it. That way they could have access to Indian wealth without openly defying the king. Often the viceregal administration would yield part but not all of what the Crown demanded. As historian John Lynch commented, "Usually there emerged a workable compromise between what central authorities ideally wanted and what local conditions and pressures would realistically tolerate."

The king appointed judges to a judicial body known as the *audiencia*, which served as Mexico's supreme court of appeals and as a consultative body. After a viceroy's death, *audiencia* judges, or *oidores*, administered the colony until the next viceroy arrived.

Districts embracing several municipalities, known either as *corregimientos* or *alcaldías mayores*, formed an intermediate administrative layer. Such districts were under the jurisdiction, respectively, of a **corregidor** or an *alcalde mayor*. These officials exercised discretionary executive and judicial powers and often engaged in the endemic corruption, bribery, and extortion that occurred at the local level. Normally such officials would serve three- to five-year terms after having been appointed or having purchased their position. Their duties included civil administration, justice, and tax and tribute collection. As with the viceroy, they also played a religious role, ensuring that Indians attended Mass and met religious obligations.

The municipality (*municipio*), which usually included a head town (*cabecera*) and outlying villages, formed the smallest significant administrative unit. Many of the early municipalities had the same boundaries as the Aztec **altepetl**, with the old ceremonial center becoming the cabecera. A municipal council (*cabildo*) of from four to fifteen members, depending on population size, presided over municipal governments. Conquistadors and holders of *encomienda* grants initially selected *cabildo* members. Later landowners and merchants made such selections. However, beginning with the reign of Felipe II, who ruled Spain from 1556 to 1598, the Crown began selling these positions, which could be inherited. By the late colonial period, a self-perpetuating oligarchy manned most municipal councils.

Rather than implementing a tax policy that would be judged sound by modern standards, the Crown obtained revenue by auctioning positions in government to the highest bidder. Buyers expected that through fees, bribes, and the ability to profit in business they would recoup their investment and make a profit. The purchase of office allowed **creoles**—those of Spanish ancestry born in the New World—to dominate municipal governments and become *alcaldes mayores* and *corregidores*.

The sale of office increased abuse, since in addition to the high costs of travel and setting up new households, office holders had to recoup the amount paid for office. Today this would be viewed as corruption. At the time, the populace regarded buying office as an investment in a revenue source that guaranteed the best men—those with a genuine stake in society—would occupy top positions. People judged officials not as honest or corrupt but by the degree to which they enriched themselves. Only flagrant excess brought condemnation.

Local officials often engaged in a practice known as the *repartimiento de bienes* (distribution of goods). They would force their constituents to buy goods on credit at a price they set and then demand the purchaser to pay back the resulting debt over time, either in kind or in cash. By opening up a market, this practice linked local economies with regional and international economies. Officials set both the price of the merchandise and of the in-kind goods offered in payment. This practice did facilitate credit for buyers, but more frequently saddled them with an overpriced item they did not really want. The Crown sought to suppress the *repartimiento de bienes*, not out of humanistic concern, but to channel more tribute to Spain.

The Habsburg colonial administration, which lasted until 1700, was a creaking cumbersome engine that consumed great quantities of paper, energy, and cash payments. These payments—bribes and the sale of offices—were essential if the system was to function. The Habsburg regimes followed the dictum of letting sleeping dogs lie. They did not entertain grand visions of social transformation, being content with limited controls and limited fiscal benefit. Typically the Habsburgs relied on consensus, using repression only in a selective fashion. Loyalty to God and king undergirded governance. This loyalty was so pervasive that during the almost 200 years the Habsburgs ruled Mexico, no concerted challenge to the Crown emerged.

THE SIXTEENTH CENTURY

> Assignment of *encomiendas* based on conquest contributions created a new gentry in New Spain including individuals who, had it not been for the chance of time and place, would never have risen above their plebeian origins.
>
> (Robert Himmerich y Valencia, 1991)

The first viceroy, Antonio de Mendoza, came from a prominent Castilian noble house, ideal for offsetting Cortés's influence. Mendoza, who arrived in 1535, invested in commerce, textile manufacturing, and agricultural enterprises, thus setting a precedent for his successors. Mendoza proved to be such an able administrator that he remained in office for sixteen years—a length of tenure that would never be equaled. At the end of his term, in recognition of his having stabilized the core and completed far-ranging reconnaissance, he was appointed viceroy of Peru.

Fierce competition between the Crown, clergymen, and Spanish settlers for a shrinking amount of Indian labor and a dwindling supply of tribute dominated early colonial history. The Crown pursued the mutually exclusive goals of humanitarian treatment for Indians and maximizing income for the mother country. Initially the Crown prohibited enslaving Indians, but reversed itself after receiving a barrage of complaints pleading the economic necessity of slavery. Similarly in 1528 the emperor prohibited the use of Indian labor in gold mines to prevent the extinction of the indigenous population—something that was already occurring in the Caribbean. However, in 1536 he revoked the decree to "insure the expanding mining industry the labor it needs."

Shortly after the conquest, Cortés began awarding grants known as *encomiendas*—a practice copied from the Spanish colonies in the Caribbean. The Caribbean grants in turn resembled the grants made to Spaniards who had captured territory from Moors during the Reconquest of Spain. Conquistadors viewed *encomiendas* as payment due them for services rendered during the conquest of Mexico.

Each *encomienda* gave Spaniards the right to collect tribute in the form of clothing, food, and other products from the Indians living in a certain area. While the grant allowed Spaniards to benefit from Indian labor, indigenous customs and local governments were largely unaffected. In exchange for receiving the fruits of Indian labor, Spaniards assumed responsibility for Christianizing the Indians included in the grant. However, the repeated sale and reassignment of *encomiendas* indicated that the Spanish viewed the grant more as an economic asset than as a religious responsibility.

The granting of *encomiendas* became a form of royal and viceregal patronage used to reward individuals who had not participated in the conquest. These grants persuaded many adventurous Spaniards to remain in New Spain. The *encomienda* enabled early Spaniards to accumulate enough wealth to establish their own enterprises. Recipients of these grants formed the first rudimentary rural administration before the establishment of conventional local government.

The first **encomenderos** enjoyed quasi-seigniorial rights and constituted an aristocracy for several decades. They not only demanded material tribute but forced Indians to transport their goods and build their houses, roads, and farm buildings. Through the mid-1500s, the *encomienda* allowed the conquistadors to survive on a plunder economy.

Early in the colonial period, the *encomienda* drew criticism. The Crown feared *encomenderos* would form a hereditary aristocracy that would threaten its power. Christian humanists pressured the Crown to lessen the abuse of Indians, noting that *encomenderos* rarely fulfilled the reciprocal duty of evangelization. *Encomenderos* collected tribute that Indians would otherwise have paid to the Crown. As a result, the king restricted the inheritability of the *encomienda*. Although Cortés's descendants retained their tribute rights, by about 1575 the descendants of most other *encomenderos* had lost their rights, and Indians paid tribute directly to the Crown. This phase-out of the *encomienda* continued into the seventeenth century.

Other factors contributed to the decline in the *encomienda*, which had dominated New Spanish society in the mid-1540s. After that date, the available tribute fell as the Indian population collapsed. Some *encomenderos* found a sedentary life uninteresting, abandoned their grants, and left for distant lands. The Crown capped the amount of tribute *encomenderos* could demand and in 1549 made it illegal to demand labor, as opposed to goods, from those included in the grant. Finally the relative position of *encomenderos* declined as new sources of income, such as silver mines, became available.

The New Laws of 1542 illustrate the conflict between the Crown's desire for humanitarian treatment of the Indian and colonial political reality. These laws prohibited enslaving Indians, even as punishment for resisting Spanish domination. They also prohibited new *encomienda* grants and stipulated that existing *encomienda* rights would terminate with the death of the current holder. Had this provision been enforced, the *encomienda* would have vanished within a generation.

In Peru, colonists rebelled and killed the viceroy sent to enforce the New Laws. Fearing such a response in Mexico, Viceroy Mendoza refrained from enforcing the new regulations. *Encomenderos*

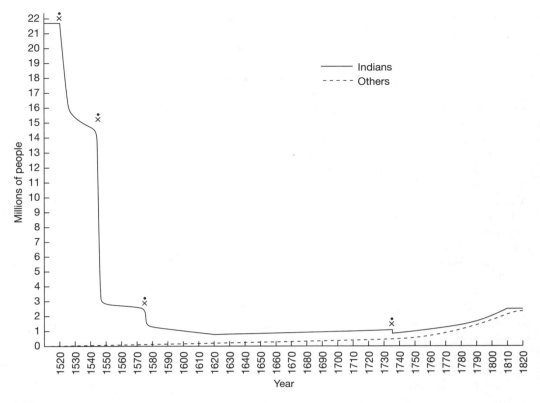

Figure 3.1 *This graph illustrates one of the great tragedies of human history—the disease-related decline of Mexico's colonial population. Despite this decline, Indians remained a majority past the end of the eighteenth century.*

Source: Adapted from Peter Gerhard, *Guide to the Historical Geography of New Spain,* revised edition (Norman, OK: University of Oklahoma Press, 1993). Copyright: the University of Oklahoma Press.

alleged they could not survive without the *encomienda*. The *encomienda* had powerful backers in Mexico, such as the Bishop of Mexico, Juan de Zumárraga, who held an *encomienda*. Given adamant opposition in the colonies, the Crown reversed itself and granted inheritance rights to the children and grandchildren of *encomenderos*.

The epidemics following the conquest caused population loss exceeding that caused by the Black Death in fifteenth-century Europe. An eyewitness account estimated 60 to 90 percent mortality from the 1545–48 epidemic alone. Compound epidemics and the rudimentary state of medical knowledge limited identification of specific diseases. Modern scholars consider the most lethal diseases to have been smallpox, typhus, measles, and influenza.

Some modern estimates put the Indian population *loss* at more than 95 percent of the pre-conquest population of central Mexico. Spanish atrocities, especially during the first wave of the conquest, lowered population, as did the incorporation of Indian women (voluntarily and involuntarily) into the reproductive system of the whites. Population loss was greatest in the low-lying tropical areas along the Pacific and Gulf coasts since people there had more contact with arriving Spaniards and the hot, wet climate facilitated the rapid transmission of newly introduced diseases. Hundreds of villages along the coasts simply ceased to exist. In addition, mortality increased as excessive labor and tribute demands by Spaniards left villagers unable to provide for themselves.

To meet their increasing labor needs at a time of Indian population decline, the Spanish adopted the *repartimiento* in 1549. This institution reflected the increasing scarcity of Indian labor and the establishment of enterprises by Spaniards who needed Indian workers. It forced Indians to work directly for Spaniards for a certain number of days a year. To meet its *repartimiento* obligation, a village supplied laborers who would march off for a week or two of work. Spanish authorities relied on Indian leaders to ensure that labor was delivered to Spanish employers. After the fulfillment of one group's labor obligation, the workers would return to their village and other workers would replace them. The Crown set the wage level for *repartimiento* workers and denied them the right to seek higher wages. During the growing season, Indian villages normally supplied from 2 to 4 percent of their adult male laborers, and at harvest time 10 percent. This institution placed Indian workers under Spanish supervision and exposed them to European agricultural techniques for the first time. However, it did not threaten the viability of the Indian community since each individual only left the community for a short period.

The *repartimiento* had replaced the *encomienda* as the main source of Indian labor by the middle of the sixteenth century. It flourished between the 1550s and the 1630s and provided the Spanish with labor during the Indian population nadir. Spanish authorities subjected Indians who tried to escape *repartimiento* service and community leaders who failed to supply the demanded number of laborers to imprisonment, fines, and corporal punishment.

Repartimiento laborers tilled Spaniards' fields, which allowed the provisioning of cities with products such as wheat, which the Spanish preferred to corn. These involuntary workers also engaged in mining and the construction of aqueducts, roads, and public buildings. Spaniards often abused their rights, forcing villages to supply more laborers than the amount legally stipulated and requiring workers to continue working longer than the law required.

THE SEVENTEENTH CENTURY

In contrast to the sixteenth century, which saw the grafting of a Spanish elite onto existing Indian societies, the seventeenth century saw a unique Mexican society emerge—an amalgam of previous cultures. Urban markets, mines, Spanish tribute demands, and a decline in the Indian population led to a relative decline in production for one's own consumption. There was a concomitant increase in the acquisition of goods through tribute, barter, and, increasingly, cash or credit.

During the early seventeenth century, the indigenous population decline continued, especially in central Mexico. Indigenous communities were impacted by the Spaniards' appropriating Indian land, the spread of grazing animals that fed on Indians' crops, and Indian males having to work to fulfill their *repartimiento* obligation rather than producing food for their own community.

By the 1620s the indigenous population began to rebound since Indians had developed some immunity to European-introduced disease. This immunity resulted from Darwinian selection and from immunity acquired as mixed-race members of the Indian community inherited immunity from Old World ancestors. The surviving indigenous population could abandon marginal lands and plant only the best Indian-held land. Indian productivity also increased as they incorporated Spanish elements into their productive system. This population recovery came too late to prevent the Europeanization of Mexico. Rather than remaining a predominantly Indian nation, such as Guatemala or Bolivia, Mexico emerged as a predominantly European and **mestizo** nation.

In 1632, the *repartimiento* was abolished except in mining districts. By then, no major social group remained dependent on that institution. Humanists saw forced labor as wrong and abusive. The *repartimiento* led to a decrease in tribute paid to the Crown since many indigenous peasants left their community, temporarily or permanently, in favor of the hacienda, the mine, and the city to avoid *repartimiento* service. Wages paid those fleeing the *repartimiento* exceeded those paid for *repartimiento* labor. At the same time, an increasing number of mixed-race individuals began working on haciendas, lessening the demand for *repartimiento* labor.

The end of the *repartimiento* reflected the Crown's declining power. Control of Indian labor passed from the hands of royal officials, who administered the *repartimiento*, to employers who became the workers' master, legislator, and judge. This shift to wage labor favored large growers since they had access to the cash needed to attract new workers by loaning them money. Laborers often remained on Spanish-owned estates because they needed wages to pay taxes or because they lacked any other attractive option. Often what passed as wage labor had little to do with cash. Landowners would provide the means of subsistence—food rations, housing, and the right to sow a plot of land—in exchange for an Indian's labor. With the possible exception of an initial loan, cash might never change hands.

THE EIGHTEENTH CENTURY

> The Bourbon reformers wanted to establish an authoritarian state, not one based on consensus.
>
> (Jaime Rodríguez O., 2012)

In 1700 Spanish King Carlos II died without leaving an heir. This gave the great European powers the opportunity to gain control of the Spanish Crown, which in turn would provide access to New World wealth. At the end of the ensuing power struggle, known as the War of Spanish Succession (1702–1713), Felipe V, the grandson of French King Louis XIV, came to the Spanish throne—the first of the Bourbon dynasty.

During the latter part of the eighteenth century, the Spanish government implemented a number of measures, generally known as the Bourbon reforms, since members of that dynasty implemented them. These reforms responded to challenges presented by the more efficient regimes emerging in northern Europe. The Crown justified the resulting increase in state power by claiming that such an increase promoted the material prosperity of its subjects. These reforms led to substantial tax increases, which offended colonial taxpayers and undermined the stated aim of improving colonists' lives.

The notion of the monarch as the promoter of public well-being replaced the notion of the monarch as a simple upholder of natural law. The Bourbon reforms centralized finance and imperial administration and eliminated corporate privilege, political autonomy, and commercial monopolies. They also favored industries, such as mining, which would provide revenue to the Crown. Bourbon rulers expected Mexico to cover its administrative costs, subsidize defense costs throughout the viceroyalty, and still transfer a substantial surplus to Spain. Fulfilling these goals required limiting the power of creoles. The Crown felt this group manipulated politics and retarded development. Administrative reforms already undertaken by the French and British provided a model for the Bourbon reforms.

In 1767, following the example set by France and Portugal, Carlos III ordered the expulsion of Jesuits from the New World and the confiscation of the order's estates and other assets. This represented an attempt by the Spanish king, who resented Jesuit wealth, power, and independence, to establish the supremacy of the state over the Church. He regarded the Jesuits as an autonomous, secretive international society in much the same way as some small nations today regard multinational corporations. At the time of their expulsion, the 678 Jesuits in Mexico maintained 41 rural estates, more than a hundred missions in northwestern Mexico, and the best schools, including 27 colleges and various seminaries.

In response to the Jesuits' expulsion, rebellion broke out in Michoacán, San Luis Potosí, and Guanajuato. These violent outbursts by people from all walks of life came after years of resistance to militia recruitment, tax increases, and revenue monopolies. The elite joined the protests of their less affluent compatriots due to the Jesuits' importance in supplying credit and educating wealthy creoles. Protesters not only supported the Jesuits, but demanded lower taxes, access to land, and an end to the tobacco monopoly. After the army quelled these protests, authorities hanged eighty-five people and sentenced many others to exile, flogging, and life in prison. The expulsion of the Jesuits made it clear that the Crown expected submission, not discussion. Viceroy Marquis de Croix ordered Mexicans to accept the expulsion since "the subjects of the great monarch who occupies the throne of Spain should know once and for all that they were born to keep silent and obey, not to discuss or express opinion on high matters of government."

In 1786, the Council of the Indies ordered that Mexico be divided into twelve new administrative districts, or intendancies, headed by an intendant. Most of these administrative units, such as Durango, San Luis Potosí, and Yucatán, remain as the modern states of Mexico. Intendants promoted economic growth, kept tabs on the Church, and oversaw public administration, finance, justice, military preparedness, public works, and revenue collection. In many cases they modernized cities with lighting, new tree-lined avenues, and improved water supplies and drainage. Since intendants reported directly to the Minister of the Indies in Madrid, rather than to the viceroy, the political links between the provinces and Mexico City were weakened. A tumultuous century would elapse before such links could be firmly reestablished.

To the modern observer, many of the changes instituted by the Bourbons appear to be the epitome of sound administration. In 1755, the first free public school opened in Mexico City. During that decade, the Crown ceased to sell public office. In 1792, the Crown founded the Royal College of Mining, the first technical school in the New World. Its professors applied recent advances in physics, mineralogy, and chemistry to mining. This mining school provided a generation of creoles with a sound technical and scientific education. In addition the Bourbons sent foreign technology and mining missions to upgrade Mexican mines. In 1804, less than a decade after the discovery of the smallpox vaccination, the Spanish government dispatched teams of medical workers to carry out a massive immunization program in Mexico. Team members not only vaccinated tens of thousands, but trained Mexican doctors and *curanderos* in the technique.

However, to the late eighteenth-century creole observer, the reforms were an unwelcome intrusion. Creoles had grown accustomed to staffing the colonial bureaucracy and resented Spaniards' displacing them from the *audiencia* and other positions. Only one of the twelve people appointed to head the newly created intendancies was a creole. Peasants, as well as the elite, resented tax increases and the extension of tribute to new groups. The Crown assumed control of community funds previously beyond the reach of officials. In the name of equality and efficiency, Indians received less special protection.

For most of the colonial period, the Spanish had not felt the need for a large standing army. Other institutions, especially the Church, maintained social control. As late as 1758, most of the 3,000 soldiers stationed in Mexico were in port cities or on the northern frontier. However, after the British occupied Havana during the Seven Years' War (1756–63), the Crown decided Mexico needed protection from other European powers. As a result, by the turn of the nineteenth century, the regular infantry had increased to 8,800 and a 22,000-man militia had been formed. The infantry was concentrated in the Veracruz area to prevent British invasion, while militia forces were organized in practically all the cities of the viceroyalty. Colonial subjects were expected to bear the costs of the militia.

As large estates devoured increasing amounts of land and the population increased, the rural poor were caught in a Malthusian vice. Population increase led to an oversupply of rural labor, which resulted in a 25 percent decrease in the buying power of wages between 1775 and independence. This produced a steady migration of unskilled workers to cities, especially to Mexico City. In 1786 Viceroy Bernardo de Gálvez declared that the many beggars, vagabonds, and unemployed in Mexico City threatened religion, the state, and public tranquillity.

Annual population growth during the eighteenth century averaged about 0.75 percent. In both 1742 and 1810, Indians comprised about 60 percent of Mexico's population, indicating that the Indian and non-Indian populations were increasing at about the same rate. Those of mixed race

Figure 3.2 *Colonial Mexican church architecture varied greatly. Pictured here is an engraving by Pedro Gualdi which depicts the sanctuary to honor the Virgin of Guadalupe.*

Source: D. A. Brading, *Mexican Phoenix* (Cambridge: Cambridge University Press, 2001), p. 241.

(*castas*) were the next most numerous group, with 22 percent, while creoles and Spaniards comprised 18 percent. Even though New Spain's population had increased to 6.1 million by 1810, it remained considerably below the pre-conquest level.

At the beginning of the nineteenth century an estimated 137,000 lived in Mexico City. The city's population increased during the late eighteenth century as many migrated from neighboring areas due to crop failures, population increase and haciendas' encroaching on village lands. By 1800, Mexico City was the largest, most prosperous city in the New World. It continued to be bicultural, although its racial proportions had shifted. At the beginning of the nineteenth century, native-born Spaniards comprised 2 percent of its population, creoles 48 percent, Indians 27 percent, and mixed-race individuals 23 percent.

THE CHURCH

> Was the religious conversion of Mexico's Indians in the sixteenth century a glorious "spiritual conquest" or a sordid story of oppression, coercion and dissimulation?
> (Alan Knight, 2002)

The notion of separation of Church and state was completely alien to colonial Mexico. The Crown micromanaged Church activity in Mexico while the Vatican provided the legal underpinning for the Spanish colony. In 1493 Pope Alexander VI responded to Columbus's first voyage to the New World by issuing papal bulls that awarded Spain and Portugal sovereignty over the Americas. The bulls drew an imaginary north–south line one hundred leagues west of the Azores and the Cape Verde islands. Spain was granted the newly discovered lands west of this line. These bulls provided the religious justification for the Spanish Conquest and control of the New World. The Spanish jurist Juan de Solórzano y Pereyra succinctly stated this rationale in his *Política Indiana*. He claimed that the Indians

> because they are so barbarous . . . needed somebody who, by assuming the duties of governing, defending and teaching them, would reduce them to a human, civil, social and political life, so that they should acquire the capacity to receive the Faith and the Christian religion.[2]

Since the Vatican did not have the resources to spread the Gospel in the New World, it transferred unprecedented control, known as the *patronato real* (royal patronage), over the Church to the Spanish monarchs as incentive for them to Christianize their colonies. In 1501, to compensate for the financial outlay required by missionary work in the New World, Pope Alexander VI allowed the Spanish monarchs to collect tithes in the New World. As a further incentive to evangelization, Spanish monarchs received the right to establish diocesan boundaries, administer church finances, nominate bishops, and review (or censor) all communications between the pope and the Church in Spanish America. While this transfer of power later had immense significance, at the dawn of the sixteenth century it did not seem as significant since little was known of the extent and wealth of the New World.

Formal missionary activity began in 1524 when twelve Franciscan friars arrived in Veracruz and walked barefoot in patched robes to Mexico City. Upon their arrival, to the amazement of nearby Indians, Cortés knelt in the dust and kissed their hands and the hems of their robes.

One of the twelve was named Toribio de Benavente. As he was walking through New Spain, he repeatedly heard indigenous people saying "motolinía." Upon inquiring what the word meant, he learned it meant "poor person." Benavente then adopted Motolinía as his name. He became a zealous missionary and an early defender of Indians against Spanish mistreatment. In 1541 he published *Historia de los indios de la Nueva España,* one of the earliest histories of colonial Mexico.

These friars began what has been called "the spiritual conquest of Mexico." By 1559, approximately 800 friars were working among a native population of 2.65 million. The mendicant orders—the Franciscans, the Dominicans, and the Augustinians—dedicated themselves to missionary work. Their devotion to preaching and teaching, and their flexibility, mobility, superior education, and intense zeal made them ideal for this task. Missionaries willingly endured harsh climate, new foods, disease, and even martyrdom. As historian Alan Knight remarked, "Like Castilian society as a whole, the Church was a crusading institution, newly invigorated by the heady triumph over Moorish Granada . . ."

Missionaries often formed the only communication channel between colonial authorities and the indigenous population. Indians were aware that conversion to Christianity allowed them to appeal to both the friars and the Crown for protection. Despite clerical efforts to isolate Indians physically and spiritually from the rest of colonial society, labor demands and the marketing of Indian products inexorably linked the two groups.

Clergymen vied with *encomenderos* for influence over Indians and protected them against extortion by merchants and abuse by *corregidores*. Priests supported the continued separation of the Indian and Spanish populations, believing they could create a new society under Church, not secular, control. The friars not only sought to uproot indigenous religious belief but to preserve the pristine, non-materialistic, and somewhat idealized Indian community. The desire to separate Indians from Spaniards reflected the clergy's concern that otherwise Spanish abuse would decimate Mexico's Indian population.

The vast area of Spanish America, which stretched from Argentina to California, presented missionaries with a monumental challenge. The area's extreme linguistic diversity compounded the difficulty of their task. Missionary priests rejected imposing the Spanish language on Indians. They argued it would be better to convert infidels by learning indigenous languages and translating

Christian precepts into these languages. Many languages they encountered lacked the vocabulary to express central concepts of Christianity such as "soul" and "devil." To facilitate their ministry, the Franciscans, who took the lead in learning native languages, published vocabularies and catechisms in such Indian languages as Tarascan, Nahuatl, Mazáhua, and Otomí.

In numerical terms, the early friars' efforts at converting Indians to Christianity proved fabulously successful. The Franciscan Fray Toribio de Benavente commented on early conversion efforts, "I believe that after this land was won, which was in 1521, up to the time I am writing this, which is in the year 1536, more than four million souls have been baptized." Another missionary, Pedro de Gante, boasted that in one day, with the aid of only one companion, he had baptized 14,000 Indians. The takeover of entire high cultures, such as the Tarascan, facilitated such mass conversion. In addition, the poverty and simplicity of the first friars impressed an indigenous population accustomed to deferring to an ascetic priesthood.

Many of those baptized had only a rudimentary understanding of Christianity. Due to the lack of personnel and problems with translation, instruction dealt only with the fundamental tenants of Christianity. In one instance, Jesuits in northern Mexico used the example of a dammed soul surrounded by rings of fire and serpents to explain the concept of hell. Indians responded with smiles, noting that in such a place surely no one would suffer from cold nights or go hungry thanks to the snakes, which they considered a delicacy.

Churchmen soon became aware that initial, euphoric conversions had been neither as pervasive nor as profound as the early missionaries had hoped. Persuading Indians to reject their old gods after they accepted the Christian one presented an enduring problem. Rather than simply switching religions, Indians frequently added or reworked Christian concepts and rituals according to their existing belief system. In 1530, Benavente commented that Indians concealed idols "at the foot of the crosses or beneath the stones of the altar steps, pretending that they were venerating the cross, whereas they were actually adoring the demon." He also noted that the Indians' acceptance of the image of Christ merely resulted in the Indians having 101 idols, where a hundred had existed before. In 1581, the Dominican Diego Durán wrote, "They *believed* in God and at the same time *practiced* the old ways and ritual of the devil." In part the Spanish were responsible for this fusion of pagan and Christian beliefs. In an effort to show the superiority of Christianity, they often built churches on top of pre-existing religious sites. Rather than indicating the superiority of Christianity, in many Indian minds this linked pre-existing and Christian beliefs.

Despite the clergy's persistent efforts to eradicate them, pagan beliefs endured throughout the colonial period. Even though the Maya were baptized and thus officially converted, they continued old family rituals in the house and agricultural rituals in the fields. In Yucatán, even the wealthiest and most influential colonists acknowledged the superior supernatural powers of the Maya belief system and sought their help when in need to exorcise a bewitched cow, to remove a curse from a field, or to cure an ailment or infertility.

In 1700, two Dominican fathers surprised the majority of the population of Francisco Cajonos, an Oaxacan village, as they sacrificed a deer and birds and said prayers in Zapotec. Two members of their own community, Juan Bautista and Jacinto de los Ángeles, had denounced them to the priests. The next day the two were savagely beaten and executed by their enraged fellow townspeople. In reprisal, the Spanish hanged fifteen people from the town.

The Church did not have a consistent policy for dealing with idolatry it encountered. In an 1819 case, Otomí near Lerma, in the present state of Mexico, set up an altar with food and danced around it in honor of Llemixuite, one of their ancient gods. They sought protection in exchange for their honoring the deity. The Indians were put on trial for this religious heterodoxy. However, the ecclesiastical judges did not punish the Indians, who were declared to have acted out of ignorance and due to "lack of instruction" in matters of faith.

Even though the early friars plunged into mission work, from a theological point of view the Indians' nature remained unclear. Some conquistadors claimed the Indians were animals. This had more than theological implications. If indeed Indians were deemed to be animals, the clergy would be in no position to check the conquistadors' abuse of Indians and their property. As a result the clergy waged a concerted effort to persuade the pope to declare unequivocally the Indians' humanity. As part of this effort, in about 1535, Julián Garcés, the bishop of Tlaxcala, lauded the Indians' intelligence and willingness to receive the faith and declared they were not "turbulent or ungovernable but reverent, shy and obedient to their teachers."

Pope Paul III responded to these efforts by declaring the Indians' humanity in a 1537 bull entitled *Sublimis Deus*. It established that "Indians are truly men and that they are not only capable of understanding the Catholic faith but, according to our information, they desire exceedingly to receive it." The bull also stated, "The said Indians and all other people who may later be discovered by Christians, are by no means to be deprived of their liberty or the possession of their property, even though they be outside the faith of Jesus Christ."

During the early sixteenth century, there existed a genuine, though unequal, alliance between missionaries and Indians. Priests defended Indian rights and served as intermediaries between village authority and civil authority at higher levels. As time passed, this alliance weakened. In 1555, the First Provincial Council of Mexico prohibited the ordination of Indians. In 1571, the Church removed Indians from the authority of the Inquisition after deeming them mentally incapable of understanding the faith.

Gradually the Church lost interest in native languages and began to doubt its ability to alter the indigenous worldview. The missionaries' initial optimism gave way to viewing Indians as idle, barbarous, and backsliding in religious matters. Priests increasingly complained that rural assignments exiled them from the civil world they had known as students. Many priests would only settle in parishes where numerous non-Indians lived. Such priests made infrequent visits to remote villages to administer sacraments. This trend became more pronounced near the end of the colonial period. In 1791, seventy-five priests lived in the city of Querétaro and only thirteen lived in the rest of the *corregimiento*, despite its having twice the population of the city. Historian Colin MacLachlan commented, "The colonial church, increasingly institutionalized, became an enclave and sanctuary of European culture amid a no longer pliable mass of Indians who had drawn a line beyond which they would not go."

The role of the Church evolved from initial conversion of Indians to ministering to long-established communities. Villagers depended on priests for spiritual consolation, for certain leadership and social welfare functions, and to mediate between community and state. These priests depended on their flock for sustenance and legitimacy.

The Bourbons were not anti-clerical in the sense of questioning the validity of Christianity. However they sought to appropriate wealth of the Church and curtail its power, which they considered politically offensive, economically retrograde, and culturally stifling. Officials felt that in many cases parish priests acted as de facto civil administrators—a usurpation of power claimed by the monarchy. As a result, priests' legal privileges—the ecclesiastical *fuero*—were reduced, and Church courts were prohibited from inflicting corporal punishment.

Shortly after the conquest, the Church viewed itself as a spiritual counterweight to the materialist Spaniards. However, by the eighteenth century it mirrored colonial society in many respects. Spaniards, rather than creoles, generally received appointment to the most desirable posts. Between 1713 and 1800, only one New World-born person presided over any of the three wealthiest dioceses of New Spain—Mexico City, Puebla, and Michoacán. The few creoles who became bishops oversaw the poorest dioceses. Priests appointed to the choice positions in cathedral chapters or who served in wealthy, urban parishes reached these positions through academic achievement, often holding doctorates in the sacred sciences. Only wealthy families could afford to keep sons in the university long enough to obtain such degrees. The few Indian priests tended to be assigned to distant rural parishes among their own people. Blacks and mulattoes were specifically barred from the priesthood.

In theory Catholicism in Durango, Mexico, was the same as the Catholicism practiced in Durango, Spain. In practice, however, Mexican Catholicism was a syncretic religion, combing orthodox Catholicism with elements of indigenous belief systems. Since different indigenous groups maintained different belief systems, the resulting syncretic, or popular, religion varied greatly within Mexico. Post-conquest syncretism continued the pre-conquest tradition of indigenous people combining their conquerors' belief systems with their own.

Popular religion, which manifested itself in innumerable festivals, came under scrutiny from both clerics and colonial officials. To the Spanish, popular practices involved excessive drinking, dancing, and fighting. The songs sung at these festivals even came under scrutiny for the taint of paganism. Indeed much of our knowledge of colonial popular religion comes from official attempts to suppress such activity.

The most conspicuous popular religious observances were Carnival and the Day of the Dead. Carnival often involved men dressing as women, the poor sporting frocked coats of the rich, and peasants dressed as priests—actions which were viewed as challenges to the social order.

Innumerable other observances rounded out the religious calendar. Colonials marched in processions and pilgrimages to honor the **Virgin of Guadalupe**. Each brotherhood, barrio, guild, institution, and village had its own patron saint. Saints days were celebrated with gusto, reaffirming the identity of the group which was celebrating.

In addition to public celebrations there were more private practices. Throughout the colonial period both *curanderos* and *hechiceros*—part medicine man and part shaman—remained influential. *Hechiceros* told fortunes and ingested psychotropic plants. Along with *curanderos*, they were often asked to cure the sick. Before the acceptance of the germ theory of disease, they were often more effective than traditional Spanish medical practitioners, given their detailed knowledge of local medicinal herbs. Due to this knowledge, mestizos and creoles as well as Indians consulted them.

The Inquisition punished *curanderos* when they were identified. They most frequently came to the Inquisition's attention when it received complaints about *curanderos'* failing to deliver promised

BARTOLOMÉ DE LAS CASAS

> If Columbus, through a daring and momentous act, lessened the geographic and cultural distances between two worlds, it fell to Las Casas, a man driven by profound Christian beliefs and untamed humanism, to attempt to bridge the informational gap created by the forced incorporation of America into the Spanish empire.
>
> (Daniel Castro, 2007)

Bartolomé de las Casas, one of the priests who influenced the pope to recognize the Indians' humanity, received an *encomienda* in Cuba. After becoming an *encomendero*, Las Casas began meditating on *Ecclesiasticus* 34:24: "He that sheddeth blood and he that defraudeth the laborer of his hire are brothers." Las Casas soon absolved his *encomienda* Indians of tribute obligations and spent the rest of his 92-year-long life defending the rights of Indians. The teachings of Las Casas, who became Bishop of Chiapas, had an impact throughout the New World and influenced the content of the New Laws of 1542.

Las Casas argued that Indians were rational beings who had the right to freely choose their religion, their place of residence, and their employment. For taking this relatively moderate stance, other Church officials, government administrators, and *encomenderos* bitterly attacked Las Casas. In some of his less moderate moments, Las Casas declared that instead of being hailed as heroes and receiving titles of nobility, Cortés and Francisco Pizarro (the conquistador of Peru) should have been hanged as common criminals. As bishop, Las Casas instructed priests not to give absolution to *encomenderos*.

The following summarizes Las Casas's views on the Indian:

> Indians are free by law and by natural right and owe nothing to the Spanish nor to any other nation. Through unjust wars they were cruelly subjugated. After thus being subjugated, they were placed in the most extreme conditions of servitude, such as the *encomienda* and the *repartimiento*. Even the devils in hell could not invent such violations of natural and divine order. *Encomiendas* are inherently depraved, perverse, and beyond the bounds of law and reason. Why should free men be distributed against their will, ordered around like a herd of cattle, even if it were for a saint?[3]

In his most dramatic effort on behalf of the Indian, Las Casas debated the renowned Spanish scholar Juan Ginés de Sepúlveda. Prior to the debate, the king ordered that all further raids and expeditions be halted until the rights of Indians could be defined. The Crown intended that the debate, which occurred in the Spanish city of Valladolid in 1550 and 1551, would clarify the legal position of Indians.

Sepúlveda based his arguments on the fifth book of Aristotle's *Politics*. He declared that: 1) Indians were barbarous and that their natural condition was that of submission to more civilized peoples; 2) they were idolatrous and practiced human sacrifice, which justified intervention to prevent crimes against natural law; 3) intervention was justified to save innocent lives; and 4) intervention would facilitate Christian evangelization.

Las Casas, in a five-day oral presentation in Latin, argued that Indians should enjoy the same rights as Spaniards. He claimed that it insulted the Almighty and bordered on blasphemy to suggest that He would have peopled an entire hemisphere with people who were as brutish and incapable as Sepúlveda claimed they were. He also emphasized that Christianity could not properly be propagated by the sword. Rather than forcing Christianity on natives, Las Casas advocated conversion as it was carried out at the dawn of Christianity, when people were slowly shown the true way.

Rather than facing each other, the debaters made oral arguments to a fourteen-man panel of judges. These judges never issued a collective decision. Sepúlveda so impressed the Mexico City municipal council that it voted to buy him 200 pesos worth of Mexican jewels and clothing to reward him for his efforts and "to encourage him in the future." Other observers felt Las Casas prevailed in the debate, noting that he could publish his views on the Conquest in 1552, while Sepúlveda did not receive permission to publish his.

Las Casas was successful in that he created a moral climate in which the Crown was forcefully reminded of its obligation to defend Indians against their oppressors and to do what it could to improve their lot. His efforts led the Crown to pass legislation favoring the Indian and to take other steps to defend the indigenous population. As historian J. H. Elliott noted, "It is not easy to find parallels in the history of other colonial empires."

After the Valladolid debate, Las Casas remained in Spain to lobby in the royal court on behalf of Indians. After realizing that the immediate abolition of the *encomienda* was a political impossibility, Las Casas sought to prevent *encomiendas* from being inherited by *encomenderos'* children. He continued his efforts on behalf of the Indian until his death in 1566.

Las Casas must be recognized as one of the most vociferous critics of the Spanish colonization project and as one of the most prolific writers of treatises, histories, and countless other documents about colonial Indoamerica. He repeatedly raised questions few of his contemporaries considered. However, when judged by modern standards, Las Casas (and his contemporaries) can be faulted on several counts. He never questioned the papal bull granting Spain ownership of the New World nor did he question imposing an alien belief system, such as Christianity, on peoples who already held well-developed theological beliefs. Although he acted on behalf of the oppressed, Las Casas never worked with the indigenous to transform them from passive objects to active subjects responsible for determining their fate.

remedies. Even if the patient recovered after consulting a *curandero*, the Inquisition could punish him or her, since the power to cure was viewed as the result of a pact with the devil. Furthermore since the Inquisition believed disease was punishment from God, it considered curing interfered with just retribution.

THE CHURCH AS AN EDUCATIONAL INSTITUTION

Ironically Church action led to much of our knowledge of pre-conquest cultures, as well as to much of our ignorance of them. Shortly after the conquest, churchmen systematically gathered and burned pre-Columbian codices. As the Bishop of Yucatán Diego de Landa stated:

> We found a large number of books in these characters [Mayan hieroglyphs], and, as they contained nothing in which there were not to be seen superstition and lies of the devil, we burned them all, which they regretted to an amazing degree, and which caused them much affliction.[4]

Subsequently, possession of such books was equated with idolatry, which was punished by hanging and burning at the stake.

The attitude of the Church soon changed, and the clergy assumed the leading role in the study of pre-conquest cultures. Fray Bernardino de Sahagún compared the study of indigenous beliefs to the study by a doctor of the cause of disease. He claimed that just as doctors needed to know the cause of disease, a priest, as a doctor of souls, needed to know the cause of idolatrous superstitions before he could cure the idolater.

Sahagún's *Historia general de las cosas de la Nueva España* (*General History of the Things of New Spain*), also known as the Florentine Codex, is the outstanding example of such studies. In compiling his work between 1558 and 1569, Sahagún used methods that foreshadowed those of the modern ethnographer, including posing the same question in Nahuatl to different informants to corroborate the responses he received. His twelve-volume encyclopedia of pre-Columbian Aztec life included information on flora, fauna, history, and religious views and ceremonies. He included a long list of dishes with the ingredients, indicating the Aztecs' wide culinary variety. Included were dozens of ways to prepare tamales. Informants' replies in Nahuatl, transcribed for the book using the Latin alphabet, were included along with a translation. Accompanying the text were 1,852 illustrations drawn by indigenous informants. (One of these illustrations appears as Figure 2.3.)

While he felt the religious practices he documented indicated that Satan had possessed the Aztecs, Sahagún described with admiration Aztec architecture, medical knowledge, educational practices, and political organization. He did not, as far as is known, either suppress or censor any responses. Mexican historian Enrique Florescano described his work as "one of the most original books human ingenuity has ever produced."

Many influential individuals in New Spain felt that Sahagún's work served to perpetuate indigenous beliefs and rites, rather than eliminating them. In 1577, as a result of these individuals' denunciations, King Felipe II forbade research on Indian history and religion, thus halting Sahagún's work. This royal disfavor delayed the publication of his study in its full form until the twentieth century.

Missionaries assumed responsibility for the early primary education of Indian children. They not only imparted a basic education but also their class and gender values. Girls' schools sought to protect Indian girls and train them to be wives and mothers. They stressed sewing, catechism, and household tasks. Girls generally remained inside. When outside, someone accompanied them. The Franciscans separated the children of plebeian and aristocratic Indians. The latter attended boarding schools, stayed in school longer, and received more religious training.

The Church was also responsible for much of the formal education imparted to non-Indians. Convents admitted elite girls both as boarders and day pupils. Thanks to the Jesuits' educating the creole elite, by the middle of the eighteenth century modest pockets of Enlightenment could be found in all major cities in Spanish America. As a result of Church efforts, along with those of private teachers and the municipal government, roughly half of Mexico City's children of primary school age were receiving education by the end of the eighteenth century.

THE CHURCH AS A FINANCIAL INSTITUTION

> The Catholic Church in the Spanish Monarchy was not a monolithic institution controlled by the pope. Rather, it was highly fragmented and decentralized.
>
> (Jaime Rodríguez O., 2012)

During the colonial period, the Church emerged as a major financial institution. In addition to offerings in cash, the Church received income from agricultural tithes, which were an involuntary tax on crops and livestock produced by haciendas and *ranchos*. Income from Church-owned property and fees charged for sacraments and Masses further increased Church wealth. Often the dying would establish a trust fund for Masses to be said for the repose of their soul. Such trust funds would generate income paid to the priest who said the Masses. Some individuals, especially those who died childless, would bequeath land to the Church. The key to Church wealth was the Church's immortality as an institution. Over decades and centuries, bequests, donations from the faithful, and sound investments increased Church wealth.

By the end of the colonial period, the Church had emerged as a major property owner. The Church rented some properties and managed others directly. At the time of their expulsion, Jesuits owned mines, large haciendas, and sugar-cane plantations. These plantations, which employed black slave labor, were among the most efficient of the colonial period. The Mexican Church's acquiring more property than any other institution did not indicate that it was being especially acquisitive. It simply followed the example set in Europe where the Church owned more than any other landowner.

As a result of donations and income from endowments, property ownership, mortgage payments, and land rental, and fees priests charged for performing rites, the Church consistently amassed large surpluses of cash. Some of these funds financed hospitals, charitable works, colleges, and missions.

Funds amassed by the Church also became the major credit source in the colony, which had no banks. Rather than Church wealth lying under a "dead hand," as critics charged, the Church kept money circulating through long-term, low-interest loans to *hacendados* and businessmen. By the eighteenth century, individual institutions—such as convents, monasteries, lay brotherhoods (*cofradías*), and Church hospitals—had become major credit facilities, handling several millions of pesos and employing trained staff who kept detailed accounts. The Marquesa de Selvanevada justified founding a convent in Querétaro specifically on the grounds that its construction would employ artisans and workers and that it would serve as a center for the circulation of money and as a stimulus to merchants, farmers, and industrialists. Such credit proved especially beneficial to small farmers in rural areas. Historian Michael Costeloe concluded, "It is difficult to imagine how any alternative credit system could have operated with greater success in the circumstances of the times . . ."

CONVENTS

Though isolated from secular life, the 57 convents established in colonial Mexico reflected colonial society as a whole. Up until 1724, admission to a convent required that women prove "cleanliness of blood," i.e. pure Spanish ancestry without any black, Indian, Moorish, or Jewish admixture. (After 1724, a handful of convents were established for elite indigenous women.) A woman's desire to become a nun initiated the entry process, even if it was against her family's wishes. Wealth was necessary for admission, since novices were required to provide the convent enough wealth—a dowry—to support them for the rest of their life. Once admitted, wealthy women were allowed to purchase elaborate multi-room cells for their personal use and owned material possessions comparable to those of affluent women in secular society. Wealthy women were allowed to have live-in servants and slaves to serve them in the convent. Unlike men who could move freely about society after they took religious vows, women never left the convent.

By the end of the colonial period, the number of nuns in New Spain exceeded 2,400. Some of the larger Mexico City convents sheltered hundreds of nuns and thousands of servants. Although only a small proportion of all women became nuns, a much higher percentage of the elite did. These elite women not only budgeted the everyday expenses of their convent, but managed a wide variety of economic assets such as mortgages and rental property. Nuns in each convent elected abbesses.

THE VIRGIN OF GUADALUPE

> The hold that the devotion to Our Lady of Guadalupe has on the Mexican people is universally recognized.
>
> (Stafford Poole, 1995)

According to Catholic tradition the Virgin Mary appeared to an Indian named Juan Diego on Tepeyac Hill, four miles north of Mexico City on December 9, 1531. Juan Diego, whose birth name was Quauhtlatoatzin, was born about 1474. When he was baptized in 1524 he took the name Juan Diego.

As he passed the hill on December 9, Juan Diego heard the sweet music of angelic choirs. He looked up and saw the image of the Virgin. A subsequent account described what he saw:

> And when he arrived in her presence, he was filled with the greatest wonder at how her perfect beauty surpassed all things. Like the sun her clothes radiated, as if throwing out rays, and with these rays the stones and rock on which she stood were radiant with light. The earth which surrounded her appeared resplendent like precious stones, as if bathed in the light of the rainbow. And the *mezquites* and *nopales* and other bushes which were there seemed like emeralds and their foliage was like turquoises, and their trunks and branches shone like gold.

The Virgin spoke to Juan Diego telling him she wanted a church built on the site of her appearance. She told him to convey that message to Bishop Zumárraga in Mexico City. Juan Diego went to the bishop, but was brushed off and told to come back later. Once again the Virgin appeared and reiterated her request. When he approached the bishop for a second time, he was told that to be taken seriously he would have to present some sign that he had actually seen the Virgin.

As Juan Diego was passing the hill on December 12, the Virgin appeared for a third time. She instructed him to pick the out-of-season flowers that had appeared on the hill and bring them to the bishop to indicate that he had indeed seen her. He then picked various flowers, including roses, carnations, lilies, and rosemary.

When he again visited the bishop, he opened his cape and the flowers fell to the floor. Zumárraga saw not only the flowers, but an image of the Virgin painted on the inside of Juan Diego's cape.

Zumárraga immediately acknowledged that Juan Diego had indeed seen the Virgin and ordered a hermitage built at Tepeyac to house the cape emblazoned with her image.

Pilgrimages soon began to visit the hermitage to honor the Virgin—known as the Virgin of Guadalupe. The initial hermitage became overcrowded. Thus the cornerstone of a new church was laid in 1600, and it was consecrated in 1622.

In 1629 the image of the Virgin was taken to the cathedral in Mexico City by canoe in response to massive flooding in the city. The image was venerated in the cathedral from 1629 to 1634. The Virgin of Guadalupe was credited with ending the flood. After the waters receded, the image was returned to Tepeyac.

Given poor communications of the time and the presence of other pilgrimage sites in Mexico, devotion to the Virgin of Guadalupe spread slowly. However, by 1688 a Jesuit chronicler noted pilgrims came from great distances to visit the Tepeyac sanctuary. He condemned many of the pilgrims' taking advantage of the festive sprit to consume great quantities of the intoxicating beverage pulque.

As crowds continued to grow, in 1695 the archbishop agreed to demolish the sanctuary completed in 1622 and erect a domed, three-nave church. This church was completed in 1709. In 1731, to celebrate the 200th anniversary of the Virgin's appearance, the viceroy headed a procession that marched from Mexico City to the sanctuary.

Devotion to the Virgin continued to increase during the eighteenth century. This devotion was shared by both the indigenous and creoles alike. Creoles found in the Virgin's appearance in Mexico a confirmation of their separate identity from Spaniards.

In 1737 the Virgin was proclaimed the principal patron of Mexico City. Other cities across New Spain made similar proclamations. These proclamations sought the Virgin's aid in halting a prolonged epidemic which caused an estimated 192,000 deaths across New Spain. In the following decade she was proclaimed patron for all of New Spain.

In 1648 the creole priest Miguel Sánchez published an account of the Virgin's appearance entitled *Imagen de la Virgin Maria, madre de Dios de Guadalupe, milagrosamente aparecida en la ciudad de Mexico* (*Image of the Virgin Mary, Mother of the God of Guadalupe, Miraculously Appeared in Mexico City*). Given the absence of written records Sánchez relied on the memory of respected elders. It is the first written account of the appearance for which an indisputable date can be attached.

The following year another creole priest, Luis Laso de la Vega, published a description of the appearance in Nahuatl. The first two words of his account are "*Nican mopohua*" (herein is recounted). Since its publication Laso's de la Vega's work has been known simply as *Nican mopohua*.

Even as devotion to the Virgin was increasing, skeptics began to question whether the Virgin actually appeared as described in the works of Sánchez and Laso de la Vega. They noted a long list of early writers who logically should have commented on the appearance of the Virgin but who failed to do so. Writers who never mentioned the Virgin's appearance include Benavente, Las Casas, and Zumárraga, who supposedly spoke with Juan Diego.

Eminent figures in the colony began to question the authenticity of the Virgin's appearance. José Ignacio Bartolache (1739–90), a physician and mathematics professor at the University of Mexico, questioned the appearance, noting that Zumárraga had never written about it and that the image on Juan Diego's cape was defective art—surely not of divine origin. Similarly a Milanese, Lorenzo Boturini Benaducci, arrived in New Spain in 1736 and spent years traveling around Mexico searching for documents that would provide a historical foundation for the Virgin's appearance. He admitted that he could find no such document.

Even though questions concerning the historical validity of the appearance have continued to the present, they have failed to undermine devotion to the Virgin. The Basilica at Tepeyac has become the most visited Catholic pilgrimage destination in the world with 20 million annual visitors. To accommodate the throngs, a new Basilica was consecrated in 1976. In 2002 Pope John Paul II canonized Juan Diego, making him the first indigenous American saint. Nobel Prize-winning writer Octavio Paz observed, "The Mexican people, after more than two centuries of experiments and defeats, have faith only in the Virgin of Guadalupe and the National Lottery."

Sources:
D. A. Brading (2001) *Mexican Phoenix*. Cambridge: Cambridge University Press. (The quotation above is from page 84.) Stafford Poole (1995) *Our Lady of Guadalupe*. Tucson: University of Arizona Press.

These elections provided one of the few examples of functioning democracy within New Spain. Even here democracy was limited—novices, servants, and slaves had no vote.

Convents played an economic as well as a religious role. Construction of convent buildings provided an economic stimulus. Once established, many convents sold produce from their orchards and gardens to the public. The wealthy endowed or bequeathed assets to individual convents. Such wealth included haciendas, ranches, livestock, sugar mills and flourmills, and, especially, urban real estate. Convents often retained and managed this urban real estate. Other property was generally sold. As a result of selling such property, donations, income from real estate, and payments made by nuns upon entering the convent, convents amassed sizable amounts of cash. This money became an important source of credit for business activity.

VASCO DE QUIROGA'S HOSPITALS

In the mid-sixteenth century, the secular priest Vasco de Quiroga, who had served as an *audiencia* judge, founded communal villages among the Tarascan Indians who lived around Lake Pátzcuaro in Michoacán. Each village, inspired by Sir Thomas More's *Utopia*, centered around a "hospital," in the medieval sense of the word. These hospitals not only cared for the sick but also welcomed the poor, the hungry, and travelers in need of shelter.

Although they were forced to renounce their old religion, village residents were housed, fed, and protected from the demands of *encomenderos*. The Tarascans could elect their own officials, and they shared communal lands. Quiroga stressed the need for all adults—men and women—to work a six-hour day and felt that well-rounded adults needed to combine urban and rural work. All residents had access to land and tools for artisanal activity. No one could hire domestic servants.

Figure 3.3 *This sixteenth-century structure, known as a "hospital," resulted from the efforts of Vasco de Quiroga. It is located in Santa Fe de la Laguna in Michoacán.*

Source: Philip L. Russell.

Each village received instruction in a particular craft, such as weaving, ceramics, or woodcarving. Assigning one craft to each village avoided competition between villages and created a trade network throughout the Tarascan area. Villagers sold their crafts to obtain cash. Quiroga established almost a hundred of these new communities, where *corregidores* and *encomenderos* could not abuse Indians.

Even though it rewarded Quiroga with a bishopric, the Crown was reluctant to extend his model since it removed Indian labor from Spanish control via the *encomienda* and the *repartimiento*. Some of the towns Quiroga founded, such as Santa Fe de la Laguna, still exist. The hospital Quiroga built there can still be seen. Today the people of Michoacán fondly remember Quiroga and still practice many of the crafts he introduced.

THE INQUISITION

In 1571, the king removed the Inquisition from bishops' hands and decreed the establishment of the Tribunal of the Holy Office of the Inquisition in Mexico. The Holy Office enforced respect for religious principles and defended Spanish religion and culture against heretical views. Heretics were assumed to be traitors, and dissenters were assumed to be social revolutionaries attempting to subvert the political and religious stability of the community. Most cases investigated by the Inquisition in New Spain concerned bigamy, blasphemy, sodomy, witchcraft, solicitation in the confessional, healing (*curandismo*), misguided interpretations of the faith, and other offenses against the Catholic religion. Virtually none of these offenses—bigamy is the exception—would be cause for judicial action in modern Spain or Mexico.

Since Protestantism had emerged from the Catholic clergy, enforcing clerical orthodoxy received special attention. This led to the Inquisition's delving into minute doctrinal matters, such as one's interpretation of the real presence in the Eucharist. In 1551 the Inquisition fined Dr. Pedro de la Torre a hundred golden pesos, exiled him from New Spain, and forced him to publicly abjure his heretical views for simply declaring that no difference existed between God and nature.

The Inquisition's interest in keeping Catholicism pure led to an ever widening circle of concern. It frequently charged people with witchcraft and sorcery, which constituted two separate offenses. Non-Indians were frequently prosecuted for idolatry after they turned to pre-Columbian indigenous traditions to improve their status or procure wealth. Possessing the Koran or the Bible in a Romance language constituted an offense.

The Inquisition created some offenses simply to facilitate its own operation. Those who failed to denounce an offense within the purview of the Inquisition could be excommunicated. Demeaning the Inquisition became an offense.

The Inquisition could impose a wide range of punishments, including fines, forced labor, seizure of property, forced public confessions, whippings, and exile. In addition, the guilty could be sentenced to obligatory service working in a hospital or convent, on a state or city project, or in galleys. The Inquisition turned unrepentant heretics over to civil authorities to be burned at the stake. However, fewer than fifty people suffered that fate in New Spain.

Although the Inquisition enjoyed extremely broad powers, the limitations imposed by its small staff and New Spain's geographical expanse restricted it. Between 1571 and 1700, it considered only 12,000 matters, of which fewer than 2,000 resulted in a trial. This amounted to only sixteen trials a year in the vast area stretching from Central America to California. Due to the Enlightenment's effect on the Spanish empire, the role of the Inquisition declined. In the 1700s, the Inquisition tried only 534 cases and put only one individual to death.

During its existence, the nature of offenses considered by the Inquisition changed markedly. Bishop Zumárraga, the outstanding figure of the early Inquisition, headed it between 1536 and 1543. During this time, blasphemy, the most frequent charge, resulted in 56 trials.

Under Zumárraga, the Inquisition also directed its attention to Indian religious practices. In one well-publicized case, the Inquisition tried Don Carlos, the *cacique* of Texcoco. He was definitely not a model citizen when judged by Spanish norms. He did not attend church and openly kept his niece as a concubine in addition to his wife. Don Carlos was convicted of declaring, "This is our land and our way of life and our possession and the rule of it belongs to us and will remain with us." The Inquisition declared him guilty of heretical dogmatism and he was burned at the stake.

Attempts to enforce religious orthodoxy peaked between 1640 and 1650. During this time, the success enjoyed by those of Jewish ancestry in Mexico caused widespread jealousy which led individuals to make false charges to the Inquisition. More than 200 individuals were tried for Jewish practices during this decade. In 1649 alone, the Inquisition had thirteen Jews burned at the stake in Mexico City.

During the late colonial period, the Inquisition focused on political matters. In 1752 unfaithfulness to the Crown became an offense. Individuals committed this offense if they indulged "in the grievous error of disobedience, unfaithfulness, or defamation of the king our lord . . ." The Inquisition scrutinized works that popularized the libertarian principles of the French Revolution and lamented the "passion for the French books which have led so many to the abysm of corruption." It prohibited and confiscated books by Rousseau, Diderot, Voltaire, and Montesquieu.

To evaluate the Inquisition, one must choose what criteria to use. The early Inquisition reflected Mexican society, which was a product of the Middle Ages. To the modern observer, the limits put on freedom of religion and expression offend human dignity. However, by European standards of the period, the Inquisition did not appear cruel. As historian William Manchester noted, at the time "men believed in magic and sorcery and slew those whose superstitions were different from, and therefore an affront to, their own."

Even when judged by the standards of the times, the Inquisition was frequently abusive. Don Carlos of Texcoco was convicted solely on the uncorroborated testimony of one neophyte who lived with the Franciscans. Don Carlos claimed he was unjustly charged. Apparently the Crown agreed, since it severely reprimanded Zumárraga for his role in the matter. The severity of Don Carlos's punishment influenced the Spanish government's decision to exclude recently converted Indians from the jurisdiction of the Inquisition. Early on, blasphemy charges against conquistadors formed part of a political campaign against Spaniards loyal to Cortés. Given the lack of safeguards to protect the accused, many individuals realized that false denunciations could be used to further their own interests. Indians falsely accused Spanish-appointed *caciques* of idolatry to deprive them of office. Convicted heretics denounced others in a desperate attempt to receive lighter sentences. Businessmen used charges of practicing Judaism to attack their competitors. Staffing the Inquisition with individuals who saw the tribunal as a path to personal wealth and selling confiscated goods to finance operations of the Inquisition also increased the possibility of abuse.

DOCUMENT 3.1: A SIXTEENTH-CENTURY CORPUS CHRISTI FESTIVAL

[Franciscan brother Toribio de Benavente wrote the following description of a Tlaxcalan pageant "Like Heaven on Earth."]

When the Holy Day of Corpus Christi arrived in the year 1538, the Tlaxcalans staged a very solemn festival that merits being memorialized because I believe that if the Pope and Emperor with their courts had attended, they would have been much pleased to see it. Although there were no precious jewels and no brocades, there were other decorations that were fine to see, especially the flowers and roses that God created in the trees and in the fields—so much that it was pleasing and worth note that a people who until now were taken for bestial, would know how to do such things.

The procession of the Most Holy Sacrament went along with many crosses and saints on portable platforms. The arms of the crosses and the adornments of the saints' platforms were made completely of gold and plumes, and so were the saints' images themselves, and they were so finely worked that people in Spain would have held them in higher esteem than those of brocade. There were many saints' banners. There were twelve Apostles; each dressed with their insignias. Many of the people who accompanied the procession carried lit candles in their hands. The whole route was covered in sedge, bulrushes, and flowers, and at one point, there were people who went along tossing roses and carnations the whole time. There were all kinds of dances that delighted the people in the procession. All along the route, one could stop at chapels with altars and beautifully adorned altarpieces from which came many singers who were singing and dancing in front of the Most Holy Sacrament. There were ten large triumphal arches that were delicately constructed. There was even more to see and to notice along the street, such as, they had divided the street along its length in the figure of the three naves of a church. In the middle, there was a space twenty feet wide, and through this space passed the Most Holy Sacrament and ministers, and crosses, and all the pomp of the procession. All the people, who were not a small number in this city and province, walked along on the other two sides that were each fifteen feet wide. This space was created by some dividing arches that had openings of nine feet. To the amazement and admiration of three Spaniards and many others in attendance who counted them, there were a total of 1,068 of these arches. The arches were completely covered in roses and flowers of every color and style, and they estimated that each arch had a load and a half of roses—understood as the load of the Indians. They estimated a total of 2,000 loads of roses for all the chapels, for all the people to hold in their hands, and the triumphal arches, which included another 66 little arches. About one fifth of them were carnations which originated in Castile, and had multiplied in such an astounding manner, that it is incredible. The groves here are much larger than those in Spain and the flower-growing season lasts year-round. There were 1,000 round shields which were woven from flowers and distributed among the arches. And the other arches did not have shields but, instead, there were great flower designs assembled like the domes of onion skins, rounded and so finely made that they shined. There was so much more that one could not count it all.

There was another thing that was amazing to see. In each of the four corners or turns of the route, they had made a mountain—and each one a great tall rock. Down below they had created a meadow with patches of grasses and flowers and everything else that is found in a wild field. The mountain and the rock [were] so natural that is was as though they had originated there. It was an amazing thing to see because there were many trees—wild, fruit, and flowering—and mushrooms, funguses, and mosses, which grow on mountain trees, in the rocks, and in old split trees. In some places it was like bushy thickets and in others it was thin. In the trees there were many birds, great and small. There were falcons, crows and owls. In the rest of the woodlands there was hunting of deer, hares, rabbits, jackals, and very many snakes. These were tamed and defanged because most of them were a type of viper, which were as long as a fathom [six feet] and as thick as a man's arm at the wrist. The Indians take them in their hands, as one would do with birds, because they have an herb that tranquilizes or numbs the ferocious and poisonous ones. This substance is also medicinal for many things; it is an herb called *picietl* [tobacco]. So that nothing would diminish the total naturalism, there were hunters very well-hidden in the mountains with bows and arrows. Those that normally play this role are from another language-group, and because they inhabit the mountains, they are great hunters. In order to see these hunters it was necessary to look very closely because they were so invisible behind all the braches and foliage of the trees; because they were so well-hidden, the hunted animals came right to their feet. They made many hand signals before they fired so that they could carefully select which of the unsuspecting animals they would hit.

This was the first day that the Tlaxcaltecans brought out their coat of arms, which the Emperor gave them when this *pueblo* [town] was designated a city, which no other pueblo of Indians had been granted. You justifiably granted this because they were a great help to Don Hernando Cortés when he won these lands for your Majesty. They had their coat of arms on flags, which also included the coat of arms of the Emperor, which they raised into the air on a very high pole. I was astonished, wondering where they could have found a pole that was so tall and slender. These banners were placed on the roof tops of the buildings of their municipal council because this is where they could be the highest. The procession left the choir and organ chapel with many singers and to the music of lutes in concert with the chorus, trumpets, drums, and large and small bells. All of this was played together at the entrance and exit of the church which made it seem all the more like heaven on earth.

Source: Nora E. Jaffary, Edward W. Osowski and Susie S. Porter (eds.) (2010) *Mexican History: A Primary Source Reader*. Boulder, CO: Westview Press, pp. 301–304.

NOTES

1   The quotation is from Enrique Florescano, *Origen y desarrollo de los problemas agrarios de México, 1500–1821* (Ediciones Era, 1976), pp. 21–22.

2   Quoted in J. H. Elliot, "Spain and America in the Sixteenth and Seventeenth Centuries," in *Cambridge History of Latin America*, Vol. I, ed. Leslie Bethell (Cambridge: Cambridge University Press, 1984), p. 304.

3   In Robert Sharer, *The Ancient Maya*, 6th ed. (Stanford, CA: Stanford University Press, 2006), p. 126.

4   *Cuadernos Americanos*, May–June (1974), p. 150.

FURTHER READING

Bakewell, Peter (2010) *A History of Latin America to 1825* (3rd ed.). Chichester, UK; Malden, MA: Wiley Blackwell.
    This study indicates how Mexico's colonial history parallels, and differs from, that of the rest of Latin America.

Castro, Daniel (2007) *Another Face of Empire: Bartolomé de Las Casas, Indigenous Rights, and Ecclesiastical Imperialism.* Durham, NC: Duke University Press.
    A discussion of Las Casas's life, the issues he raised, and his legacy.

Farriss, Nancy M. (1984) *Maya Society under Colonial Rule.* Princeton, NJ: Princeton University Press.
    As this study shows, colonial rule affected different indigenous groups in different ways.

Kanter, Deborah E. (2008) *Hijos del Pueblo: Gender, Family, and Community in Rural Mexico, 1730–1850.* Austin, TX: Univeristy of Texas Press.
    A study of how changes at the national level affected the Indian family and community in the Valley of Toluca.

Knight, Alan (2002) *Mexico: the Colonial Era.* Cambridge: Cambridge University Press.
    A concise summary of Mexico's colonial experience.

Valle, Ivonne del (2015) "Mexico's Re-Colonization: Unrestrained Violence, Rule of Law and the Creation of a New Order," *Política Común* 7.
    A consideration of how Cortés, Las Casas, and Toribio de Benavente grappled with the issues raised by the conquest and colonization.

GLOSSARY TERMS

altepetl
audiencia
corregidor
creole
curandero

encomendero
encomienda
fuero
hacendado

mestizo
repartimiento
viceroy
Virgin of Guadalupe

Chapter 4

Colonial Society, 1521–1810

TIMELINE—WORLD

1547	1558	1562	1564	1606
Birth of Spanish novelist Miguel Cervantes	Death penalty imposed in Spain for printing books without permission	Birth of Spanish dramatist Lope de Vega	Birth of English dramatist William Shakespeare	Birth of Dutch artist Rembrandt Harmenszoon van Rijn

TIMELINE—MEXICO

1531	1536	1536	1553	ca. 1620
Shipping books on history and other "profane" subjects prohibited, only books on Christian religion and virtue permitted	First book printed in Mexico	Inauguration of Indian school Santa Cruz de Tlatelolco	National University inaugurated	Indian population hits low point

Mexico is a country of inequality. Nowhere does there exist such a fearful difference in the distribution of fortune, civilization, cultivation of the soil, and population.

(Alexander von Humboldt, 1811)

1645	ca. 1650	1767	1805
Carlos Sigüenza y Góngora born	Sor Juana born	Expulsion of Jesuits	*Diario de México*, Mexico's first newspaper, published by Carlos María de Bustamante

THIS CHAPTER DESCRIBES THE SOCIETY THAT DEVELOPED during the three-century-long colonial period. This society was divided along class, ethnic, and gender lines as well as by the division between the enslaved and the free. The chapter considers the emergence of what would become the dominant element of Mexican society—the **mestizo**, or person of mixed race. It also describes how settlement inexorably crept northward, incorporating some indigenous groups and coming into conflict with others. In conclusion, this chapter considers the colony's intellectual life.

SOCIAL STRATIFICATION

After the conquest, Europeans and Indians formed the two major social groups. Europeans born in Spain held higher status than those born in the New World. The Spanish-born generally received appointments such as viceroy and archbishop, the highest positions in New Spain. All those considered European enjoyed privileged access into certain guilds and the university.

Black slaves occupied the lowest position in the social hierarchy. Although considered inferior to both Indian and European, many slaves worked in skilled occupations and served their masters in positions of trust that involved supervising indigenous workers.

In the period immediately after the conquest, children of mixed race simply moved into the community of one of their parents and did not seriously upset the system of racial classification. Later in the colonial period, mixed-race individuals formed a sizable group and generally intermarried.

Even though racial categories appeared to be rigid, in practice they could be manipulated. Individuals, or their children, would often declare themselves to be members of a racial category into which they or their parents were not born. Generally those changing racial category would declare themselves to be in the next whiter category than the one that had been ascribed to them or their parents.

Stratification by wealth existed alongside the racial hierarchy. Shortly after the conquest, Indian nobles, Spanish conquistadors, and *encomenderos* formed the elite. Eventually with the decline of the Indian nobility, Indian stratification lessened. However, as Europeans made fortunes in commerce and mining, they became increasingly stratified. A strong but not absolute correlation existed between wealth and racial classification. A few Indians became wealthy, and many Spaniards worked as bakers, barbers, cartwrights, shopkeepers, peddlers, muleteers, and artisans. Nonetheless wealth remained overwhelmingly in the hands of those of European descent. In 1792, there were only four non-whites in the 327-member elite of Antequera (today Oaxaca City).

THE SOCIAL ELITE

Colonial officials held the highest status, although not the greatest wealth. These officials not only profited from office but held significant power as well. They ceased to be household servants of the Crown and began to act as a semi-autonomous body that jealously guarded its prerogatives. These officials formed an interest group comparable to the landed aristocracy, the Church, and the urban elite. Although Spaniards almost always held the top posts, creoles provided most of the staff for the colonial administration.

Spaniards declared creoles to be their inferiors to justify the disproportionate numbers of the European-born serving as judges, provincial magistrates, chief aides to the viceroy, and leaders of missionary orders. They attributed this proclaimed inferiority to the malignant effect of New World land and climate, as well as to non-European genes among those claiming European status. Juan de Mañozca, the archbishop of Mexico from 1643 to 1650, attributed this perceived inferiority to creoles' use of Indian wet nurses, so that "although creoles do not have Indian blood in them, they have been weaned on the milk of Indian women, and are therefore, like Indians, children of fear."

Creoles' ability to comply only partially with Spanish law or to defy it outright prolonged their tolerance for Spanish domination. Those serving on town councils proved adept at resisting viceregal or even royal orders that seemed harmful to a town's (or, more exactly, the local economic elite's) interests. This maintained the empire intact for centuries, despite its undeniably exploitative nature.

With a few exceptions, European ancestry united the elite. As historian James Lockhart commented, "Wherever wealth and Europeans congregated, things happened quickly; where they did not, slowly." Both the Spanish-born and the creoles enjoyed elite status. While Spaniards controlled wholesaling, creoles dominated retail sales. Elite creoles also owned land, held positions in the colonial bureaucracy, and undertook military, professional, and ecclesiastic careers.

Many wealthy families bridged the creole–Spanish dividing line. Often newly arrived Spaniards married the daughters of wealthy creoles. The creoles' capital would finance Spanish-run ventures, which benefited from the Spaniards' family ties in Spain. Economic success relied on family ties, and old and new rich families constantly combined. As Lockhart commented, "One can emphasize either the continuity or the renewal; both are indispensable elements in the evolution of the society."

THE ECONOMIC ELITE

Mine owners' income far surpassed that of high government officials. Mine-owning families in northern Mexico would buy titles of nobility and vie socially in Mexico City with Spaniards. In a society where 300 pesos a year provided a decent living, the Mexico City home of the great silver miner José de la Borda cost 300,000 pesos. Such mine owners often provided extravagant support for charities, while remaining blind to the material needs of the mineworkers who made possible this philanthropy.

The *hacendados*—owners of large estates known as haciendas—formed another important sector of the elite. As with miners, they played a key role in the development of northern New Spain. They generally produced livestock and crops, processed what they produced, and marketed it. Wheat growers milled grain and distributed flour. Agave growers manufactured and sold intoxicants. Stock raisers slaughtered animals and sold meat. *Hacendados* created virtual feudal realms with their own jails. Owners routinely meted out corporal punishment to employees who displeased them. Typically *hacendados* established residences in Mexico City or a provincial capital and only visited the hacienda during the planting and harvest seasons. At other times, an overseer (*mayordomo*) administered the hacienda.

Hacendados developed close ties with wealthy merchants and the most powerful colonial officials. They exploited their access to capital and their local predominance to provide credit and sell manufactured items and food to those living in the region. The Sánchez Navarro family, whose holdings in Coahuila at the end of the colonial period totaled more than 800,000 acres, provides a perfect example of the *hacendado* as merchant. The family supplied the Presidio de Río Grande and exercised a virtual monopoly on retailing in the capital, Monclova.

Merchants solidified their control of urban markets by dealing only with major producers of grain, meat, and other commodities. This eliminated small producers who might undercut their prices. They lent to producers on the condition that the producer sold only to them. They also monopolized the sale of imported goods, so they could mark up the price 100 percent or more. Spanish-born wholesale merchants did not welcome the locally born, even if they were their own sons. They based their trade monopoly on their control of the merchant guild, kin ties, connections to Spain, and access to capital. Wholesale merchants only numbered 177 in 1689. That year, of the 1,182 adult male Spaniards in Mexico, only 124 served in government, compared with 628 in commerce.

Merchants in Mexico City who acted as middlemen and the Spanish who shipped goods to Mexico and withdrew cash to Spain benefited from this system. The small and mid-sized farmers and the Indian villagers who provided *repartimiento* labor and paid tribute lost out. As historian E. J. Hobsbawm noted, these merchants became the linchpin of the economic system linking Mexico and Europe:

> The key controller of these decentralized forms of production, the one who linked the labour of lost villages and back streets with the world market, was some kind of merchant . . . The typical industrialist (the word had not yet been invented) was as yet a petty-officer rather than a captain of industry.[1]

Merchants formed their own guild (the *consulado*) and invested much of their accumulated wealth in landed estates. Such estates provided a steady, if not spectacular, source of revenue. Landowning merchants could accurately assess demand and adjust production. In the late colonial period, investment in land became especially attractive as demand for food increased and labor became cheaper. Merchant capital facilitated the construction of granaries, reservoirs, and irrigation canals.

Just as with miners, merchant families occupied a precarious social position. An often-cited proverb concerning merchants commented: "*Padre comerciante, hijo caballero, nieto pordiosero*" ("Merchant father, gentleman son, beggar grandson"). As with most proverbs, it contained an element of truth. Bequests to the Church drained capital from merchant families. Division among many children, conspicuous consumption, seasonal losses, and the inability to collect debts forming part of an inheritance all dispersed capital.

Many elite families invested in mines, commerce, and haciendas. Frequently owners mortgaged their haciendas to obtain capital for commerce and mining ventures. Merchant families lacking capital frequently allied with land-owning families. This permitted land to be mortgaged to provide capital for commerce. Diversification permitted a family to retain its status in the event of a downturn in one economic sphere. It also permitted businesses to complement each other. Thus a family's haciendas might provision its mine as well as supply its store.

The economic elite's desire to have a voice in governance dovetailed with the Crown's view of the colonies as a revenue source. During the 1600s, municipal office could be bought in perpetuity. Thus wealthy creoles would not only control local government but would bequeath their positions to their children, who in turn would pass the position to the next generation. Beginning in 1687, posts in the *audiencias* were put up for sale. This allowed creoles to buy their way into the central colonial administration and reinforce their social and economic dominance.

THE INDIGENOUS POPULATION

> Regardless of how much humanitarian legislation was passed to protect the Indian, to a large extent the colonial economy was based on systematic, forced extraction of Indian wealth.
>
> (Felipe Castro Gutiérrez, 2010)

Between 1530 and 1550, the Spanish replaced the Indians' pre-conquest *altepetls* with "Indian republics" modeled on the Spanish municipality. Residents of these republics enjoyed the right to use land held communally by the republic and had their own vigorous form of self-government. Such governments, which were recognized as legal entities, would collect tribute, manage natural resources, organize worship, assemble labor for public works, and impart justice in cases involving minor offenses. The Indian republics effectively traded payment of tribute for ownership of communal land and local autonomy. This proved to be an effective survival mechanism, as the continued existence of some 4,000 Indian towns and villages through the eighteenth century indicates.

The legal status of Indians differed markedly from that of Spaniards. The Crown considered indigenous people as minors needing protection and tutelage. The colonial government sharply limited Indians' ability to buy land, receive loans, or join a guild. Spanish law prohibited Indians from wearing European-style clothing or, for security reasons, bearing arms and riding horses.

However, Indian status conferred certain advantages, such as being exempt from the compulsory tithe on agricultural produce non-Indians paid to the Church. Indians enjoyed exemptions from military service and remained outside the purview of the Inquisition. They received more lenient criminal penalties than those meted out to non-Indians. Finally, being recognized as an indigenous member of an Indian republic brought rights to farmland, to have access to water, and to hold administrative posts.

At a time when creole town councils were essentially self-perpetuating oligarchies, Indian communities held often vigorous elections to select their local officials. These officials would safeguard land titles and population registers, protect the community's historical rights, and coordinate access to land, water, and forests in the area under their jurisdiction.

Between 1592 and 1820, a special court, the *juzgado de indios*, adjudicated disputes between Indians or between an Indian and a non-Indian. The cases coming before this court mainly concerned: 1) land rights; 2) mistreatment or excessive demands made on Indians; and 3) criminal cases involving Indians.

The amount of land left in Indian hands varied according to local resources and marketing opportunities. To take advantage of the well-developed food market in the Valley of Mexico, by the end of the colonial period non-Indians had deprived Indians of virtually all their land. However, in Oaxaca, Indians retained substantial holdings due to the weak market for food and the survival of strong Indian communities to defend land titles. Of the 4,081 Indian pueblos remaining in 1803, 873 were in Oaxaca. Indians also retained more land in the south where they grew, but did not engage in the export of crops such as indigo, cacao, and cochineal.

Obligations imposed by both Church and state forced Indian peasants to earn cash. Contrary to modern notions that taxes stymie economic development, colonial officials imposed taxes to force Indians to engage in wage labor so they could meet their obligations. As long as they had access to subsistence plots, Indians doggedly (and rationally) refused to become wage laborers. Rather they sought to produce for their own consumption. In addition to producing their own food, Indians continued to weave cotton textiles on their backstrap looms, to the frustration of Spanish manufacturers, importers, and officials.

Indians quickly adapted to their new situation as colonial subjects. As historian Susan Kellogg noted, "Far from simply being passive victims of the Spanish Conquest, the Mexica and other central Mexican groups proved to be significant social actors who helped shape the history of the early colonial state." Indian leaders exercised remarkable discretion in accepting or rejecting the diverse elements of Spanish colonial culture. They soon mastered such subterfuges as hiding infants and the bodies of the dead to avoid paying baptism and funeral fees. Indian farmers improved productivity by placing metal tips on their digging sticks (*coas*) and using the plow. Indigenous people soon began raising pigs and sheep and were the sole producers of cochineal dye. Commerce at the village level, involving barter and the use of pack animals, offered employment to many Indians.

Indians engaged in the Spanish-introduced practice of litigation with considerable sophistication. Some Indian nobles went to Spain to plead their cases for land titles, tribute, or inheritance before the royal court. Litigants buttressed their cases with maps and codices produced specifically for the proceeding. If the occasion arose, Indians would even forge land titles to bolster their claims. Their success at litigation frequently vexed Spaniards, such as the curate of the Sagrario in Mérida, who complained to the government about Indians who contested land claims:

The capriciousness, malice, and dishonesty of the Indians are well recognized in the sacred laws that govern us. If royal officials do not stand firm against their feigned humility and other tricks, we Spaniards will never be able to enjoy peaceful possession of our property, especially since they are led by the detestable propositions that they are on their own homeland, that all belongs to them, and other insolent notions.[2]

In the early post-conquest period, the Spanish relied on the Indian elite to maintain order and organize production. Members of this elite were allowed to maintain their positions as long as they provided *repartimiento* labor and collected and delivered tribute to Spaniards. With their status affirmed by the Spanish, many members of the indigenous elite acquired land and diversified economically. Some adopted Spanish economic practices, such as employing other Indians to raise pigs. Others, such as the Maxixcatzin family in mid-sixteenth-century Tlaxcala, held extensive property farmed by lower-class Indian laborers. Shortly after the conquest, a significant number of Indian noblewomen married Spaniards. This not only provided Spanish men with spouses but gave them access to Indian land and labor.

As the colonial period progressed, Indian nobles became less useful to the Spanish since Indian labor became accessible through the *repartimiento* and wage labor. In many areas, such as Michoacán and the Valley of Mexico, by the middle of the eighteenth century the Indian elite had lost Spanish backing, and its members had become virtually indistinguishable from commoners. In Oaxaca, the indigenous elite retained large land holdings and high social status throughout the colonial period since they faced little competition from Spaniards. Often noble "Indian" families intermarried with Europeans and mestizos and their wealth determined their status more than their genealogy. As the status of Indian nobles declined and more Spanish women arrived, Spanish men ceased to marry Indian nobles.

The Spanish colonial regime generally respected indigenous landholdings that were cultivated. (The claims of hunter-gatherer peoples, however, were denied.) The village typically held lands communally and never placed them on the market. Its leaders assigned cropland to each household to work on an individual basis. Villagers enjoyed communal use of other lands for lumbering, hunting, and fishing. Residents sowed other plots communally to generate income to maintain the church and pay tribute.

Before the conquest, most Indians lived in scattered homes near their fields, rather than in compact villages. However, late in the sixteenth century, the Spanish forced many Indians to move from their isolated farms to grid-pattern villages. This facilitated evangelization, social control, and tribute collection. From 1596 to 1606 alone, colonial authorities forced an estimated 250,000 Indians into 190 new towns. The crowding resulting from forced urbanization made Indians much more vulnerable to European disease than those remaining in isolated homes.

This resettlement (*congregación*) played a major role in breaking down the old pre-conquest indigenous culture and creating a new, distinct Indian culture. The newly emerging Indian culture, rather than mirroring Spanish culture, borrowed from both the Spanish and pre-conquest traditions to form a unique blend. Often Indians retained their pre-Columbian festivals, but celebrated them on saints' days. Most of the ancient Indian towns that currently exist were formed by *congregación*.

A process known as *composición* facilitated non-Indians taking Indian lands. *Composición* allowed those claiming supposedly ownerless land to receive legal title to it by paying a fee. When forced to choose between the hard cash charged for legalizing such titles and the long-range desire to maintain a viable Indian community, the Crown generally chose the former. Often claims were filed on land that became vacant after the Indian population plummeted and *congregación* forced Indians out of rural areas. In other cases, officials received bribes to validate the land transfer.

Most Indians in central and southern Mexico remained in indigenous communities. However there was gradual migration to haciendas and Spanish towns to find employment and escape tribute, eroding the policy of racial separation. Abusive *encomenderos* and *corregidores*, individuals'

THE NOPAL

As is the case with amaranth, the nopal, or prickly pear cactus, has been cultivated in Mexico for several millennia. More than half of Mexico is arid or semi-arid—an ideal environment for nopal. The cactus stores large amounts of water in its thick leaves and impedes water loss with a thick cuticle. "Nopal" is something of a generic term, since there are more than a hundred distinct species of prickly pear found in Mexico—all of which are called nopal.

Various pre-conquest groups incorporated the nopal into their belief systems. Tradition holds the founding of the Aztec capital was indicated by a prickly pear. Thus the Aztec name of Mexico City, Tenochtitlan, means "prickly pear on a rock." Pre-conquest peoples used nopal widely as a food item, taking advantage of its water content, protein, sugars, minerals, fiber, and vitamins. The Aztecs also used the plant medicinally, spreading the plant's juice on burns. A beverage made from the leaf was used to induce childbirth, and its powered root was applied to limbs to speed the healing of broken bones.

Before the conquest, nopal was cultivated as a host for a small parasitic insect, the cochineal. The body fluid of this insect contains a red substance which serves as a dye. This dye was used to color food, textiles, ink, and cosmetics, and to decorate buildings. The Aztecs demanded cochineal dye as tribute from the areas producing it. The Mixtecs attributed cochineal's existence to the struggle between two gods for control of a desired nopal field. The resulting combat was so brutal that both gods died. However, according to the legend, the drops of divine blood that were shed on the cactus became the cochineal insects.

Unlike the amaranth, rather than fading out during the colonial period, nopal cultivation expanded. Also its use spread from indigenous households, which prized it, to European households. The nopal became so well entrenched that if something was considered to be very typically Mexican it was declared to be more Mexican than a nopal (*más mexicano que el nopal*).

In colonial times indigenous people expanded nopal cultivation to produce more cochineal. They sold the dye to middle men who transported it to Veracruz. From there it was exported to Europe where it was used to dye cloaks of kings and popes and redcoats of British troops at Waterloo. Between 1578 and 1598, five million pounds of this dye were exported from Veracruz to Seville. This commerce proved to be so lucrative that the Spanish attempted to conceal the origin of the dye to maintain a monopoly.

The nopal continues to be widely consumed, since the plant is a good source of fiber, is inexpensive, and is available year around. The tender leaf, known as *nopalito*, is a favorite dish. Nopalitos are opened and stuffed like a chile relleno and chopped to include in salads or to mix with scrambled eggs.

The nopal fruit, known as a *tuna* (nothing to do with the fish!), is the sixth most important Mexican fruit, ahead of grapes and peaches. Tunas are eaten fresh or processed to make marmalades and syrup. The fruit is also used to flavor pulque, an alcoholic beverage. In addition, the fruit can be fermented to produce *colonche*, consumed by some indigenous people in northern Mexico.

In northern Mexico nopal is now widely used as cattle forage. The spines are burned off the cactus and then it is fed to cattle. A milk cow can eat up to 100 pounds a day. Some believe cows fed with nopal forage produce a better-flavored butter.

During the nineteenth century, the use of cochineal plummeted, as the dye was largely replaced by synthetic dyes. However, in recent years the dye has made a comeback as synthetic food dyes were found to be carcinogenic. Ocean Spray added it to provide a more consumer-friendly color to their pink grapefruit juice.

As is the case with amaranth, there is an effort to expand the use of cochineal. A Mexican chemist Ignacio del Río y Dueñas established a demonstration farm, Tlapanochestlí, in Santa María Coyotepec, a village just south of Oaxaca City. Visitors there can buy cochineal dye and ink, and view how nopal is harnessed to feed the cochineal insect.

escaping *repartimiento* obligations, and the destruction of crops by Spanish livestock led to further out-migration. As the Indian population increased in the eighteenth century, still more Indian villagers moved to Spanish-run estates. The children of many of those who left their villages became Hispanized and joined the ranks of the mestizo, or mixed blood, population. In some cases, villagers would work seasonally on commercial estates without breaking their ties to their village.

As the urban Indian population grew, the notion of "Indian" shifted from being a racial to a social concept. Individuals who so desired could shed their Indian identity and become mestizos. Individuals who accumulated wealth or married a non-Indian could more easily shed their Indian identity. Non-Indians expressed their contempt of such ethnic shifts, but could do little to stop them. In 1692, a priest in Mexico City commented on Indians shedding their identity: "Many of them wear stockings and shoes, and some trousers, and they cut their hair shorter. The women put on petticoats, become mestizos, and go to church at the Cathedral."

CONFLICT WITH THE INDIGENOUS

Between 1700 and 1820, at least 150 village riots occurred. More than a hundred of these riots occurred after 1765, with the highest frequency between 1806 and 1810. They were generally characterized by violence, levity, and inebriation. Commonly such uprisings resulted from suppression of a local religious cult or abuses of power, often by a priest who had raised fees for baptism, marriage, burial, and the celebration of Mass. They were carried out with machetes, knives, clubs, axes, and hoes. Generally these riots burned themselves out with little intervention from the outside once they had achieved their immediate goal such as driving out a hated figure, freeing a prisoner, or getting a promise of action on a particular issue. Sometimes after particularly severe outbursts, residents would abandon a town for a time to prevent retaliation.

Increased conflict in the late colonial period reflected demographic change. As the Indian population began to increase, conflicts erupted over land. If Indians wanted to put additional land under cultivation, they had to confront the hacienda, and when haciendas expanded to meet new market opportunities, they threatened Indian interests.

Cultural and linguistic diversity and Indians' identity with village rather than with a wide-ranging cultural group, such as the Zapotecs, led most rebellions to be highly localized. The Spanish prohibition on Indians owning firearms, swords, or daggers diminished their ability to resist government force. In addition, the lack of a vigorous, surviving indigenous elite to lead rebellions, as occurred in Peru, reduced the severity of uprisings.

Authorities usually took a conciliatory stance toward such revolts, since they had limited ability to carry out counter-insurgency, sought taxes, and feared the spread of local revolts. These local revolts did not pose a major threat and generally showed a high degree of respect for the viceroy, bishops, and the *audiencia*. Anthropologist William Taylor commented on such rebels, "They did not want to take power outside the local district, and, if they had, I suspect they would not have known what to do with it."

More serious rebellions generally occurred after a miraculous occurrence, such as the claim that God or the Virgin Mary had ordered the rejection of Spanish control and had promised mystical power and the establishment of a new, divinely mandated order. A charismatic leader, often a witness to the miracle, then transmitted the message. These movements often became regionalized, and their suppression involved heavy loss of life.

In 1712, a classic case of a millenarian rebellion occurred in Chiapas. There a young Indian woman, María de la Candelaria, reported that the Virgin Mary had appeared to her and told her to build a chapel in her honor. When Spanish authorities attempted to suppress the cult that sprang up to honor the Virgin's appearance, Indians rebelled. The rebels organized their own political system and priesthood, which they reserved exclusively for Indians. They declared the Virgin to be supreme over God and heaven and that Spaniards were "Jews" who persecuted her. Members of their 5,000-man army referred to themselves as "Soldiers of the Virgin." For three months, Indians sacked Catholic churches and Spanish estates, killing Spaniards and mestizos. Colonial authorities were only able to suppress the rebellion after heavily armed Spanish troops arrived from Guatemala.

NORTHWARD

> Northern New Spain never enjoyed the long, if flawed, social peace of the centre; Spanish hegemony was, at best, patchy and frequently contested.
>
> (Alan Knight, 2002)

Spanish settlement slowly expanded northwards, largely as a result of mining operations. This led to a process that in some ways resembled the expansion of the U.S. frontier toward the west. In both cases, European settlement gradually eliminated independent Indian groups and channeled wealth into non-Indian hands. The Mexican experience differed from the U.S. experience in its emphasis on settling Indian groups and incorporating them into colonial life. The Spanish gave a major role in this process to other Indian groups that they had already dominated. Another contrast with the U.S. experience was that Spanish colonial exploration was carefully planned by the state.

As the Spaniards moved north to exploit mines in Zacatecas, warfare broke out with Indians known as Chichimeca, an Aztec term that translates roughly as "barbarian." Both the Spanish and the Aztecs used the term Chichimeca to refer to more than half a dozen distinct groups of nomadic people between San Juan del Río, Durango, Guadalajara, and Saltillo. Each group spoke, but did not write, a distinctive language. The Aztecs had never occupied the desert area the Chichimeca inhabited. The Chichimeca soon acquired horses and became expert riders. They mastered the ambush and established effective spy networks in Spanish-dominated villages, where they took advantage of the Spaniards' inability to distinguish them from other Indians. By the end of 1561, the Chichimeca had killed roughly 200 Spaniards and more than 2,000 of their Indian allies. In addition Chichimecas destroyed farms and robbed pack trains.

The wars with the Chichimeca dragged on for fifty years and provided the colonial administration with one of its greatest problems. As hunter-gatherers, the Chichimeca did not occupy a fixed location, making control extremely difficult. Before their domination, the Chichimeca cost the Spaniards more expense and lives than the conquest of the Aztecs. Peace with the Chichimeca came after Viceroy Álvaro Manrique de Zúñiga, who served from 1585 to 1590, realized that the soldiers responsible for pacifying Indians in fact exacerbated conflict. Soldiers would capture Indians and sell them into slavery. This served as the main source of income for many soldiers, who became more diligent at slaving than peacemaking.

Manrique de Zúñiga initiated a program called "peace by purchase." He provided the Chichimeca with food and clothes and encouraged them to form permanent settlements. To provide an example of settled Indians, the Spanish persuaded many Indians from Tlaxcala to settle in the Chichimeca area. Before the Tlaxcalans agreed to move, they demanded and received extensive land grants, freedom from personal tribute, and the right to carry arms and ride a horse with a saddle. As a result of the new Spanish policies, the Chichimeca and the Spanish coexisted peacefully after 1600.

Peace with the Chichimeca did not end conflict with indigenous people. In 1687, an alliance led by the Toboso people embraced thirty indigenous groups resisting Spanish intrusion. This alliance threatened security (as defined by the Spanish) in broad areas of northeastern Mexico. In 1754, the bishop of Durango lamented to the king, "I have . . . heard much about uprisings of Indians and very little about new conversions."

During the seventeenth century, settlement continued inexorably northward, driven by the discovery of new mines and the need to protect settlements further south from raids by stateless nomads. Tlaxcalans paved the way for much of this northward expansion. Newly established towns populated by Tlaxcalans supplied food and served as military outposts and centers for civilizing and Christianizing other Indians. Throughout northern Mexico, the 1600s saw repeated attempts to suppress independent Indian groups. Joining in this effort were the Spanish, Tlaxcalans, and other settled Indians who were pitted against those who did not accept Spanish sovereignty.

During the eighteenth century, northward expansion was slowed, halted, and even pushed back by stateless nomads who refused to move into permanent settlements and accept Christianity and Spanish sovereignty. Further south such renegades had been forced into submission. In the area now comprising the northern Mexican border states, however, such groups continued to live an autonomouns existence well past the end of the colonial period. Indians could successfully reject Spanish tutelage since 1) they had acquired horses and had become expert riders; 2) they could buy firearms from traders of other nations, especially the French; and 3) they had ready sources of food, such as the buffalo.

The most transformed of all Indian groups, affected by, but not dominated by Europeans, were the Comanche. The combination of the horse, the gun, and the buffalo allowed them to retain their independence. They lived a fully nomadic life, trading, raiding, and hunting buffalo. In the late 1700s, the area under Comanche control, known as the *comanchería*, covered some 240,000 square miles and created a formidable barrier to Spanish efforts to expand north and west of San Antonio. At the height of their power the Comanche boasted that they only allowed Hispanics to remain in northern Mexico so they could raise horses for them to steal.

To the west of the comanchería was the *gran apachería*, dominated by the Apache, who were divided into several independent groups sharing a common culture. This area extended from today's northern Sonora and southern Arizona to west Texas and Coahuila—750 miles from east to west and as much as 550 miles from north to south.

As historian Donald Worcester noted:

The Apaches successfully resisted all attempts to conquer them from the early seventeenth century until the last quarter of the nineteenth. They avoided pitched battles if possible, but when cornered fought to the death. As guerrilla fighters they were without peers.[3]

The cycle of raid and counter-raid continued for decades. Emphasis shifted from saving Indians' souls to killing them. Spanish punitive expeditions often struck innocent groups. The ready market for booty and slaves did not lead these expeditions to be very discriminating in their choice of targets. By the 1770s, Apaches were subjecting the entire province of Nueva Vizcaya (today's Durango and Chihuahua) to attack, and many of its villages had been abandoned. The region was described as being in a state of "permanent warfare." Governor Felipe Barri reported that between 1771 and 1776 Indian raids had resulted in 1,674 persons killed, 154 captured, 116 haciendas and ranches abandoned, and 68,256 head of cattle rustled.

The Spanish were never able to dominate either the Comanche or the Apache. By the end of the eighteenth century, they had adopted the same strategy they had adopted with the Chichimecas. They began the systematic delivery of merchandise, such as blankets, clothes, medallions, hats, cigars, pipes, candles, sugar, imported cloth, colored capes, metal tools, and gear for horses. The Apache and the Comanche concluded they were better off receiving Spanish goods than they were raiding and enduring Spanish reprisals. The key to peace was treating these indigenous groups as sovereign peoples meriting respect. Spanish gift giving formed part of a long-term Spanish strategy summarized by Viceroy Gálvez, "It is my intention to establish with the Indians a commerce which will attract them to us, which will interest them, and which in time will put them under our dependency."

AFRICAN SLAVES

Before 1519, slavery existed on the Iberian Peninsula and in Mesoamerica, where Indians enslaved people as punishment or after their capture in war. Cortés and Narváez established hereditary slavery early on, as both brought African slaves to Mexico.

During the second half of the sixteenth century, the demand for labor in commercial agriculture, urban industry, and, especially, silver mines soared, while the Indian labor supply plummeted. The lack of Indians to cultivate fields even raised the specter of famine. As a result, from about 1580 to 1620, New Spain imported more African slaves than any other locale in the Americas. The colony received approximately 36,500 African slaves between 1521 and 1594. During the seventeenth century, an annual average of 1,871 African slaves were brought to Mexico.

Residents of New Spain had few moral qualms concerning the African slave trade. In the mid-fifteenth century, papal decrees, or bulls, had proclaimed African slavery acceptable since those enslaved would be converted to Christianity. Once slavery began, slave owners rationalized the institution as a response to presumed black inferiority. A 1769 petition signed by virtually all the planters in the district of Córdoba, Veracruz, asserted: "If given freedom, blacks become increasingly more barbarous and bloodthirsty. The only proper condition for them is slavery." Free blacks and others of mixed African ancestry owned their own black slaves, indicating how widespread acceptance of slavery had become.

Arguments based on economic necessity quashed lingering doubts on the issue of slavery. During the 1665–1700 reign of King Carlos II, a report by the Council of the Indies declared:

First, the introduction of blacks is not only desirable, but absolutely necessary . . . The fatal consequences of not having them are easily deduced, for . . . they are the ones who cultivate the haciendas, and there is no one else who could do it, because of a lack of Indians.[4]

The report concluded that without the slave trade Spanish America would face "absolute ruin."

The Church, as an arm of the Crown, could not challenge slave policy. Dominicans and other orders worked African slaves on their haciendas. Other Church institutions, such as convents, owned slaves and financed others' purchase of them. In 1517, Bartolomé de las Casas, a priest who became famous for defending Indian rights, warned that unless indigenous people received some relief, they would soon disappear from Hispaniola. He proposed that each white resident of Hispaniola should receive permission to import as many as twelve African slaves.

Initially African slaves were largely employed in urban areas. However, as the Indian population declined, African slaves increasingly worked in rural areas. Many worked in the port of Veracruz and on cattle ranches and sugar plantations along the east coast. Others worked to the north and west of Mexico City on ranches and in silver mines. Between Puebla and the Pacific Ocean, slaves worked in mines, on sugar plantations and ranches, and in the port of Acapulco. Slaves would work continuously, unlike Indian *repartimiento* laborers, who returned to their communities. The number of slaves in Mexico ranged between 20,000 and 45,000, a number far fewer than the four million slaves who would later labor in the U.S. south.

Some slaves learned highly technical aspects of sugar production. Most commonly though rural slaves faced a lifetime of back-breaking labor in the fields. Slave labor came to dominate the sugar industry since the low-land Indian population had virtually vanished. The Spanish felt that Africans withstood hot, heavy work better than Indians. King Felipe III's forbidding the use of Indian labor on plantations increased the reliance on slave labor.

Creoles adamantly opposed the emergence of an Afro-Mexican elite that might compete with their own sons for the limited number of desirable jobs, such as civil and clerical appointments, so they prohibited anyone with African blood from enrolling in the university. Similarly Afro-Mexicans could not become masters in many craft guilds.

Figure 4.1 *Paintings illustrating the result of racial mixture were popular in colonial Mexico. This painting by Francisco Clapera shows the mestizo girl of a Spanish father and an Indian mother.*

Source: Jan and Frederick Mayer Collection. Denver Art Museum.

More than 200,000 slaves were imported to Mexico during the colonial period. However, slavery never assumed the fundamental role that it did in the export-oriented plantation colonies of the West Indies. In contrast to these colonies, during the eighteenth century slavery virtually vanished from Mexico. In most instances, due to increases in the Indian and mixed-race populations, it became less costly to pay wages than to import and maintain slaves.

RACIAL MIXTURE

The social position of mixed-race individuals involved several factors, which changed over time. Initially few of the parents of mixed-race children had married. Either the Indian or Spanish parent raised these children. Later as the number of mixed-race individuals increased, they intermarried and produced larger families than either Indians or creoles. Racial status varied by region. In the north, with its meager Indian population, those of mixed race occupied a position near the bottom of the social scale and worked alongside the few remaining Indians. In areas such as Oaxaca, where the overwhelming majority of the population was Indian, mixed-race individuals enjoyed a higher social position.

The various elements within the social hierarchy had differing views of it. Those forming the elite viewed racial divisions as rigid. Those at the bottom saw them as categories one could move into and out of to change status as the opportunity arose. Despite the ability of individuals, families, and even communities to change categories, especially from Indian to mestizo, these barriers were important, especially before the eighteenth century. In addition to maintaining the elite status of Europeans, the system of racial classification divided the non-European population and thus inhibited united opposition to European rule.

In the early colonial period, as many as sixteen terms, including *pardo* (black and Indian) and *morisco* (Spanish and mulatto), described racial mixtures. One category, the **casta**, eventually embraced all mixed bloods, including mestizos (Spanish and Indian), mulattos (Spanish and black), and *zambos* (black and Indian).

The elite not only held negative stereotypes of non-whites but formulated elaborate rules to prevent non-whites from competing with them for choice positions. Generally those of mixed race were not allowed to hold public office, be members of municipal corporations, join religious orders and guilds, or enter the university. In 1757, persons of color were not even allowed to own or administer grocery stores in Mexico City.

A few mestizo families, such as the Pimentel and Ixtlilxochítl families, descended on the Indian side from the royal household of Texcoco, enjoyed high social status. The majority though held much more modest status, in part due to their being barred from prestigious trades and high public posts. Mestizos often worked as shopkeepers and artisans and on haciendas where they frequently served as foremen, organizing the labor of Indians to meet the needs of Europeans. Policymakers rationalized these restrictions as a means of controlling those of bad character.

Despite the racial stereotypes and legally mandated isolation of racial groups, the actual lines became blurred. Many mestizos acquired wealth and status and gained acceptance as creoles. A legal procedure allowed people to establish "purity of blood" ("*limpieza de sangre*") by paying a fee. Such a payment enabled them to consider themselves and to be considered creole. Similarly many Indian leaders, despite their mixed ancestry, continued in their positions. Visiting Prussian scholar Alexander van Humboldt commented on the relation between race and social position: "In America, the greater or less degree of whiteness of skin decides the rank which man occupies in society. A white who rides barefooted on horseback thinks he belongs to the nobility of the country."

Table 4.1 *Colonial population, by race and ethnicity*

	1570	1646	1742	1793
Indians	3,336,860	1,269,607	1,540,256	2,319,741
Europeans	6,644	13,780	9,814	7,904
Mestizos	13,504	277,610	640,880	1,096,026
Blacks	20,569	35,089	20,131	6,100
Mulattos	2,435	116,529	266,196	369,790

Source: Gonzalo Aguirre Beltrán, *La población negra de México* (Mexico City: Fondo de Cultura Económica, 1989), pp. 210, 219, 222, 230.

WOMEN

The restrictions imposed on women in colonial Mexico reflected the value system then prevalent in the Western world, of which Spain and its colonies formed a part. Gender inequality in countries bordering on the Mediterranean, such as Spain, exceeded that of northern Europe. Spanish society viewed the family as a miniature state, which had as its head the father, who exercised complete authority over his wife and children. He was legally entitled to administer corporal punishment to his wife and children as long as he did not endanger their lives.

Urban–rural, Indian–creole (or mestizo), and slave–master divisions separated women. Some men had Spanish wives and Indian mistresses. Some women lived on the northern frontier and others resided in Mexico City. Finally the experience of women differed as the colony evolved over three centuries.

Women could not hold public office, vote, or be judges or priests. Regulations prohibited women from joining craft guilds, which prevented them from entering numerous occupations. Except for convents, women lacked groups that would further their interests in the way that the political system, the Church structure, and guilds furthered male interests.

Parents exercised authority over both male and female children until age twenty-five or until they married. After marriage women only transferred their dependence, becoming subject to their husbands' authority. Married women required their husbands' permission to carry out legal proceedings, such as selling property, borrowing money, founding a charity, or freeing a slave. During the marriage, the husband administered communal property, including any income his wife might earn. He could dispose of this property without her consent. Wives could inherit property, but husbands had the right to administer it.

Some laws did protect women's interests. Inheritance laws guaranteed female children an equal share of their parents' wealth, including land. Women could defend their interests, such as their right to an inheritance, in court. A widowed woman received half of the property accumulated during the marriage and any other personal property she might have brought to the marriage, such as her dowry.

Unmarried women over age twenty-five and especially widows enjoyed the most freedom. They could carry out their own legal transactions, manage property, and choose their residence. The 1811 Mexico City census indicated that a fifth of women aged eighteen and over, primarily widows, headed their own households. The lucky minority of widows with assets could and did administer ranches, haciendas, shops, pulque taverns, and other urban businesses. They either exercised direct control of such properties or hired an administrator.

The concept of honor exercised a strong influence on women of European ancestry, creole and Spaniard. Honor demanded that women remain virgins until marriage. Male relatives, who suffered a loss of honor if a female relative lost her virginity, kept sisters and daughters under tight control to avoid this. After marriage, to preserve a wife's honor, a life of modest withdrawal was the ideal. As a result, upper-class women, who left business matters to their husbands, remained at home and supervised family members, administered money that the husband doled out for household expenses, and inculcated acceptance of these norms in their children. In addition, they administered servants, performed domestic tasks, embroidered, and read religious works.

Income-generating activities for women, married and unmarried, varied according to class and ethnicity. The 1811 Mexico City census reported that only 13 percent of Spanish and creole women declared an occupation, while 36 percent of mixed-race and 46 percent of Indian women did. Women frequently worked as domestics or as cigarette makers, wet nurses, washerwomen, and ambulatory vendors. Mine operations depended on women serving as cooks, servants, and prostitutes. Many slave women worked in sugar mills. Indian women produced and sold poultry, vegetables, and textiles in traditional weekly markets. Poor creole and mestizo women worked as seamstresses, or sold cigars, sweets, candles, trinkets, and alcoholic beverages from small stalls. In the first half of the eighteenth century, women comprised a third of the textile labor force in Puebla. At the end of the colonial period, half of the 7,000 employees at the royal tobacco factory were women, a harbinger of the opening of salaried occupations for women in the nineteenth century.

Elite women administered family property if no adult males were available. In urban areas, women owned bakeries, print shops, and textile workshops known as *obrajes*. Sixteen of the thirty convents founded in New Spain between 1600 and the end of the colonial period were the work of women.

During the late colonial period, the Crown favored expanded female employment to increase family spending money, to provide a greater market for manufactured goods, and to free men for mining, farming, and military service. In 1799, to increase female employment, Viceroy Miguel José de Azanza decreed that women could hold a job regardless of guild rules excluding them. The percentage of the female workforce working as servants and seamstresses declined from 88 percent in 1753 to 54 percent in 1811, indicating an increase in female employment opportunities. With the exception of cigar making, women workers at the end of the colonial period predominated in the same sectors as today—domestic service, the apparel industry, and food processing and distribution.

Peasant families shared power more evenly than more affluent ones. Men cultivated the family cornfields, while women tended gardens, raised small animals, wove cloth, made clothing, and prepared meals. Peasant women often sold goods in local markets and joined husbands and children in the fields at harvest time. Landed estates mainly hired men, leaving women with increased power in the home and the community. As a result, women constituted a majority of the participants in many of the local peasant rebellions that erupted during the eighteenth century. Women often led these movements, which protested encroachments on community autonomy.

Marriage for the more affluent in colonial Mexico generally involved a dowry. The custom of providing dowries came from medieval Spain. The dowry could be in the form of cash, jewelry, slaves, clothing, household furnishings, or real estate. Upon marriage, the husband managed, but did not assume ownership of this wealth.

The dowry served as a means of parental control, since if the bride's parents disapproved of the marriage, they could deny a dowry. It also served to indicate social standing, since only the elite could afford a large dowry, which would attract a husband from a family of high standing. The dowry helped offset the cost of establishing the new household. When a couple legally separated or the husband died, the dowry reverted to the wife. As in other Latin American countries, in eighteenth-century Mexico, the use of dowries declined.

The Church required married couples to live together. Religious authorities could force a wife to live with her husband, even if both spouses preferred to live apart. However, either spouse could petition for "ecclesiastical divorce," akin to a modern legal separation. Before the petition could be granted, a spouse had to present evidence of some specific offense. Grounds for an ecclesiastical divorce included: 1) one spouse being cruel or physically abusive; 2) a spouse having an incurable contagious disease, such as leprosy; 3) one spouse forcing the other to commit criminal acts, such as being a prostitute; 4) a spouse embracing paganism or heresy; 5) adultery; or 6) abandonment by the husband. The deterioration of the relationship alone could not serve as grounds for the divorce.

This proceeding differed from divorce in the modern sense. The Church controlled both marriage and ecclesiastical divorce. Catholic doctrine regarded the couple as still married, so a spouse could only remarry upon the death of the other spouse. It did allow the spouses to establish separate households. In early nineteenth-century Mexico City, roughly 1 percent of marriages ended up in the divorce court.

Reading and writing were deemed superfluous for poor women. Even the privileged elite girls of European ancestry received only a minimal education—in reading, writing, arithmetic, and domestic arts—which was considered all the knowledge they needed. Frequently nuns in convents imparted such instruction. In other cases, lay women taught girls until the age of eleven or twelve. The low educational level of these women, known as *amigas*, prevented them from dispelling the prevailing ignorance. Only the most fortunate received instruction from the amigas. In 1753, fewer than 25 percent of girls in Mexico City received any instruction at all.

Even fewer educational opportunities existed in rural areas. Generally girls (and boys) received no formal schooling in rural Mexico, where the majority of the population lived. For Indian girls, family and community provided knowledge. Illiteracy among rural women remained the norm through the end of the nineteenth century.

Educators did not design the curricula to uplift female status, but to foster acceptance of socially assigned roles. To prepare for the woman's assigned task of providing religious training to children, girls' schools emphasized memorizing catechism. Girls' education also stressed domestic skills such as weaving, embroidery, and sewing. As historian Asunción Lavrin emphasized, "Knowledge beyond these narrowly defined parameters was not for women."

Colonial society considered marriage the norm. However, especially among the upper classes, many chose not to marry. Family wealth allowed affluent women to establish separate households. Other family members benefited by the reduction in the number of descendants who would claim the family wealth. Among the less affluent, especially those of mixed race, priests had less influence. This allowed many couples to simply begin living together. Throughout the colonial period, numerous adult women remained unmarried—living with a man, living alone, or widowed. An early eighteenth-century census in Guadalajara indicated that 64 percent of women were unmarried.

SOR JUANA INÉS DE LA CRUZ

Despite the restrictions placed on women in New Spain, Sor Juana Inés de la Cruz remains the best-remembered Mexican from the colonial period. Sor (Sister) Juana was born as Juana Inés de Asbaje y Ramírez sometime between 1648 and 1651. Her Basque father, whom she may have never met, did not marry her creole mother.

Juana spent the first years of her life in the village of Nepantla, between Mexico City and the volcano Popocatépetl. She learned to read at age three by tagging along to the reading lessons of an older sister. Juana could read proficiently before her mother even learned of her class attendance. She had the good fortune to have access to books in her maternal grandfather's library. Though far from wealthy, her grandfather had amassed one of the few private collections of books in the colony. She indicated her early devotion to learning when she unsuccessfully attempted to persuade her mother to let her dress as a male so she could enter the university, which banned women.

At age eight, Juana moved in with an aunt in Mexico City to increase her access to learning. At the age of thirteen, she received permission to live in the viceregal court as a maid-in-waiting—a common practice for favored children. During the five years she spent in court, she became an accomplished poet and the most learned woman in Mexico. Court life gave her a chance to mingle with the intellectual elite of Mexico.

When she reached adulthood, Juana faced marriage, remaining single, or entering a convent. Given the values of her age, she almost certainly could not have found a husband willing to accept her intellectual activity. Had she been wealthy, remaining single might have been an option, but her family had little money. No unmarried women intellectuals in the colony served as role models. That left entering a convent as the only alternative to marriage.

Juana entered the permissive Convent of Santa Paula of the Hieronymite order in 1669. She later wrote concerning that choice, "Given my total disinclination to marriage, it was the least unreasonable and most becoming choice I could make to assure my ardently desired salvation." She noted that another influence was her desire "to live alone, to have no fixed occupation which might curtail my freedom to study."

For the next twenty years, Sor Juana dedicated herself to intellectual pursuits. She commented on this activity:

> From my first glimmers of reason, my inclination to letters was of such power and vehemence, that neither reprimands of others—and I have received many—nor my own considerations—and there have been not a few of these—have succeeded in making me abandon this natural impulse which God has implanted in me.

Within the convent, Sor Juana amassed one of the largest libraries in New Spain. She wrote in virtually every literary genre of the time, including ballads, drama, lyrics for lay and religious songs, love sonnets, the burlesque epigram, essay, drama, and religious works. The publication of her writings in Spain gave her renown throughout the Spanish-speaking world. She remained in close contact with the viceregal court and often received correspondence from abroad. As Mexican writer Octavio Paz commented, "Throughout the eighteenth and nineteenth centuries, there is no poet who used with such exquisite mastery so much variety in meter and form."

Due to her biting comments on the subordinate role of women, many refer to Sor Juana as the first feminist in the Americas. In a frequently quoted poem, she commented on the double standard involving prostitutes:

> ¿O cuál es más de culpar,
> aunque cualquiera mal haga:
> la que peca por la paga
> o el que paga por pecar?

> Which is more to blame,
> Though each is a sinner:
> She who sins for pay,
> Or he who pays to win her?

Science fascinated Sor Juana, and she wrote concerning various physical phenomena, ranging from the spinning of a top to the chemical changes produced by cooking food. Her observations in the kitchen led her to write, "If Aristotle had been a cook, he would have written much more."

For twenty years, thanks to her ties to court and wealthy patrons financing her book purchases, Sor Juana continued her prodigious output. Her collected works total 876 pages.

Figure 4.2
The title page of this 1649 tract in Nahuatl by Luis Laso de la Vega relates the appearance of the Virgin of Guadalupe. The picture depicts the Virgin.

Source: D. A. Brading, *Mexican Phoenix* (Cambridge: Cambridge University Press, 2001), p. 82.

In 1690, the Bishop of Puebla published Sor Juana's *Carta Atenagórica* (*Missive Worthy of Athens*), her criticism of a sermon by a Jesuit priest. In addition to publishing the critique, the bishop wrote a letter criticizing Sor Juana's scholarly activity. The letter bore the signature of Sor Filotea de la Cruz, a pseudonym for the bishop. In the letter, the bishop criticized Sor Juana for failing to confine her writings to religious topics, stating: "Letters that breed arrogance God does not want in women. But the Apostle does not reject them so long as they do not remove women from a position of obedience."

The bishop's attack occurred at an inopportune moment for Sor Juana. Her benefactor, the former viceroy, had recently died in Spain. Archbishop Francisco Aguiar y Seijas, a misogynist who thought women should be scourging themselves, not writing plays and poetry, headed the church in Mexico.

The bishop, who no doubt sought a humble retraction, found himself confronted with a refutation, known as the *Reply to Sor Filotea*. In it, Sor Juana commented that she and other women were just as entitled to write as males and inquired, "Is not my mind, such as it is, as free as his, considering their common origin?" In her response she cited numerous women from classical antiquity to the seventeenth century who had written and translated religious works.

Shortly after she wrote *Reply to Sor Filotea*, Sor Juana renounced her literary activity, sold her library and musical instruments and donated the proceeds to the poor. She turned to the more conventional life of an ascetic nun. Sor Juana's renunciation of writing remains the great mystery of her life. Paz commented, "More likely it was due to the unwonted solitude in which she was living and to the anxiety caused by increasingly overt hostility on the part of her ill-wishers."

When a plague broke out in her convent in 1695, Sor Juana cared for the afflicted and contracted the disease herself. As a result, she died in the convent, after twenty-six years of being encloistered.

Sor Juana's life clearly reflects her times. She would not have been criticized if she had been a man engaged in the same pursuits. While she received severe criticism for being a scholarly woman, no one questioned the propriety of her owning the mulatto slave girl whom she brought to the convent as a servant.

THE INTELLECTUAL SCENE

With few exceptions, only those who could afford to arrange private tutors received an education. Mass education was frowned upon. In a 1785 *cédula* (decree), King Carlos IV declared that it was not desirable to "illustrate the Americans." He also proclaimed "His Majesty did not need philosophers but good and obedient subjects."

However, the need for an educated elite was recognized. In response, the Crown founded the Royal and Pontifical University of Mexico in 1553, eighty-three years before Harvard, "to serve God and the public welfare." A 1557 decree limited the number of students of mixed blood to six. In 1645, a constitution drawn up by Archbishop Palafox codified the racial make-up of the university. It excluded blacks, mulattos, slaves, Orientals, Jews, and Moors from enrollment. For the two and a half centuries following its founding, the university provided New Spain with priests, lawyers, and doctors. By 1776, the university had granted 1,162 masters and doctorates and 29,882 bachelors degrees.

Initially the university, which was modeled on the renowned University of Salamanca, concentrated on four traditional faculties—law, the arts, theology, and medicine. Except for medical classes, professors taught in Latin and students wrote exams and theses in that language. Later the university included such subjects as anatomy, surgery, mathematics, and astrology in the curriculum. Courses in Indian languages trained aspiring missionaries.

University professors received little pay, even by the standards of the time. However, along with the student body they did enjoy two privileges. The two groups formed a corporate body whose members were immune from judgment by civil authorities. Professors and students also elected the rector of the university.

In 1539, an Italian who adopted the name Juan Pablos opened a print shop in Mexico City under the auspices of the first viceroy, Antonio de Mendoza, and the first bishop of Mexico City, Juan de Zumárraga. That year, Pablos printed *Doctrina cristiana* in Spanish and Nahuatl. Between 1524 and 1572, the mendicants published 109 books facilitating evangelization in various indigenous languages. By the end of the century, roughly 220 books had been published, and eight other printers had opened shops. Initially publishing in the colony served to disseminate Christian doctrine and the king's laws. Later works included scholarly treatises and literature, including works of Sor Juana.

Figure 4.3 *Sor Juana de la Cruz, pictured here, remains the best-known Mexican from the colonial period.*

Source: Reproduced with permission of the General Secretariat of the Organization of American States.

The Mexican publishing industry grew slowly through the colonial period. In 1810, the Mexican press published 275 titles (excluding newspapers) on religion, politics, literature, and other subjects. The number of copies of each book printed ran from a few hundred to several thousand. Various factors limited further increases in book publication. The high cost of paper and competition from imports limited demand for books printed in Mexico. The small number of copies printed increased the cost of each book. Low levels of literacy limited sales. Before a book could be published, the approval of a religious censor and civil authorities was required. Priests in religious orders also needed the approval of their order before they could publish their writings. Books dealing with the New World required authorization of the Council of the Indies.

The first literature from Mexico, written by Spaniards, dealt with the conquest itself. Cortés's *Cartas de México* (*Letters from Mexico*) and Díaz del Castillo's *Historia verdadera de la conquista de la Nueva España* (*True History of the Conquest of New Spain*), the two outstanding examples of this genre, continue to be read widely. These chronicles displayed a messianic sense of history, denigrated indigenous culture, and condemned native idolatry.

During the seventeenth century, Mexico City remained the intellectual center of New Spain. Academies, literary groups, poetry readings, and musical performances complemented the university there. As in the previous century, rather than innovating, Mexico imported ideas and cultural norms from Europe. During this century, native-born creole writers replaced the Spanish immigrants who had been the dominant writers of the sixteenth century.

The expulsion of the Jesuits unintentionally resulted in the exiled Mexican priests making fundamental contributions to Mexican thought and culture. Much of their work responded to Europeans who proclaimed the "inferiority" of the geography and people of the Americas. The exiled Jesuits, who remained in Europe, compiled information on Mexico's ancient history, languages, geography, and ethnography.

The Jesuit historian Francisco Javier Clavijero, born to Spanish parents in Veracruz in 1731, was the most eloquent and scholarly of these exiled authors. While in Mexico, he learned several indigenous languages. Clavijero did not begin writing history until after the Crown forced him and his fellow Jesuits from Mexico. His works defended pre-Hispanic civilization and creole culture, which Europeans, most of whom had never even visited the New World, often misrepresented. Clavijero indicated his sympathies when he compared the Spanish destruction of Tenochtitlan to the Roman destruction of Jerusalem. His best-known work, *Historia antigua de México* (*Ancient History of Mexico*), provided a scientific description of pre-conquest cultures and nurtured creole pride in Mexico's ancient heritage.

Clavijero considered that pre-conquest Mexico was shaped by social, geographic, and political forces, rather than its being the product of diabolic influence as previous historians had claimed. He readily acknowledged the role indigenous labor played in the construction of colonial society. The tasks he mentioned as being performed by Indians, whom he referred to as *americanos*, included working the land, reaping wheat, lumbering, working stone, construction, road-building, mining, and herding.

Mexico City remained the colony's outstanding intellectual center through the end of the colonial period. Humboldt stated, "No city on the continent, without even excepting those of the United States, can display such great and solid scientific establishments as the capital of Mexico." In 1785, the Crown established the prestigious San Carlos Noble Arts Academy in the capital. There European masters, highly influenced by prevailing neo-classic styles, taught drawing, sculpture, architecture, and mathematics. From 1805 to 1812, Carlos María de Bustamante published the first Mexican newspaper, *El Diario de México*. This Mexico City paper demonstrated creole intellectual development, opening its pages to critical reflection on social and political matters as well as publishing substantial contributions concerning Indian history and antiquities.

DOCUMENT 4.1: "WHY THE INDIANS ARE DYING"

[Spaniard Alonso de Zorita began serving on the Mexico City *audiencia* in 1556. He returned to Spain in 1566 and began work on his *Brief and Summary Relation of the Lords of New Spain*, from which the text below is excerpted. Although he was writing well before the development of the germ theory of disease, he did observe how Spanish mistreatment of Indians predisposed them to disease and an early death.]

In the old days [the Indians] performed their communal labor in their own towns. Their labor was lighter, and they were well treated. They did not have to leave their homes and families, and they ate food they were accustomed to eat and at the usual hours. They did their work together and with much merriment, for they are people who do little work alone, but together they accomplish something . . .

What has destroyed and continues to destroy the Indians is their forced labor in the construction of large stone masonry buildings in the Spaniards' towns. For this they are forced to leave their native climates, to come from tierra fría [cold country] to tierra caliente [hot country], and visa versa, 20, 30, 40, and more leagues away. Their whole tempo of life, the time and mode of work, of eating and sleeping, are disrupted. They are forced to work many days and weeks, from dawn until after dusk, without any rest.

Once I saw, after the hour of vespers, a great number of Indians hauling a long heavy beam to a construction site owned by a very prominent man. When they stopped to rest, a Negro overseer went down the line with a leather strap in hand, whipping them all from the first to last to hurry them on and keep them from resting; he did this not to gain time for some other work, for the day was over, but simply to keep up the universal evil habit of mistreating the Indians. Since the Negro struck with force and they were naked, with only their genitals covered, the lashes must have caused them cruel pain; but no one spoke or turned his head, for they are ever long-suffering and submissive. It is a routine thing to drive them, to work them without letting them pause for breath, and to harass them in every possible way . . .

They have been destroyed by the great and excessive tribute they have had to pay, for in their great fear of the Spanish they have given all they had. Since the tribute was excessive and continually demanded, to make payment they sold their land at a low price, and their children as slaves. When they had nothing left with which to pay, many died for this in prison; if they managed to get out, they emerged in such sorry state that they died in a few days. Others died from being tortured to tell where there was gold or where they had hidden it. They have been treated bestially and unreasonably in all respects.

Their numbers have also been diminished by their enslavement for work in the mines and in their personal service of the Spaniards. In the first years there was such haste to make slaves that they poured into Mexico City from all directions and throughout the Indies they were taken in flocks like sheep to be branded. The Spaniards pressed the Indian lords to bring in all the slaves, and such was the Indians' fear that to satisfy the Spaniards they brought their own vassals and even their own children when they had no others to offer. Much the same thing happens today in the provision of Indians on the pretext that they had risen in rebellion, contrary to Your Majesty's orders.

They have been reduced by the thousands by their toil in the gold and silver mines; and on the journey to the mines 80 or 100 leagues away they were loaded with heavy burdens to which they were not accustomed. They died in the mines or along the road, of hunger and cold or extreme heat, and from carrying enormous loads of implements for the mines or other extremely heavy things; for the Spaniards, not satisfied with taking them so far away to work, must load them down on the way. Although the Indians brought some food from home, the amount was scanty, for they had no more; and it ran out on their arrival at the mines or on the journey home. Countless numbers died, and many fled to the woods, abandoning their homes, wives, and children, and thus the towns on the way to the mines or around them became depopulated. The Spaniards still compel the Indians to go to the mines on the pretext that they are being sent to construct buildings there and are going voluntarily; these Spaniards claim that your Majesty does not prohibit such labor, but only forbids work in the mines. In actual fact the Indians never go voluntarily, for they are forced to go under the repartimiento system by order of the Audiencia, contrary to your Majesty's orders.

Source: Gilbert M. Joseph and Timothy J. Henderson (eds.) (2002) *The Mexico Reader: History, Culture, Politics.* Durham, N.C.: Duke University Press, pp. 123–25.

NOTES

1   Eric Hobsbawm, *The Age of Revolution, Europe, 1789–1848* (New York: Barnes & Noble, 1996), p. 20.

2   Nancy Farriss, *Maya Society under Colonial Rule* (Princeton, N.J.: Princeton University Press, 1984), p. 283.

3   Donald Worcester, *The Apaches* (Norman, OK: University of Oklahoma Press, 1979), p. xviii.

4   In Hugh Thomas, *The Slave Trade* (New York: Simon & Schuster, 1997), p. 216.

FURTHER READING

Brading, D. A. (2009) "Imperial Mexico: The Viceregal Capital," in *Mexico City Through History and Culture*, ed. Linda A. Newson and John P. King, pp. 39–53. Oxford: Oxford University Press.
    A description of the outstanding city of the Americas by a noted British historian.

Farriss, Nancy M. (1984) *Maya Society under Colonial Rule.* Princeton, N.J.: Princeton University Press.
    As this study shows, colonial rule affected different indigenous groups in different ways.

Gibson, Charles (1964) *The Aztecs under Spanish Rule.* Stanford, CA: Stanford University Press.
    A classic account of how the Aztecs fared under Spanish colonial rule.

Humboldt, Alexander (1966) *Political Essay on the Kingdom of New Spain.* New York: AMS Press.
  A classic account of Mexico written by a Prussian visitor shortly before Mexico's independence.

Lavrin, Asunción (2010) "Women in Colonial Mexico," in *The Oxford History of Mexico* (rev. ed.), ed. Michael C. Meyer and William H. Beezley, pp. 235–61. New York: Oxford University Press.
  A concise description of the position of women in the colonial period.

Martínez, María Elena (2008) *Genealogical Fictions: Limpieza de Sangre, Religion, and Gender in Colonial Mexico.* Stanford, CA: Stanford University Press.
  An examination of the notion of "purity of blood" and the belief that religious preferences were passed through blood to descendants, regardless of the environment the next generation was raised in. Martínez traces this belief from its medieval Spanish origins to its application in New Spain. She also considers various aspects of Mexican colonial life including social stratification, religion, caste, and race.

Offutt, Leslie S. (2001) *Saltillo, 1770–1810: Town and Region in the Mexican North.* Tucson, AZ: University of Arizona Press.
  A description of a northern Mexican City that was founded in 1577. Unlike many northern Mexican cities which were mining centers, Saltillo was based on commerce.

GLOSSARY TERMS

casta
composición
congregación
mestizo
repartimiento

Chapter 5

From Corn to Capitalism, 1521–1810

TIMELINE—WORLD

1516 Portugal begins commerce with China	**1519–22** Magellan expedition circumnavigates globe	**1543** Copernicus publishes his theory that the Earth revolves around the sun	**1544** Silver mines of Potosí, Bolivia, discovered	**1602** Dutch East Indian Corporation established
1807 Fulton navigates steamship on Hudson	**1814** Stephenson uses first effective steam locomotive	**1820** Roughly 95 percent of energy used by humans is from wood.		

TIMELINE—MEXICO

1546 Discovery of silver in Zacatecas	**1551** Discovery of silver in Durango	**1552** Pachuca mines opened	**1553** Patio process for refining silver introduced	**1588** Guanajuato mines opened

After the Conquest, New Spain became part of a much larger whole, the Spanish empire, and, through it, the capitalist mercantile system.

(Enrique Semo, 1993)

1620	1687	1692	1776	1789
Francis Bacon's *Novrum Organum Scientiarum* paves way for experimental research	Isaac Newton's *Principia Book I* lays groundwork for modern science	Lloyd's coffee house becomes insurance office	Adam Smith publishes *The Wealth of Nations*	First manufacturing powered by a steam engine, beginning the Industrial Revolution in Great Britain

1645	1777	1784	1792	1799–1804
Sigüenza y Góngora born	Mining tribunal created	End of convoy system	Royal College of Mines founded	Humboldt travels to Latin America, including Mexico

THIS CHAPTER DISCUSSES HOW GEOGRAPHY SHAPED NEW SPAIN'S economic development. It then considers how the Mexican economy evolved over three centuries. The sixteenth century saw the introduction of new tools, plants and animals, as well as government regulations. The seventeenth saw the emergence of more Spanish enterprises while the eighteenth saw economic reforms. Next is a description of the major areas of the economy—mining, agriculture, manufacturing, and trade. The chapter concludes with discussions of New Spain's impact on the rest of the world and of colonial economic policy.

GEOGRAPHY

Geography played a crucial role in shaping colonial development. Due to soil fertility, abundant rainfall, and the availability of Indian labor, Spanish settlement was concentrated in central Mexico. Rampant diseases, to which newcomers had little resistance, discouraged European settlement in low-lying coastal areas. The aridity of the north discouraged settlement there. Relatively few areas outside the central core could be used for agriculture, as roughly 31 percent of Mexico's land area is classified as desert and another 36 percent is semiarid.

The availability of water, as well as topography, determined trade routes. In the early 1620s, Domingo Lázaro de Arregui commented on the 135-mile road from the silver-mining city of Zacatecas to the mining hamlet of Mazapil: "If you took the direct route, you would arrive in two days at Mazapil. But travelling by the water holes and along the carting road, the journey takes five or six days. Going as the crow flies, there is no road or water, which is the reason for following such a roundabout path as people use."

The lack of major rivers connecting New Spain's population centers had a profound impact on development. Transport by mule or cart was slow and expensive. As historians Arij Ouweneel and Catrien Bijleveld observed, "The severe climate, the difficult topography, the poorly paved roads, and the lack of good waterways between the population centers impeded the formation of an integrated market system." Until the advent of the railroad in the latter part of the nineteenth century, mule transport linked Mexico City with the colony's two major ports—Veracruz and Acapulco.

The transportation system in colonial Mexico stood in stark contrast to those of British North America and Western Europe, whose economies were undergoing rapid economic growth and whose broad rivers made it possible to transport bulk goods to inland population centers inexpensively. In contrast with Mexico, much of the population of both these areas was located in port cities, so goods could be exchanged by sea, and relatively flat expanses and abundant water later made it possible to extend transport networks by building canals.

Population figures illustrate the impracticality of coastal shipping in New Spain. Tampico, the only coastal town of importance north of Veracruz, had only twenty-four Spanish citizens and 226 tributary Indians in 1570. At the end of the sixteenth century, Yucatán only had 300 Spanish citizens.

Elevation change made transport difficult but yielded tremendous diversity. Thomas Gage, an English priest, traveled in Mexico between 1625 and 1636. When he passed through Jalapa, fifty miles inland from the Gulf Coast, he observed: "What makes it rich are the many farms of sugar, and some which they call *estancias*, rich farms for breeding mules and cattle; and likewise some farms of cochineal." After visiting Puebla, 100 miles further west, he commented: "Without it, there are many gardens, which store the markets with provision of salads. The soil abounds with wheat, and with sugar farms." In Oaxaca, he observed:

The valley is full of sheep and other cattle, which yield much wool to the clothiers of the City of Angeles, store of hides to the merchants of Spain, and great provision of flesh to the city of Oaxaca, and to all the towns about . . . But what doth make the valley of Oaxaca to be mentioned far and near are the good horses which are bred in it, and esteemed to be the best of all the country. In this valley also are some farms of sugar, and great store of fruits, which two sorts meeting together have cried up the city of Oaxaca for the best conserves and preserves that are made in America.[1]

THE SIXTEENTH CENTURY

Without labor, private landholding had limited value, and the accumulation of wealth, based on the utilization of economic resources, would be unlikely. The Europeans moved aggressively to establish both the concept of private property and its corollary, wage labor.
(Colin MacLachlan, 1988)

After the fall of Tenochtitlan, Spaniards began shaping the Mexican economy. The transition from feudalism to capitalism occurring in Europe and Spain's increasing insertion into the international market influenced this transformation. Spain set economic policy at all levels. The monarch set guidelines for the general course of the empire. Municipal governments allocated land, set prices, monitored markets, enforced guild regulations, and administered common land and public works.

Sixteenth-century Mexico saw sweeping changes in technology. The long list of newly introduced items includes maps, the compass, pulleys, screws, the wheel for transport, and tools for blacksmithing and carpentry. Spaniards introduced some simple items, such as the nail. Others, such as ships used in transoceanic commerce, involved a complex combination of devices.

Replacing the digging stick with the plow led to increased productivity and to more erosion as the plow loosened the entire surface of the earth. Plow-induced erosion led to the abandonment of entire estates. For example, the Jesuit-owned Jesús del Monte estate once produced 272,445 liters of wheat annually. Plow cultivation led to its fertile soil being washed away, leaving only bare rock. The Jesuits then converted the property from a wheat farm to a spiritual retreat.

The introduction of European plants and animals produced a profound biological revolution. Plants intentionally introduced from the Old World include oranges, wheat, bananas, sugar cane, and mulberry trees for raising silk worms. Animals the Spaniards brought included chickens, pigs, donkeys, goats, sheep, cattle, and horses.

European weeds proliferated and crowded out indigenous plants after Spaniards inadvertently introduced their seeds in cattle feed, horses' hooves, and cattle dung. These weeds thrived on plowed and overgrazed land. By 1600, many New World plants had become extinct, replaced by dandelions, nettles, and a host of grasses.

A biological exchange in the opposite direction benefited the Old World. Corn and the potato were native to the New World and unknown in the Old World before Columbus. Other important plants introduced from the New World include sweet potatoes, peanuts, pineapples, vanilla, chiles, tomatoes, tobacco, long-stemmed cotton, and cacao (the source of chocolate).

The Spaniards who came to Mexico during the sixteenth century had more experience with plunder, tribute, and slavery than they had with wages and market economies. The economy that emerged after the conquest reflected this. It would be centuries before the labor force freely chose jobs based on working conditions and the wages received.

In the decade after the conquest, the Spanish enslaved many Indians. However, due to their high death rate, high initial purchase costs, and the availability of Indian labor through the *encomienda* and the *repartimiento*, Indian slavery soon diminished in importance.

The Crown had a financial interest in abolishing Indian slavery since slaves did not pay tribute. A combination of financial interest and humanistic concern resulted in the New Laws of 1542, which prohibited Indian slavery. After this date Indian slavery gradually disappeared in most areas. Exceptions however persisted. In 1643, Indians were still being bought and sold for work in the mines of Oaxaca. Well into the eighteenth century northern landowners successfully veiled several forms of slavery or near slavery behind definitions of just war, penal servitude and *congregación*.

Indians not living within an *encomienda* paid tribute directly to the Spanish king. Such payments reflected the presumption that "discovered" lands belonged to the Crown. The king required the original inhabitants to pay him tribute to compensate him for generously allowing them to use his land. In 1570, roughly 800,000 Indians made such tribute payments.

Each head of a household in an Indian republic paid roughly two pesos a year tribute to the Spanish Crown. Non-Indians were exempt from this tax burden. As the Indian population declined more rapidly than the total amount of tribute demanded, per capita payments increased. This created a circular effect: more overwork, more population decline, and still more tribute per capita.

Initially Indians paid tribute in the form of food and clothing. Tribute payments in kind, such as corn, were generally sold at public auction to convert them into cash. However, most Indian-produced goods could not be readily converted to cash. As a result, treasury officials increasingly required Indians to pay tribute in cash. As this pressure increased, Indians became more integrated into the market economy, selling either their goods or their labor to raise the cash needed for tribute payments. To meet the Spaniards' cash demands, Indians produced and marketed silk, wheat, sheep, cattle, and pigs. The Spanish economy had little to offer the Indians that their own communities could not provide. The tribute requirement thus forced Indians to work for wages. In the absence of tribute, many would have produced to meet their own needs and avoided the cash economy.

Rather than being consumed by local princes and lords, post-conquest tribute embarked on a much more circuitous journey. In-kind tribute payments were sold for cash. The corn paid in tribute often nourished animals working in silver mines. Treasury officials sent the silver from the mines and cash tribute to Europe, where it circulated widely. Europeans re-exported much of this silver to the Orient in exchange for spices and other exotic imports.

Given the lack of currency, the lack of Spanish-run enterprises, and the lack of European goods Indians desired, the Spaniards could not rely on wage labor. When Indians did receive wages, as in the case of *repartimiento* workers, they did not have the choice of rejecting employment. Luis de Velasco, who became viceroy in 1550, commented, "Indians must be forced to work for wages in the fields or in the towns to stop them from becoming vagrants."

At the end of the sixteenth century, each of the major ethnic groups specialized in certain economic activities. Indians produced corn, beans, chile, and the **agave** (*maguey*). They planted with the digging stick, and the same individuals produced crops and engaged in artisanal activity. The Spanish managed silver mines and estates producing wheat, cattle, and sugar cane. Fields were plowed, and mules and wagons carried goods. Most Spanish artisans did not engage in agriculture. These two groups were linked economically through tribute, the *encomienda*, and *repartimiento* labor.

THE SEVENTEENTH CENTURY

During the seventeenth century, the pace of change slowed. In both the seventeenth and eighteenth centuries though Spanish technology continued to permeate more deeply into the warp and woof of Mexican society.

The *encomienda* ceased to be the dominant social institution. By the middle of the century, commerce, northern mines, and sugar refineries furnished considerably more revenue than the best *encomiendas*. This shift in the source of wealth led historian P. J. Bakewell to comment:

> In the sixteenth century, the white community lived on the surplus produced by a vast number of Indians working in a very primitive economic system. In the seventeenth, Spaniards lived on

the product, broadly and ultimately, of their own enterprise and of an economy that was in its general outline of contemporary European design.[2]

Mexicans invested more capital locally, leading to an increase in production for Mexican use. This benefited the colony and led to greater economic diversity and autonomy. Given the high cost of land transportation, New Spain remained a patchwork of regional economies stitched together by trade and government. High taxes, piracy, privateering, and insecurity resulting from European wars limited trans-Atlantic trade.

Between 1628 and 1724, silver production increased at an annual rate of 1.2 percent. At the same time, much to the chagrin of the Spanish, Mexicans appropriated more silver to finance their own production, administration, and defense, leaving less for the mother country. Due to increased smuggling, tax collection declined, further reducing remittances to Spain. In 1660, colonial authorities estimated that untaxed silver accounted for one-third more production than registered shipments. Finally, since Mexicans produced more goods for their own use, they sent less silver to Spain to purchase goods there.

It is hardly surprising that Mexican economic growth proceeded at a snail's pace during the seventeenth century, since that was the prevalent condition in the world to which Mexico had been linked by the conquest. Up to the beginning of the Industrial Revolution in the eighteenth century, growth was so slow that it might not be noticed within a lifetime. By one estimate, world per capita income only increased from $133 to $164 between 1000 and 1700. This imperceptible growth resulted from a very gradual increase in human population and from improvements in technology coming very slowly (by modern standards).

THE EIGHTEENTH CENTURY

> The rise in royal revenues during the eighteenth century was truly spectacular, evidence perhaps of the effectiveness of the Bourbon reforms, a flourishing mining economy, diversification of productive activity, new taxes, and a rise in the population.
>
> (John TePaske and Herbert Klein, 1981)

King Carlos III (1759–1788) emerged as the foremost proponent of economic reform during the eighteenth century. New economic ideas in vogue in France strongly influenced him. Carlos promoted commerce and production and protected national industry from foreign competition. Rather than emphasizing mining, as his predecessors had, he promoted agriculture by relaxing the restrictions on slave imports and by facilitating the purchase of agricultural implements and seeds of selected crops. He also promoted better transportation, realizing that such a measure would increase agricultural exports.

In 1777, Viceroy Antonio María de Bucareli commented on relaxed trade restrictions: "Never have the advantages been so visible as in the last few years." Due to the increased supply of labor and lower mercury prices, Mexican silver output increased substantially. In 1790, tax receipts totaled 11,493,748 pesos, 146 percent more than was collected in 1760. The mother country appropriated so much tax revenue that contemporaries spoke of a "river of silver" flowing from Veracruz to Havana and thence to Spain.

During the eighteenth century, silver production increased at an annual rate of 1.8 percent, thus enriching mine owners and their financial backers in the merchant community, expanding employment directly and indirectly, widening the market for food and services, and providing the metallic basis for the local money supply. Long-distance trade increasingly monetized the economy as payment was made in silver. Ironically even with record silver production, there were never enough silver coins since so many coins were exported.

Figure 5.1 *Aqueducts were a crucial piece of colonial infrastructure, facilitating the existence of cities. Pictured here is the Xalpa aqueduct, built in the 1700s about nine miles northwest of Tepotzotlán.*

Source: William E. Doolittle.

Economic growth resulted from eliminating restrictions on trade, the discovery of new silver deposits, an increase in agricultural production to supply mines, and increased demand generated by the creation of a standing army and an expanded government workforce. Increases in lumbering, shipbuilding, and mule transport also contributed to eighteenth-century economic expansion.

This economic growth decreased the importance of the Indian community. The share of the colonial budget coming from tribute paid by Indians reflects this decline. In the sixteenth century, tribute provided the main source of Crown income, while by the middle of the eighteenth century it provided less than 5 percent. In the latter part of that century, half of Crown income was derived from taxes on mining and tobacco.

After economic reforms were implemented, the mother country remained the main beneficiary of Spanish economic policy. In 1778, Spanish economist Gaspar de Jovellanos stated, "Colonies are useful in so far as they offer a secure market for the surplus production of the metropolis." To limit possible competition from colonial production, Spain went so far as to destroy cotton mills in its colonies. In 1801, a directive ordered Spanish colonial officials "to effect their destruction by the most convenient means they can devise, even if it means taking them over by the royal treasury on the pretext of making them productive."

THE *PARTIDO*

Throughout the colonial period, in small mines employers would supply tools, and the miner his labor. At the end of the day, the extracted ore would be evenly divided between the owner and the mine workers. As mines became larger and involved complex credit arrangements, this sharing of ore evolved into the *partido* system. The *partido* was the share of each day's ore that belonged to the mineworker. Each day an ore quota would be established. The size of the quota depended on the difficulty of extracting the ore in the particular location being mined. After enough ore had been removed to meet the quota, any additional ore would be divided equally between miners and the mine owner. Miners could sell their share of the ore to independent refiners who would process it in small charcoal smelting furnaces.

The *partido* system was well suited to the colonial milieu in which it developed. Throughout the colonial period, mines suffered from a labor shortage. The *partido* attracted scarce labor since, if a pocket of rich ore was encountered, miners, as well as owners, shared in the bonanza. The *partido* also addressed the chronic capital shortage miner owners faced. Since part of miners' compensation was paid in ore, mine owners needed less capital up front to pay wages. The details of the *partido*, such as who set the quota and whether an individual miner could choose which ore went into the share he could sell, were negotiated at each individual mine. Given the scarcity of labor, miners had negotiating leverage. Income derived from miners' selling the *partido* allowed them to earn enough to survive without having to work seven days a week. When Alexander von Humboldt visited Mexico early in the nineteenth century, he commented that, thanks to their ability to negotiate for a valuable share of the ore, Mexican miners lived better than the miners in his native Germany.

Miners felt they deserved a fair share of the wealth generated by the mine. They also felt they deserved just compensation for an occupation which was extremely dangerous and unhealthy. A contemporary mining expert wrote, "It is frightening to read the phrases that [miners] use to express the terrors of this work: the continual risks of losing one's life, smothered in a landfall, plunged down an abyss, breathing noxious fumes, contracting pestilential disease . . ." Humboldt observed that eighteenth-century miners seldom lived past the age of 35.[3]

The tenacity with which miners defended the *partido* became evident in 1766 at the Real del Monte mine, sixty miles northeast of Mexico City. Since he was fabulously wealthy, mine owner Pedro Romero de Terreros did not face a capital shortage. To increase his profits he attempted to ram through several changes to mine work rules, including increasing the amount of ore he would retain and decreasing the *partido* miners retained. Miners initially responded by sending a petition to local authorities pleading their case. Failing at this, they sent a petition to the viceroy. That too failed, so they went out on strike, killed an abusive foreman, and shut the mine down.

The official response was typical of the colonial period. Some strike leaders were sentenced to forced labor and exiled from the mine area. However most of the miners' demands were met. The viceroy mandated that harassing foremen be summarily fired, the mine speed up reversed, and pay cuts revoked. For the first time, miners' right to the *partido* was stated in writing. The viceregal response was dictated both by humanitarian concern for labor and by the desire to avoid labor unrest interrupting the flow of silver from the mine.

Even though the Real del Monte mine closed during the independence struggle, British investors reopened the mine. In 1827, miners struck when the British proposed reducing the *partido*. Miners threatened to "raze to the ground" the company headquarters. A hostile British chief officer at Real del Monte attributed the strike to instigation "by a few malicious and designing persons."

The 1827 strike for the *partido* was successful in part due to Mexican troops stationed at the mine making it clear in the event of a showdown with the British, they would side with the miners. To settle the dispute, miners and British owners signed a formal labor contract guaranteeing the *partido*. It remained in force throughout the company's existence.

Sources: Kendall Brown (2012) *A History of Mining in Latin America*. Albuquerque, N.M.: University of New Mexico Press. Doris M. Ladd (1988) *The Making of a Strike*. Lincoln, NE: University of Nebraska Press.

MINING

> A mining boom almost always caused a business upturn, but it seldom served as an instrument of structural change and intensive economic growth.
>
> (Richard Garner, 1993)

From the Spanish point of view, mining provided New Spain's raison d'être. The 1550s take-off of Mexican mining, a result of the discovery of rich lodes such as those in Zacatecas (1546), Guanajuato (1550), Durango (1551), and Sombrerete (1558), more than met Spanish expectations.

Before 1553, silver miners used a charcoal fire fanned by a bellows to heat ore and extract silver. However this process, known as smelting, required relatively rich ore to be profitable. After 1553 the introduction of a new process for refining silver paved the way for the subsequent increase in silver mining. Miners referred to the new process as the "patio process" since finely ground ore, water, mercury, and other reagents were mixed and allowed to react for weeks on the patio of the processing plant. Men or mules dragged poles through large piles of the mixture to stir it. This caused the mercury and silver to amalgamate. Refiners baked the amalgam in a kiln to drive off the mercury, leaving the silver. After the introduction of the amalgamation process, costs could be met if miners recovered only one and a half ounces of silver per hundred kilograms of ore concentrate.

After the 1550s, silver production remained a key element of the colonial economy. In large part, a viceroy's reputation was based on the level of silver output during his administration. Silver never constituted less than 50 percent of Mexico's exports to Spain, and usually exceeded that figure. In the 1670s, New Spain permanently replaced Peru as the leading source of registered silver.

For most of the colonial period, mine owners combined free and forced labor. Around 1590, there were 9,143 mine workers, of which 13.8 percent were African slaves, 68.5 percent free Indian workers, and 17.7 percent Indians working to fulfill a *repartimiento* obligation. Miners preferred to rely on forced labor, since that lowered their wage bill. However, later in the colonial period, due to the absence of docile Indian labor near the mines of northern Mexico, mine owners increasingly recruited workers though a combination of wages, often paid in advance, and a share of the ore produced. Given the wealth mines generated, they could afford to pay wages that would attract workers on a voluntary basis.

During the sixteenth century, Spaniards introduced European techniques of deep shaft mining. Mine workers extracted the ore with brute force using hammers, mallets, picks, and crowbars, some of which weighed as much as 45 pounds. Human carriers then brought the rock to the surface in sacks weighing as much as 245 pounds. After the initial wave of European innovation, mining technology stagnated and fell behind European standards. Blasting powder and the animal-powered whim (*malacate*) for lifting ore and water did not become widely used until the eighteenth century.

Mexican silver undergirded the Crown's finances. Initially, miners paid a fifth of the metal produced, without deducting for expenses, as a tax. In 1548 the Crown reduced this tax to one-tenth. Silver financed the cost of colonial administration and defense, permitted Mexico to import goods, and enabled the Crown to engage in protracted wars. The Crown obtained additional revenue from its monopoly on the sale of the mercury used to refine silver. It used its control of the mercury supply to prevent cheating by silver miners. Those who did not pay taxes on production received no mercury to continue refining.

The demand generated by the mines had an effect felt well beyond the shaft. As nineteenth-century historian Lucas Alamán commented, "The great sums poured into mining firms spread out for many leagues, promoting agriculture and industry by providing consumers for agricultural products and by the use of machinery for drainage and extracting and refining ore." Mines required mules for powering whims and for transport. The mines of Guanajuato alone used 14,000 mules in the amalgamation patios. The livestock and the workers in turn generated a demand for grain. Haciendas producing grain and livestock sprang up in mining districts. The sale of clothes to miners stimulated the textile industry. In 1802 Mexican mines consumed roughly 1.3 million pounds of domestically manufactured blasting powder. Around 1730 the Zacatecas mines annually consumed 80 tons of candle wax and more than 3,300 pounds of wick. Mine inputs also included leather, charcoal, lumber, and salt. Mine owners paid for these inputs with silver coins, which then circulated throughout the colony.

The rich silver mines of Zacatecas, located 325 miles northwest of Mexico City, stimulated colonization in the north. Within two years of its founding in 1548, Zacatecas had five churches and fifty operating mines. By the end of the sixteenth century, it vied with Puebla for the honor of being the second city of New Spain. In the early 1600s, it had a population of 1,500 Spaniards and 5,000 Indian and black laborers and supported thriving shops and markets. Later discoveries of silver at Parral, Durango, and Chihuahua led to colonization still further north. Producers of livestock and cereals followed the miners north.

In 1776 Bourbon reformers created the Mining Tribunal to distribute mercury and blasting powder and to handle educational, administrative, and judicial matters relating to mining. The Tribunal also supplied credit to mines, both large and small. It drafted the mining laws in effect until the late nineteenth century. Ironically, since California retained its Mexican mining laws after its cession to the United States, the colonial mining law remained in effect during the 1849 California gold rush.

Figure 5.2 *Miners were frisked as they emerged from the mine to ensure that they did not attempt to hide valuable pieces of ore on their body. This sketch is by famous Mexican muralist Diego Rivera.*

Source: Raquel Tibol, *Diego Rivera: Gran Illustrador/Great Illustrator* (Mexico City: Editorial RM & Museo Nacional de Arte, 2008), p. 78.

The mining industry boomed thanks to favorable legislation, such as the 1781 tax exemption on mine tools and the Crown's lowering the prices of the mercury and of gunpowder used for blasting. Mines owned by large corporations, which relied on elaborate credit networks, increasingly replaced owner-operated mines. Mine productivity increased due to new technology and increased specialization of the labor force. Between 1769 and 1804, silver mintage increased from 11.99 million pesos to 26.13 million. Mexican silver—some two-thirds of world production—facilitated the growth of international trade. Asians expanded spice and silk production to exchange for Mexican silver.

The impact of mining must be kept in perspective. In 1800, mining contributed only 8.2 percent of the colony's gross domestic product and never employed more than 50,000 people. Except for draft animals and livestock products, most of the domestically produced goods used by mines came from the immediate region of the mine. Imports, such as mercury and ironware, which constituted 18 percent of mine purchases, did little to stimulate the economy.

In the early sixteenth century, mines smelted ore—a process which required a constant supply of charcoal made from wood. Even after the patio process largely replaced smelting, wooden beams shored up tunnels, and wood fires heated the amalgam. As a result, forests around mining areas were felled, leaving barren hillsides. While the patio process reduced the demand for wood, it created a new problem—mercury pollution. Every year hundreds of tons of mercury were released into the air, water, and soil surrounding the mining areas.

Mine production by volume peaked in the 1790s, but profits peaked in the 1770s. Due to the exhaustion of rich ores, progressively more ore had to be mined to produce a pound of silver. Also, as deposits near the surface were exhausted, shafts had to be enlarged and sunk deeper. Often such deep shafts required expensive drainage operations. In the late colonial period, as costs increased, the market value of silver declined. Historian John Coatsworth noted, "Each mark of silver produced bought less and cost more to produce."

AGRICULTURE

The hacienda evolved gradually from the first estates, which were based on grazing permits, not land ownership. These initial grants did not permit the owner of the herd to deny others access. Slowly the old view of land as a common resource changed. By the mid-1600s hacienda boundaries were becoming fixed. Owners invested heavily in buildings, machinery, storage facilities, and irrigation works. The capital for the initial development of the hacienda came from the *encomienda*, public office, mining, and commerce.

In central Mexico the birth of the hacienda responded to the decline of the Indian population. The food the hacienda supplied the city on a commercial basis replaced what the Indian had supplied on a tributary basis. To the north, haciendas initially supplied mines and then became institutions in their own right, especially when the mines they had supplied ceased operation.

Early estates relied on workers who came from nearby villages—some forced by the *repartimiento* and some lured by wages. As time passed, more hacienda workers lived on the hacienda rather than in independent villages. The offer of wages and a small plot to cultivate in their free time attracted many resident workers. Others were forced from their ancestral villages as *hacendados* appropriated Indian land and monopolized water supplies to irrigate wheat and sugarcane. Hacienda employment, on either a temporary or a permanent basis, served as the chief engine of Indian acculturation.

In the 1630s, a member of the Mexico City municipal council observed that whereas fifty years earlier the city had been supplied by Indians, wealthy Spaniards had replaced them as food suppliers, and Indian cultivation had been reduced to local subsistence. As agriculture shifted from Indian to Spanish control, wheat cultivation often replaced that of corn.

Haciendas appropriated Indian grazing land, took land left ownerless after the Indian population declined and occasionally resorted to brute force to expand their holdings. They sometimes employed *composición* to gain legal title to this land. In other cases, they bought land from individual Indians or rented it from Indian nobles and later laid claim to it. Most hacienda land acquisition occurred before 1750. Land acquisition not only provided space for grazing and planting, but eliminated competition from nearby producers and forced those deprived of land to work for the *hacendado*.

Although the great estate remained a fixture on the colonial landscape, individual estates constantly shifted in terms of their size, composition, ownership and profitability. The pace of land turnover increased in the eighteenth century as swelling mercantile and mining profits found their way into landholding. Antonio de Obregón y Alcocer, owner of La Valenciana mine in Guanajuato, provides an example of such turnover. He invested his mine profits in 74,000 acres of nearby land.

The hacienda's diversity allowed its survival. A typical hacienda produced corn, wheat, barley, beans, fruit, livestock, and the agave. This enabled it to be largely self-sufficient and minimized the effect blight, draught, or frost might have on any one crop. Large haciendas also minimized damage from a localized source, such as hail, by working non-contiguous holdings.

Hacendados generally made rational responses to demographic, environmental, and economic change, effectively juggling variables to maximize profits. They would attempt to maximize income from crop sales and minimize cash outlay by operating sawmills and tanneries and producing food, building materials, and other supplies for their workers. Given their ample storage facilities, they could store corn until harvests failed and then sell their stores at inflated prices. Historian John Coatsworth described some of the reasons large estates were so profitable:

> Estate agriculture enjoyed advantages not available to Indian villagers, small landowners, or tenant farmers: economies of scale, access to outside credit, information about new technology and distant markets, a measure of protection from predatory officials, and greater security of tenure.[4]

Records from one large hacienda in Guanajuato, the Jaral, which employed 598 people, indicate the degree of internal stratification. Salaried resident administrators, a chaplain, a cashier, and storekeepers worked there. The Jaral also employed skilled workers such as bricklayers, weavers, millers, distillers, hatters, and tailors. The permanent labor force consisted of tenant farmers, wage laborers, and debt-peons.

Haciendas, which sometimes had a resident population of as many as 1,000, played a commercial role, operating a commissary store (*tienda de raya*) which served both hacienda workers and other nearby residents. Hacienda residents also formed an alternative community, bound together by informal ties of loyalty and solidarity. The labor force resident on the hacienda sometimes received a guaranteed ration, even in years of bad harvests—a frequent occurrence in Mexico's semi-arid expanses. Residents would worship together in the hacienda chapel. The *hacendado* exercised a mediating role between his domain and the outside world. Within the confines of the hacienda, the colonial state allowed the *hacendado* to dispense justice by ordering corporal punishment or confinement in the hacienda jail.

Taxes, the tithe and mortgage income paid to the Church often left *hacendados* strapped for cash. The increasingly strong position of merchants also drained cash from the hacienda. Merchants profited from selling locally produced goods in urban markets, by importing goods from Spain, and by exporting produce to Spain, leaving relatively little profit for the *hacendado*.

In the early colonial period, the *encomienda* and the *repartimiento* served to exploit Indian labor. Later large numbers of Indians came to work on haciendas. *Hacendados* could rely on Indians from nearby villages to work when labor demand reached its peak, but did not have to support them during the rest of the year (as they would with slaves). Villages sending the laborers could meet their cash needs and at the same time maintain their traditional organization.

Haciendas played an especially important role in northern Mexico since they provided vital supplies to mines and few settled Indian communities existed to dispute *hacendados'* land claims. Since there were no permanent indigenous communities nearby to supply labor, northern haciendas concentrated on raising livestock, even if water was available. Given the aridity of the north, estates needed to be larger to generate as much income as their central Mexican counterparts. In 1760, to cite an extreme case, the Marquises de San Miguel de Aguayo grazed as many as 300,000 sheep on the 15 million acres that they owned in Coahuila and Texas.

Compared with central Mexico, in northern Mexico a freer and more modern society evolved around haciendas. This unique character had limited impact during the colonial period. However, by the early twentieth century the north not only remained a center of modernization but became the locus of social revolution, overwhelming all of Mexico and having a profound impact.

In 1810, 4,945 haciendas belonged to fewer than 4,000 families. As Humboldt noted, "The property of New Spain, like that of Old Spain, is in a great measure in the hands of a few powerful families, who have gradually absorbed the smaller estates." The hacienda supplied cities with grain and mines with hides, leather, tallow for illumination, and animals for motive power. By producing virtually everything it needed, the hacienda retarded monetization of the economy, kept markets small, and led to a low level of specialization. In contrast to capitalist societies in which production was overwhelmingly geared to market demand, only part of hacienda production entered the market, while the rest was consumed on the premises. The hacienda's control of the labor supply enabled it to pay less than the market price for labor and permitted the survival of an inefficient, technologically backward agricultural regime.

Throughout the colonial period, Indian agriculture remained vigorous. Most Indians farmed on an individual basis. In addition, some village lands were communally farmed, thus giving the community cohesion and providing income for lay brotherhoods (*cofradías*).

Despite the dominance of the large estate, many smaller mestizo-owned holdings sprang up. These mid-sized holdings, known as *ranchos,* existed along aside the hacienda. By the middle of the sixteenth century, wheat was almost entirely produced on *ranchos* with Indian labor under European guidance. In northern Mexico, *ranchos* specialized in livestock.

Beginning in the 1540s, cattle spread like waves of a rising tide over the prairies of the north and the warm coastal lowlands. The number of grazing animals soared due to abundant vegetation and the lack of competition from indigenous species. As their numbers grew, cattle altered the vegetation mix, destroying plants they preferred and leaving plants such as cactus and palm. Newly arrived cattle inflicted serious damage on the Indians' unprotected crops.

Within a quarter of a century, the rapid expansion of the cattle population halted. This was largely due to the number of cattle exceeding the carrying capacity of the grasslands. In addition, the slaughter of cattle increased as more humans, especially Indians, developed a taste for beef. Cattlemen, who had an interest in limiting damage to their forage base, became more effective land managers. Regulated grazing led to mosaics in the landscape that had greater plant diversity than woodlands—the other alternative for land left idle by the declining Indian population.

Imported species had far-reaching effects. Pigs, fattened with corn that Indians paid in tribute, multiplied so quickly that, as historian François Chevalier noted, "The newcomers often had pork to eat while they were still going without bread." Animals replaced human porters, greatly increasing transport capacity. Miners relied heavily on livestock production. An *audiencia* judge wrote in 1606, "If the mines have been worked at all, it is thanks to the plentiful and cheap supply of livestock." They also created entirely new industries, as sheep provided wool and cattle provided hides. Hides became a major export, with 64,350 being shipped in 1587 alone. Large-scale producers with herds of cattle and sheep in excess of 100,000 head dominated production.

An imported species, sheep, proved especially harmful to the environment since they cropped grass close to the ground and grazed on erosion prone slopes. After the late 1570s, the sheep population plummeted since their number had exceeded the land's carrying capacity. Overgrazing permanently lowered the carrying capacity in some areas. Historian Elinor Melville described the effect overgrazing had on the Mezquital Valley north of Mexico City:

> The region was transformed from a complex and densely populated agricultural mosaic into a sparsely populated mesquite desert; and the indigenous populations were economically marginalized while the land and regional production passed into the hands of large landowners who were socially (if not always ethnically) Spanish.[5]

By the early seventeenth century, ecological equilibrium had been reestablished in Mexico. European plants had become a fixture on the landscape. Grazing animals had passed through boom-and-bust population cycles. The cattle population stabilized between 1570 and 1590, and the sheep population a little later. Indians responded to Spanish-introduced livestock by suing their owners for damages they caused, by killing the animals, and by taking advantage of their presence and using them for meat, wool, leather, and transport.

In the late colonial period, as the prices for livestock and agricultural products rose, large estates appropriated more land to service growing urban markets. A substantial increase in the rural population provided more than enough labor for these estates. Historian Eric Van Young described the result:

> Gross indicators of agricultural prosperity—rising prices, rising tithe collections, increasing stability of ownership of large estates, rising levels of profits and investment in large-scale agriculture—pointed to economic growth, but signs of rural impoverishment and a fall in living standards for the rural masses in many parts of New Spain attested to how that growth was achieved.[6]

Just as had happened in the mining sector, at the end of the colonial period Mexican agricultural technology had fallen behind that of Europe. Low wages and the abundance of land, seven persons per square mile, as compared with 127 per square mile in France, reduced the pressure to introduce new technology. As a result of this technological backwardness, expanding agricultural production required cultivating larger areas.

Despite its technological limits, agriculture remained the major economic sector. In 1800, agriculture accounted for 44 percent of the colony's production, compared with 22 percent for manufacturing and 8 percent for mining. In 1810, 75 percent of the population continued to work in agriculture.

Several obstacles prevented agriculture from expanding further. Land held by the Church and entailed estates was inalienable. Courts were inefficient, and it was impossible to foreclose on land for debts. The widespread access to public and communally held lands made it difficult to attract labor to commercial agricultural enterprises.

MANUFACTURING

Production in colonial Mexico combined indigenous and European practices. A few innovations in the artisan sector, such as the Indians' adoption of the Spanish loom, enabled them to weave wider cloth and to weave more rapidly. Generally though handicraft production retained traditional technology—and its low productivity. Early in the colonial period, Indian women produced cotton textiles to pay tribute. Throughout the colonial period, the Indian majority continued to produce most of the textiles it required. As late as 1817, the Veracruz merchant guild lamented, "The Indians spend nothing on cloth save what they make for themselves, and they produce their own raw materials." Artisan weavers consumed much of their production within their own households. However, some home production involved putting-out arrangements. In such cases, a merchant or cloth producer would supply credit and raw materials to a home weaver. Throughout the colonial period, artisans in every town dominated not only textile production, but also the production of tools, utensils, and riding gear.

Butchers, bakers, weavers, hatters, pottery-makers, silversmiths, carpenters, tanners, and blacksmiths and producers of such items as saddles, candles, confections, shoes, and silk cloth each had their own guilds. Masters in each guild hired apprentices who would later become masters themselves. Guilds established detailed regulations concerning the type of product, production techniques, prices, and marketing. The bakers' guild set the maximum number of bread shops in Mexico City at thirty-six and in Veracruz at fourteen. The needlemakers' guild limited each master to only one store and rigorously fixed the price for each type of needle. To enhance their image and eliminate competition, some guilds prohibited the admission of mestizos, Indians, mulattos, or even the descendants of Jewish or Moorish converts. Those who violated guild rules could be punished with fines, jail, whipping, destruction of tools and product, or even suspension from the profession.

Mexico City, which had a population of 113,324 in 1790, illustrates the importance of the guild. In 1788 the city's workers belonged to fifty-five guilds with a total membership of 18,624. High-status guilds, such as those for silversmiths, architects, and coach makers, existed alongside more mundane ones, such as those for water drawers and pipe layers. Masons, who numbered 2,015, formed the largest guild.

For most of the colonial period, guilds enjoyed a legal monopoly on urban production and marketing. However, in the late colonial period, guild members had to compete with an increasing number of artisans, including women, who produced and marketed their products illegally. At the same time, policymakers, influenced by the Enlightenment, increasingly questioned the guilds' economic efficiency. Others felt the guilds' employment restrictions violated individuals' natural freedom to work in any job they desired. As a result of such doubts, an 1813 decree abolished the legal monopoly enjoyed by guilds, although it did not eliminate the guilds themselves. After that date, individuals could produce items regardless of their guild membership.

Associated with each guild was a *cofradía*, or brotherhood, which organized the guild's participation in religious and civic events. Such events included the lavish ceremonies honoring the patron saint of the guild as well as guild participation in the elaborate welcomes staged for new viceroys. They also organized guild members to celebrate the birthdays of the viceroy and of members of the royal family as well as their city's saint's day. Similarly *cofradías* were responsible for arranging guild participation in religious observances such as Corpus Christi, Holy Week, and the Immaculate Conception. In these observances guild members would march together carrying a cross and the guild's unique standard. *Cofradías* provided financial aid to members who suffered accidents, supported elderly guild members, and paid for funerals of deceased members. All these activities were financed by collecting dues from guild members.

Weavers' shops known as *obrajes* produced textiles for the domestic market. *Obraje* production resembled artisan production in that some *obrajes* had as few as three workers and employed technology similar to that of artisans. Their products were, however, more widely marketed than those of artisans. *Obrajes* resembled factories in their division of labor and larger scale of production. By putting several phases of production under one roof, the costs of supervision and transportation were reduced and control over the labor force could be increased.

Obrajes differed from the factories that appeared with the Industrial Revolution in Europe in that they failed to introduce new technology. The lack of new technology limited profitability, making them unable to pay wages that would attract sufficient voluntary workers. Given their limited ability to hire voluntary workers, owners also employed slaves, convicts, vagrants, orphans, and indentured apprentices. An official eighteenth-century report on *obraje* recruitment commented on one employee: "He is in the *obraje* voluntarily, because he had nothing to eat where he came from."

In the sixteenth and seventeenth centuries, production of woolens centered on Puebla due to the availability of wool and water power and due to the market provided by nearby Mexico City and Puebla itself. Since mine labor required warm clothing produced from wool, the Crown sent Spanish artisans and sheep to Mexico and offered financial incentives for textile production. Later most production of woolens moved north, closer to wool production on the great sheep ranches of Coahuila and to the market provided by northern mines. By 1743, 22 *obrajes* operated in Querétaro, producing not only clothing but also the coarse woolen cloth used to make sacks for shipping goods.

Puebla remained as an important cotton weaving center, stimulating cultivation along the Gulf Coast. As late as 1808, the production of cottons supported some 20,000 people in the province of Puebla. Weaving in Mexico flourished since prior to the end of the eighteenth century imported textiles were beyond the reach of all but the most affluent.

At the very end of the colonial period, Mexican cotton textile production declined as English textile imports, a product of the Industrial Revolution, appeared in Mexico. Mexican textile producers had been reluctant to invest in mechanization due to Mexico's low wage levels and their ability to coerce labor. In the late eighteenth century, a striking 84 percent of goods shipped from Spain to Mexico were textiles.

In 1764 to increase revenue, the Crown established a monopoly on the manufacture and sale of tobacco products. To facilitate control, it limited tobacco cultivation to the region of Orizaba and Córdoba in the modern state of Veracruz. Monopolizing production increased royal income, as well as the income of a few privileged growers. The processed tobacco—cigars and cigarettes—could only be sold in government-licensed shops.

The monopoly reduced the income of those who had formerly grown the plant and those who had produced tobacco products. Before the Crown monopoly, many small growers and artisans had dominated tobacco growing and processing. This group lacked an effective lobby to defend their right to continue producing tobacco.

The efficiency with which cigarettes and cigars were produced demonstrated Bourbon organizational ability. Factories were located in Guadalajara, Puebla, Oaxaca, Orizaba, Querétaro, and Mexico City. The largest, in Mexico City, employed almost 9,000 workers at its peak, an extraordinary size for a factory anywhere in the eighteenth century. By the 1790s, the tobacco monopoly employed almost 20,000, making it one of the largest organized industries in the colony, along with silver mining and textile production. At the end of the eighteenth century the tobacco monopoly remained very lucrative. It accounted for almost 30 percent of government revenue, a figure surpassing silver mining, which generated 26 percent.

Management at the tobacco factories attempted to instill modern industrial labor values in workers, such as on-time arrival, not stealing materials, and abstaining from drunken or other "scandalous" behavior. It punished infractions of the rules by a stint in the factory stocks, suspension from the job, or permanent prohibition from employment.

Women were encouraged to work in the tobacco factories, since one of the goals of the monopoly was providing desirable employment for poor urban women. Managers often preferred them as employees, since they felt men should be working in mines and fields. Women readily accepted such employment since many had worked in the tobacco industry before monopolization and because work there paid substantially more than the most common female occupation of the time—domestic service.

In order to stimulate Spanish industry, Mexican producers were forced to rely on cigarette paper supplied by Spanish factories. As Spain's frequent wars interrupted the supply of paper, production declined or even halted, leaving workers jobless and the state without revenues. Despite the inescapable logic of building a paper mill in Mexico, this was never done, because it would compete with producers in Spain.

Negotiation and compromise served as the basis of labor–management relations in the tobacco factories. This resulted from: 1) there being few alternatives for semi-skilled and unskilled male workers and fewer still for women; 2) the provision of an in-house dispute resolution mechanism; 3) management's desire for labor stability; and 4) the division of the labor force along the lines of gender, status, and ethnicity. Management also benefited from a general approval of the colonial regime. This became evident after management prohibited taking rolling papers home to meet their quota. Managers soon reversed the decision, leading workers to indicate their loyalty to the regime by sending the following message to the king: ". . . only with silence can we thank you. There is no other language more meaningful for a prince as perfect as your Excellency."

The elevated price of tobacco to the consumer reflected monopoly profit. This and the illegality of growing tobacco anywhere except in a small area inevitably led to widespread illegal dealing in contraband tobacco. Officials in some cases even justified illegal production by Indians on the grounds that it enabled them to earn money to fulfil tribute obligations. Dealers in contraband tobacco often organized themselves in bands. One such band, in the Sierra de Ceutla, in the modern state of Guerrero, survived by growing tobacco and selling it to local villagers. Not surprisingly, Guerrero still produces large amounts of illegal drugs.

Further north, away from the tobacco factories, authorities and citizens alike simply ignored the monopoly. Residents of New Mexico, Coahuila, and Texas cultivated tobacco extensively and bartered with it in the frontier economy.

TRADE AND TRANSPORT

> Trade is the lifeblood of this kingdom, and from it flows the prosperity of the realm.
> (Viceroy Cerralvo, 1634)

Colonial Mexico engaged in extensive trade with the mother country and emerged as the center of a large trading region including the Caribbean and extending south to Peru and west to the Philippines. The Crown structured Mexico's foreign trade to benefit Spain, disregarding and sometimes directly opposing the needs of the colony. The then-dominant mercantilist economic doctrine served to formulate trade policy. Mercantilism, in vogue from the fifteenth to the eighteenth centuries, held that national well-being required a continuous inflow of precious metals, or goods that could be exchanged for them. The mercantilist emphasis on trade surpluses led to severe restrictions on trade between the colonies and the rest of the world.

Mercantilist thought influenced shipping regulations. For most of the colonial period, the Crown allowed only one port in Spain to trade with the colonies and required that trade to be carried in Spanish-built ships. Generally Spanish colonies could not trade directly with each other or with other nations and their colonies. Shipping regulations limited the amount of goods sent to the New World and led to the shipment of luxury goods to maximize profits from the limited space available. Mercantilist regulations and the merchants' monopoly solidified the merchants' dominant position in New Spain.

During the sixteenth century, Spain supplied Mexico with food. As creoles began to produce their own wheat and adapted to the indigenous cuisine, clothes, weapons, hardware, and tools replaced food imports. Other imported items included iron, steel, paper, honey, oils, cloth, liquors, medicines, olive oil, linen, brandy, beeswax (for candles), and spices such as cinnamon and pepper.

Silver dominated Mexican exports to Spain. For 300 years, cochineal dye was the second most important Mexican export. Ships returning to Spain also carried condiments, spices, sugar, leather, extracts, and purgatives.

For most of the colonial period, the Crown required vessels carrying goods between Spain and Mexico to sail in convoys. Initially the convoys served as a defense against pirates and later they became a means of regulating trade and ensuring that New World silver arrived in Spain. A single convoy of from sixty to a hundred vessels would leave Spain each year. En route, it would divide, with ships sailing for various Spanish American ports. Regulations required that all goods entering New Spain from Europe be unloaded at Veracruz. Between 1757 and 1776, ships arriving in Veracruz carried an annual average of 2,487 tons of merchandise.

Roughly 1,000 muleteers would meet the convoy. They then hauled the merchandise to a giant trade fair, often in Jalapa, fifty miles northwest of Veracruz and 4,700 feet above it—safely removed from tropical disease. Merchants from Mexico City bought the goods in large lots and stored them in Mexico City warehouses. They then sold their inventory through their own outlets or to other retailers and street vendors.

In order to increase the tax base and undercut smugglers, the Bourbons eliminated the requirement that ships sail in convoys. Between 1784 and 1795, 1,142 boats entered Veracruz, compared to 222 boats in the previous 12 years. This resulted in an unprecedented influx of European goods, which soon saturated markets and produced a rash of merchant bankruptcies.

Despite these reforms, heavy taxes remained on goods shipped from elsewhere in Europe to Spain and then from Spain to Mexico. This caused these items to be non-competitive with similar items shipped illegally. Spaniards, who were the only merchants who could legally ship to the New World, would declare goods to be Spanish when they had in fact been produced elsewhere. This allowed such goods to avoid the 33 percent limit placed on the shipment of foreign goods to the colonies. Foreign traders often not only supplied the goods shipped but the financing, leaving the Spanish "merchants" as only front men. Ship captains failed to list foreign goods when presenting cargo manifests and then colluded with customs guards who boarded their ships on their arrival in Veracruz.

Heavy taxes and limited local production inevitably led to widespread smuggling. This smuggling provided colonials with inexpensive goods and colonial officials with bribes, but made local production less attractive and deprived the Crown of revenue. Estimates of contraband in the Atlantic trade ranged from 10 to 100 percent of registered cargo in the years between 1670 and 1700. Smugglers were well organized and savvy. They often appeared just before the arrival of the convoy from Spain, so they could take advantage of pre-convoy scarcity and increased prices.

Often goods arrived tax-free by being shipped directly from English ports to Jamaica and then being routed clandestinely to New Spain. Silver smuggled to Jamaica to pay for these goods avoided the legally mandated taxes and duties of 10.5 percent. In other cases, Spanish American merchants illegally shipped goods up and down the Pacific Coast of the Americas. Colonial subjects rationalized such illegality, noting it was better to provide local markets with needed goods at just prices than it was to pay taxes to a corrupt empire.

Imperial reform, the general growth of Atlantic trade, and colonial prosperity created a shipping boom that lasted until 1795. New Spain's trade with the mother country increased in value from 13.3 million pesos in 1787 to 20.6 million in 1795. At the end of the century, the commercial sector comprised 17 percent of Mexico's GDP—more than that of mining. After 1795, Spain's European wars caused a decline in trade between Mexico and Spain.

The Bourbon reforms undermined the old commercial elite. Mexico City merchants had grown comfortable with rules limiting their number, with restricted supply, and with high prices. When faced with real competition and provincial merchants being allowed to legally purchase goods in Veracruz for the first time, they petitioned the Crown to re-establish the convoy system and the requirement that goods be shipped through Mexico City. Viceroy Revillagigedo responded that eliminating convoys had produced a notable increase in trade and prosperity. He also noted that some individuals had suffered due to ignorance, poor financial administration, and poor mining

Figure 5.3 *Each of Mexico's main colonial ports, Veracruz and Acapulco, were heavily fortified to prevent pirate attack. This photo depicts San Juan de Ulúa, an island fortress in Veracruz harbor. After independence, it became a notorious prison.*

Source: Condumex.

investments, but that free trade should not be abandoned because of such individual misfortune. Many established merchants moved their capital into agriculture and mining rather than facing real competition and increased volatility in prices.

Finally, it was a misnomer to describe the replacement for the convoy system as "free trade." Strict volume limits kept the fabulous potential of trade with Asia in check. Spanish merchants feared they would lose control of trade with Spanish America entirely and successfully lobbied against unlimited trade with Asia. Even more importantly, the prohibition remained on trading outside the Spanish empire, despite the North Atlantic's emergence as the hub of world commerce. These prohibitions seriously constrained Mexico's growth.

During the early colonial period, given the extreme scarcity of mules and horses, Indian bearers (*tlamemes*), as in pre-conquest times, hauled freight. Carlos V felt such a practice to be inhuman and banned it, even if the Indians worked on a voluntary basis. However, Indians continued to haul freight since no replacement for them existed. The Crown later accepted this and tried to prevent abuses. Finally in the seventeenth century, an increased supply of mules and burros allowed the replacement of human carriers.

After 1550, carts were introduced, although since they required good roads and bridges, they did not replace mules. In the north, flat land and the small number of rivers permitted the extensive use of carts. Bad roads elsewhere limited their use. A contemporary observer commented on the highway between Mexico City and Veracruz—the most important road in the colony: "It is a disgrace to the Spanish nation, that at the end of two centuries and half, this road continues to be as neglected as at the time of the Conquest, full of dangers, embarrassments, and a thousand inconveniences." The deplorable condition of the roads resulted from the great differences in altitude and torrential rains falling on areas that the roads crossed and from the Crown's failure to understand the vital role roads played in economic development.

Since carts could not traverse the roads, mules carried freight from the ports of Acapulco and Veracruz to Mexico City. At the close of the eighteenth century, 75,000 mules plied the Acapulco–Mexico City route and 70,000 hauled cargo between Veracruz and Mexico City. These beasts of burden competed with humans for available corn. Some haciendas specialized in breeding mules and growing fodder for them.

Mule teams became a feature of the Mexican landscape. Indians and *castas* found that becoming a muleteer was one of the few routes to upward mobility. Each mule carried roughly 350 pounds. Having to follow routes that provided water and pasture slowed mule trains. The trip by mule train from Veracruz to Mexico City required sixteen to twenty days.

This reliance on expensive mule transport prevented the formation of an integrated market system, added to the cost of Mexican exports, and greatly increased the prices of goods sold in Mexico. Transporting imported wine from Veracruz to Mexico City added 70 percent to its price. A third to a half of the cost of grain used in the mines of Zacatecas resulted from transport charges. Transport costs precluded the shipment of low-cost agricultural products much beyond a hundred miles. Only luxury products and high-value goods could be sold colony-wide. In addition to silver, goods transported for sale over long distances included leather and suede produced in Jalisco and woolens from Guanajuato. Further to the north, the main trade items were leather, livestock, and silver.

GLOBALIZATION

> The economy of New Spain arose from the link between two worlds, the indigenous and the Spanish, and of the insertion of New Spain into global trade.
>
> (Bernd Hausberger, 2010)

Using advances in ship design and navigation, in the late fifteenth century both Spain and Portugal sought to circumvent Venetian and Muslim middlemen who controlled imports from Asia. Iberian navigators were driven by a mix of geopolitical grand strategy, commercial profit, and the desire to undercut Muslims. By sailing around the south end of Africa, Portuguese navigators established trading ties with the Orient well before the Spanish.

Columbus set off to the west in 1492 with the same goal as the Portuguese—trade with the Orient. The unexpected presence of the New World delayed Spanish efforts to trade with the Orient until the 1570s. In that decade Manila was founded and regular trans-Pacific shipping between the Philippines and Acapulco began. For the next two centuries ships known as Manila Galleons would leave Acapulco carrying church officials, government personnel, and more than 50 tons of silver. Also in the 1570s, the Ming dynasty in China began to demand tax payments in silver, since that country's paper money had collapsed. The demand for silver coins by the Chinese was virtually insatiable, as they constituted a quarter of the world's population.

In exchange for this silver, Spaniards acquired goods only available from Asia. Each year thirty to forty Chinese junks would travel to Manila laden with silks, porcelains, linen, furniture, cotton cloth, velvet, satin, damasks, taffetas, jewelry, ivory, furniture, pearls, gold- and silverwork, and spices from the East Indies. Then the Galleons, built in the Philippines with local teak, returned to Mexico laden with some 2,000 tons of cargo brought by the junks. Upon the Galleons' arrival, from 4,000 to 9,000 merchants flocked to Acapulco to snap up the imports which were either sold locally or re-exported to Spain.

It is likely that in some years more New World silver flowed to Asia than to Spain. Rather than trying to deepen commercial ties with China—the world's largest economy—Spain sought to minimize the loss of silver to Asia. In 1593 Spain limited trade with the Philippines to two ships per year, capped the value of the goods traded, and prohibited trade between Peru and Acapulco to prevent the loss of Peruvian silver to Asia.

The Spanish silver peso, which circulated in the Americas, Europe, and Asia, became the first truly international currency. The availability of the peso stimulated monetization and commercialization in Asia and Europe. Mexican silver pesos bought textiles in India, slaves on the west coast of Africa, and Chinese tea drunk in Britain and its American colonies. The Mexican City mint, the world's largest, produced 30 million silver peso coins annually.

Given the silver peso's ubiquitous nature, the Congress of the newly independent United States adopted the Spanish peso, under the name "dollar" (which comes from the German *Thaler*) as its unit of currency. The silver content of the new U.S. currency was determined by weighing Spanish pesos. Dollar bills issued from the early 1780s stipulated that they were payable in "Spanish milled dollars." Since the silver content of the Mexican peso equaled that of the dollar, it remained legal tender in the U.S. until 1857 (as it was in Canada until 1853).

The Spanish colonization of the New World accelerated globalization. Asian-African maritime trade had persisted for centuries before Europeans rounded the Cape of Good Hope. Then, in 1498, Portuguese sailor Vasco de Gama reached India, and his countrymen began trading with Africa, India, and China. Beginning in the sixteenth century, silver, largely obtained in Peru and New Spain, linked Portuguese and Spanish commerce. The Portuguese paid for textiles in India with silver and then traded the textiles for African slaves who were brought to the New World. Later in the sixteenth century, ships sailing between Acapulco and Manila added a trans-Pacific component to globalization. New World silver also facilitated the expansion of intercontinental trade by England, France, and the Netherlands.

CARLOS SIGÜENZA Y GÓNGORA

Carlos Sigüenza y Góngora rivaled the figures of the Italian Renaissance in his domination of all branches of human knowledge. He was born in Mexico City in 1645, one of nine children. He came from a religious family, as indicated by his brother and him becoming priests, and a sister a nun. Sigüenza y Góngora took vows as a Jesuit priest at age seventeen. However, he was soon expelled from the order for an unknown disciplinary infraction. He then became a secular priest.

Sigüenza y Góngora's writings indicate the breadth of his intellectual pursuits. At age seventeen, while still a Jesuit, he wrote a poem *Primavera indiana,* which extolled the Virgin of Guadalupe. He wrote the inscription in Latin for the cornerstone of a church built to honor the Virgin of Guadalupe. After the dedication of the church, in Querétaro, he published a book, *Glorias de Querétaro,* which included a description of pre-conquest Querétaro as well as a poem he wrote to commemorate the dedication.

His later writings defy easy categorization. Many of his works deal with historical events. He chronicled the Spanish reoccupation of New Mexico after the 1680 Indian revolt which drove the Spanish out. He wrote histories of the Chichimecas and of the University of Mexico, both of which are now lost. He showed his scientific bent when he published *Philosophical Manifesto on Comets,* which explained that comets were merely natural phenomena, not auguries of doom sent by God himself. This latter belief predominated at the time.

Despite being Mexico's best-known seventeenth century savant, few of Sigüenza y Góngora's works have survived. Works by any author of the time had to face two major hurdles. First they had to be approved for publication by the Inquisition, which tended not to favor secular themes. Even if approved, the lack of funds presented another formable hurdle. As a result we only know of many of Sigüenza y Góngora's unpublished works because they were mentioned in other sources.

(Several of his surviving reports and histories appear in English translation in the book by Irving Leonard cited below.)

Sigüenza y Góngora's fame spread well beyond Mexico. Louis XIV of France offered him a position in his court. However, he chose to remain in Mexico where he enjoyed a variety of official titles and positions. In 1680 Spanish King Carlos II named him royal cosmographer. At the time this term embraced what we know today as astronomy, land measurement, and cartography. As cosmographer he produced a map of New Spain and a detailed map of the hydrology of the Valley of Mexico. Both of these served as the basis of Mexican map-making during the eighteenth century. At age twenty-seven, he became a professor of mathematics at the University of Mexico. Given his mathematical and engineering talent, he was also named artillery inspector. In that position he advised on technical aspects of the construction of fortifications. He served as chaplain of the Hospital del Amor de Dios for most of his adult life. He distributed alms to the poor in his position of almoner of the archbishop.

The viceregal administration consulted Sigüenza y Góngora on flooding in the Valley of Mexico—a problem which had existed since Aztec times. Although the problem would not be seriously addressed until the nineteenth century, Sigüenza y Góngora did determine that, despite the widespread belief at the time, there was no natural drain for the valley. He advised more effective clearing of drainage canals and the construction of dikes planted with willows to hold soil.

His description of the 1692 riots in Mexico City, which saw the burning of the viceregal palace, not only provides a detailed eyewitness account of the event, but gives insight into Sigüenza y Góngora's thinking. He blamed the riots, not on the existing grain shortage and the widespread belief that authorities were hoarding grain, but on the ready availability of an alcoholic beverage known as pulque. Commenting on this he noted that the beverage was so widely available that "there is more **pulque** consumed in one day in Mexico than there was during an entire year under idolatry." He also blamed the violence on Indians, noting they were "the most ungrateful, querulous and inquiet people that God has created."

Even though he had little sympathy for Indians who were his contemporaries, he extolled the builders of Tenochititlan. He delved into Mexico's pre-conquest past and attempted to interpret pre-conquest hieroglyphs and pictographs to determine the dates of Aztec rulers. He zealously preserved a collection of codices given to him by the mestizo historian Juan de Alva Ixtlilxóchitl. In addition he assembled an unrivaled collect of books, maps, manuscripts, and original paintings dealing with life before the Spanish arrival. Sigüenza y Góngora's pride in pre-conquest civilization influenced many eighteenth-century creoles. Their pride in Mexico's past became known as "creole patriotism" and served to distinguish Mexicans from Spaniards.

Inevitably, given the breadth of his writing, some of Sigüenza y Góngora's beliefs have not stood the test of time. He declared Mexican Indians were the direct descendants of Naphtuhim, the son of Misraim the founder and ruler of Egypt. He based his belief on similarities he perceived between Mesoamerican and Egyptian temples, pyramids, clothing, calendars, and hieroglyphics. Also as Humboldt would note more than a century later, he was more than 100 marine leagues off the mark in his attempt to determine Mexico's City's longitude.

Sigüenza y Góngora's lasting mark is in introducing modern scientific thinking in Mexico. As historian David Brading noted, "It was only his lifetime that the boundary between science and magic was clearly drawn."

Source: Irving Leonard (1929) *Don Carlos de Sigüenza y Góngora*. Berkeley, CA: University of California Press, 1929.

THE COLONIAL MODEL

> Spain never developed a coherent economic policy; the imperial bureaucracy acted simply as a conduit of wealth into Italian, South German, and Dutch coffers.
>
> (Eric Wolf, 1982)

Mexican silver underwrote Spain's cost of governance and war, formed the base of the currency, and paid for such Asian imports as spices, jewels, silks, and pepper. While mining stimulated the region adjacent to the mine, it did not stimulate the economy as a whole. Mexican mining technology changed little after the sixteenth century, so mines created less demand for iron goods, such as boilers, than mines in Europe did. Referring to eighteenth-century silver miner José de la Borda, historian Richard Salvucci commented, "Perhaps God gave to the miner Borda, and Borda gave back to God, but neither divine providence nor beautiful churches provide a basis for economic development."

During the last decades before independence, Mexico generated wealth on a scale unmatched elsewhere in Spanish America. Its diversified economy in large part served the needs of the Mexican elite, despite the Crown's attempts to shape it to meet the needs of the mother country. Between 1796 and 1820, exports only averaged 4.3 percent of the GDP.

Much eighteenth-century economic growth resulted from a doubling in population from 3.3 million in 1742 to 6.1 million in 1810. However, unlike growth in Europe at the time, Mexico did not acquire new technology. Rather, Mexico added more land and labor to increase production. With much of the domestic wealth falling into the hands of a small number of wealthy miners, merchants, and *hacendados*, little remained to trickle down. As historian Richard Garner noted, "Growth in output from mining, agriculture, and manufacturing had not visibly enhanced the material lot of the ordinary citizen."

The Bourbons administered more efficiently than the Habsburgs. They also appropriated more of Mexico's wealth to subsidize Spain, the Philippines, and Spanish colonies in the Caribbean. They remained convinced that state intervention was needed to spur economic growth and to keep the state financially solvent. In some cases, such as supplying mercury, salt, and tobacco, the state controlled economic activity directly. In most cases, though, the state influenced the economy through taxes and detailed regulations. Policymakers felt market regulation would eliminate sharp price fluctuations, shortages, and the consequent social tension. Rather than taxing wealth or income, taxes fell heavily on the movement of goods. These taxes, such as a tax on sales and barter, on the movement of goods from one tax district to another, and on exports and imports, retarded the creation of large markets.

In an exchange remarkably similar to those occurring two centuries later, miner José de la Borda argued in 1765 that a decrease in mining taxes would stimulate investment and thus increase overall tax collection. Viceroy Bucareli rejected this advice, declaring that the increase in mining that had followed a previous decline in the price of mercury resulted, not from the price decrease, but from new ore discoveries.

The society created under Spanish tutelage retarded industry. Concentrated income and high commercial profits led to an emphasis on the import of luxury goods. With the exception of tobacco and mine workers, few wage earners could afford mass-produced goods.

The Crown's policy of protecting Spanish industry retarded Mexican industrialization. Authorities tolerated some Mexican industry, such as the production of ordinary fabrics and textiles. Generally however they prohibited investment that competed with manufactured imports from Spain. Mexico was forced to rely on Spain for iron tools, rather than mining iron and making its own tools. This prohibition reflected the Crown's desire to have the colonies supply Spain with raw materials so that Spanish labor could convert them into finished goods and return them to the colonies. The Crown's protecting Spanish industry also discouraged Mexican independence by creating dependence on the mother country for manufactured goods.

In 1790, perhaps in response to the successful revolt of Britain's North American colonies, the Viceroy of Nueva Granada (today Venezuela and Colombia), Francisco Gil de Taboada, stated:

> It's clear that the security of America can be measured by the degree of dependence on the mother country, a dependency which is based on the distribution of merchandise. When the day comes that the colonies have all they need, their dependency will be voluntary, and neither the armed forces we have there, nor government generosity, nor a better system of justice will be sufficient to assure our possession.[7]

Each guild regulated in detail the type of raw materials used, the shape and form of articles produced, and the tools used. While these measures served their stated purpose of protecting consumers from inferior products, they impeded improved design and the introduction of new production technology. Guild regulations, which excluded certain racial groups, such as Indians, prevented efficient utilization of labor.

A coin shortage also affected retail trade. Due to this shortage, colonists often purchased items as insignificant as bread and clothing on credit or bartered for them. (Paper money did not exist during the colonial period.) Not only was silver hoarded but there was a massive outflow—partly to pay for imports but also because taxes and profits from government monopolies were remitted to Spain and other Spanish colonies and because wealthy Spaniards retired back to the mother country with their personal fortunes. Given the scarcity of coins, in the late colonial period an estimated two-thirds of commercial transactions involved letters of credit.

The wealthy frittered away much of the economic surplus they accumulated, rather than reinvesting it. Historian José Durand commented that among the descendants of the conquistadors, "From a very early date, riches financed such manifestations of Renaissance exquisiteness as Plateresque architecture, clothing, jewels, paintings, and the lifestyle of a courtesan." Some *hacendados* invested in ostentatious homes, titles of nobility, dowries for daughters to enter convents, and lavish social gatherings. The Church, while it did facilitate credit, also diverted much of its wealth into temples and convents adorned with paintings, altars, and images, many of which were made with precious metals and jewels that had once belonged to women of aristocratic lineage.

Between 1792 and 1820, the Bourbons transferred roughly 7.2 percent of colonial income to the mother country—a tax burden that by today's standards is remarkably light. Institutional problems resulting from Spanish colonization provided a greater obstacle to development than did taxation. These obstacles included inefficient judicial institutions and pre-modern land tenure. The existence of privileged corporate bodies, such as the military and the Church, whose members operated with their own rules and sat in judgment of one another, raised the costs and risks of enterprise for the rest of the population. The Crown failed to develop a financial infrastructure capable of supporting productive long-term investment.

Ironically, despite having the largest empire in the world, Spain failed to benefit significantly from its colonies. The 1492 expulsion of the Jews deprived Spain of much of its financial expertise, just when the inflow of New World wealth increased the need for such knowledge. Given the anti-entrepreneurial values among Spain's Castilian elite, the expulsion of Jews created a catastrophic financial vacuum. Before 1492, foreign bankers had played virtually no role in Spain. The expulsion of Spain's Jews destroyed the primary source of credit, leaving Spain completely dependent on Dutch, German, French, and Genoese bankers who charged interest rates as high as 18 percent per annum.

France, England, and the Netherlands, lacking mines, focused on obtaining gold and silver by trading and manufacturing for export. Many of the taxes and guild regulations that plagued Mexican industry of the time also stifled Spanish industry. The massive inflow of precious metals to Spain led to 400 percent inflation between 1500 and 1600, thus making Spanish goods uncompetitive internationally. Because of these factors, by 1600 the core of the world economy had shifted northward.

Spain fell further behind northern Europe in the seventeenth century, in large part due to enormous military expenditure. In the early 1600s, King Felipe IV had 300,000 men under arms. The seemingly endless wars left Spain with little to invest productively. These conflicts resulted from: 1) the Habsburg monarchy's inheriting possessions in territory now forming parts of Italy, Holland, Belgium, France, and Germany, and waging costly, futile battles to retain them; 2) the Crown perceiving its duty as combating Protestantism in Northern Europe and Muslims in the Mediterranean area; and 3) the Crown protecting its New World claims and its shipping from the French, Dutch, and English. In retrospect, imperial Spain never recovered from its wasting seventeenth-century conflicts.

Spain acted as a conduit for commerce between its colonies and the rest of Europe. Increasingly Spain bought inexpensive manufactured goods from North Atlantic nations and then shipped them to the colonies. By the end of the seventeenth century, only 5 percent of the merchandise shipped from Spain to its American colonies came from Spain. France supplied 25 percent, Genoa 22 percent, Holland 20 percent, Flanders 10 percent, Great Britain (a latecomer to trans-Atlantic trade) 10 percent, and Germany 8 percent.

By the end of the colonial period, profit-oriented Mexican entrepreneurs, who were increasingly relying on wage labor, owned and directed the major means of production. This was especially true along a spinal column of commercial capitalism that extended west from Veracruz thorough Jalapa and Mexico City and then north to the mining districts of Guanajuato, Zacatecas, and Durango.

Elsewhere in the colony, various factors prevented the formation of vigorous markets. At the end of the colonial period, most work was not performed by free wage labor. High transport costs, the Church tithe, and internal customs (*alcabala*) also hampered the development of large markets. Mexico's increasingly being milked by a greedy and belligerent metropolis further stymied the development of markets.

The colonial period saw the depletion of many of Mexico's natural endowments. Precious metals, mined and lost forever to Mexico, facilitated European development. Similarly Mexico's forest stock declined during the colonial period. Forests covered roughly three-quarters of New Spain at the time of the Conquest. By the end of the colonial period, as a result of using wood for fuel, construction, shipbuilding, and mining, forest cover had declined by one-third. This loss occurred despite efforts to protect Mexican forests. For example, in 1765, King Carlos III decreed that licenses would be required to cut wood on private as well as on common land and that for each tree cut three more had to be planted.

DOCUMENT 5.1: EARLY SEVENTEENTH-CENTURY ZACATECAS

[The following description of Zacatecas was written by the Bishop of Guadalajara, Alonso de la Mota y Escobar, in about 1605.]

One of the things for which a city may be celebrated is the great amount of gold or silver it produces. Zacatecas is renowned for the unlimited amount of silver that has been extracted from it and that continues to be extracted today . . .

At the time of its discovery, there were many forests and woodlands in this rocky land, all of which have vanished, felled when smelting was initiated, so that now except for some little wild palms, no other trees remain. Firewood is very expensive in this city because it is brought in carts from eight and ten leagues away. In the time of the heathens, the whole mountain range and its woods were a famous preserve of deer, hares, rabbits, partridges and doves, none of which had an owner in the world. The lords and *caciques* [local native leaders], whose nation and vassals were called Zacatecos, possessed and enjoyed them, and their name has stuck to this city of Zacatecas. The wood here produces a great quantity of fruit called *tuna*, which is fertilized and yields without any cultivation, and the wood also produces a great diversity of sweet-smelling flowers.

This treasure was discovered in the year 1540, in the following way. When Nuño de Guzmán, having finished the conquest of [Nueva] Galicia left there, his soldiers remained, spread out over the entire kingdom. Since no more towns remained to conquer and since they had so many Indian slaves, they devoted themselves to looking for and enriching themselves from silver mines. One of these soldiers was a *bachiller* [baccalaureate] Joanes de Tolosa, a Basque, who happened to have an Aztec among his Indian slaves. The Aztec, it is said, seeing his master so anxious to discover mines and claim silver, told him: if you so desire this substance, I will take you where you can fill your hands and satiate your lust with it. Hearing this, Joanes de Tolosa, without saying anything to his Spanish companions, left secretly and was guided by his Indian slave to this mountain range and to these minerals whereupon he started to dig out the metals and assay them. He found the hills so full of metals and of such value that there were some, although very few, with only half the silver, so that while one *quintal* [100 pounds] of earth might produce two *arrobas* [50 pounds] of silver. At the start, the smelting of each *quintal* usually produced ten, fifteen, twenty, or thirty *marcos* [marks] of silver. This caused the mines to be populated in great haste, and the first inhabitants were the soldiers who found themselves closest to the site, and at the same time many people from Mexico [City] started to come and lay claim to the silver and among them came the merchants with their merchandise . . .

The Spaniards who first populated the place never planned to remain here, but sought only to extract the most silver they could, and so they made their houses, or better said, shacks, as journeying people in the midst of their travels might. But there was so much promise in the city that they never abandoned it and have remained here with these short, low houses and with no order to their streets . . .

It is not known if His Majesty had given a land grant to assist in the foundation of this city, or if only the title of city, which does not include rent or property to cover its expenses. Zacatecas is subjected principally to the *Real Audiencia* and is governed locally by a *corregidor* supplied by the *Real Consejo de Indias* [Royal Council of the Indies] who earns one thousand ducats in salary, and a municipal council that elects two *alcaldes ordinaries* [chief municipal officers] each year. There is an *aguacil mayor* [constable] and His Majesty sells the privilege of occupying this office for nineteen thousand pesos. There are three public notaries for sale, each of which sells for six thousand pesos. This city has its own municipal buildings which house the corregidor and the place where he holds his court, the jail, and the place where the *regidores* [councilmen] meet to hold council. At present, there are four of these and they are commonly sold by His Majesty for four hundred pesos each. One of the notaries serves as the clerk of the council . . .

The houses of this city are made of adobe and mud, they all have earth floors, and few are large; some are made of stone with high roofs, but there are few of these. There are more than three hundred houses of his type . . . There is a parish church in the middle of the city dedicated to Our Lady of the Nativity because the city was conquered from the Zacatec Indians on Her day, and the regiment takes its banner from the memory of this festival day. Two beneficiary clerks serve this church, provided, according to the *Real Patronato* [Order of Royal Patronage] by the president; there are no tithes to pay because there are no residential tithes since the miners never work the soil to plant it, but only to extract metals from it. Neither do the residents provide a salary to these curates, because these latter enjoy the privileges of the citizens, sustaining themselves with some chaplaincies that have been founded in the parish, as well as from confraternities' votive masses and frequent processions . . .

This city also has three hundred large and small houses of the construction described above, it houses at least six hundred residents, more or less, and most of them are Spaniards. There are at times more than one hundred and sometimes two hundred people who come and go on business, bringing their merchandise. Sixty or seventy children of Spanish residents have been born here, some of whom are occupied in studying, others in being miners, and others in running agricultural estates. There are, according to what I know of this city, up to ten or twelve Portuguese and Italian foreigners in this city. I do not know if they have made arrangements with His Majesty about living in this kingdom. Of black slaves and mulattoes, women and men, there are about eight hundred. There are also some free blacks that come and go and rent themselves out to work in livestock, farming, mining, and commonly they are bad and depraved, these free blacks, just like the other slaves, but as it is said there "it is bad to have them, but much worse not to have them."

There are about fifteen hundred Indians of these residents in the work gangs who labor in all types of occupations in the mines, but who come and go, leaving and returning with great ease and in this way a precise number for them cannot be given, as we said earlier in the preface.

Spanish is the language that is generally spoken in this city; some Indians speak the tongues of their nations, because here there are Mexicans, Otomies, Tarascans, and those of other nations . . .

Among the noble residents, there are few who are extremely rich and those that are, are the miners; however, along the intermediate classes of people, there are many who are rich with twenty, thirty of forty thousand pesos and there are three of four individuals who possess one hundred thousand pesos, and all of these are merchants of public stores. But none of the stores are in Spain, as they call it here; rather they operate in Mexico, from where they bring all types of clothing from Castile, cloths, linens, silks, wine, oil, steel, spices and also clothing and silks from this land, and from China, all of which are transported to this city in carts. There are at least fifty merchandise stores whose worth ranges between two thousand and thirty thousand pesos. The merchants of the least value and wealth work in their own stores and the richest ones have servants and attendants working for them who are Spanish . . .

There are sufficient and necessary numbers of those who perform the mechanical offices of tailor, cobbler, ironsmith, and carpenter. Of these, there are Spaniards, mulattoes, and Indians, and those that earn the most are the carpenters and masters of making engines for mining, because these are burned and damaged continuously.

NOTES

1   Thomas Gage, *Thomas Gage's Travels in the New World* (Norman, OK: University of Oklahoma Press, 1958), pp. 111–12.

2   P. J. Bakewell, *Silver Mining and Society in Colonial Mexico: Zacatecas, 1546–1700* (Cambridge: Cambridge University Press, 1971), p. 225.

3   Miners and refinery workers suffered from a variety of debilitating if not fatal occupational diseases described in Doris M. Ladd *The Making of a Strike* (Lincoln, NE: University of Nebraska Press, 1988), p. 24 and Kendall Brown, *A History of Mining in Latin America* (Albuquerque, N.M.: University of New Mexico Press), pp. 62–63.

4   John Coatsworth, "Obstacles to Growth in Nineteenth-Century Mexico," *American Historical Review*, February (1978), pp. 87–88.

5   Elinor Melville, *A Plague of Sheep* (Cambridge: Cambridge University Press, 1994), p. 14.

6   Eric Van Young, "The Age of Paradox: Mexican Agriculture at the End of the Colonial Period," *The Economies of Mexico and Peru during the Late Colonial Period, 1760–1810* (Berlin: Colloquium Verlag, 1986), p. 82.

7   Hans Jürgen Harrer, *Raíces económicas de la revolución mexicana* (Mexico City: Taller Abierta, 1979), p. 28.

FURTHER READING

Andrien, Kenneth J. (2009) "The Spanish Atlantic System," in *Atlantic History*, ed. Jack P. Greene, and Philip D. Morgan, pp. 55–79. New York; Oxford University Press.
A discussion of the flows, human and material, across the Atlantic during the colonial period.

Baskes, Jeremy (2005) "Risky Ventures: Reconsidering Mexico's Colonial Trade System," *Colonial Latin American Review* 14 (June): 27–54.
This article discussed the interplay of credit, risk, and profit in international trade.

Brown, Kendall (2012) *A History of Mining in Latin America.* Albuquerque, N.M.: University of New Mexico Press.
A discussion of mining throughout Latin America, with emphasis on Potosí, where the Spanish faced many of the same mining problems they faced in Mexico.

Doberman, Louisa (1991) *Mexico's Merchant Elite, 1590–1660.* Durham, N.C.: University of North Carolina Press.
A study of merchants who engaged in international trade.

Florescano, Enrique (1984) "The Formation and Economic Structure of the Hacienda in New Spain," *Cambridge History of Latin America* (vol. 2), ed. Leslie Bethel, pp. 153–88. Cambridge: Cambridge University Press.
A description of the Mexican hacienda.

Humboldt, Alexander (1966) *Political Essay on the Kingdom of New Spain.* New York: AMS Press.
A classic description of Mexico written by a Prussian visitor shortly before Mexico's independence.

Melville, Eleanor G. K. (1994) *A Plague of Sheep*. Cambridge: Cambridge University Press.
    This classic of environmental history describes, as its titles suggest, the impact of sheep on the Mexican landscape.

Melville, Eleanor G. K. and Bradley Skopyk (2010) "Disease, Economy, and the Environment," *The Oxford History of Mexico* (rev. ed.), pp. 202–23. New York: Oxford University Press.
    A discussion of how indigenous people raised agricultural productivity before the conquest, followed by a discussion of post-conquest population loss and the impact of introduced Eurasian animals, plants, and germs.

Semo, Enrique (1993) *The History of Capitalism in Mexico*. Austin, TX: University of Texas Press.
    A Mexican historian traces the emergence of capitalism in Mexico.

Tutino, John (2011) *Making a New World: Founding Capitalism in the Bajío and Spanish North America*. Durham, N.C.: Duke University Press.
    A consideration of how the profit motive dominated mine production in the Bajío and how silver linked the area to world markets.

GLOSSARY TERMS

agave
alcabala
cofradía
pulque

The Nineteenth Century, 1810–1909

Chapter 6

The End of Spanish Rule, 1810–1821

TIMELINE—WORLD

1804–06	1808	1812–15	1814	1817
Lewis and Clark Expedition reaches Pacific	Napoleon invades Spain and installs Joseph	U.S. and Britain in War of 1812	Ferdinand VII regains Spanish throne	U.S. President James Monroe inaugurated

TIMELINE—MEXICO

1804	1808	1810	1810	1810
Church loans called in via Consolidation Decree	September 15 coup deposes Viceroy Iturrigaray	September 16 Hidalgo launches independence movement	September 28 Guanajuato occupied by insurgents	October 30 Battle of Monte de las Cruces

1815	1821	1821	1821	1821
November 5 Morelos captured and later executed	February 24 Plan of Iguala proclaimed	August 24 Treaty of Córdoba signed	September 27 Army of Three Guarantees enters Mexico City	September 28 Independence formally declared

Latin American independence came in the midst of an era of sweeping change in the Western world. It was indeed part of that change. The Enlightenment, in advertising the potency of human reason, had accustomed those whom it touched to the notion that change was a normal state of being; for what was dangerous, damaging, or demeaning in the human condition could be remedied by the proper application of the mind's power.

(P. J. Bakewell, 1997)

1819 Adams–Onís treaty cedes Florida to the U.S.	1820 Spanish army revolts and 1812 Constitution reinstated	1821 American citizen Moses Austin given permission to colonize Spanish Texas

1810 November 7 insurgents defeated at Aculco	1811 January 17 insurgents defeated at Puente de Calderón	1811 March 21 Hidalgo and Allende arrested and later executed	1813 September 15 insurgent congress inaugurated at Chilpancingo	1814 October 22 Constitution of Apatzingán promulgated

THIS CHAPTER FIRST CONSIDERS GRIEVANCES THAT ACCUMULATED during the first decade of the nineteenth century. These grievances led to a revolt led by two priests, Miguel Hidalgo and José María Morelos. After royalist forces repeatedly defeated rebel armies, the **insurgents** turned to guerrilla warfare. In response to the rebellion, the Crown sought to maintain, or regain, Mexicans' loyalty through such measures as abolishing tribute, allowing elections, and establishing new local governments. After more than a decade of combat a **royalist** officer, Agustín Iturbide, brought together royalist forces and rebels to form a coalition that rejected Spanish rule. This chapter concludes by considering the role of various social groups during the revolt, the economic impact of the independence struggle, and U.S. policy toward Spanish American rebellion.

EARLY NINETEENTH-CENTURY GRIEVANCES

Throughout most of the colonial period, the vast majority of New Spain's residents remained loyal to the king, just as, being good Catholics, they were loyal to the pope. Gradually, however, colonists became disenchanted with royal administration. Eventually after grievances accumulated most politically aware Mexicans welcomed a clean break with both royal administration and the monarchy.

In most instances, inefficiency, incapacity, and corruption permitted early eighteenth-century creoles considerable flexibility, autonomy, and even a modicum of self-government. The 1786 creation of intendancies directly targeted local officials and their illegal, but widely tolerated, commercial monopolies. The Bourbon state regarded the ending of creole participation and its corollary, government by compromise, as necessary steps toward control and revival. Residents of New Spain perceived these same measures as the issuance of non-negotiable demands from an imperial state. As historian John Lynch commented, "To creoles this was not reform."

In the short term royal agents successfully fulfilled their goal of increasing colonial revenue. The Bourbons increased the *alcabala* from 4 percent to 6 percent, which produced a sharp increase in the price of food and household goods. New taxes were placed on various commodities such as grains, cattle, and distilled beverages (*aguardiente*). Tax collection increased from an average of 6.5 million pesos annually during the 1760s to 17.7 million pesos in the 1790s as growth in mining, commerce, and the internal market enlarged the tax base. Between 1779 and 1820, the cost of trade restrictions and taxes equalled 7.2 percent of Mexico's income. In 1775, British colonialism only cost its North American colonies 0.3 percent of their income.

Contemporary observers felt that taxes had exceeded the prudent level. Humboldt reported that New Spain contributed ten times as much revenue to Spain, on a per capita basis, as did India to Britain. These taxes fell upon all social groups. As Lynch noted, by increasing monetary demands on New Spain, the Bourbon's "gained a revenue and lost an empire."

Creoles resented economic restrictions, such as the prohibition on producing paper, which protected Spanish producers. Except in colonies such as Cuba and Venezuela, which could produce export crops, landowners received little benefit from Bourbon trade reforms. Lowered trade barriers hurt Mexico's relatively unsophisticated manufacturers. By 1810, European imports were competing with textiles produced in Querétaro and Puebla. Finally, Spanish trade policy failed to recognize that Mexican mining, agriculture, and commerce had few economically rational links to Spain. The mother country could not supply the American market nor could it absorb goods produced in the New World.

Economic growth under the Bourbons did not translate into improved living standards for the majority of Mexicans. Higher taxes and the concentration of income left little for the majority. Cash crops increasingly relegated corn farming to marginal lands, while the population increased from 4.48 million in 1790 to 6.12 million in 1810. Not surprisingly agricultural prices rose 50 percent between 1780 and 1811. Food, housing, and clothing all increased in price more rapidly than wages after the 1780s.

FROM BAD TO WORSE

> In the wake of the Napoleonic invasion of the Iberian Peninsula, the Spanish and Portuguese territories of the New World would be forced to come to grips with what constitutes legitimate authority in the absence of the monarch.
>
> (John Schwaller, 2011)

Repeated changes in Spanish shipping policy, a result of Spain's nearly constant wars, added to resentment in the New World. From 1793 to 1795, Spain fought France in a futile attempt to reverse the French Revolution. In addition Spain and England were at war for most of the years from 1796 to 1807. When Spain and Britain were at war, the British fleet attacked ships after they left Veracruz and blockaded Spain's ports, thus interrupting trade with Spanish America. In 1797, to allow its colonies to export and receive supplies, the Spanish Crown allowed trade with neutral countries, whose ships brought badly needed cigarette paper, mercury, and textiles. Two years later, Spain prohibited such trade, claiming it only benefited Britain. In 1804 war again interrupted shipping, and Spain again permitted trade with neutrals. The legalization of neutral trade resulted in a rapid expansion of U.S. shipping to Spanish America—a harbinger of even greater influence. U.S. ships carried American flour and re-exported British textiles to Mexico.

In 1804, to ease its war-induced financial woes, the Crown ordered that all debts owed to the Mexican Church should be repaid immediately and that the funds collected should be sent to Spain. Bishop-elect Manuel Abad y Queipo of Michoacan estimated that credit extended by the Church totalled 44 million pesos, two-thirds of Mexican capital in active circulation—money used to pay salaries and grow crops. He predicted the withdrawal of this capital would severely damage agriculture, mining, and commerce. Less than a week after the publication of the decree, the Mexico City government declared the measure "totally impractical," since "it would inevitably bring ruin to these dominions and cause enormous damage to the state." The Crown's desperate need for funds caused it to ignore such warnings.

Spanish officials had assumed that the decree, known as the Consolidation Decree, would have an effect comparable to that of a similar 1798 decree issued in Spain, where the Church owned large tracts of property. However, unlike in Spain, where 90 percent of church wealth was invested in real estate and only 10 percent was liquid, in New Spain only 12 percent was invested in real estate, and the rest was liquid. Church loans financed the operations of New Spain's 200,000 entrepreneurs, only 5 percent of whom operated entirely with their own capital.

The 12 million pesos extracted from Mexico as a result of the Consolidation decree damaged the interests of miners, *hacendados*, merchants, and artisans who operated on borrowed capital. Many businesses were closed as buildings were seized and sold at auction. Medium-sized and small landowners who could not obtain cash to liquidate debts suffered the most. They were forced to sell their houses, ranchos, and haciendas to repay loans just when others' sales had cause the price of real estate to decline by half. The decree devastated schools, hospitals, and social welfare institutions, such as orphanages, which had been sustained by income from Church investment. It also embittered the lower clergy, since many of its members lived on interest from chaplaincies and loaned capital. Commenting on the European conflict that motivated the Consolidation Decree, Mexican priest Fray Servando Teresa de Mier lamented: "The war is more cruel for us than for Spain, and is ultimately waged with our money. We simply need to stay neutral to be happy."

In 1808, Napoleon sent French troops into Spain to further his imperial ambitions. He forced King Fernando VII off the throne, imprisoned him in France, and installed his own brother Joseph as the Spanish monarch.

Spaniards rejected Joseph not only as a foreign usurper but, since he came from revolutionary France, as an atheistic threat to the very foundations of Hispanic society. Soon various groups, or "juntas," sprang up in Spain to oppose Napoleon's forces. They claimed that in the absence of Fernando, whom they continued to recognize, they were the true representatives of the Spanish nation. The dominant junta represented Seville. For a brief period the invasion of Spain united New Spain. Its residents, regardless of their wealth or which side of the Atlantic they had been born on, rallied around the deposed Fernando and declared their opposition to the French occupation of the Mother Country.

To fill the power vacuum in Mexico, a junta central began meeting in Mexico City. Its members included Viceroy José de Iturrigaray, the archbishop, members of the Mexico City government, various other administrators and distinguished persons from other cities. The junta confirmed its support for Iturrigaray and announced that it would only subordinate itself to a junta in Spain that was appointed by Fernando. Since he was a prisoner in France, that was tantamount to saying the junta in Mexico City would manage New Spain's affairs until such time as the Spanish monarch returned to the throne.

Creoles who convened the Mexico City junta operated on the premise that Mexico was not a colony of Spain, but a kingdom co-equal to Spain under the monarchy. They reasoned that with the monarch absent, the link uniting Spain and New Spain had ceased to exist. They also reasoned that until Fernando's return, Mexican sovereignty resided in the representatives of the people— the cities, the tribunals, and other major corporations.

Spaniards in Mexico did their best to quash notions that Mexicans might assume sovereignty. On August 27, 1808, the Inquisition declared any theory that sovereignty resided in the corporations or the people at large to be heretical. The *audiencia* claimed that the declarations by members of the Mexico City municipal government that sovereignty was based on a pact between the governed and the monarch only served as a smokescreen for their desired independence.

Many Spanish-born people believed that Iturrigaray's cooperation with the junta indicated that he sought to separate Mexico from Spain. No evidence has been found to support that assumption, but that did not prevent Spaniards from acting on it.

Shortly after midnight on September 16, 1808, wealthy Spanish *hacendado* Gabriel de Yermo assembled an armed force numbering roughly 300. It was largely composed of immigrant Spanish merchants who swept into the viceregal palace and arrested Iturrigaray. The coup enjoyed the support of the military, the archbishop of Mexico, *consulado* members, miners, *hacendados*, representatives of the Inquisition, and justices of the *audiencia*. The plotters also imprisoned the leading figures in the municipal government. The *audiencia* then appointed seventy-seven-year-old Field Marshal Pedro Garibay as viceroy and sent Iturrigaray back to Spain to face trial for treason.

Garibay immediately recognized the junta in Seville as the legitimate ruler of Mexico and began sending it Mexican silver. In doing this, he made a giant intellectual leap. Creoles had asserted that if the monarch was absent, Mexicans were Mexico's sovereign. Garibay's recognition of the Seville junta, however, asserted that the absence of the monarch justified a self-proclaimed ruling junta of Spaniards becoming Mexico's sovereign.

In the short run, the coup was a success, since it halted the slide toward creole autonomy. However, in the long run the coup destroyed what survived concerning the mystique surrounding power. It became even clearer that naked force, not the divine right of kings, formed the basis of Spanish rule.

THE HIDALGO REVOLT, 1810–1811

In May 1810, priest, public intellectual, and eventually bishop-elect of Michoacán Manuel Abad y Queipo predicted a colonial revolt due to colonial grievances and the "electric" example of the French Revolution. He urged the Crown to appoint an enlightened military man as viceroy and that competent military officers, field cannons, cannon balls, and grapeshot also be sent to Mexico.

The warning indicated Abad y Queipo's prescience since, unbeknownst to him, residents of the Bajío region northwest of Mexico City were plotting a revolt against the government. Before 1500, the Bajío, a vast high plain in what is now the state of Guanajuato, was a little settled basin—a frontier between Mesoamerica and the indigenous people of the North American interior. By 1800, the Bajío had become one of the most prosperous and densely populated areas in Mexico. Its population, which contained few Spaniards or traditional Indian villages, was more socially mobile than the Mexican population as a whole. Its mixed economy, based on mining, herding, manufacturing, farming, and artisan production, was the most thoroughly commercial in New Spain. Numerous small farmers had been forced onto marginal lands by commercial estates. The 1808–10 draught further impoverished them.

The 1810 conspirators met regularly in Querétaro, 125 miles northwest of Mexico City, under the guise of attending a literary society. The most distinguished conspirator was Miguel Domínguez, from an elite local family, who served as the *corregidor* of Querétaro. Other conspirators included his wife, Josefa Ortiz de Domínguez ("La Corregidora"), and various lawyers, military officers, and commercial and religious figures. Neither members of the central elite nor the poor joined the Querétaro conspiracy. The conspirators hoped to strike a quick blow against the Spanish, that is, do to the Spanish what they had done to Iturrigaray. The planned uprising was initially set for December.

Miguel Hidalgo, one of the conspirators, served as the priest of Dolores, a Bajío town of 15,000. Hidalgo, the son of a hacienda manager, read prohibited books and loved wine, dance, and other worldly pleasures. He served as a one-man community development project promoting tanning, carpentry, bee-keeping, the weaving of wool, and the production of silk, pottery, tiles, and wine. In addition he produced theater, sometimes his own translations of French works. In 1804 after the recall of Church loans, the Crown temporarily seized and rented out Hidalgo's small hacienda to generate income to repay the 7,000 pesos he owed.

Spanish authorities received a report concerning the plot and sent officials to arrest the conspirators. Upon learning that the Spanish had begun arresting the plotters, Hidalgo and fellow conspirator Ignacio Allende decided to launch the rebellion immediately. On the morning of September 16, 1810, he issued his famous *Grito de Dolores* (Cry of Dolores), which set Mexico into rebellion. There are almost as many versions of what he said as there are

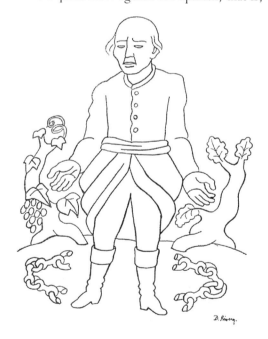

Figure 6.1
No photo or painting of Hidalgo made during his lifetime exists. This sketch by Diego Rivera conforms to the popular image of him.

Source: Raquel Tibol, *Diego Rivera: Gran Illustrador/Great Illustrator* (Mexico City: Editorial RM & Museo Nacional de Arte, 2008), p. 78.

129

historians. Most likely the *Grito* included some or all of the following, "Long Live Fernando VII! Long Live America! Long Live Religion!" and "Death to the Bad Government!" For a significant period after the *Grito* it was left unsaid if the rebellion sought a clean break with Spain or an adjustment of relations under a Spanish monarchy. The very real possibility that the French would remain to dominate the Spanish government made it difficult to formulate concrete proposals.

The people of Dolores immediately rallied behind Hidalgo, who freed and armed the seventy prisoners in the town jail. Hidalgo's hastily gathered throng of urban and rural workers then set out to liberate Mexico. They were armed with lances, machetes, rakes, slings, and sticks. His force first marched to San Miguel el Grande (today San Miguel de Allende), twenty-four miles away. Many working in the fields joined the insurgency as Hidalgo's force passed. Their standard of living had fallen, and they were suffering from unaccustomed insecurity and famine. The participation of local leaders, such as Hidalgo, indicated splits in the elite that would open a role for the masses.

Hidalgo's force took San Miguel el Grande, Allende's home, without firing a shot. The insurgents spent two days there gaining addition recruits and then marched south and took Celeya, which had been abandoned by Europeans. Hidalgo's force proceeded to plunder the homes of the Europeans.

On September 28, the insurgents, 20,000 strong, arrived at Guanajuato, a mining center of 60,000. For six days, Juan Antonio Riaño, the city's Spanish intendant, had trained militia forces and organized the digging of defensive trenches. However, at the last minute he lost his nerve and ordered wealthy Spaniards and creoles to take refuge in La Alhóndiga, a fortress-like granary. An observer noted that those taking refuge in the granary brought with them "money, silver bars, precious jewels, the most valuable goods from their chests, trunks of clothes, gold and diamond jewelry, and other valuables from their homes."

Miners and prisoners freed from the local jail joined the rebels. Riaño's decision to take refuge in La Alhóndiga intensified the class nature of the struggle, since he allowed only the wealthy inside the granary. Five hours after the insurgents attacked, they broke through the doors, killing men, women, and children and making off with clothing, bullion, and jewelry. Hidalgo's men killed at least 300 Spaniards in the granary and during the subsequent looting of the city. For Hidalgo, this was a Pyrrhic victory since the looting and brutality ended any chance of his gaining widespread creole support.

Hidalgo's force then marched to Valladolid (today Morelia), took it on October 17 without firing a shot, and looted it. The disorderly crowd that formed Hidalgo's army filed through the streets shouting, "Long live the Virgin of Guadalupe" and "Death to the Spaniards." The officers, many of whom had defected from the royalist army, commanded poorly armed and poorly dressed troops. At this stage of the rebellion, the insurgency had the festive air of a pilgrimage.

On October 29, the insurgents occupied Toluca. Hidalgo's force, the largest army assembled in Mexico since Aztec times, continued east. As the insurgent force of perhaps 80,000 approached Mexico City, it met its first major resistance from royalist forces in the Battle of Monte de Las Cruces. A force of 2,500 well-disciplined royalists with artillery almost held Hidalgo's force off. Finally after heavy losses on both sides the insurgents surrounded the royalists. The royalists then fought their way out of the encirclement, and their badly mauled force retreated to Mexico City.

Instead of proceeding on to take Mexico City, Hidalgo paused at the battle site for three days and then ordered his army back to the west. This decision remains one of the most controversial in Mexican history and probably resulted from the insurgents' lack of ammunition, the strength of Mexico City's royalist garrison, the approach of royalist reinforcements from the north, and the weakness of Hidalgo's own poorly trained army. Hidalgo may also have feared his army would loot Mexico City.

Despite massive military spending after 1762, the viceroy had virtually no forces he could mobilize against the rebels. On October 2, Brigadier Félix Calleja, the royalist commander in San Luis Potosí, wrote the intendant of Puebla: "My troops are short in numbers and of the same quality as yours. I lack artillery, infantry officers, and I am in a country so undermined by sedition that I cannot abandon it without exposing it."

Rather than wringing his hands, Calleja energetically began forming units, collecting arms, and requisitioning provisions. Only on October 24 did he march south with 3,000 cavalry, 600 infantry, and four cannons founded during the weeks after the rebellion began. Calleja mainly drew his men from the cattle estates of San Luis Potosí. Since these estates offered secure employment, employees there remained loyal to landowners and the Crown.

On November 7, soon after the insurgents turned west, they met Calleja's force at Aculco. When confronted by the royalist force, the rebels panicked and fled the battlefield, abandoning most of their artillery and supplies. The royalists at Aculco were not seasoned troops, just better disciplined and better armed than Hidalgo's.

The defeat at Aculco forced Hidalgo to the west. His force paused briefly in Valladolid. While there, the rebels marched small groups of Spaniards out of the city daily to be executed. The rebels then continued west to Guadalajara, which had already been taken by the rebel leader José Torres.

Hidalgo remained in Guadalajara from November 26, 1810, to January 14, 1811. While there, the insurgents established a rudimentary government, murdered many of the Spanish who fell into their hands, and rebuilt their army. The insurgents again found an ample supply of recruits. The hinterland surrounding Guadalajara had been subject to the same sudden commercial pressure that the Bajío had. After 1750, many villages had lost their access to land, which the elite used to grow cash crops for the Guadalajara market. This market demanded ever more produce to feed the city's mushrooming population.

After Aculco, Calleja also turned west, taking San Miguel, Dolores, and Guanajuato. In retaliation for the rebels killing so many Spaniards in Guanajuato, Calleja ordered the execution of sixty-nine Mexicans for having collaborated with the rebels. Calleja soon found that counterinsurgency presented far more of a challenge than simply reoccupying cities. He commented, "The insurrection is far from calm, it returns like the hydra, in proportion to the number of times its head is cut off."

In zones supporting the rebels, royalist commanders stripped villages, haciendas, and ranches of horses, arms, and weapons, including small kitchen knives. They rounded up all blacksmiths and destroyed forges, which could be used to make lance points and other weapons. Royalists shot individuals apprehended with arms who could not produce proper documents or who acted suspiciously. Their bodies were displayed at the point of execution. Such tactics terrorized some people into compliance, while others became even more implacable foes of the regime.

When he learned of Calleja's approach, Hidalgo ordered his army out to meet the royalists. The insurgents had 80 cannons, 3,500 soldiers, 2,000 mounted ranch hands armed with lances, and 50,000 men on foot with lances, slings, and bows and arrows. Calleja commanded 6,000 men, mostly cavalry, and had ten cannons. The battle near the Puente de Calderón (Calderón Bridge) lasted all day, January 17, 1811, and involved hard fighting on both sides. The royalists finally managed to fight their way up onto the high ground occupied by the insurgents, at which point Hidalgo's force fled. Historian Christon Archer remarked, concerning both Aculco and Calderón: "The insurgent commanders committed the tragic error of believing that they could engage in conventional battle with the royalist army. They lacked the arms, leaders, and discipline." This defeat ended the threat to the Crown posed by Hidalgo.

With their force in disarray, Hidalgo and Allende retreated north through Aguascalientes and Saltillo. Feeling Hidalgo had bungled the military campaign, the rebels stripped him of his military command, but kept him as a figurehead. This reflected the conflict between Hidalgo and Allende, who, as a military officer, had consistently advocated the use of a smaller, more disciplined force. Subsequent observers have seconded Allende's judgment, noting that Hidalgo lacked an overall military strategy and did not carry out tactical maneuvers in battle. His inexperienced generals had neither seen combat nor studied military tactics.

While the initial leaders of the movement fled north, many others, inspired by Hidalgo's example, continued to fight. They did not attempt to confront the royalist forces directly, but carried out fragmented, regionalized campaigns.

On March 21, 1811, north of Saltillo, royalists captured the remnants of the insurgent army as its leaders attempted to reach the United States and obtain sanctuary and support. A former rebel officer, who had been angered by his failure to receive a promotion, facilitated the capture.

Royalists shot several hundred of the captured rebels and condemned others to presidios or assigned them to labor in haciendas and mines. Royalists took Hidalgo to Chihuahua, where a court composed of four Spaniards and five creoles tried him. Members of the court unanimously voted to execute him. Authorities placed his head and those of three other executed rebels, including Allende, in metal cages on the granary in Guanajuato as a warning to potential rebels.

It is difficult for modern readers to interpret the insurgents' declarations since "Mexico" is a post-independence construct. At the dawn of the nineteenth century, the area now forming Mexico was a conglomeration of cities, towns, and Indian villages with no clearly defined northern or southern boundary. Similarly the term "independence" is ambiguous, since some used it to refer to Mexican independence from Spain, while others used it to refer to the Spanish empire's independence from France and Great Britain. At the time, "independence" was also used to refer to "autonomy."

Hidalgo and his close allies had hoped for a creole coup, but failed to attract sufficient military support for that. Hidalgo praised Fernando VII and condemned Spaniards and the French, declaring them to be enemies of God and humanity. Religion, as well as Enlightenment ideals, served to justify the revolt.

Hidalgo issued several reformist decrees, which increased his lower-class following. On October 19, 1810, he decreed the abolition of slavery and threatened those not emancipating slaves with the death penalty. The next month he decreed an end to the tribute paid by Indians and mulattos, and abolished the monopoly on tobacco and gunpowder production. In December, he abrogated existing agreements for the rental of Indian land, since renters often used such agreements to usurp Indian holdings. Hidalgo never controlled sufficient territory to implement these policies. Nor did he ever issue decrees dealing with such basic issues as wages and land ownership.

Hidalgo relied on a mass-based movement that he could not or would not discipline. He and his subordinates had no way of anticipating that his rebellion against Spanish rule would become a class war that threatened both the creoles and others who aspired to replace the Spanish. Arousing the poor to revolt and placing all property and established social relations in jeopardy drove Spaniards and creoles alike into the royalist camp. Hidalgo condoned pillaging by his forces and the murder of numerous Spanish prisoners as a legitimate means to attract new recruits and retain his followers.

Had Hidalgo concentrated solely on independence and guaranteed the lives and property of creoles and Spaniards, he would doubtlessly have won. Calleja, who later served as viceroy, commented:

This vast kingdom weighs too heavily upon an insubstantial metropolis; its natives and even the Europeans themselves are convinced of the advantages that would result from an independent government; and if the absurd insurrection of Hidalgo had been built upon this base, it seems to me as I now look at it, that it would have met with little opposition.[1]

Hidalgo presents historians with sharply conflicting images, just as the slave-owning Thomas Jefferson as an advocate of democracy does. Historians on both sides of the Rio Grande have criticized Hidalgo. For example, Mexican historian and politician Lorenzo de Zavala (1788–1836) wrote: "He operated without a plan, a system, or a fixed objective. Viva la Señora de Guadalupe was the only basis of his campaign; the national flag on which her image was printed, his code of law and institutions."

THE MORELOS REBELLION, 1811–1815

The executions of Hidalgo and Allende shifted the focus of the insurgency to southern Mexico. There José María Morelos y Pavón, a priest from Carácuaro, a backwater, hot-country village in Michoacán, led the struggle. Morelos, the mixed-race son of a carpenter, came from more humble origins than the original leaders of the rebellion. He had worked for years as a mule driver before entering the priesthood at age thirty-two. This experience gave him an intimate knowledge of southern Mexican terrain.

Figure 6.2 Morelos, pictured here, was the most successful of the insurgent leaders, but ultimately failed to free Mexico from Spain.

Source: Reproduced courtesy of the Benson Latin American Collection, the University of Texas at Austin.

Morelos, a former student of Hidalgo's, met with him as the rebel army marched east toward Toluca and then joined the insurgents. Hidalgo ordered him south, where he proved to be an astute guerrilla leader. The social programs he proposed went beyond Hidalgo's. Morelos called for racial equality, declaring, "Slavery will be forbidden forever, as well as caste distinctions, leaving everyone equal, and the only thing that will distinguish one American from another is vice and virtue." Morelos's emancipation proclamation facilitated his recruiting the large Afro-Mexican population in his area of operations. Morelos absolved creoles of paying debts to Spaniards, but left unaffected debts owed by Spaniards to creoles. He said agriculture should be

> many cultivating small plots separately, with their own industry and labor, with no one individual having large expanses of unused land and enslaving thousands to work that land which was cultivated.[2]

The rebellion reached its high point between 1812 and 1814, with insurgents operating over much of southern and western Mexico. During these years, rebels felt they could destroy the colonial government by conquering increasing amounts of territory and establishing civil administration in the areas they controlled.

Both sides followed a scorched-earth policy that destroyed substantial wealth. The insurgents burned haciendas, looted towns, and drove off cattle in areas supporting the Crown. The royalists, in turn, burned villages and crops in areas supporting the insurgents. Historian Lucas Alamán reported that every day in the early months of 1814 an average of twenty-five insurgents, or suspected insurgents, faced firing squads. Many Spanish officers excelled at counterinsurgency since they had been guerrillas during the Spanish struggle against the French. Royalist officers recognized that effective counterinsurgency demanded mobility, speed, and flexibility. They combined the use of exemplary terror and "flying detachments," which chased down and punished guerrilla bands and the civilian population that supported the insurgency. The royalist captain general of **Nueva Galicia**, Brigadier José de la Cruz, wrote in April 1811, "We must spread terror and death everywhere so that not a single perverted soul remains in the land . . . These bandits will learn what war to the death really means." Despite the terror, the royalists found that the traditional social ties and habits of obedience, once broken, could not be reestablished.

Morelos's small army, which never exceeded 6,000 men, attacked swiftly and then vanished in classic guerrilla style. In coastal areas Morelos's ability to recruit blacks and mulattos who were already skilled with firearms contributed to his success. Morelos energetically suppressed any outbreak of looting or racial warfare. The insurgents had learned that they could not challenge disciplined royalist units in conventional battles, and so there were no battles such as occurred at Aculco.

By the end of 1812, the insurgents controlled territory stretching north from the Isthmus of Tehuantepec to Acapulco (under siege) and toward Veracruz, Puebla, and Mexico City. In November of that year, the rebels had taken Oaxaca. Morelos's mountainous domain provided an ideal location for waging guerrilla war. It contained a large Indian and mixed-race population and few creoles.

During 1813, the rebels consolidated their gains. However, the following year, a royalist offensive penetrated deep into rebel territory and recaptured Oaxaca and Acapulco. In addition, the rebels lost key leaders. Other rebel leaders began to act independently of Morelos.

In an attempt to unite the scattered insurgent groups and to project a favorable image to creoles outside rebel territory, insurgent leaders convened a Congress on September 15, 1813, at Chilpancingo, the capital of the modern state of Guerrero. At its inauguration, Morelos declared that indigenous leaders such as Montezuma, who had resisted Cortés, were national heroes. He linked Montezuma and the independence movement, referring to the latter as "the auspicious movement in which your illustrious children have gathered to revenge the outrages and abuses committed against you and free ourselves from the grasp of the tyranny . . ." The unelected Congress never actually legislated. Given the military situation, elections could be held for only two of its members, while the rest were appointed to represent areas where the rebels could not hold elections.

On November 6, 1813, the Congress issued a declaration of independence, definitively laying to rest the notion that the rebels were fighting for Fernando VII. This declaration does not seem to have either attracted or alienated many potential followers. In social matters, the Congress generally ratified decrees Morelos had already issued concerning the abolition of class distinction, slavery, and tribute.

The Congress did write a constitution, which it promulgated on October 22, 1814 at Apatzingán, where it had been forced to flee by royalist forces. The document declared all Mexicans to be legally equal. The drafters' fear of absolutism led them to grant the legislative branch the power to choose a three-man executive and appoint justices of the supreme court. The document resembled the Spanish constitution in that it declared the Catholic Church as the official and only religion of Mexico. Given that the rebellion was in decline by the time of its promulgation, the constitution never served as the law of the land.

Despite Morelos's efforts to prop up a civilian administration, the Congress never managed to unite the scores of guerrilla bands and military satrapies resisting the colonial regime. Rather than enhancing the rebels' stature, it weakened them by introducing politics, debate, and divisions within rebel ranks and by weakening Morelos's position.

During 1815, the rebel Congress spent much of its time fleeing from one small town to another to avoid royalist troops. In the fall of that year, Congress members decided to seek refuge among rebel forces in the Puebla–Veracruz area. In November, royalists captured Morelos while he was fighting a rearguard action to protect the Congress during its move.

The Inquisition tried Morelos on twenty-six charges, which included: 1) carrying out priestly functions after being excommunicated; 2) attacking the king and his ministers; 3) executing prisoners; 4) possibly being tainted with atheism for espousing principles of anti-Catholic authors and of the U.S. Constitution; 5) imitating Luther and other heretics in criticizing the Church; and 6) sending his thirteen-year-old son to the United States, where, it noted, there was religious toleration. The indictment declared that Morelos's low birth (baja extracción) aggravated the charges. The court convicted Morelos on all counts, defrocked him, and sentenced him to death.

Morelos and Hidalgo failed to impose modern values on a colonial, politically underdeveloped, conservative society. Morelos failed to attract substantial creole support, even though he sought such support by preventing peasant land-takeovers, which would have alienated wealthy creoles, and by promising to give creoles high military and civil posts. Morelos's elimination of racial categories and his proclaiming the right of Indians and peasants to land prevented creoles from embracing his cause. Even though Morelos retained control of his army, creoles did not trust it. A royalist soldier held prisoner by Morelos commented on the social background of his force: "None of them came from a decent family . . . there are Indians, Negroes, mulattos, and delinquents, fugitives from their homelands." The issues Hidalgo and Morelos raised would not be seriously addressed until a century later in the Mexican Revolution.

HEARTS AND MINDS

Even before the Spanish could seize the military initiative, they acted to quell the rebellion. In October 1810, without waiting for permission from Spain, Viceroy Francisco Javier de Venegas, who had taken office only forty-eight hours before Hidalgo launched his rebellion, abolished tribute for Indians and those of mixed race. He ordered that the decree abolishing tribute be published in Nahuatl, as well as Spanish, so that the literate Indian elite could read it in their own language.

The church hierarchy consistently backed the royalist cause. The Archbishop of Mexico declared Hidalgo the "precursor of the Antichrist." In 1816, when it became apparent that Spanish American rebellions would continue, Pope Pius VII issued the encyclical *Etsi longissimo*, which urged bishops and clergy in Spanish America to inform the faithful of the dreadful consequences of rebellion against legitimate authority.

Given the prevailing illiteracy, information (true and false) propagated at markets, drinking establishments, and areas where women drew water and washed clothes. The difficulty either side had in communicating with the rural population was compounded by the inability of many indigenous people to speak Spanish.

Most creoles supported the Crown. However, a small group of rebel sympathizers known as the Guadalupes met secretly in Mexico City. Its members acted as an informal political party during the 1813–14 elections for the Spanish parliament (Cortes). They helped elect sympathetic creoles, whom they felt could further the cause of Mexican independence while serving in the Cortes. They also helped obtain a printing press and materials for insurgent publishing operations, sheltered refugees, furnished recruits, provided information, and smuggled arms to insurgents. They infiltrated the viceregal palace and pilfered correspondence from the office of the viceroy's secretary. The Guadalupes' activities so peeved Viceroy Calleja that he referred to them as a "diabolic assembly."

The most famous member of the Guadalupes was Leona Vicario, a member of an elite creole family who received a good education by the standards of the time. She began to aid the independence movement by using her Mexico City home as a meeting place for insurgent sympathizers. She later sent arms to rebels, used her family inheritance to finance the insurrection, and recruited and armed rebels. Late in 1813, authorities intercepted letters she had written the rebels, investigated her activity, and confined her under the authority of nuns at the Colegio de Belen.

A group of rebels soon freed Vicario, enabling her to join the insurgents. After joining Morelos's army, she administered its finances and supervised care of the ill and injured. She soon married another rebel, her uncle's former law clerk, Andrés Quintana Roo, and gave birth to their first child in a cave in Achipixtla. Royalist authorities responded by confiscating her goods and declaring her a traitor.

THE WAR DRAGS ON

Following Morelos's death, the nature of the independence struggle changed dramatically. No formal structure united the rebel groups. After the rebel Congress arrived in Puebla, the local rebel commander refused to accept its authority and simply dissolved it. The movement became more atomized, more rural, and

Figure 6.3
Leona Vicario, pictured here, was one of the best known of the women who participated in the independence struggle.

Source: Reproduced courtesy of the Benson Latin American Collection, the University of Texas at Austin.

THE VIRGIN AT WAR

> Sharply divided by race, class, customs, and even language, the inhabitants of New Spain had little to bind them together save their common identity as children and subjects of our Lady of Guadalupe.
>
> (David Brading, 2002)

During the war for independence the perception of the Virgin of Guadalupe changed radically as she became associated with patriotism. As Hidalgo passed through Atotonilco, between Dolores and the rebels' first major destination, San Miguel el Grande, he appropriated an image of the Virgin and used it as a battle standard. The Virgin soon became the symbol of the insurgency and a potent force for mobilizing people for independence.

The image of Guadalupe, which depicted her with dark skin, especially appealed to indigenous people since her skin tone contrasted with the more European features of religious images associated with royalists. Guadalupe not only adorned battle standards but was frequently invoked in seditious verses, battle cries, and insurgent proclamations. Often rebel sentries would challenge unidentified individuals with a "who goes there?" Frequently the correct response would be "Our Lady of Guadalupe." Her image often appeared on rebels' hats.

In September 1813 Morelos presented his political program, known as *Sentimientos de la Nación*, at the inaugural meeting of the rebel congress at Chilpancingo. It included the following: "Let a constitutional law establish the celebration of December 12 [the date of the Virgin's appearance] in all villages as a feast day consecrated to the Patroness of our Liberty, Holy Mary of Guadalupe."

The role of the Virgin went well beyond serving as a logo for the rebel movement. She lent the insurgents the appearance of religious sanction and was widely seen as supporting the poor against the wealthy. Rebel victories were attributed to her miraculous intervention, just as Spanish victories had been attributed to Santiago during the Conquest. Captured rebels testified emphatically that King Ferdinand had appeared in New Spain by the miraculous intercession of the Virgin.

Rural priests supporting the insurgents were often viewed as mediators between parishioners and supernatural powers represented by God, Jesus, and the Virgin. Such an association greatly facilitated mobilizing large numbers of rural people.

While most rebels viewed the Virgin as a religious figure supporting the insurgency, others simply saw her in political terms. Thus as religious skeptic Simon Bolivar noted:

> Happily, the leaders of the independence movement in Mexico have profited from the fanaticism with the greatest skill, proclaiming the famous Virgin of Guadalupe, the queen of the patriots, invoking her name at all difficult moments, and bearing her image on their flags. With all this, political enthusiasm has formed a mixture with religion, which produced a vehement fervor for the sacred cause of liberty.

Not surprisingly given the Virgin's hold on the population of New Spain, royalists also attempted to appropriate her image. On occasion those supporting the royalists, such as indigenous combatants in Zacapoaxtla, attributed their victories to her. Such isolated examples, however, did little to diminish the widely held perception that the Virgin supported the insurgency, leaving Spaniards to turn to their own Virgin of Remedios for spiritual sanction.

In 1822, after independence was finally won, Manuel de la Bárcena, archdeacon of Michoacán, delivered a sermon which declared if Mexico "breathes liberty, we owe everything to the Virgin of Tepeyac." Since then, as anthropologist Eric Wolf observed, "The Guadalupe symbol links together family, politics and religion; colonial past and independent present: Indian and Mexican . . ."

lost its appeal to the urban elite. Guadalupe Victoria, in the Puebla-Veracruz area, and Vicente Guerrero, in Oaxaca, commanded the most substantial rebel forces. In 1818, royalist commanders still reported that bands of 200 to 300 insurgents attacked Querétaro haciendas almost daily. Other small units operated in Veracruz, Michoacán, Guanajuato, Puebla, the Mexico City area, and in the Pacific lowlands in the modern states of Michoacán and Guerrero.

Rebels employed guerrilla tactics and took advantage of terrain to avoid royalist soldiers. They attacked, withdrew, and then hit another place. In each locale, if the royalist army showed signs of weakness, guerrilla bands would reemerge and operate again. Due to both geography and the aspirations of local leaders, the rebels never managed to coalesce over large areas. This weakened them militarily, but made it impossible to snuff out the insurgency.

After 1815 royalist officers assumed de facto control of many areas, displacing civilian officials. As historian Virginia Guedea commented, "Civil order ceased to exist and the armed struggle, the guerrilla war, became the new way of life for everyone." Legality became a victim of the war effort. The viceroy tolerated royalist officers who confiscated and sold property of supposed rebels, keeping the proceeds for themselves. Others traded with insurgents and pocketed special taxes they levied. Authorities tolerated all but the most egregious cases of royalist enrichment. By the end of the decade, this process resulted in regional commanders having created a series of semi-autonomous military satrapies.

The number of unemployed increased as commercial traffic and industrial output declined during the war. Many who lost their jobs joined the rebel cause. Others joined the insurgents after fleeing royalist tax collectors who were desperately attempting to finance the war effort. De facto redistribution of land abandoned by *hacendados* repeatedly occurred as individuals moved into rebel zones to be able to farm and raise stock. The expulsion of wealthy *hacendados* and their overseers did not always result in declining production. Royalist officers on long-range patrols expressed shock at re-entering insurgent-controlled districts and finding the countryside well ordered and sometimes apparently more prosperous than before 1810.

Many observers dismissed the remaining insurgents as "bandits." As historian Eric Van Young noted, "In the revolutionary period, the rather fluid boundary between crime and rebellion was continually crossed back and forth by thousands of Mexicans." The elite considered any act of collective appropriation, destruction of property, or violence against royalists as "banditry." In contrast, when viewed from below, in social terms, vague but discernible notions of social justice, retributive or redistributive in nature, generally sustained these attacks.

DEMOCRACY, SPANISH STYLE

In September 1808, a Junta Central was formed to coordinate resistance to the French. While Spanish aristocracy and royalty had controlled previous governments, the Junta Central attracted the most liberal elements of Spanish society. The Junta desperately needed support, especially silver, from Spanish America, so it elevated the Spanish colonies to the same legal status as that enjoyed by Spain.

In January 1810, a five-man Regency replaced the Junta. As French forces advanced, its members fled southwest to Cádiz, where the British fleet protected them. The most memorable act of the Regency was convening a Cortes, or parliament, to write a constitution for the Spanish empire. The municipal governments of Mexico's provincial capitals chose twenty-one representatives who served in the Cortes. Of these, fourteen were ecclesiastics, three government officials, two military men, and two merchants. These representatives, along with others from the New World, played a major role in shaping the new constitution, especially in matters concerning the expanded franchise for males and the creation of local governing institutions.

The Cortes took several steps to keep the colonies loyal. In October 1810, it ended tribute for Indians and *castas* and declared the judicial equality of inhabitants of Spanish America and the

Spanish mainland. In November 1812, the Cortes prohibited the *repartimiento* and all other forms of personal servitude and ordered the distribution of Crown lands to married Indians residing on them.

The Cortes sought reform, but not an end to colonialism. Although their number varied, roughly 158 deputies represented Spain while only fifty-three came from the Americas. This did not reflect the relative population of the two areas. The population of Spanish America totalled roughly 16 million, compared with only 10.5 million in Spain.

In 1812, the Cortes promulgated a new constitution. Drafters of the constitution granted Indians the right to vote, since they felt indigenous people were fully capable of integration into the mainstream of society and that the material progress of Spanish America required such integration. However, the constitution denied those of African descent the right to vote. Such individuals could be granted that right on an individual basis, based on meritorious service. The failure to enfranchise those of African descent reflected politics as well as prejudice. Since most people of African descent lived in the colonies, enfranchising them en masse would tip the scales toward New World control.[3]

The constitution eliminated literacy and property restrictions for voting and so restrained the king that it virtually created a republic. It also established freedom of the press and provided for the election of all municipal officers and the removal of those who had inherited or bought seats on municipal councils. Indian tribute, forced labor, and the Inquisition were eliminated. In a major concession to tradition, Article 12 declared Catholicism the one official religion and prohibited the exercise of any other religion.

Several rounds of elections in Mexico chose representatives to the Cortes and to institutions created by the constitution. In November 1812 the first popular elections in Mexican history selected twenty-five electors to choose members of the Mexico City municipal council. There was widespread grassroots participation, including the successful candidacy of those who had headed the recently disbanded Indian community governments. All those chosen as electors in Mexico City were born in Mexico and favored political change.

Once again, the residents of New Spain received a lesson in realpolitik. Claiming electoral fraud, the viceroy and the archbishop simply nullified the elections. It became apparent though that the birthplace of those elected and their political sympathies, not voting irregularities, caused the annulment.

In December 1812 elections selected representatives for the ordinary session of the Cortes. Each parish chose one elector for each 200 citizens in the parish. These electors met at the district level to choose district electors, who met in the provincial capital and selected a representative to the Cortes. Once again, the electors did not choose a single Spaniard. The Spaniards' failure to be elected, despite their efforts to gain office, reflected: 1) resentment due to the 1808 coup; 2) the increasingly repressive nature of the colonial government fighting the insurgency; 3) voters' sympathy with the insurgents; and 4) support for candidates known to favor autonomy.

These elections were allowed to stand, and the duly elected deputies took their seats in the Cortes. The three main issues raised by the New World deputies were: 1) the reserving of half of all offices for creoles; 2) opening colonial ports to foreign shipping; and 3) extending voting rights to all those born in the New World, including those of African descent. Spaniards not only opposed a further expansion of voting rights but bitterly resented the expansion that had already occurred. The Spanish-dominated Mexico City *consulado* declared New Spain to be "a province the home of five million automatons, of a million disloyal vassals, and of a hundred thousand citizens addicted to order."

To decentralize the formerly monolithic Spanish governing structure, the 1812 constitution created provincial deputations to administer local affairs and report directly to the government in Spain. The Spanish considered the six provincial deputations in New Spain merely as advisory bodies without legislative power. However, Mexicans felt they represented the will of each province's citizens. The seven Mexicans elected to each provincial deputation performed many local administrative, judicial, and fiscal functions and served as advocates for their provinces' interests.

In addition to creating provincial deputations, the 1812 constitution granted municipalities with a population of more than 1,000 the right to elect their own town councils. As a result, by 1814, the number of town councils in Mexico had increased from a mere fifty-five to nearly 900. Most of the newly created councils were in indigenous and mestizo communities. These elections not only created new town councils but transformed previously established ones, since from the early seventeenth century on, they had become closed, self-perpetuating oligarchies.

After prolonged resistance, the French withdrew from Spain due to: 1) the success of Spanish guerrillas; 2) victories by Portuguese troops under British command who fought Napoleon's troops; and 3) Napoleon's 1812 defeat in Russia. Without a French force to sustain him, Joseph abdicated on January 7, 1814, paving the way for Fernando to reclaim the throne. Both sides of the Atlantic rejoiced when the recently released Spanish monarch assumed full powers in May.

This rejoicing came to an abrupt end when Fernando abolished the Cortes, which he claimed had usurped his power and forced a constitution on the Spanish people. He assumed absolute power and abolished all the institutions, such as the provincial deputations and elected municipal governments, created by the 1812 constitution. Policymaking became dominated by hardliners who rejected compromise with Spanish America. Indians were once again required to pay tribute. Many liberal leaders, including some of the Mexican deputies, were jailed.

In the final months of 1819, Fernando ordered Spanish troops to Cádiz so they could be deployed to the New World to suppress independence movements that had broken out there. Rather than engaging in a colonial war, the troops rebelled. Major Rafael Riego, the rebel leader, argued that the New World insurgencies would cease if the constitution were restored. Rebellious military units joined forces with liberals opposed to Fernando's absolutism. By March of 1820, they had gained sufficient strength to force the reestablishment of the Cortes and the restoration of the 1812 constitution.

The 1820–21 session of the reconvened Cortes saw Spain fail to seize upon its last chance to keep the empire intact. In June 1821, the Spanish American deputies presented a *plan* that would have created a new *corte* (parliament) in Mexico and two new ones in South America. This would have in effect created three new governments, which would have been presided over by Bourbon princes and which would have been free to trade with any nation. They would have maintained commercial and foreign policy ties to the Spanish Crown, which they would help finance. The deputies making this proposal cited Canada as an example of an area that had administrative autonomy without rejecting its sovereign.

Spanish merchants, liberals, and absolutists agreed upon one thing—the ports of Spanish America must remain closed to all except Spanish ships. They rejected the proposal of the New World deputies and in the process made a mockery of the vaunted equality—proclaimed by the Cortes—of Spaniards and overseas citizens.

The 1812 constitution served to convert Mexicans from subjects to citizens. Between 1810 and 1822, Mexico held five elections for deputies to the Spanish Cortes, each of which was held at three levels. In addition, Mexicans elected municipal councils and provincial deputations. Those elected learned parliamentary procedure, the value of compromise, and debating skills, and voters learned to value the ballot. The twenty-two Mexicans who served in the Cortes occupied important positions and gained invaluable experience. Freedom of the press exposed Mexicans to new ideas. Documents published in the Mexican press included the U.S. Constitution and the manifesto of the government of independent Buenos Aires.

BREAKING THE STALEMATE

The 1820 reimposition of the 1812 Constitution exacerbated royalist financial woes. Royalist revenue collection had already declined from 28 million pesos in 1809 to less than 9 million in 1817. The newly reconstituted municipal governments further decreased royalist income by refusing to impose taxes to fund counterinsurgency efforts. Royalist Colonel José Barradas, serving in Veracruz, reported that the "constitutional municipalities have openly refused me any aid . . . I only receive frivolous excuses." The lack of local financial support caused the disbanding of many militia units that had been engaged in counterinsurgency operations.

Early in 1821, virtually no constituency favored the status quo. Royalist forces were suffering from battle fatigue and a lack of finances, which literally reduced some units to rags. Military levies and continued destruction prevented economic recovery. The creole elite and the ecclesiastical hierarchy, both staunch opponents of the insurgents, felt the re-imposition of constitutional rule in Spain threatened their privileges. Surviving rebel units were still far from victory. The moribund economy and the mass mobilization prevented countless Mexicans from obtaining jobs and getting on with their everyday lives.

Agustín de Iturbide, the son of a noble Basque merchant in Valladolid, facilitated the break-up of the political-military logjam. His father-in-law was the wealthiest and most powerful man in that city. When the independence war began, Iturbide was serving as a lieutenant in the Provincial Regiment of Valladolid. He cast his lot with the royalists and established himself as an effective counterinsurgency fighter who rose rapidly through the royalist ranks until 1816. That year he was relieved of command for financial impropriety and cruelty to non-combatants.

Denied the opportunity to advance his military career, Iturbide turned increasingly to politics. In November 1820, four years after being relieved of his command, Viceroy Apodaca appointed him as Commander of Southern Mexico, hoping this would enable the royalists to defeat Guerrero's forces.

Rather than pursuing military victory, Iturbide sent Apodaca false reports about his "progress" and requested additional troops and supplies. At the same time, he corresponded extensively with various factions of the urban elite in Mexico City and Veracruz, sounding out the possibility of a political solution to the military stalemate.

On February 24, 1821, after it became apparent that a political solution was viable, Iturbide signed a document stating his intentions in Iguala, a village in the modern state of Guerrero. On March 1, Iturbide formally presented his new proposal, known as the Plan of Iguala, to his officers. Iturbide and his men then took an oath to support the independence of Mexico. The ceremonies ended with a Te Deum chanted at the local church.

The Plan of Iguala called for an extremely broad coalition, including both royalists and insurgents, to unite against Spain to achieve Mexican independence. Article 1 of the Plan of Iguala established the Roman Catholic Church as the official religion "to the exclusion of all others." Article 2 proclaimed the "absolute independence" of Mexico. Article 3 called for Mexico to be ruled by a constitutional monarchy. Article 4 invited Fernando, a member of his family, or a member of another ruling dynasty to govern. Article 5 established an interim government until a *corte* could meet. Article 12 granted citizenship to "all the inhabitants" of New Spain. Article 14 guaranteed the special legal status (*fuero*) and property of the clergy.

The Plan of Iguala was as conciliatory as possible in keeping with its goal of independence. To attract conservatives, it declared Spain to be the "most Catholic pious, heroic, and magnanimous nation on earth." The Plan offered each interest group some of what it desired. It offered all citizens, including Spaniards, security of property. Government, military, and religious officials accepting the Plan could continue in their posts. The most radical proposal, in addition to that of independence itself, was civil equality for all ethnic groups. This served to win over insurgents, many of whose bloodlines had previously been declared to be inferior.

With the advantage of hindsight, one can marvel at the political acumen of the Plan of Iguala. However, early in 1821 the response to Iturbide's Plan remained in doubt. In many places people evaluated Iturbide's program and his capacity to win a definitive victory. Slow communications gave the newly announced Plan the appearance of having settled in limbo. The Puebla newspaper *La Abeja* partly resolved Iturbide's problem with disseminating the Plan when it printed it "by mistake."

On March 10, insurgent leader Vicente Guerrero announced his alliance with Iturbide. After having exacted an assurance that citizenship would be extended to men of all races, Guerrero declared the former royalist to be *"primer jefe de los ejércitos nacionales"* ("commander-in-chief of the national armies") and placed his forces at Iturbide's disposal. Then on March 19 a leading royalist commander Colonel Anastasio Bustamante (later to serve three times as president of Mexico) joined the cause. Still, at the end of March, Iturbide's troops numbered only 1,800, many of whom were irregulars who had served in Guerrero's force.

Once it became apparent that the Plan of Iguala would attract officers of Bustamante's stature, an avalanche of royalist defections followed. Sometimes officers joined Iturbide, bringing their units with them. In other cases, royalist units simply melted away. At the beginning of March 1821, the royalist force in Valladolid numbered more than 3,500, but by April 4, only 1,500 remained.

As both royalist and insurgent forces joined Iturbide's movement, they formed the Army of Three Guarantees (*Ejército Trigarante*). This force took its name from the three main provisions of the Plan of Iguala—the guarantees of independence, of the Roman Catholic religion, and of civil equality. This army won repeated victories, not so much due to its effectiveness but to the collapse of the royalist forces. As historian Christon Archer observed, "Exhausted by eleven years of conflict, the old order simply crumbled without much fighting and faded away." During April, May, and June of 1821, large parts of the Bajío and Nueva Galicia accepted the Plan of Iguala. On June 14, Guadalajara signed on to the Plan and at the end of July Puebla did.

Viceroy Apodaca was an able administrator, but proved to be a poor military commander. Initially he responded to Iturbide by concentrating his veteran troops in Mexico City in anticipation of an attack. This enabled Iturbide to build his forces with little opposition. Apodaca could not even trust the loyalty of the troops he commanded.

Military officers were attracted by Iturbide's offer to let them keep their rank and by his pledge to reestablish the military *fuero*, which had been abolished by the Cortes. Many creole officers, such as Antonio López de Santa Anna, switched allegiance, feeling they had been neglected in the provinces and often left without pay. Many Spanish soldiers accepted the Plan, too, since it promised them safe conduct back to Spain. Other Spanish officers, who had been in Mexico so long that they had developed extensive financial interests, joined Iturbide with the intention of remaining in Mexico. Others disliked the anti-military aspects of the reimposed 1812 constitution.

Juan O'Donojú, the last viceroy sent over from Spain, arrived on July 30, 1821, just as royalist forces were on the verge of collapse. By August, the Army of Three Guarantees controlled almost all of Mexico except Mexico City, the port of Veracruz, Acapulco, and the fortress of Perote. O'Donojú, a liberal who had been jailed after Fernando reimposed absolutism in 1814, realized he could not save Mexico as a colony.

O'Donojú accepted Iturbide's invitation to meet in the town of Córdoba on August 23, 1821. The following day, the two signed the Treaty of Córdoba. As Iturbide later commented, O'Donojú accepted his proposal "as if he had helped me write the plan." With the treaty, O'Donojú felt he could save Mexico for the Bourbon dynasty, if not for Spain, and lay the foundation for cordial relations between the two nations. He was promised a lifetime pension, allowing him to remain in Mexico rather than returning to Spain where he would be stigmatized for having lost Mexico.

The seventeen articles of the Treaty of Córdoba largely reiterated the provisions of the Plan of Iguala. Article 2 declared that Mexico would be governed by a moderate constitutional monarchy. Article 8 provided for the immediate establishment of a Governing Provisional Junta, to include O'Donojú, which would function until a Mexican *corte* could be convened. Article 11 provided for a three-man regency to serve as the executive power. O'Donojú agreed to use his authority to persuade Spanish troops in Mexico City to lay down their arms.

The Spanish force in Mexico City presented the only remaining obstacle for the Army of Three Guarantees. On September 14, O'Donojú informed its commander that, under Spanish law, he remained subject to the viceroy and that resistance was absurd. The commander then ordered his men to lay down their arms. As his final official act, O'Donojú assumed responsibility for marching Spanish troops out of the city.

On September 27, 1821, Iturbide's thirty-eighth birthday, he and his 16,000-man Army of Three Guarantees triumphantly entered Mexico City, passing under a magnificent triumphal arch constructed for the occasion. Also present, commanding a division, was Vicente Guerrero. A huge popular festival celebrated independence. Indians danced in streets strewn with flowers. Official Mexico celebrated with a Te Deum and a banquet. After Iturbide's arrival, Mexico enjoyed a period of euphoria, rejoicing, and hope.

On the following day, September 28, 1821, the Governing Provisional Junta issued a formal Declaration of Independence. Thirty-eight people signed it, none of whom were former insurgents. However, some of the signatories included members of the Guadalupes, former deputies to the Cortes, and a member of the feisty 1808 Mexico City municipal council.

Iturbide provided a political program around which various groups could rally to end the war. As historian Timothy Anna noted:

> In the short run, the Plan of Iguala swept the whole nation before it precisely because it was a workable compromise. Of course, different adherents to the Plan had different motives for supporting it and different ideas about what form of government should be created.[4]

SOCIAL ROLES

> To interpret any process of large-scale, protracted political violence or nation-building as monolithic . . . whether or not a revolution in the classic sense of the term, is folly.
> (Eric Van Young, 2001)

Internal divisions and opinion shifts complicate any discussion of the role groups played in the independence struggle. The Enlightenment influenced some members of the elite. Other Mexicans reflected the thinking of another era. For example, insurgent troops commanded by General Mariano Matamoros fought under a banner inscribed "Die for ecclesiastical immunity," an expression of their demand that special legal privileges be restored to the clergy. In so far as the rebels fought for the concept of a nation, it was a creole notion, since *castas* had at best a vague notion of nationhood, and Indians and blacks none at all. Indian communities, which supplied the majority of insurgent troops, were deeply conservative and sought to defend community lands and other assets that were under pressure from commercial agriculture and increased taxes. Sometimes one community would support the insurgency largely because an adjacent, rival community opposed it.

The failure of the creoles, by and large, to rally behind Hidalgo prolonged the independence struggle. The examples of creole rebellion provided by Hidalgo and Allende were the exceptions, not the rule. Even Hidalgo's own brother José María Hidalgo fought in the area of Pénjamo, Guanajuato, as a royalist officer. In contrast to the elite in the thirteen British North American colonies, the creole elite lived in a predominantly non-white society. While they sought autonomy, its members did not necessarily wish to sever their ties with the mother country. They not only respected the monarchy but feared that radical change might upset the existing social hierarchy that placed them close to the top of the social order.

The Plan of Iguala united creoles and many Spaniards. Conservatives, including upper clergy and *audiencia* members, who had steadfastly supported Spanish colonization found that those ruling Spain were no longer sympathetic to their goals. They also saw that Iturbide's Plan did not endanger their wealth and social position. This led them to make common cause with Mexican liberals. While the two groups differed radically on the type of economy and society they sought, in the interim they could agree on independence.

Generalizations about the rural lower class are hampered by the extreme variation of its members and their not having left as abundant a written record as members of the elite. Much of what we know of their thinking was recorded in their testimony when royalists put them on trial for having joined the insurgents.

Most of the population of late colonial Mexico did not have a worldview that extended far enough beyond their own locality to even conceive of a state, let alone contemplate the nature of the state they desired. Evidence from trials of rebels fails to indicate that the notion of "autonomy" made its way down to rural combatants. Indians and *castas* fought in the hope that their lot in life might in some way improve. Rather than a cohesive rebellion Mexico saw regional insurrections motivated by myriad grievances explode in thousands of directions at once. None of these insurrections responded to any such thing as "Mexico." Rather than fighting for land per se, as revolutionaries would a century later, rural insurgents concentrated more often on defending themselves from voracious administrators and their representatives and protecting existing land holdings and water and grazing rights. Although a majority of the population was poor, only a minority joined Hidalgo's rebellion or later uprisings.

Indian attitudes ranged from support for the insurrection, loyalty to the Crown, and indifference. The Indian community had become highly dependent on Church and Crown for its existence, so colonial ties were not cast off lightly. Generally the more "Indian" individuals were in culture and self-identification the less likely they were to move much beyond their villages for collective political action.

Some Indians joined the insurgents to preserve the autonomy of their communities from new market and fiscal pressures and based their actions on entirely different assumptions than the elite. Indian insurgents of both sexes captured in November 1810 clearly believed they were following the orders of the king of Spain, who was physically present in Mexico, riding about the countryside in a mysterious black coach. They testified that he had commanded Father Hidalgo to take up arms against the Spanish colonial authorities. Furthermore they believed that the headman of their village had ordered them to kill the viceroy and all other Spaniards and divide their property among the poor. Some of the testimony supported the notion that the Virgin of Guadalupe was working hand in hand with Fernando.

Some Indians supported the royalist cause using slogans similar to those of the rebels. At the village of San Miguel Tomatlán, near Orizaba, patriotic Indians and mestizos volunteered to serve in royalist militias shouting, "¡*Viva la religión, Viva el rey, Viva la patria, Muera todo traidor!*" ("Long live religion, Long live the king, Long live the homeland, Death to Traitors!").

The clergy formed a pivotal grouping in the insurrection. One study found that priests comprised 27.5 percent of the rebel leadership, the largest single occupational group. By 1815 more than a hundred priests had been executed for supporting the insurgency and many more had been excommunicated. Regardless of whether they joined the insurrection or served in elected positions, priests generally acted as individuals, rather than representing the interests of the Church as an institution.

In contrast to the lower clergy, the ecclesiastical hierarchy, almost all of whom were Spaniards, feared they would lose their status and supported the Crown until the issuance of the Plan of Iguala. While many priests actively supported the insurrection, not more than a tenth of them played an active role on either side.

After the proclamation of the Plan of Iguala, the clergy rallied around Iturbide's cause since he promised them the ecclesiastical immunity that had been abolished by the Spanish Cortes in 1820. The Cortes had also restricted the right of the Church to own property. Soon churchmen were preaching sermons denouncing the Spaniards and announcing that the war for independence would be a religious war to defend the old order.

JOSEFA ORTIZ DE DOMÍNGUEZ

Josefa Ortiz de Domínguez, who is likely the best-known woman of Mexican history, is generally referred to simply as *La Corregidora* (the *Corregidor*'s wife). In 1773 she was born in Valladolid (today Morelia), the daughter of a military officer. Even though her father was killed in the line of duty while she was still a girl, her family had enough resources to enroll her in Mexico City's Colegio de las Vizcaínes. Miguel Domínguez, an administrator of the school's endowment, met her there while she was still a student. He was smitten by her and married her in 1791. In 1802 the viceroy appointed Miguel as Corregidor of Querétaro—a prestigious position. Josefa energetically plunged into her expected social welfare role as First Lady of Querétaro, caring for the poor and sick.

After almost a decade as First Lady, she joined the "Literary Academy of Querétaro," the group serving as a smokescreen for the plot to rebel against Spanish rule. When Miguel found out that authorities had learned of the plot and that arrests were imminent, he went into damage control mode. He locked Josefa in her bedroom to prevent her from doing anything that could endanger her or confirm her participation in the plot.

Undaunted, Josefa began to pound on the floor of her bedroom to attract the attention of jailor Ignacio Pérez, who lived immediately below her in the city hall. She informed Pérez, a fellow conspirator, that their cover had been blown and that immediate action was necessary. Pérez, acting on that information, rode twenty miles to San Miguel el Grande, the home of conspirator Ignacio Allende. When he found that Allende was out of town, he contacted another conspirator, Juan Aldama. Aldama then took the news that arrest was imminent to Hidalgo who was in Dolores. Acting on this information, Hidalgo uttered his historic Grito de Dolores.

Josefa was imprisoned for her presumed role in the plot. However, when she was placed on trial there was insufficient evidence to convict here, so she was released. (No doubt her high social standing aided her case.)

Undaunted, she continued to support the insurgency, activity that resulted in her being rearrested. In December 1814 a church official wrote the viceroy informing him that Josefa was an "active, impudent, effective, audacious, incorrigible insurgent agent" who took advantage of every possible opportunity to "inspire hatred of the king, of Spain, and of the just and legitimate decisions of his kingdom." In conclusion he stated that she was a true Anne Boleyn. In her second trial, there was ample evidence of her support of the insurgency and she was sentenced to four years confinement in the convent of Santa Clara de Sena.

In 1817, as the insurgency wound down, she was released. Once Mexico had become independent, Emperor Iturbide offered her the position of lady-in-waiting for his wife. Being of firm republican convictions, she refused the honor saying she was too busy at home caring for her eleven children. In 1824 she refused a cash payment the government offered those involved in the insurgency and declared that serving the cause of independence was a duty which she had willingly fulfilled.

Josefa lived in Mexico City until 1829, when she died of pleurisy. She has received a variety of posthumous honors for her role in the independence struggle. In 1878 the Querétaro Legislature declared her *Benemérita* (Meritorious) and ordered her name inscribed in gold letters on the wall of the legislative chamber. Her most conspicuous honor is having her portrait placed on Mexico's five-peso bill.

Between 1810 and 1821, given the absence of males who had been mobilized to fight, women were thrust into overseeing farms and businesses. As with other groups, Mexican women lent support to both sides of the conflict. Their involvement led to a permanent shift in socially accepted roles for women. Some took up arms, such as Manuela Medina, an Indian from Taxco, who reached the rank of captain fighting with the insurgents. More commonly women smuggled messages and weapons under their full skirts. In one celebrated instance a group of women, accompanied by children and picnic baskets in a carriage, smuggled a printing press out of Mexico City so rebels could publish a newspaper. Other women served as spies, accompanied troops to prepare food and care for the wounded, and made cartridges for insurgent combatants. Royalists executed many women for supporting the independence cause. While the total number of women involved in the independence struggle remains unknown, almost 250 have been identified.

In 1815, Leona Vicario accepted a royalist pardon, which permitted her and her husband to survive until independence. In recognition of her contribution to the independence cause and to compensate her for the financial losses she had suffered, the first Congress of independent Mexico granted her a hacienda and several houses in Mexico City. When Vicario died in 1842, President Antonio López de Santa Anna led her funeral procession.

Women also actively supported the royalist cause. In late 1810, when Hidalgo was poised to take Mexico City, they formed the first known secular female organization in Mexico, the Patriotas Marianas. Its more than 2,000 members watched over the image of the Virgin of Remedios, the patroness of the royalist army, and sewed banners with her image. This group later raised funds for the royalist cause and published pamphlets proclaiming their loyalty to the Crown.

There is little evidence that agrarian conflicts were the driving force of the independence war. Although rebels would frequently farm abandoned land, they never clearly called for the systematic transfer of land from *hacendados* to the landless, as Emiliano Zapata would a century later.

During the war years, rural residents acquired arms, fighting experience, and above all consciousness of their strength. Municipalities proliferated and appropriated judicial and fiscal powers. This allowed their residents to play an essential role in Mexican political life in subsequent years.

The independence war in Mexico was much more bitter than the U.S. war for independence due to the lack of consensus among the elite, which led to mass rural insurrection and class and racial conflict. The struggle in Mexico lasted longer than the U.S. war for independence due to Mexico's lack of foreign support. The forces fighting for U.S. independence had the assistance of 10,000 French troops. In addition, Spanish and French ships neutralized the British fleet, while Spanish troops attacked the British in the Mississippi Valley. Throughout Spanish America, pro-independence forces were unable to pit other European powers against Spain.

Estimates of the number who died during the Mexican independence conflict range from a low of 200,000, or 3 percent of the population, to 600,000, or 10 percent of the population. In any case, Mexico paid an inordinately high price. The movement led by Iturbide was essentially a counter-revolution designed to defend the established order, which was no longer guaranteed by its traditional protector, the Spanish Crown. For almost half a century, generals whose careers began with the independence struggle would rule Mexico. With changed names and slightly altered institutions, Mexico began its independent life without having solved any of the basic questions behind the struggle. These remained for the future.

THE ECONOMIC IMPACT

The great future predicted by Alexander von Humboldt in the last decade of the eighteenth century ended in civil war, destroying much of 300 years of economic progress.
(Colin MacLachlan and William Beezley, 2010)

Even before the Grito de Dolores, the Mexican economy was in trouble. To maintain mining output at a high level, the Crown provided massive financial subsidies for the purchase of the mercury used to refine silver. As trade barriers were lowered, legally imported textiles, as well as smuggled ones, ruined local producers. Buyers found imported British cottons especially attractive since the mechanization of carding and spinning reduced the cost of producing them—and therefore their market price—by nearly 70 percent between 1790 and 1812. The 1804 Consolidation Decree eliminated the major source of credit. After that date, miners lacked the capital needed to sink deep shafts, could not purchase drilling equipment, and had difficulty buying supplies from merchants.

After the Grito de Dolores, the insurgency damaged the economy in innumerable ways. Well before rebels appeared, mine owners would flee to cities controlled by royalists. Mine workers joined the rebels, died, or moved away. Many wealthy Spaniards not only departed but took their capital back to Spain with them, exacerbating the credit crunch. Higher taxes to finance the royalist war effort increased costs. Royalist officers speculated with merchandise under their control, further increasing prices and damaging the economy.

The independence struggle most affected mining, with its complex system of supply and financing. Since the insurgents were especially active in mining areas, these areas suffered a precipitous withdrawal of capital. To finance the war, the Crown shifted from subsidizing mining to heavily taxing it, further exacerbating the capital shortage. In 1811 the Crown ended its monopoly on the supply of mercury. However, to the mine owners' chagrin, private suppliers charged as much as five times more to supply mercury than the Spanish government had charged. Also private vendors ceased to provide mercury on credit, as the Crown had. The isolation of mining towns not occupied by rebels often prevented them from obtaining supplies. The population of the mining-dependent Guanajuato area decreased from 70,600 in 1802 to 35,733 in 1822. As production declined, the price of silver in London increased by 10 percent.

As with mining, the textile industry depended on extended raw material and marketing networks. *Obraje* owners complained of an "almost absolute lack of necessary materials" because of the "present barbarous and destructive insurrection" that had "annihilated the ranchers that supplied the wool" and obstructed the roads for the transport of what little remained. Given their isolation from *obrajes*, many ranchers began to rely on homespun wool. In the fifteen months after the Grito de Dolores, the number of *obrajes* in Querétaro fell from nineteen to eight. Machine-made fabrics from Europe and cheap cloth from the Orient displaced local production after they entered Mexico in substantial quantities without the heavy duties established under Spanish trade regulations. As a result of tariff-free textile imports through Pacific ports, Guadalajara's cotton textile industry was virtually eliminated.

Some of the richest agricultural areas, such as Jalisco and the Bajío, also saw some of the heaviest combat and destruction. Hacienda owners often fled to the safety of the city, and many of their workers joined the insurgent cause. Rebel bands in Querétaro killed hacienda administrators, ran off livestock, and pillaged, leaving many haciendas ruined. As mines closed, small farmers lost their markets and left the land. Morelos's troops specifically targeted Veracruz tobacco fields for burning, since they supplied the royal tobacco factory, a major revenue source for the Crown. Agricultural production during the insurgency fell by roughly 50 percent.

The insurgency disrupted trade routes for prolonged periods. Many small villages were abandoned to the insurgents. After royalist troops garrisoned cities, their residents complained about the loss of contact with rural areas. As early as 1811, the Chihuahua municipal government noted the interruption of trade had led to shortages of clothing, paper, sugar, chocolate, medicine, and even tobacco, which led to the smoking of local herbs. Due to rebel activity, bullion often could not be shipped to Mexico City to be minted, so the viceroy authorized regional mints to convert bullion into coins.

Traders who remained in business had to pay the high cost of military escorts to accompany mule trains. As many as 1,000 soldiers guarded the caravans that carried goods from Veracruz to Mexico City. Muleteers operating without royalist military escort often had to pay rebels protection money. The scarcity of beasts of burden and of coins to pay for goods further reduced trade. During the second decade of the nineteenth century, foreign trade declined by 41 percent. As a result, between 1810 and 1818, the population of Veracruz declined from 15,000 to 8,934.

In Mexico, the independence conflict resulted in economic and fiscal changes that lasted longer than mere physical destruction, which could be repaired in a relatively short period (witness post-World War II Europe). Local officials spent more on defense than before the Grito de Dolores. The Guanajuato district transferred roughly 80 percent of all taxes to Mexico City between 1791 and 1807. However, between 1812 and 1816, since tax receipts declined to half the pre-war level and military spending soared, only 28 percent were transferred to Mexico City. Eliminating Indian tribute deprived the government of 2 million pesos a year. Military spending by the provinces deprived the central government of both resources and political power. Reestablishing the fiscal ties with the provinces that had existed for almost three centuries presented a monumental challenge for nineteenth-century Mexico.

The interruption of trade routes also deprived Mexico's core of its traditional power. Tariff revenue fell as foreign trade declined. Since transport through central Mexico was often impossible during the war, new trade routes opened. Spanish, Panamanian, and South American merchants flocked to the Pacific port of San Blas. These merchants, with commercial ties to Kingston, Jamaica, and access to British capital, provided a preview of the economic forces that would shape post-independence Mexico. Opening new trade routes decentralized power and the tax base.

THE U.S. REACTION

The war of 1812 minimized the U.S. ability to play a role in the Latin American independence struggles. Combat at home and British control of the seas left the United States with little influence over Spanish America. During the war the British had an almost entirely free hand in consolidating their political and economic influence throughout Latin America. British diplomacy effectively headed off Spanish attempts to secure the intervention of other European powers. Such intervention might have prevented the loss of Spanish sovereignty and the increase of British influence in the Americas.

While the independence struggle was being waged in Mexico, the United States and Spain negotiated a border treaty known as the Adams–Onís Treaty. The treaty, signed in 1819, recognized the Spanish claim to Texas in exchange for Spain's ceding to the United States its claim to Florida, which it obviously could not defend. The newly delineated boundary separating New Spain and the United States ran along the present east boundary of Texas, up the Red River, and then north along the one-hundredth meridian (the present east boundary of the Texas panhandle) to the Arkansas River. It followed the Arkansas to its headwaters and then ran to the forty-second parallel and then west along that parallel (the present northern boundary of California) to the Pacific.

The treaty pleased both the Spanish and U.S. governments. Spain secured its claim to Texas and lost only Florida, which it had in fact already ceased to control. The United States obtained not only title to Florida but its first solid claim extending to the Pacific. Previously Spain had claimed territory north of the forty-second parallel. Since the treaty gave the United States access to the Pacific, it is also referred to as the Transcontinental Treaty.

Other European powers lost out as their prospects for acquiring territory on the Pacific Coast dimmed. Of course the area's indigenous population suffered the biggest loss. Without even their knowledge, much less their consent, those of European descent divided their land among themselves.

The unwillingness to jeopardize the delicate negotiations that led to the Adams–Onís Treaty shaped the U.S. response to the Spanish American independence struggle. The two-year delay between the 1819 signing of the treaty and its ratification by Spain ensured that the United States would not openly support pro-independence forces. Also after 1776 Cuba's trade with the United States surpassed Cuba's trade with Spain. The United States was unwilling to risk being excluded from the Cuban market by supporting independence struggles in other Spanish colonies. By 1821 U.S. exports to Spanish America had reached $8 million a year, or 13 percent of all U.S. exports.

Officially the United States remained neutral during the struggle for Spanish American independence. However by allowing roughly thirty-seven insurgent-flagged privateers to operate from U.S. ports and prey on Spanish commerce, President James Monroe virtually recognized the rebels' belligerency. Spain urged that these rebel ships be considered as pirate ships, just as many Americans during the U.S. Civil War felt Confederate cruisers should be treated as pirates.

Despite the U.S. government's declared neutrality, American citizens generally sympathized with the cause of Spanish American independence. They sold weapons to insurgents and sent propaganda and copies of the U.S. Constitution south. Roughly 90 percent of the captains who carried letters of marque for the government of Buenos Aires were U.S. citizens. Prominent U.S. politician Henry Clay described the Spanish American independence movement as a "glorious spectacle of eighteen millions of people, struggling to burst their chains and be free."

Since the United States and Britain both sought to control Spanish American markets and keep the French out, they maintained very similar policies toward independence movements. The British and the Americans largely formulated policy for the Spanish empire as a whole and only rarely designed measures directed specifically at Mexico. Since both the United States and Great Britain were formally allied with Spain, they sought to maintain at least the appearance of neutrality. The British enacted laws making it almost impossible for British subjects to render any assistance to Spanish American rebels, then demurely ignored the systematic violation of these laws. In 1818 alone, six expeditionary forces illegally departed from Britain to South America's north coast.

DOCUMENT 6.1: THE TREATY OF CÓRDOBA

Art. 1: This American nation is sovereign and independent and will henceforth be called the Mexican Empire.

Art. 2: The government of the empire will be a moderate constitutional monarchy.

Art. 3: As provided in Article 4 of the Plan of Iguala, the throne will be offered first to Fernando VII, the Catholic King of Spain. If he declines, then it will be offered to his brother the infante Don Carlos; if he declines, then to the infante Francisco de Paula; if he declines then to Carlos Luis, Spanish infante, former heir to Tuscany, and now to Lucca. If he declines, the throne will be offered to the person the Cortes designates.

Art. 4: The emperor will locate his court in Mexico City, which will serve as the capital of the Empire.

[Art. 5 details how the treaty is to be presented to the Spanish Cortes and the infantes.]

Art. 6: In keeping with the spirit of the Plan of Iguala, a junta made up of the leading men of the empire will be designated immediately. Their selection should be based on their virtues, profession, fortune, authority, ideas, and high public esteem. Their number will be sufficient to ensure prudence in exercising the powers provided in the following articles.

Art. 7: The junta described in the previous article will be named the Provisional Governing Junta.

Art. 8: Given the advantage of having a person of his stature playing an active role in the government, Lt. Gen. Juan O'Donojú will be a member of the junta . . .

Art. 9: Members of the Provisional Governing Junta will select its president. They are free to select either a Junta member or a non-member. If no individual receives a majority of the votes in the first round of voting, the two persons receiving the most votes will compete in a second round of voting.

Art. 10: After its first meeting, the Provisional Governing Junta will inform the public of its goals and priorities and provide details as to how the members of the Cortes will be elected.

Art. 11: Following the election of its president, the Provisional Governing Junta will name a three-man regency selected from either its members or non-members. The regency will govern until a monarch is crowned.

Art. 12: Once the Provisional Junta is constituted, it will govern on an interim basis according to existing law, provided such law is not contrary to the Plan of Iguala. Existing laws will remain in force until the Cortes drafts a Constitution.

Art. 13. The regency, as soon as it is named, will convoke a Cortes, whose method of selection will be determined by the Provisional Governing Junta. It will govern in accordance with Article 24 of the Plan of Iguala.

Art. 14. Executive power will be vested in the regency, while legislature power will be vested in the Cortes. However since it will be some time until the Cortes meets, in order to avoid these two powers being vested in the same body, the Junta will exercise legislative power. This will allow necessary legislation to be enacted before the Cortes meets. After that the Junta will play an auxiliary, consultative role.

Art. 15: All people belonging to a society that has changed its system of government or which has passed from one power to another enjoy a natural right to move and take their wealth with them. There is no reason to deprive them of liberty, unless they have contracted a debt to the society to which they belong. This debt may result from a crime or from another cause recognized by legal authorities. Europeans living in New Spain and Americans living on the Peninsula will be free to remain as citizens of either nation. They are also free to request their passport, which may not be denied them. They can leave within a specified time, taking with them their family and their goods. However they will be subject to any laws governing exports which have been established.

Art. 16: Military men and public officials who are known opponents of Mexican Independence will not be offered the option provided in Article 15. They will leave the empire with their effects, on the terms that the regency establishes, paying the export duties mentioned in the previous article.

Art. 17: The Spanish troops occupying the capital prevent implementation of this treaty. The commander-in-chief of the imperial army has more than enough resources to overcome them by force. However he prefers, as does the Mexican nation, not to remove them forcibly. These valiant, loyal Spanish troops cannot maintain themselves under the new regime. Don Juan O'Donojú has offered to use his authority to withdraw these troops, who can surrender honorably, without shedding blood.

DOCUMENT 6.2: THE SEPTEMBER 28, 1821 DECLARATION OF INDEPENDENCE

The oppression, which the Mexican nation has suffered for 300 years without being able to act freely or express itself, ends today.

The heroic efforts of its sons have concluded. The eternally memorable undertaking of a genius who is beyond all praise and admiration, acting for the love and glory of his country, has been completed. This undertaking, began in Iguala, was completed by surmounting almost insuperable obstacles. The rights, granted by the Author of Nature and which are recognized as inalienable and sacred by the civilized nations of the world have been restored throughout the North [of Spanish America]. The nation is now free to constitute itself in the manner which maximizes its well being. Its representatives can make known their programs and ideas and employ their precious talents. It is now free to form the government which will best ensure its well-being. The Supreme Imperial Junta solemnly declares *that Mexico is a sovereign nation and independent of Old Spain.* In the future its ties with the mother country will be limited to close friendship whose terms will be established by treaty. Mexico will establish amicable relations with other powers on the basis of mutual respect. It will now constitute itself according the provisions of the Plan of Iguala and the Treaty of Córdova, wisely established by the commander of the Imperial Army of Three Guarantees. In short, it will resolutely sustain, sacrificing the property and lives of its citizens (if it proves necessary), the solemn declaration` made in the capital of the Empire on September 28, 1821, the first day of Mexican independence.

NOTES

1   In Timothy Anna, *The Fall of the Royal Government in Mexico City* (Lincoln, NE: University of Nebraska Press, 1978), p. 138.

2   Enrique Semo (ed.) *México: un pueblo en la historia*, vol. 2 (Mexico City: Alianza Editorial Mexicana, 1989), p. 156.

3   The office of viceroy, whose duties changed and whose official title became "*jefe político superior*," was restructured. To avoid confusion, the term "viceroy" will continue to be used in this chapter.

4   Timothy Anna, *The Mexican Empire of Iturbide* (Lincoln, NE: University of Nebraska Press, 1990), p. 8.

FURTHER READING

Anna, Timothy (1978) *The Fall of the Royal Government in Mexico City*. Lincoln, NE: University of Nebraska Press.
   A description of how the old order crumbled, with emphasis on the 1808–13 period.

Archer, Criston (2008) "Royalist Scourge or Liberator of the Patria?" *Mexican Studies/Estudios Mexicanos* 24 (Summer), pp. 325–61.
   This article discusses Iturbide's role from 1810 to 1821.

Hamill, Hugh M., Jr. (1968) *The Hidalgo Revolt*. Gainesville, FL: University of Florida Press.
   A classic study of Hidalgo's movement.

Henderson, Timothy J. (2009) *The Mexican Wars of Independence*. New York: Hill & Wang.
   An easily accessible summary of events leading to Mexican independence.

MacFarlane, Anthony (2014) *War and Independence in Spanish America*. New York: Routledge.
   MacFarlane considers events in Spain leading to conflict with the colonies and then describes the various movements struggling for independence in Mexico and South America.

Rodríguez O., James E. (2012) "*We Are Now the True Spaniards.*" Stanford, CA: Stanford University Press.
   A detailed account of Mexico's independence struggle, focusing on the political values of the various interest groups and the political institutions created.

Anna, Archer, Rodríguez O., and Eric Van Young have written or edited numerous worthwhile works on Mexican independence.

GLOSSARY TERMS

insurgents
Nueva Galicia
plan
royalists

Chapter 7

Nationhood, 1821–1855

TIMELINE—WORLD

1820	1820	1823	1824	1825
China produces 32.9 percent of world GDP, Europe 26.9 percent, India 16 percent, and the U.S. 3 percent	First iron steam ship in Britain	Monroe Doctrine issued	Bolívar defeats Spanish royalists at Ayacucho, Peru, dooming Spanish colonialism on the American mainland	Stockton and Darlington Railway, first British steam railway

TIMELINE—MEXICO

1822 (May)	1823 (March)	1823 (November)	1824	1829 (January)
Itrubide declared emperor	Iturbide abdicates	Constitutional convention convenes	Guadalupe Victoria becomes President	Congress declares Guerrero President

1853	1854	1855		
Santa Anna sworn in as president for last time	Plan of Ayutla	Santa Anna ousted for last time		

After eleven years of war, the militarization of society, and the fostering of deeply entrenched guerilla and bandit traditions, Mexico needed a long stretch of peace in which to settle divisions, establish institutions, and make fundamental assessments directed at the formulation of the nation. Sadly, Mexico did not get peace.

(Christon Archer, 2010)

1836	1850	1855
Spain recognizes the independence of Mexico	California becomes a U.S. state	English engineer Henry Bessemer invents process of converting iron into steel

1829 (December)	1833	1838	1841	1846–48
Guerrero ousted	Santa Anna elected as president for first time	Pastry War	Congress of Yucatán declares itself independent	Mexican American War

THIS CHAPTER DESCRIBES ONE OF THE MOST COMPLICATED PERIODS in Mexican history. The first three sections consider the post-independence period chronologically. A separate section then discusses why early nineteenth-century Mexico was so unstable. Following that are descriptions of the post-independence Catholic Church and post-independence Mexican society. There follows a discussion of why early Mexican history did not parallel that of the United States. The chapter then considers Mexico's post-independence economy and why it failed to meet the optimistic predictions concerning it. A final section considers United States policy toward its newly independent southern neighbor.

A NATION IS BORN, 1821–1823

In accordance with the Treaty of Córdoba and the Plan of Iguala, elections were held for a unicameral Congress, which first met in February 1822. As had been the case with the Cortes, three-tier elections selected Congressional representatives. Common citizens only voted for electors, who then chose another elector at the district level. Electors chosen at the district level then met to choose a representative to Congress. Those establishing these rules assumed that members of local elites would be chosen in the first round of voting and that these electors would keep power in the hands of the elite. This permitted the enfranchisement of the masses without their empowerment.

On May 19, responding to pressure from the military and crowds in the streets, Congress declared Iturbide emperor of Mexico. Congress's embracing of Iturbide reflected the prevailing national mood. Liberal historian Lorenzo de Zavala reported that support for Iturbide's becoming emperor came from "the clergy, the miserable nobility of the country, the army in its greater part, and the common people who saw in that chief nothing more than the liberator of their country." As has been repeatedly noted since, that constituted the majority of Mexico's population.

Congress had assumed Iturbide would serve as a constitutional monarch. However, after his coronation Mexico's new emperor proved incapable of restraint and plunged into partisan politics. He became one of the first Latin American military dictators and soon began closing critical newspapers and jailing dissenting writers and legislators.

Eight months after its convening, Congress had made no progress at writing a constitution nor had it devised a way to finance the newly independent government. Since Iturbide considered Congress obstinate, unrepresentative of the national will, and incapable of directing the nation, on October 31, 1822, he simply dissolved it, threatening the use of military force if its members did not accept his decree.

During 1822, Emperor Iturbide received many letters accusing Brigadier Antonio López de Santa Anna, the commander of the port of Veracruz, of insubordination, unjust acts, and embezzlement of regimental funds. In response, Iturbide summoned Santa Anna to Jalapa, located between Mexico City and the port of Veracruz, and personally informed him that he had been relieved of his command. Iturbide felt he had resolved the matter, not realizing that he had come up against the all-time political survivor of Mexican history.

Before news of his having been relieved of command arrived in Veracruz, the twenty-eight-year-old Santa Anna raced back to the port and launched a rebellion. Iturbide ordered General José Antonio Echávarri, who commanded troops nearby, to capture the port of Veracruz, which Santa Anna continued to control. Rather than attacking Santa Anna, Echávarri issued the Plan of Casa

Mata, which called for the election of a new Congress, with one deputy for each 100,000 population. By basing representation on population he sought to eliminate the overrepresentation Mexico's sparsely populated north had enjoyed in the initial Congress. Significantly, rather than calling for Iturbide's removal, his **Plan** only sought to limit his power.

The Plan of Casa Mata rapidly attracted followers, just as the Plan of Iguala had two years earlier. After issuing his Plan, Echávarri joined forces with Santa Anna. Many regional commanders supported the Plan because it decentralized the army command, facilitating the advancement of junior officers. The Plan not only challenged Iturbide's absolutism, but represented a major power shift from the old colonial center of power, Mexico City, to the provinces.

The conflicting demands on Iturbide complicated his response. Some sought the restoration of the dissolved Congress; others demanded that a new Congress be elected. The emperor decided not to fight the rebels. His war record clearly indicates his decision did not result from cowardice. Perhaps his decision reflected his fear of anarchy, of plunging the nation into civil war.

On March 19, 1823, Iturbide submitted his abdication. Even though none of the forces opposing him had demanded his removal, when faced with the choice of compromise or abdication, Iturbide chose the latter. Iturbide fell from grace so rapidly and so completely because he had forgotten where independence had come from and what had caused it. He turned his back on the provinces and threatened provincial autonomy, especially by dissolving Congress, which represented the interests of the provincial elites.

Mexicans remember Iturbide more for his faults than for his contribution to their independence. His household expenses were nearly five times those of the viceroys. His dissolving Congress not only indicated disdain for democracy but provided a concrete issue for his enemies to rally around. He compounded the new government's financial problems by lowering taxes to increase his popularity.

Iturbide faced many grave problems, such as financing his government, that would stymie Mexico's leaders until the latter part of the century. None of the governments in succeeding years managed their finances more effectively, but at the time this could not be foreseen. After Santa Anna challenged him, the provincial elite, which correctly perceived the Plan of Casa Mata as their key to empowerment, overwhelmed Iturbide's support among senior army officers, high clergy, the colonial nobility, and Mexico City plutocrats.

Figure 7.1

Throughout Spanish America military leaders known as caudillos dominated the early post-independence period. The most famous Mexican caudillo was Antonio López de Santa Anna, pictured here.

Source: Reproduced courtesy of the Benson Latin American Collection, the University of Texas at Austin.

BEFORE SANTA ANNA, 1823–1833

In late March 1823, the Congress that Iturbide had dissolved was reconvened. Initially its members assumed that they would write Mexico's first constitution. However, some states, including Jalisco and Zacatecas, withdrew support from Congress and declared they would not be bound by its actions. This led to Congress's agreeing to new congressional elections. Congress hoped this concession would avoid the disintegration of the country—a highly probable event.

Elections then chose representatives to Mexico's second Congress, which convened in November 1823 specifically to write a constitution. The new Congress found favor in the hinterlands because it represented the provincial elite rather than the Mexico City elite. Most deputies favored federalism and rejected a monarchy.

The second Mexican Congress drafted a new constitution, which it promulgated in 1824. Mexico's first constitution, modeled on the 1812 Spanish constitution, abolished the monarchy and shifted power to the states. The military and the Church retained special privileges such as their *fueros*. The constitution prohibited all religions except Roman Catholicism. The framers were so sure they were on firm religious ground that they specifically prohibited amending the article concerning religion. States received the exclusive right to administer affairs within their borders. This reflected the consensus that, due to Mexico's enormous size and geographic diversity, local problems could be best addressed locally.

Between 1824 and 1835, as a result of the constitution's enfranchising males without regard to wealth, literacy, or ethnicity, Mexico enjoyed broader suffrage than the United States, France, and Great Britain—the nations usually cited as the maximum achievement of liberal democracy in the early nineteenth century. Each state legislature chose two members of the national senate and elected supreme court justices. The state legislatures also elected the president, with each state casting one vote, regardless of its population. Given the framers' fear of absolutism, they created a weak presidency and a weak federal government that was dependent on states for troop recruitment and tax collection.

In 1824 Guadalupe Victoria, a respected insurgent combatant, was elected Mexico's first president. Due to Victoria's non-assertive political style, to this day he remains something of a cipher. During his term, the real initiative in public affairs did not lie in Mexico City. The 1824 constitution, which created a weak presidency, left initiative to the states. Victoria's outstanding grace was his willingness to respect state autonomy, just as the constitution mandated.

In 1829 President Victoria completed his term, an event that would not occur again for decades. The stability that enabled Victoria to finish his term resulted from the acceptance of his cabinet choices and his actions by most members of the elite. The receipt of $17 million in British loans, which temporarily filled government coffers, also increased stability.

The 1828 presidential election pitted General Manuel Gómez Pedraza, a former royalist officer who had joined Iturbide, against the former insurgent commander, Vicente Guerrero. During the campaign, Guerrero's opponents referred to him as "El Negro," a comment on his dark skin. Centralists supported the more moderate Gómez Pedraza, a rich, cultivated creole.

As was mandated in the constitution, each state legislature cast one vote for its preferred candidate. Gómez Pedraza received eleven votes, while Guerrero received nine. This procedure, while strictly legal, did not reflect popular will, in that Guerrero, a hero of independence, was far more popular than his opponent.

Rather than accepting defeat, Guerrero decided to take the presidency by force. From his power base in Veracruz, Santa Anna supported Guerrero's assuming the presidency, charging that "pro-Spanish" interests had backed Gómez Pedraza. Then the two main military commanders in Mexico City seized the Acordada Armory and called for Guerrero to assume the presidency. Soon crowds took to the streets in support of Guerrero, charging Gómez Pedraza with fraud.

In January 1829, Congress, responding to both military and mass support for Guerrero, annulled votes for Gómez Pedraza, confirmed Guerrero as president, and installed Anastasio Bustamante as vice-president. Guerrero served as president from April 1, 1829, to December 28 of that year. His presidency represented the high-water mark for the locally based, non-white, populist forces that Hidalgo had mobilized.

During the Guerrero administration, decentralization of power reached its high point. Municipalities demanded and received the same rights to participation and autonomy over their affairs and resources that states had demanded in 1823. This municipal autonomy reaffirmed the traditional role played by the village, dating from the colonial period and before.

The abolition of African slavery remains as Guerrero's major accomplishment. By 1800, for economic reasons, slavery had fallen into disuse in all but a handful of areas. High slave mortality, their high initial purchase costs, and the uncertainty of future slave purchases led to a reliance on Indian and mestizo wage labor.

Shortly after independence, a national commission on slavery estimated that only 3,000 slaves remained. In contrast to the United States, the 1829 abolition of slavery produced little controversy, given the small slave population. Again in contrast to the experience of the United States, the role of blacks in the post-slavery era has not been a significant issue. Miscegenation has so thoroughly blurred the differences between blacks and other mixed-race Mexicans that the number of Mexicans with identifiable African ancestry has become socially insignificant.

The other major social enactment of the 1820s—the expulsion of Spaniards—was far more controversial. Resentment against Spaniards had its roots in their haughty treatment of Mexicans during the colonial period. Counterinsurgency campaigns during the war for independence exacerbated anti-Spanish sentiment. Spain's rejection of the Treaty of Córdoba and its continued occupation of San Juan de Ulúa, the island fortress offshore from Veracruz, increased resentment. Mexicans regarded Spanish merchants remaining after independence as usurious and monopolistic and felt their massive imports threatened the livelihood of artisans. The discovery of an 1827 plot by the Spanish friar Joaquín Arenas to restore Spanish rule exacerbated such fears. Nationalist creoles found Spaniards a satisfying scapegoat for Mexico's post-independence economic decline. Congress passed the first of several Spanish expulsion laws in 1827. Such laws, which required Spaniards to leave Mexico, continued to be in force until 1836, when Spain finally recognized Mexican independence. As a result of expulsion legislation, roughly three-quarters of the 6,600 Spanish men in Mexico departed between 1827 and 1834. While the granting of many exemptions permitted some Spaniards to remain in Mexico, the expulsion virtually eliminated Spaniards from the military, government service, the mining industry, and the Church. Spaniards managed to survive, to a degree, in commerce and as property owners.

Forcing Spaniards out of Mexico impoverished the economy since those expelled took substantial specie with them, as well as their productive energy. Expelled Spaniards, though a small percentage of the workforce, were among the most experienced and highly trained of the professional, commercial, and artisan classes. Ironically, the Americans, the French, and the British, but not the Mexicans, filled the gap left by departing Spanish merchants.

In response to the small Spanish-led invasion that sought to re-establish a colony, Congress granted emergency war powers to President Guerrero. Once he assumed these extraordinary powers, which he used to abolish slavery, he refused to relinquish them even after the invaders had surrendered. This provided the military, leading clerics, and business interests with a rationale for ousting him and installing Vice-President Anastasio Bustamante.

Conservatives had several reasons for ousting Guerrero. His Finance Minister, Lorenzo de Zavala, had announced a progressive income tax, which left the poor untaxed and imposed a 10 percent tax on rent for property worth more than $500. The elite considered the measure dangerous populism. It was also concerned that Indian peasants in the present-day state of Guerrero interpreted anti-Spanish legislation as authorization to expel non-Indians from their lands, continuing their long struggle over land rights. Guerrero's support for village autonomy also threatened elite interests. The military turned against Guerrero, not on ideological grounds, but because its pay was in arrears due to the lack of government funds.

Mexicans still honor their second president for his prominent role in the independence struggle. Historian Justo Sierra wrote this epitaph for Guerrero, who came from a humble background and had virtually no formal education: "Ambitious partisans had tried to make a politician out of a man who was only a great Mexican."

Bustamante's assumption of the presidency gave conservatives their first opportunity to curtail the political role of the common man and peasant communities. Lucas Alamán, who served as Bustamante's minister of interior and foreign affairs, emerged as the driving force behind the administration. Since the constitution vested so much power in state legislatures, Alamán concentrated on deposing legislatures hostile to the conservative agenda. He would induce elements of the state militia to revolt against state governments. Since the states were not organized to defend their interests, they could be picked off one by one.

Bustamante established an authoritarian, elitist, pro-clerical, highly centralized government that alienated many by arresting and imprisoning critics. To allay the rising fear of the upper classes, Bustamante curtailed peasant movements and used the colonial administration as a model for his own. He promised to cut government deficits through efficient management rather than new taxes. However. he spent more on the army than his predecessors—spending that he financed by secretly borrowing from domestic moneylenders (*agiotistas*). The Bustamante administration closed the lively newspapers of the republic's early days if they opposed the president.

In 1832, the Jalisco state government issued a call for other states to rebel in defense of states' rights. Santa Anna was asked to lead the rebellion, which was financed by Veracruz and Tampico customs receipts and backed by state militias. The rebellion, under Santa Anna's leadership, quickly gathered support since Bustamante was viewed as arbitrary and despotic. Bustamante soon saw that his position was untenable and abandoned the presidency.

Santa Anna, rather than assuming power, ensured that Gómez Pedraza served the last months— December 1832 to April 1833—of the 1829–33 term to which he had been elected. This created the façade of legality and left Santa Anna's reputation unsullied. Santa Anna received almost all the credit for overthrowing the Bustamante regime, and as a result enjoyed overwhelming popularity.

LUCAS ALAMÁN

Lucas Alamán was born into a prosperous Guanajuato mining family in 1792. Up until age 18, Alamán lived a privileged existence as he grew up in Guanajuato. However, Hidalgo's sacking of his hometown, which he witnessed firsthand, marked his political thinking for life. After that attack Alemán's family joined many other families in moving to Mexico City in search of security. Alamán continued his education in Mexico City, studying chemistry and mineralogy at the mining school.

Alamán was selected as a member of the Mexican delegation serving in the Spanish Cortes. There he promoted measures favoring Mexico, such as removing limitations on trade and the lowering of mining taxes. He also promoted the creation of three New World *cortes*, or congresses, designed to preserve the Spanish empire yet allow Spanish America to administer its own affairs.

During the Guadalupe Victoria administration (1824–29), at age 31, Alamán served as foreign relations minister. While he held this position, the U.S. accepted the boundary defined by the

Adams–Onís Treaty, thus establishing the border (temporarily as it turned out) between the rapidly expanding U.S. and newly independent Mexico. Alamán sought to reinforce ties to Europe and other Latin American nations to prevent Mexico from being overwhelmed by the United States. As a cabinet member during the Bustamante administration (1830–32) he sought to concentrate power under the executive since he was convinced Mexico was unsuited to U.S.-style federalism.

Unlike most political figures of the period, Alamán also played a major role as an entrepreneur. After returning from his term in the Spanish Cortes, he directed the United Mining Company, which operated with British capital. Although the company failed to find a rich lode, it paved the way for the entry of British capital into mining. After 1830, he shifted his entrepreneurial energies to industry. Alamán founded crystal and porcelain factories in Mexico City, as well as a foundry and paper and textile factories elsewhere. He stated that if Mexico did not protect domestic industry with tariffs, "We will remain as a ruin in the desert of the past, boring through mountains like moles to extract gold and silver to send abroad."

In addition to his entrepreneurial activity, Alamán remained a fixture on the political scene, serving repeatedly as foreign minister and also as general director of industry. In 1851 he was elected to congress to represent Jalisco and in 1853 he joined the last Santa Anna administration for a final stint as foreign minister. He died a month after taking office, depriving Santa Anna of his most capable cabinet member.

Alamán strongly supported centralism, feeling that federalism undermined national unity. Given his privileged background, he not surprisingly failed to identify with Hidalgo, whose followers he claimed were given free rein to rob and murder. He shared with his fellow conservatives a favorable impression of Iturbide, noting his backers supported civilization, order, and prosperity. Again in keeping with most conservatives, he supported maintaining the strong position of the hacienda, which he saw as the key to maintaining rural social order. He also joined conservatives in supporting the traditional role for the Catholic Church, stating it was "the only common bond which unites all Mexicans when all other ties have been broken and the only one capable of sustaining the Spanish American race and protecting it from the great dangers to which it is exposed." Finally he joined fellow conservatives in feeling democracy would not serve Mexico, which he described as a nation "where the people don't take part in public affairs, and politics are dominated by ambitious social climbers with links to dubious interests."

Despite his having been a public figure almost two centuries ago, many of the matters Alamán dealt with still confront modern politicians. He felt the government should promote industry through tariffs and other measures. He was instrumental in the founding of the Banco de Avío, a forerunner of Mexico's current development bank, the Nacional Financiero. Industry, he stated, "should not only be considered as a producer of public wealth, but also as a powerful tool to improve the behavior of the population, promoting its welfare and all of the advantages of civilization." He supported immigration, since he felt that with a larger population Mexican agriculture would prosper. He claimed a liberal immigration policy was the reason the United States had made "such rapid progress in civilization, industry and commerce."

In a throwback to colonial times (and also anticipating the twenty-first century) Alamán favored special legal status to protect what he characterized the "weaker oppressed races." Unlike many conservatives he did not feel Indians' poverty reflected their inferiority.

Alamán was a strong advocate of public education. While serving as general director of industry he emphasized the importance of technical schools for the preparation of artisans and farmers. He also fostered what would today be called professional schools in fields such as medicine, mining, and law. Traditional courses, such as theology, which he felt provided little benefit for the nation, were eliminated. In addition to his public service and entrepreneurial activity, Alemán published extensively. Alamán's best-remembered work is his 3,352-page, five-volume *Historia de México*. Reflecting conservative sensibilities, he saw Mexico's origin in the conquest, which created the Mexican nation by uniting disparate indigenous groups. By the time he finished his *Historia* in 1852, he shared many Mexicans' disillusionment with their country which he described as "completely lacking public spirit, which has caused the disappearance of all national character."

The 1832 war to oust Bustamante left Mexicans exhausted in spirit and pessimistic about the future. It also made it abundantly clear that continued state autonomy required state-controlled militias and that those controlling the instruments of force would determine Mexico's future.

ANTONIO LÓPEZ DE SANTA ANNA

The leader of the 1832 rebellion, Antonio López de Santa Anna, was born in Jalapa, Veracruz, the son of a minor official in the colonial administration. In 1810, at age sixteen, he joined a Veracruz-based infantry militia unit. He fought pro-independence forces in northeastern Mexico and later commanded 500 troops in the Veracruz area. In contrast to many of his timid colleagues in the royalist officer corps, Santa Anna was a vigorous commander. On his own initiative, he made land available to amnestied insurgents to provide them with an alternative to warfare.

Santa Anna showed a charismatic quality of leadership and the ability to gain control of the Veracruz customs receipts. He first rose to prominence when he called for limits on Iturbide's power. His leading the forces which defeated the 1829 Spanish invasion and his role in the revolt that ousted President Bustamante further increased his stature. Before he passed from the political scene, Santa Anna had served as president of Mexico six times.

In 1833, Mexico's state legislatures provided Santa Anna with sixteen of the eighteen votes cast, thus electing him president for the 1833–37 term. He immediately put his personal stamp on the presidency by retiring to his 220,000-acre Veracruz hacienda, Manga del Clavo (Clove Spike), and leaving governance in the hands of Vice-President Valentín Gómez Farías. This enabled Santa Anna to avoid instituting the reforms his liberal constituency expected. Such reforms would inevitably divide society and undermine his popularity.

Gómez Farías and his allies in Congress introduced sweeping changes affecting the whole society. Following liberal tenets, he shifted the responsibility for education from Church to the states and secularized Franciscan missions in the north. He made payment of agricultural tithes to the Church voluntary. To replenish the national treasury, the government ordered the Church to sell all non-essential property and levied a 6 percent tax on such sales. Priests were forbidden to bring politics into their sermons. Gómez Farías canceled the *fueros* of both the Church and the army. He also reduced the size of the military, placed governors in command of military forces serving in their state, and strengthened state militias. Finally, he launched an intense propaganda campaign against wealthy aristocrats, claiming that wealth should circulate and not remain in the hands of the few.

By 1834 Gómez Farías had not only instituted sweeping change but had accumulated a formidable list of political opponents without having consolidated a power base. To devout common people, his measures affecting the Church constituted rampant anti-clericalism. The Church and the military resented both the end of their *fueros* and their reduced role in society. Many wealthy individuals, who in the abstract supported free enterprise, resented their loss of monopoly and privilege.

Santa Anna possessed a keen sense of the politically possible that bore no relation to ideology. In 1834, he seized upon opposition to Gómez Farías and staged a coup. The elite, the military, and the clergy supported the coup. Santa Anna also drew support from some individuals who had previously favored federalism, but who had decided Mexico required a strong central government to maintain control of Texas, impose order, adequately finance the government, and keep the nation whole. In April 1834, Gómez Farías resigned and left the country, ending the first great attempt to reform the Church and the army.

Santa Anna then began to restructure government in a manner more sweeping than Gómez Farías had attempted. He dissolved Congress after it granted him the power "to make as many changes in the Constitution of 1824 as he should think needful for the good of the nation without the hindrances and delays which that instrument prescribed."

A new constitution, promulgated in 1836, required voters to have an income of at least a hundred pesos a year or "honest, useful" employment. Such a requirement reduced male suffrage by 60 percent. The constitution also introduced a minimum income requirement for members of the chamber of deputies, senators, and the president. States, which lost their political and financial autonomy, were downgraded to "departments," whose governors were appointed by the president. State legislatures were eliminated. Officials appointed by department governors assumed most municipal functions, greatly limiting peasants' ability to compete for local power and protect their interests. Federal army officers took command of state militias, rendering these forces incapable of defending state interests.

Santa Anna's scrapping of the federalist political structure won him the support of a broad range of interests. The army and the Church supported him for having returned to them the power and privilege that they had previously enjoyed. *Hacendados* supported him for his having denied peasants access to local political power. The Mexico City elite supported him because he restored power to the capital, enabling them to protect their interests in the provinces. Many others supported Santa Anna simply because he promised an end to insecurity and political strife.

As has so often been the case, those promising to rule with a firm hand to end strife have only increased conflict. Provincial interests in Yucatán, Zacatecas, and Texas refused to accept Santa Anna's centralization of power. Many Yucatecans considered Mexico a greater liability than Spain since it lacked the mother country's wealth, stability, and trade connections. Zacatecas sought to keep the federal government at arm's length so more wealth from its rich silver mines would remain in the state, rather than disappearing into federal coffers. In Texas, Anglo settlers who had been allowed to colonize the area after Mexican independence formed the nucleus of the opposition. Some in Texas preferred to remain a part of Mexico, but under the decentralized government provided by the 1824 constitution. Others saw their opposition to Santa Anna as a wedge issue they could use to wrest sovereignty from Mexico and join the United States, from where the overwhelming majority of the colonists had come.

Santa Anna's decisive responses to these movements left permanent changes in the map of Mexico. Since Zacatecas was the closest of the upstarts, he advanced on the state with a 4,000-man force and delivered an ultimatum declaring that the state militia should lay down its arms or be attacked. Zacatecans rejected the ultimatum since they knew Santa Anna would abolish their state militia, and by so doing render the state unable to resist the new order. Santa Anna's forces took the state capital in a pre-dawn surprise attack. He not only allowed his troops to plunder the city but removed Aguascalientes from the jurisdiction of Zacatecas, making it a federal territory. Zacatecas never again played a major role on the national political scene.

Following his unsuccessful attempt to control **Anglo** colonists in Texas, Santa Anna returned to Manga del Clavo—as often occurred when his fortunes declined. In 1838 luck favored Santa Anna in the form of a French invasion. As was the norm in international diplomacy of the time, the French government demanded the payment of damage claims made by its citizens against the Mexican government—a sum of $600,000. These claims included compensation for a French-owned pastry shop destroyed in 1829 by a mob demanding that Guerrero become president. When the bankrupt Mexican government failed to honor the claims, France landed troops in Veracruz. This incident is known as the Pastry War because of the pastry shop claim.

Santa Anna assembled a force that pushed the French back to their ships. Mexico later met the French monetary claims, but did not yield to other French demands. This action came at a high personal cost for Santa Anna, since French artillery riddled his leg with shrapnel. Doctors amputated his left leg below the knee after it turned gangrenous. However, Santa Anna's rallying of troops to save Mexico's honor did restore his reputation.

Having redeemed himself politically, Santa Anna returned to the presidency in 1839. To consolidate his position, he attempted to muzzle the press, referring to reporters as "a race of delinquents" and urging state governors to "take the most energetic measures available . . . to purse and apprehend" those responsible for all "seditious" printing.

Neither Santa Anna nor any other Mexican could effectively govern. Between 1839 and 1847, there were twenty-one presidencies, with Santa Anna repeatedly returning to the National Palace. Since presidents came and went with such frequency, none could reshape Mexico. A new constitution, promulgated in 1843 in an attempt to correct the flaws in the two previous constitutions, failed to provide stability.

During these revolving presidencies, ceremony replaced substance. In 1842, Santa Anna staged an elaborate funeral parade to Santa Paula Cemetery, where his severed leg was solemnly interred. The next year, Santa Anna was serving as president when the new constitution was proclaimed. A day-long round of parades, processions, and speeches, a Te Deum, and a bull fight were capped by filling the fountains of the Alameda park with sangría so the poor could celebrate publicly while the wealthy held private parties.

An 1844 coup ousted Santa Anna, who had fallen out of favor due to the bankrupt state of the treasury, his despotic measures, excessive military spending, and the lack of progress on retaking Texas, which was the rationale for increased taxes. Mobs then invaded the Santa Paula Cemetery, destroyed the cenotaph marking the resting place for Santa Anna's leg, and gleefully dragged the leg through the streets.

Santa Anna continued to swirl into and out of the presidency, and, when his fortunes plummeted, into exile. He assumed personal command of the army facing the U.S. forces during the Mexican–American War. With Mexico's defeat and its loss of New Mexico and California, Santa Anna again went into exile.

Following the Mexican–American War, Mexico hit a low point. Losing half its territory demoralized the nation, Yucatán was in rebellion, there were revolts in the heartland, and the Apache and Comanche raided far into northern Mexico and took refuge north of the newly established U.S.–Mexican border. Communications remained poor, and little industry had developed.

This formed the backdrop for a victorious conservative rebellion in 1852. Conservatives claimed that embracing foreign ideas such as federalism and rejecting Mexico's Spanish heritage had resulted in the moral and political disintegration of the nation. The victors wanted to create a government modeled on the old colonial order and saw Mexico's defeat in the Mexican–American War as validation of their views. They also felt that economic growth required a strong central government.

In March 1853, given the power vacuum, eighteen of the twenty-three state legislatures voted to select Santa Anna as president. He returned to the presidency, established a military dictatorship, and promised stability. On this basis, most of the elite backed him. All state legislatures and most town councils were abolished. Santa Anna governed without a constitution and became a monarch in all but name, assuming the title of "His Extremely Serene Highness." During one eight-month period, military spending accounted for 93.9 percent of the government budget. In trying to resurrect the old colonial model, Santa Anna reestablished compulsory payment of agricultural tithes to the Church.

His Extremely Serene Highness tolerated no political dissent and exiled those who refused to kowtow to him, including the liberal governor of Oaxaca, Benito Juárez. In 1854, John Black, the American consul in Mexico City, commented on the Santa Anna administration: "There is no doubt generally speaking that it is the most unpopular government that has ever existed in this country since their independence, although nothing dare be said against it."

Santa Anna's final administration did improve highways, reform the judicial system, and promote education. Medals were given to outstanding educators. Visiting Spanish poet José Zorrilla wrote that all bandits had been caught and executed, leaving only Santa Anna to rob.

Once again, dictatorial control imposed by Santa Anna led to revolt. Juan Álvarez, who had fought royalists in the area now forming the state of Guerrero, led the rebellion. From 1820 to

1862, Álvarez controlled this area, maintaining a political fiefdom. During this period, he protected Indian land rights and provided tax relief. Those he protected formed his power base.

The rebels' March 1854 manifesto became known as the Plan of Ayutla. It promised the removal of Santa Anna, the writing of yet another constitution, and constituting the nation "in a stable lasting manner" to guarantee individual liberty.

Santa Anna's intemperate spending for government and the military made inevitable the imposition of new taxes, which further undermined him. These taxes fell on, and alienated, landowners and the Church. By the early 1850s, many moneylenders had invested in factories and sought stability and access to national markets. When they realized that Santa Anna could not guarantee these, they supplied funds to Álvarez. At the same time, thousands in small towns and villages rallied against Santa Anna in the hope that the Plan of Ayutla would allow the restoration of federalism.

In August 1855, as his elite support crumbled and the heterogeneous coalition of creoles, Indians, and mestizos opposing him continued to grow, Santa Anna resigned and made his final trip into exile. In 1874, he was allowed to return to Mexico, where he died two years later impoverished and nearly forgotten.

The rebels' 1855 victory represented the triumph of the periphery over the center, of militia units over the regular army, and of the countryside over the city. A broad coalition facilitated victory, and like all such alliances, once it had accomplished its original purpose, it required some sorting out to determine its direction. What distinguishes the Ayutla movement from other uprisings of the period was that its triumph ushered a new political generation into power. This group would radically change existing political structures.

Santa Anna understood the importance of propaganda in a way none of his antagonists did. He and his followers converted his campaigns into epic legends and his questionable triumphs into dazzling victories. His political longevity did not result from military prowess, since his defeats outweighed his victories. However, his showering the military with promotions, pay raises, pensions, and prestige during each of his administrations facilitated his repeated return to power. Finally, his strong regional base in Veracruz gave him control over the Veracruz customs receipts, upon which the national government depended.

At the end of his final presidency in 1855, many held Santa Anna responsible for Mexico's impoverishment, its being decreased in size by half, and its being overwhelmed by economic woes and profiteering. As a result, Santa Anna has joined the man he helped depose, Iturbide, in Mexico's pantheon of anti-heroes.

However, Mexico's early nineteenth-century ills were more of a reflection of the times than of Santa Anna, who occupied the presidency for a total of less than six years. Almost all other Spanish American republics experienced similar shake-out periods. The collapse of colonial control led to a power vacuum that Santa Anna repeatedly filled. In a similar manner, *caudillos* filled power vacuums from Guatemala (Rafael Carrera) to Argentina (Juan Manuel de Rosas).

CAUSES OF INSTABILITY

> Just after independence Mexico covered an enormous area and had a very small, poorly distributed population, inadequate transportation, and extreme linguistic, economic and cultural diversity.
>
> (Moisés González Navarro, 1952)

Between 1829 and 1855, there were forty-eight changes in the presidency and 319 in the four-member cabinet. However, since the executive branch had not become the all-pervasive hydra it was to become in the twentieth century, such changes were not as devastating as they might appear. While the executive resembled a merry-go-round, members of the national Congress demonstrated considerable courage and determination to sustain the independence of the legislative branch, often in the face of open hostility from the military men who dominated the executive.

State governments, which affected individuals more directly, were neither chaotic nor anarchic. After independence, the national government often did not have sufficient strength to challenge village councils and mayors, leaving them with a high degree of local autonomy. While those applying European notions of sound governance saw only chaos, the regions functioned with far more efficiency. Regular elections were held at the state and local level. As historian Timothy Anna observed:

> One has the strongest sense that it mattered very little who occupied the National Palace and that brief sojourns in office should not be counted as "regimes" . . . It is not clear if any president could get his orders obeyed beyond the outer patio of the palace.[1]

Despite its remoteness from the lives of most Mexicans, it is worth considering why the executive branch remained so unstable.

REGIONAL INTERESTS

> The history of Mexico is a history of its states and regions; its identity is an identity based on states and regions.
>
> (Timothy Anna, 1998)

At the time of independence, Mexico, in the sense we normally use the term today, did not exist. In 1821, the people of central Mexico, where Aztec culture had held sway, were the only people considered "Mexicans." Further from the capital, people tended to identify with their own locality, often referred to as a *patria chica* (little homeland). There, family, community, and ethnic group mattered far more than an abstraction called Mexico. It would take centralizing forces decades to extend the notion of being "Mexican" to outlying regions. The lack of a term to address citizens of the new nation is illustrated by the Plan of Iguala, which opened by addressing "*americanos*," not "*mexicanos*."

For decades, the provincial elites felt that there were no advantages to be gained by submitting to a strong central government. Rather than submitting, as historian David W. Walker noted, "*empresarios* and other groups that made up the emerging dominant class in Mexico ruthlessly manipulated the state for private gain, to the detriment of class interests, economic growth, and political stability."

Eventually these regional elites did accept that a strong national government would be advantageous. As a result, after the middle of the century, they sought to forge a nation, just as, over the centuries, the kingdoms and provinces on the Iberian Peninsula were forged into the Spanish nation.

CENTRALISTS VS. FEDERALISTS

> Conflict ensued between the newly empowered provincial elites, who sought to institutionalize local control, and the national elite, which insisted on maintaining power in the center.
>
> (Jaime Rodríguez O., 2012)

Much of the instability of the early republic resulted from the Mexico City elite's attempting to concentrate power in the capital. Opposing them were the provincial elites who felt that shifting power from Madrid to Mexico City was only a marginal improvement over colonialism. This latter group wanted regional centers, not the old viceregal capital, to exercise power. The conflict between Mexico City and Guadalajara, which had long chafed under control from the viceregal capital, was especially pronounced.

Those desiring devolution of power to regions were known as federalists. They assumed they were victorious when the 1824 constitution placed extensive power, including electing the president, in the hands of state governments. However, powerful interests representing Mexico City—the centralists—were far from vanquished. Beginning in late 1823, the federal government began sending military forces against state governments, especially those in Puebla and Jalisco, which appeared to pose the greatest challenge to centralized power.

Even after the scrapping of the 1824 Constitution, federalists remained more numerous then the centralists. However, since they were never unified, their strength did not match their numbers. This permitted the centralists to increase their strength by abolishing state militias, increasing the strength of the federal army, and allying with the Church.

The center's efforts to reassert hegemony over all aspects of government in the early republic became the major cause of political turmoil. Nothing indicates that the federal government was more socially enlightened than state or local governments in this period. The federalists attempted to thwart centralizing efforts by: 1) maintaining control of revenue sources; 2) fracturing the political power of the center by separating the Federal District from the State of Mexico; 3) expelling the Spanish who were seen as a major source of the central elite's power; and 4) maintaining state-controlled militias.

The 1824 constitution created a de jure federalist system. However, federalism lasted only five years since centralism was so deeply rooted, as was the tendency to depend on the will of a single man. During the Victoria and Guerrero administrations, the states never acted in concert against the center, state militias were unable to confront the central government's army, and the clerical and military *fueros* lent strength to centralism. Guerrero did not build an organized base of support during his short administration. This left his federalist administration easy prey to a centralist coup. Once in power, centralists, with the support of the Church, the military, and wealthy property owners, used the state to solidify their control.

FINANCIAL CRISES

> The new republic was caught in a vicious cycle: financial problems caused political turmoil, which in turn unsettled an already shaky economy.
>
> (Ruth Olivera and Liliane Crété, 1991)

A lack of revenue severely constrained government effectiveness and the incumbents' ability to resist challenges to their power. When revenues fell, the government could not meet defense costs and became vulnerable to challenge by regionally based military strongmen. If taxes on outlying areas were increased, those being taxed might rebel. If the government could not meet its international financial obligations, it risked foreign intervention to collect debts owed to foreigners.

In 1825, President Victoria's budget totaled 21 million pesos, of which the military received 90 percent. This proposed expenditure amounted to four times government income, since between 1806 and 1824, government revenue declined from 39 million pesos to 5.4 million. To further add to its financial woes, the national government accepted the debts of the colonial administration. Even after dubious claims were disallowed, the colonial debt assumed by the republic totaled 45 million pesos. Accepting the colonial debt favored those who had lent the most to sustain the colonial regime—the Church and the elite.

The traditional sources of revenue the colonial government had relied on were either greatly reduced or unavailable. Both the mining tax and Indian tribute, which together had supplied 30 percent of colonial revenue, were abolished. In addition, the *alcabala* and the pulque tax were transferred from the federal to state governments. Customs receipts formed the only reliable source of federal government revenue. However, the government pledged much of these receipts to liquidate debts, leaving little for day-to-day operations. When protectionists were ascendant, imports declined, reducing tariff collection. Smuggling and the seizure of customs receipts by military officers to pay troops further decreased tariff revenue. Also, since Mexican exports did not generate enough revenue to finance large-scale importation, there were few imports to levy tariffs on. Imports fell at an average rate of 3 percent a year from the mid-1820s to the mid-1840s, thus undermining customs duties as a revenue source.

Financial solvency was undermined by the fallacious assumption that the tax structure that had functioned so well during the colonial period could finance the republic. Officials simply assumed that the new government would inherit the legitimacy of the Crown. However, the elite, which had willingly financed the Crown, refused to pay taxes since it regarded the newly created federal government as a greedy consumer of its wealth, not as a partner in the development of the nation. Between 1824 and 1867, financial policy was in constant flux, as is indicated by the terms of finance ministers averaging less than five months.

Since the old colonial tax collection system had collapsed, states assumed the responsibility for collecting taxes and then transferring revenue to the federal government. However, this often resulted in delayed payment.

For a brief period in the 1820s, the government remained solvent by borrowing aboard. However, after it defaulted on its foreign loans and could no longer borrow abroad, it turned to domestic moneylenders (*agiotistas*). The *agiotistas* produced a vicious cycle of mortgaging future income to secure funds at ever higher interest rates. This reduced even further the revenue available for daily needs and necessitated increased borrowing from the moneylenders.

In the context of a shrinking economy, government borrowing at annual interest rates sometimes exceeding 300 percent created a veritable Ponzi game. Since the government had no solid revenue base, it used new loans to liquidate old debts. Since the loans were so risky, interest rates were exorbitant. When the amount borrowed reached untenable levels, as it frequently did, the whole system would collapse. Sometimes new governments would repudiate loans to previous governments. In other cases, they lowered interest rates by decree. Often, when all obligations could not be met, certain sets of lenders were paid, and others were not. Lenders would use all their political leverage, domestic and foreign, to ensure they were among those repaid.

The *agiotistas* became one of the most influential groups, utterly unaccountable to any constituency. They would lend money to those contemplating a coup if they felt that their chances of having previous loans repaid would be enhanced by the coup. In 1844, historian Carlos Bustamante observed they constituted a "class of people cursed by God and abhorred by the whole nation."

THE MILITARY

> The praetorian bands of Mexico like those of Rome must have money and indulgences and those who promise fairest secure their aid, until one promise fails or a better one is made.
>
> (Anthony Butler, U.S. Chargé d'affaires, 1830)

The military impaired government effectiveness by consuming the majority of government revenue. Officers repeatedly installed governments that they felt would better serve their financial and other interests. The military's size alone made it inevitable that it would be a major consumer of government income. Both the insurgent and royalist forces were kept under arms after independence, yielding a force of some 75,000. The 22,750 men still under arms in 1825 continued to place a tremendous drain on government finances.

Valid reasons existed for maintaining military strength. Until 1825, the Spanish continued to occupy San Juan de Ulúa and interfere with operations of the port of Veracruz. Even after that date, the military faced the real threat of Spanish reconquest. Soon after Spain recognized Mexican independence and the danger of reconquest faded, Mexicans expected the military to reoccupy Texas.

However, military spending and influence went far beyond Mexico's needs. Between 1821 and 1851 only six civilians served as president—for a total of 947 days—while fifteen generals occupied the presidency. A high level of spending—48 percent of the budget between 1822 and 1855—was required to prevent officers from revolting and installing a patron who would provide increased funding. A saying of the time reflected this, "When salaries are paid, revolutions fade."

The many coups of the period mobilized no more than a few thousand men, and none attracted mass popular support. A successful coup provided virtually the only access to the presidency. Junior officers would support coups in response to explicit promises of promotions and wealth if the coup succeeded. Coups were not formed exclusively within the army. Regional factions of army officers formed alliances with tobacco and cotton farmers, textile manufacturers, and merchants, promising them the requisite government permits to ensure their business success in exchange for their support.

In addition to seeking financial favor, the military establishment openly opposed the maintenance of state militias, which it saw as a threat to its privileged status. This led to conflict, since outside Mexico City, people considered militias to be protectors of states' rights and checks on the power of the army.

Despite its massive consumption of government revenue and its strong political role, the army never formed an effective fighting force as became apparent during the Mexican–American War. While officers used the military as a path to wealth and political power, its ranks were formed by the forced enlistment of vagabonds and criminals in cities and Indians from rural areas. Before the middle of the century, the military never emerged as a cohesive body.

CAUDILLOS

> There was a ruralization as well as a militarization of power, which represented a shift in the center of political gravity from the city to the countryside, from the intellectuals to the interest groups, from the bureaucrats to the rural militias, and from the politicians to the caudillos.
>
> (John Lynch, 1994)

The weakness of the central government and a decline in the unifying power of the Church created a political vacuum filled by regional strongmen known as *caudillos*. They were generally of humble origins and had achieved prominence by leading their men in combat, especially in isolated rural areas. The most famous of all the *caudillos*, Santa Anna, expanded his influence from his Veracruz power base to the national scene.

Caudillos exercised so much power at the local and regional level that they undermined the authority of the central government. Often they defended local interests that the national government either ignored or opposed. Juan Álvarez, the insurgent leader from Guerrero, maintained regional power to the almost total exclusion of the national government. Eventually, he used his home region as a power base to oust Santa Anna. *Caudillos* retained local power and aspired to national power by promising offices and other rewards to followers once they triumphed.

DIVIDED ELITES

> It is precisely because no school of thought, no ideological force, decisively carried the field in nineteenth-century Mexico that unanimity and consensus were not possible.
>
> (Timothy Anna, 1993)

The elite lacked consensus on the direction the country should move in. During the early post-independence period, it formed factions that became known as federalists and centralists. Mexicans who had favored continued colonial rule generally advocated a monarchy after independence. When they failed to establish a monarchy, they became centralists. Those who had favored independence from Spain sought a republic after the end of Spanish rule. After the establishment of the republic, they advocated federalism.

The centralists advocated a strong central government with Mexico City in control, as in colonial times. They felt the army and the Church should play major political roles. The centralists were generally supported by the military, which could count on receiving a large part of the revenues raised by centralist governments. Centralists also advocated developing industry, rather than purchasing manufactured goods aboard. As Lucas Alamán noted, "Manufacturing stimulates agriculture just as mining does, but in a more stable manner."

The federalists wanted to loosen the old system so they might advance more rapidly. State governments tended to be federalist, since they wanted power to be exercised at the state level, rather than at the national level. They wanted colonial institutions reformed and special privileges for the Church and the army abolished. Federalists turned their back on their Spanish heritage, claiming it should be put behind them. When in power, federalists often acted like centralists in an attempt to spread their notions nationwide. As with most of the interest groups of the time, federalism was based on broad, heterogeneous, shifting alliances.

By the middle of the century, the federalists and centralists had evolved into groups known, respectively, as liberals and conservatives. The term "liberal," as used in nineteenth-century Mexico, meant limited government, a capitalist economy, and a low level of government regulation, especially of foreign trade.

The free individual, unrestrained by government or corporate bodies and equal to his fellows under the law, was the liberal ideal. They felt a constitution should limit government authority and advocated the strengthening of state-controlled militias to break the regular army's control over politics. With such limits, liberals felt, the individual would thrive after being freed from the constraints imposed by traditional corporate entities—the Church, the army, guilds, and Indian communities. Since the Church was the strongest of these entities, liberals targeted its wealth, judicial privileges, and control over education and the events of life itself—birth, marriage, and death. Similarly they felt that restrictions affecting the sale of property should be removed, including those imposed by the traditional Indian community.

The conservatives continued the centralist tradition and were backed by *hacendados*, militarists, monarchists, and the Catholic hierarchy. They felt their social position reflected their better bloodlines and their natural superiority over those with non-European ancestors—the majority of the nation. They looked to Europe as a model for development, rather than to the United States.

Conservatives advocated a strong military and the maintenance of Church privileges. They also felt that the government should play a major role in determining the course of economic development. Power, conservatives felt, should be in the hands of the prosperous class, the group they perceived as most able to manage the affairs of state. To keep power there, they advocated restricting access to the ballot box through such means as property requirements for voting.

Although liberals and conservatives considered themselves as being at opposite ends of the political spectrum, they agreed on more than they disagreed. Leaders of both groups came from the urban middle and upper classes, roughly the top 20 percent of the income strata. Neither group sought to build a base among the rural majority.

The elite also agreed that the hacienda should remain intact. Most *hacendados* were conservatives, so conservatives not surprisingly supported the institution. Liberals were reluctant to force the subdivision of the hacienda, feeling market forces would best harmonize the interests of the individual and society. They failed to realize the contradiction in their own beliefs. They accepted the Jeffersonian dream of agrarian democracy. However, since they failed to force the partition of haciendas, little land was available for small farmers.

THE PLAZA

Historian Robert Ricard commented on the importance of the plaza, "A Spanish American city is a main plaza surrounded by streets and homes, rather than a group of streets and houses around a main plaza." Linguistic use reinforces the centrality of the plaza. In Spanish, terms such as "control of the plaza" or "capturing the plaza" refer not just to one city block, but the city as a whole.

The modern Mexican town plaza is a felicitous merger of two cultural traditions. Mesoamerican plazas date back at least to 1200 BC. These open areas, surrounded by temples and other buildings, are thought to have symbolically represented the mythical primordial sea—the source of life itself. These plazas served as a sacred space for spiritual rites and rituals. In addition, they functioned as a *tianguis*, or market.

European notions of urban design date back at least to ancient Greece and Rome. The Old World plaza, as did its Mesoamerican counterpart, served for meeting, marketing, and staging rituals. Spaniards introduced their design practices to Mexico. They laid out streets in a grid pattern emanating from a central open space—the plaza.

Early on the plaza in New Spain assumed many of the roles which had been assigned to Mesoamerican plazas. Civic events, markets, and social exchange took place there. Surrounding the secular plaza was usually a church, the city hall, shops, and residents of affluent citizens. Often the strictly religious aspects of community life took place in front of the church in an open *atrio* which was separate from the secular plaza.

Plazas remained a key part of Mexican existence into the twentieth century. Anthropologist Robert Redfield described the plaza in 1920s Tepoztlán, Morelos:

> Everywhere the plaza dominates the town; the only large buildings are there; it is the center of social life. Even in unimportant towns like Tepoztlán the two market days break the week into two periods of lull separated by two days of special interest and attention. On these days the Tepoztecans come to the plaza to exchange not only goods but information.

Architect Logan Wagner, who grew up in Mexico, commented: "When you grow up in Latin America, plazas are in every town and city; they are part and parcel of daily life. Plazas were taken for granted in my world; I thought everyone had one."

Visitors to Mexico also become enthralled by the plaza. American Jal Box commented on his stay in San Miguel de Allende, "For the twelve years I lived in San Miguel, I visited the plaza almost every day for one reason or another, at times for no reason other than to enjoy being in that special communal open space, the place where something is always happening."

While small-town plazas still have a timeless quality, modernity has not been kind to many large-city plazas. As a result of rapid urbanization and sprawl, a high percentage of the urban population is spatially removed from the central plaza. In cities, automobiles flock to central plazas, creating traffic jams and making the plaza less pleasant for those outdoors. In some cities, such as Oaxaca, cars have wisely been banned from the central plaza, restoring nineteenth-century tranquility.

NATION VS. VILLAGE

Much of the early nineteenth-century instability resulted from unsuccessful attempts to reconcile two powerful ideals—the sovereignty of the nation and the sovereignty of villages. Neither centralists nor federalists were able to create a functional national government and simultaneously respond to villagers' desire to control their own resources. Elites of any persuasion seeking power often mobilized locally based militia forces to claim power. After the elites took power, the communities that had been mobilized would retain their arms and demand concessions, such as the confirmation of community lands and municipal sovereignty, which those in power were loath to grant.

THE CHURCH

> For many liberals, the Church embodied all the fundamental obstacles to change—a position diametrically rejected by conservatives.
>
> (Colin MacLachlan and William Beezley, 2012)

As with other institutions in Mexico, independence had a profound impact on the Church. Its financial strength had been undermined by the 1767 seizure of Jesuit property, the 1804 Consolidation decree, and war damage to remaining Church property. The Church also suffered because of the close association between the Church hierarchy and the Crown during the independence struggle.

Even though its wealth had declined, the Church did retain title to vast properties, urban and rural. It continued to charge fees for marriages, baptisms, and other religious services and receive the agricultural tithe. To the extent it was possible with its diminished resources, the Church continued to provide credit. In addition, as in colonial times, the Church maintained birth, marriage, and death records. The number of clergy fell from 9,439 in 1810 to 3,232 in 1851.

The Church emerged as one of the few cohesive forces in Mexico, transcending regional and class differences. Lucas Alamán commented that the Church formed "the only common bond which united all Mexicans, when all the rest have been broken."

To fend off liberal attacks, the Church allied with political conservatives and became more conservative itself. Since conservatives felt the Church provided spiritual certainty and bore a long social and cultural tradition that bound society together, they responded vigorously to attacks on the religious establishment.

MEXICAN SOCIETY AFTER INDEPENDENCE

> With a soil and climate scarcely equaled in the world she [Mexico] has more poor and starving subjects who are willing to work than any country in the world. The rich keep down the poor with a hardness of heart that is incredible.
>
> (Ulysses S. Grant, 1848)

THE NEW ORDER

After independence, Article 12 of the Plan of Iguala, which declared all Mexicans to be legally equal, guided government policy. Not only were Mexicans legally equal but all official usage of racial categories was discontinued. Though race disappeared from official documents, not surprisingly it did not vanish as a social concern. Race simply became an unwritten component of Mexican culture, with roughly the same significance as before. In the 1840s, U.S. Ambassador Waddy Thompson remarked, "At one of these large assemblies at the President's palace, it is very rare to see a lady whose color indicates any impurity of blood."

The abolition of racial categories did provide for increased social mobility. Mestizos began to take advantage of new opportunities to rise on the social scale. Non-whites, in general, could obtain better jobs and interact more freely with other groups at all but the upper levels of society. Former slaves and their descendants began to vote, run for, and be elected to public office. A few Indians, most notably Benito Juárez, also took advantage of increased opportunity for social mobility.

In rural areas, most large estates remained in the hands of a relatively small group of creoles who dominated rural labor and resources. In most of rural Mexico, as throughout Spanish America, the new order brought little in the way of improved material circumstances, let alone electoral democracy.

Debt peonage increased after independence due to a labor scarcity resulting from the number of war dead. Historians' interpretations of debt peonage vary. Some see it as an oppressive force trapping rural workers in a never-ending cycle of poverty and exploitation. Others see it as reflecting rural workers having sufficient bargaining power to demand a cash advance during times of labor scarcity. At the time, a few liberals, such as Melchor Ocampo, denounced the immorality of debt peonage. However, he and other liberals were afraid of social conflict, so they took no action on the issue.

Policymakers embraced laissez faire economic policies, assuming that a free market would enable all citizens to prosper. However, as historian Richard Graham noted, "Those reformers could not have been expected to know that when superimposed on still remaining hierarchical and elitist traditions, these policies would mean merciless exploitation."

The government did make a valiant attempt to provide universal public education, although such an undertaking clearly exceeded the resources available. An 1842 law made education obligatory for boys and girls aged seven to fifteen. As has often been the case in Mexican history, this law reflected more a statement of good intentions than a change in educational practice. Schools were simply not available for all the children the law compelled to attend. In 1844, only 4.8 percent of children were in school.

Between independence and the middle of the nineteenth century, Mexico's population grew slowly due to war, famine, poor sanitation, lack of medical care, and the failure to attract immigrants. During this period, births equaled roughly 4 percent of the population each year, while deaths equaled 3 percent. Between 1820 and 1854, Mexico's population increased from 6.2 million to 7.9 million.

As people fled the tumult of the independence wars, Mexico City's population mushroomed from about 100,000 in the 1790s to 167,000 in 1821, preserving the capital's position as the largest city in the Western Hemisphere. The city's population growth continued, reaching 200,000 in 1857. However, its relative importance had diminished. The growth of Mexico City, and of Mexican cities in general, slowed as Spaniards departed from urban areas, political power shifted to *hacendados*, and commerce increasingly bypassed the capital.

Mexico's arid north remained sparsely populated. Before the coming of the railroad, travel from Mexico's major population centers to the north remained difficult. Persistent attacks by stateless nomads discouraged further settlement. Between 1820 and 1835, Apache raiders killed an estimated 5,000 Mexicans along the frontier. In the twelve years before the Mexican American War, the Comanche and their allies slew another 2,000. Historian Brian DeLay observed that this led to "an exodus from many of northern Mexico's smaller towns and rural settlements into larger northern cities or else southward, out of the region altogether." In 1850 the four border states (plus Baja California) comprised 41 percent of Mexico's land area, yet the 459,000 people living there accounted for only 6 percent of its population.

Most of Mexico's mestizo population lived in rural areas or in small villages. Such villages had dirt streets, few amenities, and were dominated by the village church, both architecturally and spiritually. Retail sales were largely transacted in weekly open-air markets held in the principal square. As was the case in Indian villages, residents of mestizo villages had little contact with the outside world, which increased the difficulty of inculcating a sense of national identity. Village life had changed little since the late colonial period.

The collapse of colonial rule ended royal efforts to protect Indian lands. However, a weakened central government gave villagers more room to maneuver. Their goals included minimizing taxes, protecting individual and collective land holdings, and limiting interference in village life by state and national governments.

About 1850, Carl Sartorius, a German who had lived in Mexico for decades, described a typical rural home:

> Inside the hut, upon a floor of earth just as nature formed it, burns day and night the scared fire of the domestic hearth. Near it, stand the *metate* and *metlapil*, a flat and a cylindrical stone for crushing the maize, and the earthen pan (*comal*) for baking the maize bread. A few unglazed earthen pots and dishes, a large water pitcher, a drinking cup and dipper of gourd-shell

Figure 7.2 *The material culture of many people changed little with independence. Many traditional housing construction practices persisted well into the twentieth century, as is indicated by this hut near Córdoba, Veracruz.*

Source: Reproduced courtesy of the Benson Latin American Collection, the University of Texas at Austin.

constitute the whole wealth of the Indians' cottage, a few rude carvings, representing saints, the decoration. Neither tables nor benches cumber the room within, mats of rushes or palm leaves answer for both seat and table. They serve as beds for their rest at night, and for their final rest in the grave.[2]

In dry areas, homes were often built of adobe. Few homes were made of wood, since, due to its scarcity, it was too expensive. The price of wood, the only available fuel, also made the use of kiln-baked bricks prohibitively expensive. In wetter areas, logs often supported a thatched roof while wickerwork, which allowed air and light to enter, formed the walls.

Cities differed from villages not only in population size but in the number of amenities, the presence of retail shops, and in their having a substantial creole population. The affluent lived near the central square in multistory houses. The sides of the main square not occupied by the church or official buildings had ground-floor arcades where warehouses, wine and coffee shops, and retail stores supplied a wide variety of goods, many of which were imported.

The one-story dwellings of the less affluent stood further from the city square. As in colonial times, the poorest residents occupied city fringes. Sartorius commented on these outlying areas:

In Mexico, the suburbs are mean and dirty, and inhabited by the lowest classes. Refuse and filth, carcasses of animals and rubbish of buildings are found piled up at the entrances of the streets, by the side of wretched hovels, the abode of ragged vagabonds or half naked Indians.[3]

POLICY TOWARDS THE INDIGENOUS

In keeping with Enlightenment ideas, Indians (but not the military or priests) were declared legally equal to other citizens. Official documents referred to residents of the abolished communities as "those previously called Indians." Such equality rang especially hollow after 1835 when minimum income requirements for voting disenfranchised virtually all Indians.

Many viewed ending the special status enjoyed by Indians as the elimination of a pernicious colonial legacy. Benito Juárez, as governor of Oaxaca, claimed that the Indian community must be broken at all costs, so that individual initiative and modern forms of representative government could prevail. Liberal Gómez Farías viewed the existence of different races in the same society as an eternal cause of conflict. Not only did he refuse to recognize distinctions between races but he sought to hasten the fusion of Indians with the rest of Mexican society.

Changes in the status of the Indian were significant not only because of the radical change demanded in the lives of these affected but because, as late as 1850, Indians constituted roughly half of Mexico's population. As municipal governments replaced Indian community governments, Indians had less direct control over their everyday affairs and had to share administration with others who were more powerful and more knowledgeable in the mechanisms of formal electoral government.

Not only were indigenous people denied separate status, but their communal land-holding system came under legislative attack. An 1826 Veracruz law decreed that "all the land of indigenous communities, forested or not, will be reduced to private property, divided with equality to each person . . . who belongs to the community." By the late 1820s, twelve Mexican states, including the central highland states of Mexico, Puebla, and Michoacán, had passed laws mandating the division of communal holdings into private plots.

Despite the enactment of privatization legislation, states were politically divided, so they could not implement the radical changes in land tenure they had mandated. States' legislating for changes in land tenure rather than the federal government indicates the active role played by state governments of the period.

Although legislators claimed legal equality would benefit the Indians, the reality was far from that. In general terms the nation preserved the social structure built up over the previous three centuries. Indigenous communities saw little formal education, use of Spanish, or Western medical practices. Farmers' ties to the cash economy were minimal. As in colonial times, indigenous people produced textiles and pottery, raised animals, worked for wages, and traded in petty commodities. In 1841, Fanny Calderón de la Barca, the wife of the first Spanish ambassador to Mexico, wrote: "Certainly no visible improvement has taken place in their condition since independence. They are quite as poor and quite as ignorant and quite as degraded as they were in 1808 . . ."

THE INDIANS' RESPONSE

As non-Indians extended their landholdings at the expense of indigenous communities, Indians turned from formal protests to rebellion. In northern Veracruz, Indian rebels successfully fought government forces to a stalemate, thus ensuring continued control of their land and the survival of the tropical forest in which they lived. Usually, though, Indians did not prevail. In 1832, dozens of villages revolted, beginning with Nochistlan in Oaxaca. The revolt spread to southern Guerrero and Michoacán before it was finally suppressed. As historian John Lynch succinctly stated, "The Indians were losers from independence."

Ten years later an even more serious revolt spread over 60,000 square miles, extending from Michoacán to the Isthmus of Tehuantepec. Indians violently rejected the changes in language, ecosystem, diet, work regimen, religion, politics, and local autonomy associated with commercial agriculture. In 1845, General Nicolás Bravo described the rebels as "miserable Indians, incapable of understanding the benefits of civilization, returned to a barbarous state worse than that of savage tribes."

In 1847, the most serious nineteenth-century Indian conflict broke out in Yucatán as the Maya also took advantage of the opportunity presented by the Mexican–American War. There the lines were still sharply drawn between dominant creoles and indigenous Maya. Debt servitude and civil and religious taxes were forced on the indigenous population. Creoles were rapidly increasing the area planted in sugar cane and **henequen**. They were also producing increased amounts of food for Yucatán's expanding population. Creoles asserted control over land and water holes (*cenotes*) to which the Maya had previously enjoyed unrestricted access. This expansion of commercial agriculture deprived the Maya of land for growing corn.

An indigenous rebellion known as the War of the Castes broke out. Its goal was to expel or kill all whites. By 1848, Indians controlled four-fifths of the Yucatán Peninsula, and had Mérida, the capital, under siege. The Maya in Yucatán could effectively resist the creole elite since they had access to rifles smuggled in from British Honduras (today's Belize).

Just when the Maya forces appeared to be on the verge of taking Mérida and some creoles were fleeing by boat, the rebels turned back, for reasons that are still poorly understand. Suggested explanations include: 1) Maya peasants wanting to return to their fields at the beginning of planting season; 2) disagreement on goals; 3) the whites having received shipments of rifles, artillery, food, and money from Cuba, Veracruz, and New Orleans; and 4) the distance from Maya supply sources in British Honduras.

Creole-led forces eventually drove the Maya into the jungle with the aid of guns from Spain and a shipment of U.S. arms and munitions brought from Veracruz by Commodore Matthew C. Perry—later to gain fame by opening up Japan to U.S. commerce.

As advancing troops of the Yucatán government pushed the Maya back, Indian rebels embraced a Maya–Christian religious cult that had as a central icon a cross representing the ancient Maya world tree or flowering cross. They believed their crosses spoke, issuing instructions to followers of the movement. The crosses, called *santos*, were dressed in Maya garments, replacing the images of saints with Caucasian features and European clothing, which had previously been venerated.

Inspired by the voices from the crosses, the Maya retired into the jungle of the eastern Yucatán peninsula and maintained their independent existence. Fighting continued at different levels of intensity for decades, with raids, massacres, and reprisals occurring repeatedly. The indigenous there were not subjugated until 1901, when Porfirio Díaz's machine-gun-equipped army occupied the last independent rebel town, Santa Cruz. The severity of the struggle is indicated by the fall in Yucatán's population from 582,173 in 1837 to 320,212 in 1862.

WOMEN

The Mexican government redefined the status of both Afro-Mexican slaves and Indians. In contrast the legal status of women during the early nineteenth century underwent only slow evolution. Sometimes this benign neglect, such as the continued enforcement of the Spanish law guaranteeing women and men equal inheritance rights, favored women. In most cases though it hurt women. A woman's only remedy to a failed marriage remained, as in colonial times, an ecclesiastical divorce—a form of Church-sanctioned separation.

The labor of poor, rural women played a crucial role in the economy, even though their efforts never appeared in the detailed hacienda account books of the period. Wives rose before dawn to prepare tortillas for the family. Once that was done, they tended gardens, raised small livestock, and "helped" work the estate fields, with their labor being credited to the accounts of their fathers, sons, or husbands. They earned cash by spinning; in the household they converted crops to food, wool to yarn, and yarn to family clothing, and they raised the next generation.

In Mexico City, women over age eighteen who worked outside the home increased from 32 percent of the labor force in 1811 to 37 percent in 1848. Throughout the early nineteenth century, domestic service remained the main source of female employment. Domestics were often on call twenty-four hours a day, and many received only room and board. An endless stream of young women coming from rural areas ensured that pay for domestics remained low. As other opportunities for women became available, the percentage of Mexico City's female labor force working as domestic servants declined from 54 percent in 1811 to 30 percent in 1848. Increasingly women were being hired in commerce, food preparation, and service industries. Seamstresses increased from 3 to 14 percent of Mexico City's working women during this period. Women prepared food for sale, sewed, opened small retail establishments, peddled in the streets, and sold in local markets, where they dominated.

In 1836, Mexican writer and politician José María Luis Mora noted that "the progress of Mexican civilization is especially evident in the Fair Sex." He also noted that women's education had improved since colonial times when instruction was "reduced to the barest essential required to fulfill domestic obligations."

Entrenched male attitudes toward women changed slowly. In 1843, the liberal writer Guillermo Prieto expressed a widely held view when he described an ideal wife, "She should know how to sew, cook, sweep . . . find pleasure and utility in virtue, [and] be religious, but never neglect my dinner for mass . . . The day she discusses politics, I'll divorce her." Many believed that ending wives' subordination to husbands would upset the social order.

THE PRESS

The benefits of independence were most readily apparent in the press, as Mexicans took advantage of their newly acquired freedom of expression. Newspapers published in Mexico City became increasingly influential. The openly partisan papers of the era, such as *El sol de México*, favored centralism, while others, such as *El águila mexicana*, advocated provincial autonomy. The best-known paper of the period, *El siglo XIX*, promoted expanded suffrage and a federal republic.

As remains the case today, Mexico City papers were the most influential. Nonetheless, provincial papers proliferated. In 1847, German botanist Karl Heller visited Mérida, Yucatán, population 25,000, and noted that the city supported four newspapers as well as two book printers.

Incumbents paid lip service to freedom of expression and repeatedly infringed upon it, jailing editors and banning certain publications. Often political cartoons expressed notions that, if openly stated, would result in censorship. The chorus of anti-government publications became so strident under Bustamante that he began to subsidize pro-government papers—a tactic widely used by his twentieth-century successors.

THE MEXICAN ETHOS

Early Mexican history differs sharply from that of the United States, which had become independent less than half a century earlier. In New Spain, the entire government had been built on a top-down basis, with power coming from the Crown. When this single legitimating institution disappeared in 1821, nothing bound Mexicans together. Not only did Mexicans have to create new institutions, but people had to learn to respect them.

In British North America, there had been a significant degree of self-government. The institutions the British created, such as J.P. courts, country courts, houses of burgesses, and town meetings in New England, remained intact after U.S. independence and provided a stable framework for the new government. Economic diversity—shipbuilding, farming, and some manufacturing—led to internal trade ties that held the former colonies together. Britain's 1783 recognition of U.S. independence minimized the danger of recolonization and decreased the need for military spending. Finally, the elite in the United States enjoyed a high degree of cohesion through the first five U.S. presidencies.

The English settlers in North America brought with them the ideals of the Reformation and the Enlightenment. By the time of their arrival, the power of the British monarchy had been limited, a robust private sector flourished, and the religious monopoly of the Roman Catholic Church had been broken. Mexico lacked these influences since the Spanish settled New Spain earlier and then closed it to new ideas.

The United States was relatively homogeneous in the early nineteenth century as a result of the English having eliminated or pushed aside the indigenous population and then created small farms. After independence townships organized and funded basic public education. In contrast the Spanish superimposed themselves on the existing Indian population. After independence the small creole population maintained its privileges, denying power to the vast majority and refusing to finance a broad-based educational system.

The differences between Mexico and the United States at independence reflect more their economic foundations than any grand colonial design. Given New Spain's endowment of precious metals, fertile tropical land, and a sedentary indigenous population, the Spanish constructed the highly inegalitarian society that Humboldt commented on. In contrast, in British North America, the colonizers found neither precious metals, nor a subordinate labor source comparable to the Mesoamericans, nor land suitable for crops such as sugar, best produced on plantations. This resulted in a society where land ownership was more equitable. The examples of Jamaica and other British Caribbean islands, where harsh slave regimes prevailed, indicates that what shaped New World colonies was not an abstract colonial model but the nature of the colony's economy.

Mexican writer Carlos Fuentes commented on the differences between Mexico and the United States:

> We did not acquire freedom of speech, freedom of belief, freedom of enterprise as our birthright, as you did. The complexity of the cultural struggles underlying our political and economic struggles has to do with unresolved tensions, sometimes as old as the conflict between pantheism and monotheism, or as recent as the conflict between tradition and modernity. This is our cultural baggage, both heavy and rich.[4]

THE DAWN OF INDUSTRIALIZATION, 1821–1855

Mexico could not get needed capital without stability, it could not establish stability without capital.

(Daniel Levy and Kathleen Bruhn, 2001)

EARLY OPTIMISM

The euphoria surrounding political independence also extended to economic matters. Since Mexico had been the jewel of Bourbon Spain's American empire, most observers assumed it would soon recover from the ravages of the independence war. In addition to its endowment of natural riches, independence allowed Mexico to use foreign capital to accelerate economic recovery, to sell in the best-paying markets, and to buy where prices were lowest. Tribute formerly paid to Spain could be invested in Mexico. The stability of the four-year-long Guadalupe Victoria administration increased this optimism and attracted foreign investors.

MINING

Mines were the source of much of the 1820s optimism concerning Mexico's economy. Mexican mines, such as La Valenciana, had become worldwide symbols of wealth. Humboldt's description of late colonial Mexico had been disseminated widely in Europe, further enhancing Mexico's image as a mother lode of silver.

Figure 7.3 *Foreign investment in mining helped revive the mining industry after independence. The British invested heavily at Real del Monte, where "La Dificultad" mine was located.*

Source: Reproduced courtesy of the Benson Latin American Collection, the University of Texas at Austin.

Clearly considerable effort would be required to restore the mining industry to its former glory. The mines themselves had suffered from more than a decade of cave-ins and flooding. On the surface, financiers and suppliers had disappeared, and skilled labor had dispersed. The mines still operating were only a shadow of their former selves. By 1822 employment at La Valenciana mine had declined from more than 3,000 to 1,000.

In 1823 since Mexico lacked capital to quickly rehabilitate mines, the government enacted legislation opening mining to foreign investment for the first time. A modest 3 percent tax on silver production replaced the burdensome colonial taxes on mining. Another law permitted the tax-free importation of mercury to refine silver.

This welcoming of foreign mining investment occurred at a propitious time. In 1824 and 1825, a wave of speculative interest carried capital from a prosperous Britain throughout the world. By 1827 seven British, one German, and two American mining companies had begun operations in Mexico. British investment alone totaled some £3 million. In addition to capital, England sent negotiators, mine experts, skilled mine workers, and a variety of tools, implements, vehicles, and machines to Mexico.

Beginning in the 1830s, the rehabilitation of old mines and the opening of new ones resulted in a slow recovery of silver production. By the middle of the century, Mexican silver production approached pre-independence levels. At this time, Mexico produced 50 to 60 percent of the world's silver.

The decline and slow recovery of silver mining reduced both mine employment and the silver-based money supply. During the first half of the nineteenth century, mining contributed between 8 and 9 percent to Mexico's gross domestic product (GDP).

MANUFACTURING

In the early post-independence period, entrepreneurs wishing to reestablish and expand their facilities faced capital shortages, political instability, and poor transport. In addition, manufacturers faced competition from imports, which caused a decline in Mexican textile production during the 1820s.

After independence, the position of shop artisans and self-employed craftsmen became increasingly precarious. They faced competition from imports, *obrajes*, and the few mechanized factories established after independence. The guilds, which no longer enjoyed legal protection, declined. Even the strongest guilds, such as those of the goldsmiths and silversmiths, passed out of existence before the middle of the century.

During the middle of the nineteenth century, due to the lack of modern factories and the high cost of shipping goods from Veracruz to central Mexico, production by artisans continued to dominate Mexico City manufacturing. Artisan shops failed to evolve into true factories since they lacked capital and the necessary political clout to obtain favorable tariff policies. Moreover, they relied heavily on family labor, which limited their size. As a result of this reliance on artisanal techniques, much of the labor force had a very low level of productivity.

Mexican liberals felt that the country could rely on export revenue to purchase manufactured goods from abroad, and that, in any case, the market would resolve production problems. In contrast, conservatives favored deliberate government action to stimulate industry. In 1830, to further industrial development, the Bustamante administration founded a government-owned industrial development bank known as the Banco de Avío. Tariffs levied on imported cotton goods financed the bank. The government directed the bank to lend money to Mexican entrepreneurs so that they could establish factories, especially textile mills, improve technology, and make Mexico less dependent on imports.

Before its liquidation in 1842, the Banco de Avío had lent $509,000 for textile mills in Puebla, Veracruz, Querétaro, and the State of Mexico. It lent to thirty-one enterprises, of which twenty-one became operational, ginning cotton and producing lumber, honey, silk, paper, glass, earthenware, and textiles. Of the enterprises the bank financed, 65.8 percent produced cotton textiles and 14.3 percent produced iron and machinery.

The problems of the Banco de Avío were representative of early nineteenth-century Mexico. Liberals opposed it, claiming it distorted the market. The government had so little cash that it ceased providing funds to the bank years before formally liquidating it. Its record keeping led one inspector to conclude that the bank "had never been staffed by employees even modestly trained in the principles of bookkeeping." The bank also suffered from its inability to rely on courts to recover from defaulting borrowers and from political pressure determining who would receive loans.

During the 1830s, thanks to tariffs and the introduction of mechanized mills, textile production rebounded. As a result of British investment, as well as that of the Banco de Avío, Mexico possessed the most highly developed textile industry in Latin America and became almost self-sufficient in cotton textiles. Between 1837 and 1845, the number of spindles in Mexican mills increased from 8,000 to 113,813. Due to high transport costs, foreign textiles could not compete with domestic production.

In 1854, the 10,316 textile workers wove 5,482 tons of cotton into cloth. The cotton-textile industry produced $12 million worth of fabric, roughly equal in value to the mintage of precious metals—quite an accomplishment in a nation where mines were universally regarded as the principal source of wealth.

As in the rest of Latin America, extremely low manufacturing productivity increased the cost of goods at a time when the population had little buying power. At the same time, the high cost of transporting goods over poor roads created many small markets. State and local governments continued to impose regional trade taxes (the *alcabala*), which further reduced market size. This served to protect local producers and fill local government coffers, but made economies of scale impossible.

AGRICULTURE

The independence struggle resulted in extensive damage to the dams, wells, and aqueducts that had provided water for Mexico's 1,729,000 irrigated acres. Even haciendas that remained physically intact suffered from a loss of markets as the buying power of miners and city dwellers declined. However, as an institution the hacienda emerged unscathed after independence. Since mining and commerce were largely in the hands of foreigners, generals and politicians often invested their newly acquired wealth in haciendas. In the 1850s, liberal Ponciano Arriaga commented on the *hacendado*:

> With some honorable exceptions, the rich landowners of Mexico . . . resemble the feudal lords of the Middle Ages. On his seigneurial lands, with more or less formalities, the landowner makes and executes laws, administers justice and exercises civil power, imposes taxes and fines, and has his own jails and irons, metes out punishments and tortures, monopolizes commerce, and forbids the conduct without his permission of any business but that of the estate.[5]

These estates were largely self-sufficient, with resident artisans producing saddlery, furniture, tiles, and pottery. Such production further reduced the incentive to invest in industry.

The hacienda continued to be the dominant rural institution. The well-documented hacienda El Maguey in Zacatecas, which covered 416 square miles, was only the seventh or eighth largest in the state. It centered around a cluster of stone buildings, where most of the 500 to 900 employees lived. In 1835, 89,000 sheep, 4,000 horses and mules, 12,000 goats, and a hundred head of cattle grazed on El Maguey. Workers lived on hacienda land and worshiped in its chapel. Their children attended the hacienda school. El Maguey sold wool as well as goat and sheep tallow used to make candles to illuminate mines. The hacienda attracted and kept labor by offering security in an insecure rural environment.

Further north, where there was abundant land and few if any sedentary Indian communities, even larger estates predominated. After the Sánchez Navarro family bought out the Marquisate de Aguayo in 1840, their holdings totaled at least 25,780 square miles—an area larger than Connecticut, Massachusetts, New Jersey, Rhode Island, and Delaware combined. As part of the purchase, the buyers acquired not only land, buildings, and livestock but also indebted workers. By way of comparison, the fabled King Ranch of Texas covered only 1,719 square miles. In 1846, an American army captain commented on the Sánchez Navarro ranch, whose size was extensive even for Mexico, "More than half the whole State of Coahuila belongs to the two brothers Sánchez, who also own some thirty thousand peons."

Mid-sized holdings, or ranchos, mostly owned or rented by mestizos, existed alongside the large estates. The rancho differed from the hacienda in that the owner lived on his land and relied on his own labor and that of his family and of seasonal employees. Unlike the *hacendados*, who were often seen as vain and idle, rancho owners were widely admired.

Between independence and the mid-nineteenth century, the number of ranchos increased substantially. Some Mexicans, taking advantage of the instability of the period, moved into isolated uplands and established ranchos. In other cases, people bought plots from financially weak haciendas, converting them into *ranchero* communities. By 1854, there were 15,085 ranchos.

Small farms recovered from the independence war relatively rapidly. As early as 1824, future U.S. ambassador[6] Joel Poinsett noted, "The buildings are in ruins, yet the country appears to be cultivated as extensively and as carefully as ever." Reduced demand in cities and mines did not have a significant effect on small farmers, since they mainly produced for local markets or their own use. The vitality of this sector is indicated by the degree to which multi-village peasant movements, in alliance with other actors, became a major force shaping the Mexican state in the nineteenth and early twentieth centuries.

As in colonial times, agriculture remained the most important sector of the economy. Between 1810 and 1860, it provided roughly 45 percent of gross domestic product. Between 1822 and 1858, the area cultivated increased from 530,304 to 929,145 acres.

TRADE

The British merchants who arrived in the 1820s succeeded due to their access to capital. They could pay for goods they bought in Mexico with cash. More importantly, they could extend long-term credit. They replaced the Spanish at the top rung of the distribution system, but would often sell to a Spanish middleman, who in turn would sell to retailers and peddlers. By virtue of being British citizens, these merchants could live a relatively normal life, even in the midst of political turmoil. They were generally protected by the widespread fear of British retaliation against those who harmed them or their property.

Given these advantages, between 1819 and 1825 the value of Mexico's trade with Great Britain soared from £21,000 to more than £1 million. By 1831, more than twenty British import-export houses were operating in Mexico. These commercial houses remained dominant from the 1820s to the 1850s. During this period, British merchants were among the wealthiest individuals in Mexico. In describing Jalapa, Fanny Calderón de la Barca remarked on the expensive homes with "the best as usual belonging to English merchants." British merchants even replaced their Spanish counterparts in matrimony. They would marry into leading Mexican families, creating win–win marriages that matched British capital with the local contacts of the bride's family.

In the early nineteenth century, neither France nor the United States ever threatened British commercial dominance. The British supplied the elite with a wider variety of manufactured goods of better quality, at lower prices, and usually on better terms, than any other merchants.

Gaining access to Spanish American markets became a key element of British foreign policy. George Canning, who served as British Foreign Secretary from 1822 to 1827, proclaimed, "The deed is done, the nail is driven, Spanish America is free; and if we do not mismanage our affairs sadly, she is *English*." To bolster their exports, the British promoted free trade, an advantage to their already established industries. They opposed tariff protection for industries being established in Latin America. They would respond to trade restrictions by threatening to press for debt payments, impose economic sanctions, suspend relations, or invade.

Once freed from Spanish regulation, trade flourished on the Pacific Coast. Acapulco, the port of the Manila Galleon, was forgotten in its tropical splendor, since few affluent buyers lived in the hinterland adjacent to it. Further north, San Blas served Jalisco, Mazatlán served Sinaloa, and Guaymas served Sonora. The principal Asian goods shipped to these ports were textiles from Calcutta and Canton.

Despite this trade diversification, Veracruz remained Mexico's principal port and maintained close shipping links with Havana and New Orleans. Its continued prosperity resulted from it being the closest port to the locus of Mexican population, economic activity, and politicking.

The same items were traded as in colonial times. Silver accounted for 70 percent of exports, followed by cochineal dye, which accounted for 7 percent. During the first sixty years of independence, 90 percent of imports were consumer goods for the wealthy, including textiles, wine, food, perfume, hats, and some durables, such as furniture and mirrors.

Foreign trade had a mixed impact. Consumers benefited from cheaper goods. Due to technological progress, in 1850 inexpensive imported cotton cloth cost only a quarter of what it had cost between 1810 and 1820. Import tariffs also provided the government with an easily collected source of revenue that created little popular protest. Trade also created jobs. Dressmakers and tailors fashioned imported textiles into clothing for the elite. Foreign trade meant travel, so more innkeepers and others catering to the traveler found employment.

Foreign trade also carried liabilities. To pay for imports, scarce coinage left the country, thus depriving Mexico of a medium of exchange. The British Industrial Revolution reached out to ruin textile artisans in Puebla, Querétaro, and Oaxaca. Between 1800 and 1827, the number of working looms in Oaxaca declined from 800 to thirty. Unlike Europe, where factories offered jobs to displaced artisans, there were few factory jobs available.

Once foreigners quit lending to Mexico, the nation's ability to import was largely determined by its production of the silver used to pay for imports. During the 1820s, international trade totaled only 67.1 percent of the 1801–10 level. At mid-century, Mexico's annual exports totaled only $3.20 per capita, well below the Latin American average of $5.20.

With most of its production and population in the central volcanic belt or in the mountainous south, Mexico could not rely on water transport for domestic trade, as was occurring in the United States and Western Europe. That left traders dependent on roads, which were generally in poor condition, if in fact any roads existed at all. Road conditions were so bad that it was cheaper to import wheat flour from Kentucky and Ohio to Veracruz than to transport it from central Mexico. In the early nineteenth century, as a result of poor roads, mules continued to haul the bulk of Mexican goods.

Mexico continued to be divided into numerous small markets. As economist Clark Reynolds observed, "It is highly probable that interregional trade and internal commerce in Mexico were more highly developed at the time of the Aztecs than they were in mid-nineteenth century." Mexico would have to await the arrival of the railroad in the late 1870s for its national market to achieve the integration it had enjoyed in 1800.

DASHED HOPES

> Mexico lagged behind Chile, Brazil, or Argentina because of its cycle of civil wars and foreign invasions was more severe and protracted, while its economy and topography were more resistant to commercial penetration.
>
> (Alan Knight, 2008)

The early optimism concerning Mexico's economy soon turned to despair as Mexico found itself in a downward spiral. The lack of domestic capital presented a seemingly insurmountable obstacle to growth. After Mexico defaulted on the bonds sold in the 1820s, foreign investors were loath to lend. Without growth, the government would remain weak, so it could not defend itself from internal or external attack. This inability to defend the nation exacerbated the very conditions that retarded growth. Between 1800 and 1850, the per capita GDP declined at an average rate of 0.7 percent.

The reestablishment of a sound legal climate was long delayed. The ponderous and exacerbating colonial judicial system was a model of efficiency compared with the process following independence. The break with Spain destroyed many of the institutions that provided credible commitments to rights and property within the Spanish empire. The wealthy preferred keeping their wealth in cash or exporting it, rather than investing it where property rights were insecure. Some of the laws that would have stimulated investment were simply not on the books. For example, only in the 1890s did the government pass legislation permitting the formation of a limited liability corporation.

The Mexican economy suffered from losing its sophisticated colonial financial markets, especially those based on Church lending. With interest rates on government loans generally fluctuating between 30 and 200 percent, capital was siphoned away from long-term productive investment. As was the case in most of Latin America, through the middle of the century Mexico was plagued by a lack of banking institutions and the non-existence of formal stock markets.

Railroads would have lowered transport costs and created a national market. However, the attempts at railroad building only indicated the ineffectiveness of both government and private enterprise. In 1837, the government granted Veracruz merchant Francisco Arrillaga the first concession to build a railroad from Veracruz to Mexico City. It canceled this concession in 1840, since he had failed to lay a single mile of track. A new concession was granted in 1842 and was then canceled in 1849 since only three miles of track had been laid. By the time another decade had passed, only fifteen miles of track had been completed.

In the early nineteenth century, the British were the world's supreme industrial power and the only naval power. Backed by this strength, the British Foreign Office often used its power to support British businessmen in Mexico, usually at the expense of Mexican development. While Mexicans considered building factories, British consuls situated at ports encouraged smuggling. When the Mexican government urged the creation of a national bank, British merchants actively opposed the measure so they could continue lending to the Mexican government. Such loans and the diplomatic power to enforce their repayment weakened Mexico's fragile fiscal structure. As historian Barbara Tenenbaum concluded, "The British in Mexico in pursuit of riches for themselves, only made Mexico poorer and more powerless."

Early nineteenth-century Mexico underwent little environmental change. The ecological equilibrium of the late colonial period continued through the first half of the nineteenth century. This ecological balance resulted from the lack of large enterprises and the reliance on traditional technology rather than from environmental awareness. Most labor continued to be performed with simple hand tools.

Some enterprises, however, proved to be highly destructive. Operators of the Real del Monte Mine in Hidalgo cut so much wood that it became necessary to fell trees as far as twenty miles away to obtain fuel and timbers. In 1848 the company's three steam engines were burning 2,600

350-pound loads of wood a month. Heating the ore required another 1,200 loads. This reliance on wood highlights yet another problem facing Mexico at the time—its lack of industrial fuels.

The first half century after independence had a marked influence on Mexico's subsequent economic relationship with the United States. In 1800 goods and services produced in the United States had twice the value of those produced in the area which would become Mexico. By 1867 U.S. production of goods and services was valued at eight times that of Mexico. Since then, Mexico has grown at roughly the same rate as the United States, but it has never been able to close the income gap that opened up before 1867.

JOCKEYING FOR POSITION

On April 23, 1822, U.S. Secretary of State John Quincy Adams wrote José M. Herrera, Mexico's secretary of foreign affairs, stating President James Monroe's willingness to receive an envoy from Mexico. In response Emperor Iturbide dispatched José Manuel Zozaya to Washington. On December 12, 1822, Adams presented Zozaya to Monroe as envoy extraordinary and minister plenipotentiary from the Mexican empire. With that ceremony, the United States formally acknowledged the independence of Mexico. The United States was the first nation to recognize Mexico, a reflection of the U.S. fear that if it did not move quickly, a strong Great Britain would replace a weak Spain, leaving little benefit for Americans.

In 1825, Joel Poinsett arrived as ambassador carrying a triple mandate: 1) to negotiate a treaty of commerce; 2) to obtain territorial concessions from Mexico; and 3) to foster democratic institutions. He faced a difficult situation. Mexican officials were already suspicious of U.S. territorial aspirations. The fact that Poinsett arrived after Henry Ward, Britain's highly effective chargé d'affaires in Mexico, also left him at a disadvantage. Ward had already negotiated a commercial treaty with Mexico and did his best to prevent the Mexican government from granting the United States any privileges not accorded Britain.

The British were generally more successful at advancing their trade interests since the finished goods and low-cost capital they exported were in greater demand than the raw materials and foodstuffs exported by the United States. In addition the British were simply better diplomats. As Mexican historian Josefina Vázquez noted, "They were good observers, and they learned to utilize friendships and pressure to achieve their demands, without violent confrontations, and thus functioned efficiently in Mexican political circles."

While the British were advancing their trade interests, Poinsett was repeatedly offending Mexicans by offering to buy their territory rather than accepting the existing boundary between the United States and Mexico. This insistence was hardly Poinsett's fault since Washington repeatedly instructed him to buy land.

Poinsett did successfully negotiate a commercial treaty. During negotiations, the question arose as to whether Mexico should return runaway slaves to their U.S. owners. Poinsett argued that if Mexico did not return them, respectable people, that is, slave owners, would not settle near the border. The Mexicans responded that a free republic should never assume the role of sending slaves to their merciless and barbarous masters in North America. The treaty was finally ratified under Poinsett's successor, with the United States dropping its demand that runaway slaves be returned. Mexico agreed not to give any other nation more favorable trade privileges than it gave the United States.

Poinsett was replaced by Anthony Butler, who served from 1830 to 1835. While Butler served in Mexico, U.S.–Mexican relations deteriorated. The Mexican ambassador in Washington, José María Tornel, reported that the United States was openly advocating the acquisition of Texas without considering Mexican rights. Since it was public knowledge that Butler was attempting to buy Texas, he was not popular in Mexico.

None of the other U.S. ambassadors to Mexico before the Mexican–American War left much of a mark. Butler's successor, Powhatan Ellis, devoted himself to collecting damage claims filed against the Mexican government by U.S. citizens. The claims issue was closely tied to the territorial issue. Many Mexicans felt that claims against Mexico had been deliberately inflated to force Mexico into ceding territory to settle them.

EVOLVING TRADE RELATIONS

Trade between the United States and Mexico increased after Mexican independence. The United States replaced Spain as a transshipment point for British goods, which arrived in Mexico via New York or New Orleans. Flour and cotton were the major U.S. exports to Mexico.

In 1835, U.S. exports to Mexico reached $9 million, or 7 percent of all U.S. exports. U.S. imports from Mexico were not as significant. Before the Mexican–American War, Mexico only supplied about 1 percent of U.S. imports. As conflict over Texas intensified, trade between the two nations declined and remained low for decades.

DOCUMENT 7.1: PLAN OF THE STATE OF ZACATECAS

[In the early nineteenth century states assumed a wide variety of powers, such as land reform, more commonly associated with federal governments. As the "Plan of the State of Zacatecas" indicates, states also raised armies and denied recognition to the government at the federal level.]

Plan of the State of Zacatecas

July 10, 1832

The Secretary of the Congress of the Free State of Zacatecas, considering:

First: that when the States adopted the Plan proclaimed in Jalapa by the Army in Reserve, it was under the impression that through it the constitutional order of the Republic would be re-established.

Second: That far from re-establishing the constitutional order as he had promised in his pronouncement, General Bustamante occupied the Presidency unconstitutionally, and that to maintain himself in office the constitution has been violated several times.

Third: That to obtain his removal, a civil war has been necessary, which has caused lamentable damages.

Fourth: That the war cannot cease except by giving the government a general constitutional character, which it cannot have until his Excellency Manuel Gómez Pedraza is recognized as its legitimate president. In September 1829 he obtained the absolute majority of the votes of the States and has been already called by General Santa Anna and many commanders and officers to take possession of this office. It is hereby decreed:

1st. The State of Zacatecas recognizes as constitutional President of the Republic His Excellency Manuel Gómez Pedraza.

2nd. This recognition will continue in effect even if the Chamber of Deputies of the national Congress does not attest the votes emitted by the legislatures of the States in the year 1828 since it is unquestionable that General Pedraza obtained the absolute majority of said votes and he had the constitutional requisites at the time of elections, and considering the present representatives of the nation without the necessary freedom to concern themselves with this matter.

3rd. The government of the State will proceed with its foreign relations in conformity with this decree, and to maintain its position it can raise up to six thousand men of the civil militia and underwrite all the expenses judged necessary. The state government will be informed and it will publish, print and circulate this Plan and will ensure that it be duly complied with.

Given in the Chamber of Sessions of the honorable Congress of Zacatecas.

Signed,
Antonio Eugenia de Gordoa, Deputy President.

Source: Thomas D. Davis and Amado Ricon Virulegio (eds) (1987) *The Political Plans of Mexico*. Lanham, MD: University Press of America, pp. 251–52.

DOCUMENT 7.2: PLAN OF AYUTLA

[The Plan of Ayutla marked the end of ideological indecision. After the defeat of Santa Anna, liberals assumed control of government and reshaped it.]

Plan of Ayutla

The political leaders, officers, and individual members of the troops undersigned, being called together by Col. Florencio Real, in the town of Ayutla, district of Ometepec, of the Department of Guerrero:

WHEREAS:

1) D. Antonio López de Santa Anna's remaining in power is a constant threat to the liberties of the people. Under his administration individual guarantees that are respected even in the least civilized countries have been trampled under foot.

2) Mexicans, so zealous of their liberty, find themselves in imminent danger of being subjugated by the absolute power exercised by a man to whom both generously and deplorably they entrusted the destinies of the Fatherland.

3) Very far from responding to so honorable a challenge, he has oppressed and vexed the people, burdening them with onerous taxes without consideration for the general poverty. He has used tax revenue for superfluous expenses and amassed a personal fortune.

4) The Plan proclaimed in Jalisco, which opened the gates of the Republic to him has been betrayed in spirit and purpose, and is contrary to public opinion which was suffocated by arbitrary restriction of the press.

5) He has violated the solemn obligation which he contracted with the nation on returning to native soil when he offered to forget personal resentments and not favor to any one party.

6) Although he was obligated to maintain the territorial integrity of the Republic, he has sold a considerable part of it and has sacrificed our brothers on the northern border who will be foreigners in their own country and will be dispossessed as happened to the Californios.

7) The nation can no longer continue without establishing itself in a stable and durable manner nor can it depend for its existence upon the capricious will of a single man.

8) Republican institutions are the only ones that are suitable to the country, to the absolute exclusion of any other form of government.

9) And finally, since national independence is threatened by the dominant party led by Gen. Santa Anna:

Using the same rights which our fathers used in 1821 in order to win liberty, those undersigned proclaim and promise to support to Death itself, if it should be necessary, the following Plan:

1st. Antonio López de Santa Anna and the rest of the functionaries, who like him have betrayed the confidence of the people, and all those opposed to this Plan shall be removed from public office.

2nd. When this Plan has been adopted by the majority of the nation, the ranking General among its supporters will call a representative from each State and Territory to meet in a convenient location to elect an interim President of the Republic. The representatives shall serve as an executive committee during his brief term.

3rd. The interim President will defend national territory and administer other branches of government.

4th. In the States which support this Plan, the ranking commander of the forces backing it, along with seven persons chosen by him, will meet and promulgate within a month provisional laws which will govern in their respective State or Territory. These laws will ensure the nation is and always will be one, indivisible, and independent.

5th. Within two weeks of assuming office the interim President shall summon a special congress based on the law which was issued with the same purpose in the year 1841. The Congress shall occupy itself exclusively with forming a republican, representative, popular government and shall consider the acts of the provisional executive as mentioned in Article 2.

6th. Since the army must support order and social guarantees, the interim government will take care to conserve it and to attend to its needs as is due this noble institution . . .

8th. All who are opposed to the present Plan or who lend direct aid to officials whom it no longer acknowledges will be treated as enemies of the Nation.

[Points 7 and 9 deal with administrative details such as passports and modifications of the plan.]

Ayutla, March 1, 1854

Source: Thomas D. Davis and Amado Ricon Virulegio (eds) (1987) *The Political Plans of Mexico*. Lanham, MD: University Press of America, pp. 500–03.

NOTES

1 Timothy E. Anna, "Review of *Mexicans at Arms* by Pedro Santoni," *American Historical Review*, 103 (April 1998), p. 627.

2 Carl Sartorius, *Mexico about 1850* (Stuttgart: Brockhaus, 1961), p. 69.

3 Ibid. p. 102.

4 Carlos Fuentes, *Myself with Others: Selected Essays* (New York: Farrar, Straus and Giroux, 1988), p. 205.

5 Benjamin Keen, *A History of Latin America* (5th ed.) (Boston: Houghton Mifflin, 1996), p. 188.

6 In this book the contemporary term "ambassador" is used instead of "minister." Poinsett's official title was "envoy extraordinary and minister plenipotentiary." The first U.S. diplomatic representative to Mexico who officially bore the title "ambassador" was Clayton Powell, who served from 1899 to 1905.

FURTHER READING

Anna, Timothy E. (1998) *Forging Mexico, 1821–1835*. Lincoln, NE: University of Nebraska Press.
    A detailed description of Mexico's first fourteen years of independence.

Calderón de la Barca, Frances (1982) *Life in Mexico*. Berkeley, CA: University of California Press.
    An insightful first-hand description of life in Mexico, written by the wife of Spain's first ambassador to Mexico.

Fowler, Will. (2007) *Santa Anna of Mexico*. Lincoln, NE: University of Nebraska Press.
    An account of the *caudillo*'s life and how he reflected the instability of early nineteenth-century Mexico.

Guardino, Peter (2005) *The Time of Liberty: Popular Culture in Oaxaca, 1750–1850*. Durham, N.C.: Duke University Press.
    Independence affected each area of Mexico differently. Guardino describes how Oaxaca changed over a century.

MacLachlan, Colin and William Beezley (2010) *Mexico's Crucial Century, 1810–1910*. Lincoln, NE: University of Nebraska Press.
    A highly readable description of the major social and political trends of the nineteenth century.

Martin, Luis (1975) "Lucas Alamán: Pioneer of Mexican Historiography," *The Americas* 32: 239–56.
    A description of Lucas Alamán's classic history of Mexico, its author, his conclusions concerning his newly independent nation, and others' opinions of the book.

Olivera, Ruth R. and Liliane Crété (1991) *Life in Mexico under Santa Anna, 1822–1855*. Norman, OK: University of Oklahoma Press.
    A description of everyday life in Mexico in the decades after independence, touching on village life, Mexico City, transport, labor, festivities, and the indigenous population.

Poinsett, Joel R. (1969) *Notes on Mexico Made in the Autumn of 1822. Accompanied by an Historical Sketch of the Revolution*. New York: Praeger.
    The future U.S. ambassador to Mexico's description of the independence war and of his 1822 travel in Mexico.

Randall, Robert W. (1972) *Real del Monte: A British Mining Venture in Mexico*. Austin, TX: University of Texas Press.
    An account of how British capital and technology revolutionized Mexican mining, but failed to benefit investors.

Rugeley, Terry (2009) *Rebellion Now and Forever: Mayas, Hispanics, and Caste War Violence in Yucatán, 1800–1880*. Stanford, CA: Stanford University Press.
A discussion of how political and social change led to violence in Yucatán and how the war impacted elements of Yucatecan society.

Tenenbaum, Barbara (1986) *The Politics of Penury: Debts and Taxes in Mexico, 1821–1856*. Albuquerque, N.M.: University of New Mexico Press.
An account of Mexico's early financial problems and of its ties to international finance.

Wagner, Logan, Hal Box, and Susan Kline Morehead (2013*) Ancient Origins of the Mexican Plaza*. Austin, TX: University of Texas Press.
A detailed study of the plaza. Its profuse illustrations depict many plazas and much of traditional life in Mexico.

GLOSSARY

agiotista
Anglo
caudillo
empresario
henequen
plan

Chapter 8

Shifting Boundaries, 1823–1854

TIMELINE—WORLD

1825	1825–29	1837	1841–45	1845 (March 1)
Erie Canal opens	John Quincy Adams U.S. president	Republic of Texas recognized by U.S.	John Tyler U.S. president	U.S. formally annexes Texas

TIMELINE—MEXICO

1823	1834	1835	1836	1836
Stephen F. Austin given permission to settle Texas	Santa Anna institutes centralized regime	(Dec. 5–11) Anglo-Texans take San Antonio	(March 2) Anglo-Texans declare independence	(March 6) Santa Anna takes Alamo
1847	1847	1847	1847	1847
(February 20–23) Battle of Buena Vista	(March 9) U.S. troops land at Veracruz	(April 18) Battle of Cerro Gordo	(September 13) Battle of Chapultepec	(September 14) U.S. forces enter Mexico City

1845–49	1848	1849–50	1854
James Polk	Gold discovered	Zachary Taylor	U.S. Senate
U.S. president	in California	U.S. president	approves Gadsden
			Purchase

1836	1846	1846	1846	1846
(April 21)	(April 25)	(May 8–9)	(May 13)	(September
Houston defeats	Attack on U.S.	Battles of Palo	U.S. declares war	20–24)
Santa Anna	troops between	Alto and Resaca	on Mexico	Battle of
	the Rio Grande	de la Palma		Monterrey
	and the Nueces			

1848	1848
(February 2)	(July 15)
Treaty of	Last U.S. troops
Guadalupe	leave Mexico
Hidalgo is signed	

CHAPTER EIGHT CONSIDERS HOW, BEGINNING IN THE 1820S, a flood of settlers came from the United States to Texas, then a part of northern Mexico. These settlers—some arriving legally and some illegally—became the dominant population group. Resentment against Mexican control built up, leading to a successful rebellion in 1836. The chapter then considers how the United States annexed Texas, which had existed as an independent republic for nine years. Shortly after annexation U.S. Present Polk ordered troops south of the **Nueces River**—historically the southern boundary of Texas. Combat between U.S. and Mexican forces soon erupted, giving the United States a *causa belli*. American troops then drove deep into northern Mexico, marched west to California, and after an amphibious landing at Vera Cruz, fought their way inland to Mexico City. To end hostilities, the two nations signed the Treaty of Guadalupe Hidalgo, which ceded to the United States territory which became the states of New Mexico, Arizona, and California.

TEXAS

In 1823 the Mexican government gave Missourian Stephen F. Austin permission to bring colonists to settle in Texas. In retrospect this appears to be a colossal Mexican blunder. However, at the time Mexicans felt that if Texas remained sparsely populated U.S. encroachment was inevitable. Very few Mexicans were moving north to populate Texas. Colonists, it was believed, would become loyal to Mexico and thus maintain Mexican control over the area. Mexican observers also saw that immigrants were fueling rapid economic expansion in the United States and felt that they would do the same in Texas. Finally, Mexicans believed Texas settlements would form a shield that would protect those further south from attack by indigenous people such as the Comanche.

At least twenty-four additional grants calling for the settlement of more than 8,000 families in Texas were signed after 1823. By 1830 more than 20,000 settlers had arrived. Many brought black slaves with them to provide labor needed for raising cotton. Even though slavery had been abolished by President Guerreo, a special exception was made to allow settlers in Texas to continue using slave labor.

Anglo settlers arrived, drawn by the offer of inexpensive land. Few pondered on the political arrangement offered by Mexico. However, after they arrived certain aspects of this arrangement vexed settlers. They resented the lack of trial by jury and the need to travel to distant Saltillo, the state capital, for many legal matters. Mexico's attempt to collect customs duties on trade with the U.S. caused resentment, as did an 1830 ban on further immigration—passed when Mexicans realized their control over Texas was slipping away. (Anglos ignored the ban and continued arriving.) Finally, slave owners were worried that eventually the Mexican prohibition on slavery would be extended to Texas.

Santa Anna's 1834 centralization of power produced a strong reaction in Texas. Anglo settlers formed the nucleus of the opposition. Some in Texas preferred to remain a part of Mexico, but under the decentralized government created by the 1824 constitution. Others saw their opposition to Santa Anna as a wedge they could use to wrest sovereignty from Mexico and unite Texas with the United States, from where the overwhelming majority of immigrants had come.

Settlers in Texas formed a militia, just as had occurred in Zacatecas. They attacked the main Mexican military force in Texas, which was quartered in San Antonio. After five days of combat, they defeated the Mexican force, commanded by General Martín Perfecto de Cos, Santa Anna's brother-in-law.

In response, President Santa Anna marched 6,000 troops north through the central Mexican desert and arrived in San Antonio in February 1836. There, a defiant, overwhelmingly Anglo force held an old mission now known as the Alamo. Santa Anna's forces stormed the Alamo on March 6, killing all its 188 defenders.

Meanwhile, settlers meeting at Washington-on-the-Brazos, 150 miles east of San Antonio, formally declared that Texas was independent from Mexico. Santa Anna, feeling his Alamo victory ended the Anglo military threat, very unwisely divided his forces so they could drive Anglos east into Louisiana.

On April 21, his 1,200-man force was camped at San Jacinto, near present-day Houston. There 910 Texas rebels under the command of Sam Houston routed his force in a surprise attack. Santa Anna was captured and, in order to secure his release, he agreed to recognize Texas's independence from Mexico. Even though the Mexican government refused to recognize Texas's independence, Texas had become de facto independent.

Most Anglos in Texas favored immediate annexation to the United States. However, the United States resisted annexation due to opposition by anti-slavery forces and fear it would lead to war with Mexico. For the next decade, Texas existed as an independent republic. In 1837, the United States extended diplomatic recognition to Texas. Later Great Britain and France both recognized Texas's independence. The French Legation, built during the independence period, still stands in Austin.

LORENZO DE ZAVALA

Generally the reputations of historical figures such as George Washington and Miguel Hidalgo are the same regardless of borders. A conspicuous exception to this is Lorenzo de Zavala, who was instrumental in establishing two republics within a dozen years.

In 1788, Zavala was born was born into a creole family in Yucatán. By eighteenth-century Yucatecan standards, he received a good education at the Tridentine Seminary in Mérida. As a student he demonstrated what would become a life-long trait—challenging recognized authority. He corrected widely accepted, but erroneous scientific statements made by priests instructing him. After finishing his education, he commented, "No useful truth, no principle, no axiom capable of inspiring noble or generous sentiments was heard in these schools of Jesuitism."

After finishing seminary, his more affluent classmates continued higher education in Mexico City. However since his family could not afford to send him there, he plunged into the two activities that would occupy him for the rest of his life—politics and writing.

Between 1810 and 1813 he wrote for local publications, some of which he founded. His writings condemned the forced collection of tithes from Indians, virtually all of whom were mired in poverty. He also strongly supported the 1812 Spanish constitution, which in the conservative milieu of late colonial Yucatán, was a bold position. During this period he served as secretary of the Mérida city government. In 1814 he was elected to the upcoming session of the Spanish Cortes.

After Fernando returned to the Spanish throne and abolished the Cortes, Zavala was imprisoned for having expressed such heretical notions as constitutional rule and ending abuse by priests. Ironically his first trip out of Yucatán was to the prison fortress of San Juan de Ulúa in Veracruz. He was released from prison in 1817 and returned to Mérida to practice medicine—a subject he had learned by reading books in prison.

Zavala's medical career was cut short by his being elected to the restored Spanish Cortes. After the promulgation of the Plan of Iguala he returned to Yucatán and was elected to Mexico's first congress. He was also elected to the second congress and served as president of that body. In this position he oversaw the drafting of the federalist 1824 constitution. Under President Victoria he served in the senate, of which he was also president. While serving in congress, articles he published in *El Águila mexicana* between 1823 and 1828 won him renown as a journalist.

In 1827 Zavala was elected as governor of the state of Mexico. He felt that Mexico should not simply accept the pattern of land ownership inherited from its colonial past. He presciently warned a "new entirely different revolution based on the inegalitarian distribution of land inherited from the colonial period was building." Zavala foreshadowed Mexico's twentieth-century land reform by dividing lands worth almost a half million pesos among more than forty Indian villages in the Valley of Toluca. In 1833, he expropriated lands belonging to the Dominican order and divided them into plots large enough to support a family. In addition to distributing land, he established a college, which offered courses in French, Latin, Spanish grammar, philosophy, political economy, and civil and canon law. As governor, he also oversaw the creation of a state library, a mint, a tobacco factory, and a canal from the city of Texcoco to Lake Texcoco.

While serving as governor Zavala also served as secretary of the treasury in the short-lived Guerrero administration. To address Mexico's fiscal needs, he proposed and congress passed a progressive income tax that only applied to the affluent—those making more than 1,000 pesos a year. This drew the wrath of wealthy individuals, the Catholic Church, foreign merchants, and powerful journalists and contributed to Guerrero's ouster.

In 1833 Zavala was appointed as Mexico's first ambassador to France. His diplomatic career was distinguished by its brevity. He resigned his post as ambassador in August 1834 to protest Santa Anna's seizure of powers. Rather than returning to a politically inhospitable central Mexico, he settled in Texas, arriving in July 1835.

The reasons for his choosing Texas remain unclear. He declared that he simply wanted to make money to support his family—a not implausible proposition since in 1828 he received a grant to bring colonists to Texas. His biographer Raymond Estep suggested the he might also have planned to use Texas as federalist stepping-stone to return to Mexican politics.

He became economically and politically tied to Texas as he acquired both a home and land there. He met with Anglo settlers in October 1835 in what has been called a consultation. There he espoused the Mexican federalist position—Texas would remain a part of Mexico, but would not be bound to obey Mexico City until the 1824 federalist constitution was reimposed. This was the position adopted by the consultation.

In March 1836, after combat between Texans and Mexicans broke out, the colonists met again and declared Texas to be independent. Regardless of Zavala's original intention in coming to Texas, he signed the declaration of independence along with two Texas-born Hispanics (*tejanos*) and fifty-six Anglo immigrants. Since he had more political experience than anyone else in Texas he helped draft the constitution of the new republic and was chosen as its first vice-president. Less than a month after he was replaced by an elected vice-president, his rowboat in Buffalo Bayou overturned. As a result he caught pneumonia and died November 15, 1836 at age forty-eight.

For Zavala's having sided with the Texas rebels, Mexicans to this day regard him in much the same way as Americans regard Benedict Arnold. However, in Texas he remains an honored founding father, and a county, the state archives, and innumerable schools are named for him.

Zavala consistently defended federalism and, despite his being a devout Catholic, opposed privileges of the Church and its influence over politics. He never amassed great wealth and did not use his numerous public positions to enrich himself. Finally, he was a tireless journalist. As Estep noted, "Few men of his time in America understood better or made fuller use of the newspaper as an instrument of public opinion."

In 1844, Great Britain's decision to broker peace between Texas and Mexico caused the United States to re-evaluate annexation. That year James K. Polk campaigned for the U.S. presidency advocating the annexation of Texas. After Polk won the election, President John Tyler felt this was a mandate and started the formal annexation process before he left office.

Annexing Texas deprived the British of an opportunity to extend their influence in North America. An expected negative aspect of annexation, a strong Mexican response, failed to materialize. Mexico's ambassador to the United States called the annexation "an act of aggression, the most unjust which can be found recorded in the annals of modern history" and left Washington, severing diplomatic relations. However, Mexico did not respond militarily.

THE MEXICAN–AMERICAN WAR

THE OUTBREAK OF WAR, 1845–1846

Once Texas was annexed the question arose—what was the border between Texas and Mexico? The United States claimed the Rio Grande was the boundary based on: 1) the claim the United States had obtained via the Louisiana Purchase; and 2) the December 1836 claim by the Texas Congress that the Rio Grande formed the border. The Adams–Onús Treaty extinguished whatever rights might have been acquired via the Louisiana Purchase. The claim by the Texas Congress neither reflected the historic boundary of Texas nor the de facto situation during the existence of the Republic of Texas. Even after the U.S. annexation of Texas, Mexicans continued to collect customs duties at Point Isabel (today's Port Isabel), north of the Rio Grande.

Events in Mexico made it appear that war could still be avoided. Despite his having made bellicose statements, President Mariano Paredes took no action, since he lacked an effective army and the money to finance one. Eventually, after harsh criticism in the press, he sent troops north under the command of General Pedro Ampudia. They reinforced the Mexican position on the lower Rio Grande, but did not cross to the north side of the river.

If the Polk administration intended only to bluff the Mexicans, it pushed the situation too far. On January 13, 1846, after receiving word that Mexicans were unwilling to negotiate other matters before settling the Texas question, Secretary of War William Marcy ordered Gen. Zachary Taylor to move his 4,000-man force to "positions on or near" the Rio Grande.

Regardless of whether Mexicans considered Texas to still be a part of Mexico, the virtually unanimous opinion in Mexico was that the State of Tamaulipas extended more than 100 miles north of the Río Grande to the Nueces River. In this light, Mexicans viewed Polk's actions as an invasion, or a provocation, or both.

As U.S. troops reached the north bank of the Rio Grande across from Matamoros, Mexican cotton farmers living there fled to the south side. In the U.S. Senate, anti-slavery Ohio Senator Thomas Corwin commented that Mexicans successfully grew cotton there without slaves. By Mexican reckoning, the land they farmed on the north side of the river did not lie in Texas, but in the Mexican state of Tamaulipas.

On April 4, in response to what Mexicans considered an invasion and to Taylor's refusal to withdraw, Minister of War and Marine General José María Tornel ordered an attack on U.S. forces along the Rio Grande.

On April 26, Taylor ordered an eighty-man detachment to investigate a report that Mexican troops had crossed to the north side of the Rio Grande upstream from his position. The 1,600 Mexican soldiers who had indeed crossed the river then ambushed the detachment fifteen miles upstream from present-day Brownsville, Texas, killing or wounding seventeen Americans and taking the rest prisoner.

News of the incident arrived in Washington on May 9, leading Polk's cabinet to unanimously vote to support a declaration of war. On May 11, Polk submitted a war message to Congress, noting that Mexicans had "shed American blood on American territory." In addition to simply assuming that "American territory" extended to the Rio Grande, Polk rewrote history when he stated, "It is absurd for Mexico to allege as a pretext for commencing hostilities against the United States that Texas is still part of her territory." It was the U.S. occupation of the area between the Nueces and the Rio Grande, not Mexico's claim to Texas, that led to war.

Paredes stated his motives for not accepting U.S. occupation of this area:

The defense of Mexican territory which the troops of the United States are invading is an urgent necessity, and my responsibility before the nation would be immense if I did not order the repulse of forces which are acting as enemies.[1]

Since not all members of the U.S. Congress favored war with Mexico, the declaration of war was included with the same bill that appropriated funds to support Taylor's force. Those voting against a declaration of war also voted to deny support for American forces under attack. This was likely unnecessary, since the declaration of war passed overwhelmingly. Only fourteen of the 188 votes cast in the House, all of them by abolitionist Whigs, were against the declaration. In the Senate, the declaration passed by a vote of forty to two, with three abstentions.

THE MONTERREY CAMPAIGN, 1846–1847

When Taylor learned that additional Mexican troops were crossing to the north side of the Rio Grande, he withdrew to Point Isabel on the Gulf of Mexico and waited for supplies and reinforcements.

On May 7, 1846, after receiving the supplies and reinforcements, Taylor started back toward the Rio Grande. Before reaching the river Taylor's force fought two battles. In the first, at Palo Alto, highly mobile U.S. artillery led to an American victory. The next day the Mexicans regrouped at Resaca de la Palma, an old channel of the Rio Grande. The outcome of the battle there was still in question until U.S. troops found a trail around the west end of the Mexican line. When they appeared at the Mexican rear, the Mexicans broke and ran for the Rio Grande.

Matamoros, on the south side of the Rio Grande, was fortified. However, Mexican troops withdrew, permitting U.S. forces to enter it on May 18, 1846, without firing a shot. Upon occupying the city, the Americans found 400 sick and wounded Mexican troops that had been abandoned.

After waiting until September for additional supplies, Taylor's force moved south to Monterrey, a city of 10,000, which guarded a key mountain pass through the Sierra Madre Oriental. Beyond that pass lay Saltillo and the interior of Mexico. After meeting stiff resistance in the city, Taylor settled for less than total victory. He permitted the Mexicans to retreat to Saltillo with their arms, rather than fighting to the last man. Taylor's forces were running low on ammunition and had suffered 120 killed and 368 wounded, or 8.5 percent of the men fighting. This exceeded the Mexican casualty rate of 5 percent.

From his exile in Cuba, Santa Anna convinced President Polk that if he was allowed to return to Mexico, he would arrange for a cession of territory and a peaceful settlement of the conflict. Thus Polk allowed Santa Anna to pass through the U.S. blockade of Veracruz. Almost immediately after his return, Santa Anna once again became president.

Two weeks after his arrival in Mexico City, on September 28, 1846, Santa Anna ordered the Mexican army north toward Taylor's force. This act added Polk to the long list of those betrayed by Santa Anna.

Santa Anna's force approached Taylor's position at Buena Vista, ten miles south of Saltillo. The ensuing battle of Buena Vista lasted two days, February 22 and 23, 1847. On one occasion, the Mexicans broke through the U.S. line. Reinforcements thrown into the breach saved the Americans. Later Mexican attacks were turned back by light artillery, which proved decisive due to its ability to shift rapidly to check Mexican infantry advances. Finally after two days of hard fighting and heroism on both sides, Santa Anna's forces turned back. Taylor lost 272 killed, the highest U.S. death toll of any battle in the war. The Mexicans lost more than twice that number.

Strategically the battle accomplished little, since both armies returned to their initial positions, Santa Anna in San Luis Potosí and Taylor in Saltillo. However, the battle did stir the fires of patriotism in the United States as reports arrived of Taylor's turning back of Santa Anna's superior force.

FROM VERACRUZ TO MEXICO CITY, 1847

The battle at Buena Vista left the Americans in a quandary. Taylor's campaign had permitted U.S. forces to occupy territory from the Gulf of Mexico to Saltillo. However, it did not immediately lead to peace, since distance prevented U.S. forces from pressuring the central government in Mexico City. Polk's hopes for a short, neatly executed war were never met. Even though they had defeated the Mexicans on the battlefield, after almost a year peace was still elusive.

Even before Buena Vista, Polk had decided on an amphibious invasion of Veracruz followed by an attack on Mexico City, with the invaders retracing Cortés's footsteps. Taking Veracruz would prevent the Mexican government from importing arms and deny it revenue from the Veracruz customs house. Polk selected General Winfield Scott to lead the force invading Veracruz.

Scott was general-in-chief of the army and had served in the military for almost thirty-seven years. As a result of his distinguishing himself as a commander in the War of 1812, he was promoted to brigadier general at the age of twenty-nine. Later he remained in the limelight as an Indian fighter. In choosing Scott to command the invasion force, Polk, a Democrat, attempted to neutralize Taylor's popularity. Nonetheless Taylor parlayed his military victories into the 1848 Whig nomination and was elected president.

On March 9, 1847, the campaign to take Veracruz began with an amphibious landing three miles south the city. At the time, it was the largest amphibious landing in the annals of war. More than 10,000 troops went ashore in sixty-five heavy surfboats towed close to the shore by steamers. In addition, artillery and supplies were landed. Horses were thrown overboard and forced to swim.

Rather than attacking Veracruz from the sea, as the Mexicans had anticipated, the Americans encircled the city after they landed, cutting off supplies. Then, rather than storming the city and suffering heavy casualties, Scott ordered a prolonged shelling. The shelling lasted four days. Finally, after 6,700 rounds—463,000 pounds—had been lobbed into the city, Veracruz surrendered. During the siege some 600 Mexican soldiers and 400 to 500 civilians died. U.S. dead numbered only about thirteen.

On April 8, after Scott's force had acquired sufficient mules and wagons, his troops began to move toward Mexico City. At Cerro Gordo, fifty miles northwest of Veracruz, Scott found his way blocked by a Mexican force commanded by Santa Anna. The situation was the reverse of Buena Vista. Santa Anna was entrenched on high ground, while U.S. forces were coming from below. The Mexicans trained their artillery on the road, assuming that the U.S. force, with its heavily laden supply wagons, would follow it inland.

On April 17, rather than pushing through the concentrated fire directed toward the road, the Americans turned north. Troops under the command of a young captain named Robert E. Lee pushed their way through ravines and thickets north of the road. This permitted them to occupy the top of a hill, Cerro Atalaya. Then with artillery support from Cerro Atalaya, U.S. troops stormed up another hill, Cerro Gordo, which overlooked Mexican forces. Other U.S. troops continued through woods and across ravines behind Cerro Gordo. As they emerged behind the Mexican line, Mexicans, feeling American forces would envelop them, broke and ran.

The Battle of Cerro Gordo lasted only three hours. There were 431 U.S. casualties, while Santa Anna lost more than 1,000. Scott's force took more than 3,000 prisoners, so many that they could not be cared for, so they were released. Santa Anna barely escaped capture.

Rather than immediately following Santa Anna into Mexico City, Scott stopped in Puebla, where the clergy welcomed him. No one attempted to organize a defense of the city. Scott remained in

Puebla for nearly three months, while he awaited supplies and additional troops. His forces were low on ammunition, and many of his men were wounded or sick. Others had enlisted for only a short period and returned home.

On August 7, after deciding he could not obtain peace through negotiation, Scott ordered his 10,738-man force to advance on Mexico City. To many, Scott's mission seemed impossible. A force of 30,000 troops on their own ground was defending his objective—a fortified city of 200,000. As in Aztec times, lakes and swamps protected Mexico City.

A series of battles ensued, which resulted in heavy casualties. This allowed American forces to approach the city. A final obstacle, Chapultepec Castle, stood in their way. Despite its impressive appearance, perched high on a hill, Chapultepec Castle had been built as a summer home for the viceroys, not as a heavily constructed fort. On September 13, the U.S. attack began with more than twelve hours of artillery bombardment followed by an infantry assault. After intense hand-to-hand combat, the Americans prevailed.

The battle at Chapultepec has been immortalized in both countries. Mexicans annually commemorate the valor of the *niños héroes*—the cadets at the military academy located in the castle. The U.S. Marine Corps hymn keeps the battle alive in American memory with its reference to "the halls of Montezuma."

Santa Anna still had roughly 12,000 troops in Mexico City. Rather than defending the capital, he marched his troops out of the city. As a parting gesture, he opened the prisons, loosing hundreds of felons on the populace and the invaders.

The entire world recognized Scott's defeat of Santa Anna as an impressive military feat. The Duke of Wellington, Europe's most distinguished solder, commented, "His campaign was unsurpassed in military annals."

Figure 8.1 *This painting by Carl Nebel of General Scott riding into Mexico City's main square has become the iconic image of the Mexican–American War. The cathedral is at the center and to the right is the Presidential Palace, over which flies a U.S. flag.*

Source: Reproduced courtesy of the Benson Latin American Collection, The University of Texas at Austin.

The war, which also included a U.S. force that marched west to occupy New Mexico and California, resulted in the deaths of 10,000 Mexicans, of whom 4,000 to 5,000 died in battle. U.S. combat deaths numbered 1,721, while another 11,155 died from accidents, disease, and other causes. This gave the Mexican–American War the dubious distinction of being the deadliest war the United States ever fought in terms of the percentage of troops who died. In this war, 15.3 percent of U.S. troops died. In the next most deadly U.S. conflict, the Civil War, 9.8 percent died.

PEACE

After American forces occupied Mexico City, the remnants of the Mexican government fled northwest to Querétaro. A period of political instability followed. No Mexican wanted to take responsibility for admitting defeat and signing away territory.

LOS *NIÑOS HÉROES* (THE HEROIC BOYS)

After Mexico became independent, a military academy was established in Chapultepec Castle. On September 13, 1847, at least forty-seven cadets from the academy, as well as regular Mexican troops under the command of General Nicolás Bravo, defended the castle. After intense hand-to-hand combat, Bravo ordered a retreat. Six of the cadets, rather than retreating, fought to the death. One of them, Juan Escutia, is popularly believed to have wrapped himself in a Mexican flag and leaped to his death from the castle.

Escutia, along with the other five, Vicente Suárez, Juan de la Barrera, Fernando Montes de Oca, Agustún Melgar, and Francisco Márquez, who died at age thirteen, now symbolize Mexican heroism in the war.

Initially the Association of Ex-Cadets organized an annual commemoration of the event. However, such ceremonies were too politically valuable to leave to civil society, so the War Department assumed responsibility for organizing them. Soon the presence of the president was de rigueur.

The War Department-sponsored commemorations served to buttress President Díaz. They conveyed the message that if the cadets had sacrificed themselves for their government in the early nineteenth century, late nineteenth-century Mexicans should do no less.

The passing of the Porfiriato was reflected in the commemoration of the *Niños Héroes*. In 1910 Díaz attended, while in 1911 interim President De la Barra did. The following year Madero did, then in 1913 Huerta did.

President Ávila Camacho downplayed the commemoration. He did not want to offend the United States, with which he was strengthening ties, by bringing up past conflict.

In 1947, the *Niños Héroes* were back in the news when U.S. President Truman, during the first U.S. presidential visit to Mexico City, laid a wreath at the monument to the six. At the time he pledged invasion would never again be used to settle disputes between the two countries.

In 1952, the *Niños Héroes* again emerged into the limelight. Their bodies had been buried in the grounds surrounding the castle. After the remains were found and identified, they were moved to the monument honoring them and re-buried.

The monument to the cadets, built at the foot of the castle, is the most conspicuous of the many honors they have received. In the center of the monument is a statue of a woman, representing the Nation, with a boy in her arms and another at her side. Flanking the statue is a curved marble wall with six granite columns, each two meters in diameter and 28 meters high. In the center of the wall the names of the cadets appear along with the date September 13, 1847.

Other cities, such as Guadalajara, also have monuments. In addition, many songs and poems have been composed in honor of the *Niños Héroes*. Numerous schools throughout Mexico, as well as a Mexico City metro station, also bear the name.

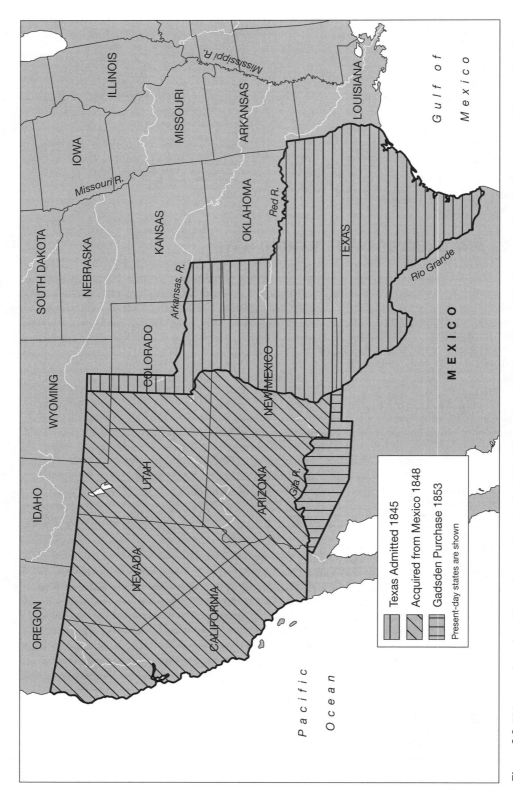

Figure 8.2 *This map shows how Mexico lost territory to the United States in 1845 (Texas), 1848 (Mexican–American War), and 1853 (Gadsden Purchase).*

Source: Reproduced by permission of HarperCollins Publishers.

Polk had sent Nicholas Trist, the chief clerk of the State Department, to Mexico along with Scott's force. Trist, whose position today would be called under-secretary of state, was authorized to negotiate a peace treaty. Polk's negotiator, who spoke Spanish, carried with him a draft treaty. He could offer $15 million for California and New Mexico, the minimum territorial concession acceptable to Polk. If Baja California and transit rights across the Isthmus of Tehuantepec were also ceded, he could offer $30 million. Before the transcontinental railroad and the Panama Canal, the Isthmus of Tehuantepec provided a relatively easy way to cross from the Gulf of Mexico to the Pacific.

The Mexican delegates negotiating the peace treaty did their best to minimize territorial loss. They held Trist to his minimal demand and preserved for Mexico a land bridge between Baja California and Sonora. Given that the United States could have taken whatever it wanted, limiting U.S. acquisitions constituted a triumph for Mexican diplomacy.

Mexican negotiators not only had to defend Mexican interests against Trist, but had to contend with the *puro* (pro-war) faction in Mexico, which advocated continued war against the United States, not only to avoid loss of territory but to bring about economic and political reforms. The pro-peace faction finally prevailed, arguing that failure to ratify a peace treaty would result in continued American military occupation, the probable loss of additional territory, and prolonged financial disaster for the Mexican government, which received no customs receipts from American-occupied ports.

On February 2, 1848, a peace treaty was signed in the village of Guadalupe Hidalgo, four miles north of Mexico City. The Treaty of Guadalupe Hidalgo established a new U.S.–Mexican boundary which included Texas (whose southern boundary was defined as the Rio Grande), most of New Mexico and Arizona, and California.

Mexico received $15 million, and, in addition, the Mexican government was relieved of responsibility for meeting past damage claims filed by U.S. citizens. Throughout the war, Polk had insisted that Mexico should cede territory to the United States to pay for the war it forced the United States to fight. At the same time, the United States wanted to avoid the appearance of stealing land, so it paid for the territory it acquired. U.S. historian Glenn Price noted, "It was all very odd logic." At the time, Mexican President Manuel de la Peña y Peña commented that Mexico did not cede California and New Mexico for $15 million but rather to get U.S. troops out of Mexican cities and ports.

The Treaty of Guadalupe Hidalgo gave the roughly 85,000 Hispanics in the area transferred to the United States the option of moving to Mexico to keep their Mexican citizenship. If they remained for more than a year in the territory acquired by the United States, they automatically became U.S. citizens and were guaranteed possession of any property they owned.

Mexicans were lucky to retain as much territory as they did. A strong "all of Mexico" movement in the United States advocated taking the entire country. Advocates of the "all of Mexico" position were not confined to the United States. Some Mexican liberals who admired the United States proposed to General Scott that he should become dictator of Mexico. They wanted that to be the first step towards annexation by the United States.

Proponents of seizing "all of Mexico" did not prevail for a variety of reasons. Former ambassador Poinsett warned that taking all of Mexico would require a large occupation force and would inflame Mexican nationalism, increasing resistance to the United States. Since the legality of slavery in former Mexican territory had not been settled, abolitionists opposed absorbing Mexico since they feared that all the land annexed would become slave territory. Others opposed annexation because they did not want 7 million Mexicans of mixed race to be cast into the U.S. racial melting pot. William Prescott, author of the classic account of the Spanish conquest of Mexico, commented, "The Spanish blood will not mix well with the Yankee."

BEHIND THE U.S. VICTORY

> Mexico's weakness with respect to the United States which lay at the root of the conflict was no one's fault, but was rather the result of a long and complex history
>
> (Tim Henderson, 2007)

The Mexican press limited the possible actions of Mexico's leaders by urging war on them and whipping up public sentiment to favor war. Mexicans' failure to accurately assess the relative military strength of the United States and Mexico impaired their decision-making ability. Finally, many in Mexico felt that if Mexico did not take a strong stance against its northern neighbor, the United States would continue to press claims forever, nibbling away at Mexican territory until the nation ceased to exist.

Given that the United States had long supply lines, a pre-industrial economy, and a small standing army, and that it was forced to attack the strong defensive position offered by the Sierra Madre Oriental, it is worth considering why the United States triumphed over Mexico. The U.S. victory amazed European observers. A British journalist commented, "There must be some mystery—some leading cause, imperfectly understood on our side of the Atlantic."

Factors contributing to the U.S. victory include:

- The U.S. population at the time of the war consisted of 17 million whites and 3 million slaves, more than double the number of Mexicans. This enabled the United States to draw on a much larger population for soldiers and war production.
- The United States made extensive use of light "flying" artillery that could be moved rapidly, keeping up with the troops and advancing to fire on Mexican positions. Artillery officers were permitted to move and fire without having to wait for orders from a central command. The U.S. artillery played a crucial role in several battles, such as those as Palo Alto, Monterrey, and Veracruz. At Buena Vista, General John Wool stated, "Without our artillery we would not have maintained our position a single hour."
- The smooth-bore muskets that were the standard U.S. infantry weapon were among the world's most advanced shoulder weapons. The milling machines used in their manufacture produced interchangeable parts and uniform barrel diameter. U.S. muskets had a range of 220 yards, considerably greater than the hundred-yard range of the Mexicans' muskets.
- By the time of the Mexican–American War, the majority of the lieutenants and captains were West Point graduates. Years of campaigning against elusive Indian guerrillas on the western frontier accustomed these officers to rapid, decentralized decision-making. Such officers were especially valuable when U.S. forces were operating in small units.
- The élan of the all-volunteer U.S. force was crucial. Many existing militia units volunteered en masse, reinforcing camaraderie. Initial American victories lifted spirits and additional triumphs kept them high.
- The U.S. economy, unlike the Mexican economy, which had yet to recover ground lost during the struggle for independence, was beginning its industrialization. The United States could achieve what, for the times, were prodigious logistical feats. For example, within a four-month period, forty-nine ten-inch mortars and 50,000 shells were ordered, manufactured, and transported to Veracruz.

A number of factors contributed to the Mexican loss:

- The Mexican population of seven million was substantially smaller than the U.S. population. Only a small proportion of Mexico's population was mobilized, some 70,000 out of 7 million, or 1 percent. This contrasts with the U.S. Civil War in which roughly 3 million, or 10 percent of the population, were mobilized for the Union and Confederate armies.

- Mexican statesmen failed to realize in time that the United States constituted a threat to Mexico. As late as 1825, the Mexican government convened a special commission to advise on developing California. It warned not of danger from the United States, but from Russia.

- The frequent changes in government in the mid-1840s undermined the government's already weak financial structure. The U.S. occupation of the Veracruz, Tampico, and Matamoros customs houses further impoverished the government.

- The actions of individual Mexican states also weakened the war effort. Yucatán declared itself independent on January 1, 1846. This renegade state not only failed to contribute to the war effort but sold supplies to U.S. naval forces blockading Veracruz before the invasion. By default, much of the defense burden fell on the individual state being invaded. Puebla failed to accept this defense burden, and the State of Mexico, which U.S. forces had to pass through to enter Mexico City, declared itself to be neutral. Many state governors were reluctant to raise militia units due to the long-standing perception that military commanders were abusive and authoritarian. Conservative governors were reluctant to see militia units recruit politically unreliable members of the lower classes. The Mexico City municipal government opposed attempts to fortify the city.

- Many wealthy Mexicans not only failed to contribute to the war effort but actually welcomed the invaders. Often merchants preferred Scott to Santa Anna and his forced loans. Santa Anna complained that the wealthy went into hiding as U.S. troops approached Mexico City, so they could avoid contributing to its defense.

- Unlike slaves in America, Mexican Indians, roughly half the population, produced little surplus that could support the war effort. They had little in common with the rest of Mexico and little sense of belonging to a "nation." Taking advantage of the national crisis to advance their own causes, indigenous people staged widespread uprisings in the central and southern regions following the U.S. invasion. In northern Veracruz, Indians under pressure from encroaching cattlemen rose up, burning towns and haciendas. *Hacendado* Manuel Soto wrote, "Blood ran in torrents, and for ten months the Huasteca [region of Veracruz] was the stage for the most horrible scenes." Suppressing such uprisings diverted men and arms away from fighting Americans.

- Prolonged conflict with independent Indian groups such as the Apache had left large areas of northern Mexico unable and unwilling to resist the U.S. army. American troops frequently encountered abandoned homes, overgrown fields, and hastily finished graves—a result of Indian raids—in the parts of northern Mexico they occupied. Prior to the Battle of Buena Vista, the states of Chihuahua, Durango, and Zacatecas ordered soldiers to remain at home to protect against Indian raids.

- The civilian population frequently reacted as if the war was being waged by two foreign powers. U.S. officers and Mexican landowners frequently fraternized. Other landowners, such as the Sánchez Navarro family in Coahuila, sold massive amounts of livestock, corn, and wheat to the U.S. army. To insure that the U.S. forces did not antagonize landowners, Generals Scott and Taylor insisted that all food and supplies needed by U.S. troops were paid for in voluntary, negotiated sales. Other Mexicans served U.S. troops as guides, teamsters, and spies and supplied them with mules, cattle, and corn.

- The army reflected the chronic financial problems of early nineteenth-century Mexican governments. The lack of finances resulted in an army that was poorly equipped at the outbreak of hostilities and made it difficult to amass war materiel later on.

- The professional army that defended Mexico reflected Mexican society as a whole. The army was poorly led, since individuals with little military training used bribes or political influence to obtain leadership positions. The officer corps was conservative and elitist. Of the 137 most senior officers, all but about twenty had fought on the Spanish side in the independence struggle.

Changes in government generally resulted in changes in the army's command structure. These repeated personnel shifts impaired fighting ability. The British ambassador wrote home in 1846 that the army was "the worst perhaps to be found in any part of the world."

- Morale among Mexican troops was low, since they were often impressed or taken from prisons. They received little training and, as a result, could not perform tactical maneuvers in large groups.
- The effectiveness of Mexican cannons was limited by their being of a variety of calibers and by poor logistics. The solid shot used by Mexicans was less effective than the grape and canister shot used by Americans. Mexican muskets had been purchased from British stocks after they had been declared obsolete and often unserviceable.
- Mexican officers tended to view battles like chess games. They expected events to unfold within a clearly defined area. The Americans would repeatedly extend the limits of the battlefield, and win.
- Many of Mexico's problems resulted from its failure to have formed a national consciousness in the quarter century after independence. In 1848, statesman Mariano Otero commented, "There has not been, nor could there have been a national spirit, for there is no nation."

To this date, Mexicans resent the loss of roughly 40 percent of "their" territory. However, just as was the case with the Adams–Onús Treaty, those most affected by the Treaty of Guadalupe Hidalgo were not the roughly 85,000 Hispanics on land ceded to the United States but the 160,000 Indians whose ancestral lands passed to U.S. control without their having been consulted.

In Mexico, the war was a painful but perhaps necessary shock to the nation, provoking self-examination. The questions raised by the war shaped a new generation and led to a consolidated state and increased nationalism, evident in the 1860s during the struggle against Maximilian. In the aftermath of the war, the dominance of the army, the Church, and *hacendados* began to be questioned more strongly than ever before.

For most of the twentieth century, the Mexican Revolution of 1910–17 overshadowed the Mexican–American War. However, by the end of that century the effects of the Revolution had largely run their course. The results of the Mexican–American War, in contrast, remain glaringly apparent. The four states—California, Arizona, New Mexico, and Texas—that form the bulk of the territory lost to the United States had a GDP almost four times that of Mexico in 2000.

THE LAST STEP OF MANIFEST DESTINY

After the Mexican–American War, U.S. planners began to consider possible transcontinental rail routes. One of the most promising routes lay in the area, still in Mexican hands, just south of the Gila River in what is today southern Arizona. Mexico came under intense pressure to cede this territory to the United States. In 1853, President Franklin Pierce appointed James Gadsden, a prominent railroader and proponent of a southern transcontinental rail route, as U.S. ambassador to Mexico. He was instructed to negotiate a treaty with Mexico that would move the border south to include the future rail route.

Mexicans greeted renewed U.S. territorial demands with resignation. They could do little to stop the United States since the government teetered on the edge of bankruptcy and lacked popular support. President Santa Anna commented on the situation he faced, "Our neighbors to the north were threatening another invasion if the boundary question was not settled to their satisfaction." Santa Anna desperately needed money to fight Álvarez's rebels. He rationalized the loss of further territory by claiming that it was of little use to Mexico.

Given Santa Anna's desperate financial situation and his inability to confront the U.S. militarily, he signed what is known as the Gadsden Treaty, which the United States ratified in 1854. For $10 million, Mexico ceded 29,640 square miles that now form southern New Mexico and Arizona, including Tucson. Since this was the last land acquisition by the United States at Mexican expense, it has been referred to as the final step of **Manifest Destiny**.

Mexico and U.S.–Mexican relations both underwent major changes in the 1850s. After the 1850s, the Mexican government became more stable thanks to revenues obtained from the export of raw materials. At the same time, the U.S. interest in territorial acquisition waned. Instead the United States sought to acquire raw materials and invest in the mines that produced them and in the railroads that transported them to the United States.

DOCUMENT 8.1: POLK'S JUSTIFICATION FOR THE MEXICAN–AMERICAN WAR

[On May 11, 1846 President Polk sent a long war message to congress to justify a declaration of war. In it he declares the Rio Grande, which he refers to as the Del Norte, to be the southern boundary of Texas.]

Upon the pretext that Texas, a nation as independent as herself, thought proper to unite its destinies with our own, she [Mexico] has affected to believe that we have severed her rightful territory, and in official proclamations and manifestoes has repeatedly threatened to make war upon us for the purpose of reconquering Texas. In the meantime we have tried every effort at reconciliation. The cup of forbearance has been exhausted, even before the recent information from the frontier of the Del Norte. But now after repeated menaces, Mexico has passed the boundary of the United States, has invaded our territory, and shed American blood upon American soil. She has proclaimed that hostilities have commenced, and that the two nations are now at war.

As war exists, and, notwithstanding all our efforts to avoid it, exists by the act of Mexico herself, we are called upon by every consideration of duty and patriotism to vindicate with decision the honor, the rights, and the interests of our country . . .

In further vindication of our rights and defense of our territory, I invoke the prompt action of Congress to recognize the existence of the war, and to place at the disposition of the Executive the means of prosecuting the war with vigor, and thus hastening the restoration of peace.

Source: James D. Richardson (1917) *A Compilation of the Messages and Papers of the Presidents* (vol. 5). New York: Bureau of National Literature, pp. 2292–93.

DOCUMENT 8.2: MEXICAN DECLARATION OF WAR

A special session of Congress has decreed the following:

Article 1: The government, in defense of the nation, will repel the aggression the United States has initiated and is sustaining against Mexico, by invading various departments.

Article 2: To accomplish this, the government is authorized to use its power to bring up to strength the permanent active militia. It may also form new units and spend what is necessary to prosecute the war. Newly formed units will be disbanded once peace is reestablished.

Article 3: The government will make known throughout the Republic and to friendly nations the justifying causes which compel it to defend its rights, repelling with force the violent aggression of the United States.

Mexico City: July 2, 1846.

Source: *Colección completa de las disposiciones legislativas*, Vol. 5. Mexico City: Imprenta de Comercio, 1876, p. 136.

DOCUMENT 8.3: TRIST'S FEELINGS CONCERNING PEACE NEGOTIATIONS

[Nicholas B. Trist who negotiated the Treaty of Guadalupe Hidalgo on behalf of the United States later reflected on his feelings at the conclusion of the negotiations.]

Could these Mexicans have seen into my heart at that moment, they would have known that *my* feelings of shame as an American were far stronger than theirs could be as Mexicans. For although it would not have done for me to say that in *there*, that was a thing for every right-minded American to be ashamed of, and I *was* ashamed of it, most cordially and intensely ashamed of it. This had been my feelings at all our conferences, and especially at moments when I felt it necessary to *insist* upon things which they were adverse to. Had my course at such moments been governed by my conscience as a man and my sense of justice as an individual American, I should have *yielded* in every instance. Nothing prevented my doing so but the conviction that the treaty would then be one which there would be no chance for the acceptance of by our government. My object throughout was not to obtain all that I could, but on the contrary, to make the treaty as exacting as little as possible from Mexico, as well as compatible with its being accepted at home.

Source: Josefina Zoraida Vázquez (2000) "Causes of the War with the United States," in *Dueling Eagles*, ed. Richard V. Francaviglia and Douglas W. Richmond. Fort Worth, TX: Texas Christian University Press, pp. 60–61.

NOTE

1   David Pletcher, *The Diplomacy of Annexation* (Colombia, MO: University of Missouri Press, 1973), p. 439.

FURTHER READING

Bauer, Karl Jack (1974) *The Mexican War, 1846–1847*. New York: Macmillan.
    A comprehensive military history of the war.

DeLay, Brian (2008) *War of a Thousand Deserts*. New Haven, CT: Yale University Press.
    A discussion of Mexican and U.S. relations with stateless Indians in the years before the Mexican–American War. A virtual prequel to *Empire of the Summer Moon*.

De Paulo, William A. (1997) *The Mexican Army, 1822–1852*. College Station, TX: Texas A&M University Press.
    A discussion of the army facing U. S. forces—and its many problems.

Greenberg, Amy S. (2012) *A Wicked War: Polk, Clay, Lincoln and the 1846 Invasion of Mexico*. New York: Knopf.
    A description of how the three individuals named in the title responded to the drift into war.

Henderson, Timothy J. (2007) *A Glorious Defeat*. New York: Hill & Wang.
    A history of non-military events relating to the war, concentrating on the Mexican experience.

Vázquez, Josefina Zoraida (1997) "The Colonization and Loss of Texas: A Mexican Perspective," in *Myths, Misdeeds and Misunderstandings*, ed. Jaime E. Rodríguez and Kathryn Vincent, pp. 47–77. Wilmington, DE: Scholarly Resources.

—— (2000) "Causes of the War with the United States," *Dueling Eagles*, ed. Richard V. Francaviglia and Douglas W. Richmond, pp. 41–65. Fort Worth TX: Texas Christian University Press.
    Both of these works by a distinguished Mexican historian describe events as perceived south of the Rio Grande.

GLOSSARY

Manifest Destiny
Nueces River

Chapter 9

Juárez and Díaz, 1855–1909

TIMELINE—WORLD

1851 Isaac Singer patents sewing machine	1856 English engineer Henry Bessemer developed	1856 Bessemer process to convert iron into steel	1859 First commercial oil well, Titusville, Penn.	1860 Abraham Lincoln elected
1879 Edison produces incandescent lamp	1898 Spanish–American War	1900 World population reaches 1.55 billion	1900 US produces 24 percent of world's manufactured goods	1900 Great Britain produces 19 percent, Germany 13 percent

TIMELINE—MEXICO

1854 Plan of Ayutla issued	1855 Santa Anna goes into exile	1855 Comonfort becomes president	1857 New constitution promulgated	1858 Zuloaga ousts Comonfort and claims presidency
1864 Maximilian and Carlota arrive in Mexico	1867 (March 11) Last French troops leave Mexico	1867 (May 15) Querétaro falls to forces of the Republic	1867 (June 19) Maximilian executed	1872 Juárez dies
1907 U.S. recession spills over into Mexico	1907 Rio Blanco strike	1910 Díaz re-elected president	1910 Madero calls for uprising on November 20	

1861	1862	1865	1869	1876
U.S. Civil War begins	Homestead Act accelerates westward expansion of U.S.	U.S. Civil War ends	U.S. transcontinental railroad completed	Alexander Graham Bell delivers first telephone message

1900	1903	1904	1908	
Russia produces 9 percent, and France 7 percent.	Wright brothers make first flight	Panama Canal begun	Ford introduced Model T	

1858	1859	1861	1861	1862
Juárez establishes a liberal government in Veracruz	Juárez nationalizes Church property	Juárez returns government to Mexico City	Congress suspends debt payments	French defeated at Puebla (Cinco de Mayo)

1873	1876	1880	1884	1906
Mexico City–Veracruz railroad inaugurated	Porfirio Díaz becomes President	Díaz leaves presidency	Porfirio Díaz begins second term	Strike at Cananea

THIS CHAPTER CONSIDERS THE SECOND HALF-CENTURY of Mexico's independent existence—a period which began tumultuously and then became all too stable. Early 1860s tumult resulted from a civil war which pitted modernizers vs. traditionalists. Later in the 1860s the French established an empire in Mexico. National icon Benito Juárez successfully led opposition to the empire. Then, following Juázez's presidency, Porfirio Díaz became president, dominating Mexico from 1876 to 1911. The chapter then considers changes in Mexican society and economy as the nation industrialized and was knit together by the railroad. Finally, there is a description of how the United States inexorably increased influence over Mexico.

CONSOLIDATING THE REPUBLIC, 1855–1910

The New Order, 1855–1857

Santa Anna's overthrow in 1855 ended the alternation between liberal and conservative governments that dominated the first years of Mexico's independence. A liberal juggernaut that soon linked its fortunes to the rapidly increasing export of minerals and agricultural products overwhelmed the conservatives, who still looked back to the Spanish colonial model. Even though they had vanquished the conservatives, uniting their country provided liberals with a formidable challenge. At mid-century, the trip from Mexico City to the capital of Sonora required two weeks, and the trip to Yucatán, which included a voyage by sea, required a similar time.

As their power grew, the liberals sought to dismantle the system based on the Church, the army, and *caudillos*. In its place, they sought to establish civil liberties, build railroads, break down barriers to internal commerce, and put the immense land holdings of the Church and Indian villages on the market. Liberals saw themselves as nation-builders, feeling Mexicans' principal allegiance should not be to villages, communities, or corporate bodies, including the ecclesiastical estate, but to the nation. For the liberals, allowing males to vote without income restrictions was the sine qua non of democracy. The liberal ideal was a Jeffersonian agrarian democracy where large numbers of smallholders formed a stable citizenry. The liberal program, as well as that of the conservatives, lacked any measure to address extreme inequalities of wealth.

After the liberal army overthrew Santa Anna, a group of liberals met in Cuernavaca and, on October 4, 1855, chose Juan Álvarez, the leader of the revolt against Santa Anna, to be Mexico's next president. As a life-long resident of rural, southern Mexico, Álvarez, who had only three years of formal schooling, never felt at home in the capital.

In December 1855, Álvarez, who had no ideological axe to grind, realized that fighting suited him better than governance and resigned. He turned the presidency over to Ignacio Comonfort, a moderate liberal who, as a Puebla *hacendado* and retired militia colonel, functioned more effectively in Mexico City than Álvarez.

The month before he resigned, Álvarez implemented by decree the Juárez Law (*Ley Juárez*), named for his appointee as secretary of justice, ecclesiastical affairs, and public instruction, Benito Juárez. The law provided that priests and the military charged with common crimes or facing civil suits were tried in ordinary courts.

The next major enactment, the Lerdo Law (*Ley Lerdo*), also affected the Church, which owned roughly a fifth of national property, including half the houses in Mexico City. This law, named for Miguel Lerdo de Tejada, the secretary of development who drafted it, prohibited both the Church and Indian villages from owning land. The law did not affect Church property used for strictly religious purposes, such as monasteries, convents, and church buildings. Liberals felt both indigenous communities and the Church stymied development and curbed individual initiative by removing land from commerce. The Lerdo Law provided that tenants could buy Church land they were renting. The government auctioned Church property tenants could not or would not buy and turned the proceeds over to the Church, after collecting a 5 percent tax. Many of the Church's tenants refused to buy the land they were legally entitled to purchase because they felt such a purchase would be a betrayal of their religious faith. As the liberals intended, the Lerdo Law reduced Church power, increased government revenue, and placed land on the market.

However, most land sales failed to benefit the small farmer and rancher, whom the liberals proclaimed to be the basis of the ideal society. Wealthy landowners, including some of the liberal legislators who voted for the Lerdo Law, acquired most of the large tracts that were auctioned.

In many cases Indian communal lands were transferred to individual community members. This allowed wealthy *hacendados* to acquire this land, plot by plot. As a result, Indian poverty increased— just the opposite of what liberals had anticipated. Within a generation, many Indian villages that had lost their land also lost their indigenous identity.

In February 1856, 157 deputies, mostly young liberal lawyers, met to draft a new constitution. Despite their being considered anti-Catholic by many, all but one (a deist) were professing Catholics. Since conservatives had opposed the coalition toppling Santa Anna, they were largely unrepresented in the constitutional Congress. The new charter, drafted by some of the best liberal minds of the period, was promulgated on February 5, 1857. It created a state that claimed power based on popular will, not on divine right or the pope's blessing. Since only half of the political spectrum drafted it, not surprisingly, the document did not produce political consensus.

Mexico's new constitution removed the prohibition against religions other than Roman Catholicism, which had been included in the 1824 constitution. The constitution also guaranteed freedom of press, of association, and of travel, and protected the right to bear arms.

The constitution's lofty ideals and its provision for the separation of powers never had much to do with reality. Despite its positive provisions, such as civil liberties and voting rights for males without regard to land ownership or wealth, it failed to deal with Mexico's single greatest problem—the grossly inequitable distribution of land. Liberals felt that a constitution alone would reform a society composed of people who for the most part could not read and whose life was governed by tradition, not by legislators seated comfortably in Mexico City.

The delegates debated the land question. Liberal Ponciano Arriaga stated that society had granted the right of land ownership and could withdraw this right. He advocated government action to subdivide haciendas, declaring: "A few individuals have immense uncultivated tracts of land, which could support many millions of men. This leaves the overwhelming majority of the citizens to languish in the worst squalor, without property, home, or job." The liberals, given their respect for private property, took no action on Arriaga's proposal, hoping market forces would eventually lead to the subdivision of the hacienda.

Conservatives felt liberal measures, such as abolishing the clerical *fuero* and the forced sale of Church property, were attacks on religion. They wanted a strong role in society not only for the Church but for the army. They felt the constitution should have imposed wealth restrictions on suffrage. Governance was best accomplished, they felt, by a strong executive, just as it had been in colonial times.

The Conservatives Strike Back, 1858–1860

In January 1858, a coup, led by General Félix Zuloaga, deposed Comonfort. Given the opposition of conservatives and weak support from his own liberal base, Comonfort resigned and went into exile. This marked the demise of the broad alliance of anti-Santa Anna forces that had supported Álvarez.

Conservatives and the regular army supported the coup and recognized Zuloaga as president. However, the 1857 constitution provided that Benito Juárez, who was serving as the chief justice of the Supreme Court, should assume the presidency. Juárez had been elected to this position during the Comonfort administration. Soon both Zuloaga and Juárez were claiming the presidency.

Juárez's birthplace, the isolated Oaxacan village of Guelatao, had neither a school nor a church. As was the case with the other twenty families in the village, the family of Mexico's future president spoke the Zapotec Indian language, not Spanish. Juárez overcame these obstacles by moving to Oaxaca City and getting an education. He briefly studied for the priesthood, but soon enrolled to study law at Oaxaca's Institute of Arts and Sciences, a hotbed of liberal ideas. Beginning in 1832, with his membership in the Oaxaca City municipal council, Juárez rose steadily through public-sector positions. By the middle of the century, Juárez had broken with the indigenous world into which he was born and had adopted the worldview of the Hispanic city of Oaxaca. From then on, Juárez was viewed, and viewed himself, not as an Indian, but as a liberal Mexican.

During his last presidency, Santa Anna sent Juárez, who was serving as governor of Oaxaca, into exile in New Orleans. After Santa Anna went into exile and Juárez returned from it,

D. BENITO JUAREZ.

Figure 9.1

Of the historical figures between independence and the revolution, Benito Juárez, pictured here, has by far the best reputation.

Source: Reproduced courtesy of the Benson Latin American Collection, the University of Texas at Austin.

Álvarez appointed the Oaxacan as his minister of justice, ecclesiastical affairs, and public instruction (one of only six cabinet positions). His subsequent election as chief justice of the Supreme Court placed him first in the line of presidential succession.

The strongest support for the conservatives came from Mexico City, Querétaro, and traditionally conservative Puebla. In addition many rural people supported the conservatives because they resented urban, liberal lawyers imposing their views on others through legislation. Conservatives drew support from the Church, military officers, and Indian villages wishing to retain communal land holdings. Residents of central Mexico, especially *hacendados*, hoped conservatives would perpetuate that region's dominance of the periphery.

The Veracruz customs house, the major source of government revenue, financed the liberal cause. Juárez, who had limited support in Mexico City, set up his government there. Liberals used customs duties to purchase foreign arms, which were shipped to Veracruz.

In July 1859, Juárez nationalized all remaining Church lands without compensating the Church. He blamed the civil war on the Church and accused it of financing the conservative war effort with income from its land holdings. Liberals also nationalized the Church's investment capital, which exceeded the value of its real estate. These measures and the changes embodied in the 1857 constitution are known as the *Reforma*, for which Mexico City's Paseo de la Reforma is named.

The liberal government hurriedly sold nationalized Church property to finance the war. Since the sales were so hasty and the titles so shaky, in many cases the government received only a quarter or a third of the value of the land. Liberals made no provision for instalment buying or subdividing large tracts seized from the Church. As a result, only the already wealthy could afford the single payment required to purchase a large tract.

Liberals recruited those favoring the abolition of compulsory military service, freedom of commerce, army reorganization, and, in areas where the Catholic clergy had lost its legitimacy, religious liberty. Eventually, liberal tenacity, the support of state militias, and the arms bought with Veracruz customs revenues overwhelmed the conservatives. Liberal commander Santos Degollado suffered repeated defeats. However, after each defeat he would rally his forces, suffer another defeat, and then rally his forces once again.

Liberal forces reoccupied Mexico City on Christmas Day of 1860, thus ending the War of the Reform, as the 1857–60 civil war is known. Once again, war had devastated the country. The U.S. consul at Veracruz reported, "Haciendas are abandoned, *ranchos* deserted, and even whole villages pillaged and sacked, leaving nothing but desolation wherever the armies of the contending parties have made their tracks."

The Second Empire, 1861–1866

The victory over the conservatives allowed Mexico to hold elections. Three candidates presented themselves—acting president Juárez, Miguel Lerdo de Tejada, author of the Lerdo Law, and General Jesús González Ortega, a hero of the War of Reform. Based largely on his reputation from the War of Reform, Juárez won the election.

Given wartime destruction and bands of conservative irregulars who refused to demobilize, Mexico could not make payments on its public debt. In July 1861, the Mexican Congress recognized this and, as an emergency measure to permit internal reconstruction, unilaterally suspended payments on its debts for two years. However, it did not repudiate the debts. This act gave Europe the pretext for massive intervention in Mexico.

Spain, Britain, and France formed an alliance to collect the debt and landed troops in Mexico. The French, who were already expanding their empire into Algeria and Indo-China, had the most far-reaching plans. French Emperor Napoleon III planned to impose a monarchy that would provide France with markets and raw materials and prevent the spread of U.S. influence into Latin America. The British and Spanish soon realized that the French were planning a much greater undertaking than debt collection and departed.

Mexican conservatives welcomed France's monarchical pretensions. Having lost in the War of Reform, they were more than willing to allow foreigners to restore them to power. They felt the early 1860s were an ideal time to install a monarchy since the United States, preoccupied with its own civil war, could not oppose an empire to its south.

The French commander, General Charles Latrille, Count of Lorencez, began an advance on Mexico City. On April 25, 1862, he wrote his minister of war, "We are so superior to the Mexicans in race, organization, morality, and devoted sentiments that I beg your Excellency to inform the Emperor that as head of 6,000 soldiers I am already master of Mexico."

Ten days after this was written, the French force fought its first major battle at Puebla. After 475 of the attackers were killed, wounded, or taken prisoner, the French force withdrew. Mexican casualties totalled 227. The victory at Puebla remains the outstanding military victory in Mexican history. Each year Mexicans, and many Americans, celebrate the Cinco de Mayo (Fifth of May).

After their defeat at Puebla, the French retreated and awaited the arrival of reinforcements. By January 1863, the interventionist force totalled 30,976. Then the French advanced on Mexico City. As the French approached, Juárez abandoned the practically defenseless capital and moved his government north. For the next three years, he would govern by decree to prosecute the war.

After arriving in Mexico City, the French created an interim government. Its officials invited all Mexicans to unite around it and urged them to cease considering themselves liberals or conservatives. Conservatives forming the interim government felt a foreign Catholic monarch would bring Mexico's polarized society together. As a result, they invited the Austrian archduke Ferdinand Maximilian to become emperor of Mexico.

The future emperor of Mexico accepted the offer. In April 1864, he signed a secret treaty with the French, making Mexico a virtual French colony. He agreed to pay not only the inflated debt claims of the French but also the cost of French troops occupying Mexico. Napoleon agreed to keep French troops in Mexico until 1870.

Even before arriving in Mexico, Maximilian began courting liberals by granting pardons to republican prisoners and reducing their prison sentences. To broaden his support, he shifted tax burdens to the rich and ended debt servitude. He also showed his moderate European liberalism by refusing to return to the Church the property it had formerly owned and by allowing freedom of worship. He abolished corporal punishment and limited child labor and work hours. Maximilian also mandated a minimum wage for agricultural workers and ordered those employing more than twenty families to provide free primary education. He anticipated twentieth-century **land-reform** efforts by ordering that unused government land should be provided to the landless. Maximilian's failure to embrace the conservative agenda reduced his conservative backing and won him few liberal supporters. His enactments might have been sound policy. However, quite often imperial hegemony did not extend beyond the edge of Mexico City, leaving his decrees unenforced.

After occupying Mexico City, the French moved north, taking Saltillo and Matamoros. Juárez retreated, eventually taking refuge in Paso del Norte (today, in his honor, Ciudad Juárez). By 1865, all state capitals flew the imperial flag. Imperial forces totaled 60,000 troops, of whom 30,000 were French, 24,000 Mexican, and the rest Austrian and Belgian. These forces confined Juárez's regular forces to a small area bordering on west Texas and New Mexico. In addition, 200 to 300 men in Guerrero and Oaxaca, led by the wily guerrilla fighter Porfirio Díaz, supported Juárez. Unlike Santa Anna in the Mexican–American War, Juárez realized that guerrilla warfare was the only way to confront a powerful foreign army.

The French occupation made elections impossible when Juárez's presidential term expired in 1865. Juárez used the extraordinary powers granted him by Congress in 1861 to simply extend his term. Some liberals, especially those seeking power themselves, criticized this as a violation of liberal principles.

Even though Juárez's regular forces verged on annihilation, the French could not extend their control into the countryside. As soon as their troops withdrew, popular uprisings occurred. French-organized counter-guerrilla forces were effective, but lacked sufficient numbers to dominate an area as large as Mexico.

In 1866, Napoleon decided to withdraw French troops from Mexico. His decision resulted from: 1) the high cost of the war in Mexico; 2) its unpopularity in France; 3) Maximilian's failure to develop an independent base; 4) the fear that the United States would support Juárez after its own civil war ended; and 5) Napoleon's need for troops in Europe to respond to the threat posed by an increasingly militarized Prussia.

The last French forces sailed from Veracruz in March 1867—three years earlier than the departure date agreed to by Napoleon. After the French departure, Maximilian's empire began to disintegrate with increasing rapidity. Juárez's forces, taking heart at the French withdrawal, moved south, aided by U.S. arms and Union veterans who appeared in Mexico after the end of the U.S. Civil War.

The imperial forces made their final stand at Querétaro. In February, General Mariano Escobedo besieged the city with 30,000 liberal troops. Maximilian came north from Mexico City to personally lead his 9,000-man force. The siege lasted until May, when liberals captured the city and took

Maximilian prisoner. Shortly afterward, Porfirio Díaz came from the east and captured Mexico City for the liberals.

Juárez ordered that Maximilian be tried by court martial. The former emperor faced the same criminal charges of rebellion that he had decreed Juárez's supporters captured in battle should face. The court found him guilty and sentenced him to be executed by firing squad, along with two of his generals, Tomás Mejía and Miguel Miramón. Juárez resisted intense pressure from around the world to issue a pardon, feeling that a live Maximilian would only serve to promote further uprisings and prolong internal strife. Juárez knew that conservatives pardoned after the War of Reform had supported the empire.

In July 1867, after an absence of four years, Juárez returned to Mexico City. His wife Margarita Maza de Juárez, who had spent the war years in the United States, soon rejoined him. During these years she had rallied support for the liberal cause in Washington.

Compared with Mexican resistance in the Mexican–American War, resistance to the empire was, as historian Alan Knight noted, "more prolonged, dogged, and above all, successful." Liberal strongmen provided Juárez with crucial support at the regional level, just as they had in defeating the conservatives during the War of the Reform. Rural people generally supported the liberal cause, feeling liberalism offered greater local autonomy. Much of Juárez's appeal was based not on his program but on his once having been a poor Indian who rose thorough the ranks to govern the country.

The forging of a Mexican national identity, a spirit sorely lacking in 1847, forms a lasting legacy of the struggle against the French. After the collapse of the empire, creoles no longer defined Mexican nationality. This role shifted to Juárez's generation of mestizo politicians, journalists, writers, poets, legislators, and historians. They created republican institutions and a wide range of newspapers, magazines, and scientific and literary academies.

The Restored Republic

With Maximilian's defeat, many felt that internal stability was finally at hand. Liberalism had become a unifying myth almost synonymous with patriotism, since it had been the liberals' tenacity that had defeated the French. However, once liberals no longer faced a common enemy, forging a consensus became a major challenge. The following constituencies vied for influence in the restored republic: 1) landowners who wanted to acquire Church and Indian lands; 2) the middle class; 3) workers, including textile workers, blacksmiths, and artisans; and 4) peasants who had supported the 1855 revolt against Santa Anna.

The 1867 presidential elections involved indirect voting, as was provided in the 1857 constitution. Juárez, who was at the peak of his popularity, obtained 72 percent of the 10,371 electoral votes cast. His young rival, General Porfirio Díaz, who only obtained 26 percent of the votes, found he could not convert military prowess into electoral victory.

The hoped for post-war calm never became a reality. Rather the years after the liberal victory were ones of rebellion, with men being pressed into military service, civil discord, and the opposition of almost all the press to Juárez. National guard officers, who resented demobilization, led many uprisings. Disgruntled peasants and demobilized soldiers, lacking land, often turned to banditry. Congress granted Juárez extraordinary powers, allowing him once again to govern by decree, so that he could suppress bandits and guerrilla movements.

The failure, once gain, to address the land issue, increased unrest. At the time Juárez could have distributed unused national lands or lands that had been owned by the Church, villages, and conservatives such as the Sánchez Navarros. However, authorities either returned confiscated estates to conservatives or sold them to politically powerful liberal landowners. In addition the government retained ownership of extensive tracts in the hope that they could be used to attract

European immigrants. The inability of the landless peasant and the demobilized war veteran to obtain land contrasted sharply with the U.S. experience after the Civil War. The Homestead Act there provided free public lands to settlers.

The war-ravaged economy yielded little tax revenue, and the army devoured much of the government budget. Although $45 million worth of Church property had been nationalized, less than $2 million had reached the treasury, and that was soon spent.

Between 1867 and 1877, the federal government repeatedly intervened to suppress insurrections mounted by villages and districts to assert local sovereignty. Such conflicts only subsided after Porfirio Díaz assumed the presidency and successfully centralized power.

In 1871, against the advice of many friends, Juárez sought re-election. The propriety of his re-election became a major issue. Even though the 1857 constitution did not prohibit re-election, many felt it ran counter to the liberal ethos. Only in 1878 did a constitutional amendment prohibit immediate presidential re-election.

Juárez faced challenges by two of his former supporters, Porfirio Díaz and Sebastián Lerdo de Tejada, whose brother wrote the Lerdo Law. Both of his opponents attacked Juárez's re-election, after thirteen years in office, as a violation of liberal principles. Díaz claimed that Juárez's mission had been fulfilled after Maximilian's defeat and that he was attempting to personalize the presidency.

In the 1871 election, whose fairness was questioned, Juárez received 5,837 electoral votes, Díaz 3,555, and Lerdo de Tejada 2,874. The law stipulated that if no candidate received a majority of the votes, Congress would select the next president. Juárez retained office when Congress selected him for the 1871–75 term.

In 1872, Juárez died of a heart attack in the National Palace. During his fourteen and a half years as president, Mexico underwent greater change than under any previous president.

Juárez strengthened Mexicans' feelings of nationhood and unity. Rather than seeking vengeance on Maximilian's vanquished supporters, he implemented a broad amnesty that embraced all but those who had held the highest positions in the empire.

During his presidency, Juárez greatly expanded the power of the federal government as he confronted not only foreign invasion and civil war, but the task of unifying his fragmented nation. The Juárez presidency began a trend towards a strong executive with little regard for the written constitutional model. By the end of the Juárez administration, power had shifted from the Church, *caudillos*, and the military establishment to a modern nation state. Power also shifted from states to the federal government. Under Juárez, the presidency became the lynchpin of the political system—perhaps his most lasting legacy.

Since his death, Juárez has been regarded in much the same way as Lincoln in the United States. His austere lifestyle stood in sharp contrast to Santa Anna's and Maximilian's profligacy. However, Juárez never presented a concrete program for dealing with social inequality. Rather he merely declared all men to be equal before the law. This reflected the emphasis classical liberalism placed on the role of the individual in society, while failing to present a positive theory of government.

Juárez viewed the elementary school as a means of transferring Mexicans' primary loyalty to the republic from corporate and ethnic groups and kin and patron–client networks. In 1867 the First Law of Public Instruction established free, compulsory primary education for "the poor" and specifically excluded religious instruction from the curriculum. Despite Juárez's vision of education as a force of change, the reality of recurrent insurrection and financial limitations prevented widespread provision of secular schooling. During his presidency, school attendance increased from 10 percent to 15 percent of school-age children.

The next in line of presidential succession upon Juárez's death was the chief justice of the Supreme Court, Sebastián Lerdo de Tejada. Lerdo de Tejada took office in July 1872 and called elections for October. He won these elections with 92 percent of the vote.

Lerdo's 1872–76 term was more peaceful than Juárez's last term. Economic development and the completion in 1873 of the Veracruz–Mexico City railroad added to Lerdo's prestige. He continued the trend towards a strong presidency.

Porfirio Díaz Ascendent, 1876–1884

Porfirio Díaz became president of Mexico in 1876. Mexico's new president was born in 1830, the son of a modest mestizo innkeeper and an Indian mother. The turmoil in the decades after his birth permitted social mobility. He followed the career path of his fellow Oaxacan Benito Juárez and began studying for the priesthood. Also like Juárez he later studied law at the Institute of Arts and Sciences in Oaxaca City.

Díaz practiced law briefly, but was forced into hiding in 1854 for opposing Santa Anna. He joined a group of Indians combating the dictator and proved to be a brilliant guerrilla fighter. In 1862 his reputation reached almost mythical proportions when as a young general he led a cavalry charge during the Battle of Puebla.

When President Lerdo de Tejada announced his intention to stand for re-election in 1876, Díaz responded with his Plan of Tuxtepec, which emphasized "No re-election." Díaz's manifesto claimed that Lerdo de Tejada had trampled on the constitutional rights of Mexican citizens. He claimed that by preventing Lerdo de Tejada from serving another term, he would spare Mexico another experience with prolonged one-man rule.

For symbolic reasons Díaz named his *plan* for the small Oaxaca town of Tuxtepec, even though his revolt began in Brownsville, Texas. Some Texas landowners and U.S. railroad tycoons, bankers, and holders of Mexican bonds who felt Díaz would pave the way for their future operations in Mexico openly supported him with arms and cash. Americans made up as many as half of the armed force that Díaz led into Mexico.

Díaz's ability to wage prolonged guerrilla warfare undermined the already bankrupt Lerdo de Tejada government, which was unable to obtain loans to purchase arms. Given the multiple centers of rebellion, Lerdo de Tejada's government could not suppress the revolt. As members of the provincial elite saw that he could not suppress the revolt, they began to jump on Díaz's bandwagon.

In November 1876, Lerdo de Tejada resigned, and Díaz assumed power as a hero of the popular resistance to the French intervention. The general, who enjoyed the support of various regionally based movements that had grown up in the power vacuum left by Maximilian, then called for elections to legitimize his rule. Díaz, who ran unopposed, was elected to serve the 1877–80 term. As president, he faced the challenge of establishing peace and stability in a nation plagued by poverty, illiteracy, social inequality, political turmoil, financial penury, and a woefully inadequate infrastructure—the same problems Juárez and Lerdo de Tejada had faced.

At the end of his term, Díaz abided by his "no re-election" pledge. However, he did promote a stand-in to succeed him in 1880. He showed his political savvy by choosing not a general who might build his own independent power base but General Manuel González, one of his least able protégés.

During González's term, the first rail line to the United States was completed, linking El Paso and Mexico City. Various trends emerged during his administration that would characterize Mexico for the rest of the century. The executive became increasingly important, eclipsing Congress. The press and political opponents came under increasing attack, and the economic elite's influence over the government increased. Finally foreign investment began to enter Mexico at an ever-increasing rate.

The Porfiriato, 1884–1900

> Himself a Mixtecan from Oaxaca who had risen through local and provincial office, both civil and military, Díaz had a profound understanding of how Mexico functioned at its most basic levels. Mexico City-based intellectual and political figures rarely understood this.
>
> (Brian Hamnett, 1999)

Díaz's re-election in 1884 allowed him to assume the presidency again. During his extended administration, known as the **Porfiriato**, Porfirio Díaz created a political apparatus over which he kept tight personal control. For decades the smooth functioning of this machine indicated his political genius. Díaz atomized power so no individual could challenge him. Power at the regional level was divided among governors, military commanders, and 300 district chiefs, known as *jefes políticos*. All owed their position to Díaz. The responsibility for maintaining order was divided between two separate bodies, the army, under the secretary of war, and the *rurales*, under the secretary of the interior. The *rurales* dated back to 1861 and were modeled on the Spanish Civil Guard.

The army received the latest European military technology, which made it prohibitively expensive for local warlords to challenge Díaz. The creation of a national rail network permitted Díaz to deploy troops to distant trouble spots and nip opposition in the bud. During the Porfiriato, the army provided the order necessary for economic development, and economic development provided the revenues necessary to keep the army loyal and well equipped.

Díaz let bygones be bygones. He accepted liberals, conservatives, and the clergy alike into his ruling coalition. These groups, along with military leaders, landowners, foreign investors, and positivist intellectuals, formed a coherent dominant class. Even Díaz's later rival Francisco Madero conceded that Díaz was "quite successful at eliminating old hatreds."

In 1887, near the end of his second term, Díaz ensured the passage of a constitutional amendment allowing a single consecutive re-election, thus paving his way for his election to the 1888–92 term. In 1890, with his position secure, he ensured that yet another amendment eliminated all restrictions on presidential re-election. During the Porfiriato, it was Díaz's will, not the constitution, that determined the course of political events.

In appearance the old federal structure was maintained. However, Díaz held all the reins of power. The courts simply responded to the dictates of the president, the governor, or the local *jefe político*. As the Porfiriato wore on, congressmen, whose positions were virtually assured for life, aged. After 1886 Congress became for all practical purposes a rubber stamp. Díaz approved congressional candidates before their election or re-election. As historian Alan Knight observed, "A large proportion of Porfirian governors—maybe 70%—were presidential favourites, imported into alien states, where their prime allegiance was to their president and maker, rather than to their provincial subjects."

Despite power being concentrated in the federal executive, as historian Michael Johns noted, "No other Latin American country combined the oppression of dictatorship with such an obsession for the appearance of legality and legitimacy." Election fraud became a way of life, a ritual to sanctify an incumbent, not a method of selecting a leader. Once this became accepted practice, it was hard for Mexico to shake it during the twentieth century.

Unlike earlier liberal presidents, Díaz had the financial wherewithal to reward large numbers of potential rivals. By the late nineteenth century, transport facilities and soaring world demand permitted massive raw material exports. Between 1876–77 and 1892–93, federal tax revenue rose from 17.2 million pesos to 38.6 million, vastly increasing Díaz's power. By 1894 the government began to run a budget surplus. Mexico was finally able to break out of the vicious cycle of weak government leading to chaos, leading to reduced revenue, leading to weak government.

A small group of advisors called *científicos* surrounded Díaz and formulated policy. They were so named because of their supposedly "scientific" management practices. Díaz and the *científicos* set policy for decades. They emphasized that wealth had to be created before it could be divided, thus rationalizing its concentration. The *científicos* argued that the country's problems could be solved by the application of statistics and rational thought. The very small number of *científicos* exercised enormous power due to their holding top government positions and thus controlling government economic policy. They had close dealings with major industrial and commercial firms and often were important businessmen in their own right.

By the end of the nineteenth century, positivism had replaced liberalism as the guiding philosophy of the Mexican political and economic elite. Auguste Comte (1798–1857), the French social philosopher who formulated positivist doctrine, believed that societies passed through three stages—the early primitive stage, then the metaphysical stage, and finally the scientific or positivist stage. The positivist stage was based on reason and empirically verifiable scientific knowledge. Comte considered the advanced nations of the nineteenth century were entering the positivist

Figure 9.2 *Few artists in history have matched José Guadalupe Posada's number of drawings or the range of subjects. The slogan below this drawing of Porfirio Díaz reads, "Something is rotten in the state of Denmark."*

Source: Reproduced courtesy of the Benson Latin American Collection, the University of Texas at Austin.

stage. In Mexico, positivism's greatest impact was in shaping the higher education curriculum. Positivist educators stressed science and mathematics, while downplaying the arts and social and religious studies.

By the turn of the century, Díaz had already ruled Mexico longer than anyone before, including Santa Anna. His lengthy tenure in office resulted from, above all, the overwhelming desire for peace. Writing in the 1890s, historian Justo Sierra commented: "The country's real desire, manifested everywhere, was peace . . . Seldom in history has there been a people with a more unanimous, more anguished, more determined aspiration."

Initially it appeared that Mexico could have both democracy and peace. Díaz pledged no re-election in 1876. Then in 1884 he was elected for a single additional term. By 1888 when it had become obvious that he intended to remain in the presidency, re-election seemed a small price to pay for peace and economic growth.

Rather than trying to oust Díaz or modify his policies, humble Mexicans shared a deep belief in Díaz's enormous power and often assumed that his personal will was all that was needed for their needs to be met. Supplicants wrote him letters, often accompanied by a photo, to ask for a favor or a job, just as they wrote viceroys in colonial times. Government employees sought back pay or promotions. Aging soldiers or their widows requested pensions. Impoverished students sought scholarships. Litigants sought his intervention to obtain favorable judicial rulings. Some wrote simply to reiterate their loyalty to him.

Porfirio Díaz Descendent, 1901–1911

The first decade of the twentieth century saw the decline of the Porfiriato. Until then a combination of economic growth and repression had prevented nationwide opposition to the dictator. However, after 1900 splits among the elite, economic recession, and jockeying for presidential succession undermined the Díaz regime.

As Díaz aged, those he had placed in high positions not only aged but acquired an air of permanence. By 1910, of Mexico's twenty-four governors, only one was under fifty, and sixteen were over sixty. The chief justice of the Supreme Court was eighty-three, and six of the ten justices were over seventy. Ignacio Mariscal had served as secretary of foreign relations since 1885, and José Yves Limantour had served as treasury secretary since 1893. Fresh blood was seldom infused into Díaz's inner circle. This extended tenure in office reflected the changed nature of the Díaz regime. It had shifted from reliance on regional strongmen and peasants who had fought alongside Díaz early in his career to reliance on a Mexico City-based entrepreneurial class and the foreign investors associated with it.

Newly affluent industrialists, merchants, professionals, and intellectuals, the product of economic growth, were excluded from political power, as were miners, industrial workers, and schoolteachers. The generation coming of political age at the turn of the century no longer viewed Díaz as the national hero who had saved Mexico from France, but as an aging tyrant clinging to power. Aspirations rose along with educational levels. As historian Roger Hansen noted, "The co-opted grew richer and older; the outsiders grew older and increasingly resentful."

In response to what he felt was ill-advised tolerance of Church activity, liberal Camilo Arriaga called for like-minded Mexicans to form liberal clubs. By the end of 1900 fifty such clubs had been founded in thirteen states. Members of liberal clubs formed part of the elite, as 68 percent of their members had professional training in law, engineering, or medicine, and another 16 percent were teachers.

The liberal clubs never assumed a prominent political role, in large part due to their focus on enforcing anti-clerical laws, long after popular concern had shifted to political democracy and economic issues. The rapid proliferation of the clubs reflected the degree to which modernization had broadened the set of political actors.

In February 1901 club members held a convention that drew fifty-six delegates—fifty-two men and four women—representing forty-nine clubs and four newspapers. The delegates founded the Mexican Liberal Party (PLM—Partido Liberal Mexicano). The PLM provided a forum for a variety of individuals, many of whom did not represent the elite. One of Díaz's strongest critics at the convention was Ricardo Flores Magón, who was born to Indian parents in Oaxaca. He soon became cut off from his Indian roots as his family sent him to Mexico City to receive the best possible education. At the convention he attacked the status quo and demanded justice, democracy, and freedom of speech and press. He described the Díaz administration as a "den of thieves." By the middle of the decade, he had became Díaz's foremost opponent.

Under the influence of younger, less affluent leaders, such as Flores Magón, the PLM soon became far more radical than the Juárez liberals ever had been. The party advocated forcing those who invested in Mexico to become Mexican citizens, ending presidential re-election, and land reform. It targeted industrial workers by demanding the eight-hour day, a minimum wage, equal pay for equal work, accident compensation, and other reforms workers themselves had been seeking. *Regeneración*, which Flores Magón founded, became the unofficial journal of the party. This paper dealt with such politically volatile issues as the administration of justice, freedom of the press, and labor conditions. Flores Magón was soon jailed for his criticism of the regime.

In 1904, Flores Magón was released after spending twenty-two months in jail. He went into voluntary exile in the United States, where he and a small group of followers resumed publication of *Regeneración*. Although the paper was banned in Mexico, 25,000 copies of each issue were smuggled in and circulated widely.

A number of factors limited the effectiveness of the PLM. As it became increasingly radical, affluent members who had financed the publication of *Regeneración* left the party. Mexicans associated with Díaz forced the closing of *Regeneración* by suing for libel in U.S. courts. PLM organizing, following more of a European intellectual tradition, relied heavily on the written word, which was effective with workers but almost totally bypassed the illiterate rural majority. Finally, the PLM call for a revolt in 1907 came during an economic boom. For many industrial workers and dissatisfied members of the middle class, economic opportunities diminished the oppressive burden of government policy.

In 1906, workers went on strike at the copper mines in Cananea, Sonora, twenty-three miles south of the Arizona border. The mines there had contributed to the rapid change characteristic of Mexico's northern border. As with so many Mexican mines, the Cananea mine was owned by an American, Colonel William Greene. As was the case with many foreign investors, Greene enjoyed a cozy relationship with local officials.

On June 1, 1906, rather than allowing the company to lay off miners and accept a shift from hourly wages to piece work, workers called a strike, demanding equal pay with Americans, access to American-held jobs, the eight-hour day, and the dismissal of an abusive foreman.

After fire hoses were turned on the strikers, generalized violence erupted, resulting in the death of half a dozen Americans and thirty Mexicans. Rafael Izábal, the governor of Sonora, called in 275 armed American volunteers from Arizona. The volunteers remained in Cananea for only a few hours, since the 2,000 Mexican troops and *rurales* who were sent to the area had no trouble restoring order.

The strike collapsed after General Luis Torres, who commanded the Mexican troops sent to the scene, gave striking workers an ultimatum—return to work or be drafted into the army to fight Yaqui Indians. Except for the dismissal of one foreman, none of the workers' demands were met. A number of strike leaders were sentenced to the notorious San Juan de Ulúa prison from which they only emerged after Díaz's fall.

The presence of armed American volunteers inflamed Mexican nationalism. Díaz's failure to take action against the governor who allowed armed Americans to enter Mexico indicated to the public that the aging dictator supported foreign investors, not Mexicans.

In January 1907 Díaz issued an arbitration decree that sought to end a textile workers' strike that protested new management-imposed work rules. Workers were scheduled to return to the mills on January 7. However, when the steam whistle summoned workers back to the Santa Rosa mill in Río Blanco, Veracruz, some workers refused to accept the arbitration decree. Soon several thousand workers gathered outside the mill. Stone throwing began, and a group of workers headed for the company store a block away. Employees inside the store panicked and fired on the unarmed workers, killing several and converting a hostile crowd into a raging mob that looted and burned the store. Troops were called in, and before calm returned between fifty and seventy workers were killed, including some taken prisoner and summarily executed.

Díaz's failure to resolve labor conflicts peacefully tarnished his image and weakened him politically as his regime later went into crisis. Negotiation and compromise, which had characterized the early decades of Díaz's administration, were conspicuously absent. The regime had apparently lost its ability to adapt.

The 1907 recession in the United States spread to Mexico, threatening banks and causing the finance minister to tighten loan requirements. Restricting credit lowered mine output, as did reduced demand in the United States. The effects of the crisis were most keenly felt in the north, which had the closest ties to the U.S. economy. The mills, mines, railroads, and cattle ranches of northern Mexico all began laying off workers. In 1907 a draught-induced crop failure resulted in soaring food prices. Resentment against Díaz increased as the *científicos* were held to blame for economic problems.

As Díaz prepared for the 1910 elections, he found his traditional supporters divided. Since Díaz obviously would not live forever, the question inevitably arose concerning the transition from one-man rule to the rule of law in a nation where only 22 percent of the population over age ten could read and write.

Díaz set the stage for the 1910 presidential elections by telling journalist James Creelman that he would not be a candidate. The interview containing this statement appeared in the March 1908 issue of *Pearson's Magazine* and was widely reproduced in Mexico.

Later Díaz let it be known, the Creelman interview notwithstanding, that he would be a candidate for the 1910–16, term. This produced a challenge from Francisco Madero, a member of one of the oldest aristocratic families in the north. As with so many elite families in the north, the Maderos were being challenged by foreign investors. Madero family interests included the largest Mexican-owned smelter, which competed directly with those of the Guggenheims—a U.S. family that owned mining and smelting interests around the world. The Madero family also invested in banking and agriculture.

Madero first achieved national prominence with the 1909 publication of his 321-page book *Presidential Succession in 1910*. The book criticized the lack of democracy in Mexico. Madero's repeated reference to the "government of the center" indicated his regional viewpoint. Finally, his quoting from Montesquieu and making repeated references to classical antiquity indicated his elite background.

Madero began campaigning for the presidential nomination. He organized something unheard of in Mexico—campaign tours across the country. These tours, financed with personal funds, drew large crowds of disenchanted industrial workers, intellectuals, schoolteachers, members of the middle class, and even *hacendados*.

As Madero toured the country, it became clear that he enjoyed widespread support. Many members of the urban middle class, who had seen their income decline due to the 1907 recession, joined his campaign. Support came from groups that had long felt shut out of power and opportunity. Students, seeing little future under the old regime, flocked to his cause. Industrial workers around the nation generally favored him. He sought labor support by visiting Orizaba, Veracruz, a textile-mill town where he pledged support for workers' freedom and their right to unionize. Madero was the first Mexican to awaken popular consciousness in thirty years.

Tolerance turned to repression as Madero's campaign gained momentum. Municipal officials denied him permission to hold rallies, and police broke up the crowds that did appear. Authorities warned newspapers not to give him coverage and closed them if they failed to heed the warning. By May numerous leaders of Madero's movement had been jailed or sent to military service in Quintana Roo. By June repression, which specifically targeted Madero's working class followers, had increased. That month, authorities arrested Madero himself, charging him with fomenting rebellion and insulting authorities.

Madero remained in a San Luis Potosí jail on election day, June 26, 1910. By the official count, Madero received the votes of only 221 electors nationwide. Díaz, credited with the votes of 18,829 electors, began his eighth term as president of Mexico. Once the elections were over, authorities released Madero from jail, assuming that he no longer posed a threat. Unwilling to give up the struggle against Díaz, Madero crossed the border into Texas and began to organize a movement to oust Díaz.

Mexican Society

Social Change

With the exception of the creole replacing the Spaniard at the top of the social order, as historian Francisco Pimentel observed in 1864, the colonial social order remained largely unchanged. He described the enormous social chasm separating creoles and the indigenous:

> One speaks Spanish and French; the other expresses himself in more than 100 distinct languages. The white is Catholic or indifferent; the Indian is idolatrous. The white is the owner; Indians are the workers. The white is rich; the Indian is poor and miserable. Descendents of Spaniards have at their finger tips modern knowledge and scientific discoveries, which Indians are unaware of. The whites' clothing, made of rich fabric, follows the latest Parisian fashions. The Indian goes about practically naked. The white lives in majestic urban homes; the Indian lives in isolated, rural huts. . . . There are two different peoples living in the same land, and what is worse, to a certain extent they are enemies.[1]

Tradition maintained a strong hold on Mexican society. More than 80 percent of the population was rural, working in agriculture outside the cash economy. They made little use of fossil fuel and produced few exports. In 1861, there were only 443 engineers and architects in the country, while there were 9,344 priests and 42,578 in the military.

Slowly tradition yielded to modernity. By the late 1890s, roughly 1 percent of the population formed the upper class, while the middle class encompassed 8 percent. The remainder included soldiers, miners, industrial workers, vendors, hacienda workers, sharecroppers, and beggars. By the dawn of the twentieth century, Mexico, rather than simply replicating mid-nineteenth-century society, albeit with more population and wealth, had produced a qualitatively different society.

As artisan production declined, and, as Church, Indian, and untitled lands (*baldío*) were transferred to private ownership, migration from rural areas to Mexico City and other urban areas increased. However, as late as 1900, 72 percent of Mexicans still lived in communities of fewer than 2,500, down from 92 percent a century earlier. That year, in addition to Mexico City, only four cities—Guadalajara, Puebla, Monterrey, and San Luis Potosí—had as many as 50,000 residents.

A number of factors caused newly created wealth to be highly concentrated. As Mexico entered the world market, fewer artisans produced for home or local use, while the wealth of factory owners and merchants increased. Population increase put downward pressure on wages, as did the expropriation of village land, which forced peasants into the labor market. New technology, while increasing productivity, displaced labor with machines.

Rather than trickling down to workers, wealth trickled upward. Historian Moramary López-Alonso, who studied the heights of individuals born between 1850 and 1890, illustrated the impact of concentrated wealth. Adult height is a good indicator of the amount of nutrition received, or in other words, the level of well being. As indicated by military induction records, the heights of those born after mid-century declined by as much as three centimetres. During this same period, the height of passport holders—the middle class and the elite—increased, indicating improved living standards for the few.

During the first decade of the twentieth century, economic conditions worsened. Between 1903 and 1910, the average cost of corn, beans, rice, wheat, sugar, and coffee rose by 20 percent. Between 1895 and 1907 agricultural wages declined by 17 percent.

In the north, after attacks by nomadic Indians ceased, the railroad facilitated the export of crops, cattle, and minerals. Population increase there surpassed that of Mexico as a whole. Between 1877 and 1910 the population of the border states increased by 227 percent. In 1910, 31.7 percent of the population of Coahuila had been born outside the state. The same individuals often moved from mine labor to agriculture to the railroad in search of employment.

In central Mexico, cities underwent the most conspicuous change. There electricity, street cars, paved streets, street lamps, the telephone, sewage treatment plants, the sewing machine, and drinking water systems resulted in urban life being qualitatively different from what it had been in the early nineteenth century. The telegraph vastly increased the speed and volume of long-distance communication between both businesses and private citizens. Mexico's newly created wealth was most prominently displayed in these urban areas.

While change swept into urban areas and the north, tradition continued to exercise a strong grip on rural central and southern Mexico. Most of those living in rural areas rarely saw a mine, a railroad, a foreigner, a Mexico City resident, or a politician.

During the later part of the nineteenth century, in most rural areas, the means of communication remained excruciatingly slow. Most people traveled only to nearby towns and markets and only rarely to state capitals. As historian Alan Knight observed, even as late as 1910 Mexico was "less a nation than a geographic expression, a mosaic of regions and communities, introverted and jealous, ethnically and physically fragmented, and lacking common national sentiments."

In 1910, while Mexico's elite enjoyed a lavish government-financed celebration of the centennial of Hidalgo's Cry of Dolores, much of village Mexico was still infused with traditional values and practices. Colorful pre-Hispanic markets, or *tianguis*, with their profusion of herbs, crafts, and foods, supplied villagers.

Eventually even small towns began to feel the winds of change. One of the first harbingers of change in rural areas was the increased use of basic consumer goods, which indicated that a substantial number of individuals were joining the money economy. The number of non-agricultural jobs increased. Traveling salesmen appeared in villages with increasing frequency, selling not only traditional goods but such technical innovations as Singer sewing machines. Postal service was established, and newspapers, phonographs, cameras, and factory-made goods made their appearance.

To a greater or lesser degree, all areas underwent transformation. The Reform era in the middle of the century brought into prominence a generation of mestizo and Indian leaders. Beginning in the last third of the nineteenth century, income generated by the export of coffee, sugar, and copper enabled those who benefited from this trade to import the goods needed to enter the European world of fashion. As an increasing percentage of the population was integrated into the national and international economy, caste identity was supplanted by class identity. Many ethnically distinct Indians were transformed into an ethnically indeterminate peasantry. At the dawn of the twentieth century, the railroad had eroded if not broken rural isolation, the printed word had become far more influential than before, thanks to an expanded educational system, and Mexicans had become more conscious of being Mexicans.

The Elite

Díaz wooed the upper classes with riches beyond the imagination of previous generations. Many Mexican members of the new elite bore foreign names, such as Creel, Limantour, and Braniff. Wealthy members of the French, American, British, and Spanish communities resident in Mexico also formed part of the elite.

Those enjoying Díaz's favor received public positions, which enabled them to increase their wealth. Control of state governments, or the favor of those who did exercise control, allowed the purchase of public lands and former Church and Indian lands at bargain prices. A privileged few received lucrative government contracts, tax exclusions, tariff exemptions, favorable judicial rulings, and concessions to exploit natural resources. Well-placed members of the upper class, including state governors, federal cabinet members, and Díaz's family members, received high salaries for serving on boards of directors of foreign corporations.

The Díaz administration sought to keep wages depressed, feeling that would attract foreign investors. Low wages permitted high profits. The company owning the Santa Rosa textile factory in Río Blanco paid 12 to 14 percent dividends between 1902 and 1907. Profits could be further increased by the use of forced labor. Olegario Medina, who had grown fabulously wealthy in the henequen business in Yucatán, used his position as minister of development to arrange for the deportation of Yaqui Indians, who were resisting the takeover of their lands, to work in the henequen fields of his home state.

Control of vast amounts of land formed one of the keys to elite wealth. The size of land holdings increased substantially during the late nineteenth century. Landowners used their already immense power to acquire land put on the market as a result of the Reforma. To further increase their holdings, they would seize the lands of peasant villages. After the defeat of the Yaqui Indians who had previously lived on the land, a single company, the Compañía Constructora Richardson, acquired 993,650 acres.

The Middle Class

Porfirian schools were more important in their production of middle-class talent for the post-revolutionary educational and cultural efforts than they were in transforming popular behavior and eradicating illiteracy.

(Mary Kay Vaughan, 2006)

During the Porfiriato, the middle class included physicians, lawyers, engineers, midwives, pharmacists, petty merchants, rancho owners, journalists, politicians, the lower clergy, and junior military officers. Government employees also joined the middle class in increasing numbers. Between 1876 and 1910, the government payroll increased by 900 percent.

The 1907 depression closed the gates for social mobility and undercut the middle class, whose members disproportionately lived in the hard-hit northern states. Foreign-owned corporations cut wages and jobs, and small merchants went out of business. Widespread bank failures occurred after growers failed to make mortgage payments. Unemployment, lower wages, and a sharp rise in the cost of living threatened to pull many down from middle class status.

The middle class resented its inability to gain access to public offices held by Díaz's cronies and to mid-level private-sector jobs held by foreigners. White-collar workers resented receiving wages only slightly above those of industrial workers. Modest middle-class incomes were heavily taxed, since the government kowtowed to the domestic oligarchy and foreign investors, leaving them virtually tax free. After 1907, the specter of downward mobility increased discontent. For these reasons, members of the middle class ultimately rebelled against the regime that had fathered them.

Workers

> No longer ignored, the men and women who made up Mexico's first generation of industrial workers demanded not only higher wages and better working conditions, but respect from their fellow citizens as well.
>
> (Rodney D. Anderson, 1976)

With some notable exceptions, during the Porfiriato, the government assumed a hands-off stance in labor disputes. In 1877 Interior (and later Treasury) Minister Trinidad García expressed this view, "The government should grant private enterprise complete freedom of action with respect to labor." Nonetheless, labor leaders, realizing that they could never match the economic power of industrialists, frequently demanded government regulation of labor relations in hopes of improving their bargaining position.

With a virtually inexhaustible labor supply, management felt little pressure to increase wages or even to keep them abreast of inflation. Wages for the unskilled plateaued just above subsistence. In 1893, a newspaper in the textile town of Orizaba, Veracruz, noted: "There is poverty, great poverty, and the struggle for a living is . . . painful (but not so for those who have capital). In addition to this, the cost of living increases daily, and labor is compensated disgracefully." The worst conditions existed in urban areas where workers were crowded together with no plumbing or safe water supply, amid filth and diseases.

In addition to low wages, labor had a number of grievances. In the 1890s, with the advent of electric lighting in mills, the fourteen-hour day became common and the sixteen-hour day was not unusual. Miners and textile workers were often paid in script only redeemable at the company store. Despotic treatment by supervisors, many of whom were foreign, produced widespread resentment. Workers' safety, especially in mines, emerged as an issue, since the lack of workers' compensation laws provided management with little incentive to invest in safety.

At least 250 strikes occurred during the Porfiriato. Workers in textile mills and cigarette factories—two groups with a long labor tradition—went out on strike most frequently. Miners and rail workers also used the strike to further their demands. Workers often went out on strike, not to demand increased wages, but to prevent wage cuts. Most of these strikes failed due to the workers' lack of strike funds.

By the turn of the century, labor militancy was increasing. As manufacturing shifted from artisan shop to factory, increasingly large numbers of workers were thrown together, thus facilitating a higher degree of working-class consciousness, much of which was tinged with nationalism—a response to the abuses of foreign owners. More workers were the children of other workers, not transplants from rural areas. These second-generation workers measured their lot in life not by comparing themselves with agricultural workers but by comparing their situation with that of the Porfirian elite. Mexican workers also protested that they were being discriminated against in their own country. As U.S. investment increased, especially in railroads and mining, Mexicans often found themselves working alongside U.S. workers. Almost invariably, the best jobs were reserved for Americans. U.S. workers also received substantially higher pay for doing the same work as Mexicans.

Until the end of the Porfiriato, the government officially maintained its hands-off attitude toward labor disputes. This attitude was justified by writer and presidential advisor Francisco Bulnes, who declared:

> The words "just remuneration" have no meaning in political economy. In political economy nothing is just or unjust as far as remuneration is concerned. Labor is a product, like any other, such as corn, wheat, flour, and is subject to the law of supply and demand.[2]

Official declarations notwithstanding, organized labor repeatedly suffered repression. Such oppression frequently occurred in the mining industry where workers were often concentrated in isolated areas, removed from the public view, and where mining companies were wont to share their wealth with local officials. One mine manager wrote:

> There is no objection to a man or any number of men striking, but the moment these began to interfere with other men taking their places, or the moment they began to destroy property, the Federal Government takes a hand, and the leaders will, in all probability, be shot without trial.[3]

During the Porfiriato, many first-generation workers maintained the rural tradition of short-term wage labor. Later as an increasing number of workers were the children of other workers, Mexican labor became more stable, and workers increasingly viewed themselves as full-time industrial workers, not as farmers sporadically working in industry to supplement their income. By 1910 the nearly 750,000 workers in modern industry, frustrated in their efforts at reform, came to favor Díaz's removal.

Rural Mexico

During the late nineteenth century, agricultural workers were linked to the land through a variety of arrangements. Some, known as *peones acasillados*, lived full time on haciendas. Others lived in villages that owned land that they could cultivate. A few villages retained enough land to support all their residents. More commonly villagers would work part time for wages on a nearby hacienda to earn cash, which allowed them to purchase what their village plot could not provide them. The landless formed the lowest rung of the rural social ladder. The number of landless rural laborers regularly exceeded the demand for their labor, leaving them with little bargaining power. These workers, known as *jornaleros*, frequently moved from region to region to find work. Increasingly, the landless migrated to the United States in search of work, and, after 1910, joined revolutionary armies.

Porfirian economic development did not produce a uniform transformation from communal landholding to wage labor. Peasants were most likely to lose their land in states such as Veracruz, Morelos, and Chiapas, where there was a rapid expansion of capitalist agriculture. While many villages lost land, 92 percent of the villages of Oaxaca retained communal lands in 1910. This was especially true in isolated regions that offered few marketing opportunities.

In areas where there were few dispossessed peasants, plantation owners sometimes resorted to forced labor. Muckraking investigative reporter John Kenneth Turner, who visited Oaxaca posing as a potential investor, exposed the forced labor system on Valle Nacional's tobacco plantations. He described the abuses he witnessed there in his book *Barbarous Mexico*. Workers would be attracted by false promises of high salaries, shanghaied off the streets of urban centers, or sent from jails.

Through their access to political leaders and their ability to summon armed force, *hacendados* exercised power that extended well beyond the market. They maintained close ties to the local priest, supported the hacienda school, meted out their own justice, and brought in the only merchandise available, which was supplied at the hacienda store. The hacienda set the pattern for rural wages and working conditions generally. The hacienda also formed the principal link between rural Mexico and the city.

As Díaz built a stable, solvent regime, his need for rural backing diminished, and the paternalism he had shown rural people faded. Throughout Mexico, the railroad provided distant markets for agricultural produce, thus providing an incentive for the appropriation of village land. After 1870 the growth of the market became a bigger threat to the village than liberal legislation. The seizure

225

of village land by sugar-producing *hacendados* in Morelos so they could meet increased market demand provides a classic example of this. Such a fragment of economic history would be long forgotten if it had not been for Emiliano Zapata, who rebelled in defense of these lands.

In Chihuahua, many lived in communities that had been established in the eighteenth century as a means of defending against Indian attack. By the end of the nineteenth century, the Chihuahuan elite no longer needed military colonies to defend against Indians. As a result, a 1905 law permitted wealthy ranchers, *hacendados*, and public officials to purchase the land of these villages, including house lots where people lived. This created bitter enemies who would bring down Díaz in 1911.

Rural Mexico, whose inhabitants were overwhelmingly illiterate, hungry, ill-housed, and marked for an early death due to disease, bore the brunt of the Porfirian economic development model. Rural people not only lost land but control of their community and social life.

As a result of increased corn prices, increased population, and more workers seeking wage labor after losing access to land, the purchasing power of agrarian wages declined 17 percent between 1895 and 1910. In that last year, peasants, more than 70 percent of Mexico's population, received only 3.3 percent of Mexico's national income.

The Indigenous Population

With the exception of using the military against Indians in northern border states, Mexico did not have a coherent Indian policy in the late nineteenth and early twentieth centuries. Liberals associated the white man with technology, a spirit of enterprise, good manners, and progress. They associated the Indian with lethargy and treachery. Policymakers felt that the Indians' extensive land holdings formed the patrimony of all Mexicans and resented Indian attempts to cling to their ancestral domains.

Some explanations for the income disparity between indigenous people and non-Indians were based on race. In 1910 papers presented at the Seventeenth Congress of Americanists meeting in Mexico City expressed the academic consensus that Indians were racially inferior, as indicated by bone measurement of their skulls. Writer Francisco Bulnes claimed that Indians' poverty resulted from a lack of energy-releasing nitrogen in their corn-based diet. Positivist Luis Mesa claimed the Indian suffered from the negative impact of the Church, and suggested the Indians' redemption lay not in more nitrogen but in less religion. Others, such as Justo Sierra, felt Indian poverty resulted from inadequate education. He stated that "given the equality of circumstance, of two groups of people, the one that is less educated is inferior."

Elite discourse centered on bringing the Indian into contemporary society. Historian and philologist Francisco Pimentel stated that Indians must "forget their customs and even their language." Mestizos and creoles felt assimilation would benefit not only the Indian but also the nation as a whole, since cultural homogenization would lead to true nationhood. As was the case with most liberals, Juárez himself believed that full citizenship for indigenous peasants could only be achieved by cultural assimilation, as he had shown with his own example.

Efforts at Indian education were generally limited to teaching Spanish. Expressed interest in Indian education remained largely intellectual rhetoric. While most Mexicans at least paid lip service to the desirability of educating Indians, others, such as Francisco Cosmes, editor of the positivist daily *La Libertad*, stated that Indians should not be subjected to compulsory education laws, since they were "impervious to all civilization." Cosmes also stated the state should not deprive Indian families of child labor in a futile effort to educate them.

Depriving villages of communal lands and the Indians' increased incorporation into the national market caused many Indians to lose their Indian identity and to be considered henceforth mestizos. As a result, after the middle of the nineteenth century, the Indian population began to decline. In 1877, 38 percent of Mexico's population spoke an Indian language, while, in 1910, only 13 percent did.

Mexico's indigenous people did not reject the varied forces of modernity outright, but negotiated, innovated, and adopted those that they felt would meet their needs. Growing coffee is an example of an innovation that Indians wholeheartedly embraced. Under Indian control, raising coffee became an important income source. As a result of this selective embrace of elements of alien cultures, the designation "Indian" did not automatically denote a poor peasant. In some areas, especially in Oaxaca, there were comfortable indigenous artisans and wealthy indigenous landowners.

Women

As a result of the 1857 constitution's remaining silent on gender-related issues, women remained disenfranchised. Given the tumult of the 1860s, only in 1870 did a national civil code define the status of women.

The 1870 Civil Code left most of the colonial practices concerning women intact. They remained excluded from politics and were punished for transgressions, such as adultery, according to a double standard. As historian Silvia Arrom observed, "The new codes often repeated ancient patriarchal provisions almost verbatim."

The 1870 legislation not only wrote into law the long-standing inferior social position of women but attempted to enforce a nuclear family prototype with a single line of inheritance. As historian Carmen Ramos-Escandón noted, "The liberal model for the family, one in which the family is formed solely by a monogamic couple and its children, was not prevalent in Porfirian Mexico, and legalized marriages were not the rule."

Canon law governed marriage until 1859, when the Law of Civil Matrimony became effective. The new legislation provided little change, even though the power to define marriage shifted from Rome to Mexico City. The law declared marriage to be a civil contract. However, it continued Catholic practice by declaring that neither party could remarry until the death of the other party in the marriage. This gave the contract the unique status of not being rescindable even though both of the parties to the contract might desire its rescission. The law included a passage, known as the Epistle of Melchor Ocampo, whose reading was required at all civil marriage ceremonies. It included the following passage: "The woman, whose principle sexual endowments are self-denial, beauty, comprehension, perspicacity, and tenderness, should and will obey the husband and provide pleasure, assistance, consolation, and counsel."

Laws such as the 1857 constitution, the 1859 law on matrimony, and the 1870 Civil Code lagged behind changing Mexican social reality. Though denied the vote, women repeatedly took part in political movements. More than 1,000 women signed a petition opposing the freedom of religion that the 1857 constitution provided for. In 1879 Carmen Huerta was elected president of the General Congress of Workers, a position to which she was reelected in 1880. In 1900 a number of women answered Arriaga's call to become active in liberal clubs. In Veracruz an all-women liberal club was formed with Concepción Valdés as president.

More women joined the labor force, since few urban male workers could support a family on one income and many single or widowed women sought employment. Increased migration from rural to urban areas undermined the traditional nuclear family. In Mexico City, 70 percent of births were to unmarried women. The low rate of marriage also reflected the high cost of a formal marriage and the slow acceptance of civil, as opposed to religious, marriage.

Women's educational opportunities expanded as their role in society evolved. As late as 1874, education remained not only a preserve of the elite, but of males, as only 22 percent of students were women. Only in 1892 did the Escuela Normal de Profesores in Nuevo León accept women. Between 1878 and 1907, the number of teachers' colleges increased from twelve to twenty-six. At the same time other professions were slowly opening to women. In 1886, the first woman dentist graduated, and in 1887, the first surgeon did.

Economic expansion greatly increased the need for education, and, as in the rest of the Western world, teaching became one of the first professions to open its doors to women. By 1910, 64.4 percent of teachers were women. Many middle-class women found jobs in the growing commercial sector and in government, working as clerks, secretaries, typists, and bookkeepers.

The number of women enumerated as a part of the formal labor force increased to 872,978 in 1900. Then with the economic downturn, the decreased cost of male labor removed the economic incentive to hire women who previously had been willing to work for even lower wages than men. As a result, the number of working women declined by 1910.

Women were almost entirely excluded from some areas of the economy, such as mining. However in the industry of transformation, which included textile and cigar factories, women comprised a third of the workforce. As women increasingly joined the industrial labor force, the idealized notion of a woman evolved from that of a frail, helpless person to one who should be allowed to work as long as her job did not interfere with her domestic duties.

While some women moved into new areas of employment in the professions and industry, many others continued to work in traditional occupations. The 1895 census found 190,413 women (and 82,887 men) working in domestic service. Indigenous women in urban areas, who were frequently separated from their families and cultures, often worked as domestics. They worked in an environment where they received little pay, toiled long hours, and were vulnerable to sexual abuse. Home sewing was another common form of female employment. Many other women worked as street vendors and tortilla makers.

The 1910 census indicated that women made up only 14 percent of the work force. This figure in part reflects employment practices in still largely rural Mexico. The low percentage of women reported to be in the labor force also indicates census takers' blindness to many economic activities undertaken by women but not generally included in employment statistics.

During the Porfiriato, Mexican feminists concentrated on eliminating the inferior status for women codified in the civil code and in expanding women's access to education. Even these rather tepid, by modern standards, demands put women on the defensive. In response to the charge that such changes would destroy the family, women noted that increased education would allow them to obtain better jobs and thus improve their families' living standard.

The changing role of women inevitably produced a backlash. In 1909, Horacio Barreda, whose father founded the National Preparatory School, declared that feminism, by preaching the equality of rights for men and women, "threatened to uproot the very foundation of the family and society."

Population

Between 1855 and 1875 Mexico's population only increased from 7.5 million to 8.4 million, or 0.6 percent a year, reflecting the toll taken by war and instability. Later population growth accelerated due to political peace, medical advances, improvements in sanitation, railroads moving grain during times of famine, and improved living conditions for some sectors of the population. Between 1875 and 1910, the population increased from 8.4 million to 15.1 million—an increase of 1.7 percent a year. This moderate population increase almost entirely resulted from the birth rate exceeding the death rate. During the first decade of the twentieth century, the birth rate was 46.3 per 1,000, while the death rate was 33.2 per thousand. In 1900, despite the government's having promoted European immigration for decades, 99.5 percent of Mexico's residents were native born.

Due to improved transportation and communication during the Porfiriato, Mexico City dominated Mexico as never before. In 1856, Mexico City's population was 185,000, or 2.4 percent of the national population. By 1910, it had risen to 471,066, or 3.1 percent of national population. The city's increased population resulted from in-migration. Between 1869 and 1886 there were 30,472 births in the city and 165,823 deaths. In the 1880s life expectancy in Mexico

City was 24.5 years, while in Paris it was 46.6 years. At the turn of the century, the newspaper *El País* referred to Mexico City's working-class neighborhoods as "centers of sickness and death."

The Church

Opinion became so polarized by the middle of the nineteenth century that Catholicism ceased to be the principal factor of national unity.

(Anne Staples, 1989)

Most of the drafters of the 1857 constitution were Catholics who wanted to end close Church–state ties. They felt that only by eliminating the Catholic Church as a political and economic force, though not as a religious one, could Mexico become a modern nation. Others thought the Church too prone to support abusive centralized power.

The Church responded as if the authors of the constitution belonged to a satanic cult, when in fact they had taken their oath to the constitution before a crucifix and the first line of the document mentioned God. The Church also condemned the 1857 religious toleration implied (but not explicitly stated) by the 1857 constitution.

The Church subsequently made what were, from a political point of view, two disastrous mistakes. Its rejection of the reform laws led to the War of Reform. Then the Church responded to the liberal victory in the War of Reform by promoting French intervention, hoping to regain from a Catholic prince what it had lost to Mexican liberals.

After Maximilian's defeat, the Church's standing plummeted, since it not only lost its material wealth but was stigmatized for having cast its lot with those whom the victorious liberals branded as reactionary enemies of the state.

Before the Church's wealth was nationalized, much of it had been used to support social services. Many of these assets were transferred to the landed classes, leaving the poor without hospitals, foundling homes, schools, and orphanages. In early independent Mexico, priests had been an integral part of public life. After the French intervention, priests, who were among the best educated in Mexico, were denied a political role.

During the Porfiriato, toleration and reconciliation between Church and state reflected Díaz's general policy of not letting old antagonisms needlessly interfere with current governance. By 1907, the Church was operating 586 primary schools. That same year, the old Palafox Seminary became a degree-granting Catholic university. The Church maintained loose links with more than twenty-three newspapers. By the end of the Porfiriato, the Church had again become a landowner, with lands and buildings registered in the names of intermediaries. Whenever Díaz dedicated a government project, a robed priest stood at his side to add his blessing. The number of clergy increased from 3,576 in 1895 to 4,533 in 1910. Díaz's approach to improved relations with the Church was typically Mexican: he did not repeal anti-clerical legislation— he simply did not enforce it.

While doctrinaire liberals continued to demand suppressing the Church as a reactionary body, within the Church a current developed in response to the social problems of emerging industrial societies. This current became known as the Catholic Social Action Movement. It originated during the last years of the nineteenth century and drew inspiration from Pope Leo XIII's 1891 encyclical *Rerum Novarum*, which called for Catholics to combat the evils of both "savage" capitalism and socialism. Rather than accepting either ideology, it proposed a third path based on small and medium-sized family properties.

As American influence increased and religious freedom was allowed by the 1857 constitution, Protestantism became a significant religious force in Mexico. Hundreds of American lay preachers took up residence in Mexico. By 1910 an estimated 700 Protestant congregations with roughly 70,000 members had been established. They were concentrated in major urban areas and in areas where economic transformation had been most profound, especially those areas associated with the railroad and mining. Protestants embraced not only different religious beliefs, but modernity, education, and the view that the world was an orderly place marching to progress. Díaz actively encouraged Protestantism since he felt it would break the Catholics' religious monopoly and that the presence of Protestant churches would make U.S. investors feel more welcome.

The Intellectual Scene

Following a brief press renaissance during the restored republic under Juárez, Díaz began to either punish or reward newspapers, depending on the coverage he received. A writer could be jailed and a newspaper closed for even the mildest criticism of his regime. Newspaperman Filomeno Mata was jailed thirty-four times.

Díaz's approach to the press was sometimes more subtle than merely jailing writers and raiding print shops. Papers providing favorable coverage, such as *El Universal*, received subsidies of as much as 70,000 pesos a year. Writers who praised the regime often received well-paying jobs. Eventually massive subsidies to pro-Díaz papers made financial survival for those not receiving subsidies difficult, if not impossible.

Journalists responded to the dictatorship in a variety of ways. Some, such as Filomena Mata, doggedly continued to criticize and be jailed. Some writers published under pseudonyms. The political cartoon flourished, since much could be alluded to in pictures that could not be explicitly stated.

Justo Sierra (1848–1912) was perhaps the Porfiriato's most influential man of letters. His prolific work included poetry, literature, essays, plays, and history. In typical Latin American fashion, he played a major role in government, serving as secretary of public instruction and fine arts. He believed virtually all people, including Indians, could be educated and that without effective, free, compulsory education, corruption and tyranny would prevail.

Sierra become something of an in-house historian for the Porfiriato and promoted the notion that liberalism was the equivalent of the Mexican nation and that conservatism and Catholicism had become discredited, dead-end branches of the Mexican family tree. The last sentence of Sierra's best known work, *The Political Evolution of the Mexican People*, indicates that he did not entirely buy into official dictum, "Mexican social evolution will have been wholly abortive and futile unless it attains the final goal: liberty."

Another important commentator was Andrés Molina Enríquez, who is best known for his *Los grandes problemas nacionales* (*The Great National Problems*), which was probably the second most important book of the Porfiriato (after Madero's *Presidential Succession in 1910*). In this book, he anticipated various post-revolutionary points of view. He viewed the Mexican mestizo as a new race, endowed with its own character and inner force. He noted that the low wages Mexican workers received would not create a vibrant domestic market and that the reliance on exports exposed Mexico to boom-and-bust cycles. He anticipated the land reform by calling for wide-spread government-mandated changes in Mexico's land ownership. Molina Enríquez even warned that the concentration of wealth, especially concentrated land ownership, could lead to violence if not remedied.

A few Mexican painters, such as José María Velasco (1840–1919), broke with convention and painted typically Mexican themes. Velasco, who specialized in magnificent landscapes of the Valley of Mexico, is considered to be Mexico's most important nineteenth-century artist. He left a strong artistic legacy and, as an instructor at the San Carlos Fine Arts Academy, taught Diego Rivera.

Mexican leaders had long paid lip service to education. However, only during the Porfiriato did mass education become a reality. Between 1878 and 1907, primary school enrollment increased from 141,178 to 657,843. In 1910, Mexico's 21,017 teachers outnumbered doctors, lawyers, and priests combined. Between 1878 and 1910, states increased their education spending from 10.52 percent of their budgets to 23.08 percent, making education the largest budget item. Outstanding students in rural areas received scholarships to be trained as teachers. As a result of the increased emphasis on education, by 1910 literacy increased to 37 percent.

Despite such increases, the educational effort fell far short of what was needed to sustain economic growth. In part this resulted from the government's having broken what it considered a "clerical monopoly" on education. After largely forcing the Church out of education, the government failed to fill the vacuum. The rural and urban poor had little opportunity to attend school at all. The educational opportunities that did exist were highly truncated. In 1910, the state of Puebla had 1,091 schools offering grades one to four, but only one offering grades five and six. The lack of funding remained as a permanent obstacle to expanding the school system.

JOSÉ GUADALUPE POSADA

Printmaker José Guadalupe Posada (1852–1913) was the son of a baker in Aguascalientes. Rather than formally studying graphic design, he apprenticed himself in a lithography shop at age sixteen. Posada later became one of the most prolific artists in history. His work appears as chapbook covers, cartoons, announcements, newspaper and magazine mastheads, and even cigar-box lids.

In 1888 Posada moved to Mexico City, well before advent of photography into printing. He began going door-to-door with his engraving block. On the spot he would produce an illustration on any subject a publisher was covering. He eventually established his own studio where he prepared illustrations for broadsheets and small papers.

His illustrations almost always were linked to text they were published with. His work frequently appeared alongside *corridos* (narrative ballads) which might describe a cockfight, a stabbing, or the merciful intervention of the Virgin of Guadalupe on behalf of a wronged peasant. Many *corridos* dealt with famous bandits of the day, who often ended up before Díaz's firing squads. Perhaps his most common theme was the suffering of common people.

His work forms a virtual illustrated encyclopedia of turn-of-the-century Mexico. He depicted the arrival of the electric train, the bicycle, the auto, and various women's fashions. He illustrated publications announcing such political events as the death of former President González and Francisco Madero's triumphant 1911 arrival in Mexico City.

One of Posada's trademarks was the *calavera* (skeleton) which served as a vehicle to depict either well-known individuals, recognizable by facial characteristics and accoutrements, or social classes, such as peasant or politician. His best known *calavera*, who appeared repeatedly, was the Calavera Catrina—an elegantly dressed lady. His use of the *calavera* builds on the Day of the Dead tradition of puppets, masks, and figures depicting skeletons and skulls.

Although the common people were a frequent theme, he never used them to express any political leanings. Unlike many twentieth-century artists, he never lent his work to further a political party or movement.

Although his prints appeared frequently in journals and on thousands of broadsides which were recognized throughout Mexico, as a person he lived a very modest, sedentary life. When he died, he was buried in a pauper's grave by his neighbors, only one of whom could sign his name.

The great mural painters Diego Rivera and José Clemente Orozco both credit Posada's art with inspiring them when they were children. This influence was acknowledged when Rivera included a robust portrayal of Posada and his Calavera Catrina in his famous mural *A Sunday's Afternoon's Dream in Alameda Park*.

Posada was unappreciated by the artistic community during his lifetime, was little collected, and never had a show. After the Revolution, as Mexican muralists stimulated interest in the country's art, Posada became the subject of academic study and numerous books were published on his life and art. He finally got his shows, including one at the U.S. Library of Congress.

Educational spending strongly favored the already educated. In 1900, the government spent twenty centavos per primary school student, 105 pesos per secondary student, and 126 pesos for each person enrolled in higher education. Such spending provided a sizable government subsidy for the few who could afford to remain in school for an extended period.

While teachers outnumbered other professionals, their status and wages lagged behind considerably. Teachers' wages barely exceeded those of factory workers and hacienda day-laborers. Not surprisingly, scores of teachers became leaders in the Revolution, including future presidents Álvaro Obregón and Plutarco Elías Calles, as well as Otilio Montaño, who helped Emiliano Zapata draft the Plan de Ayala in 1911.

PLUNGING INTO THE INTERNATIONAL MARKET, 1856–1909

> Where the Bourbon boom depended upon Spanish demand for bullion, coupled with Mexican demographic growth, the Porfirian boom derived from the far more potent stimuli of a global—though primarily North American—industrial economy, richly endowed with capital and technology and greedy for industrial raw materials and consumer goods.
>
> (Alan Knight, 1998)

Breaking with the Past

The victory over Maximilian did not automatically lead to economic development as the liberals had hoped. Mexican society remained very traditional, with 61 percent of its workers employed in agriculture and mining. Some 64,000 artisans dominated manufacturing. Church wealth, which liberals had hoped would provide a stimulus to the economy once it was transferred to private hands, had been largely dissipated by war.

Juárez felt economic development would create a strong state that could defend Mexican interests. Given the lack of local capital to spur development, his administration sought foreign investment. That led to a conundrum—how to attract foreign capital without inviting the foreign intervention that development was designed to prevent.

Throughout Latin America, the elite shared the view that economic development would occur by Latin American nations': 1) exporting commodities, 2) receiving foreign investment, and 3) attracting European immigrants. Before 1880, the Mexican government did not assume an active role in the development process due to the general feeling that development would be almost spontaneous. Even if it had desired to do so, the government's meager budget would not have allowed it to play an active economic role.

Díaz pulled Mexico out of a self-replicating cycle of violence, predation, and zero growth by granting special privileges to certain businessmen. These special privileges, such as protecting bankers from competition and establishing high tariffs on imports competing with Mexican producers, allowed the operations of certain individuals to be so profitable that they assumed the risk of investing in Mexico. Díaz ensured that the property rights of those enjoying his favor were respected. As these privileged individuals prospered, they provided financial and political support for Díaz, enabling him to defeat or buy off his rivals.

After 1880, the Mexican economy began sustained economic growth. U.S. investment began flowing into Mexico, in part due to an effective public relations campaign undertaken by the Mexican government. Increased mining activity became economically feasible due to the construction of railroads to haul ore and metal to foreign markets. These foreign markets were especially buoyant, because the demand for raw materials was soaring as the North Atlantic nations were undergoing rapid industrialization.

Technological change played a major role in the post-1880 economic expansion. Steamships facilitated the export of raw materials and the import of machinery. By 1888 the American-organized Mexican Telegraph Company had installed more than 19,200 miles of telegraph line. Later in the Porfiriato, the introduction of electricity revolutionized the mining and textile industries. Electricity also allowed for streetcars, which made large cities workable. By 1905, Mexico City's 190-mile long streetcar system had an annual ridership of 48,000,000.

After 1880 the government began to play a more active role in promoting development. Under the González administration (1880–84), for the first time the budget of a government agency—the Department of Development (*Fomento*)—exceeded the budget of the War Department. Legislative changes encouraged investment. The 1884 commercial code paved the way for joint-stock companies (*sociedades anónimas*). This legislation limited investors' liability to the amount invested in the corporation. Until that time, an investor's entire assets were liable in case of corporate loss or damage claims. By 1900 some twenty-five large joint-stock companies operated in the tobacco, textile, brewing, and metallurgy sectors.

The formation of the Banco Nacional de México (Banamex) in 1884 provided the government with access to funds, including money to subsidize the construction of railroads. To induce it to lend to the government, Banamex was allowed to manage the mint and collect customs and excise taxes. The government protected Banamex by not granting charters to rival banks and allowing it to avoid taxes and reserve requirements imposed on other banks. Only two banks—one of which was Banamex—were allowed to branch freely across state lines. These privileges made it well worth Banamex lending to the government. The bank averaged 30.5 percent profits on equity between 1885 and 1898.

After returning to power in 1884, Díaz established a solid reputation as a friend and protector of investors, and by the dawn of the twentieth century that image provided a strong inducement for investment. To maintain his investment-friendly image, Díaz offered investors low taxes, liberal concessions, cheap labor, police protection, predictably pro-business judicial rulings, and laws adjusted to the international legal order of the developed countries. In 1895 American mine operator Alexander Shepherd proclaimed Díaz to be the greatest man in North America because he had made property "twenty times safer in Mexico than it is in the United States."

Banks played a major role in economic development by providing long-term, low-interest financing for cotton-textile factories, metallurgical firms, and railroad companies. Their issuance of banknotes freed commerce from its old bugaboo of lacking a medium of exchange. Between 1882 and 1897, the amount of paper money in circulation increased by 21.5 percent a year.

The 1907 recession notwithstanding, the elite expressed satisfaction with the course of Mexican development. Mexico was enjoying low-cost credit as Treasury Secretary José Limantour had balanced the budget and renegotiated Mexico's foreign debt. Also under Limantour, the *alcabala*, a form of internal tariff, was abolished, facilitating the creation of a national market. Foreign investment increased from $200 million at the beginning of the Porfiriato to between $1.5 billion and $2 billion at its end:

In sharp contrast to the period before 1870, during the Porfiriato Mexican economic growth exceeded that of the United States. In 1870, Mexican gross domestic product (GDP) per capita was 27.6 percent of that of the United States. By 1910, it had risen to 34.1 percent.

Railroads

> Railroad construction did not take off until the Porfirian state seized the initiative by providing hefty subventions to encourage British and U.S. investment and by promoting the development of the North.
>
> (Allen Wells, 2000)

During the nineteenth century, the railroad occupied the same position that steel plants would occupy in the twentieth—it symbolized a better tomorrow. Rail fever swept over Mexico. In 1881, the *Diario Oficial* noted that it "was indeed with the greatest of enthusiasm that, in all sections of the country, the building of the railroads is being prosecuted."

The Mexican private sector proved incapable of carrying out railroad construction. Between 1860 and 1880 eleven concessions were awarded to private Mexican interests to build railroads. Only one, in Hidalgo, was completed. Despite attempts to raise money through such novel means as a lottery, the capital and managerial requirements of rail construction overwhelmed Mexican builders, private and public.

By the end of Díaz's first term, it had become apparent that if Mexico was to have railroads within the near future, foreign interests would build them. The government attracted foreign rail companies by offering subsidies that ultimately paid a quarter to a third of construction costs. In addition to cash subsidies, rail builders were promised bonds, generous land grants, and certificates that could be used to pay customs duties.

Since Mexicans could not finance rail building and Europeans were reluctant to invest in Mexico, the United States supplied 80 percent of the capital used to build Mexico's major railroads. By 1883, the Central Railroad Company was employing 22,000 workers in rail construction. Employing such large numbers of workers on projects before they began to yield revenue required access to vast financial resources. The amount required exceeded the resources of individual U.S. companies. The Central Railroad and the National, which received the concession to link Mexico City and Laredo, Texas, sold shares on the Boston and New York exchanges to raise capital. When funds raised there proved insufficient, they turned to the London exchange.

Once the decision had been made to allow foreigners a dominant role in rail construction, rail mileage soared. When Díaz first took office, Mexico had only 416 miles of track. In 1884, Mexico City was connected with El Paso, Texas, amid predictions that the new line would stimulate the Mexican economy and open new markets for U.S. products. By 1910 rail mileage had reached 11,954 as political stability and generous government subsidies attracted foreign capital and innovations in metal production (such as the Bessemer process) reduced the cost of steel.

Between 1878 and 1910, the railroad produced a dramatic decrease in freight costs. Thanks to the railroad, the cost of shipping a ton of cotton goods from Mexico City to Querétaro declined from $61 to $3 between 1877 and 1910.

Only with the coming of the railroad did Mexico regain the degree of economic integration that it had enjoyed in 1800. Although railroads were largely foreign-built, they did link most inhabited regions, crossed the best agricultural districts, and reached the richest mineral deposits. The railroad's linking of different areas not only allowed shipment of agricultural surplus from one area to another but also created a synergistic effect. New firms created new demand and new products. To supply railroad builders, Monterrey's steel mills produced rails. In northern Mexico, coal mines supplied locomotive fuel, and ranches expanded so they could supply the U.S. market. As a result, between 1883 and 1911, rail freight increased at an average annual rate of more than 10 percent.

Small farmers and artisans often suffered as the railroad led to ruinous competition with large-scale producers. Preferential shipping rates for exporters and high-volume shippers put the small producer at an even greater disadvantage. In the 1880s and 1890s, as marketing opportunities provided by the railroad led to an increase in cash crops, many subsistence farmers were forced off the land they had occupied. Some cities and regions lost out as trade patterns changed. Guaymas

Table 9.1 *Miles of railroad in Mexico, 1870–1910*

Year	Number of miles
1870	259
1880	666
1890	5,917
1900	8,441
1910	11,954

Source: William R. Summerhill (2006) "The Development of Infrastructure," in *The Cambridge Economic History of Latin America*, vol. 2: *The Long Twentieth Century*, ed. Victor Bulmer-Thomas, John Coatsworth and Roberto Cortes-Conde. Cambridge: Cambridge University Press, p. 302, Table 8.1

Figure 9.3 *The railroad not only transformed the Mexican economy, but provided the average Mexican with unprecedented mobility. Depicted here are rail passengers at Amemeca.*

Source: Photo by Summer Matteson, reproduced courtesy of the Science Museum of Minnesota, photo #A 84: 16: 29.

was displaced as the main supplier of imports to Sonora after rail lines connected the state to the United States via Nogales. In the 1870s, Tampico suffered economic collapse due to competition provided by the opening of the Veracruz–Mexico City line. In 1890, the city enjoyed an economic revival after rail service was established. This allowed the transshipment of European coal to foundries in Aguascalientes, San Luis Potosí, and Monterrey.

Railroads consumed enormous amounts of wood for station construction, ties, bridges, posts, and fuel. An 1880 circular published by the Secretariat of Development reported that forest destruction had caused erosion, climate change, air pollution, increased flooding, the drying up of springs, and the loss of agricultural land.

Foreign Trade

> Too often the expansion of the export sector was achieved on the back of the rural poor, at the expense of traditional landholding arrangements, and was dominated by foreign capital. The social dislocations and resentment were severe and widespread.
>
> (Edward Beatty, 2000)

Several factors contributed to the dramatic increase in Mexico's foreign trade during the Porfiriato. The booming North Atlantic economies drew in raw materials to manufacture a wide range of new goods, including electrical machinery, chemical dyes, and vehicles with internal combustion engines. The demand for raw materials continued to increase as the rising population of the industrialized nations led to ever increasing consumption.

Mexican exports increased as transport improved. Between 1815 and 1900 freight rates for shipping commodities across the Atlantic declined almost 95 percent due to innovations such as the screw propeller, the compound engine, steel hulls, larger ship size, and shorter turn-around time in port. The port of Veracruz was modernized to facilitate trade with Europe, thus offsetting U.S. influence, which was increasing as a result of the railroad.

The mines of northern Mexico exported to the United States by rail. Products such as coffee and vanilla from southeastern Mexico were distributed to U.S. and European buyers. Although exports were more varied than in colonial times, precious metals continued to dominate. In 1913, 75.2 percent of Mexican exports went to the United States, followed by the United Kingdom, which absorbed 13.5 percent.

Increased exports generated revenue that was shared by merchants, bankers, landowners, the urban middle class, and especially, the government. Export revenue partially financed rail construction and increased the capacity of the government, allowing it to promote industrialization.

International, national, and regional elites concurred in orienting Mexico's economy towards the export of minerals and agricultural raw materials. The assumption prevailed that in some ill-defined fashion export growth would enhance productivity and lead to structural change throughout the economy. Little consideration was given to just how the rest of the economy would be transformed, even though the domestic sector produced far more and employed far more people than the export sector.

Government officials favored exports since export taxes on silver, gold, and copper formed an important element of public finance. Revenue earned by exports allowed the purchase of imports, which then could be subjected to a tariff, providing another politically acceptable source of government revenue. At the turn of the century, customs revenue provided 44 percent of government income.

Mexico experienced positive trade balances every year from 1892 to 1910. In the heyday of Mexico's export growth—1890 to 1912—Mexico's exports increased at an annual rate of 5.2 percent. During the Porfiriato, foreign trade played an ever increasing role in Mexican development. In 1860, the sum of exports and imports equaled only 9.8 percent of GDP. This figure increased to 30.5 percent by 1910.

Mining

After the War of Reform and the French intervention, mines were again flooded, labor had dispersed, and investors were lacking. As late as 1884 mining remained at a virtual standstill. American companies were working only forty mining concessions. The British had become so disillusioned that they had largely withdrawn from mining.

By 1904, miners were working 13,696 active concessions that covered 552,534 acres. Silver exports, a third of all exports, increased from 607,000 kilograms in 1877–78 to 2.3 million in 1910–11. In 1911 Mexican mines produced 32 percent of the world's silver, 11 percent of its lead, and 7 percent of its copper.

This boom in mining combined all the elements that led to rapid economic growth in other sectors. Before 1884 all mineral wealth belonged to the nation. Those wishing to begin mining were required to obtain government permission. Government control over minerals represented a continuation of the colonial tradition.

The Mining Law of 1884 allowed private ownership of subsoil mineral and oil deposits—ownership rights that were separate from those of the surface owner. An 1892 law allowed miners to claim as much land as they could pay taxes on and to open or close mines as they saw fit. As a result of these laws, which followed the U.S. model, not only was the right to exploit mineral wealth granted to private individuals but it could also be sold on the open market independently of the ownership of the surface property.

British investors returned to Mexico, drawn by this legislation, as well as political stability and favorable publicity in England. Americans invested even more, especially in the north. By 1902, Sonora had become Mexico's most prosperous state and received more U.S. mining investment— $27.8 million—than any other state. By 1910, U.S. mine investment totaled $200 million, while the British had $50 million invested.

The introduction of electricity into the mines produced huge savings in hoisting, drilling, and illumination. Electricity permitted the use of winches, hoists, electric locomotives, and pneumatic drills. As historian Marvin Bernstein noted, "Peons no longer had to carry 200-pound loads up ladders in suffocating temperatures; hoists did the lifting and ventilating fans could make the mines more liveable."

The use of cyanide revolutionized the refining of silver ore. To extract the silver, ore was crushed to a powder and then mixed with water and cyanide. The silver bonded with the cyanide. Then zinc was added to the mixture, causing the silver to precipitate out. The use of cyanide permitted the recovery of as much as 92 percent of the silver contained in the ore, compared to 60 percent with the patio process. It also made it economically feasible to mine ores with a lower silver content and to rework previously accumulated mine tailings that still contained substantial amounts of silver. This new refining technique, which almost entirely replaced the patio process, reduced costs and processing time.

Although cyanide did not last long in the environment, its short-term impact could be disastrous. Mining journals frequently discussed cyanide poisoning of miners. The American-owned El Rey del Oro Mining Company discharged waste near the town of Mulatos, Sonora, causing the death of cattle that drank the water. The village mayor filed a complaint with the superintendent of the mine. When the superintendent failed to respond to the complaint, the mayor ordered the company to either shut down or build a pipeline so the poison would at least be discharged downstream from the town. In response, the mine owners visited Sonora's governor, who overruled the mayor and allowed the mine to continue operating and discharging waste in the same way as before.

In 1910, mining produced 8.4 percent of the GDP, roughly what it had produced at the end of the colonial period. At its peak, the industry employed 126,900 miners.

Increased mining led to increased deforestation. In 1865, a member of the scientific commission of Pachuca, Hidalgo, commented that "the axe of the woodcutter has become a terrible enemy of these forests." He noted that the Real del Monte Mining Company caused the most deforestation and that, as a result, springs were drying up. Later the mining boom in Sonora produced wholesale deforestation, which led to desertification. Sonoran mining also left the countryside dotted with mountains of mine waste and allowed the toxic chemicals used to process ores to seep into aquifers.

Industrialization

> Before 1870 markets were still too small, the energy supply too unreliable, and transport costs too high to permit more than a handful of large-scale factories to be built to serve the home market.
>
> (Victor Bulmer-Thomas, 1994)

In 1862 there were more than 20,000 artisan shops in Mexico, while only 207 factories operated. Toward the end of the nineteenth century, artisan production began to decline as railroads brought inexpensive imports into the Mexican interior and Mexican factories began production. Few artisan shops evolved into modern factories since their owners lacked access to capital, had little political clout to influence public policy, and often relied on a very limited supply of family labor.

In the 1880s, tariffs were repeatedly reduced on certain raw materials, while duties were increased on such products as textiles, beer, cement, and iron and steel to encourage their

Figure 9.4 *During the Porfiriato the working class emerged as an important element in society. As this photograph of a cigarette factory indicates, many workers were women.*

Source: Reproduced courtesy of the Benson Latin American Collection, the University of Texas at Austin.

production in Mexico. Several other factors favored industrialization. Displaced artisans and agricultural laborers provided an abundant supply of inexpensive labor. Railroads allowed factory-produced goods to be distributed nationwide. As the value of the silver-based Mexican peso declined relative to the gold-based North Atlantic currencies, imports cost more, thus encouraging domestic production. Finally, between 1877 and 1900, industry benefited from the introduction of new manufacturing technology and steam and hydroelectric power.

Between 1895 and 1910, manufacturing increased by 106 percent. During that period, the number of industrial workers only increased from 45,806 to 58,838, indicating an increase in productivity associated with new technology. Consumer-oriented industries produced textiles, beverages, clothing, paper, soap, footwear, and food and tobacco products. Factories produced cement, bricks, paints, chemicals, and iron and steel for use in extractive and manufacturing processes.

Mexican textile factories, which employed 32,147 workers in 1910, were the largest modern enterprises in Mexico. Rail transport made larger mills profitable, and electrically powered looms and spindles replaced water powered ones. French investors, who supplied almost 80 percent of the capital in the industry, facilitated this expansion. The expansion of the textile industry did not lead to increased employment since the number of handloom weavers declined from 41,000 to 12,000 between 1895 and 1910.

The textile industry produced inexpensive cotton cloth for Mexico's expanding work force, successfully combining foreign capital, transport, and imported technology. In 1901 it transformed 43,040 tons of cotton into cloth, up from 5,842 tons in 1854. In 1899, 32 percent of the textile products consumed in Mexico were imported, while in 1911, only 3 percent were imported.

Mexico's lack of energy sources hampered industrialization. Domestic coal and hydropower only partly met industrial energy needs. Some coal was imported. At the very time energy needs were increasing, the supply of wood, the traditional fuel source, was becoming exhausted. It became increasingly costly to bring in wood from ever-greater distances as nearby supplies were exhausted. As historian Fernando Rosenzweig noted: "Deforestation occurred around the large cities where demand was greatest and along the principal transport routes."

By 1910, Mexico's manufacturing base contributed 10 to 12 percent of the national economy and employed roughly 10 percent of the labor force. Between 1876 and 1911, as more items were produced locally, consumer goods fell from 75 percent of Mexico's import bill to 43 percent. In 1910 Mexican manufacturing produced $713 (in 1970 U.S. dollars) per worker, far above the production of agricultural workers. When the Revolution broke out, Mexico was well ahead of other Latin American nations in developing its paper, cigarette, glass bottle, and basic chemical industries.

Despite its impressive gains, Porfirian industry failed to achieve the synergy found in the industrialized nations. Typically, almost everything in a factory was imported. For example a new textile factory would incorporate imported construction materials, spindles, and looms.

Low demand presented the single biggest obstacle to industrialization. Peasants' low income largely excluded them from the cash economy. The oversupply of industrial labor and its repression eliminated upward pressure on wages. For individual industrialists, this meant higher profits. However, for the nation as a whole it limited further industrialization. Despite Adam Smith's notion of the invisible guiding hand, as historian Alan Knight noted, "Individual profit will not redound to collective development."

Agriculture

The agricultural sector was divided between those who produced primarily for their own consumption, that is, the subsistence sector, and those who produced for sale. Commercial agriculture increased in importance during the Porfiriato as the railroad opened the way to distant markets and exports. The subsistence sector was closely associated with the small farmer, while commercial agriculture was closely associated with the roughly 7,000 *hacendados* in Mexico. Some 50,000 *rancheros*, who worked, but did not necessarily own, properties in the 100 to 1,000 hectare range (247 to 2,470 acres), formed a middle stratum.

A variety of factors led to the increased concentration of land ownership during the Porfiriato. The railroad increased marketing opportunities and provided incentive to displace peasants. Lands that in the past had been set aside to attract colonists to fight Indians were no longer needed for that purpose. Díaz's advisors believed that large landowners, particularly those who engaged in commercial agriculture, were more efficient and productive custodians of land than Indian villagers and peasants. They reasoned that for nature to be transformed and for the economy to be developed, both the land and the labor of the peasant had to be placed on the market.

The actual mechanism for transfer of property to large landowners varied. Sometimes property was simply purchased. In other cases, individual landowners illegally appropriated land. The government intervened to remove the Yaqui and open the way for commercial agriculture in Sonora. Sociologist Andrés Molina Enríquez noted that some *hacendados* simply litigated spurious claims until the legitimate, but financially strapped, owner was overwhelmed.

Laws passed in 1883 and 1894 allowed privately owned surveying companies (*compañías deslindadoras*) to identify unclaimed lands, survey them at their own expense, and then turn two-thirds of the land surveyed over to the national government. To compensate the surveying companies for their efforts, the remaining third would become company property, which was usually sold. The government felt that the surveying process would: 1) promote growth by attracting capital once titles were regularized; 2) raise money for the government, which could auction the two-thirds of surveyed land it received title to and later collect taxes on all the land surveyed; 3) attract European immigrants who could be lured by secure land titles; and 4) attract Mexicans to border areas by offering land with clear titles.

During the Porfiriato, the surveying companies received 52 million acres of land in compensation, that is, 10.7 percent of Mexico's territory. This implies that 157 million acres, 32 percent of Mexico's territory, were surveyed under the program.

The transfer of this surveyed land to private individuals represented a tremendous concentration of wealth, and, as was desired, served to create a modern capitalist economy. Without secure titles, no one would invest in natural resources or agriculture.

As an institution, the hacienda rebounded from its post-independence slump due to: 1) political stability; 2) the markets offered by mines and cities; 3) railroads to move crops and cattle; 4) access to bank credit; and 5) access to land provided by reform laws and surveying companies. Generally *hacendados*, or their administrators, quickly adjusted to new markets offered by the railroad and brought in machinery on the same railroad tracks that carried away their crops.

Hacienda agriculture differed from U.S. agriculture, which faced a labor shortage. In the United States, farmers made massive investment in labor-saving technology. This resulted in the United States becoming a world leader in the design and production of farm machinery and provided a stimulus to the U.S. capital goods industry. In Mexico, the solution to agricultural labor shortages in areas such as Valle Nacional was not to introduce better technology but to coerce labor.

During the first decade of the twentieth century, agricultural exports totaled more than a third of export value, which was amazing considering the resurgence of mining. This agricultural boom was closely associated with the railroad. Before the building of the railroad, *hacendados* lobbied to have a rail line built near their land and subsequently they lobbied the government to mandate lower freight rates for their produce.

At the beginning of the Porfiriato, Mexico was still relying on such agricultural exports as vanilla and tobacco. This changed as the railroad opened new marketing opportunities. Between 1891–92 and 1901–02, cattle exports increased by 493 percent, rubber by 95 percent, and beans by 127 percent. Growers in Mexico's Pacific Northwest appropriated Indian lands and constructed irrigation works, allowing them to use the railroad to supply U.S. markets with sugar and fresh vegetables.

Unlike mining and manufacturing, technological change did not revolutionize agricultural production. It did, however, influence the demand for Mexico's agricultural exports. The discovery of aniline dyes in 1856 eliminated the demand for cochineal dye. As a result of the development of the mechanical reaper/binder in the United States, Yucatán began exporting **henequen**, a fiber obtained from an agave, a cactus-like plant. Binders used twine made from twisted henequen fibers. Between 1900 and 1910, as a result of cheap labor and a booming international market, profits on henequen investments ranged between 50 and 600 percent. U.S. and Canadian binders consumed an average of 235,000 tons of twine a year between 1900 and 1930.

As with most agricultural commodities, henequen came at a steep price. Growers used state power to break down communal village land ownership and coerce the Maya to produce the fiber, which permitted the use of labor-saving reaper/binders in Canada and the U.S. Midwest. To limit their mobility, henequen workers were encouraged to take on debt. England's Anti-Slavery and Aborigines Protection Society reported that henequen workers toiled "in a bondage at once as cruel and hopeless as almost any form of slavery within knowledge of the society."

Henequen cultivation shifted 9,000 square miles from more biologically diverse cattle and corn-raising to mono-crop plantations. The steam-powered machines used to extract the fiber from

PULQUE

Archeological evidence indicates that Mexicans have been producing pulque for roughly 2,000 years. This beverage, made from fermenting the sap of a cactus-like plant known as **maguey**, was so much a part of Aztec life that they had distinct words for sweet pulque, spoiled pulque, high-alcohol pulque, and so on. As with much else in the Aztec life, a special deity Tepoztecatl was dedicated to pulque. One can still visit the god's temple, perched high on a hill overlooking Tepotzlán, Morelos. While pulque was an accepted part of Aztec life, strict laws prohibited its abuse.

The widespread consumption of pulque continued through the colonial period. Not only did people enjoy drinking it, but colonial authorities found it to be a good source of tax revenue. Others found they could profit handsomely from producing and selling pulque.

Colonial political and religious authorities attempted to limit the consumption of pulque, citing "the continual inclination of Indians for the vice of drunkenness." Pope Pius V even weighed in on the issue, ordering bishops to "avoid drunkenness to which the generally lazy Indians are inclined."

Various observers, including Sahagún, Clavijero, Humboldt, and Calderón de la Barca, commented extensively on pulque, indicating how important it has been. Calderón de la Barca noted its continued economic importance, "The maguey is a source of unfailing profit, the consumption of pulque being enormous, so that many of the richest families in the capital owe their fortune entirely to the produce of their magueys."

The railroad revolutionized pulque production, since it allowed the rapid transfer of pulque barrels to Mexico City and other points. Entire haciendas were dedicated to maguey cultivation. Production was so lucrative that owners of the estates producing pulque were referred to as the pulque aristocracy. Per capita consumption of pulque doubled during the Porfiriato. An estimated 2,000 pulque bars, or *pulquerías*, operated in Mexico City alone. Authorities proclaimed pulque to be sinful and harmful and to interfere with production since workers often missed work due to their having consumed it.

In the early nineteenth century all social classes consumed pulque. However, toward the end of the century it became associated with lower social strata. For the financially challenged, it was not only a cheap way to drink but provided a source of carbohydrates, vegetable protein, and vitamins B and C.

Among the lower classes an elaborate culture developed around pulque, the consumption of which was de rigueur at a variety of events such as baptisms. Pulquerías were typically elaborately painted, inside and out, and had striking names. A few names preserved include El Cañón de Largo Alcance (Long-Range Artillery), El Emperador de China (the Emperor of China), and Los Recuerdos del Porvenir (Remembrances of the Future). Innumerable drinking songs and card games added to patrons' enjoyment. Drinking glasses even had their own typology, with a variety of sizes, each with a name. The large glass was named the *camión* (truck).

Connoisseurs of the beverage recognized subtle changes in pulque based on the differing varietals of maguey, just as oenophiles recognize different varietals of grape. (A maguey varietal is used to produce tequila—a product of both fermentation and distillation.) Additives, such as fruit, added further nuances.

Unlike many cash crops, maguey production has little impact on the environment. Pulque-producing magueys are generally grown on land not suitable for other crops, especially in arid parts of Tlaxcala, Hidalgo, and the State of Mexico. The hardy plants are able to withstand hail, draught, and the cold found at the relatively high altitudes where they are grown. They also require limited care, so there is little negative impact from pesticides and chemical fertilizers. The plants not only produce sap (*aguamiel*) which is fermented, but yield construction material and food, as various parts of it are eaten. Magueys are frequently planted to limit erosion on sparsely vegetated soil.

Unlike beer, large corporations have never dominated pulque production and distribution. The drink never stops fermenting, so it has limited shelf life. While individual pulquerías were well known, there were no pulque brands. By the end of the twentieth century, brand names, heavy advertising, and pulque's lower-class stigma all led to its being largely replaced by beer.

However, just as most observers declared that pulque was about to go the way of the typewriter, it has staged a revival. A Google search turns up several pulquerías in Mexico City. Indicating the new life the beverage has taken on, many patrons are in their twenties and could easily afford other beverages.

the henequen leaf were fueled by wood, which in turn led to deforestation and erosion on additional land.

U.S. investment in land came late in the Porfiriato. Between 1902 and 1912, such investment increased from $30 million to $80 million. In 1910, Americans held about 130 million acres, or 27 percent of Mexico's surface area. Fewer than a hundred American interests held nearly 90 million of these acres in tracts larger than 100,000 acres.

In 1910 Mexico had 3,581,000 people in its agricultural labor force, or 63.7 percent of workers. However, due to their low productivity, they only produced 24.0 percent of GDP, an average of only $230 per capita (in 1970 U.S. dollars). The almost universal illiteracy of agricultural workers made increasing their productivity difficult.

While agricultural exports boomed, production for domestic use was neglected. Between 1877 and 1907, per capita corn production declined from 282 kilograms to 144. Imports from the United States made up part of this shortfall. However, few mechanisms existed to match grain supplies with the increased number of people thrust into the grain market.

Oil

The Porfirio Díaz dictatorship (1876–1911) had strong incentives to develop this industry because Mexico faced high energy costs.
(Stephen Haber, Noel Maurer, and Armando Razo, 2003)

After A. A. Robinson, the president of the Mexican Central Railroad, informed independent American oilman Edward Doheny that oil was seeping from the ground near Tampico, Doheny made a trip to Mexico, prospecting for oil from the back of Robinson's private rail car. Doheny considered the area so promising that he began to buy land near the seeps to obtain oil rights. He soon purchased 450,000 acres of land and leased an additional million acres. As he later admitted, he often bought land for $1 an acre from owners who knew nothing of its oil prospects.

In the northern Veracruz region, known as the Huasteca, where Doheny prospected, as late as 1885 a majority of the population spoke an indigenous language. Many lived within a tropical forest, replete with vines and epiphytes. In 1909, travel writer Philip Terry described the Huasteca as a "primitive biblical region flowing with milk and honey."

The indigenous population readily agreed to lease their land to oil companies since, before drilling began, petroleum extraction did not seem as invasive as the corn-eating cattle from nearby haciendas. Oil company agents offered undreamed-of cash payments for leases and promised residents they could continue their slash-and-burn agriculture. If Indian residents refused to sign, companies were not averse to resorting to violence to obtain the leases they sought. Local *hacendados*, who understood the notion of land titles, oil leases, and royalties far better than the indigenous population, sold or leased their property simply because the sums oil companies offered far exceeded the potential income from cattle raising.

Before it marketed any crude, Doheny's company, the Huasteca Petroleum Company, laid 125 miles of eight-inch pipe and constructed ten pumping stations and twelve 55,000-barrel steel tanks. For a time, Doheny's drilling at El Ébano, forty miles west of Tampico, produced only dry holes. As Doheny teetered on the verge of bankruptcy, well number six came in at 15,000 barrels a day and soon filled all available storage facilities. Then number seven came in at 60,000 barrels a day. When workers tried to cap it, oil sprung forth from a fissure in the earth 300 feet from the well. Workers feverishly constructed a 750,000-barrel earthen reservoir to contain the oil.

Doheny signed a contract to supply the Mexican Central Railroad with 6,000 barrels of fuel a day and soon began supplying Mexican smelters. After investing more than $4 million, and nearly going bankrupt, Doheny began to earn $10 million a year from his Mexican oil holdings.

The Mexican government welcomed Doheny's oil venture since domestic oil production replaced expensive imported fuels. To stimulate oil investments, the government waived import duties on machinery and granted a ten-year exemption on all taxes except the stamp tax.

Although the Díaz administration welcomed Doheny's efforts to produce Mexican petroleum, it felt that Mexico was becoming dangerously dependent on the United States and sought to offset U.S. influence by turning to Weetman Pearson, a successful British businessman and engineer. Pearson first visited Mexico in 1889, at age thirty-three, and for more than twenty years continued to spend considerable time there. In England, where he held a seat in the House of Commons, Pearson was known as the "Member for Mexico," which is also the title of his biography by Desmond Young.

To encourage Pearson, who had no prior oil experience, Díaz granted him a fifty-year oil concession on national lands, lakes, and lagoons in six states including oil-rich Veracruz. By 1906, Pearson reported owning "about 600,000 acres of land in the oil country and hav[ing] royalty leases for 200,000 or 300,000 acres." Pearson's early wells were dry holes, just as Doheny's had been. He began to make a profit from oil production only after investing £5 million of his own money.

In 1908, one of Pearson's wells blew in at Dos Bocas, midway between Tampico and Tuxpan. His next big strike came on a hacienda named Potrero del Llano, fifty miles northwest of Tuxpan. In 1910, a 250-foot gusher erupted there. The 100,000 barrels a day that shot out of the well flowed into the Tuxpan River and fouled the Gulf Coast as far as Tampico, 200 miles to the north. More than 3 million barrels of oil were lost. When it was finally controlled, the well produced 30,000 barrels a day, more than many entire fields. That single well became the most productive well in the world, yielding 117 million barrels of oil in twenty-eight years.

Pearson, who is said to have made more money in Mexico than any foreigner since Cortés, enjoyed access to Mexico's political insiders. He learned such social graces as leaving a case of whisky with the appropriate Mexican officials. His firm paid retainers to prominent politicians not only to ensure cooperation but also to avoid making political enemies. His leasing land from elite families, including Díaz's in-laws, ensured that he would not fall from official favor.

By the end of the Porfiriato, the oil industry had become Mexico's star economic performer. In 1901, only 10,345 barrels were produced. By 1911, production had reached 12.6 million barrels. Doheny and Pearson together controlled 90 percent of this production.

By the end of the Porfiriato, Mexico had become the fourth largest oil producer in the world. The petroleum industry bolstered Mexican development in a number of ways. Railroads and other industries could operate at lower costs thanks to the use of petroleum fuels and lubricants. Paying workers in cash stimulated the development of local industry.

However, much of the potential stimulus to the economy was never realized. As with railroads, most of the equipment used in the production of oil was produced outside Mexico. Even many of the oil workers' daily necessities were imported, since most of the work occurred near a port. As with the mines, profits were sent out of Mexico, rather than being reinvested locally. Finally, the bulk of oil produced in Mexican fields during the first decade of the twentieth century was refined in the United States.

The Porfirian Model

Between 1877 and 1910, Mexico's per capita income (expressed in 1950 U.S. dollars) increased from $62 to $132. From 1860 to 1910, Mexico's rate of per capita economic growth exceeded that of such economic powers as France, Germany, and Great Britain. This economic growth resulted from: 1) railroads lowering transport costs; 2) political stability; and 3) banks supplying credit to both private interests and the government. Between 1877 and 1910, federal government revenue increased by 437 percent, while the population only increased by 60 percent.

Mexico's exports were too low to lift the whole economy, as occurred in Argentina, Latin America's star economic performer. In 1890, Mexico exported $4.40 per capita, while Argentina exported $32.40 per capita. In addition, Mexico's exports generated relatively few jobs and had limited links to other sectors of the economy. Exports were often generated in rather small enclaves, such as mines.

The government's failure to invest in educating the labor force prevented sustained economic growth. In the short term, this kept taxes low and made enterprises profitable. However, in the long term it choked off development by denying Mexico a skilled labor force that could absorb technical innovation from advanced countries and produce manufactured exports.

While Mexico had no clear alternatives to the acceptance of foreign investment, such investment could have been more effectively regulated. The elite rationalized the virtual carte blanche given to foreign investors as a necessary measure to attract foreign capital. The experience of Brazil and Argentina, however, contradicted this. These two countries not only had more nationalistic investment policies but also received more British investment than Mexico during the Porfiriato.

While some statistics paint a positive picture of the Porfiriato, others indicate the opposite. Mexico failed to break out of the colonial development model. As late as 1910, three metals—gold, silver, and copper—comprised almost three-fifths of Mexico's exports. That year, 67 percent of the labor force remained in the primary sector (agriculture, cattle, forestry, hunting, and fishing).

At the end of the Porfiriato, the roughly $2 billion of foreign investment denied Mexicans control of mining, oil, banking, commerce, public utilities, cattle ranching, and railroads (until their nationalization). This led historian James Cockcroft to conclude, "The single most influential economic group was neither a rural aristocracy nor an urban bourgeoisie, but rather a *foreign* bourgeoisie."

Some problems that became apparent during the Porfiriato have yet to be adequately addressed. Factories, mines, and other extractive industries could not absorb the surplus of workers produced by land consolidation, population increase, and the declining need for artisans.

Regional disparity increased during the Porfiriato. Electricity permitted the location of industry in Mexico City, rather than near sources of hydropower. Chihuahua, Sonora, Coahuila, and the Federal District alone received 86 percent of foreign investment. Government investment was concentrated in Mexico City. This left many entire states with little benefit from Porfirian economic development. As historian Leticia Reina commented, "The majority of people were left out of the national project."

A fatal flaw in the way Mexico based development on industrialization, commercialization of agriculture, and internationalization of capital was that the lower classes were denied returns to labor commensurate with the new wealth being created. As historian Mark Wasserman stated, "Mexico's last and greatest civil war, the Mexican Revolution (1910–1920) was essentially a protest against this system."

A WORLD POWER EMERGES NEXT DOOR, 1856–1909

> Prior to the Civil War, the United States had constructed an empire on the North American continent; following the conflict, the focus shifted to a "New Empire" of foreign trade. By the 1890s, the makers of U.S. foreign policy sought markets rather than extensive new territories.
>
> (Joseph Fry, 1996)

The War of Reform, 1857–1860

During the War of Reform U.S. Present James Buchanan sent Robert McLane to Mexico as U.S. ambassador and instructed him to recognize whichever of the two governments in Mexico offered the best prospects for acquiring Baja California and transit rights across Mexican territory. McLane landed in Veracruz, and, since the liberal government there appeared willing to negotiate, McLane recognized it in April 1859

The positive liberal response to McLane reflected Juárez's realization that support from Washington could be a decisive advantage. Juárez felt that obtaining U.S. recognition would not only allow his beleaguered government to receive economic aid but would also guarantee maritime security in the Veracruz area.

McLane and liberal Foreign Relations Minister Melchor Ocampo negotiated a treaty on transit rights, known as the McLane–Ocampo Treaty. The transit rights enumerated in the treaty reflected not the liberals' desire to open Mexico's doors to unregulated crossings of its territory but the financial and military pressures they felt at the time of McLane's arrival and their hope that signing the treaty would be the key to obtaining U.S. aid.

The McLane–Ocampo Treaty granted the United States perpetual transit rights: 1) across the Isthmus of Tehuantepec; 2) from the lower Rio Grande to Mexico's west coast; and 3) from Guaymas to Nogales, Arizona. Americans not only viewed these transit rights as desirable but also felt they would pave the way for the formal incorporation of these areas into the United States. The treaty granted the United States the right to intervene militarily to protect people and goods in transit along the routes included in the treaty. In exchange for these rights, the United States was to pay the liberal government $4 million, of which $2 million was to be retained to settle damage claims against Mexico filed by U.S. citizens.

Fortunately for Mexico and Juárez's historical reputation, the U.S. Senate rejected the McLane–Ocampo Treaty. Senators from northern states felt slave interests would benefit if U.S. influence extended into Mexico.

Late in 1860, Juárez's army took Mexico City. In January 1861, John Weller, the new U.S. ambassador, presented his credentials and a long list of damage claims filed by U.S. citizens.

The Second Empire

After Maximilian's arrival in Mexico City, the European powers soon recognized his government. However, the United States maintained diplomatic relations with Juárez throughout the intervention. Even though the Juárez government enjoyed U.S. recognition, the outbreak of the American Civil War thwarted Juárez's hopes for U.S. aid.

The blockade of Confederate ports during the Civil War led to a commercial boom in northeastern Mexico. In exchange for cotton, Mexico sent the Confederacy flour, hides, wool, lead, silver, salt, footwear, cloth, blankets, gunpowder, and potassium nitrate (to produce gunpowder). Monterrey served as the distribution center for Mexican goods bound for the Confederacy. Thousands of carts carried goods between Monterrey and Texas.

The Restored Republic

After peace was re-established in Mexico, relations between Mexico and the United States were as warm as they had ever been. U.S. Ambassador Marcus Otterbourg, who arrived in 1867, was instructed not to press the damage claims of U.S. citizens so that the liberals would have time to put their affairs in order. The liberals, firm believers in international trade, sought U.S. investments and technology to develop the Mexican economy.

During the early 1870s, border conflict began to undermine the existing goodwill between Mexico and the United States. From an American perspective, border conflict resulted from Mexican cattle rustlers who would cross to the north side of the Rio Grande, steal cattle, and retreat back across the river. U.S. forces repeatedly crossed the border into Mexico in "hot pursuit" of rustlers and raiders during the Lerdo de Tejada administration

Relations between the United States and Mexico remained almost quaintly simple. In 1873, when U.S. Ambassador John Foster (the grandfather of John Foster Dulles) arrived in Mexico, only 130 American adults lived in the Federal District. Ships sailing at what Foster described as "rare intervals" provided communication between the two nations. That year, trade with Mexico only accounted for about 1 percent of U.S. foreign trade. In the 1870s, U.S. exports to Mexico totaled between $6 million to $8 million a year, below the peak reached before the Mexican–American War. The United States imported from Mexico even less—never more than $5 million a year in the 1870s.

The Homestead Act, post-Civil War reconstruction, rapid industrialization, and the shifting of the United States' attention to its own west absorbed vast amounts of U.S. capital and human resources, reducing expansionist pressure. Neither the Republican nor the Democratic platforms of 1868, 1872, 1876, and 1880 contained a word about Latin America.

Recognizing Díaz

When Rutherford Hayes was inaugurated as U.S. president in March 1877, Díaz, who came to power the previous November, remained unrecognized. Díaz mounted a publicity offensive in the United States to promote trade with and investment in Mexico. He invited American investors to Mexico and granted them huge concessions and subsidies. Not surprisingly, these investors then lobbied in the United States for improved relations between the two countries. In 1878, Díaz sent Manuel Zamacona, an experienced diplomat, to the United States to publicize Mexico's resources. He also hired two American journalists to produce books and articles supporting the recognition of Mexico.

Recognition finally came on April 9, 1878. The pressure of American bankers, miners, and potential railroad investors played a major role in the decision to recognize the Díaz administration. U.S. efforts to force Díaz into making concessions backfired, since Mexico's president refused to concede on any of the U.S. demands, such as the right to "hot pursuit," an end to forced loans from American citizens living in Mexico, and the elimination of the duty-free zone along the border. U.S. pressure, which Mexicans viewed as heavy handed, soured U.S.–Mexican relations. Díaz enhanced his already solid record as a patriotic war hero by standing up to the United States.

By the 1870s, recognition by the United States had become a key to stability throughout Latin America. Such recognition signaled that it was safe to make investments and that nations enjoying recognition might obtain loans. It was presumed that the United States would not actively undermine administrations it recognized. Lack of recognition indicated instability and inadvisability for investment, and the possibility of dissidents obtaining U.S. aid to topple the incumbents. The United States, realizing that its recognition had become a valuable commodity, began to charge accordingly.

The Porfiriato, 1884–1908

> The most powerful foreign influence in Mexican affairs was of course the United States, whose proximity and overwhelming superiority in wealth, technology, and population were both welcomed and feared.
>
> (Robert Holden, 1994)

During the Porfiriato, U.S.–Mexican relations became more complicated. New concerns arose as trade and investment increased. Trade between the two nations, which only totaled $4 million in 1855, soared to $117 million by 1907. The number of Americans living in Mexico steadily increased, reaching 75,000 by 1910. In 1911, more than 45 percent of total U.S. foreign investment was in Mexico.

Since France, Spain, and Great Britain lacked diplomatic relations with Mexico after the fall of Maximilian, the United States had little difficulty increasing its trade with Mexico. By 1885, the United States had replaced Great Britain as the main supplier of goods to Mexico.

In 1900, the United States supplied 51.1 percent of Mexico's imports, while Great Britain supplied 17 percent, and Germany supplied 11.5 percent. During the next decade, as U.S. manufacturing increased and rail transport improved, the United States supplied between 55 and 60 percent of Mexico's imports and absorbed between 65 and 75 percent of its exports.

From the 1870s to roughly 1912, Mexico absorbed more U.S. direct foreign investment than any other country. Thanks to legal reforms south of the border that replicated institutional structures in the north, the border nearly ceased to exist as an obstacle to trade and investment. By 1910 the United States, which accounted for 38 percent of total foreign investment in Mexico, had surpassed the British, who supplied 29 percent. Mining, railroads, and the petroleum industry accounted for roughly 80 percent of U.S. direct investment. As U.S. investment increased, U.S. investors developed a vested interest in stability and in Díaz remaining in office. In 1907, Secretary of State Elihu Root declared Díaz to be "one of the great men to be held up for the hero worship of mankind."

By the end of the Porfiriato, as historian W. Dirk Raat noted, "U.S. capital and markets had created the commercialization of agriculture, the proletarianization of the peasantry, and the expansion of an export-oriented economy." In general Mexicans' desire for better-paying jobs outweighed any doubts they had about the foreign influences accompanying U.S. trade and investment. In northern Mexico, the upper class often sent its children to the United States so they could learn English and receive a good education.

Don Porfirio Teeters

> It is not clear that the Taft administration [1909–1913]—or the U.S. interests it sought to represent—stood to gain from the ouster of Díaz, or that they rejoiced at his fall.
>
> (Alan Knight, 1998)

In the early twentieth century, Díaz attempted to balance U.S. and European investment to prevent Mexico from becoming too dependent on its northern neighbor. Also, for historical reasons, Mexican politicians did not want to appear to be dominated by American interests. Loans were placed with European banks, and the British-owned El Águila Oil Company was favored over its American competitors. This search for European investment indicates that Díaz's action was not motivated by opposition to foreign capital per se.

At the turn of the century, the United States did not have separate polices for each Latin American nation. President Taft, like Roosevelt, sought to maintain existing markets and find new outlets for U.S. capital and goods. The U.S. government saw its role as protecting private American entrepreneurs threatened by local political crisis. In the United States, this appeared to be a very even-handed approach. To Latin American countries, the United States appeared to be overwhelming them, often earning itself the "imperialist" label.

In 1910, after Madero fled to the United States, the U.S. government was noticeably lukewarm in the application of U.S. neutrality laws to Madero's supporters. However, little evidence indicates that the U.S. desired Díaz's removal. The tension resulting from Díaz's pro-European tilt notwithstanding, the U.S. delegation to Mexico's 1910 centennial celebration declared: "Just as Rome had its Augustus, England its Elizabeth and Victoria, Mexico had Porfirio Díaz. All is well in Mexico. Under Porfirio Díaz, a nation has been created."

Emigration

Although it was only a trickle compared to a century later, the latter half of the nineteenth century saw sustained Mexican emigration to the United States. The railroad not only facilitated passage across the northern Mexican desert but also permitted easy access to New Mexico, Arizona, and California. The railroad also permitted the shipment of minerals and produce from the U.S. southwest to the eastern United States, causing the demand for labor to soar.

Labor recruiters in Mexico, known as *enganchadores*, aggressively recruited workers for the rail companies and other U.S. enterprises that they represented. There was no shortage of Mexicans willing to come north since the railroads offered $1 a day, a princely sum for those used to receiving the $0.12 to $0.15 a day *hacendados* paid.

Opposition to this migration largely came from south of the border, where the loss of low-cost labor was viewed with concern by landowners. In 1906, *El Correo de Chihuahua* reported with alarm that 22,000 Mexicans had entered Texas through Ciudad Juárez. As would be the case well into the twentieth century, the overwhelming majority of these emigrants came from rural areas.

Between 1900 and 1910, the number of Mexican-born residents living in the United States increased from 103,393 to 221,915. By 1912, Mexicans had become the main source of labor on railroads west of Kansas City. Some of the suggested reasons for Mexican emigration include: 1) political repression; 2) the high birth rate in Mexico; 3) easy access to the United States by rail; 4) higher wage levels in the United States; and 5) escaping the rigors of hacienda life.

Through the first decade of the twentieth century, the U.S. government adopted a neutral policy on immigration from Mexico, trying neither to stimulate it nor limit it. American employers welcomed Mexican workers since they assumed them to be temporary sojourners who would not aggressively demand better wages and working conditions.

In 1908 a U.S. Bureau of Labor Statistics researcher estimated that 60,000–100,000 Mexicans crossed the border each year to work in the United States. The researcher observed, "Except in Texas and California, few Mexicans become permanent residents and even in those two states, a majority are transient laborers who seldom remain more than six months at a time in this country." Employers came to depend on seasonal Mexican labor for certain tasks, such as clipping sheep.

Up until 1890 it was the responsibility of individual U.S. states to enforce existing legislation concerning immigrants. An 1891 federal law provided for the deportation of immigrants who became a public charge within a year of their arrival or who belonged to an excluded group, such as Chinese contract laborers.

Those who had spent more than a year in the United States could not be deported. In 1917 the period of deportability was extended to five years. Even then those who had been in the United States for more than five years were not deportable. Mexicans were not even required to pass through official ports or inspection points until 1919.

DOCUMENT 9.1: THE CANANEA STRIKE: WORKERS' DEMANDS

Memorandum:

1. Working people declare a strike.

2. The workers will labor only under the following conditions:

 I. The firing of Luis the overseer (Level 19).
 II. Minimum wage for a worker will be five pesos for an eight-hour workday.
 III. The Cananea Consolidated Copper Co., throughout its entire work force, will employ 75% Mexicans and 25% foreigners, for the former have the same aptitude as the latter.
 IV. Honorable men are placed in care of the cages, in order to avoid any sort of conflict.
 V. All Mexicans employed to work by this company will have the right to promotions as long as they are qualified.

Mexican workers: A government elected by the people so that it guides them and satisfies their needs in as much as possible: Mexico does not have this.

Furthermore: A government that is made up of ambitious men who tire the patience of the people with their criminally self-interested activities, elected by the worst of them in order to help then get rich: Mexico does not need this.

The people elect their representatives to govern them, and not to ridicule and humiliate them; that is a Republic.

People, rise up and go forward. Learn what it seems that you have forgotten. Gather together and discuss your rights. Demand the respect that is owed you.

Each Mexican who is mistreated by foreigners is worth the same or more than them, if he unites with his brothers and demands his rights.

It would be an unheard of exaggeration to say that a Mexican is not equal to a Yankee, a Negro, or a Chinaman, in the very land of Mexicans. That this might otherwise be the case is because of the worthless government that gives advantages to adventurers and in doing so devalues the true owners of this unfortunate land.

Mexicans, awake, unite. The Fatherland and our dignity demand it.

Source: Nora E. Jaffary, Edward W. Osowski and Susie S. Porter (eds.) (2010)
Mexican History: a Primary Source Reader. Boulder, CO: Westview Press, p. 271

DOCUMENT 9.2: THE CREELMAN INTERVIEW

[Díaz's 1908 declaration that he would not be a candidate for president in 1910 opened the way for challenges to his administration.]

I have waited patiently for the day when the people of the Mexican Republic would be prepared to choose and change their government at every election without danger of armed revolutions and without injury to the national credit or interference with national progress. I believe that day has come . . . I retire when my present term of office ends, and I shall not serve again.

We were harsh. Sometimes we were harsh to the point of cruelty. But it was all necessary then to the life and progress of the nation . . . It was better that a little blood should be shed that much blood should be saved. The blood that was shed was bad blood; the blood that was saved was good blood.

Source: James Creelman, "President Díaz: Hero of the Americas," *Pearson's Magazine*,
March (1908), pp. 237, 242, 244.

NOTES

1   Francisco Pimentel, *Memoria sobre las causas que han originado la situación actual de la raza indígena de México y medios de remediarla* (Mexico City: Imprenta de Andrade y Escalante 1864), pp. 217–18.

2   Rodney Anderson, *Outcasts in Their Own Land* (De Kalb, IL: University of Northern Illinois Press, 1976), p. 37.

3   E. A. H. Tays, "Present Labor Conditions in Mexico," *Engineering and Mining Journal*, 84 (October 5, 1907), p. 624.

FURTHER READING

Altamirano, Ignacio Manuel (1961) *Christmas in the Mountains*. Gainesville, FL: University of Florida Press.
   This novel, by one of Mexico's outstanding nineteenth-century writers, makes obvious the author's opposition to the military draft, poor schools, and the clergy's failing to serve rural communities.

Anderson, Rodney (1976) *Outcasts in their Own Land: Mexican Industrial Workers, 1906–1911*. DeKalb, IL: Northern Illinois University Press.
   Describes the working class at end of Porfiriato.

Bernstein, Marvin D. (1964) *The Mexican Mining Industry, 1890–1950*. Albany, N.Y.: State University of New York Press.
   A description of the modernization and subsequent decline of mining.

*Coatsworth, John (1974) "Railroads, Landholding, and Agrarian Protest in Early Porfiriato," *Hispanic American Historical Review*, February, pp. 48–71.
   The rural response to introducing a new technology

—— (1981) *Growth against Development*. DeKalb: Northern Illinois University Press.
   The impact of the railroad on Porfirian Mexico.

Fowler-Salamini, Heather and Mary Kay Vaughan (eds.) (1994) *Women of the Mexican Countryside, 1850–1990: Creating Spaces, Shaping Transition*. Tucson, AZ: University of Arizona Press.
   Essays on rural women during and after the Porfiriato.

González, Luis (1974) *San José de Gracia: Mexican Village in Transition*. Austin, TX: University of Texas Press.
   The history of the author's small hometown, indicating how it reflected change occurring throughout Mexico.

Hamnett, Brian (1994) *Juárez*. London: Longman.
   A biography of the president.

*Katz, Friedrich (1974) "Labor Conditions on Haciendas in Porfirian Mexico: Some Trends and Tendencies," *Hispanic American Historical Review*, February, pp. 1–47.
   The lot of rural labor during the Porfiriato.

López-Alonso, Moramay (2012) *A History of Living Standards in Mexico, 1850–1950*. Stanford, CA: Stanford University Press.
   The author's study of the height of late nineteenth-century Mexicans indicates the negative impact industrialization had on most Mexicans.

McAllen, M. M. (2014) *Maximilian and Carlota: Europe's Last Empire in Mexico*. San Antonio, TX: Trinity University Press.
   A study of Mexico's imperial first couple, illustrated with many photos from the period.

Pani, Erika (2002) "Dreaming of a Mexican Empire: The Political Project of the Imperialists," *Hispanic American Historical Review*, February, pp. 1–31.
   A consideration of those who, feeling Maximilian's empire offered solutions to long-standing problems, served in his civil administration.

Turner, John Kenneth (1969) *Barbarous Mexico*. Austin, TX: University of Texas Press.
   This account, originally published in 1910, of appalling working conditions was influential in shaping U.S. opinion about Mexico.

* Both of these authors have written and edited numerous works on the Mexican economy.

Wasserman, Mark (2000) *Every Day Life and Politics in Nineteenth-Century Mexico*. Albuquerque, N.M.: University of New Mexico Press.

A concise description of life during the nineteenth century.

—— (1984) *Capitalists, Caciques and Revolution: the Native Elite and Foreign Enterprises of Chihuahua, Mexico, 1854–1911*. Chapel Hill, N.C.: University of North Carolina Press.

A description of a state dominated by a single family and the state's revolutionary response.

GLOSSARY TERMS

científico
henequen
land reform
maguey
Porfiriato
plan
rural (pl. *rurales*)

The Early Twentieth Century, 1910–1940

Chapter 10

The Mexican Revolution, 1910–1916

TIMELINE—WORLD

1911	1912	1913	1914	1914
U.S. Supreme Court orders dissolution of Standard Oil Co.	Republic of China formed with Sun Yat-Sen as president	Woodrow Wilson becomes U.S. President	First ship passes through Panama Canal	Archduke Franz Ferdinand, Crown Prince of Austria, assassinated, setting off World War I

TIMELINE—MEXICO

1910 (Nov. 20)	1911 (May 10)	1911 (May 21)	1911 (May 25)	1911 (May–Nov.)
Uprisings against Díaz begin	Villa and Orozco capture Ciudad Juárez for Madero	Treaty of Ciudad Juárez signed	Díaz resigns and goes into exile	Interim presidency of Francisco León de la Barra
1914 (April) US troops land in Veracruz	**1914 (June)** Villistas take Zacatecas	**1914 (July)** Huerta resigns and goes into exile	**1914 (Oct.)** Aguascalientes Convention convenes	**1915 (April–June)** Obregón defeats Villa in series of battles extending from Celaya to Aguascalientes

1916
Columbus, New
Mexico attacked
by Villistas

1916
Albert Einstein
publishes his book
*Relativity: The
Special and
General Theory*

1911
(Nov. 6)
Madero becomes
president

1911
(Nov. 28)
Zapata issues
Plan of Ayala

1913
(Feb.)
Madero murdered

1913
(Feb.)
Huerta seizes
presidency

1913
(March)
Carranza issues
Plan of
Guadalupe

1916
(Sept.)
Carranza calls for
constitutional
convention

THIS CHAPTER CONCERNS AN EVENT THAT WOULD FORM THE BACKDROP for Mexican politics throughout the twentieth century—the Mexican Revolution. The Revolution began with the 1911 overthrow of Díaz and the election of Francisco Madero. Mexico's elected president was challenged by several armed groups and finally removed from office by a 1913 military coup. The coup installed a military regime headed by General Victoriano Huerta. Armed groups in northern Mexico sprang up in opposition to the new regime. These challengers drove Huerta from office but then began to fight among themselves for power. Finally after bitter fighting, forces led by Venustiano Carranza emerged victorious. The chapter concludes with descriptions of the economic impact of the Revolution and of how the United States repeatedly attempted to determine its outcome.

THE FALL OF THE DÍAZ ADMINISTRATION

In October 1910, after fleeing Mexico and taking refuge in San Antonio, Texas, Madero issued his Plan of San Luis Potosí, which called for a revolt against Díaz on November 20, 1910, free elections, and a legal review of previous land thefts.

The most successful of the uprisings that occurred in response to Madero's Plan were in Chihuahua, where the initial revolt spread. Soon more than 1,000 men were fighting under the command of Pancho Villa and a prosperous muleteer named Pascual Orozco.

Rural lower-class leadership of the revolt in Chihuahua came as a surprise to Madero. He had assumed the November 20 revolt would be an urban affair that would soon topple Díaz and permit a smooth change at the top.

On February 14, 1911, Madero returned to Mexico from the United States to assume command of the Revolution. By April 1911, insurrection had spread to eighteen states and most of the countryside was in the hands of revolutionaries.

On May 10, rebel troops under Villa and Orozco captured Ciudad Juárez, across the Rio Grande from El Paso, Texas.

While Madero was challenging Díaz in the north, resistance was developing in the state of Morelos, just south of Mexico City. Anenecuilco, Morelos, a village that had appeared on Aztec tribute lists before the Spanish Conquest, was the home of Emiliano Zapata. By 1910, all the lands of his village, in an area where land had traditionally been communally owned, had been appropriated by sugar planters.

In 1909, at age thirty, Zapata was chosen as chief of village defense. Along with eighty armed men, he began reclaiming and distributing to villagers land usurped by *hacendados*. Zapata's example spread to other parts of the state.

After the defeat of Díaz's forces at Ciudad Juárez, his traditional power base began deserting him. As large parts of the countryside fell under the control of revolutionaries, *hacendados* and the financial elite decided that they would undercut the more radical rural *insurrectos* by yielding to Madero's political demands.

Díaz's abandonment by his traditional power base led him to agree to the Treaty of Ciudad Juárez, which called for him to resign and go into exile. The treaty stipulated that Díaz's federal army would remain intact, while the rebel forces that had supported Madero would be disbanded. This agreement, which sought to end the Revolution, disarm the peasants, and maintain the social system upheld by the federal army, did not mention land reform.

Díaz agreed to the treaty due to the hemorrhaging of his support and his desire to resign and leave in dignity, rather than facing rebel hordes at the gates of Mexico City.

Figure 10.1 *The Revolution went through several phases. The initial democratic phase was led by Francisco Madero, pictured here.*

Source: El Paso Public Library, Aultman Collection, photo #A 1458.

With the benefit of hindsight, Madero has frequently been criticized for allowing Díaz's legislature, judiciary, and, most significantly, his army to remain intact. However, he sought to reform, not destroy, Mexico's socioeconomic system. He felt this could be accomplished by reopening the political process.

Díaz kept his word, resigned on May 25, 1911, and went into exile. Unlike the typical Latin American dictator, Díaz did not loot the treasury, and he lived to the end on the charity of friends. In 1915 he died in exile in France.

As revolutionary General Felipe Ángeles observed:

Díaz was a glorious soldier who struggled for independence and national sovereignty. He was an able administrator, but took advantage of his prestige as a caudillo and used the army to impose his will on the nation. He did not respect our democratic institutions nor did he obey the law. He usurped authority and became a dictator.[1]

THE MADERO YEARS, 1911–1913

In October 1911, voters selected Madero president. Pro-Madero sentiment was overwhelming. While the elections were free, they served only to ratify what had been achieved earlier by force of arms.

By the time Madero assumed the presidency in November 1911, popular enthusiasm had already waned. As president, rather than dismantling the old Porfirian bureaucracy, Madero merely changed the personnel at the top. At the same time, millions of peasants continued stoop labor on the haciendas of the Terrazas, the Creels, and other *hacendados*, just as they had under Díaz.

Given Madero's failure to initiate land reform, in late November 1911, Zapata issued his Plan of Ayala, which withdrew recognition from the president and called for his overthrow. The Plan charged Madero with abandoning the Revolution and siding with *hacendados*. It reflected the enormous gulf between the elite, literate, legalistic Madero and the parochial, egalitarian, and largely illiterate **Zapatista** movement.

The Plan of Ayala declared that peasants should take the initiative to reclaim stolen lands and defend them with armed force. In addition one-third of each legally owned hacienda was to be purchased for the landless. The Plan did not demand political power for Zapata's followers. Rather it called for elections to select a new government after Madero's overthrow.

In addition to the Zapatistas, Madero faced other challengers. In December 1911, former governor of Nuevo León Bernardo Reyes launched a rebellion. In March 1912 his former supporter Pascual Orozco, rebelled in Chihuahua, charging him with having betrayed the principles of the Plan of San Luis Potosí. In October 1912 Porfirio Díaz's nephew Félix Díaz rebelled in Veracruz. Together these rebellions sapped government resources and undermined Madero's credibility.

To add to Madero's woes, peasant-initiated violence continued to sweep the country. Díaz's many-layered repressive apparatus was too damaged and overextended to respond to these peasant initiatives. In the countryside the revolution had mutated and taken root among people with no patience for parliamentary procedure, little interest in candidates and ballots, and scant faith in politicians.

Deep crisis gripped the Madero government by the end of 1912. Madero could not satisfy the aspirations of peasants and industrial workers without betraying his closest associates. Throughout rural Mexico, strikes and spontaneous land seizures challenged his administration. Industrialists, landowners, and foreign investors felt their property was unprotected. Army officers considered Madero a non-military upstart.

On February 9, 1913, military officers responded to what they felt to be Madero's inability to govern. They initiated a coup and released from jail Félix Díaz and Bernardo Reyes, whom they planned to install as president. Reyes was killed as he approached the National Palace on horseback, thinking it was in rebel hands.

Félix Díaz and his fellow rebels took refuge in the Ciudadela, a stoutly built Mexico City fortress that contained most of the local supply of artillery shells. Madero appointed General Huerta to crush the rebels. However, Huerta had little sympathy for Madero and deliberately protracted a military stalemate. The rebels remained in the Ciudadela for ten days, a period known in Mexican history as "La Decena Trágica" ("The Ten Tragic Days"). During this period, the two forces engaged in artillery duels in downtown Mexico City, carefully avoiding the cannons of the "enemy" and creating a climate in which the population would welcome any settlement.

Finally, General Victoriano Huerta and Félix Díaz formally agreed to join forces. Huerta was to be the interim president until elections could be held to elect the younger Díaz as president. Madero and his vice-president were arrested.

On February 22, while being taken from the National Palace to prison, Madero and the vice-president were killed, although it remains unclear just who gave the orders to kill them.

Madero failed to solve Mexico's social problems due to his sharing with the *científicos* the belief that the existing socioeconomic system was the only rational one and that it should be preserved. Preservation of the system required suppressing radical peasant movements that demanded immediate land reform. To accomplish this he left the federal army intact,

During his brief administration, Madero permitted the formation of political and labor organizations, shortened the workday, and outlawed punishment by factory owners. He instituted Mexico's first taxes on producing and exporting oil and made Spanish the official language of the Mexican railway system, replacing English. Congressional elections in 1912 allowed the election of Madero opponents as well as supporters. Unlike so many movers and shakers of Mexican history, Madero is still remembered favorably. Historian Stanley Ross wrote of Madero, "His martyrdom accomplished, at least for a time, what he had been unable to do while alive: unite all the revolutionists under one banner."

THE HUERTA DICTATORSHIP, 1913–1914

Huerta established a government with the backing of *hacendados*, bankers, rich merchants, high clergy, the federal army, British oil interests, and the U.S. business community. Huerta's backers felt that Mexico needed a firm hand like Díaz's and that Madero had failed due to too little repression, not too little reform.

Initially, Huerta's administration did not swing sharply to the right. His educational budget exceeded that of Díaz. However, the exigencies of war soon led to increased repression, forced military recruitment, and attempts to squeeze more resources out of the citizenry to wage war.

Response to the coup was not long in coming. In the northern state of Coahuila, Venustiano Carranza, a *hacendado*, declared Huerta's government to be illegal. Carranza's distance from Mexico City afforded protection that permitted his survival. Carranza, then fifty-three years old, had flowing white whiskers worthy of an Old Testament prophet. He stood over six feet tall and very much fit the image of a revolutionary leader.

In March 1913 Carranza issued a written call for resistance to Huerta known as the Plan of Guadalupe. The Plan, named for the hacienda where it was drafted, deliberately avoided all social issues in order to build the broadest possible coalition against Huerta. Its sole demand was that constitutional rule, usurped by Huerta, be reestablished. The Plan provided for the formation of an army, whose members were known as **Constitutionalists**, with Carranza as its commander

Huerta's coup brought peasant leaders into the forefront, removing them from the obscurity to which years of Díaz oppression and Madero inaction had condemned them. In the south, Zapata continued to defend his version of the Revolution.

In Chihuahua, Pancho Villa built a force of artisans, workers, shopkeepers, small farmers, miners, peasants, muleteers, peddlers, bandits, and the unemployed. Residents of Chihuahua's military colonies joined Villa in hopes of reasserting their old position.

Villa was of the same background as his followers. In 1878 he was born into a sharecropper family on a hacienda in the state of Durango. Before answering the call to join Madero's November 20 uprising, Villa seems to have lived in the twilight zone between legal occupations and cattle rustling.

As Villa's army gained strength, another general, Álvaro Obregón, organized anti-Huerta forces in Sonora. Obregón was a self-made man, typical of northern Mexico. After working as a carpenter and mechanic, he became a small-scale chickpea farmer. After Madero's overthrow, Sonora's governor appointed Obregón to command the state's military forces. It soon became apparent that he was a self-taught military genius.

By early summer, rebellion had broken out in thirteen states in addition to Sonora, Chihuahua, and Coahuila. As these rebellions spread, the anarchy that the Huerta coup was supposed to end inexorably increased.

As opposition mounted, Huerta increased the federal army to more than 200,000. He kept his regime in power through systematic assassination of dissenters and press censorship.

In large part due to income from confiscated Chihuahua estates, Villa's army became the strongest and best equipped of the armies opposing Huerta. Selling cattle from these estates allowed him to make payrolls at a time when jobs were scarce. Arms purchased in the United States permitted a rapid southward advance that gave Villa and his army, the **Northern Division**, fame as the strike force of the Revolution. At the height of his power in October 1914, Villa commanded 40,000 men. His popularity, and thus his ability to raise large armies, resulted from his appearance

Figure 10.2 *The railroad provided revolutionary forces with unprecedented mobility. Villa's forces, pictured here, used trains extensively.*

Source: El Paso Public Library, Aultman Collection, photo #A 2457.

of invincibility, his extensive distribution of goods and money to the lower classes, his promise that veterans would receive land after Huerta's defeat, and the perception that he could not lose due to U.S. backing.

As Villa's forces moved south, antagonism between him and Carranza increased. Historian G. M. Joseph contrasted the two leaders' forces, noting that Villa's were "underdogs and outcasts of the great Chihuahuan expanses. They espoused a freewheeling brand of populism that clashed with Carranza's more gradualist, aristocratic notions of reform."

In June 1914, Villa's 22,000 men then attacked Zacatecas's 12,500-man garrison, producing the largest and bloodiest battle that occurred during the revolt against Huerta. The fall of Zacatecas, which produced 5,000 casualties, sealed the fate of the Huerta regime.

After the victory at Zacatecas, Carranza and Villa remained openly at odds, even though they were both fighting to topple Huerta. Subsequently Carranza denied Villa ammunition and the coal his locomotives required to move further south, thus preventing him from taking Mexico City.

The federal army backing Huerta was never defeated in set battle. Rather it was simply undermined by surprise attacks and the frequent defection of garrisons. Seeing the inevitable, Huerta resigned on July 15, 1914 and went into exile.

With Villa immobilized by a lack of coal for his locomotives, Obregón continued to advance down the west coast. He captured Guadalajara, turned east, and triumphantly marched into Mexico City in August.

The Constitutionalists demanded and obtained the unconditional surrender and disbanding of the federal army that had served under Díaz, Madero, and finally Huerta. As Obregón's troops entered Mexico City, the national government ceased to exist.

At this point, Mexico was again rid of a dictator, but the major leaders—Zapata, Villa, Obregón, and Carranza—strongly disagreed on the kind of society to construct. This reflected their different class origins and the varied social and economic make-up of the regions from which they came.

CIVIL WAR, 1914–1916

> Once Díaz and Huerta were removed in 1914, the Revolution lacked any national goal.
> (John S. D. Eisenhower, 1993)

In an attempt to resolve the question of who should head the government that was to replace the Huerta dictatorship, a convention was called at Aguascalientes, midway between Mexico City and Villa's Chihuahua bastion. It opened on October 10, 1914, with representatives of the armies of Obregón, Villa, and Carranza declaring the Convention sovereign and beholden to none of the leaders who had sent representatives. Delegates then invited the Zapatistas to Aguascalientes.

During the Convention, the most revolutionary, popular, and democratic debates of Mexican history occurred. Issues such as women's rights and an activist, interventionist state were seriously considered for the first time in Mexican political history.

The Convention resolved that Villa and Carranza should resign their commands simultaneously. Villa agreed to resign, but was challenged by Carranza, who questioned whether he had actually relinquished command of his forces. Carranza refused to recognize the Convention's authority and recalled his representatives. The Convention then declared Carranza to be in rebellion and reinstated Villa as head of the Northern Division. With his mantle of legality restored, Villa advanced on Mexico City.

Following Carranza's withdrawal, Mexico City was occupied by the armies of Villa and Zapata in the legal role of representatives of the Convention government. On December 4, 1914, Zapata and Villa met at Xochimilco on the outskirts of Mexico City. After the meeting, Villa and Zapata decided to abandon the center of the country and return to their own regions whose limited horizons they had never been able to overcome.

Figure 10.3 *This classic photo of the Revolution shows Pancho Villa and Emiliano Zapata (with hat).*
Source: El Paso Public Library, Aultman Collection, photo #A 5648.

This decision not to advance on Carranza is one of the most important of the Revolution. Villa's army numbered roughly 40,000, Zapata's 25,000, and another 20,000 or 30,000 were loyal to the Convention. These troops far outnumbered those serving under Carranza.

Within a week of Carranza being declared in rebellion by the Convention, almost all the important military leaders of the northwest and northeast, including Obregón, had joined him. Most of these men were up-and-coming entrepreneurs and public officials.

Carranza was hemmed in on the Gulf Coast without a political base. However, he had a worldview that was both national and international in scope. He had access to income from Veracruz customs duties, the sales of Yucatán henequen, and Gulf Coast oil—revenue sources that would not run short as did the revenue Villa obtained from selling cattle to the United States.

Carranza's first major move was political. On January 6, 1915, he announced his own land reform. Carranza's land reform differed from Zapata's Plan of Ayala in that it called for the reform to be implemented by local, regional, and national agrarian commissions, not peasants themselves—a difference that proved to be fundamental.

Once they had reorganized in Veracruz, the Constitutionalists launched a military offensive. In late January 1915, Obregón moved west and occupied Mexico City, left practically defenseless by Villa's withdrawal to the northwest. He then advanced northwest to fight Villa. By this time Carranza had established an appreciable following. He signed a formal alliance with the organized working class, which saw little in the programs of Villa and Zapata that would benefit them. Many members of the middle class, who saw Carranza as a promoter of economic development, supported him. Similarly many *hacendados* and wealthy city dwellers backed the Constitutionalists.

Carranza drew peasant support in many areas where Villa and Zapata were seen as far removed from local affairs and lacking a land-reform program such as Carranza's, the "legality" of which was constantly emphasized. ("Legality" meant it was in written form to guide authorities.)

The impending conflict between Obregón and Villa would result in a qualitatively different type of warfare—that of professional armies in conventional battles. Charisma counted for less, and there was no guarantee the most popular leader would win.

In three months of fighting, Obregón advanced 150 miles from Celaya to Aguascalientes. Villa suffered his greatest losses at Celaya where he repeatedly ordered his cavalry to charge Obregón's force, which was protected by elaborate barbed-wire networks and the then-novel machine gun. In these battles, more than 50,000 men were involved on both sides, and 20,000 were killed or wounded. Cool generalship triumphed over élan. After a final defeat at Aguascalientes, the remaining elements of Villa's force straggled back to Chihuahua, where they reverted to guerrilla warfare.

With Villa's army out of the picture, the Constitutionalists turned their attention toward Morelos, where events had gone almost unaffected by the Carranza–Obregón-Villa struggle.

While the Constitutionalists were fighting the Villistas, the Zapatistas turned inward and began to create the society they had long envisioned. The Zapatistas administered Morelos as they saw fit. Reforms went far beyond the Plan of Ayala. Entire haciendas were expropriated without compensation. Each village in Morelos carried out land reform on its own. While Mexico City verged on starvation, people in Morelos were eating more food than in 1910—and paying less for it. This resulted from shifting land from sugar production to food crops that supplied not only villages but guerrilla forces.

In April 1916, Carranza ordered his forces into Morelos. The 30,000-man army advancing into Morelos differed little from Díaz's army of the previous decade. Its troops came not to liberate, but to conquer the local population, which at best were treated as prisoners of war.

By July 1916, all towns in Morelos were occupied, and the Constitutionalist commander reported the campaign concluded. Zapatistas again waged effective guerrilla warfare, despite their constant currency and ammunition shortages. The Zapatistas fought with the aid of the population, who served as observers, informers, and suppliers of food and shelter, as well as combatants who would take up arms for a battle and then return to their farms.

By December, the 30,000-man Constitutionalist army that had occupied Morelos was demoralized and disintegrating. By year's end, Carranza's army had been forced to evacuate Morelos.

Even though the Zapatistas continued to control Morelos, after Villa's defeat Carranza was without political commitments and free of opponents who threatened his regime. The Constitutionalist leader differed from Madero in that he felt that Mexico would not progress until it modernized economically. This was a major departure from Madero's call for "Effective suffrage" and "No re-election."

The year 1916 saw the end of major combat and the implantation of a coherent national policy by the triumphant Constitutionalists. Once he no longer faced military threats, Carranza halted his reforms. He returned confiscated property to the Porfirian elite. The Constitutionalists crushed

JUAN PÉREZ JOLOTE

Juan Pérez Jolote was born in Chamula, an indigenous village in Chiapas, presumably in the 1890s. He never knew the year of his birth. As was the case with many indigenous, he did not grow up speaking Spanish. His mother tongue was Tzotzil, the Mayan language of his village. The village itself straddled two worlds—that of the subsistence corn farmer and that of the international capitalist economy.

As he approached adulthood, he engaged in a traditional rite of passage—leaving the village to perform wage labor on a nearby coffee plantation. While working there he was a bystander when a fellow worker was murdered, so he was arrested as the presumed guilty party and jailed without trial for almost a year.

During the Huerta administration, authorities arrived at the jail and conscripted all the able-bodied men for the army. They placed him and other "recruits" in a boxcar and shipped them to Mexico City. Then he was sent north to face Villa's forces at Zacatecas. He was one of the many casualties of the battle there and was still in a Mexico City hospital when Constitutionalists took the city.

After his recovery Pérez Jolote did odd jobs, often for only room and board. Seeing that he was at a dead end, he decided to volunteer for the army—this time Carranza's. As a Carrancista he was stationed in Pachuca, 50 miles northeast of Mexico City. He was still there when Villistas overran the town. Pérez Jolote described his exchange with the Villistas:

They asked us why we'd become Carrancistas, and I said: "The Huertistas made us go with them, and when Carranza started winning we had to change sides . . ." An old man with a big moustache said, "Well, what do you want to do now?" I said, "I just want to be on your side . . ." They signed us up and gave us weapons and five pesos each, and that made us Villistas.

Shortly after his becoming a Villista his commanding general arrived and said there was no money, the unit was being disbanded, and all troops were free to leave. After a stint working in Veracruz, Pérez Jolote returned home.

After reintegration into his community, Pérez Jolote lived the life of a typical Chiapas Indian. He married, started a family and spent long stretches working on coffee plantations to earn money to maintain his family.

Pérez Jolote served in a variety of village positions. He was selected as *fiscal* based on his ability to read. In this position he scheduled religious festivals and answered questions concerning the significance of various saints. He later served as *sacristán*, caring for the church building, and as *alférez,* caring for figures of saints in the church.

In addition to being honored by his village with various positions, anthropologist Ricardo Pozas honored Pérez Jolote by compiling his biography, which is the source of information presented here. An English translation of the biography was published as *Juan the Chamula: An Ethnological Recreation of the Life of a Mexican Indian* (Berkeley, CA: University of California Press, 1962).

strikes and allowed land reform to endure only in those states where governors had already committed themselves to such policies, certainly a tiny minority nationwide.

The new Constitutionalist administration began rebuilding a centralized state—a task that required decades. In many places, crop failures led to widespread food scarcity, and government authority was lacking. Transportation was uncertain, and bands of disgruntled, leaderless revolutionaries marauded the countryside.

To implement Carranza's policies, Constitutionalist officers, who overwhelmingly came from northern Mexico, assumed governorships and other top posts throughout central and southern Mexico. Often these northern officers were viewed not as liberators but as carpetbaggers attempting to impose unwanted, alien values. Anyone who opposed or openly questioned them was branded a "reactionary." Carranza's northern officers so widely abused their positions that a new term was coined, *carrancear*, meaning to sack, pillage, confiscate, and rob.

THE OUTCOME

The Constitutionalists won because they planned on a national level and used populist tactics to broaden their support. Their control of Tampico, Veracruz, and Yucatán, all of which generated substantial export revenue, allowed the purchase of arms from abroad. The Plan of Ayala did not address the needs of the more heterogeneous population, including artisans, laborers, itinerant merchants, and others with an urban orientation, outside the state of Morelos. Finally, along with the rest of the Western world of the period, the Constitutionalists adopted mass war as a means to power. By 1917, Carranza's army alone totaled 147,000, seven times the number who served in the army at the end of the Porfiriato.

The Revolution's having been initiated by a section of the elite with little interest in social reform limited revolutionary potential. It was led in Coahuila by Carranza, a conservative *hacendado*. In Sonora upwardly mobile members of the middle class, who would become the next generation's elite, provided leadership. In tiny Morelos, with its broad revolutionary base, the goal was an idealized past of communally held village land.

The very concept of "Mexican Revolution" only developed after the fact. There were various revolutions and movements. Some lost, some won. Before 1920, people spoke of the Madero Revolution, the Constitutionalist Revolution, and Zapata's Southern Revolution. Only after 1920 did the term "Mexican Revolution" gain acceptance.

The Revolution dramatically increased the power of the state. This is ironic, since one of the principal causes of the rebellion, especially in the north, was the desire for more local autonomy. Post-revolutionary governments accepted responsibility for some of the social costs of development, such as education and health care, and assumed new roles, such as implementing land reform and arbitrating labor disputes.

The *soldadera* forms the most enduring image of women in the Mexican Revolution. As in the nineteenth century, the revolutionary armies generally did not have troops assigned to tend the wounded and secure and prepare food. These tasks fell on female auxiliaries who accompanied the forces, usually linked to a husband or lover.

Soldaderas served for a variety of reasons. Often service provided a way to keep a family intact or to avoid being left alone and unprotected in perilous times. Some became *soldaderas* to earn a living, given the prevailing economic hardship of the time. When a *soldadera* served, she and her children simply accompanied her man.

In addition to serving as *soldaderas*, women were active in a variety of revolutionary activities. Some served full-time as combatants, while others smuggled arms and ammunition across the U.S.–Mexico border. Upper-class women often volunteered to serve in organizations such as the Red Cross. Still others served as couriers, spies, and political organizers, building support for the revolutionary leaders they supported.

On January 15, 1915, Carranza issued his one significant decree affecting women. For the first time in Mexico, it allowed divorce, in the modern sense of the word. This decree reflected not grassroots pressure but the anti-clerical sentiments of the revolutionary elite.

As historian Alan Knight noted, "Out of the maelstrom of revolution . . . emerged a society which, compared with pre-1910, was more open, fluid, mobile, innovative and market-oriented." Society opened more fully to mestizos. Those with battlefield experience and a working-class background assumed leadership positions that previously had been reserved for those with a college education and civilian institutional experience.

CORRIDOS

The *corrido* is a form of narrative ballad which has roots in both indigenous and Spanish culture. *Corridos* were created and performed in response to events affecting local communities. The subjects of the *corrido* were as varied as life itself and included war, crime, and love. Through the early twentieth century *corridos* functioned as an oral newspaper, providing information to an illiterate society. *Corridos* typically took the viewpoint of the underdog.

One of the oldest recorded *corridos*, "*Adiós mamá Carlota*" dates from the Maximilian era. By the beginning of the twentieth century the genre reached its peak as is indicated by the number of *corridos* published along with illustrations by José Guadalupe Posada. *Corridos* were influential during the Mexican Revolution. They functioned in parallel with the printed media of the time which addressed a conservative, literate audience. *Corridos* in contrast extolled leaders such as Villa and Zapata. The best known of the Revolutionary *corridos* is "*La cucaracha*" (the Cockroach) which celebrated the exploits of Villa's Northern Division.

Below are lines from a *corrido* commenting on the assassination of Pancho Villa:

Pobre Pancho Villa.	Poor Pancho Villa.
Fue muy triste su destino.	His fate was a sad one.
Morir en una emboscada.	To die in an ambush
Y a la mitad del camino.	in the middle of the road.
Ay, México está de luto.	Ay, Mexico is in mourning
Tiene una gran pesadilla.	It has a great nightmare
Pues mataron en Parral	Because they killed in Parral
al valiente Pancho Villa.	The brave Pancho Villa.

By mid-twentieth century literacy, radio, and increasingly television had reduced the *corrido* from its role in subverting the established order to folklore status. However conflicts of the late twentieth century gave it new life. Luis Váldez's Teatro Campesino employed the *corrido* to mobilize the largely Mexican and Mexican-American farm workers in California during the 1960s. Later it galvanized Mexican Americans demanding civil rights. Further south the *corrido* gave voice to the 1970s Sandinista Revolution in Nicaragua.

As a result of the drug war in Mexico, the *corrido* has been rebranded as the *narcocorrido*. These new manifestations of the *corrido* describe, often approvingly, illegal activities such as murder, torture, extortion, and above all drug smuggling. Frequently those performing *narcocorridos* are viewed as being in the employment of an individual drug smuggler or as sympathizing with him. As a result between 2006 and 2008 more than a dozen prominent Mexican musicians were murdered. Given *narcocorridos'* glorification of lawbreakers and their precipitating violence, authorities have engaged in an ongoing battle to prohibit the distribution and radio-play of *narcocorridos*.

[*Corrido* stanzas and translation from Friedrich Katz (2007) *The Face of Pancho Villa*. El Paso TX: Cinco Puntos Press. p. 32.]

Between 1910 and 1921, Mexico's population declined from 15.1 million to 14.3 million, thus providing a measure of the Revolution's impact. This population decline only in part resulted from battlefield fatalities, the execution of prisoners, and wounds that often proved fatal due to poor medical care. This decline also resulted from a lowered birth rate, increased emigration, and a lower living standard, which made people more susceptible to diseases such as typhus. The 1918 "Spanish flu" epidemic killed as many as 400,000. The 1920 U.S. census enumerated 486,418 U.S. residents born in Mexico, compared to 221,915 in 1910.

During the period of the armed struggle, 1910–17, the goals of the Revolution lacked clarity since there was no overall coordination of combatants, some of whom fought for opposing goals. In the aftermath of the Revolution, a consensus emerged concerning what the Revolution stood for. These goals, some of which were only inserted into the revolutionary portfolio well after the last battle, included: 1) replacing the Díaz dictatorship with democracy; 2) supplying land to the tiller; 3) the creation of a new government with a strong executive; 4) nationalism; 5) uplifting labor; 6) a coherent state-led development strategy; 7) mass education; and 8) support for Mexico's indigenous population.

DESTRUCTION AND DEVELOPMENT, 1910–1916

The economic impact of the Revolution varied widely by place, year, and type of industry. As a whole, the economy performed well through 1914, after which militarization and destruction took their toll. Destruction associated with the Revolution was highly regionalized, with the north-central and south-central regions being especially hard hit. Coastal areas, the far south, and Mexico City suffered far less. Industries closely tied to the railroad, such as mining, were devastated, while producers of commodities exported by ship, such as oil, bananas, and henequen, prospered.

Economic Decline, 1911–1916

As security conditions deteriorated, a decline in new investment halted economic growth. Beginning in 1912, many U.S. investors curtailed and, if possible, repatriated their investments in railroads, mining, land, and utilities. By 1914 only the oil industry was attracting new investment.

As a result of the Revolution, rail service was severely curtailed. All factions seized rolling stock, which was diverted from passenger and freight service to military uses. Given the interruption of fuel supplies, locomotives were converted to burn wood. To meet immediate fuel needs, stations were sometimes dismantled and burned as fuel.

In a three-year period, 1912 to 1915, silver production declined from 2,526,715 kilograms to 712,599. As late as 1921, mine output remained 40 percent below the 1910 level.

Between 1910 and 1915, the volume of agricultural production fell by 24 percent. Between 1910 and 1921, the number of cattle in Chihuahua declined from roughly 1.2 million to 60,000.

Few factories and cotton mills were destroyed during the Revolution, since most were located in Monterrey, Mexico City, and the Veracruz–Puebla corridor—areas that saw little combat. All factions considered factories as economic assets to be taxed and thus spared them from attack. Factory production plummeted, though, as rail service declined, making it difficult to market goods or obtain spare parts and raw materials.

The lack of a stable currency added to Mexico's economic woes. To finance their war efforts, both Villa and Carranza turned to the printing press. By mid-1915, the Constitutionalists had printed 672 million pesos, compared with the 193.2 million pesos that were in circulation in 1910.

In 1916, as a result of runaway inflation, the peso–dollar exchange rate shifted from 22.72 to 1 to 217.39 to 1. There was widespread reversion to a barter economy, except in export enclaves and border areas where foreign currency circulated.

In 1916, with victory in hand, the Constitutionalists began the massive minting of gold and silver coins. Paper money would not circulate again in large amounts until 1931.

Revolutionary Development, 1911–1916

While rail service was interrupted, marine commerce was largely unaffected by the Revolution. Thanks largely to maritime commerce, U.S. imports from Mexico, which totaled $57 million in 1911, increased through 1916, when they reached $105 million.

After 1911 the oil industry boomed, the Revolution notwithstanding. By 1915 Mexico had become the world's second largest oil producer, behind only the United States. The following year production reached 40.5 million barrels, up from 12.6 million in 1911. Between 1910 and 1921, the population of Tampico, the major oil center, increased from 23,310 to 94,667. With soaring production levels, the weak Mexican market was soon saturated, causing oilmen to turn to exports.

As a result of oil, Mexico became more closely linked than ever to the United States. In 1911 Mexico only supplied 1 percent of U.S. petroleum needs. By 1919 Mexico supplied 14 percent of the greatly increased U.S. demand. More than two-thirds of the petroleum was exported as crude oil, with little value added.

Given its isolation from combat zones, henequen production was not interrupted. The United States had become so dependent on henequen twine for its wheat harvest that when unrest threatened to interrupt supply, President Wilson ordered U.S. navy ships to Yucatán. These vessels brought the gold used to pay for the henequen and then returned to U.S. soil with the fiber. As historian Gilbert Joseph commented, "While the rest of the Republic made war, Yucatán made money."

Given the disruption of the war years, Mexico did not carry out a census until 1921. Based on this census data, between 1910 and 1921, the economy shrank from 11,650 to 11,273 million 1950 pesos.

TRYING TO PICK A WINNER, 1910–1916

> U.S. efforts to interfere notwithstanding, the Revolution was started by Mexicans, conducted by Mexicans, and resolved in a wholly Mexican fashion.
>
> (John S. D. Eisenhower, 1993)

Taft and Díaz, 1909–1911

By the end of the Porfiriato, the United States and Mexico were inexorably linked. Henry Lane Wilson, who presented his credentials as ambassador in March 1910, reported that the U.S. embassy in Mexico City generated 33 percent of all State Department correspondence, which was handled by "as many as six clerks."

The embassy served the needs of some 70,000 Americans living in Mexico and of U.S. investors who had roughly $800,000,000 invested there. With this large stake in Mexico, it became clear that the United States could never again be truly neutral in matters concerning Mexico. Recognizing Mexican governments put the U.S. stamp of approval on them and discouraged rebels. Non-recognition encouraged rebels. The U.S. also exerted influence over Mexico by making or withholding investments and loans, by raising or lowering tariffs, and by selling or embargoing arms.

In 1910, most American businessmen remained pro-Díaz. U.S. journalist John Kenneth Turner observed that due to the availability of cheap labor in Mexico, "American capitalists support Díaz with a great deal more unanimity than they support Taft."

U.S. tolerance of Madero's insurrectionary activities contributed to his victory. As would be the case throughout the Revolution, the U.S. government did not act with a single mind. Officials on the border tolerated arms smuggling into Mexico, Ambassador Wilson felt keeping Díaz in power was the key to Mexican stability, and Taft professed neutrality.

The United States and Madero, 1911–1913

U.S. President William Howard Taft quickly recognized Madero's government. However, the honeymoon between the United States and Madero ended after it became apparent that Madero could not quickly suppress the Orozco and Zapata uprisings. This called into question Madero's ability to maintain law and order. U.S. Ambassador Henry Lane Wilson was especially shrill in his condemnation of Madero, since he felt not only that Madero was unable to maintain order but also that he was a naive dreamer.

In June 1912, when Madero instituted a $0.015 per barrel tax on oil, U.S.–Mexican relations took a turn for the worse. Oilmen clamed the tax was confiscatory and equaled 17 percent of their profits. This was an outrageous lie, but it made good newspaper copy. The oil companies finally negotiated a lower tax rate.

The oil tax and Madero's permitting trade union organization turned U.S. businessmen against him. After decades of Díaz's accommodating attitude, the U.S. business community refused to accept any tinge of nationalism. This became self-defeating. As successive revolutionary leaders emerged, the United States came into conflict with each of them as they adopted nationalist policies.

When Félix Díaz and Bernardo Reyes revolted against Madero, Ambassador Wilson's actions reflected not U.S. policy but his personal opinion of Mexico's president. On his own initiative, Ambassador Wilson arranged for General Huerta, still ostensibly fighting to preserve Madero's presidency, to meet secretly with Félix Díaz in the U.S. embassy. There they signed the Pact of the Embassy, the agreement that Huerta would betray Madero and become the provisional president.

After helping arrange this unholy transfer of power, Ambassador Wilson informed Washington, "Our position here is stronger than ever." The day Madero and his vice-president were arrested, Wilson hosted a reception at the U.S. embassy attended by both Huerta and Díaz. The U.S. ambassador did not realize that, rather than restoring order, the coup he was involved in would lead to even more massive bloodshed.

Author Carlos Fuentes expressed the widely held Mexican view of Ambassador Wilson: "Madero respected free elections, a free press, and an uncontrolled Congress. Significantly, he was promptly overthrown by a conspiracy of the American ambassador, Henry Lane Wilson, and a group of reactionary generals."

The United States and Huerta, 1913–1914

The U.S. business community in Mexico welcomed Huerta, feeling the country needed a new strongman and that Huerta would fill that role. However, his government had not received U.S. recognition by March 4, 1913, when Woodrow Wilson, a former political science professor at Princeton, assumed the presidency. He believed that Christian virtues were as applicable to the conduct of foreign affairs as to personal conduct. This led him to remove Ambassador Wilson (no relation to the president) whom he felt was morally implicated in Madero's murder.

In applying his interpretation of morality, Wilson refused to recognize Huerta's government. To end the supply of arms to Huerta, on August 17, 1913, Wilson decreed an embargo on all arms sales to Mexico.

Throughout his presidency, Wilson came under intense pressure from railroaders, oilmen, and cattle barons such as William Randolph Hearst to intervene directly in Mexico to restore peace, order, and security. Wilson would decline, noting, "I have to pause and remind myself that I am the President of the United States and not of a small group of Americans with vested interests in Mexico."

On April 21, 1914, U.S. troops landed in Veracruz. As Secretary of Navy Josephus Daniels later wrote, "The purpose of the landing was accomplished in the weakening and the undoing of Huerta's reign of terror." Secretary of Navy Josephus Daniels's message to Rear Admiral Frank Fletcher, anchored off Veracruz, stated: "Seize the custom house. Do not permit war supplies to be delivered to Huerta government or any other party." Before the U.S. forces took control of the port, seventeen Americans and 126 Mexicans had been killed.

The landing at Veracruz had its intended effect. The U.S. occupation of the port denied the Huerta administration arms shipments and customs revenue, hastening its collapse. The United States collected and retained customs duties while it occupied the port.

Wilson and the Constitutionalists, 1914–1916

With Huerta gone, the Wilson administration no longer had a rationale for occupying Veracruz. Thus U.S. troops withdrew on November 23, 1914, after having made substantial sanitary improvements. As U.S. troops departed, they turned over to Carranza war material seized when U.S. troops landed, other arms intended for Huerta that had arrived after the U.S. landing, and arms brought by U.S. troops and not removed. This material, which included cars, trucks, radios, artillery, machine guns, 12,000 rifles and carbines, 3,375,000 rounds of ammunition, and 632 rolls of barbed wire, was used by Obregón to rout Villa's force.

After Huerta's fall, Carranza was the only viable elite leader left in Mexico. His return of confiscated estates to their former owners and his lack of close ties to Europeans raised his standing in the United States. Carranza sent agents to the United States to promote the Constitutionalist cause and to pay for favorable publicity.

The impending Great War began to dominate U.S. thinking, leading policymakers to seek a rapid end to hostilities in Mexico. As war began to loom in Europe, the United States decided to pick a winner, propel him to a rapid victory, and thus prevent Germany from taking advantage of ongoing conflict to meddle in Mexican affairs. On October 10, 1915, Secretary of State Lansing wrote in his diary, "Our possible relations with Germany must be our first consideration; and all our intercourse with Mexico must be regulated accordingly." Nine days later the Wilson administration granted Carranza de facto recognition. That same day, an embargo was placed on the sale of arms to all other factions.

The Columbus Raid and Wilson's Response

On March 9, 1916, about 500 Villistas raided Columbus, New Mexico, four miles north of the U.S.–Mexican border. Eight U.S. soldiers and nine civilians died. Roughly sixty Villistas were killed in Columbus and about seventy more died as they were chased back to Mexico.

The U.S. response to Villa's raid was outrage. Wilson, facing re-election in 1916, was conscious that he could not look "weak" to the electorate. Given this political imperative, he ordered General John "Black Jack" Pershing into Mexico "for the sole purpose of capturing the bandit Villa." Pershing's force crossed the border with 5,000 men, including cavalry, infantry, engineers, artillery units, and the entire U.S. air force—eight Curtiss Jenny biplanes—for reconnaissance. Later the strength of his force was increased to 10,000 men. These mounted troops made several indecisive contacts with Villistas, who broke and scattered.

Whether war with Mexico would have broken out if Wilson had had a free hand is unclear. In any case, as the Great War loomed, U.S. concerns in Europe prevailed over those in Mexico. Wilson was aware that intervention in Mexico would turn the rest of Latin America against the United States. As a result, Wilson recalled Pershing's force, which, although it did not capture Villa, did disperse his major troop concentrations. The last U.S. soldier departed Mexico on February 5, 1917.

Nationalism and Anti-Americanism

All in all, the Mexican Revolution was neither pro- nor anti-American. The United States as a nation and U.S. citizens were simply judged by what they did. For example, when American agricultural colonies were attacked, it was often due to their owners' having appropriated land without having provided jobs. American *hacendados* often protected themselves from anti-American outbursts by paying their employees higher wages than those paid on Mexican-owned estates. In general American businesses were not attacked since they were a prized source of well-paying jobs. In the free-ranging debate at the Aguascalientes Convention, the occasional references to the United States were generally favorable.

Emigration

Throughout the armed phase of the Revolution, violence and declining employment in Mexico and continued U.S. economic prosperity led to a sharp increase in emigration. Mexicans easily found employment in the United States, since the outbreak of the Great War in late 1914 halted European emigration. In the decade 1911–1920, 219,004 legal immigrants entered the United States from Mexico. Another 628,000 Mexicans came as temporary workers, and countless others came as refugees or undocumented workers.

At the time, Americans simply regarded Mexican workers as a needed source of labor for agriculture, mining, railroads, and smelting, and their presence produced little controversy. For the first time, a sizable number of *hacendados*, middle-class professionals, and intellectuals emigrated north along with the rural poor. They abandoned Mexico because they feared for their safety at the hands of revolutionaries due to their wealth or their having supported a losing political faction.

DOCUMENT 10.1: PLAN OF AYALA

[After listing what they considered Francisco Madero's failings as president, the Zapatistas in their Plan de Ayala, declared:]

Sr. Francisco I. Madero is no longer recognized as Chief of the Revolution and as President of the Republic, for the reasons already expressed, in order to overthrow this official.

The illustrious General Pascual Orozco, the second of Don Francisco I. Madero, is recognized as Chief of the Liberating Revolution, and in case he does not accept this difficult post, recognition as Chief of the Revolution will go to General Don Emiliano Zapata.

The Revolutionary Junta of the State of Morelos manifests to the Nation under formal oath; that it adopts as its own the plan of San Luís Potosí, with the additions expressed below, for the benefit of the oppressed pueblos, and it will make itself the defender of the principles it upholds until victory or death.

The Revolutionary Junta of the State of Morelos will not allow agreements or compromises until it achieves the overthrow of the dictatorial forces of Porfirio Díaz and Francisco I. Madero, for the Nation is tired of false men and traitors who make promises as liberators, and who upon arriving in power forget them and become tyrants.

As an additional part of the plan, we give notice: the pueblos or citizens who have legal title to real estate will take possession of the lands, forests, and water, which, in the shadows of corrupted justice, landlords, científicos, or bosses have usurped, maintaining at any cost with arms in hand the mentioned possession; and the usurpers who believe their old rights to these properties will be heard before the special tribunals which will be established upon the triumph of the revolution.

Since the immense majority of Mexican pueblos and citizens are owners of no more than the land they walk on, suffering the horrors of poverty without being able to improve their social condition in any way or to dedicate themselves to Industry or Agriculture, because lands, timber and water are monopolized in a few hands, for this cause there will be expropriated the third part of those monopolies from the powerful proprietors, with prior indemnification, in order that the pueblos and citizens of Mexico may obtain ejidos, colonies, and foundations for pueblos, or fields for sowing or laboring, and the Mexicans' lack of prosperity and wellbeing may improve in all and for all.

The landlords, científicos, or caciques who directly or indirectly opposed the present Plan, shall have their property nationalized, and the two thirds parts which otherwise would belong to them will go for indemnifications of war, and pensions for widows and orphans of the victims who succumb in the struggle for the present Plan.

In order to carry out the procedures regarding the aforementioned properties, the laws of disentailment and nationalization will be applied as appropriate: as norm and example, shall be those laws put into effect by the immortal Juárez regarding ecclesiastical properties, which punished the despots and conservatives who have always sought to impose upon us the ignominious yoke of oppression and backwardness.

After declaring who will be judged as traitors and how war expenses will be met, the Plan calls for:

Once the revolution we carry out is realized, a junta of the principal revolutionary chiefs from the different States will name or designate an interim President of the Republic, who will convoke elections for the organization of federal powers.

Ayala, November 15, 1911

Liberty, Justice and Law

Source: Nora E. Jaffary, Edward W. Osowski and Susie S. Porter (eds.) (2010) *Mexican History: A Primary Source Reader*. Boulder, CO: Westview Press, pp. 301–04.

NOTE

1 Odile Guilpain, *Felipe Ángeles y los destinos de la Revolución mexicana* (Mexico City: Fondo de Cultura Económica, 1991), p. 10.

FURTHER READING

Azuela, Mariano (1992) *The Underdog*. Pittsburgh, PA: University of Pittsburgh Press.
This classic novel of the Revolution, rather than glorifying war, emphasizes its futility.

Gonzales, Michael (2002) *The Mexican Revolution, 1910–1940*. Albuquerque, N.M.: Univeristy of New Mexico Press.
A summary of events during the armed struggle and in subsequent decades.

Katz, Friedrich (1998) *The Life and Times of Pancho Villa*. Stanford, CA: Stanford Univeristy Press.
The definitive study of the man and his role in the Revolution.

Knight, Alan (1986) *The Mexican Revolution*. Cambridge: Cambridge University Press.
The comprehensive study of the Revolution.

Richmond, Douglas W. and Sam Hayes (eds.) (2013) *The Mexican Revolution: Conflict and Consolidation, 1910–1940*. College Station: Texas: A&M University Press.
Essays discussing changes in Mexico between 1910 and 1940 and their impact on U.S.–Mexican relations.

Womack, John (1986) *Zapata and the Mexican Revolution*. New York: Vintage.
The classic description of Zapata and his movement.

—— (1986) "The Mexican Revolution, 1910–1920," *Cambridge History of Latin America*, Vol. 5, pp. 79–153.
A consideration of the forces, foreign and domestic, shaping the Revolution.

GLOSSARY

Constitutionalist

Northern Division (División del Norte)

Zapatista

Chapter 11

The Post-revolutionary Years, 1917–1940

TIMELINE—WORLD

1917	1918	1919	1920	1921
Russian Revolution	Armistice ends World War I combat	Treaty of Versailles sets out terms of peace, including saddling Germany with reparations	Prohibition begins in the United States	Warren Harding inaugurated U.S. President

1933				
Prohibition ends in the United States				

TIMELINE—MEXICO

1917	1920 (April)	1920 (May)	1920 (December)	1923
New Constitution promulgated	Plan de Agua Prieta against Carranza	Carranza murdered	Obregón inaugurated	De la Huerta Rebellion

1934	1936	1938	1940	
President Cárdenas inaugurated	Calles exiled	Oil expropriation	President Ávila Camacho inaugurated	

1923	1927	1929	1929	1933
Harding dies in office, Vice-President Calvin Coolidge becomes U.S. President	World population reaches 2 billion, 123 years after reaching 1 billion	Wall Street collapse begins Depression	Herbert Hoover becomes U.S. President	Franklin D. Roosevelt becomes U.S. President

1924	1928	1928	1930	1932
Calles inaugurated	Obregón re-elected and assassinated	Provisional President Portes Gil inaugurated	President Ortiz Rubio inaugurated	President Abelardo Rodríguez inaugurated

THIS CHAPTER DESCRIBES HOW MEXICANS CREATED A NEW POLITICAL SYSTEM and restored their war-ravaged economy—the same problems they faced a century earlier after independence. The first major step in this rebuilding process was the promulgation of the 1917 constitution which in theory would provide structure for the new political order. Political order however was slow in coming. During the 1920s, at both the national and local level, armed force, not ballots, determined who held office. The creation of the National Revolutionary Party (PNR) in 1928 laid the groundwork for more orderly political succession. Under the aegis of the PNR Lázaro Cárdenas was elected president for the 1934–40 term. He carried out the most far-reaching reforms associated with the Revolution. The chapter then considers how the economy began to recover from wartime damage, only to be confronted by the Depression. A final section considers how the U.S. government attempted—ultimately unsuccessfully—to impose its interpretation of investor rights and subsurface mineral (i.e. oil) ownership.

INSTITUTIONALIZING THE NEW REGIME, 1917–1940

The Carranza Administration, 1917–1920

To consolidate and legitimize his power, in September 1916 Carranza called for a constitutional convention. The next month Mexicans elected delegates to the Convention. Carranza stipulated that those who had aided any other faction in the Revolution or who had served Huerta would be ineligible to become a delegate. This provision prevented any delegates from representing Villa or Zapata.

Despite having dictated the process for selecting Convention delegates, Carranza proved unable to dominate the Convention once it convened. A radical majority emerged that sought a strong federal government that could challenge the Church and implement social reform.

Article 3 of the completed constitution decreed education would be compulsory and without charge. As with other articles, it was out of touch with Mexican reality. With just over 1 percent of the budget earmarked for education, for most Mexican children school attendance was only wishful thinking. The article left education in the hands of states and municipalities, the entities least able or willing to implement it.

Article 27 granted the government the power to control land use for "public utility," thus providing the legal basis for Mexico's far-reaching land reform. This article also declared the government, not the surface landowner, owned oil in the ground.

Article 123 contained a rich lode of labor rights, including the right to unionize and strike, the eight-hour day, and equal pay for equal work regardless of one's gender or nationality. This article also ignored Mexican reality. It prohibited child labor in an economy where such labor was essential for the survival of many families. Miner Nicolás Cano, one of the few workers at the Convention, was prescient in noting that by protecting only "legal" strikes, Article 123 left the door open for business and government to jointly declare strikes illegal and oppress labor.

Article 83 prohibited both immediate presidential re-election and a later return to the presidency à la Porfirio Díaz in 1884. This reflected the belief that the ills of the Porfiriato resulted from Díaz's repeated re-election.

In March 1917, elections were held to legitimize Carranza's presidency. There was no organized opposition, and Carranza received more than 97 percent of the vote.

Carranza faced a number of challenges once he assumed the presidency. The large standing army, which received two-thirds of the federal budget, was reluctant to disband. Peasants and workers, having been mobilized by the Revolution, demanded that the government take measures to meet their aspirations. Given Mexico's economic disarray, merely feeding the population presented a major challenge.

Carranza shared the conviction of the Porfirian elite that land reform would be a disaster for the Mexican economy and that it would sharply reduce agricultural production. In keeping with this notion, he returned many seized estates to their pre-revolutionary owners. He felt this would increase tax collection and food production and win the political support of those who recouped their land.

Carranza decided it was not militarily feasible to eliminate Zapata's guerrilla force in Morelos, so he set a trap. Jesús Guajardo, a Carrancista colonel, claimed that he wanted to defect from Carranza and join the Zapatistas. He promised to bring along badly needed troops and munitions. Guajardo met Zapata at Chinameca hacienda in Morelos. Upon entering the hacienda courtyard on April 10, 1919, Zapata was cut down by gunfire from an ambush that Guajardo had laid for him.

Carranza's civilian appointees began a trend toward personal enrichment through public office on a scale previously unmatched. The tone of government changed so radically that by 1920 it was difficult to see any relation between government action and the 1917 constitution. Carranza, like Madero before him, had no desire to implement sweeping changes.

By 1919 Obregón had allied himself with middle-class military men who were dissatisfied with the tenor of Carranza's government. His new allies resented the unfulfilled promises of the Revolution and the increasing power of *hacendados*. The enrichment of Carrancista officials, widespread repression, and the assassination of Zapata only served to increase their dissatisfaction.

As Obregón drew broad-based support, Carranza's power base began to crumble. The United States opposed him due to his nationalism. Peasants and labor unions failed to rally behind him due to his opposition to land reform, unions, and strikes.

In 1919, Carranza attempted to impose his ambassador in Washington, Ignacio Bonillas, as his successor. Carranza thought he could control Bonillas even after his term was over and thus maintain de facto power. He knew he could not control the outstanding general of the Revolution, Obregón.

In June 1919, Obregón announced his own presidential candidacy. His whistle-stop tours around the country drew enthusiastic crowds. Fearing he would be arrested if he continued campaigning, he formed an alliance with remnants of the Zapatista movement and called for revolt against Carranza. Obregón had the backing of reform-minded military men, peasants, and workers, who saw in him the hope for change. He also had strong backing in his home state of Sonora, where on April 23, 1920, two generals, Plutarco Calles and Adolfo de la Huerta, issued the Plan of Agua Prieta, which repudiated Carranza's government.

On May 7, 1920, realizing that he had little support, Carranza fled toward Veracruz. Before reaching that port, Carranza found rebels had blocked the rail line. He abandoned the train and reached the village of Tlaxcalantongo, Puebla, on horseback. There he was ambushed and killed by troops under the command of a general in Obregón's employ.

Carranza's strongest legacy is providing an institutional framework—the 1917 constitution—which his successors could build on. Carranza's nationalism forms another part of his legacy. He increased the taxes on oil companies seven-fold between 1917 and 1920. He was not anti-capitalist or even anti-foreign and did not seek to eliminate foreign investment, but to control it.

The Sonoran Dynasty, 1920–1928

Following Carranza's death, Congress selected Adolfo de la Huerta, a former governor of Sonora, as provisional president to serve the remainder of Carranza's term. Since de la Huerta had not been a military rival of Villa, he was able to persuade Villa to surrender. In exchange for his surrender, Villa was given Canutillo Hacienda, a 163,000-acre spread in Durango.

On September 5, 1920, Obregón, facing only nominal opposition, received 94 percent of the votes for president. Bonillas had withdrawn his candidacy. As would be the case throughout the 1920s, the election served not to select a president but to legitimize a military victor.

Obregón did not attempt to contain the masses through repression as Huerta had. Rather, reform—or the promise of reform—was used as a means of political control. Obregón's indulging in radical rhetoric served to whet appetites and make workers and peasants look to his administration for change. The terms "class struggle," "socialism," and "anti-imperialism" flowed easily from officials' tongues

By the time Obregón took office, it had become clear that Mexico was failing to meet its educational goals. In many cases, school attendance was below the rates of the Porfiriato. To address this issue, Obregón pushed through a constitutional amendment that granted the federal government the right to build and administer schools. In 1921, he established a new cabinet post, the secretary of public education, which oversaw federal schools, libraries, and the fine arts.

By the time Obregón left office in 1924, only 3.5 percent of agrarian land had been distributed. In contrast, as late as 1925, some 79 million acres were foreign owned. Obregón stated that subdividing estates would reduce production. He felt that if haciendas were subdivided, "We would put to flight foreign capital, which at this moment we need more than ever."

Obregón increased social mobility for the middle class. Its members enriched themselves quickly, taking advantage of the power the government gave them. During the 1920s, they became virtually indistinguishable from those whom they had fought during the Revolution. Often their wealth was based on public works contracts or simply on pillaging the public treasury.

Obregón initiated the decades-long task of converting the military from the destroyer of governments to their protector. He increased military pay scales and founded a national military academy that stressed military subordination to civilian government. During the first three years of the Obregón administration, the number of soldiers declined from more than 100,000 to 40,000, and military spending declined from 61 percent to 36 percent of the federal budget. Since military conflict appeared unlikely soldiers were assigned to build highways, streets, reservoirs, schools, hospitals, and airports, and to carry out reforestation projects. Given the lack of law and order in the 1920s, soldiers were often stationed to maintain peace on highways, haciendas, and towns.

On July 20, 1923, as former interim president de la Huerta's presidential ambitions began to pose a serious threat to the government, gunfire riddled Villa's car as he drove into town from Canutillo, killing him instantly. In his magisterial biography of Villa, historian Friedrich Katz concluded, "There can, on the whole, be little doubt that the Mexican government was not only implicated in but probably also organized the assassination of Villa." Likely Obregón took seriously Villa's boast that he could mobilize 40,000 men in forty minutes and feared that they would be mobilized in favor of de la Huerta.

During his term, Obregón personally chose those who would serve as congressmen, senators, and governors. His departure from the presidency began another Mexican political tradition—the out-going president's selecting his successor without popular involvement.

Obregón chose Plutarco Elías Calles, another general from Sonora, to succeed him. When Calles's nomination was announced in 1923, General Adolfo de la Huerta, who had served as Obregón's secretary of finance, attempted a coup.

De la Huerta's revolt drew some 50,000 followers, mainly in the north, and had the backing of conservatives, *hacendados*, Catholic leaders, and half the army's generals. Obregón's alliance with peasants, a product of his populist style, served him well. Feeling that Calles offered the best hope of land distribution, 120,000 peasants attacked de la Huerta's lines of communication, sabotaged supplies, and formed small military units. Support from organized labor and U.S.-supplied arms, ammunition, and airplanes also contributed to de la Huerta's defeat.

When elections were finally held, Calles received 84 percent of the vote. Most Mexicans showed little interest and abstained.

Obregón was a pragmatic president with few political ideals. Assassinating Villa and creating schools were exceptions to what was generally a non-activist presidency. Most of the large estates that existed during the Porfiriato were intact at the end of Obregón's term, although ownership of many of them had passed to generals. In 1924 Mexicans probably ate less, had fewer jobs, and enjoyed no greater political rights than they had before the Revolution. Obregón did have the distinction of being the first Mexican president in generations to complete his term and leave office.

Obregón's successor, Calles, was the third president in a row from Sonora—thus the term Sonoran dynasty. In 1915 Carranza appointed him as interim governor of Sonora. While serving as governor (1915–16, 1917–19), Calles opened 127 primary schools, organized a congress on education, and inaugurated a teachers' training school. He later served as Carranza's secretary of industry, commerce, and labor and as Obregón's interior secretary.

Calles campaigned for the 1924 presidential election affirming support for Article 27 and other reformist provisions of the 1917 constitution. He portrayed himself as an advocate for the "landless classes." In October 1924, as president-elect, Calles muted his populism when he spoke at New York City's Waldorf-Astoria Hotel. He declared the goal of the Revolution was "to secure the social and economic elevation of 12 million submerged Mexicans, but at the same time invite the cooperation of capitalists and industrialists of good will."

Obregón administered as if the Revolution had ended. However, Calles, resurrected the concept of "the Revolution" and used it as a political tool. Calles defined himself and his followers as true "revolutionaries" and labeled opponents as "conservatives" and "counterrevolutionaries."

Calles was most progressive with regard to land reform. From 1924 to 1928, he distributed 7.3 million acres of land. This was more than twice the amount distributed between 1915 and 1924. Early in his term he used land reform to build a power base among those who received land. Once he had consolidated his power, land distribution slowed dramatically.

Even though Calles substantially increased the amount of land distributed, he viewed the *ejido* (the communal farm formed by those receiving land) as a transitory institution incapable of meeting Mexico's agricultural needs. The Sonorans placed their faith in privately owned farms—the dominant agricultural model in their home state. They increasingly turned their attention to making the land more productive, not distributing it. Land reform was viewed as the means to correct past injustices or simply as a political necessity in areas where peasants were militant and mobilized.

By the end of his term, Calles had become quite conservative. In 1927, he announced, "The Government will do everything in its power to safeguard the interests of foreign capitalists who invest in Mexico." This conservative shift reflected not only the increasing wealth of Calles and his followers but also the close ties the president had developed with U.S. Ambassador Dwight Morrow. A fall in oil and silver prices and in the volume of oil exports also caused Calles to scale down his attempts to effect change. Efforts to suppress religious-based rebels known as *cristeros* sapped further energy for reform. Finally, low levels of production on land already transferred to peasants as part of the land reform led Calles to bring the program to a near halt.

Calles continued Obregón's effort to expand the educational system—an imperative given that literacy was below 25 percent. Between 1920 and 1928 primary school enrolment increased from 743,896 to 2,402,731. As a result of this increase, in 1928, 46 percent of school-aged children attended school. For all but a privileged few, education stopped with the elementary school. In 1928, there were only 16,024 enrolled at the secondary-preparatory level and 9,763 in professional schools.

The members of the Sonoran dynasty—de la Huerta, Obregón, and Calles—rebuilt the government bureaucracy and returned power to Mexico City. During this recentralization, revolutionary leaders gained power, the military lost it, and peasants became marginalized.

Many supported this recentralization of power since they felt it would lessen anarchy and political violence. Between 1921 and 1930, government employment increased from 1.4 percent of the labor force to 2.9 percent.

During the 1920s at lower levels of government the diverse political forces seeking political control often took up arms, just as those seeking the presidency did. Between 1920 and 1930, Puebla had nineteen governors. Similar instability existed at the local level. In the two decades after 1920, forty-two men served as mayor of Ciudad Juárez, Chihuahua.

The generals forming the Sonoran dynasty brought to the presidency a set of values alien to central Mexico. The north never had a village-oriented society. The Catholic Church in Sonora was not the major institution it was in central Mexico. Agricultural development in northern Mexico was the forerunner of today's agribusiness and often involved irrigation and other government-financed projects. While Zapata had looked to the Indian village with its communal lands as his model, the Sonorans, who were largely removed from the radical ideological influences of central Mexico, saw Californian agriculture as their model. They felt that the Mexican government had to assume an active role in promoting economic development.

As the end of Calles's term approached, it became clear that Obregón wished to return to the presidency. Calles backed Obregón's re-election, likely feeling that Obregón would return the favor at the end of the 1928–34 term. The constitution was amended to permit non-consecutive re-election. Another amendment extended the presidential term from four to six years—its current length. (The amendment permitting re-election was repealed in 1933.)

Generals Francisco Serrano and Arnulfo Gómez, who had presidential aspirations of their own, became convinced that the 1928 presidential election would not be fair. Acting on this belief, they planned a coup to thwart the anticipated succession of Obregón. Within two months both had been captured and executed. Twenty-five other generals were placed before firing squads for their participation in the plot.

Obregón campaigned on a platform of fulfilling revolutionary promises and uniting the forces of the Revolution. He faced no opposition candidate, although a broad range of public opinion opposed Obregón—or anyone else—being re-elected president. In 1928, after closely observing Mexican elections, U.S. historian Ernest Gruening concluded the elections "reveal irrefutably the utter failure to date of any growth of democratic practice."

By 1928, it appeared that presidential succession had been, if not democratized, at least institutionalized, with the incumbent selecting his successor. This perception was shattered when president-elect Obregón was assassinated by José de León Toral, a person generally described as a Catholic fanatic.

The assassination placed Calles in a quandary. Some of his backers wanted him to extend his term to prevent the chaos resulting from not having a president. Others wanted him to leave the presidency as scheduled, since they feared Obregón's supporters would revolt if denied power.

Calles's political ability prevented frustrated Obregón backers from taking up arms to gain the power they considered rightfully theirs. On September 1, 1928, in his last annual address, Calles announced not only that he would leave the presidency as scheduled but that it was time to make presidential succession an orderly process. He noted that Mexico lacked *caudillos* and declared: "This should, and will, permit us, once and for all, to direct the national political process toward institutional rule. Mexico will forever cease to be, as it has been historically, a nation led by a 'strongman' and will become a nation of institutions and laws."

The Maximato, 1928–1934

With Calles's blessing, Congress designated Interior Minister Emilio Portes Gil as provisional president. Portes Gil was ideal for defusing the political crisis generated by Obregón's assassination. He had close ties to both Obregón and Calles, and as a civilian his temporary presence in the seat of power ameliorated rivalries between numerous generals, each of whom felt they should replace Obregón. Portes Gil took office at the end of Calles's term and remained until a special election could be called to fill the remainder of the 1928–34 term to which Obregón had been elected.

The choice of Portes Gil made Obregón loyalists feel that the way was still open for them to assume power. The new president had a progressive reputation, since as governor of Tamaulipas he had distributed more than 494,000 acres of land to peasants on his own initiative. On December 1, 1928, given his acceptability to all major factions, Portes Gil peacefully assumed the presidency.

Shortly before the end of his term, Calles called for the creation of a national political party. This party, the National Revolutionary Party (PNR), served to dominate ambitious *caudillos*, each striving for national power. The PNR differed from conventional political parties in that it was created to conserve power, not contest it. The creation of the party ten years after the Constitutionalists' victory in the armed struggle highlights the differences between the Mexican Revolution and the revolutions in Russia and China, where pre-existing parties guided the post-triumph course of development.

There was no grassroots participation in choosing representatives to the party's 1929 founding convention in Querétaro. If its founding had occurred in the United States, its organizers would have been referred to as a bunch of good old boys in a smoke-filled room.

The regionally based *caudillos* who formed the initial cadre of the party were guaranteed control over their local fiefdoms if they backed the party's presidential nominees. Most of these *caudillos*, aging and quite wealthy, were more than ready to accept mediation by the new party.

In addition to bringing together generals, the PNR incorporated all the political parties claiming their origins in the Revolution. In 1929 these parties, which numbered more than 1,000, were mostly regional and generally were linked to one political figure. Existing parties were allowed to preserve their local and regional autonomy if they adhered to decisions of the PNR on national matters. Thanks to its building on existing parties, within a few months the PNR had a functioning nationwide network in place.

Calles selected officials to lead the PNR, which remained an extension of his personal power. Both state and federal governments provided funds to the party, while opposition parties were forced to rely on private funds. The rough-and-tumble battles to decide who would exercise power at the local level soon shifted to struggles for power within the PNR. In 1933 Calles pushed through a constitutional amendment to prohibit immediate congressional re-election. This made those wishing to serve in Congress dependent, not on constituents they had served, but on Calles's approving their nomination. Left outside the party were workers, peasants, and members of the middle class. Politics became a game played exclusively by the closed circle around Calles.

Calles continued as a highly influential figure during Portes Gil's interim presidency, which extended from December 1928 to February 1930. The Sonoran orchestrated the nomination of Pascual Ortiz Rubio as presidential candidate for the remainder of the term to which Obregón had been elected. In 1926 Ortiz Rubio had been appointed as Mexican ambassador to Brazil. He was attractive to Calles since by virtue of his having been abroad he had no power base and was totally dependent on Calles.

The designation of Ortiz Rubio triggered Mexico's last widespread revolt, led by generals Jesús Aguirre and José Gonzalo Escobar, who had their own presidential aspirations. They had hoped to attract the broad coalition that had been held together by Obregón's strong personality. However, without its leader the coalition had disintegrated. Thus they were soon defeated by Calles, who stepped in as secretary of war. Irregular rural forces, whose members had either received land in the land reform or hoped to in the future, contributed significantly to Calles's victory, as did the U.S. government, which supplied the Mexican government with arms.

As a result of the revolt, forty-seven generals were shot or exiled and 2,000 combatants died. The failure of the revolt delivered a clear message—from then on, the route to power was through official channels, not through toppling the by-then-entrenched government.

Another feature of the PNR became apparent on election day. The party counted the votes. Despite Ortiz Rubio being virtually unknown, he was credited with 1,825,732 votes. The better-known educator José Vasconcelos officially received only 105,655 votes nationwide. Individual Vasconcelos rallies in Mexico City had attracted more than 100,000 supporters. It was clear that Calles and the generals supporting him were unwilling to lose at the ballot box what they had won by force of arms. As historian Jean Meyer commented, the elections were "quite manifestly fraudulent." The main result of the election was increased cynicism about democracy among an entire generation of middle-class Mexicans.

Ortiz Rubio served as a figurehead president from February 1930 to September 1932. His dependency on Calles—who lived directly in front of the presidential residence in Chapultepec Castle—was so great that Mexicans would point to the castle and proclaim, "*Aquí vive el presidente, él que manda vive enfrente*" ("Here lives the president, the boss lives in front").

Calles ousted his own choice as president when Ortiz Rubio disagreed with him on policy and choice of cabinet members. To finish the presidential term ending in 1934, Calles selected Abelardo Rodríguez, a typical millionaire general. From 1923 to 1929, as governor of Baja California Norte, Rodríguez had loyally served Obregón and Calles. He had enriched himself by promoting gambling and prostitution.

Calles's role as the dominant political figure earned him the title of *Jefe Máximo* (top chief). In 1929 he stated that in the future any land taken for land reform would be paid for in cash. Given the lack of funds in the Depression-wracked treasury, Mexicans generally viewed that statement as signaling the end of land reform. After that date, agricultural production, not distributing land to the landless, was emphasized. This reflected Calles's view that agriculture should be left to commercial farmers receiving government guarantees and incentives.

Agricultural workers were eating less than in 1896, and the low wages paid them in 1910 would have looked magnificent in 1934. The country was still suffering from the Depression. Labor unrest was increasing, and foreign observers spoke of the likelihood of new peasant wars.

In response to these conditions a faction opposing Calles formed inside the PNR. Its members were of middle-class origin, felt dispossessed, and were in disagreement with the ruling faction. Weak in itself, this faction found support in workers and peasants, whose aspirations it had raised.

The leader of this faction was a general of humble origins, Lázaro Cárdenas. His ancestry was mixed at a time when other leading political figures were of higher social status and had lighter skins. He joined the Revolution as a teenager after only four years of formal education. Cárdenas advanced rapidly through the ranks of the army and was promoted to general at age twenty-five. Between 1925 and 1928, he served as a military zone commander on the oil-rich Gulf Coast, where he witnessed firsthand the squalor and inequality of oil camps and the companies' cynical disregard of the host population. Such abuses would later come back to haunt these firms.

Calles, taking into consideration the broad support for Cárdenas, approved his candidacy for the 1934–40 term. He felt he could control Cárdenas, as he had controlled his immediate predecessors, and that power would inevitably make Cárdenas more conservative. Calles assumed that since Cárdenas was not only his friend but had also served as 1) head of the PNR, 2) a revolutionary general, 3) interior minister, 4) and governor of Michoacán, he was as much a part of his system as one could be.

Even though he lacked significant opposition, Cárdenas undertook a marathon campaign, traveling more than 17,000 miles by car, rail, airplane, boat, and horse. This served not to convince voters—his election was assured—but to give him the opportunity to learn about Mexico's problems, to familiarize people with his ideas, and to build a base of support.

The election, in which Cárdenas ran virtually unopposed, aroused little interest. Only 14 percent of the electorate bothered to cast a ballot to select Cárdenas for the 1934–40 term.

During the **Maximato**, the PNR simply incorporated *caudillos* into its ranks. Its goal was to maintain consensus and eliminate violence as a way to settle disputes among the elite. The PNR regularly won elections since it had the backing not only of *caudillos* but also of government arms and financing. As a result membership in the PNR became an indispensable requirement for political success. No one from the outside could be elected to or volunteer for PNR leadership. In its attempt to satisfy the contradictory demands of labor, business, and peasants, the party called upon these groups to oppose "reactionary forces," whose identity was never precisely spelled out.

The Cárdenas Administration, 1934–1940

> When General Cárdenas took office as president, he was firmly convinced that to achieve a lasting peace, he had to anchor his administration in a sweeping social-justice program on behalf of the most beleaguered: the workers and peasants.
>
> (Carlos Martínez Assad, 2013)

Cárdenas refused to accept the role of puppet that Calles had assumed he would. He immediately began to build a broad coalition to challenge Calles's power. By the end of 1935, the government had distributed more than 6.7 million acres of land to more than 100,000 families. This land transfer not only won support for Cárdenas but also undermined the power of Calles's wealthy backers. The provision of increased agricultural credit and extension services further cemented peasant loyalty.

Cárdenas shuffled army commands to get his loyalists in key positions and moved pro-Calles generals to positions of less power. Military men who had fallen out with Calles, including Zapatistas, Carrancistas, and Villistas, were rehabilitated. Cárdenas further bolstered his support by offering loyal officers seats in Congress.

When Cárdenas learned Calles was trying to organize a new political party, he acted. By this time, Cárdenas had the backing of the military, workers, peasants, and some churchmen. In April 1936 he ordered Calles onto a chartered Ford Trimotor which flew him to exile in the United States. Upon arriving in Dallas, Calles told reporters, "I was expelled from Mexico for fighting Communism."

Removing Calles from the political scene united party and government authority under one individual—a pattern that was to endure for the rest of the century. Despite his vastly increased power, Cárdenas set a less imperial tone for the presidency, moving the official residence from Chapultepec Castle to nearby Los Pinos—the current presidential residence. He also accelerated his reforms.

Cárdenas's reforms, in contrast to the "revolutionary" rhetoric of the previous regimes, had a profound impact throughout

Figure 11.1
Lázaro Cárdenas not only served as president at the same time FDR did but, as is the case with Roosevelt, is generally regarded as the greatest twentieth-century president of his country.

Source: Reproduced courtesy of the Benson Latin American Collection, the University of Texas at Austin.

the country. His reforms relied on state intervention in labor relations and land reform. Cárdenas explained the rationale for these reforms: "The modern view of the state and of labor legislation requires that doubtful cases be resolved in favor of the weaker party. To grant equal treatment to unequal parties is not justice, nor is it equitable."

Land reform, for which he is still remembered, was Cárdenas's most ambitious program. From 1910 to 1930, only 3.9 percent of Mexico's land surface was distributed to the landless, two-thirds of the large holdings were untouched, and only 780,000 of Mexico's 3.6 million peasants were in permanent possession of any land.

Table 11.1 *Land reform, 1917–40*

President	Area Distributed (in acres)
Carranza	414,801
de la Huerta	83,229
Obregón	2,717,288
Calles	7,343,003
Portes Gil	4,218,142
Ortiz Rubio	2,333,008
Rodríguez	1,953,014
Cárdenas	46,401,743

Source: *Estadísticas Históricas de México* (Aguascalientes: INEGI, 1994), p. 381.

Cárdenas began the rapid transfer of land to peasants. Some of those receiving land claimed it on the basis of its having been usurped illegally by *hacendados*. Others received land from nearby haciendas after filling a petition declaring their village lacked sufficient land. Recipients benefited from larger plots than had previously been distributed and from new schools, improved social services, and the increased availability of credit. Rather than viewing the *ejido* as a transitional stage towards privately owned farms, as his predecessors had, Cárdenas believed the *ejido* should form the basic unit for rural development.

The official party, the PNR, was still closely associated with Calles and remained in the hands of the political elite. In yet another of his sweeping reforms, Cárdenas transformed the party, which was renamed the Mexican Revolutionary Party (PRM), dividing it into four major sectors—peasants, the military, organized labor, and a "popular sector." Initially most members of the popular sector were civil servants. Thanks to its corporate structure, one joined the party not as an individual but as a member of an officially recognized group.

This reorganization came just twelve days after the nationalization of the oil industry and allowed Cárdenas to mobilize mass support against external political and economic pressure. By virtue of these sectors, which automatically incorporated soldiers, government workers, trade union members, and land-reform beneficiaries, the party could claim more than 4 million members, out of a total population of slightly less than 19 million.

Despite the party being renamed and given a new slogan, "For a workers' democracy," it remained an undemocratic institution. The restructuring of the official party shifted power from regional interests to Mexico City. As was the case when the PNR was founded, there was no public debate about restructuring the party. Cárdenas simply decreed the change was to occur. Also, as with the PNR, the citizenry was excluded from selecting candidates for public office. Mexico's national leaders, from Carranza to Cárdenas, all rejected Madero-style democracy as a source of instability and as the preamble to being overthrown. Madero had become a figure who was revered but not imitated.

By 1938, the Depression in the United States had spilled over into Mexico. Following the oil nationalization, there was massive capital flight and reduced private investment. As a result, tax receipts fell. Government spending soon exceeded income by 15 percent. To meet this shortfall, the government printed paper money, increasing inflation. Late in the Cárdenas administration, this inflation led to a decline in the buying power of wages. As the end of Cárdenas's term approached, money to finance additional restructuring was lacking.

Given financial constraints, mounting domestic opposition, and pressure exerted by U.S. and British corporations, the pace of land reform drastically slowed and other reforms largely ceased. Despite the urgings of radical elements, after the nationalization of the oil industry, Cárdenas showed no interest in nationalizing any other industries.

As the end of Cárdenas' 1934–1940 term approached, he faced the prospect of either selecting a PRM presidential candidate who would implement further change or one who would guarantee the reforms he had carried out would not be reversed. Cárdenas and his backers had little maneuvering room since conservatives were launching a strong electoral challenge.

Cárdenas selected Manuel Ávila Camacho as his successor. Ávila Camacho, who was serving as Cárdenas's secretary of defense, at most stood for maintaining intact the reforms that Cárdenas had instituted. By the end of Cárdenas's term, Ávila Camacho was known as an honest functionary and as a middle-of-the-roader. The political establishment backed him and no group strongly opposed him. By virtue of his having served as secretary of defense, he could hold the army within the PRM coalition.

Cárdenas's choice reflected the conservatives' strength and his desire for peace and stability. Mexico's president realized that he had bumped up against what political scientist Nora Hamilton termed the "limits of autonomy," that is, he had instituted as much change as the international capitalist system was willing to accommodate.

For the 1940 elections, conservatives rallied around General Juan Andreu Almazán, the military zone commander of Nuevo León. Almazán enjoyed the support of surviving hacendados, oil interests, high clergy, many military officers, and even some dissident PRM members. Many in the middle class, who had largely been ignored by Cárdenas and who resented official anti-clericalism, supported Almazán. His supporters were hard to pigeonhole ideologically. They included workers and peasants resenting corruption, high inflation, and having their leaders imposed on them by the PRM. The revolutionary muralist Diego Rivera supported Almazán, characterizing the PRM as "fascism with a socialist mask."

The election was the most violent in recent history. In Mexico City alone, twenty-seven died on election day and roughly 150 were wounded. According to official returns, Ávila Camacho received 2,476,641 votes. Almazán was credited with only 151,101 votes nationwide—fewer than the number attending his Mexico City rallies. It was clear in 1940—as it had been when Vasconcelos was a candidate—that the official party was unwilling to let elections be used to oust the political elite from power and that the common citizen had very little to do with choosing leaders.

After Ávila Camacho's inauguration, Cárdenas remained a public figure, but in no way attempted to maintain political power as Calles had. He overcame the legacy of the fraudulent 1940 elections and became a symbol of Mexico's hopes for electoral democracy and civil liberties. His leaving of both the presidency and power completed the institutionalization of the Revolution and is one of the central elements of Cárdenas's legacy. For more than half a century, Cárdenas's successors would follow his example of selecting a successor and then relinquishing power.

While Cárdenas failed to make progress at instituting political democracy, he made huge strides in promoting "social democracy." This concept is defined in Article 3 of the 1917 constitution: "Democracy shall be considered, not just in juridical and political terms, but as a social system based on constant economic, social, and cultural improvement." A variety of statistics indicate Cárdenas's success at promoting social democracy. In addition to distributing land, during his term 3,000 schools were constructed and 100,000 teachers trained. Between 1930 and 1940 there was a 22 percent increase in the number of literates over age ten. Social spending, which included health and education, reached an unprecedented 18 percent of the federal budget. As political scientist Lorenzo Meyer observed, "The Mexico Cárdenas left in 1940 was doubtlessly more just than the one he received in 1934."

Cárdenas retained immense moral influence up until his death in 1970. Writer Carlos Fuentes commented on his presidency:

I have known all of the presidents of Mexico from 1934 to the present. Some have been more intelligent than others, some more politically astute, some more cultivated; but only one has attained true greatness: Lázaro Cárdenas. By greatness I mean, over and beyond tactical skill, energy, and determination, the concept of nationhood, the lofty vision that Cárdenas had of Mexico, its people, its history and culture, its destiny. He never thought small; he never belittled Mexico or its people.[1]

Mexican Society

Changes in political leadership were much more dramatic than changes in living standards. The year 1917 was not the year of the constitution for most Mexicans, but rather one of hunger. The government, burdened with enormous debt and without access to internal or external credit, had difficulty buying grain to feed the population. Unemployment was rising, and the country lay in ruins. Just as the Mexican population was beginning to benefit from economic recovery, the Depression halted progress in health and education. Annual per capita consumption of corn, the mainstay of the popular diet, fell from 300 pounds in 1928 to 194 in 1930.

At the time of Cárdenas's inauguration, rural life had changed little. Many small towns, accessible only by mule trail, lacked schools, churches, and running water. In his classical study of Tepoztlán, Morelos, anthropologist Robert Redfield observed that in the late 1920s the town lacked electricity and power tools. Even though the village was only fifty miles from Mexico City, because of the rough, rocky roads, humans and a variety of quadrupeds carried all the cargo coming to town.

In contrast to the Sonora dynasty, which focused on economic progress promoted by the state, Cárdenas used the state to promote social justice. The major agents of change were education and land reform. Improved communications also facilitated change, as Cárdenas donated radios so residents of every agricultural and workers community in Mexico could listen to three state radio stations—one belonging to the education ministry and two to the official party. By 1940, Mexicans were benefiting from thousands of new schools, innumerable public services, and extensive new irrigation projects. Government-run stores opened in urban areas, selling food at reduced prices. As Carlos Fuentes noted, "Even if the upper and middle classes were favored, the working and peasant classes received larger slices of the national pie than they had before or ever have had since."

As the Revolution faded into history, it became increasingly difficult to isolate what emanated from the Revolution and what was attributable to change sweeping all of Latin America. Motor vehicles, for example, had an impact far more diffuse than that of the railroad, which left the vast majority of Mexico's villages just as isolated as they had been in colonial times. As novelist Aldous Huxley noted:

> Over and above their material freight, the Fords will carry an invisible cargo of new ideas, of alien, urban ways of thought and feeling . . . Along the metalled roads the Fords will bring, not only reading matter, but also notions that will make the printed words fully comprehensible.[2]

Rustic village shops increasingly stocked such city-made goods as matches, candles, beer, and even canned foods. Other changes included increased state bureaucracy, extension of tax powers, and more mass participation in politics. These changes were occurring not only in revolutionary Mexico but also in non-revolutionary Argentina, Brazil, and Chile.

While change was indeed occurring, the Mexico of 1940 in many ways had more in common with the Mexico of the late nineteenth century than that of the late twentieth. The population remained small, rural, and agricultural. Although there was steady population increase and migration from rural to urban areas, the rate of change was quite low compared with the rate later in the century. In 1921, 68.8 percent of the population was rural, and by 1940, 64.9 remained so.

The Elite

Though vastly diminished in power, even after Cárdenas's massive land reform many members of the agrarian elite remained wealthy. Those who had been unable to convert their land to cash and invest elsewhere were allowed to retain 370 acres of irrigated land or its equivalent in dry land. Often they controlled milling, credit, agricultural inputs, and marketing outlets and, through these channels, profited from dealings with the direct beneficiaries of land reform.

At the end of Cárdenas's presidency, the industrial elite was in an advantageous position. Cárdenas's support for labor had its greatest impact on foreign capitalists, not Mexican ones. The state had financed infrastructure with internal and external debt, not higher taxes. The oil nationalization held the promise of an inexpensive fuel supply. With the government having vastly enlarged the domestic market with land reform, rosy days lay ahead for businessmen, especially during the World War II-induced boom.

Figure 11.2 *During the 1920s many individuals took advantage of the power thrust on them by the Revolution to enrich themselves while doing little for the poor. This sketch by Diego Rivera highlights the contrast between the new rich and the rural poor.*

Source: Stuart Chase, *Mexico: A Study of Two Americas* (New York: Macmillan, 1935).

Workers

> Organized labor's entry into national politics was among the most significant consequences of Mexico's 1910–1920 social revolution.
>
> (Kevin Middlebrook, 1995)

Even when it was protected by state legislation, labor organizing was fraught with difficulties. In 1921 Mexico remained a largely rural society, with 71.4 percent of its work force in agriculture, forestry, hunting, and fishing. Organizing was complicated by the dispersal of the labor force into many small work sites. Few large concentrations of workers existed outside mining, railroads, oil, textiles, and the public sector.

With Carranza's backing, the governor of Coahuila sponsored the organization of a national labor federation in an effort to preempt an anticipated independent organization. Luis Morones was selected as secretary general of the new organization, the Regional Confederation of Mexican Workers (CROM). The CROM sought to ensure the labor provisions of the 1917 constitution were enforced. Morones urged that workers take a moderate stance since labor was too weak to win radical demands and such demands could provide the United States with a pretext to intervene in Mexico.

Given Carranza's lack of support for labor, CROM leaders sought other leadership, which they found in Obregón, who was viewed as a friend of labor for his having championed the inclusion of pro-labor provisions in the 1917 Constitution. In August 1919 the CROM signed a secret pact with Obregón, in which it agreed to mobilize support for Obregón in the 1920 presidential election. In exchange it was to receive privileged political access, the creation of a separate labor ministry with CROM influence over it, and presidential support for statutory law implementing the provisions of Article 123.

The CROM was amply rewarded for its support of Obregón. Under his administration, the CROM could organize freely. In 1921 there were more than 300 strikes involving 100,000 workers. The government began to impose settlements favorable to labor, thus permitting the CROM to win the majority of its industrial disputes between 1920 and 1924. The workers most favored were those that the government needed as allies to ensure political stability. As it became obvious that joining the CROM provided material rewards, its membership soared from 300,000 in 1920 to 1.2 million by 1924.

With the benefit of hindsight, many have criticized CROM leaders for having allowed themselves to fall under state control. However, at the time there were numerous reasons for welcoming an alliance with the state. Labor justified cooperation with the government by declaring that the main enemy of the Mexican working class was international capital, which both the government and labor should confront. It was also obvious that labor was weak numerically and organizationally and that it needed to build alliances to meet its goals. Collaboration with the government yielded government subsidies for labor organizations. Labor also cooperated with industrialists since both constituencies supported high tariffs, the former to protect their jobs and the latter to protect their profits.

In 1924, the CROM backed Calles's presidential candidacy, a move for which it once again received ample reward. Between 1924 and 1928, Morones served as minister of industry, commerce, and labor and became one of the most powerful politicians in Mexico. Other CROM members received congressional seats. The CROM repeatedly won enforcement of legally mandated seniority rights, minimum wages, and severance pay and gained control over labor conciliation and arbitration boards through which it could force settlements favorable to labor. Workers affiliated with the CROM enjoyed higher wages and had more rights than did members of independent unions. By virtue of its obvious government support, the CROM could claim two million members in 1928.

Obregón's assassination shattered the cozy relationship between Morones and the government. Obregón supporters widely believed Morones had masterminded the assassination since he had his own presidential ambitions. For self-preservation, Calles distanced himself from Morones, forced him from his cabinet, and withdrew government support from the CROM.

Once it became apparent that the CROM no longer enjoyed government support, trade unions began to desert en masse. The number of affiliated organizations declined from 1,172 in 1928 to 349 in 1932. Portes Gil removed CROM members from the government and used army troops against CROM unions.

In 1936, more than 3,000 labor representatives met and created the Mexican Workers Federation (CTM), which included several existing labor organizations. The CTM soon claimed 3,594 affiliates and 946,000 members, dwarfing the remaining labor groups. Reflecting the radical thinking of the period, the CTM statutes declared, "The working class of Mexico must never forget that the final aim of its struggles is the abolition of the capitalist regime."

Membership in the CTM continued to increase since the federation was successful at gaining increased wages, collective contracts, and compliance with federal labor law. The CTM enjoyed obvious government support in the form of a cash subsidy, protection for CTM activities, and the persecution of the CTM's enemies. The CTM's close relationship with the Cárdenas administration was formalized in 1938, as the CTM voted to become part of the Partido Nacional Revolucionario (PNR). At the time, CTM leaders felt they could maintain their autonomy.

As historian Joe Ashby noted, "Under the Cárdenas regime, the Mexican labor movement attained its highest form of organization, prestige, and influence in national economic policy." The number of officially recognized strikes rose from thirteen in 1933 to 833 in 1937. Since such labor actions had government support, during Cárdenas's term, there was a 43 percent increase in real wages and an improvement in working conditions. In 1930, 5.5 percent of the labor force was unionized, while by 1940, 14.5 percent was.

Rural Mexico

After the Revolution, three competing notions of land ownership emerged. One—similar to that then prevailing (and still doing so) in the United States—held that individuals were entitled to own as much land as they wanted (and could afford). The second view, adopted by the Zapatistas, was that justice demanded that peasants have land to sow and that the peasants themselves, guns in hand if necessary, should transfer land from large estates to the tillers. The third view agreed with the second in its belief that justice demanded that peasants be given land to sow, but held that the government should determine which land was transferred to peasants, when it was transferred, and which peasants would receive it.

Even though Zapatismo disappeared as a movement after Zapata's assassination, many still accepted the premise that peasants should claim land on their own. The General Federation of Workers (CGT), an anarchist labor federation, openly advocated peasants taking land on their own initiative. This approach to land reform remained a potent force for decades, especially as peasants saw that government-sanctioned land reform was agonizingly slow and corrupt or excluded them for a variety of reasons.

The third view was accepted by government policymakers as a way to control peasant movements and as an orderly way to transfer land to the rural poor. It gained widespread acceptance among peasants since when they attempted to claim land on their own violent clashes frequently ensued.

To implement land reform, the government created a new institution known as the *ejido*. To establish an *ejido*, the government would designate a certain extension of land as having surpassed the legal ownership limit. Typically land would be transferred from private ownership to the *ejido* and then would be divided into plots that would be distributed to male heads of families included in the *ejido*. The plot could be farmed by the family, but not legally sold, rented, or mortgaged.

This provision prevented the reconcentration of land into large estates. *Ejido* land could be inherited by family members, thus keeping the institution viable for generations.

Before the Cárdenas administration, those receiving *ejido* land usually did so only after large-scale mobilizations to pressure authorities. These mobilizations were subject to violent repression by *hacendados*. Leaders of such movements were often rendered ineffective by providing them with employment in state peasant organizations. In other cases, leaders were simply murdered.

Even after those soliciting land had received it, *hacendados* continued to resort to violence in an attempt to drive them off and deter others. Authors Nathaniel and Sylvia Weyl describe one such effort in Michoacán:

> After the distribution of lands in Langostura, the "white guards" of the *hacendados* attacked the *ejidatarios* in the fields. The men and women of the village repelled the invasion. Mauser [rifle] in hand, the members of the feminine league stood guard over the fields while their husbands worked.[3]

Just as earlier attempts at land distribution had met with armed force, Cárdenas's efforts were opposed by *hacendados*' hired gunmen. In a three-month period in 1936, 500 peasants were killed in land disputes. However rather than backing down to the show of force by landowners, Cárdenas armed some 60,000 peasants.

During the Cárdenas administration, land was distributed to 728,847 peasants. As a result, in 1940, *ejidatarios* cultivated 17.3 million acres, while private farmers cultivated only 16.8 million. Since corn required relatively little capital to grow and techniques for growing it were familiar to many, *ejidatarios* concentrated on producing it. Between 1930 and 1940, Mexico's corn production increased by almost 50 percent.

The land reform increased the standard of living of its beneficiaries, weakened the *hacendado* class, preserved rural political stability, and increased peasant self-esteem. American hacienda owner Rosalie Evans commented on the psychological impact land reform had had on her hacienda workers, "The Indians are in appearance as you know them, but are no longer apathetic, they are insolent and aggressive."

Given that land tenure was only part of Mexico's agricultural problem and that Cárdenas's efforts were thwarted by resource limitations and by domestic and foreign opposition to land reform, in 1940 numerous problems remained in rural Mexico. One of the most significant of these problems was an excess of rural labor. Some 50 percent of the agricultural work force remained landless when Cárdenas left office.

With the hacienda largely out of the picture and with the countryside more peaceful that it had been for generations, by 1940 life in rural Mexico had indeed changed. However, the *ejido* only addressed the concentration of land ownership. Rural Mexico continued to face numerous other problems, such as a lack of credit, the lack of competitive advantage in basic grain production, an underdeveloped market, and the poor quality of much cultivated land. Even in relatively modern areas, such as the Laguna, 73 percent of agricultural workers were illiterate. The Weyls described the farm technology used in the late 1930s as "contemporary with the Egyptian pharaohs."

Following the Revolution, much of Mexico fell under the control of *caciques*, or regional strongmen, who ensured stability and kept peace—tasks which were beyond the power of the still weak federal government. They were expected to demonstrate loyalty to the incumbent regime in Mexico City. As long as they maintained relative peace, gross abuses of power were tolerated. They controlled city governments, state legislatures, political parties, and dispensed government jobs. Some *caciques* were popular leaders who defied local landlords, priests, and elites. Others simply enriched themselves and their supporters. Although *caciques* inevitably fell from power, just as absolute rulers at the national level did, many *caciques* retained influence in their local fiefdoms well past the 1930s.

The Indigenous

Except for its effect on those who actually fought in revolutionary armies, the Revolution was slow to impact indigenous communities. The delegates to the 1917 Constitutional Convention did not debate indigenous rights, and there is no indication that Indians concerned them. No specific rights were granted indigenous people based on their identity. At the time the indigenous population remained reliant on craft production, poorly remunerated labor on haciendas, and the use of low-yield agricultural techniques on often poor land. This use of poor land reflected the process by which non-Indians, beginning in colonial times, had inexorably appropriated the best Indian lands.

Despite the constitution's silence on the matter, during the 1920s the government began devoting more resources to improving the lot of Mexico's indigenous population than it had during the Porfiriato. Unlike land reform, the government was not responding to popular pressure from below. Rather, the non-Indian intelligentsia imposed reform from above. Advocates of new government policies, known collectively as *indigenismo*, rejected nineteenth-century notions that Indians were biologically inferior. Such beliefs were replaced by the notion that Indian poverty resulted from their cultural values, the social structure of the Indian community, and the domination, exploitation, and oppression embedded in relations between Indians and non-Indians.

Indigenismo advocated the voluntary integration of the Indian into Mexican society, especially through education. Its supporters claimed that Indians could become educated, bilingual, and politically mobilized and at the same time sustain their distinctive language, dress, religion, and mores.

Indigenismo was formulated without the participation or even awareness of most Indians. Its implementation involved establishing schools in isolated Indian villages. The primary goals of these schools were teaching Spanish and incorporating Indians into the national culture. In addition to being woefully underfunded in relation to the large indigenous population, the program had limited impact since its monolingual Spanish curriculum was detached from Indian reality.

Rather than rushing to join the Mexican nation, many Indians consciously withdrew from it, since they felt they generally came out the worse when they worked for or sold goods to non-Indians. The indigenous community of Chamula, in Chiapas, even prohibited the selection of a mayor who spoke Spanish. Chamulans felt that mayors who spoke only the village language, Tzotzil, would be unable to sell out village interests to non-Indians.

During the Cárdenas administration, the programs that had the greatest impact on Indians were those that affected all Mexicans. Land reform increased access to land for Indian as well as non-Indian. Similarly both Indians and non-Indians enjoyed increased access to water, credit, and technical aid. Such programs also lessened local autonomy as they tied Indians more closely to state and federal governments through labor unions, land-reform offices, and local branches of the PRM.

On the abstract level Indian "integration" remained a goal during the Cárdenas administration. However, at the more practical level it became apparent that programs tailored for the non-Indian population were not addressing the needs of Indians. This led to the 1936 creation of the Department of Indian Affairs. Its agents represented Indians in matters involving land, taxes, and labor rights. It managed vocational schools for Indians that taught agricultural techniques to boys and homemaking to girls. The agency gave free legal advice to indigenous communities and sought to guarantee labor rights for Indians employed on plantations. It organized co-ops, taught Spanish, and promoted government construction of roads, reservoirs, and schools. The agency also coordinated its work with that of other government agencies, such as the Education Ministry, whose work affected Indians.

Between 1921 and 1940, the proportion of the population over five years of age that spoke an indigenous language only varied slightly, declining from 15.1 percent to 14.8 percent. Precise figures on the number of Indians are lacking since enumeration was so subjective. There was no agreement on what physical or cultural characteristics marked one as an Indian. To further complicate the quantification of Mexico's Indian population, beginning in 1930 racial categories were removed from the census since officials felt that the important social divisions were no longer ethnic or racial but socioeconomic.

Women

At the 1917 constitutional convention, the citizenship committee declared women would not be allowed to vote, since: "The fact that some exceptional women have the qualifications necessary to exercise political rights satisfactorily does not justify the conclusion that these should be conceded to women as a class." While the 1917 constitution did not enfranchise women, it did guarantee women equal pay for equal work.

During the 1920s and early 1930s, little official attention was paid to women's rights, since few male leaders were concerned with the issue and they were burdened with what for them were more pressing issues. During this period Mexican women more than made up for their male leaders' inactivity by plunging into a plethora of organizing efforts. In fact, the multiplicity of groups and issues addressed, as well as divisions along class, ethnic, religious, and ideological lines, limited their ability to achieve their goals. Women's groups promoted temperance, addressed labor and agrarian issues, and formed mothers' clubs, consumption cooperatives, and labor unions. While lay groups demanded recognition of women as wage earners, the largest Catholic women's organization defined them as "the paradigm of purity, abnegation, and sublimity."

During the late 1920s and early 1930s, while systematically denying them leadership roles, both the revolutionary state and the Catholic Church sought to enlist women to support their respective causes. The males leading the government assumed that women would overwhelmingly support the very clerical elements they were seeking to control and thus denied women suffrage. The males leading the Church, acting on the same assumption, favored women suffrage.

Cárdenas's open support for women suffrage galvanized the United Front for Women's Rights (FUPDM), organized in 1935. This group served as an umbrella organization including some 800 feminist organizations that claimed 50,000 members. The front embraced women from a broad political spectrum, ranging from the Mexican Communist Party to the official PNR and included rural and urban women, professionals, and workers. In addition to promoting its central issue— women suffrage—the Front pressed for expanded employment opportunities, lower rents, lower electric rates, lower taxes for women market vendors, the establishment of day-care centers, and granting women the same rights to *ejido* land as men enjoyed.

In November 1937 Cárdenas's secretary of the interior sent Congress a draft constitutional amendment that provided for women suffrage, along with a message stating that women would be more subject to Church influence if they remained outside the electoral process than if they were included.

Both houses of Congress soon approved a constitutional amendment enfranchising women. By May 1939, the legislatures of all twenty-eight states had ratified the amendment. However, one step remained—Congress had to tabulate the votes of the legislatures and declare the amendment to be in effect.

At this point, the political momentum toward enfranchising women faltered. Politicians considered women to be overly influenced by the Church. As Almazán's candidacy gained strength, PRM leaders felt that if women were enfranchised, they would back Almazán.

Since Cárdenas, on his own initiative, had accelerated land reform, transformed the PNR, and nationalized the oil industry, he could presumably have pushed though women suffrage if he had still supported it. At the end of Cárdenas's term, feminists Adelina Zendejas and Concha Michel concluded: "Cárdenas felt that women were controlled by the clergy, and said, 'If they have the vote, then we'll be beaten, because they are a majority.' That's why they never declared the passage of the suffrage amendment."

The failure of the PRM leadership to enfranchise women by no means brought to a halt the social forces that were, willy-nilly, changing women's role in Mexican society. Women not only received more education but increasingly imparted it. The opportunity to become a rural schoolteacher provided many young women with professional identities and modest incomes. However, women were still denied equal access to education, due to the widespread belief that highly educated women would not be able to find males willing to marry them and due to families with limited income only investing in educating male children.

After the Revolution female employment increased rapidly in the state sector, especially in agencies concerned with social welfare, such as health and education. During the early 1920s, an unprecedented number of careers opened to women. They worked in medicine, law, accounting, and real estate, and served as stenographers and telephone operators.

Even though new areas of employment were opening for women, between 1921 and 1930 female employment declined from 6.7 percent of the workforce to 4.6 percent as women were disproportionately laid off during the Depression and as demobilized revolutionary veterans rejoined the labor force. By 1940, as Mexico began to urbanize and recover from the Depression, female employment increased to 7.4 percent of the labor force.

Perhaps the biggest change of all in the lives of women resulted from the widespread introduction of *molinos de nixtamal* (corn mills) powered by internal combustion engines. Since pre-historic times, grinding the corn kernels used to make tortillas had been culturally defined as women's work. Mechanical mills, which began to appear in the 1920s, freed women from rising before dawn and spending tedious hours on their knees grinding corn. In petitions listing a community's needs, women often placed a mill above schools, clinics, and water rights. In some cases, mills even produced a male backlash, since they dramatically changed women's daily routine. Men in Tepoztlán commented that the flavor of tortillas coming from the mechanical mill was inferior, and repeatedly opposed the mills on the grounds that women would use their increased free time for gossip, idleness, and—so it was believed—infidelity.

Population

Death rates remained high, especially for children, well into the post-revolutionary period. In 1930, more than half the population still lacked safe drinking water sources. Medical care remained beyond the reach of most Mexicans. Mexico City had one doctor for every 679 inhabitants, while the predominantly indigenous state of Oaxaca had one for each 18,107.

The government sought to accelerate the rate of population increase, reflecting its longstanding pro-natal views that resulted from the teachings of the Catholic Church, from the lesson drawn from the Mexican–American War, and from the desire to compensate for population loss resulting from the Revolution. Between 1921 and 1940, Mexico's population increased from 14.3 million to 19.7 million.

After the Revolution, Mexico's northern border region flourished due to massive government-funded irrigation works and U.S. tourists who flocked to border towns in search of alcohol—unavailable north of the border due to Prohibition. During the 1920s, the population of Juárez more than doubled while Tijuana's more than octupled. Between 1921 and 1940, the population of the border states (plus Baja California) grew from 1,717,442 to 2,617,723.

Between 1920 and 1940, the area of Mexico City expanded from eighteen square miles to forty-five. The city's population almost tripled, rising from 4.3 percent of the national population to 9.2 percent. As Mexico's largely rural population increased, it found few rural job opportunities. Many rural areas remained insecure well after the major armies had ceased to fight. As haciendas went bankrupt or were converted into *ejidos*, many lost jobs. These factors resulted in migration to the capital. Also high government spending, at least until 1934, generated jobs in Mexico City and made it a more pleasant place. After 1934, the federal government increased its role, adding employment in the bureaucracy. Finally, as industrialization increased, new, relatively high-paying jobs were created in the city.

Education

Along with land reform, education was one of the great transforming forces of the post-revolutionary period. Article 3 of the 1917 constitution guaranteed free public education. However, just as was the case with land reform, this constitutional mandate was not immediately implemented.

By the time Obregón took office in 1920, it had become obvious that Mexico was failing to meet its educational goals. To fill this gap, Obregón pushed through a constitutional amendment that granted the federal government the right to build and administer schools. By 1923, educational spending had risen to a record 9.3 percent of the federal budget. Between 1921 and 1924, more schools were built than had been built during the previous fifty years. More than 1,000 of these schools were in rural areas. Teachers sometimes rode by horseback for days from the nearest railroad station to their assignment.

Figure 11.3 *Of the various reforms carried out in the name of the Revolution, education enjoyed the broadest support. This photo by Mariana Yampolsky shows a school for the Mazahua, an indigenous group from the State of Mexico.*

Source: Mariana Yampolsky. Escuela Mazahua, 1979/Mazahua School 1979. Estado de México/State of Mexico. Silver gelatin print. D. R. © 2015 Mariana Yampolsky, Cultural Foundation, Mexico.

Photograph courtesy of The Witliff Collections, Alkek Library, Texas State University.

JOSÉ VASCONCELOS

José Vasconcelos, the son of a customs agent, was born in 1882. His family repeatedly moved around Mexico as his father was assigned to different customs houses. In 1899, he enrolled in Mexico City's National Preparatory School. There he and his fellow students founded the Athenaeum of Youth, a literary salon that rejected positivism due to its failure to embrace arts and humanities. The talented students in the salon would dominate Mexican intellectual life for a generation.

Vasconcelos subsequently graduated from law school and began practicing law in Mexico City. In 1909, he joined Madero's campaign to oust Díaz. He became editor of the pro-Madero journal *El Anti-reeleccionista*. Díaz closed the paper and Vasconcelos fled to the United States to avoid arrest.

After an amnesty was declared, he returned to Mexico City and joined a group planning an armed uprising in support of Madero. When the plot was discovered he fled the country again and did not return until after Díaz went into exile.

He became one of Madero's closest advisors and was jailed briefly by Huerta after Madero was murdered. After his release, he established ties with Carranza and was sent to Europe as a secret agent. While in Paris, he persuaded the French secretary of treasury to have Huerta's bonds removed from the French stock exchange.

Once Huerta was defeated, he returned to Mexico City, where Carranza appointed him to head the National Preparatory School. His tenure at the school only lasted a few months since he failed to demonstrate sufficient loyalty to Carranza. He was removed from the school and briefly jailed.

Vasconcelos escaped from jail and fled to Aguascalientes, where the Convention government appointed him secretary of education. Convention President Gutiérrez later sent him to the United States to lobby for the Convention government. Having burned his bridges with Carranza, Vasconcelos remained outside Mexico from 1915 to 1920.

In 1920, he returned to Mexico and was met at the train station by Obregón, who appointed him rector of the National University. In that position he launched a national adult literacy campaign, declaring, "To truly resolve our educational problem, we must involve the public and create missionary fervor, just like that of the Christian missionaries who spread the faith."

The following year Obregón appointed Vasconcelos to the newly created position of secretary of public education. He continued the "missionary teacher" campaign and launched a campaign to build schools and libraries throughout Mexico. Given limits on the education budget, he diverted funds from the University, attended by the affluent, to broaden access to elementary education nationwide.

Vasconcelos linked the notions of social justice and education. He emphasized that without the latter, the former would remain wishful thinking. He also viewed education and culture as a way of incorporating the peasantry and urban workers into the post-revolutionary reconstruction of Mexico. Thousands of small libraries throughout Mexico were stocked with inexpensive editions of social science works and European and Mexican literature. Painters assumed a central role in this process, legitimizing revolutionary policies by fusing myths of the national past with visions of the revolutionary future. Under Vasconcelos's patronage, three artists—Diego Rivera, José Clemente Orozco, and David Alfaro Siqueiros, who became known simply as the Big Three—were put on government salary to paint murals.

In 1929, Vasconcelos challenged Ortiz Rubio in the presidential election. Vasconcelos ran as a reformist, criticizing public office being used for private gain. He advocated a literacy program and an expansion of the educational system. Another plank of Vasconcelos's platform called for granting the vote to women. Many saw Vasconcelos, who stressed the need for democracy, as a new Madero. In contrast to Madero, Vasconcelos advocated accelerating land reform.

During his campaign, Vasconcelos, who enjoyed strong urban support, drew large crowds. He was hampered by having to rely on private funds while the PNR enjoyed access to public funds.

Pro-government goons repeatedly attacked his rallies. This violence continued through election day, when nine died and nineteen were wounded in Mexico City alone.

Vasconcelos denounced the official results, threatened revolt, and took refuge in the United States. However it was clear that since Ortiz Rubio had the backing of the army, Calles, and both the U.S. and Mexican governments, rebellion would be futile.

The 1929 campaign ended Vasconcelos's political career, but not his extensive scholarship which includes magazine and newspaper articles and roughly sixty-nine books. His oeuvre ranges widely, including essays, fiction, history, and philosophical treatises.

The concept for which Vasconcelos is best remembered is that of the Cosmic Race, his term for the mestizo. He felt the mestizos of Mexico, by combining the best of the Indian and the European, were humans superior to their ancestors. He predicted that mestizos would dominate the world in the twentieth-first century due to this superiority. In the 1960s, this concept became influential with the Chicano movement in the United States, since it told Mexican Americans that their mixed-race heritage, rather than being a liability, was indeed an asset.

Teachers were instructed to organize festivals commemorating patriotic holidays such as the Cinco de Mayo and the births and deaths of such figures as Hidalgo, Juárez, Morelos, and Madero. Educators felt these holidays offered attractive alternatives to religious festivals. Teachers were instructed to change the way people farmed, marketed, consumed, and organized their households. They were to do this by visiting mothers in homes and forming cooperatives and hygiene brigades.

The next wave of educational reform came during the Cárdenas administration. The month Cárdenas took office, Article 3 of the constitution was amended to read:

Education imparted by the State will be socialist, and, in addition to excluding all religious doctrine, it will combat fanaticism and prejudice, to which ends the school will organize teaching and activities to permit the formation in the youth of a rational and exact concept of the universe and of social life.

This amendment led to a debate about what the term "socialist education" actually meant. Some thought it required praising the Soviet Union and singing a communist anthem known as the "Internationale." In practice, socialist education embodied new textbooks promoting land reform, the dignity of labor, a materialist approach to history, and the Mexican national identity.

The key to educational success in the 1920s and 1930s was the willingness of teachers to accept low pay and difficult living conditions. Parallels were often drawn between the missionary task of rural teachers and the efforts of the Franciscan missionaries in the sixteenth century. Teachers persisted despite the violent opposition of local landowners and political bosses who did not want their workforce educated, literate, and informed about new revolutionary laws.

From 1935 to 1940, the number of children enrolled in primary school increased from 1.7 million to 2.2 million, and educational spending accounted for between 12 and 14 percent of the federal budget. Between 1910 and 1940, male literacy increased from 32 to 50 percent, while female literacy increased from 24 to 42 percent.

The Church

The 1917 Constitution reflected the anti-clericalism of convention delegates. Article 3 prohibited the Church from imparting primary education. Article 24 outlawed outdoor religious services. Article 27 prohibited the Church from owning any property, even if it was dedicated to worship. Article 130 provided for extensive regulation of the Church. It denied the Church standing as a legal entity. Priests and ministers were declared to be professionals subject to regulation, just as physicians and lawyers were. State legislatures were granted the power to limit the number of priests in their respective jurisdictions. Priests were denied the right to vote, hold office, or criticize laws or government officials.

Both Carranza and Obregón, intent on consolidating their regimes, looked the other way as the Church hierarchy ignored the restrictions the 1917 constitution had placed on religious activities. Since there was no feasible alternative to religious education, the Church continued to administer a fifth of Mexico's schools.

State-level autonomy on religious matters was most conspicuous in Tabasco. The state remained under the control of Tomás Garrido Canabal from 1920 to 1935. The virulent anti-clericalism of Garrido Canabal, the son of a *hacendado*, has never been explained. Garrido Canabal, who served two terms as governor, closed all churches in the state, required all priests to be married, and prohibited the display of religious images.

In contrast to Carranza and Obregón, Calles came to the presidency with a well-deserved reputation for being militantly anti-clerical. In 1916, while governor of Sonora, Calles referred to priests as "inciters of illiterates and fanatics."

By the beginning of 1926, Church and state were engaged in low-intensity conflict. The Church prohibited its members from joining the CROM. Early in 1926, the state of Hidalgo limited the number of priests in the state to sixty. Some of the Catholic hierarchy publicly (and according to the 1917 constitution, illegally) criticized this limit. In January, the bishops stated, "We must collectively declare that these measures and any others that violate religious freedom cannot be respected by the prelates and the clergy."

Historian Jean Meyer suggests that Calles rejected his predecessors' peaceful co-existence with the Church because he felt the Church threatened his power. His biographer Jürgen Buchenau commented, "Calles' hatred of the Church ran so deep that it defied structuralist explanations of his behavior, confounding historical analyses to the present day." In any case, Calles's obtuse anti-clericalism soon led the nation to civil war.

On July 25, the Mexican Episcopate, with Papal authority, ordered that all Catholic churches be closed and public worship suspended to protest Calles's anti-clerical measures. Calles remained unmoved and referred to his dispute with the Church as "the struggle of darkness against light." In fact Calles welcomed the suspension of religious services, which began on July 31, since he assumed that if religious practice was suspended, people would gradually forget about the Church and become non-religious.

The response of Mexico's devoutly Catholic peasantry caught the government, the army, and the Church completely off guard. By the spring of 1927, sustained rebellion was occurring in Jalisco, Michoacán, Colima, Guanajuato, and southern Zacatecas. Since the rebels used the battle cry of "*¡Viva Cristo Rey!*" ("Long Live Christ the King!"), they became known as Cristeros, and the uprising as the Cristiada.

The composition of Cristero forces varied widely from place to place due to differing local histories and interests. In general though they included the landless, smallholders, sharecroppers, tenants, and members of corporate Indian communities. Some former Zapatistas participated in the Cristiada, viewing themselves as simply continuing their struggle for justice and religious liberty. Generally priests did not participate in, or even actively support, the Cristiada. There were some exceptions, such as Father Vega, who became such an effective rebel leader that he was known as "Pancho Villa in a cassock." Cristeros were united in wanting to overthrow the government and eliminate any semblance of official anti-clericalism and socialism.

The Cristiada lasted for three years as mounted guerrilla forces dodged more than 70,000 federal troops. The federal army adopted tactics resembling those of the Spanish during the war for independence. It established concentration camps and declared that anyone found outside them would be subject to summary execution. Rather than reducing support for the Cristeros, the brutality of this policy generated yet further resistance to the state, and rebel ranks swelled accordingly. After three years, federal forces had made little progress at suppressing the rebellion. They would leave their barracks, travel down rail lines and highways, and launch futile attacks against an enemy whose high degree of mobility allowed him to avoid superior federal forces.

Cristeros's control in broad areas allowed them to establish a civil government that operated print shops, delivered mail, managed schools, and collected taxes. Since so many men had joined Cristero forces, women assumed many traditionally masculine roles. They worked the land to ensure a food supply and directly contributed to the war effort by carrying messages, bringing food to Cristero forces, smuggling in ammunition, and caring for the wounded.

The number of insurgents reached 50,000, spread over seventeen states. By mid-1929, it was obvious to the Mexican government, the Episcopate, and the Vatican that the Cristiada had turned into a hopeless stalemate. Through the good offices of U.S. Ambassador Morrow, who feared Mexico would plunge into chaos, an agreement was reached between the Episcopate and the government. On June 21, 1929, President Portes Gil announced that the government would pardon all Cristeros, return church buildings to the Church, and allow Catholics to engage in educational and social welfare activities, and that persecution of the Church would cease.

The total number of deaths resulting from the Cristiada, including both civilians and the military, reached almost 200,000. In addition, since the rebellion occurred in the heart of Mexico's granary, cereal production plummeted by almost 40 percent between 1926 and 1929.

The Church–state cooperation that began in 1929 set the tone for the following decade. During the Cárdenas administration, Church–state relations further improved, since Cárdenas wanted Mexico to be undivided by religious issues so Catholics would rally around him when his reforms were challenged. With moderate leaders at the helm of both the government and the Church, an officially acknowledged modus vivendi was established.

Cárdenas's overtures to the Church yielded results, as the hierarchy supported his land reform and the oil nationalization. After the oil nationalization, Archbishop of Mexico Luis María Martínez stated: "There is no reason why Catholics should not cooperate with the government effort to pay the indemnification to the oil companies. This is not a political issue, in which we would not become involved, but an issue of patriotism."

The Intellectual Scene

Print Media

The literary depiction of the Revolution gained ground in 1924 with the "discovery" of *Los de Abajo*, which had been originally published in 1915. This novel by Mariano Azuela, a physician who served with Pancho Villa, described the suffering and killing of the Revolution by depicting the exploits of a band of peasant revolutionaries led by Demetrio Macías. In *Los de Abajo*, which was translated in 1929 as *The Underdogs*, one of the rebels declares, "The revolution is the hurricane, and the man who surrenders to it is no longer a man, he's a poor dead leaf tossed about in the gale . . ." In addition to emphasizing the lack of clear motives behind the Revolution, Azuela focused on its cruelty, plunder, and betrayal of popular ideals. Some of Azuela's later novels dealt with the middle and upper classes, which he also criticized for their cynicism and venality.

The other great novelist of the Revolution was Martín Luis Guzmán, a journalist and one-time secretary to Pancho Villa. His 1928 novel *El Águila y la Serpiente*, translated in 1930 as *The Eagle and the Serpent*, is a memoir of the author's experiences with Villa. Guzmán's other major literary work *La sombra del caudillo* was not published in Mexico until 1938. Unlike previous novels of the Revolution, it deals with events after 1920, depicting an unnamed *caudillo* who employed treachery and murder to install his chosen candidate as his successor.

Unlike many revolutions, the Mexican Revolution did not lead to a loss of press freedom. Papers such as *El Universal*, which began publishing in 1916, and *Excélsior*, which began publishing the following year, offered views independent of the government. Generally these papers were more conservative than the government and criticized what were perceived as its leftist excesses. However *El Machete*, the official organ of the Mexican Communist Party, criticized government conservatism.

Newspapers flourished during the Cárdenas administration as is indicated by their annual sales rising from 140 million in 1935 to almost 200 million in 1937. Even though the Cárdenas administration faced significant opposition, it preserved press freedom, which allowed many papers and columnists to endorse Almazán's presidential candidacy.

While post-revolutionary papers were freer than they had been under Díaz, they were not demonstrably less venal. In 1940, German Minister to Mexico Baron Rüdt von Collenberg-Bödigheim lamented that a lack of funds prevented him from getting Axis views aired in the Mexican press. He observed, "In this country all newspapers and most journalists expect cash for cooperation, as obviously the other side is offering plentiful."

DIEGO RIVERA, JOSÉ CLEMENTE OROZCO, AND DAVID ALFARO SIQUEIROS

The Big Three mural artists, Diego Rivera, José Clemente Orozco, and David Alfaro Siqueiros, were hired by Vasconcelos and began their work at the National Preparatory School and in the process launched an artistic movement that would dominate Mexico for a generation. The muralists, who would embellish dozens of public buildings in Mexico, celebrated the mestizo, Mexico's Indian roots, and the long struggle for social justice against rich Mexicans and foreign imperialists. Not only were their murals politically charged but, unlike Mexico's previous Eurocentric artistic creation, they depicted people who looked like most Mexicans—brown-skinned peasants—rather than idealized Greek figures. Their murals incorporated scenes from everyday life, landscapes, the Revolution, patriotic heroes, and religious celebrations. A final element of the mural movement was a faith in progress. Rivera's biographer Bertram Wolfe commented on government art policy, "It spread out magnificent frescoes before the gaze of a people to which it could not offer sufficient books or literacy, nor guarantee a wage sufficient for the purchase of a daily newspaper."

As with most sweeping changes, controversy swirled around the shift from reproducing European fashions in easel art to depicting Mexican-looking figures in murals while at the same time attacking the economic status quo. Egged on by a conservative press, students at the National Preparatory School defaced some of the murals and demanded that the work at the school cease. The writer Salvador Novo called the murals repulsive and designed to awaken in the viewer not an aesthetic emotion but "an anarchistic fury if he is penniless or, if wealthy, to make his knees buckle with fright." The vilification of mural art only ceased after critics in Paris and New York began to praise the murals. By the end of the 1920s, the muralists had emerged as cultural heroes, much as movie stars of a later generation, and just as with movie stars, their turbulent private lives became highly public.

After Obregón and Vasconcelos left office in 1924, official sponsorship of the muralists ended and each of the Big Three went their separate ways. Only Rivera remained in government employment, painting 235 panels in the building of the Secretary of Education. These murals form only a small part of his enormous artistic legacy, which despite his focusing on Mexican themes, brought in the latest European influences.

Rivera's legacy includes murals at the National Agriculture School at Chapingo and scathing visual representations of the new political class in his mid-1930s frescos in the National Palace.

Rivera left behind not only a wealth of great paintings but also the very idea of a people's art, inspiring others to paint with a social consciousness. Rivera's biographer commented, "It was Diego's hope that an illiterate people who had been told the stories of the saints through the painted image would respond to this new secular myth of the Revolution and its promises for man's life on earth."

During the 1920s, the mural renaissance, with its static visual imagery, could still exercise a compelling effect on Mexico's population, since both cinema and radio were in their infancy. By the 1930s, radio and cinema were the harbingers of mass media. Their impact during the Cárdenas administration far outstripped the static visual didactics of the revolutionary muralists, whose work was seen only by a relatively small fraction of the population.

Despite their critiques of capitalism in general (both Rivera and Siqueiros were members of the Mexican Communist Party) and of the revolutionary nouveau riche in particular, by the end of their careers the Big Three had been firmly embraced by the political establishment. In 1949, a fifty-year retrospective of more than 1,000 Rivera art works opened at the Palace of Fine Arts. At its inauguration, Mexican President Miguel Alemán referred to Rivera as a national treasure. In 1956, the government declared Rivera's seventieth birthday as a day of national homage. When Rivera died the following year, he was buried in the Rotunda of Illustrious Men in Mexico City's Dolores Pantheon. Upon his death in 1949, Orozco was also accorded high honors. Siqueiros was the last of the Big Three to be embraced by the establishment. He was jailed from 1960 to 1964 for his efforts on behalf of political prisoners and his criticism of the government. His fate shifted between 1967 and 1971 when he was commissioned to decorate the massive exterior panels and the interior dome of the Polyforum, part of a privately owned development project—today's World Trade Center in Mexico City. At the 1971 inauguration of the Polyforum, President Luis Echeverría hailed Siqueiros's work as a fitting monument to fifty years of muralism in Mexico.

There are two striking contrasts between the Revolution as depicted by the muralists and by novelists. The muralists, excepting Orozco, portrayed the Revolution as the dawn of a better tomorrow, made possible by harnessing machines in a new social order. In contrast, the novelists' view of the Revolution was much more pessimistic. The other contrast is the impact of the two mediums. While the murals and the muralists became known internationally, the novels of the Revolution had a much more restricted audience.

Radio

In the nineteenth century and early twentieth century, newspapers circulated among the literate elite, leaving it to radio to become Mexico's first mass media. It could fill this role since it was free (except for the set) and it did not require literacy or the land distribution channels that newspapers used.

Commercial radio first appeared in Mexico in the 1920s. Early on the government decided to follow the U.S. model, that is, to have programming paid for by selling ads. Some of the early stations were owned by the companies that sought to market their products. El Buen Tono, a cigarette manufacturer, owned a station and then created a cigarette brand, El Radio, to market on the air.

Radio came of age in 1930 with the inauguration of XEW, a 200-kilowatt station, the most powerful in the Western Hemisphere. This station, owned by Emilio Azcárraga Vidaurreta, was known as "The Voice of Latin America." Azcárraga used his business talents and his marriage into the Monterrey industrial elite, which gave him access to capital, to build a radio-based media empire.

During the 1930s, radio became increasingly influential. By 1935, there were eighty radio stations and 250,000 sets. In 1937 the government began to produce a weekly program, which it mandated that all stations play at the same time. This program, known as "*La Hora Nacional*" ("The National

Hour"), combined government messages and, to attract listeners, music. It was one of the first cultural phenomena to link the entire nation. Cárdenas effectively used radio to broadcast his speeches and rallies and even announced the nationalization of the oil industry on the radio.

PICKING UP THE PIECES, 1917–1940

The Economy, 1917–1929

The commodity boom induced by World War I favored the Mexican economy. As a result of increased prices for metals, oil, and henequen, exports nearly doubled in value between 1916 and 1920. Once the war was over, the received wisdom in the United States and Great Britain was that it would be best for the world to simply return to the old economic system. Carranza's Secretary of Industry and Commerce Alberto Pani shared this view, advocating a continued reliance on raw material exports, albeit with further processing in Mexico.

Restarting the economy presented myriad challenges. Many *hacendados*, businessmen, and professionals had fled, lessening human capital. Wealthy Mexicans shied away from new investments, deterred by continued political instability, the radical tone of the 1917 constitution, and the increased strength of labor organizations. Since Mexico was already in default on its foreign loans, there was little likelihood of obtaining loans outside Mexico. Given the lack of other sources, there was general agreement that Mexico would have to rely on private foreign investors to rebuild the economy.

A few days after he took office in 1924, Calles declared, "The revolutionary movement has entered its constructive phase." This "constructive phase" was based on private enterprise and a continued reliance on exports and foreign investment. A central bank, modeled on the U.S. Federal Reserve Bank, was created in 1925. Until its creation, private corporations, many of them foreign, dominated the Mexican banking system. As a result, there was little the government could do to insure that banking activity conformed to its economic goals. To entice Mexican bankers back into the market, they were virtually allowed to write banking regulations themselves.

During the Calles administration (1924–28), Mexico began to shift away from its reliance on mining, oil, and subsistence agriculture towards manufacturing and commercial agriculture—the sectors that would undergird the economy in the latter half of the twentieth century. Calles felt that, in the absence of other sources of investment, the state should create banks, reservoirs, and roads. Officials frequently used the term "businesslike" untranslated in Spanish documents.

The combination of political order, a revamped banking system, and government austerity began to attract foreign investors, including Ford, Palmolive, and Dupont. Such investment was welcomed since the political elite felt that if the country relied exclusively on domestic investment, development would be postponed indefinitely. Mexico's wealthy also became confident enough to begin investing. Calles's Treasury Minister Alberto Pani referred to Mexicans who invested productively as "revolutionary capitalists."

Pani's phrase notwithstanding, there was little one could call revolutionary about the Mexican economy. Mexico was tied more closely than ever to the United States by trade. Many members of the old Porfirian business community had survived and even prospered, working in cooperation with the state. Oil, silver, and industrial minerals accounted for up to 80 percent of exports. Large estates remained intact. Between 1919 and 1929, U.S. direct investment in Mexico increased from $644 million to $709 million. In 1935, foreigners controlled 98 percent of mining, 99 percent of the oil industry, 79 percent of the railroad and trolley system, and 100 percent of electrical power generation. Export industries created little consumer demand, since in 1930 mining and oil together employed only 1 percent of the work force. Labor was distributed in much the same way it had been thirty-five years earlier. In 1930, agriculture employed 68.7 percent of workers,

299

compared to 66.5 percent in 1895. Manufacturing employed 9.9 percent of workers, down from 11.5 percent in 1895.

Between 1921 and 1929, the economy grew at 1.7 percent a year. This growth largely resulted from raw material exports. In 1929, exports were 265 percent above the 1909–10 level. Mineral exports had increased by 336 percent and agricultural exports by 190 percent.

The Depression, 1929–1934

Between 1929 and 1932, as the international demand for raw materials plummeted, the value of Mexican exports declined from $274 million to $96.5 million. Since the government was heavily reliant on export taxes, there was less money for public works. In 1932, Mexico's gross domestic product (GDP) was 24 percent below its 1926 peak.

The Depression resulted in massive job loss, plus the return of 300,000 Mexicans who had been working in the United States. However the impact of the Depression was not as severe as in some industrialized nations since only 3 percent of the non-rural labor force worked in oil and mining. These sectors produced 65 percent of exports. The Depression also had limited impact on the large number of people engaged in subsistence agriculture.

Beginning in 1931, to stimulate the economy the government sharply increased its spending and the money supply. To fill the void left by the lack of foreign credit and investment, in 1934 the Nacional Financiera, a government investment bank, began issuing bonds to finance agricultural and industrial projects.

Higher government spending and an increase in oil and silver prices aided Mexico's recovery from the Depression. Between 1932 and 1935, as traditional foreign markets recovered from the Depression, Mexico's exports doubled in value. By 1935, production had passed the 1929 level.

Throughout Latin America, as a result of the Depression, the volume and price of exports declined and the large influx of foreign investment ceased. New development strategies created in response to the Depression emphasized greater state intervention in the economy and a focus on the domestic market.

The Cárdenas Years, 1934–1940

Cárdenas faced a dual challenge—rebuilding the Depression-ravaged economy and making it responsive to Mexican needs rather than foreign ones. During his administration (1934–40), the share of the federal budget devoted to economic development increased from 22 to 38 percent. Unlike his predecessors, Cárdenas felt that social justice would facilitate economic development rather than retard it.

During his administration, there was a sharp drop in foreign investment as the oil industry and railroads were nationalized. Cárdenas's nationalism deterred new foreign investment. In 1940, U.S. investment totaled only $300 million, down from more than $1 billion in the 1920s. In 1939, the principal investors were the state, which accounted for 39 percent of new investment, and Mexican citizens, who accounted for 46 percent. Even though he was a nationalist, Cárdenas did not oppose foreign investment. As long as investors did not expect special privileges, they were welcome.

Rather than relying on exports, as Mexico had for the previous half century, economic recovery resulted from increased internal demand, stimulated by the land reform and wage increases. Between 1932 and 1939, annual economic growth averaged 6.2 percent. During the Cárdenas administration, manufacturing increased by 51 percent, commerce by 41 percent, and construction by 40 percent. Despite the almost total lack of new foreign investment, the economy not only expanded, but became more diversified and more integrated.

By 1940, the state had emerged as an important economic actor, with a major if not exclusive role in finance, railways, petroleum, electrical energy production, road building, and the expansion of irrigation works. Public expenditure per capita during the Cárdenas administration was 41 percent above the previous six-year period.

Cárdenas's policies set the stage for unprecedented subsequent expansion. Hacienda labor became more mobile. With land reform, the old order crumbled, and rural people began to examine their options. Some farmed for themselves, others decided the city had more to offer and sought industrial jobs. Increased investment in education and health care, although slow to pay economic dividends, was crucial to subsequent development. As anthropologist Oscar Lewis observed, consumption patterns shifted:

> More and more people sleep on beds instead of on the ground, wear shoes instead of huaraches or going barefoot, use store-made pants instead of home-made white cotton calzones, eat bread in addition to tortillas, grind their corn in the mill instead of by hand, drink beer instead of pulque, use doctors instead of curanderos, and travel by bus or train instead of on foot or by burro.[4]

Roads

Before the Revolution, the railroad led to a transportation revolution. However, even the great nineteenth-century railroad building boom left most areas isolated. In the early 1920s, France had eight times as many kilometers of railroad per square kilometer as Mexico did, while the United States had five times as many.

After the Revolution, road building created another transportation revolution. Calles initiated a massive road-building program that integrated isolated rural areas into the national economy and facilitated sanitation and health programs. A variety of interests—including construction companies, auto manufacturers, and auto dealers—lobbied for increased highway construction.

During the 1930s, agrarian expert Eyler Simpson described Mexican goals and needs as "roads and schools, Fords and books." Cárdenas shared this view, devoting 26.6 percent of government investment to road building, literally paving the way for subsequent development. Between 1930 and 1940, road mileage increased from 884 miles to 6,156. During this same period, the number of motor vehicles increased from 85,535 to 149,455. By 1940, highways linked eleven of Mexico's twelve largest cities.

By reducing transportation costs, new roads facilitated a consumer invasion that included Frigidaires and Palmolive products. They also increased personal mobility, taking villagers to the city. Many, especially the better educated, never returned.

Elaborate celebrations marked the opening of new highways, just as they had marked the opening of new rail lines in the nineteenth century. To celebrate the completion in 1939 of the Pan American Highway from Laredo, Texas, to Mexico City, a celebrity motorcade wended its way from the border to the capital.

Agriculture

> The leaders of the Mexican Revolution were seldom economic or political theorists and left no clear statement of the ultimate ends they sought to gain via land reform. In fact, the objectives were constantly changing, sometimes without a recognition that such a change was occurring.
>
> (Robert Edminster, 1961)

For Obregón and Calles, land reform was a political instrument for maintaining the loyalty of peasant groups, manipulating and subordinating them. The Sonorans' aim was to encourage the kind of entrepreneurial, market-orientated, and mechanized farming that Obregón had engaged in personally. They placed more emphasis on irrigation works and the promotion of commercial agriculture than on changing land tenure.

One of Calles's main concerns was agricultural production. Between 1907 and 1929, corn production had declined 40 percent and bean production by 31 percent as producers either ceased farming or switched to more lucrative crops. Meanwhile the population had increased by 9 per cent. Given the desperate need to increase food production, by the end of his term, Calles, like Carranza, favored reliance on the hacienda. As late as 1930, the agricultural sector employed 69 percent of workers, but produced only 22 percent of gross domestic product.

Between 1907 and 1929, land ownership became more concentrated, with a mere 1.5 percent of landowners owning 83 percent of private farmland. Agriculture also became polarized geographically, with production in the north increasing by 430 percent. Northern agriculture was in the hands of aggressive entrepreneurs who employed modern technology to produce high-value crops for distant markets. The problem in the north was distributing everything that was produced.

In central Mexico, agriculture—which was at the subsistence level and relied on traditional, labor-intensive methods—declined by 38 percent between 1907 and 1929. There was little investment in producing corn—the main staple. The government imported food to make up for the decline in food production there.

Figure 11.4 *Impoverished peasants sought land yet many conservative clerics told them land reform was theft. This Diego Rivera sketch appeared on a poster promoting acceptance of land reform. The poster proclaimed: "Distributing land to the poor is in accord with the teachings of Our Lord Jesus Christ and the Holy Mother Church. The Mexican people fought and suffered for ten years seeking the word of Our Lord Jesus Christ."*

Source: *Vida mexicana: Revista mensual de ideas sobre asuntos de interés*, December 1922, vol. 1, no. 1.

Despite the promises of land reform made in the heat of battle, the main trend in the 1920s was not a radical land reform but a mixed economy based on small and medium-sized plots in addition to the hacienda. In part this backtracking occurred due to revolutionary military leaders allying with *hacendados* and their appropriating some haciendas themselves. Landed interests sought to prevent land distribution and to have the federal government provide them with roads, subsidized credit, and irrigation works. Except in the area dominated by the former Zapatista leaders, during the 1920s the federal army did more to block land reform than further it. By 1928, only 4 percent of all agricultural land had been distributed as part of the land reform.

Cárdenas differed from his Sonoran predecessors in that he viewed the *ejido* as the key to social justice *and* as a viable form of rural production. He realized that to be successful *ejidos* would require improvements such as electricity, roads, potable water, and schools, just as large commercial farms required them. The January 1, 1934 entry into his diary stated it was the responsibility of the present generation to distribute land to villages that lacked it and provide them with the necessary credit to cultivate it: "The Revolution requires ejidos and the subdivision of great estates. This will expand production, increase the purchasing power of the rural masses, and benefit the economy as a whole."

Cárdenas addressed this responsibility by distributing almost 10 percent of Mexico's total land area to 723,000 families. As a result, in 1940 *ejidatarios* cultivated 17.3 million acres, while private farmers only cultivated 16.8 million. In 1930, only 13.1 percent of irrigated land was included in the *ejido* sector, while by 1940, 57.4 percent was. In addition to land, during Cárdenas's term *ejidos* received credit, machinery, marketing assistance, and agricultural extension services.

Since the beginning of the land reform, the *ejido* has been subjected to criticism for being "inefficient." However, it was well suited to the times in that it utilized what was in abundance— land and labor—and required relatively little scarce capital. In addition, it increased security for larger producers whose fears of peasant takeovers were quieted. Cárdenas's efforts notwithstanding, *ejidos* suffered from having less water, fertilizer, fixed capital, and financing than privately owned farms.

Industry

> Within the revolutionary leadership, political factions oriented toward a broad variety of urban populations prevailed, to the exclusion of campesinos [peasants], such that the development policy of choice in those critical early years after the Revolution was urbanization-led industrialization, not rural development.
>
> (Diane Davis, 1994)

The destructive effects of the Revolution on Mexican industry were so short and mild that Porfirian industrial growth largely merged with post-revolutionary growth. Unlike the landed elite, the barons of industry remained wealthy and powerful after peace returned.

To promote industry during the 1920s the government sharply increased tariffs. Tariffs on clothing and textiles, which ranged between 40 and 100 percent, were the highest. Government-mandated subsidies for the cotton used to produce textiles provided a further incentive for production. These measures greatly increased mill owners' profits, some of which were passed on to labor, causing the number of strikes to decline.

The presence of foreign manufacturers became highly controversial. Critics called such investment a "menace" to Mexico that would lead to foreign domination and corrupt Mexican culture. They felt it would be better to forgo such investment and grow more slowly, but on a sounder basis. Advocates of foreign investment felt foreign capital would create more jobs and increase wages. They felt American companies, with their enormous increases in efficiency and output, held the promise of seemingly endless improvements in material well-being.

Up until the Depression, industrialization continued at about the same rate it had under Díaz. From 1901 to 1910, manufacturing had increased by 3.1 percent a year. From 1922 to 1935, it grew at 3.8 percent a year. Traditional industries continued to dominate. In 1926, only 0.8 percent of manufactured products were exported. Most industry remained in the hands of artisans. The average number of workers per industrial establishment was only six. As had been the case under Díaz, the government protected industry from foreign competition. Industry continued to be stymied by the export-dominated economy not creating a dynamic consumer market.

By drastically reducing the amount of foreign currency Mexico received from its exports, the Depression forced Mexico to produce what it could no longer afford to import. In addition, as President Ortiz Rubio noted in his 1930 Annual Address, he increased tariffs "to stimulate various sectors of the national economy." The Depression shocked Mexican leaders out of thinking they could rely on raw material exports forever. To secure a reliable supply of manufactured goods, they decided they would have to produce them domestically. The fatalistic notion of "natural comparative advantage" was rejected. It became official dogma that it was not the Creator's design that Mexico produce raw materials while other countries industrialized. Policymakers felt that with modern technology and transportation systems, Mexico could manufacture what it needed.

A variety of government polices stimulated Mexico's still-weak industries. Between 1929 and 1933, the peso was devalued by 64 percent, making it much more expensive to import manufactured goods. The 1936 Law of Industrial Saturation closed entry to branches of industry with excess capacity. In 1937, there was a 26 percent tariff increase. After the 1938 oil nationalization, there was further devaluation of the peso. Government deficit spending increased the demand for industrial goods. Cárdenas also granted new industries a five-year tax exemption.

Between 1932 and 1940, as a result of both policy shifts and changed conditions in Mexico, industrial output increased by 6.1 percent a year, with industry for the first time becoming the most dynamic sector of the economy. With profits soaring, Mexican industrialists began to update their facilities. Output per industrial worker increased 37 percent in the 1930s. Between 1929 and 1940, manufacturing increased from 11.9 percent of gross domestic product to 24.2 percent, while agriculture declined from 23.7 percent to 14.6 percent.

Almost all of this industrialization was financed domestically. Both the old landed classes and the new political class invested their wealth in industry. Most foreign investors remained on the sidelines while Cárdenas was in office. However, General Motors and Chrysler did open plants during his term.

Oil

During the Carranza administration (1917–20), the oil industry boomed. In 1918, Mexico became the world's largest oil exporter and its second largest oil producer, behind only the United States. In 1920, Mexico pumped 25 percent of world production. At their peak oil taxes accounted for a third of government income.

Several features of the Mexican oil industry remained constant through the 1920s. Most of the production was exported, mainly to the United States and Britain. In 1926, only 10.5 percent was retained for Mexican use. Ownership of the industry remained overwhelmingly foreign. As before the Revolution, the oil industry imported almost all the equipment it needed.

At its peak, the oil industry provided 40,000 jobs to unskilled and semi-skilled Mexican workers, who found better pay than otherwise available. The oil labor force was highly stratified, with the best jobs, housing, and salaries reserved for foreign employees who were not interested in learning Spanish or in sharing their technical know-how with Mexicans.

During the 1920s, Mexico's oil boom turned to bust. Annual production fell from 193.4 million barrels in 1921 to 44.7 million in 1929. Few new wells were found to replace exhausted ones, despite extensive exploration efforts. Between 1921 and 1929, oil declined from 76 percent of Mexican exports to 15 percent. Although the oil companies were often accused of reducing production in response to Mexican nationalism, it was geology, not politics, that caused production to decline.

After 1921, as production declined, foreign oil companies came to be regarded as despoilers of the land rather than as agents of progress. Increasingly attention focused on polluted streams and on the large areas of deforested land blanketed in oil. Along the coast, there were oil-fouled oyster beds, shrimping grounds, and mangrove swamps. Roads, telegraph lines, and some 2,589 miles of pipeline, which ruptured with regularity, cut though what had been tropical forest. Rivers were so polluted that they sometimes caught fire.

UNCLE SAM CONFRONTS REVOLUTIONARY NATIONALISM, 1917–1940

Carranza and the United States, 1917–1920

Even before the promulgation of the 1917 Constitution, the United States made it clear that it would not accept Mexico's desire to restructure its society as justification for overriding the rights the United States claimed under international law. In 1916, Secretary of State Robert Lansing warned that Carranza's refusal to guarantee U.S. investment would lead to "the gravest consequences." Such statements indicated a contradiction in U.S. foreign policy. President Wilson publicly urged redistribution of wealth in Mexico but would not countenance any change involving wealth belonging to Americans.

Mexican leaders never foresaw their country developing in isolation from the United States. Rather they wanted to redefine Mexico's relations with the Colossus of the North. Mexican policymakers sought to: 1) protect and regulate the exploitation of Mexican natural resources; 2) regulate the activities of foreign businesses and investors; and 3) increase the government's economic role. Carranza did not oppose U.S. investment as long as investors did not demand special privileges. In 1917, he pledged "all the security and guarantees granted by Mexico's laws" to U.S. investors.

During World War I, President Wilson attempted to safeguard U.S. investments in Mexico without driving Mexico into the hands of Germany. At the same time, Carranza remained neutral in World War I, demonstrating his independence from the United States.

The seriousness of the German threat to the United States was emphasized by the Zimmermann telegram, sent to Mexico in February 1917 by German Foreign Minister Arthur Zimmermann. This coded message proposed that Mexico join the war on the German side and fight the United States. In exchange Mexico would be allowed to regain Texas, New Mexico, and Arizona from the United States. Carranza, realizing that Germany was distant and thus unable to provide effective support, did not accept the proposal.

The Zimmermann telegram backfired after the German code was cracked by British intelligence, which passed the contents of the telegram to the U.S. government. When the message was published in the United States, it turned public opinion strongly against Germany and influenced Wilson's decision to declare war.

It was U.S. investment in Mexico, not German–Mexican relations, that produced conflict with the United States during Carranza's 1917–20 term. U.S. investors controlled 78 percent of the mining industry, 72 percent of smelting, 68 percent of rubber production, and 58 percent of the oil industry. Their investments were worth more than the combined total of all other foreign investments.

In April 1917, Carranza increased the tax on oil to 10 percent of the value of oil exported. U.S. companies denounced the tax as illegal, since their concessions acquired before 1910 specifically granted them relief from such taxes. Furthermore they claimed that the tax was "excessive beyond the point of being confiscatory."

In his dealings with foreign oilmen, Carranza clearly came out a winner concerning taxation. Between 1914 and January 1, 1920, he vastly increased the share of oil wealth remaining in Mexico by raising the oil tax from an almost trivial 60 centavos per ton to 10 percent of the value of the oil.

Carranza's ability to make such increases resulted from the U.S. preoccupation with World War I. President Wilson also contributed to Carranza's success in that, even though Wilson ordered the landing at Veracruz and the Pershing expedition, he was not as pro-intervention as many of his U.S. contemporaries. While World War I gave Carranza some latitude vis-à-vis U.S. interests, the presence of a powerful, foreign entrepreneurial sector did form one of the real limits on the alternatives open to the Mexican Revolution.

Obregón and United States, 1920–1924

After World War I, the United States definitively replaced Great Britain as the major economic power throughout Latin America. As in the rest of Latin America, the United States increased its dominance over Mexico's foreign trade. By 1922, the United States was selling ten times as much to Mexico as Great Britain and buying four times as much.

The United States also replaced Great Britain as the main source of foreign investment. In 1913, the United States and Great Britain were virtually tied with $800 million each in direct investment in Mexico. By 1926, British investment had risen to $1 billion, while U.S. investment had increased to $1.5 billion. In 1928, U.S. investments in the oil industry totaled $408 million, followed by $391 million in mining and smelting, and $300 million in railroads. As these figures indicate, U.S. investment was still overwhelmingly involved in producing raw materials and shipping them out of the country, not in producing for the Mexican market.

When he took office in December 1920, Obregón sought to normalize relations with the United States. However before extending recognition, U.S. President Warren Harding demanded guarantees for foreign property rights—in effect, the abandonment of Article 27. Charles Evans Hughes, Harding's Secretary of State, declared that to gain recognition Mexico had to promise not to "cancel, destroy or impair any right, title, or interest in any property" held by Americans in Mexico.

In 1921, progress began on breaking the impasse on recognition. In August, the Mexican Supreme Court, following Obregón's wishes, ruled that oil lands acquired before 1917 could remain in oil company hands if improvements, known as "positive acts," had been made on them. The most common such act was drilling a well.

In response to U.S. pressure, in 1922 Mexico agreed to a meeting to resolve the debt question. The Mexican negotiator was Adolfo de la Huerta, then Obregón's Secretary of Finance. De la Huerta emphasized that Mexico was willing to recognize its pre-revolutionary debts, but that the government would not sacrifice the well-being of the Mexican people to make immediate payments.

The negotiator for the International Committee of Bankers, representing U.S. and British interests, was Thomas Lamont, of J. P. Morgan Company, the most powerful American financial house. The Committee's leaders met frequently with the U.S. State Department and had its blessing in dealing with Mexico.

De la Huerta's arguments did not persuade Lamont. As a result, there was no compromise on the debt. The negotiated result, known as the Lamont–de la Huerta Agreement, committed Mexico to pay the entire foreign debt contracted by Obregón's predecessors, as well as a considerable part of the interest accrued.

Signing the Lamont–de la Huerta Agreement led bankers to support diplomatic recognition of Obregón. They felt that if Obregón fell, the agreement would be rejected and debt payments would cease. The agreement drove a wedge between oilmen and bankers in that it guaranteed payment of past debts with future taxes on oil exports.

Obregón's seeking U.S. recognition was sound from both the economic and political point of view. With recognition would come—Obregón hoped—loans and protection from being toppled by revolts organized in the United States. U.S. Undersecretary of State Robert Olds commented on the importance of U.S. recognition, "Central America has always understood that governments which we recognize and support stay in power, while those we do not recognize and support fall."

In 1923, Obregón, still unrecognized, agreed to hold talks with the United States. From May to August 1923, U.S. and Mexican representatives met in Mexico City. Given the relative strength of the two parties, not surprisingly, virtually all U.S. demands were met. In an understanding known as the Bucareli Accords, Obregón reaffirmed the Supreme Court decision on positive acts to property acquired before 1917. Its practical effect was to grant in perpetuity oil concessions made between 1876 and 1917. Mexico agreed to the formation of a claims commission to settle damage claims by U.S. citizens against Mexico.

The Lamont–de la Huerta and Bucareli Accords led to U.S. recognition of the Obregón administration on August 31, 1923. In their 1924 platform, the formerly bellicose Republicans stated that "our difficulties with Mexico have happily yielded to a most friendly adjustment."

For Obregón, the most immediate benefit of recognition was access to U.S. arms. When de la Huerta revolted, the United States supplied the Mexican government with sixteen aircraft, rifles, ammunition, and permission to move Mexican troops through Texas.

Calles and the United States, 1924–1934

Shortly after Calles took office in 1924, U.S.–Mexican relations began another downward spiral. Calles declared that the Bucareli Accords had been merely informal arrangements between Obregón and the United States and therefore were not binding on his administration. A law promulgated in 1925 limited concession acquired before 1917 to fifty years, even if positive acts had been performed.

The oil issue dragged on into 1927, with both sides refusing to give ground. Mexicans viewed Calles as a dedicated nationalist. Americans considered him as anti-capitalist. Mexicans viewed oilmen as foreigners exploiting non-renewable resources and leaving behind only ruined land. Oil companies portrayed themselves as creators of jobs and as taxpayers.

A definitive shift in the tone of U.S.–Mexican relations came with the mid-1927 appointment of Dwight Morrow as U.S. ambassador. Morrow, an Amherst College classmate of Coolidge, had served as a corporate lawyer and partner in the banking firm of J. P. Morgan.

Morrow's instructions from Coolidge were short and to the point: "Keep us out of war with Mexico!" As a friend of Coolidge's, Morrow had more leeway than most diplomats. He also had a knack that was rare for diplomats of the time—he could see both sides of an issue.

Morrow's appointment reflected the shift that was occurring in U.S. Latin American policy. Before arriving in Mexico City, Morrow had stated unequivocally that private debts ought not to be collected by government coercion.

Morrow soon began traveling around Mexico with Calles as a friend and advisor, and he became a major influence on the Mexican president. His greatest success at persuasion was ending the impasse created by the 1925 oil law. Morrow suggested that a face-saving solution could be arrived at if the Mexican Supreme Court would declare the law to be *ex post facto* and therefore illegal. Such a ruling would defuse the situation, without Mexico recognizing a U.S. veto power over Mexican legislation.

Calles passed Morrow's suggestion on to the Supreme Court, which was not noted for its independence. Within a month, Calles had the ruling he wanted. The following month, January 1928, a new oil law took effect that reflected this decision, thus ending the oil crisis. The 1928 law declared that lands improved before 1917 would remain in oil company hands indefinitely.

Morrow did not betray U.S. interests, even though his detractors often accused him of that. He only defended a broader set of interests than oil. He commented on his surprise at the "extent to which responsible oil companies seem to believe it is the duty of the State Department to run their businesses in foreign lands." He balanced the interests of oilmen, bondholders, and those who had lost land to the land reform while exacting payment of as much of Mexico's foreign debt as its weak economy could bear. Unlike his predecessors who had ignored Mexican interests, he observed, "It would be short-sighted policy for the creditors to insist that they be paid at whatever the cost to the people of Mexico."

In his last annual address, Calles stated that the Mexican government was "free of all vexatious difficulties with the neighbor republic of the north." Between 1928 and 1934, relations between the two countries remained cordial due to Calles's increasing conservatism and the settlement of conflicts to both U.S. and Mexican satisfaction.

Throughout the 1920s, U.S. influence continued to increase. In 1928, trade between Mexico and the United States totaled $241 million. That year the United States accounted for 68 percent of both Mexican exports and imports. In addition, the Mexican elite increasingly sent their children to college in the United States. This trend was decried by nationalists and Hispanophiles alike— former Education Secretary José Vasconcelos commented that children of the elite were sent to study in the United States "so they might become lackeys of imperialism."

Roosevelt and the Good Neighbor Policy

Thanks to the warm relationship established between Morrow and Calles, no serious problems clouded U.S.–Mexican relations when Franklin D. Roosevelt took office in March 1933. Throughout Latin America, relations with the United States were improving as FDR avoided military intervention and adopted a more conciliatory approach known as the Good Neighbor Policy.

After FDR took office, U.S. policy in Latin America shifted from the defense of U.S. investment in extractive industries to promoting trade. Also as World War II approached, hemispheric defense became an increasingly important concern. At this time, the United States switched from defending its interests in Latin America with armed force to using its economic power, such as withholding loans from the Export–Import Bank.

In 1933, to implement his Good Neighbor Policy, Roosevelt appointed Josephus Daniels as ambassador to Mexico. As ambassador, Daniels attempted to implement Roosevelt's Good Neighbor Policy, which often produced conflict with the more traditional State Department. Daniels felt U.S. interests in Mexico could be reconciled with Mexican interests. He was not anti-business but saw reforms as a way to provide Mexicans with greater purchasing power, which would make them more stable neighbors and greater consumers of U.S.-made goods.

In early 1936 the stage was once again set for conflict when the national oil workers union demanded a 30-million ($8.3 million) wage increase and increased control over the workplace.

Negotiations between oil workers and oil companies began in July 1936. The companies claimed that since they were paying among the highest wages in Mexico, further wage increases were unwarranted. Labor claimed that their high profits justified the workers' demand for increased wages and benefits.

Before weighing in on the wage increase, the Federal Board of Conciliation and Arbitration appointed a panel of Mexican experts to review oil industry operations. In August 1937, the experts issued a 2,700-page report that recommended that oil workers be granted a wage-and-benefit package worth 26 million pesos. The panel of experts based the 26-million-peso figure on its finding that annual oil company profits amounted to 79 million pesos. The experts noted that Mexican workers received a third or a quarter of what U.S. oil workers received but produced twelve times as much oil per worker.

Once again Ambassador Daniels assumed a position closer to the Mexican one than to that of the State Department. In September 1937, he noted:

> Having made big money on absurdly low wages from the time the oil gushers made Doheny and Pearson rich, all oil producers oppose any change in taxes and wages, and resent it if their Governments do not take their point of view. Mexico can never prosper on low wages and we must be in sympathy with every just demand.[5]

On December 18, 1937, the Arbitration Board followed the recommendation of the experts and awarded oil workers a 26-million-peso wage-and-benefit package. The oil companies immediately appealed the ruling to the Mexican Supreme Court. On March 1, 1938, the Supreme Court ruled that the decision of the Board was binding on the oil companies.

On March 15, oilmen announced: "The companies are unable to put the award into effect. It would ruin their businesses." The oil companies' intransigence in Mexico sought to send a message to Venezuela where production had become much more profitable than it was in the largely exhausted Mexican fields. They felt that, based on anticipated U.S. government support, flaunting Mexican law would not have serious consequences.

On the night of March 18, 1938, in a nationwide radio address, Cárdenas announced the nationalization of the oil industry:

> This is a clear-cut case which forces the government to apply the existing Expropriation Act, not only to force the oil companies to obey and submit, but due to the labor authorities' having declared void the contracts between the companies and the workers. An immediate paralysis of the oil industry is imminent. This would cause incalculable damage to the industry and to the rest of the economy.[6]

The popularity of the move resulted not from abstract nationalism but from the sordid reputation of the oil companies in Mexico. In the 1920s, when Cárdenas was stationed in the oil-producing area, he observed that oil companies acted as if they were operating in "conquered territory." Oilmen formed company unions, dismissed union organizers, and hired goons to harass and assassinate independent labor leaders. The 1920s decline in oil production was considered oil-company skullduggery.

Cárdenas justified the nationalization of the oil companies on the basis that they had violated the labor provisions of Article 123. He promised compensation for nationalized property, but not payment for oil in the ground. By the Mexican interpretation of Article 27, such oil had always belonged to the Mexican government.

Massive demonstrations in support of the nationalization sent a clear message to the United States—an attack on Cárdenas would be an attack on the nation as a whole. Historian Frank Tannenbaum commented on the psychological effect of the nationalization, "If one is to mark a date in Mexico when the nation felt itself in possession of its own house at last, it was the day of the expropriation of the oil wells."

FDR encouraged oil companies not to try to recover their property but to negotiate terms for compensation. He felt that American companies were only entitled to payment for total investment less depreciation. Such a figure would not include prospective profits from oil in the ground.

A number of factors restricted U.S. government action. A week before the nationalization, Hitler had invaded Austria, so war in Europe shaped the U.S. response. FDR, when forced to choose between maintaining the Good Neighbor Policy throughout Latin America and taking a hard line on Mexico, chose the former. Since most of the expropriated oil belonged to Holland and

Britain, the U.S. response was more moderate. The United States realized that if too much pressure was placed on Cárdenas, his government might fall. If Cárdenas had fallen, he would likely have been replaced by a pro-fascist regime.

While various U.S. interests vied to have their preferred policy implemented, Mexican policymakers masterfully averted a confrontation with Washington by emphasizing that they would provide compensation for land taken for the agrarian reform as well as oil company assets as soon as possible. They effectively stalled for three years, all the while telling the Roosevelt administration what it wanted to hear concerning land reform, bilateral trade, and the fight against international fascism.

While pressure was being exerted from abroad, Mexico faced the problem of managing the oil industry. Foreign technicians had been withdrawn. Mexico could not replace aging oil field equipment and lacked workers trained in technical roles. Nevertheless, to the oil companies' astonishment and dismay, Mexicans were able to resume production. Within three months, production reached 65 percent of the pre-nationalization level.

As a result of World War II, the U.S. government intervened to resolve the oil dispute and thus eliminate a potential source of conflict with its southern neighbor. In November 1941, the U.S. and Mexican governments, acting without the oil companies' consent, appointed experts to evaluate the expropriated properties. The experts placed the value of the oil holdings, which the oilmen claimed to be worth more than $260 million, at just over $29 million.

Mexico signed an agreement which stipulated that Mexico was to pay $9 million immediately, with the rest to be paid in installments. The oil companies were not actually forced to accept the settlement. However, they had little choice. The United States announced that it would no longer support oil-company claims.

Mexican writer Carlos Fuentes commented on FDR's role in the settlement: "Instead of menacing, sanctioning or invading, Roosevelt negotiated. He did not try to beat history. He joined it."

Immigration, 1917–1940

The Immigration Act of 1917 restricted the flow of Mexican workers coming to the United States by adding a literacy requirement and a head tax of $8.00. These requirements could be waived in case of emergency.

The World War I-induced labor shortage justified the emergency waiving of the literacy requirement and the head tax. This allowed Mexican agricultural workers to fill jobs vacated by Americans who were fighting or who had gone north to work in well-paying industrial jobs. Rail and mine workers as well as other industrial workers were later admitted on similar emergency exemptions. From 1917 through 1921, 72,862 Mexicans took advantage of these exemptions to enter the United States. Given the cumbersome paperwork required to hire workers under these emergency measures, many growers preferred to hire workers who had entered the United States illegally. As a result, illegal entrants likely outnumbered legal ones during this period.

After World War I, given the poor economic situation in Mexico and the reluctance of Americans to perform unskilled, backbreaking jobs at the wages offered, the northward flow of Mexicans continued. From 1919 to 1921, 112,937 Mexican immigrants legally entered the United States. Except in New Mexico with its long-established Hispanic population, new arrivals soon outnumbered long-established Spanish or Mexican residents.

In 1924, the Border Patrol was established to enforce immigration laws, thus driving undocumented workers into clandestinity. The number of Mexicans deported in the four years prior to the founding of the Border Patrol was 5,096, compared with 15,434 in the following four years. These numbers represent only a small fraction of those who entered illegally and found employment. Both U.S. officials and Mexican workers understood that it was the demand for labor in the

Southwest, not laws drawn up in Washington, that defined Mexican immigration to the United States.

During the 1920s, given the cost of legal immigration and the reluctance of some U.S. officials to issue visas to Mexicans, an estimated five Mexicans entered the United States illegally for each one who entered legally. By making unauthorized entry illegal, without making it illegal to hire undocumented immigrants, the U.S. government shifted power even further in favor of U.S. employers. Strike leaders and labor organizers could be targeted for deportation. Growers could report Mexican workers to the Border Patrol if they pressed demands concerning wages or working conditions. Some growers would simply inform the Border Patrol where it could find their undocumented employees rather than paying them. This ambiguous status was used at the local level to lower wages. At the national level, it served as a valve. When the demand for labor rose, enforcement declined. When there was an oversupply of labor, enforcement increased. Thanks to a provision of the 1924 immigration law, immigrants could be deported regardless of how long they had lived in the United States.

Between 1921 and 1930, 459,287 Mexicans, 11.2 percent of all legal U.S. immigrants, came from Mexico. The rate at which Mexicans entered the United States during the late 1920s would not be equaled again until the 1990s. The 1930 census reported 1,422,533 persons who were Mexican-born or of Mexican ancestry, compared with 700,541 in 1920.

New York Congressman Florello La Guardia was very candid when asked why, if Mexicans caused problems, they were not excluded. He replied, "Because the influence of the sugar-beet growers and railroads is too strong."

When the Depression hit, Mexican workers in the United States found themselves unwelcome. By January 1930, there were more than six million unemployed Americans. Not only did many of the jobs held by Mexicans vanish but the unattractive jobs they still held were being sought by Americans, desperate for work. Generally Mexican workers were the first laid off. To add insult to injury, Mexicans found themselves blamed for U.S. joblessness.

Between 1929 and 1931, many Mexicans returned to the country of their birth, arriving with their cars piled high with their belongings. Others boarded special trains to the border at collection centers such as Detroit, Chicago, St. Louis, Denver, Phoenix, Oklahoma City, and Los Angeles. Ships carried additional repatriates from New York and California.

After 1931, it became obvious that the Depression was not just a temporary recession. This resulted in a more concerted effort to drive Mexican workers out of the United States. Secretary of Labor William Doak, who took office in 1930, spearheaded this effort, promising to provide jobs for Americans by deporting illegal aliens.

Most Mexicans were not deported in the legal sense of the word. In addition to being denied relief benefits, they were told that if they did not leave voluntarily, they would be deported and thus be ineligible to ever return to the United States.

By 1934, the massive expulsions were largely over. The grapevine spread the word in Mexico that there were no jobs in the United States and that Mexicans were unwelcome, so Mexicans largely stopped emigrating. As the U.S. government assumed an increased share of relief efforts, there was less pressure at the local level to force out remaining Mexicans.

By 1937, the often contradictory nature of Mexican employment in the United States was manifest. Some Mexicans were still returning to Mexico in desperation. Other Mexicans, just as desperate, were leaving Mexico to find work in the United States. Between 1931 and 1941, only 22,319 Mexicans legally entered the United States.

The total number of Mexican returnees in the 1930s has been placed at between half a million and one million. These figures include some returnees who had intended to return to Mexico even before the onset of the Depression, as Mexicans had been doing for generations. The effect of the Depression is clear from U.S. census data. While the 1930 census showed 639,107 Mexican-born people in the United States, the 1940 census found only 377,433.

DOCUMENT 11.1: ARTICLE 27 OF THE MEXICAN CONSTITUTION

[Article 27 of the constitution is quite lengthy and considers many questions such as land rights, church land ownership and ownership of petroleum. Provisions in the article include:]

Ownership of the lands and waters within the boundaries of the national territory is vested originally in the Nation, which has had, and has, the right to transmit title thereof to private persons, thereby constituting private property.

Private property shall not be expropriated except for reasons of public use and subject to payment of indemnity.

The Nation shall at all times have the right to impose on private property such limitations as public interest may demand, as well as the right to regulate the utilization of natural resources which are susceptible to appropriation in order to conserve them and to ensure a more equitable distribution of public wealth. With this end in view, necessary measures shall be taken to divide up large landed estates . . . Centers of population that at present either have no lands or water or that do not possess them in sufficient quantities for the needs of their inhabitants, shall be entitled to grants thereof, which shall be taken from adjacent properties, while respecting the rights of small land holdings in operation.

Direct ownership of the following is vested in the Nation: all minerals or substances which in veins, layers, masses, or beds constitute deposits whose nature is different from the components of the land, such as minerals from which metals and metalloids used for industrial purposes are extracted; beds of precious stones, rock salt, and salt lakes, formed directly by maritime waters, products derived from the decomposition of rocks, when their exploitation requires underground work, mineral or organic deposits of materials which may be used for fertilizers, solid mineral fuels; petroleum and all hydrocarbons—solid, liquid or gaseous.

Religious institutions known as churches, regardless of creed, may in no case acquire, hold, or administer real property or hold mortgages thereon. Such property held at present directly or through an intermediary shall revert to the Nation . . . Places of worship are the property of the Nation, as represented by the Federal Government, which shall determine which of them may continue to be devoted to their present purposes.

Source: Gilbert M. Joseph and Timothy J. Henderson (eds.) *The Mexico Reader: History, Culture, Politics* (Durham, N.C.: Duke University Press, 2002), pp. 398–400.

DOCUMENT 11.2: CALLES'S 1928 DECLARATION THAT HE WOULD RELINQUISH THE PRESIDENCY

[The following is Calles's statement that he would not extend his term to fill the poser vacuum opened by Obregón's assassination:]

I consider it absolutely essential that I digress from my brief analysis to make a firm and irrevocable declaration, which I pledge upon my honor before the National Congress, before the country, and before all civilized peoples. But first, I must say that perhaps never before have circumstances placed a chief executive in a more propitious situation for returning the country to one-man rule. I have received many suggestions, offers and even some pressures—all of them cloaked in considerations of patriotism and the national welfare—trying to get me to remain in office. For reasons of morality and personal political creed, and because it is absolutely essential that we change from a "government of caudillos" to a "regime of institutions," I have decided to declare solemnly and with such clarity that my words cannot lend themselves to suspicions or misinterpretations, that not only will I not seek the prolongation of my mandate by accepting an extension or designation as provisional presidency, but I will never again on any occasion aspire to the president of my country.

Source: Nora E. Jaffary, Edward W. Osowski, and Susie S. Porter (eds.) *Mexican History: A Primary Source Reader* (Boulder, CO: Westview Press, 2009), pp. 325–26.

NOTES

1   Carlos Fuentes, *A New Time for Mexico* (New York: Farrar, Straus and Giroux, 1996), p. 156.

2   Aldous Huxley, *Beyond the Mexique Bay* (New York: Harper, 1934), pp. 237–38.

3   Nathaniel Weyl and Sylvia Weyl, *The Reconquest of Mexico* (New York: Oxford University Press, 1939), pp. 79–80.

4   Oscar Lewis, "Mexico since Cárdenas," *Social Research* 26 (Spring 1959), p. 20.

5   E. David Cronon, *Josephus Daniels in Mexico* (Madison, WI: University of Wisconsin Press), p. 171.

6   In "Un manifesto del Sr. Presidente a la Nación," *Excélsior*, March 19 (1938), p. 4.

FURTHER READING

Bantes, Adrian (1997) "Cardenismo; Interpretations," *Encyclopedia de Mexico*, ed. Michael Werner. Chicago: Fitzroy Dearborn, pp. 195–99.
  As with many great presidents, there are conflicting views about Cárdenas.

Buchenau, Jürgen (2007) *Plutarco Elías Calles and the Mexican Revolution* (Lanham: MD: Rowman & Littlefield).
  An account of Calles's presidency and the Maximato.

——— (2011) "The Sonoran Dynasty and the Reconstruction of the Mexican State," in *A Companion to Mexican History and Culture*, ed. William Beezley, pp. 407–19. Malden, MA: Wiley Blackwell.
  An account of how the Sonorans rebuilt a centralized government.

——— (2011) *The Last Caudillo: Álvaro Obregón and the Mexican Revolution*. Malden, MA: Wiley-Blackwell.
  An account of Obregón's presidency and his re-election.

E. David Cronon (1960) *Josephus Daniels in Mexico*. Madison, WI. University of Wisconsin Press.
  A biography of the ambassador who implemented the Good Neighbor policy in Mexico.

Delpar, Helen (2010) "Mexican Culture, 1920–45," in *Oxford History of Mexico*, ed. William H. Beezley and Michael C. Meyer, pp. 508–34. New York: Oxford University Press.
  A description of Mexican mural painting, music, photography, and literature in the decades after the Revolution.

Freidrich, Paul (1977) *Agrarian Revolt in a Mexican Village* (2nd ed.). Chicago: University of Chicago Press.
  The history of a Tarascan (Purépecha) Indian village that underwent agrarian reform.

Greene, Graham (1970) *The Power and the Glory*. New York: Viking.
  A novel inspired by Tomás Garrido Canabal's anti-clericalism in Tabasco.

Knight, Alan (1994) "Cardenismo: Juggernaut or Jalopy?" *Journal of Latin American Studies* 26 (Feb.), 73–108.
  An article discussing the degree to which Cárdenas controlled events.

Olcott, Jocelyn (2005) *Revolutionary Women in Postrevolutionary Mexico*. Durham, N.C.: Duke University Press.
  A discussion of women's participation in educational, labor, agrarian, and feminist organizations in post-1917 Mexico.

GLOSSARY TERMS

ejido
ejidatario
Maximato

The Late Twentieth Century, 1941–2000

Chapter 12

After Cárdenas, 1940–1970

TIMELINE—WORLD

1937 War begins between China and Japan, a prelude to World War II	1939 Germany invades Poland, launching World War II in Europe	1941 U.S. declares war after Pearl Harbor	1944 Normandy invasion	1944 Bretton Woods Conference sets pattern for postwar monetary and financial affairs
1950 North Korea invades South Korea, beginning Korean War, which lasts until 1953	1953 Democratically elected Iranian prime minister Mohammad Mosaddegh ousted in CIA-organized coup	1954 Democratically elected Guatemalan president Jacobo Arbenz ousted in CIA-organized coup	1959 Rebels led by Fidel Castro oust Cuban dictator Fulgencio Batista	1960 World population reaches 3 billion, thirty-three years after having reached 2 billion

TIMELINE—MEXICO

1940 Ávila Camacho inaugurated as president	1942 Mexico declares war on Germany	1942 *Bracero* (guest worker) program allows Mexicans to work in the U.S. legally	1946 PRM reorganized as PRI	1946 Miguel Alemán inaugurated as president
1965 Border industrialization program announced	1965 It allowed for border assembly plants (*maquiladoras*)	1968 Tlatelolco massacre of students		

1945	1945	1947	1947	1948
World War II ends	U.N. Conference negotiates U.N. Charter in San Francisco	U.S. President Truman announces "Truman Doctrine" to Congress	General Marshall outlines Marshall Plan for European recovery	Founding conference of Organization of American States in Bogatá, Columbia

1961	1962	1963	1965	1969
John F. Kennedy inaugurated as U.S. President Bay of Pigs invasion	Cuban Missile Crisis	Kennedy assassination, after which Vice-President Lyndon Johnson becomes president	U.S. combat units deployed to Vietnam	Richard Nixon inaugurated as U.S. president

1952	1954	1958	1964	1964
Adolfo Ruiz Cortines inaugurated as president	Women receive right to vote in national elections	López Mateos inaugurated as president	Gustavo Díaz inaugurated as president	*Bracero* program ended

THIS CHAPTER CONSIDERS MEXICO'S SHIFTING FROM REFORM AND SOCIAL
JUSTICE to economic development. Mexico joined the Allies in World War II. The official
political party changed its name to the Revolutionary Institutional Party (PRI) and built
a virtually unbeatable political machine. Dissent was forced into the streets and plazas,
where tragically students were gunned down in 1968. Society urbanized, was educated,
and grew in numbers—all at unprecedented rates. Several elements came together to
produce rapid economic growth—a phenomenon known as the Mexican Economic Miracle.
Finally, the chapter considers how relations warmed between the United States and Mexico
as wartime alliance and cooperation on issues such as immigration led to mutual benefit.

TURNING RIGHT, 1940–1952

In his 1940 inaugural address Manuel Ávila Camacho stated that entrepreneurs would find
"institutional guarantees." Rather than extolling land reform, he pledged protection for private
landowners "not only to protect those holdings which now exist, but to stimulate the formation
of new private holdings on vast uncultivated expanses."

As president-elect, Ávila Camacho pledged that Mexico would remain neutral in World War
II. However, after German submarines sank two Mexican tankers, public opinion turned against
Germany, and Mexico declared war.

Ávila Camacho's policies were much more conservative than Cárdenas's had been. A number of
factors permitted Ávila Camacho to shift to the political right. Since Cárdenas had moderated his
policies at the end of his term, the shift in government policy was not as sharp as it would have been
had Ávila Camacho initiated the shift. During the war former president Cárdenas was placed on
active duty, so he was under military discipline and thus was not in a position to challenge Ávila
Camacho's move to the right. The pro-Soviet left was neutralized as it urged war production to aid
the Soviet Union, even at the cost of a lowered standard of living for Mexican workers. The presence
of pro-Axis elements in Mexico allowed Ávila Camacho to be viewed as a moderate between the
left and right. Within the PRM, he held the middle ground between the conservative *caudillos* of the
Revolution and backers of Cárdenas and leftist labor leader Vicente Lombardo Toledano.

Ávila Camacho's ability to withdraw support from labor and peasants without entailing organized
resistance indicated the control established over these groups during the Cárdenas administration.
Labor was immobilized as Fidel Velázquez, a pliant ally of the government, was installed to head
the official labor federation, the Mexican Workers Federation (CTM).

In early 1946, his last year in office, Ávila Camacho presided over the reorganization of the official
party, which was renamed the Revolutionary Institutional Party (PRI). This reorganization resulted
in the labor, peasant, and popular sectors having a reduced role. Power was further concentrated
in the hands of the president and the party's National Executive Committee. As had occurred with
the founding of the National Revolutionary Party (PNR) and the PRM, decisions concerning the
formation of the PRI were made from the top down. In one day, the party's convention agreed
on an already drafted declaration of principles, program of action, and statutes. *Ejidatarios* and trade
union members continued to be automatic party members.

Ávila Camacho's choice of his Interior Secretary Miguel Alemán to be the first PRI presidential
candidate signaled a continuation of the conservative trend in government. In his speech accepting
the PRI nomination, Alemán emphasized agricultural and industrial development. Alemán, a career
bureaucrat, was the first of a string of professional politicians who would dominate Mexican
political life for the rest of the century.

The outlines of a new Mexican political system were clearly visible by the end of Ávila Camacho's term. He established cordial relations with the Church and the United States. Presidential power had greatly increased, accumulated on the pretext of wartime emergency but retained after the war. The government and business began a close alliance that was to transform Mexico socially and economically over the course of the next thirty years. Foreign business interests became active participants in this alliance. Workers and peasants were left leaderless as their nominal leaders looked increasingly to the government rather than their base. Ávila Camacho and his successors, rather than admitting a change in direction, extolled economic nationalism and industrialization—all of which was cloaked in the symbolism of the Mexican Revolution.

Many welcomed Alemán as a charismatic young leader with something of a playboy image. The average age of his cabinet members, who were largely civilian university graduates like the president himself, was forty-four—the first cabinet formed by the generation that had grown up under the Revolution. Military men headed only the secretaries of national defense and navy. Alemán's rise to the presidency made it clear that the military no longer provided entry into the political establishment. Graduation from the National University and a career in government had become the route to the presidency.

Alemán forced all elements of the PRI and the labor movement to accept his anticommunist ideological position. Alemán-like political clones replaced the center-left to center-right coalition that had existed under Cárdenas. He further marginalized the military, which for the first time since the Revolution received less than 10 percent of the federal budget.

Even though Alemán began his administration with a pledge to fight corruption, graft became more firmly entrenched than ever in the Mexican political system. By one estimate, during his term Alemán and his associates "plundered" $800,000,000. Historian Daniel Cosío Villegas observed, "It has been the dishonesty of the revolutionary governments, more than anything else, which has cut off the life of the Mexican Revolution . . ."

Alemán accelerated industrialization and increased agricultural production by promoting an alliance between the state and foreign and domestic capital. If he felt the left or independent trade unions stood in the way of achieving these goals, they would be violently suppressed.

In October 1951, it was announced that the PRI presidential candidate would be Adolfo Ruiz Cortines, Alemán's colorless interior secretary. Since he exuded honesty and austerity, he was an ideal candidate to offset Alemán's corruption and profligate spending.

Ruiz Cortines faced an electoral challenge by General Miguel Henríquez Guzmán, a wealthy contractor with impeccable establishment credentials. He drew a substantial following including Cardenistas excluded from the Alemán coalition, military men who resented being replaced by younger civilians, members of the middle class wanting multi-party democracy, and peasants resenting government aid going to landowners with political ties rather than to poor farmers. Most of Henríquez Guzmán's support was concentrated in urban areas—a harbinger of the long-term decline in the PRI's urban strength.

Henríquez Guzmán directly criticized the lack of social justice. He noted that rising living costs had hurt the majority, that government agricultural policy had left peasants in misery, and that there was no democracy. He also criticized government control over organized labor and Mexico's increasing dependence on the United States.

Henríquez Guzmán supporters called for a victory rally in the Alameda, a park in downtown Mexico City. The day after the election, thousands gathered there to celebrate the "victory," even though official election returns had not yet been released. Police and army troops attacked the Henríquez Guzmán supporters, leaving dozens dead and wounded and as many as 500 arrested. The message was clear—the government was unwilling to tolerate independent political activity.

LIFE UNDER THE PRI, 1952–1970

> By the 1960s, Mexico's regime enjoyed a reputation as the most stable, most centralized, and strongest government in mainland Latin America.
>
> (Thomas Rath, 2013)

By the time Ruiz Cortines took office, presidents, rather than innovating, simply maintained the political system. As with other incoming presidents, Ruiz Cortines was presented to the Mexican people as the solution to his predecessor's excesses. His belonging to the same party as the incumbent and his being chosen by him were not stressed. Rather, he was assumed to be capable of remedying the problems his predecessor was unable to solve or had in fact created.

After 1955 there was a shift in public policy. Along with economic development and retaining power, a major goal of PRI administrations was stability and social peace. In the face of rising criticism and social unrest, social spending rose under Ruiz Cortines. During his term, the government expanded the social security program and constructed rural clinics and hospitals. To combat inflation, price controls were placed on basic necessities. After 1955 the government ensured that the buying power of organized labor would increase. This met little opposition since the Mexican economy was growing rapidly at the time.

On November 4, 1957, the Secretary General of the National Peasant Confederation (CNC) announced that Labor Secretary Adolfo López Mateos would be the PRI presidential candidate, since "the absolute majority of ejido committees, agrarian executive committees, regional committees, leagues of agrarian committees, and other agricultural groups have chosen him." No one was impolitic enough to inquire just when representatives of these groups had made such a momentous decision.

On November 15 and 16, 1957, there was a PRI convention to ratify the president's choice and make López Mateos the official PRI candidate. In eighteen minutes, the nearly 5,000 delegates meeting in the Cine Colonial in Mexico City voted unanimously for López Mateos. The result was such a foregone conclusion that banners extolling López Mateos had been hung even before the meeting began.

Then as happened every six years a massive government-financed public relations campaign began to sell the candidate to the public. As an American observer noted, "Half the stone walls are painted with giant signs of public support; all the mass media are alive with eulogies." Before television came to dominate the political scene, so many walls were painted to promote PRI candidates that it was said that U.S. paint manufacturer Sherwin Williams was the main beneficiary of Mexican elections.

The 1958 election, which credited López Mateos with 90.5 percent of the vote, proceeded smoothly. Henríquez Guzmán's potentially divisive Federation of Parties of the People had been ruled off the ballot.

Between 1958 and 1994, there was relatively little change in PRI candidate selection. Presidential aspirants were expected to give the public appearance of meekly awaiting the president's designation of his successor. The president would decide who would be the PRI candidate, a choice known as the *dedazo* (finger pointing). A trusted functionary then revealed the choice—an announcement known as the *destape* (the unveiling). Once this occurred, the PRI establishment would jump on the bandwagon. Even bitter rivals of the nominee, the *destapado* (the unveiled), were expected to swallow their pride and affirm that the president's choice was the best man for the job. To do otherwise would be to fall out of favor and lose the chance for a desirable position during the next presidential term.

More than any other president before him, López Mateos brought Mexico onto the international stage. During his term, Mexico received visits from eighteen heads of state. López Mateos's travels took him to sixteen nations in Asia, Europe, and the Western Hemisphere. These trips provided him with the opportunity to proclaim Mexico's non-alignment in the Cold War and his country's adherence to the policies of self-determination and non-intervention. Mexico's president traveled so widely that he was nicknamed "López *paseos*" ("López's promenades").

López Mateos instituted reforms, but always on his own terms. Between 1958 and 1964, social security coverage (which included health care) increased from 7.7 percent of the population to 15.9 percent. After a rail strike was crushed, the government increased wages, not only for rail workers but also for teachers, electrical workers, and oil workers. Social spending under López Mateos increased to 19.2 percent of the federal budget.

The reform measures chosen by López Mateos reflected a major change in Mexico. For the first time, the 1960 census indicated that a majority of Mexicans lived in urban areas. After 1960 the promise of land reform would mean little to the majority.

Figure 12.1 *This poster was produced in conjunction with the 1968 student movement. The slogan is "Freedom of Expression." The small lettering on the padlock reads "Made in USA." This reflects the general anti-American tone of the movement.*

Source: Philip L. Russell, *Mexico in Transition* (Austin, TX: Colorado River Press, 1977), p. 133.

López Mateos's designated successor was his Interior Secretary Gustavo Díaz Ordaz, who had the reputation of being an anti-communist hard-liner. His candidacy received support from the Church and former President Alemán, the leader of the conservative faction in government.

López Mateos left office a popular man. He was the last president to do so for decades. Economic growth and government benefits provided during his term created optimism for the future. His public support for the Cuban Revolution was well received, since it was viewed as a sign of his standing up to the United States.

When Díaz Ordaz took office in 1964, few anticipated significant social strife. In a book published the previous year, U.S. historian Howard F. Cline noted, "The PRI is now so secure that it can afford to relax and does not need many of the repressive measures it earlier took in dealing with the opposition."

The chain of events for which Díaz Ordaz will always be remembered began on July 23, 1968. There was a street fight between students from two high schools in Mexico City. Police broke up the fighting and chased the students into a school building, clubbing everyone in sight, including students and teachers who had nothing to do with the fighting. This produced a typical response— a march three days later to protest police brutality. Police, rather than ignoring the protestors, again waded in with clubs. This resulted in more protest and more repression.

The National University, the National Polytechnic Institute, and their affiliated high schools went out on strike to protest the military occupation of the university-affiliated high schools, which was seen as a violation of university autonomy. On August 1, Javier Barros Sierra, the rector of the National University, led a 100,000-person demonstration. A second demonstration on August 13 saw 150,000 march and chant insults to the press, the police, and the president. At a third demonstration on August 27, there were 200,000, including many non-students. On September 13, 100,000 marched in complete silence to demonstrate that the movement was disciplined.

The students compiled a list of demands including the arrest and trial of public officials guilty of abuse and the release of political prisoners. It was not these specific demands, however, that caused political, economic, and religious leaders to oppose the students. The perceived threat came from festive, insolent, anti-authoritarian young people effectively calling into question the legitimacy of the existing order.

A march scheduled for October 2 had been prohibited by the government, so strikers decided to hold a rally near the center of Mexico City "to avoid violence." As 5,000 to 10,000 were peacefully listening to speakers in the Plaza of Three Cultures at the Tlatelolco housing project, 5,000 soldiers surrounded them. Then heavy gunfire broke out. As people tried to flee, they were cut down by bullets.

Estimates of the number killed at Tlatelolco run into the hundreds. Bodies were burned to avoid a politically embarrassing string of funerals just before the Olympics. Ironically, the 1968 Olympics—the first held in the underdeveloped world—were to have shown the great progress Mexico had made. The desire to establish peace before the opening of the Olympics, even if it were the peace of Porfirio Díaz, partially explains the brutal actions at Tlatelolco.

Documents drawn up by then-Secretary of Defense Marcelino García Barragán and only made public after his death indicate that during the rally marksmen from the presidential guards stationed in adjacent apartment buildings fired on army troops surrounding the rally. This caused the army troops to fire on the students in what they considered to be self-defense, thus creating plausible deniability for military authorities while smashing the student movement. Forces from the Interior Ministry, the military, and the presidential guards were present. In theory, the chain of command for all three forces led back to the president. It remains unclear if Díaz Ordaz knew in advance of the positioning of the presidential guards to fire on the army or if rogue elements orchestrated the operation. Declassified U.S. Defense Department documents state that the firing by the marksmen resulted from military insubordination, with officers ordering the shooting without the knowledge or consent of the president or the secretary of defense.

The attack at Tlatelolco marked the end of the student movement. According to a then-secret government security report, by the afternoon of October 3, 1,043 had been arrested. Arrests of activists continued for weeks. Students who only weeks before had believed in a democratic Mexico had no response.

The 1968 student movement reflected the government's inability to respond to the needs of the middle class. Protests also reflected dissatisfaction with Mexico's skewed distribution of wealth. At a time millions were being spent on the Olympics, university budgets were declining even as enrolments were burgeoning.

While the students' demands remained unmet, many participants in the movement later played leading roles in urban, peasant, and trade union movements that contributed to eventual democratic change. Some, despairing of democracy, formed Marxist guerrilla groups operating in urban and rural areas.

Nobel Prize-winning author Octavio Paz commented on the impact of the Tlatelolco massacre:

> At the very moment in which the Mexican government was receiving international recognition for forty years of political stability and economic progress, a swash of blood dispelled the official optimism and caused every citizen to doubt the meaning of that progress.[1]

The economy grew at an annual rate of more than 6 percent during Díaz Ordaz's term. This insulated the president from much of the criticism by students. In addition government social spending increased under Díaz Ordaz, as it had during the previous two administrations. The government portrayed social welfare spending and economic growth to be as the fruits of the more just, nationalistic order ushered in by the 1910–17 Revolution.

The Military

After Mexico entered World War II, the state of readiness of its army became a matter of national concern to the United States. To increase Mexican military capabilities, the United States provided arms, including coastal artillery and 305 aircraft, and sent officers to teach in Mexican military schools. Select Mexican officers came to the United States for advanced training.

As the economic and social role of the Mexican government increased, the percentage of the budget devoted to the military declined. Under Ávila Camacho (1940–46) military spending accounted for 18.85 percent of the federal budget. By Díaz Ordaz's term (1964–70), it had declined to 2.63 percent.

After World War II, the number of military officers holding important civilian positions declined. Beginning in 1946, each president was a civilian. Military men regularly headed the PRI until 1964. In 1940 fifteen governors were military men, while between 1964 and 1985 only one was. Similarly, with the exceptions of the secretaries of defense and navy, civilians held all cabinet positions. By 1970, the control of politics had definitively shifted to civilians.

After World War II the army repressed dissent and provided intelligence on political and social disturbances. In 1956 soldiers occupied the National Polytechnic Institute to suppress student protests. The army remained active in rural policing. Generally the press ignored military repression, although some incidents were too big to cover up. Thus the army's 1946 killing of seventy unarmed political protestors in León did receive press coverage.

Following World War II the Mexican military maintained ties with the U.S. military. However these ties were weak compared with the ties the U.S. established elsewhere in Latin America. Between 1946 and 1971, U.S. military aid to Mexico only totalled $17.6 million, less than 1 percent of the Latin American total. During the 1950s and 1960s the United States trained 61,000 Latin American troops. Of these, only 659 came from Mexico.

The Opposition

Through 1970 opposition parties served more as pressure groups than as real alternatives to the official party. PRI presidential candidates won by overwhelming majorities—85.8 percent in 1970. PRI candidates for lower offices usually won by similar margins.

Since it was clear that elections did not lead to changes in government, the role of opposition parties was unclear. Many felt the primary purpose of opposition parties was legitimizing the PRI. The raison d'être of the opposition political parties was further clouded by some of them regularly backing the presidential candidates of the PRI.

A variety of motives prompted recognized opposition parties to continue to present candidates. Election campaigns allowed opposition parties to enunciate their views and lobby for concessions. A few opposition victories at the mayoral and congressional level whetted the political appetites of would-be challengers to the PRI. Finally, even if the opposition parties could do little for the average Mexican, they did benefit party officials and the handful of opposition party candidates who held office. This select group received recognition, contracts, loans, services, and political training for a more auspicious political future. Sociologist Pablo González Casanova observed that the masses "learn that the opposition parties solve the problems of opposition politicians, not those of the masses."

The Political Left

> The Mexican security services are so effective in stamping out the extreme left that we don't have to worry. If the government were less effective we would, of course, get going to promote repression.
>
> (Former CIA agent Philip Agee, 1975)

The enormous flexibility of what was called the ideology of the Mexican Revolution made it very difficult for the left to present programs that were perceived by their potential followers—peasants and workers—as something strikingly different from what the progressive wing of incumbent administrations espoused. Much of the economy was already under state control. Incumbents would frequently advocate land reform, labor rights, and the struggle against imperialism. Since incumbents had the power to implement the changes they spoke of, their positions appeared more credible than those of the left. In addition, the PRI and the government so predictably hired talented members of the minuscule Communist Party that PRI functionary Guillermo Martínez Domínguez declared the party to be the training school for PRI staffers.

The Political Right

The PAN

The National Action Party (PAN) was founded in 1939 to oppose rigged elections, government anticlericalism, and what was viewed as excess government intervention in the economy. Its initial base included businessmen, intellectuals, members of Catholic organizations, and other middle-class Mexicans. Given the ephemeral existence of many parties formed at election time, mere survival presented the PAN with a serious challenge.

During the first years of its existence, the PAN had to face numerous unfavorable (for the party) trends. As the government became increasingly pro-business, businessmen abandoned the PAN. Similarly as government anti-clericalism declined fewer were drawn to the party for religious reasons. Also the PAN had to live down its initial enthusiasm for Spanish dictator Francisco Franco and its initial lack of support for World War II.

After 1946 the party made municipal independence from central control a major issue. In 1949 the PAN issued a call for the enfranchisement of women at the federal level. The party became a moral crusade, attacking the legitimacy of the ruling group, which it branded as undemocratic and corrupt.

During the 1940s, the meager results produced by participating in elections presented the party with a dilemma—it was far removed from power, yet its participating in elections made the PRI look democratic. Many within the party felt the PAN should abstain from elections to protest election fraud.

By the end of the 1940s, the PAN had emerged as an independent, loyal Mexican political alternative to the Revolution. Catholic faith replaced a professional degree as the salient characteristic of PAN members, especially after women received the vote in 1953 and increased their role in the party. All the party's presidents through 1972 had their initial political formation in openly Catholic organizations, such as the National Catholic Student Union, and then moved into the PAN. The party's very existence remained in question, as Soledad Loaeza noted in her magisterial history of the party, "For the PAN, the decade of the 1950s was a long crossing of the desert, during which time it was barely able to make its presence felt at election time."

In the early 1960s, various tendencies existed within the PAN. Leftwing Christian Democrats and Social Christians demanded massive redistribution of income and socialization of property. Secular PANistas opposed what they viewed as an overly intrusive government, but did not ground their views in Catholicism. More conservative PANistas were primarily concerned with defending property rights.

In 1963, the conclusions of the Catholic Church council known as Vatican II were published. After these conclusions were released, the PAN abandoned its traditional defense of the status quo and became a champion of human rights, promoted a more active social role for the government, and was influenced by liberation theology. Vatican II served to invigorate party members and recruit newcomers. In 1969, the party advocated a third path of development between capitalism and socialism, called "*solidarismo*," which has been described as "political humanism."

By 1970 the PAN had established a significant electoral base. Despite its repeatedly charging vote fraud, the PAN continued to field candidates. Vote totals credited to PAN presidential candidates increased steadily from 7.8 percent in 1952 to 14.0 percent in 1970. PAN members soldiered on, viewing their central mission not as obtaining power via elections but as inserting morality into politics, educating citizens, and inculcating them with a set of principles that would guide their political actions.

From the outside, such goals appeared to be illusory. The PAN suffered constant financial problems. After the 1970 elections, historian Daniel Cosío Villegas wrote, "Since the PAN is not gaining strength, it is hard to believe that in the foreseeable future the party will be able to serve as a restraining wall for the overwhelming power of the government and its party."

The "Perfect Dictatorship"

> By the middle of the last century the Mexican Revolution had died, and "Revolutionary" rhetoric had become a hollow shell.
>
> (Lorenzo Meyer, 2014)

After the collapse of the Soviet Union, the PRI became the world's longest-running political act. Since 1934 all its presidents had come and gone every six years as scheduled. Between 1946 and 1973 the party won 98 percent of all mayoral and congressional elections. In 1991 Peruvian novelist Mario Vargas Llosa visited Mexico and observed that its government was a "perfect dictatorship." He noted that the PRI political machine had overcome the fatal flaw of Porfirio Díaz's earlier political machine—the lack of a succession mechanism. By choosing a new president every six years in theory the PRI machine could last forever.

One of the keys to Mexican political stability was rigid adherence to the "no re-election" rule for the president. The forced retirement of the president every six years kept the politically ambitious in check by providing them with a chance at power six years later. They remained in the PRI since they knew the party was the only route to high public office. In theory the regular changing of administrations provided a chance for the talented to move up to higher positions in the public sector and for the incompetent to be winnowed out.

Another key to Mexico's long-term political stability was the concentration of power in the president. The Mexican president exercised the powers normally associated with the president of a constitutional democracy, such as being commander-in-chief of the armed forces. In addition he exercised a wide variety of other powers, referred to as "metaconstitutional" powers. Given the lack of checks and balances, no person, group, or institution could challenge the president when he exercised these powers. In addition to choosing his successor, an outstanding metaconstitutional power was the president's control over the PRI. Exercising his metaconstitutional power, the president would name the president of the PRI. This enabled him to make crucial decisions on PRI nominees for Congress, governors, and sometimes mayors.

The key to presidential dominance over Congress was the legal prohibition against the immediate re-election of congresspersons. This meant that congressional representatives had to look to the president for their next position in the public sector. Having served one's constituency admirably had nothing to do with a congressperson's ability to continue in public service.

Since Mexico lacked a tradition of an independent judiciary, presidentially appointed judges, who were approved by the presidentially controlled Congress, lacked independence. Legislation passed in 1949 prevented the Supreme Court from hearing disputes involving elections. This prevented aggrieved candidates from raising legal challenges to electoral fraud, as had happened earlier in the 1940s.

Another factor contributing to the durability of the "perfect dictatorship" was sustained economic growth. Between 1950 and 1970, Mexico's per capita GDP increased at an average annual rate of 3.35 percent—well above the Latin American average of 2.40 percent.

While the fruits of this growth were inequitably distributed, economic development between 1940 and 1970 did result in improved living standards for a substantial majority of Mexicans. As a result life expectancy increased from forty to sixty years between 1940 and 1970 and those born in the late 1930s and 1940s grew taller than the previous generation. Improved living standards produced genuine support for the PRI. Journalist Alma Guillermoprieto commented:

> For all its inefficiencies and other faults, the patrimonial system worked well enough to pull a largely rural and illiterate population into the twentieth century, insuring levels of education, health care, public services, and social mobility which comparable societies (Peru, Brazil, and Colombia, say) never achieved.[2]

Even though the PRI was not involved in choosing its own presidential candidates, it performed a number of functions that maintained the system. Its sectors gave average citizens, such as street vendors, factory workers, or *ejidatarios*, at least the perception that there was an official channel that would respond to their complaints. The PRI recruited political cadres, controlled mass organizations, carried out social and welfare roles, and organized elections to legitimate the regime. The party was so effective at organizing elections that through 1970 it never lost a presidential, gubernatorial, or senatorial election. A 1964 CIA report observed: "The party-government complex has become so large and intricate in the attempt to be all things to Mexicans of all political views, that its orientation defies conventional definition."

The PRI worked closely with the government to keep the peace and stage elections. It enjoyed a multiplicity of resources to ensure its candidates won. If one tactic failed or seemed imprudent, it had many alternatives.

In shantytowns, PRI municipal governments provided clinics, schools, lighting, water, land titles, and street paving on a discretional basis. Residents were expected to show support for PRI candidates and attend rallies in an implicit quid pro quo for obtaining these services.

Once important decisions had been made and personnel selected to fill public offices, elections were staged with great fanfare. Millions would be spent to hold campaign rallies, often using rented trucks and busses to haul in people to create the appearance of widespread support for the PRI. A single 1961 PRI rally in San Luis Potosí cost $74,520 to stage. The largest single cost was $2 paid to each of the 15,000 attendees.

If the outcome of an election was in the slightest doubt, the PRI had a multi-layered defense to guarantee victory. Through its control of election machinery, polling places could be established far from areas known to favor the opposition or such polling places could be given insufficient ballots or opened late and closed early. After the polls opened, the PRI had several colorfully named methods of enhancing its vote count. A "taco" was simply a wad of ballots already marked for the PRI candidate that a single voter would deposit in the ballot box. A "pregnant ballot box" was one filled with ballots marked for the PRI before the voting started. "Flying squads" went from polling place to polling place to repeatedly vote for the PRI. Little subtlety was needed for such scams, since election judges were under PRI control.

If, due to some oversight, after polls closed the outcome of the election was still in doubt, it was not too late to snatch victory from the jaws of defeat. In Baja California, PAN candidate Salvador Rosas Magallón noted that after polls closed in his 1959 gubernatorial race, soldiers appeared and carried the ballot boxes back to their barracks. A PRI victory was later announced without PAN members having any idea of how the announced vote totals were determined. If all else failed, elections could be annulled, as occurred in 1968 when the PRI-controlled Baja California legislature annulled municipal elections in Tijuana and Mexicali, where PAN candidates presumably won.

If attempts at co-opting regime opponents failed, the result was frequently violence. Small-scale violence was especially common in rural areas as a repressive tool. At least twenty-two members of Henríquez Guzmán's party were murdered during his presidential campaign. The mass repression of the 1968 student movement reflected the government's inability to either co-opt or repress individual leaders, whom the students frequently rotated in their positions to prevent just that.

Those firing on political protestors, those running election-day scams, and those engaged in the massive transfer of wealth from the public sector into the hands of well-connected individuals all relied on one factor—impunity. Since the government, the PRI, the Congress, the president, and the judicial system formed a seamless whole, political control and loyalty to the system could be maintained. Spanish human rights activist Carlos Castresana commented, "It is useless to pretend that democracy can take root in nations, such as Mexico, where there is systematic impunity with respect to the most serious, repeated violations of human rights."

A final key to regime survival was ideological flexibility. As historian Jesús Silva Herzog noted, even the president considered to be the most conservative, Miguel Alemán, would "oscillate to the right or left, according to both international events and to the internal pressure of the most active political parties and social organizations . . ." Examples of major policy shifts include Ávila Camacho's decision to ally with the United States during World War II and Alemán's decision to emphasize industrialization. Essayist Jorge Castañeda commented on Mexican presidents, "Conventional wisdom notwithstanding, they have proved remarkably successful at changing just as much as necessary to ensure the system's survival."

Mexican Society

> Rural emigration—which is a continuous flow—has simply transferred poverty and underemployment from the countryside into the cities.
>
> (Rodolfo Stavenhagen, 1975)

The pervasive social and economic forces unleashed during the 1940s produced more change in Mexico than the earlier revolutionary programs that had social change as their object. Change resulted from World War II, population growth, rural-to-urban migration, and decisions made by private investors. Between 1940 and 1970, Mexico's population increased by 145 percent, its urban population increased by 296 percent, while the share of total production contributed by industry rose from 25 to 34 percent.

Gone were the days when revolutionary leaders sought to modify the economic and political structures to improve the lives of poor Mexicans. The growth of industry and commercial agriculture replaced full employment, higher wages, social welfare, and more equitable income distribution as top government priorities.

Rural-to-urban migration in search of jobs and education caused millions to pack their meager belongings and move to the city. The grapevine told of many newly created industrial jobs. The locus of government investment shifted from rural areas to the city. In addition most of the new jobs in the burgeoning government bureaucracy and in commerce were added in cities. City life appeared especially attractive since urban residents received almost six times the per capita income of rural people.

Between 1940 and 1970, the large cities—Mexico City, Monterrey, and Guadalajara—absorbed more than 60 percent of rural-to-urban migration. In 1950, 4.9 million Mexicans held agricultural jobs, while 3.4 million worked in urban jobs. Twenty years later, the number of agricultural jobs had only increased by 0.2 million, while the number of urban jobs had increased by 4.6 million.

During the 1960s, the number of urban workers increased by 2.673 million, but the number of industrial jobs increased by only 600,000. This imbalance between the increase in the urban work force and the number of industrial jobs forced many into commerce and other services, where they were often underemployed and impoverished.

Many newly established industries exacerbated employment problems since the number of artisans they displaced exceeded the number of jobs created in capital-intensive factories. To cite one example, in 1949 there were 290 factories and workshops producing soap. Colgate Palmolive, which had a national distribution system and a nationwide advertising campaign, soon forced all but a handful out of business.

Massive migration to urban areas, natural population increase in cities, and a continuing scarcity of well-paying jobs led to rings of owner-built housing surrounding major cities, inhabited by those who could not afford other accommodation. Frequently would-be homeowners would descend on vacant land and overnight erect houses built of scrap lumber and cardboard. Authorities would often allow squatters to remain on land they had occupied since they realized good housing alternatives simply did not exist and eviction efforts would lead to violent confrontation. Once it became clear that they would be allowed to stay, improvised shanties were slowly replaced by solidly built cinderblock structures.

Distribution of Wealth

Since at least the time of Humboldt, it was evident that there was widespread poverty in Mexico. However, it was only around the middle of the twentieth century that sufficient data became available to measure the distribution of income statistically. In 1970 the poorest 30 percent of families received 7.2 percent of income, while the wealthiest 30 percent received 66.2 percent of income.

The obvious reason for the maldistribution of income was the maldistribution of wealth. In each sector of the economy, ownership was not only highly concentrated but also becoming more concentrated as years passed. The 1965 industrial census indicated that the largest 1.5 percent of industrial firms accounted for 77.2 percent of capital and 75 percent of industrial production. In 1960, the largest 0.6 percent of commercial establishments controlled 47 percent of capital and generated 50 percent of income from sales. In 1960, the top 0.65 percent of producers held 30 percent of the cultivated land, while the bottom 50 percent only cultivated 12 percent.

Increases in productivity per worker were largely captured by business owners, further concentrating income. Between 1940 and 1970, the productivity of industrial workers increased by 200 percent, while the buying power of their wages increased by only 8 percent.

As a result of population growth, the supply of labor in both rural and urban areas exceeded demand, which was an additional factor concentrating income. By the 1960s, 400,000 new workers a year were coming into the labor force—an influx that depressed wages, as most employees signed on not with union contracts but as individuals, leaving them at the mercy of their employers. As capital was replacing labor throughout the economy, employers prospered, some workers earned a steady wage, and millions of others joined the marginal population.

Regardless of whether the income of the poorest was rising or falling, it was clear that many millions of Mexicans, often referred to as the marginal population, were mired in poverty. Political scientist Lorenzo Meyer observed:

Marginality, that is, the low productivity which results from underemployment, was a phenomenon found both in rural areas and in the city. The enormous slums surrounding major cities indicate that population growth long ago surpassed the capacity of the urban economy to absorb available labor, a product of births in the cities and of migration from rural areas to the city.[3]

The Elite

The primary fact of life in contemporary Mexico is that although the government has a political monopoly it does not control the economy. Seven banking groups in Mexico are as strong in the economic life of the nation as the PRI is in the political life.

(Stephen Niblo, 1975)

After 1940 the business elite grew more powerful, reflecting the increased wealth of its members, who diverted substantial human resources from production to lobbying for government favors, to making personal contacts with the political elite, and to maintaining such business organizations as the National Federation of Industrial Chambers (CONCAMIN). Political discourse pointedly ignored the intimate links between the PRI and big business. Government subsidies, trade protection, and other government benefits became the key to success, not lower production costs and higher quality goods.

Membership in a business group increased an individual's political clout, which was key to prospering in Mexico's highly regulated economic atmosphere. Business groups had enough power to prevent the implementation of progressive tax schemes, which could have laid the groundwork, via investing in education, for higher future economic growth. The failure to implement substantial tax reforms in the early 1960s would have far-reaching consequences since it forced the government to finance later increases in social and infrastructural spending by borrowing abroad. This would contribute to the debt crisis of the 1980s.

Through the 1960s, the political and economic elites existed harmoniously since, as political scientist Lorenzo Meyer observed:

For the private sector, regime legitimacy depended not on its democratic merits, which it never had, but on its capacity to maintain workers under its control, as well as to develop a system of tariff protection, with fiscal incentives, subsidies, and the construction of infrastructure, which permitted investors an acceptable profit rate.[4]

The Middle Class

By one estimate, between 1940 and 1970, membership in the middle class increased from 16 to 29 percent of Mexico's population. The increased size of the middle class was closely tied to increased industrialization and expanded access to education. The middle class, whose earnings were well above the national average, was largely made up of professionals, managers, office workers, small-scale entrepreneurs, and some unionized workers in strategic industries.

During the prolonged economic growth of the 1950s and 1960s, upward social mobility was a reality. In 1962, sociologist Pablo González Casanova commented: "In Mexico, which is industrializing and urbanizing, there is permanent social mobility. Yesterday's peasants are today's workers, whose children can become professionals."

During the 1960s, the very success of the middle class produced contradictions that would lead to change. The political system, which had been structured in the 1930s to accommodate workers and peasants, failed to provide a political role for members of the middle class, aside from those actually holding office. Also by the 1960s the number of aspirants to higher education exceeded capacity. These tensions formed the backdrop for the 1968 student movement, which cost the political loyalty of middle-class members whose parents had strongly supported the system that had provided them with upward mobility.

Labor

> The history of Mexican trade unionism has oscillated between two extremes: the submission of trade unions to the state and the repression of the independent movements which have tried to extricate themselves from that situation.
>
> (Raúl Trejo Delarbre, 1976)

After the Cárdenas administration, policymakers felt control over labor was necessary for capital accumulation, which is a prerequisite of industrialization. The government adroitly combined legal, financial, and political controls in its effort to provide a cheap, docile labor force to industrialists. Between 1939 and 1946, as a result of this control, it was possible to lower the buying power of industrial wages via inflation. Industrial wages did not recover their 1939 level until 1968.

Government authorities orchestrated the takeover of key unions by PRI party loyalists, known as *charros*, who were willing to restrain labor militancy in exchange for perks and power. *Charro* control over labor organizations made it attractive for entrepreneurs, foreign and domestic, to invest in industry. This control also enabled the PRI to mobilize labor at election time, to receive its support in times of crisis, and to control inflation by keeping wage demands in check during periods of economic instability.

A key element to government control over labor was Fidel Velázquez. In 1941, President Ávila Camacho supported Velázquez, a former milkman, to head the main labor federation, the CTM. The new CTM head slavishly allied himself with incumbent presidents to suppress rival leaders and labor organizations. Except for the years 1947–1950, he remained in this position until his death in 1997.

The government had a wide variety of tools at its disposal to maintain its control over labor:

- The Labor Department had the legal power to deny registration to any labor union. If unions were not registered, they could not call legal strikes, enter into arbitration proceedings on behalf of their members, negotiate labor contracts, or appoint members to government wage commissions.

- The legality of each strike had to be recognized on a case-by-case basis. If a strike was not declared legal, workers were subject to firing and replacement by strike-breakers.
- If workers could not be co-opted, they were repressed. In the late 1950s rail workers carried out a series of strikes for increased wages and against government-imposed union leaders. The strikes were broken up when the government sent in military forces. Thousands of rail workers were arrested and dismissed. Some of the leaders were imprisoned for eleven years.
- So long as labor leaders followed the PRI party line and kept their rank-and-file in line, the official party would ensure their tenure in office. Such leaders could aspire to PRI posts and elective office at the local, state, and federal level. Dozens of seats in the Senate and Chamber of Deputies were reserved for labor. As they became a moneyed elite in their own right, labor leaders came to share interests not with the workers they nominally represented but with management.
- During the Cold War era, labor insurgency was frequently labeled "Communist," thus delegitimizing workers' demands and making repression more politically acceptable.
- Relatively few workers were unionized at all. In 1970, only 14.8 percent of the labor force belonged to a union. In the most unionized sector, industry, 37.2 percent belonged to unions, while only 12.9 percent of service workers were unionized. Union members received higher wages than non-union workers. In addition, they had written contracts and benefited from social security (which included health care) and government-subsided pensions, commodities, and housing. Non-unionized workers often received below the legally mandated minimum wage and lacked such benefits as social security health care.
- The PRI's protectionist policies shielded Mexican manufacturers from foreign competition. This allowed manufacturers to pay above average wages and pass the cost on to consumers. Since the PRI was strongly identified with industrial protectionism, labor had good reason to support that party. Autoworkers for example received wages five times the average, generous welfare benefits, and scholarships for their children. Similarly public-sector workers received above-average wages and benefits, so they backed the official party.

A quiescent labor force undergirded industrial development. A 1956 article in *Fortune* magazine commented:

> Indeed it might be correctly said that the true hero of the Mexican investment boom is the ordinary Mexican worker, whose acceptance of a declining real income has in effect "subsidized" much of the nation's building . . . It is a token of Mexico's political stability that this program of inflation has been accompanied by no political disorders or even by any notable diminution of the party in power.[5]

Even though their demands were moderated by *charros*, in the twenty years following 1956, workers enjoyed more job security and received more material gains than any generation of Mexican workers, before or since.

Rural Mexico

> With the one major exception of Lázaro Cárdenas (1934–40), Mexican presidents regarded land distribution more as a way to pacify the peasantry and ensure their support rather than as a central component in an integrated rural development program.
>
> (Tom Barry, 1995)

After World War II, rural Mexico saw a communications revolution. The village of Tepoztlán in Morelos was typical. In 1943, only four villagers there had a radio. By 1958, there were eighty battery-powered sets, and, by 1964, after electricity was introduced, only the very poor lacked radios. During the same period, rural transportation was shifting from muscle power to fossil fuels. In 1940, people overwhelmingly walked or rode carriages, horses, or *burros*. During the next decades, there was a massive shift to cars and busses as new roads made this alternative feasible.

Rural Mexicans suffered from the combined effects of soaring population, government neglect, and low productivity. In 1969, the value added per agricultural worker was only 30 percent of the average for all Mexican workers. Population growth overwhelmed the tepid efforts at land reform. Between 1940 and 1970, the number of agricultural workers increased from 3.8 million to 7.8 million, while the number of land reform beneficiaries only rose from 1.5 million to 2.1 million. During this same period, the cultivatable area per agricultural worker declined from 3.0 to 1.5 acres. In 1970, 49 percent of rural households were below the poverty line.

Beginning in the 1940s, successive Mexican governments favored privately owned agricultural properties, not the *ejido*. Each new government would reaffirm that land reform was a "major goal" of the Revolution and then lavish benefits on commercial farmers, especially those producing for export.

After World War II, it became obvious that land distribution per se was not producing equality in the countryside. *Ejidatarios* and small farmers found themselves caught in a vicious cycle. They had low educational levels, small plots, and little access to capital. As a result of using antiquated technology on land that was often poor to begin with, yields per acre were low. Their meager income was further reduced by their relying on others to transport and warehouse crops. While the rural population was rapidly increasing, job loss occurred as capital-intensive agricultural technology was transferred from developed countries to rural Mexico and land was shifted from labor-intensive crops to raising cattle.

In the 1930s, the *ejido* provided a quick response to the Depression, combining land and labor, both of which Mexico had in abundance. Transferring land to the *ejido* alleviated immediate employment problems, but in the process created obstacles to increased agricultural production. Corruption undermined the efficiency of many *ejidos*. Article 27 of the constitution not only provided the legal basis for the *ejido*, but prohibited corporate investment in land, thus limiting capital available for both private and *ejido* land. Over the years, the division of land among many children led to plots so small that it was impossible to achieve economies of scale and apply modern technology. Given differences in plot size, soil fertility, and water availability, some *ejidatarios* prospered and escaped poverty, but many did not.

Despite the numerous grievances of the rural population, the government effectively headed off rural unrest. One factor enabling the government to contain peasant unrest was the lack of effective rural organization. From its inception under President Cárdenas, the National Peasant Confederation (CNC) relied on patron–client relationships with those it organized. Under Cárdenas, the CNC offset the power of the landed elite and channeled goods, services, and land to the peasantry. However, after 1940 as the government's commitment to land reform waned, the CNC maintained the rural status quo rather than promoting land reform or redressing the imbalance of power between peasant producers and the small elite of commercial farmers. Credit and infrastructure projects were allocated on a discretional basis, leading most peasants to continue looking to the CNC to improve their lot in life.

The CNC retained its influence by channeling government resources to *ejidos*. It remained as the only channel available for receiving land via the land reform. If peasants bypassed the CNC to make demands, they were ignored or repressed. The CNC depended on the PRI and various government agencies for its operating expenses. In exchange for this subsidy, the CNC faithfully delivered the peasant vote for the PRI. As one former secretary of agriculture commented, "Mexican peasants are organized to vote, not to produce."

With the official peasant organization intent on maintaining the status quo, landless peasants repeatedly turned to extralegal methods in their quest for land ownership. Their most frequent tactic was moving onto land they felt exceeded the limits imposed by the land reform law and laying claim to it—a process knows as a land invasion. By doing so, they kept alive Zapata's notion that land reform should be carried out by peasants without state intervention.

The Indigenous Population

Based on the number of people speaking an Indian language, census authorities reported that the Indian population over age five increased from 2.5 million in 1940 to 3.1 million in 1970. Non-linguistic methods were also used to determine Indian identity. Sociologist Pablo González Casanova defined an Indian as an individual with an "awareness of belonging to a community which is different and isolated from the national culture . . ." By applying that definition, he calculated that in 1960 the number of Indians was between 6 million and 7.5 million, or 20 to 25 percent of the national population.

From the end of Cárdenas's term until 1988, the Indian faded from official discourse and party platforms. Intellectual discourse concerning the Indian increasingly focused on how the poverty of the Indian community resulted not from Indians' biological endowments or their social organization, as had been often argued in the past, but from mistreatment and neglect by the rest of Mexican society. Closer integration to the Mexican nation was viewed as the best way to address pervasive Indian poverty. In 1967, influential anthropologist Gonzalo Aguirre Beltrán voiced this view of *indigenismo*, the term used to describe the government's Indian policy, "The ultimate goal of indigenismo is not to capture the attention of the Indians and improve their lot, but to achieve a much loftier goal: the integration of the Indian, under socially just conditions, so that Indian and non-Indian are really free and equal citizens."

Government programs dealing with the Indian were coordinated by the National Indigenous Institute (INI), which was founded in 1948. In regions with a high indigenous population, the INI established "coordinating centers." These centers drew on the services of physicians, agronomists, veterinarians, engineers, and lawyers. Complementing the efforts of the non-Indian professional was the bilingual teacher, or "*promotor*." The promotor was a member of the indigenous community who could speak the local Indian language as well as Spanish and who was trained as a bilingual teacher.

While these efforts were a well-meaning attempt to end the poverty in which most Indians found themselves, they never addressed the question of whether Indian cultures could be preserved while at the same time being integrated more closely to the national culture. It also remained unclear just who received the most benefits from the increased integration of the Indian with the national economy. As anthropologist Cynthia Hewitt de Alcántara noted, "Rural roads ran in two directions, and the greater experience and economic power of many inhabitants of the urban terminal gave the latter a definitive advantage over the peasantry in putting the new means of communication to profitable use."

Women

Congress's failure to implement the women's suffrage amendment at the end of the Cárdenas administration caused women's organizations to shift their attention to other goals, such as providing for child care, the establishment of cooperatives for indigenous women, guaranteeing maternity leave, and passing legislation to protect domestic servants.

Even though women's organizations lost momentum during the 1940s, the suffrage issue was not forgotten. In 1952, suffragist Amalia Caballero de Castillo Ledón interviewed PRI presidential candidate Adolfo Ruiz Cortines. He promised her that if she could gather the signatures of half a million women (out of a population of 30 million), he would grant women the right to vote. She launched a successful petition drive, and Ruiz Cortines pushed though an amendment

Figure 12.2 *The 1958 presidential election was the first in which women were allowed to vote. To the surprise of many, female voters voted similarly to male voters.*

Source: Reproduced courtesy of Archivo General de la Nación.

to Article 34 of the constitution. That article was revised to state that both men and women (*los varones y las mujeres*) had the right to vote in national elections.

In the 1958 presidential election, 7,845,400 votes were cast. This was more than twice the total cast in 1952, reflecting not only population increase but also the enfranchisement of women. Contrary to the predictions made by opponents of women suffrage, there was not a marked increase in the vote for the PAN. By and large, women voted for the PRI, just as men did. In response to the enfranchisement of women, the PRI did establish female organizations within the party and allowed the election of a handful of female deputies.

During the 1950s and 1960s, women reshaped the Mexican labor force. As Mexico urbanized and industrialized, the percentage of women in the labor force increased from 7.4 in 1940 to 19.0 in 1970. Many of those joining the labor force had migrated from rural areas. Women migrants to the city, drawn by jobs in education, commerce, and domestic service, outnumbered men.

Generally women found employment in jobs that were an extension of their traditional roles in the home. They worked as domestics (cleaning and cooking) and in food service (cooking), the garment industry (sewing), hospitals (caring for the sick), and schools (caring for children). In 1970, 69.6 percent of the 2.5 million women in the formal labor force worked in the service sector. Of these, 488,344 were domestics.

Population

As late as 1940, Mexican birth rates and death rates remained high compared to the levels found in the North Atlantic nations. After 1940, birth rates remained high while death rates plunged, leading to a population surge. Immigration had scant impact on Mexico's population between 1940 and 1970—the surge in population resulted from births far exceeding the number of deaths. Between 1940 and 1970 Mexico's population increased from 19.7 to 47.2 million.

FRIDA KAHLO

Of the artists in the post-mural movement, Frida Kahlo became the most widely recognized in the United States. Her father, Guillermo Kahlo, was a German-Jewish expatriate of Hungarian descent who was commissioned by Porfirio Díaz to photograph major architectural monuments for the 1910 centennial celebration. Her mother was of mixed Spanish and Indian heritage.

When she was six, Kahlo contracted polio, which left her right leg shorter than her left. Then at age eighteen she was involved in a near fatal bus-trolley accident that crushed her spine and pelvis, leaving her with pain for the rest of her life. She began painting while convalescing.

In 1929, Kahlo married muralist Diego Rivera, who was twenty-one years her senior. Her parents described the marriage between the expansive Rivera and the diminutive Kahlo as a "marriage between an elephant and a dove." During their marriage, Rivera and Kahlo each took many lovers and she became involved with both men and women, thus providing ample fodder for the press.

Politically. Frida (as she is almost universally known) was influenced by her celebrity husband, and she joined the Mexican Communist Party in which Rivera was active. Significantly though she did not adopt a single element of Rivera's artistic style. In her self-portraits, which introduce Catholic symbolism, pre-Columbian imagery, and fantasy, she typically appears wearing the headdress of the indigenous women of Tehuantepec.

Given her husband's celebrity status, Kahlo had difficulty emerging as an artist in her own right. She produced her best work in the 1940s. However, during her lifetime Frida had only two one-woman gallery shows, and her work was mainly bought by her friends.

After her death in 1954, her casket lay in state in the rotunda of the Palace of Fine Arts. Many prominent figures attended her funeral, including Lázaro Cárdenas. Even in death she could not escape from the shadow of her husband. When Cárdenas commented on her passing, he referred to her simply as "the wife of my friend, the excellent painter Diego Rivera, whose art has given such glory to Mexico."

In contrast to Rivera, whose artistic legacy came to be viewed with less enthusiasm in the late twentieth century, Kahlo became an icon for feminists as well as for art lovers everywhere. A single 1997 review essay considered nine works concerning her that were published in the United States between 1991 and 1996. At least six films have been made on her life, including the 2002 release *Frida*, starring Salma Hayek. A 2014 MIT study found her to be the most famous Mexican worldwide. (Rivera didn't even make the top ten.)*

---

* Rounding out the top ten were Montezuma, Emiliano Zapata, Carlos Santana, Anthony Quinn, Carlos Slim, Octavio Paz, Francisco "Pancho" Villa, Antonio López de Santa Anna, and Porfirio Díaz.

Continuing a trend begun in the 1930s, between 1940 and 1970 the death rate plummeted from twenty-three per thousand population to eleven per thousand. During this period, the government vaccinated children, built rural and urban health centers, provided drinking water systems and sewage treatment plants, and applied DDT to eradicate malaria-carrying mosquitoes. A higher standard of living, increased access to markets, and improved diets further reduced mortality. Mexico acquired the technology to prevent and treat infectious and parasitic diseases that had caused a large proportion of deaths, especially in children. Thanks to antibiotics, the proportion of deaths attributable to infectious and parasitic diseases declined from 42.6 percent of total deaths in 1930 to 23.1 percent in 1970.

During the late 1960s, as a result of the imbalance between births and deaths, Mexico's annual population growth rate reached 3.6 percent, one of the highest in the world. Within a thirty-five-year period—1940–1975—Mexico's population tripled. The previous tripling, between 1820 and 1940, had required 120 years.

Much to virtually everyone's surprise, population increase began to affect almost every aspect of Mexican life. By 1970, 46 percent of Mexico's population was below age fifteen. This required increased educational budgets—capital that might otherwise have resulted in new investments or in educating a smaller number of children longer, thus making them more productive. In 1958, President López Mateos noted that 300,000 new jobs were needed annually to accommodate job seekers who were born in the 1940s. Eventually the number of new job seekers entering the labor force annually would exceed one million.

The locus of new job creation was Mexico City. Between 1940 and 1970, Mexico City's population increased from 1.8 million to 8.8 million due to the high birth rate of its residents and rural-to-urban migration. During the 1940s, 612,000 migrated to Mexico City. The number of migrants increased to 800,000 during the 1950s and 2.8 million during the 1960s. In the 1960s, a major attraction of the Federal District was an income level 185 percent above the national average, which translated not only into more spending money but also into access to education, health care, clean water, sewers, and electricity.

Education

After 1940, the educational system was increasingly seen as the key to economic development, not as a vehicle for instilling new values in students. In 1946, Article 3 of the constitution was amended to state that education should stimulate "love of country and international solidarity." The reference to "socialism" was deleted from the article.

Even though overt political messages were dropped, schools continued to foster change. This was especially true of female students. As corn-grinding mills, sewing machines, store-bought utensils, and water sources close to home were introduced, girls had more time to attend school. As it became apparent that schooling increased the productive capacity of family members both on and off the farm, parents became increasingly willing to permit rural girls to attend school. Anthropologist Robert Redfield felt education was the key to the changes he observed after 1931 in the village of Chan Kom, Yucatán. He commented on the young women who had attended school there: "She speaks up when spoken to and has not the shy, almost voiceless and completely unassertive manner which prevailed among young women in former generations."

After 1950, due to population increase, a tidal wave hit the educational system. The number of Mexican children attending elementary school increased from 2.7 million in 1950 to 8.5 million in 1970. At the same time, with increased prosperity, many children could afford to stay in school longer. As a result, while primary enrollment increased by 3.7 percent a year between 1950 and 1970, secondary enrollment increased by 16.9 percent a year. In response to increased enrollments, the education budget rose from 7.8 percent of federal spending under Alemán (1946–52) to 13.2 percent under Díaz Ordaz (1964–70). Even with increased budgets, new enrollments strained the system. The average number of children per classroom increased from forty-five during the Díaz Ordaz administration (1964–70) to fifty-three during the Echeverría administration (1970–76).

Between 1940 and 1970, as a result of both adult literacy programs and the increased education of children, the percentage of illiterates in the population decreased from 58 to 28. The workforce continued to reflect past limitations on educational opportunity. In 1970, 67 percent of the population over twenty-four had three years or less of formal education and only 9 percent had attended secondary school.

In many ways, the educational system reinforced existing social inequality. In 1970 rural Mexico, home to the majority of Mexico's poor, accounted for 42 percent of the school-age population but only 9 percent of those finishing primary school. Government allocation of resources reinforced rural poverty. In rural areas, 74 percent of schools offered only grades one to four. Money and the best teachers flowed to areas that already had above average income.

Figure 12.3 *The library on the newly constructed campus of the National University became an instant icon. The mural decorating the building is by Juan O'Gorman.*

Source: Reproduced courtesy of the Benson Latin American Collection, the University of Texas at Austin.

There was a very close, circular relation between education and poverty. In families classified as poor, 47.7 percent of family heads had no formal education and only 2.8 percent had continued beyond elementary school. Since children in these families could not afford to remain in school for long, they formed another poorly educated generation on its way to poverty.

For those fortunate enough to attend collage, the future appeared bright. In the early 1950s, the National University moved to a new campus on the southern fringes of Mexico City. The new campus, whose buildings were decorated with mosaics and frescos by David Alfaro Siqueiros, Diego Rivera, and Juan O'Gorman, boasted some of the finest examples of modern architecture anywhere. An imposing statue of President Alemán towered over the grounds of the campus whose creation he had ordered.

The National University entered its golden age after moving to the new campus. Its graduates dominated Mexico's cultural, political, and entrepreneurial elite. Alliances made while on campus served politicians and bureaucrats as they moved up the political ladder. All Mexican presidents from Alemán (1946–52) through Salinas (1988–94) were graduates of the National University.

The National University experienced the same accelerated growth that lower levels of the educational system did. Between 1950 and 1970 its enrollment increased from 24,929 students to 106,038.

While the National University continued to dominate higher education, other institutions were founded, diversifying higher education. The Colegio de México, which was formalized in 1940, specialized in the social sciences and history and benefited from Spanish refugees on its faculty and funds from the Rockefeller Foundation. To this day this unique public–private hybrid produces outstanding social science works. In 1943, to ensure a continued supply of technicians for Garza

Sada enterprises, Eugenio Garza Sada, a second-generation member of the Monterrey elite, spearheaded the creation of the Monterrey Institute of Technology. It became a highly regarded technical training center modeled on MIT, of which Garza Sada was an alumnus.

By 1960, twenty-two state universities had been established. As a result of these new campuses, total enrollment in higher education rose from 29,892 in 1950 to 252,200 in 1970–71. Between 1960 and 1970, the number of degrees granted by universities rose by 12.4 percent a year. A college degree, which had been the key to upward mobility in the 1950s, became a source of discontent in the 1960s, as the number of college graduates exceeded the number of professional jobs being created.

Even though university enrollment was increasing faster than the population as a whole, access to higher education remained sharply tilted toward economically and geographically privileged males. The average family income of National University students was 3.2 times the national average. In 1963, only 17 percent of those enrolled in higher education were women. The next year, a survey found that only 18 percent of National University students had a worker or peasant background. As was the case with so many aspects of Mexican life, the Federal District was over-represented. The National University and the National Polytechnic Institute, founded in Mexico City by Cárdenas to provide technicians sympathetic to his development goals, together accounted for 49 percent of the university students in Mexico.

Religion

After 1940 anti-clerical legislation remained on the books, but was unenforced. Mexico remained staunchly Catholic. In the 1970 census, 96 percent of the population identified themselves as Catholic. The Church faced the same demographic pressures faced by the educational system. In 1940, there were 3,863 priests, or one per 5,088 Mexicans. In 1967, there were 7,922 priests, or one per 5,765 Mexicans.

During the 1940s, Church–state collaboration ceased to be covert as presidents and bishops openly participated in joint ceremonies. The Church increased its influence by controlling important centers of secondary and higher education that were attended by middle- and upper-class students. The Church lobbied the government, especially on matters concerning private education. It used a wide variety of magazines, books, and other publications to disseminate its views. In both the number of people organized and in the volume of its publications, the Church was second only to the government.

The Church became more critical of social conditions and began to use the social sciences to critique the Mexican development model. It did not challenge capitalism as an institution—only its excesses. Church officials spoke out against corruption in government and the inequitable distribution of income. In addition to criticizing the government and the economic system, the clergy attempted to influence attitudes towards such innovations as movies, the mambo, and women's sleeveless dresses—all of which were denounced.

Between 1940 and 1970, the number of Protestants in Mexico rose from 177,954 to 876,879. Membership in Protestant groups rose in part due to an influx of U.S. Protestant missionaries, many of whom had been displaced from Asia by World War II. In other cases, Mexicans working in the United States during the war underwent conversion to Protestantism and then returned to Mexico.

The Intellectual Scene

Painting

In 1940, the Revolution remained the dominant theme of public art, reflecting the state's willingness to subsidize muralists in an effort to keep alive the image of the Revolution. By 1950 mural art had become an obstacle to Mexican artistic development. As Octavio Paz commented: "Muralism died of an ideological infection. It began as a search and ended as a catechism."

Younger artists rebelled against muralism. Rufino Tamayo, a member of the new generation of artists, commented, "Mexican peasants triumphed only in the murals." In the most publicized criticism of muralism, painter José Luis Cuevas charged in a 1956 essay, "The Cactus Curtain," that the continued ascendancy of the Mexican mural school stifled creative freedom and kept the nation isolated from artistic developments in other countries. Cuevas declared, "What I want in my country's art are broad highways leading out to the rest of the world, rather than narrow trails connecting one adobe village with another."

Eventually Mexican artists did break away from the muralist school. This was formally acknowledged when the works of a new generation of artists were included in a 1966 exposition at the Palace of Fine Arts entitled "*Confrontación '66*." This exhibit was later sent to Montreal to be exhibited at the 1967 world's fair. Unlike the mural movement, there was little to unite the post-mural generation. Its members worked in a variety of individual, almost isolated styles.

The Literary Boom

During the 1960s, Mexico became caught up in what is known as the Latin American literary boom. Essayist Carlos Monsiváis commented on it:

> As never before, Spanish-language readers were confronted by the intense and complementary correspondence between literature and reality. In the midst of every sort of transition (towards fascism, towards revolutionary nationalism, towards the incongruous practices of Third Worlders), readers clung to these books as a means of escaping, not a cultural tradition, but the oppression of underdevelopment.[6]

The boom transcended the boundaries of Latin America and reading Latin American fiction soon became fashionable among the cultural elite of the United States and Europe.

Carlos Fuentes's 1958 novel *La región más transparente* (*Where the Air is Clear*, 1960) is one of the novels that launched the boom. It brought instant recognition to Fuentes, the son of a Mexican diplomat. His novel evoked the Mexico City of the 1940s and 1950s, where the aggressive capitalism of Ávila Camacho and Alemán clashed with the idealist revolutionary rhetoric of an earlier period. Fuentes set his story in urban surroundings, as was characteristic of boom writers, whose primary reality was the city and its inhabitants.

In 1971, Fuentes published *Tiempo Mexicano*, a collection of his best essays and reporting from the previous decade. He described the Revolution not as a historical event but as a myth. He stated, "We are a dependent nation, semicolonial, we have no more room to maneuver than Poland." In *Tiempo Mexicano*, Fuentes criticized "development for the sake of development." As with many intellectuals of his generation, he felt the solution to Mexico's problems was "an energetic intervention by the state in Mexico's economic life."

The 1950s were one of the most productive periods for Mexico's great man of letters, Octavio Paz. Paz, the son and grandson of revolutionary intellectuals, is best known in the United States for his *El laberinto de la soledad* (1950; *The Labyrinth of Solitude*, 1961), the definitive study of what it meant to be a Mexican. In it, he delved into what he believed were Mexicans' feelings of inferiority and resignation. Paz also published poetry and essays, lectured on and presented new poets and painters, and founded journals and a theater group. Later he joined the diplomatic corps, and in 1962 he was appointed ambassador to India.

When Paz learned of the 1968 student massacre, he resigned his ambassadorship in protest. The next month he commented on the massacre in *Le Monde*: "If there were any hopes the PRI could be reformed, they have become absurd after the events of October 2. The only solution is to criticize it from the outside and remove it from power." In 1970, Paz published *Posdata* (*The Other Mexico*, 1972), a revaluation of Mexican reality in light of the 1968 student movement. In this book, Paz described two Mexicos, one modern and one underdeveloped. He felt this duality was "the result of the Revolution and the development that followed it: thus, it is the source of many hopes and, at the same time, of future threats."

Print Media

After the middle of the century, the newspaper industry boomed, driven by cheaper printing technology, government-subsidized newsprint, greater affluence, and a thriving ad industry tied to mass-produced consumer goods. In 1970, 7.7 million newspapers were printed daily in Mexico, or one paper for every 4.2 citizens over age ten.

Despite the large number of papers published, as historian Enrique Krauze noted, "It was a given that the press did not honestly, thoughtfully, or independently report on political events or politicians." Even though the government lacked the formal legal power to censor print media, it had numerous more subtle means of control.

From 1960 to 1970, the government placed 20 to 30 percent of all advertisements. By simply withholding its ads, the government could exert pressure on publishers. Papers providing favorable coverage would receive sufficient ad revenue to wipe out debts resulting from unpaid contributions to the government-run social security system. Often government ads made the financial survival of a publication possible.

Even though the mass media was almost uniformly uncritical, decades before vote totals began to show the PRI was losing its grip, academics were undermining its foundations. In 1943 economist Jesús Silva Herzog wrote an article entitled "The Mexican Revolution in Crisis." In it, he criticized the failure of the government's economic model to improve the lives of broad sectors of the population. He recommended a continuation of the land reform, denounced corrupt labor officials, and advocated an increased emphasis on education.

In 1947, historian and economist Daniel Cosío Villegas provided another critique. In an article entitled "Mexico's Crisis," he stated, "The men of the Revolution can be judged now with certainty—they were magnificent destroyers, but nothing they created to replace what had been destroyed has proven indisputably better." He noted that the political system was rife with corruption, that crimes were committed with impunity, and that the population was so accustomed to the press mouthing the government line that readers instinctively assumed to be true the opposite of what the press claimed. Finally, he concluded, "The men of the Revolution have exhausted their moral and political authority."

In 1965, sociologist Pablo González Casanova published *Democracy in Mexico*, the most devastating critique yet of the direction the Revolution had taken. In his work, he applied sociological methodology to official statistics and concluded that after World War II Mexico had generated substantial economic growth but had not lessened dependency, underdevelopment, or inequality.

Broadcast Media

In 1940, Mexico had ninety commercial and twelve government radio stations and an estimated 450,000 radio sets. By 1960, there were more than 3 million radios, five or six times the number of TV sets. In 1961, radio accounted for 36 percent of the $120 million spent on advertising in Mexico, while television accounted for only 6 percent. Radio had a nationwide cultural influence and served to popularize dances such as the samba and the rumba.

Radio reached its zenith about 1970, when there were 17 million sets. Even though the law restricted station ownership to Mexicans, radio paved the way for increased foreign influence. A 1971 study found that 84 percent of the products advertised on XEW, one of the most influential radio stations, were produced by foreign-controlled firms.

THE GOLDEN AGE OF MEXICAN CINEMA

As a result of both U.S. and Mexican government support and lessened competition, Mexican feature film production soared from twenty-nine in 1940 to eighty-five in 1944. By 1943, the quality of Mexican films had risen so much that *Variety* suggested they could be thought of as "arty" replacements for French films, which were unavailable due to the war. In 1946 motion picture theaters numbered almost 1,000, more than double their number in 1940. Film had a much greater cultural impact than the static revolutionary murals.

World War II ushered in what is known as the Golden Age of Mexican cinema. Film momentum continued after the war, and by 1947 four studios employed 32,000 people to produce films. In the early 1940s, the *comedia ranchera*, set in rural areas, was a dominant theme. Singing cowboys Jorge Negrete and Pedro Infante invoked a safely romanticized rural past as millions were moving to the cities. Other films, especially those directed by Emilio "El Indio" Fernández, romanticized and attempted to dignify the life of the Indian. Even films sympathetic to the Indian created a false image of a simple, unspoiled life. In *María Candelaria*, the star, Dolores del Río, who portrays a poor Indian, always emerges from her hut with dress and coiffure immaculate. Nonetheless, this film did accurately portray how Indians lived at the mercy of non-Indians.

In the late 1940s, as Mexico continued to urbanize, directors increasingly chose urban settings. In both life and film, Mexico City sparkled as the shining star on Mexico's horizon. A genre known as the cabaret film dealt with the tragic life of the naïve country girl who went astray and ended up in a brothel. If the *comedia ranchera* stood for traditional values, the cabaret film dramatized the breakdown of these values as Mexico urbanized and corruption flourished.

After World War II, Hollywood films began to flood the Mexican market again. In 1953, 226 U.S. films premiered in Mexico, while only eighty-seven Mexican ones did. The inescapable U.S. film presence in Mexico led journalist Paulo Antonio Paranaguá to comment, "Poor Mexico, so far from God and so close to Hollywood."

After Mexico attempted to protect its domestic market by taxing the exhibition of foreign films. In response the United States slapped a retaliatory tax on Mexican films, depriving Mexico of the lucrative U.S. market. Hollywood filmmakers not only had much larger budgets than their Mexican counterparts but also had the active support of the U.S. State Department to regain export markets. In order to receive allocations of still-scarce raw film for its domestic film industry, Spain had to grant U.S. film exports privileged access to its domestic market. This effectively shut out Mexican exports.

Films remained politically bland since the government had the legal right to prohibit the production or exhibition of any film. Julio Bracho's 1960 film *La sombra del caudillo*, a lightly fictionalized account of the ugly power struggle among ex-revolutionaries, was immediately censored and remained unseen for thirty years.

During the 1960s, the immense popularity of the TV soap opera undermined the film industry as resources were shifted from local film production toward TV, which, since it was not competing directly with Hollywood, was highly profitable.

By 1968, television had replaced radio as the main source of home entertainment and had surpassed radio in ad sales. Even though there was no formal mechanism of censorship, as there was with movies, concentrated media ownership stifled diversity of opinion. Advertisers' opinions and interests shaped content. As a result, as Octavio Paz observed in 1975, "Freedom of the press is more a formality than a reality; radio and television are in the hands of two or three families who are more interested in earning money by brutalizing the audience than in analyzing the country's problems honestly and objectively."

THE MEXICAN ECONOMIC MIRACLE, 1941–1970

The War Years, 1940–1945

While Mexico was only marginally involved in World War II militarily, it was heavily involved economically. The Mexican and U.S. governments worked closely to coordinate Mexican production for Allied war needs. Production rapidly increased as lead, iron, zinc, and copper mines operated twenty-four hours a day. Since mining was already largely under the control of U.S. corporations, it was easy to integrate mining into the U.S. war effort.

During the war, the government increased its role in the economy and shifted economic priorities. An emphasis on industrialization regardless of social cost replaced Cárdenas's vision of prosperous peasants working their own land. To promote industrialization, the government tightened its control over labor, provided favored entrepreneurs with credits and other financial incentives, kept taxes low, and increased investment in infrastructure. Between 1941 and 1945, the government was responsible for 58 percent of all investment. Road building and irrigation projects absorbed 44 percent of this investment. Between 1940 and 1946, as a result of federal investment, the area irrigated increased from 293,200 acres to 882,300.

Between 1940 and 1945, as a result of wartime demand and increased government economic support, Mexico's gross domestic product increased by 6 percent a year. Industrial production expanded at 10 percent, while exports rose at an annual rate of 11.7 percent. During the war years, there was an 850 percent increase in manufactured exports as Mexican textiles, chemicals, and processed food replaced production by the great powers, whose industrial capacity was diverted to military needs. The World War II boom was almost entirely domestically financed. Foreign direct investment declined from 30 percent of gross domestic product in 1940 to 10 percent in 1946.

High inflation resulting from the wartime boom, weak labor leadership, and a lack of government support for labor resulted in a 37 percent decline in workers' buying power between 1940 and 1944. Wealth was quickly shifted to business owners.

Import Substitution Industrialization, 1946–1954

Even as Mexico rode the Korean War (1950–53) raw material export boom, the government officially embraced an economic development strategy known as import substitution. Its proponents believed that the traditional strategy of underdeveloped countries—exporting raw materials and importing manufactured goods—led to an economic dead end. Planners also noted that the failure to develop local industry limited job creation. Import substitution shifted the central focus of development policy from the international market to the domestic market.

Various social groups favored this emphasis on industrialization. They included government policymakers, an urban population little interested in land reform, workers in industries protected from foreign competition, and owners of industry, who had emerged during the Second World War as a major interest group.

The views of government policymakers were shaped by the experience of the Depression (when Mexico could not afford manufactured imports due to a decline in its raw material exports) and World War II (when the Allies limited the export of manufactured goods due to wartime priorities). To Mexican planners, industry was the key to both economic autonomy and the new technology needed to increase productivity. Industrialization was made almost synonymous with national sovereignty and economic development. U.S. historian Lesley Byrd Simpson compared the zeal of industrial planners to that of the sixteenth-century missionaries. Simpson noted that both groups felt that they had the solution to Mexico's problems in hand.

The existing pro-industry views of Mexican manufacturers, government planners, and urban residents were reinforced by an emerging Latin American consensus on development. Argentine economist Raúl Prebisch, who served as executive secretary of the U.N. Economic Commission for Latin America (ECLA) between 1949 and 1963, observed that the already developed nations were extracting wealth from Latin America by buying inexpensive raw materials and then supplying the region with costly manufactured goods. He also believed that the prices of raw materials were rising more slowly than those of manufactured goods. ECLA doctrine formally abandoned the nineteenth-century notion of free markets and replaced it with the notion that governments should ensure sound development.

Mexican government officials, following Prebisch's reasoning, encouraged the production of manufactured items that had been previously imported. A 1946 law empowered officials to decree certain industries "new and necessary." Tariffs would then be levied on the type of goods these industries produced. In some cases, the government would prohibit the importation of an item or impose an import quota. As imports were restricted, Mexican entrepreneurs would begin production, often taking advantage of low-interest loans from the government development bank, Nacional Financiera. Thanks to tariffs and import prohibitions, they would not have to worry about foreign competition. New industries received a five-to-ten-year exemption on taxes and a duty-waiver to import manufacturing machinery. Autos, refrigerators, and electrical products were among the items whose import was restricted in an attempt to stimulate their domestic production.

Even though President Alemán was a staunch advocate of private enterprise, he felt government should make key investments to further the development process. The areas targeted for such investment were those with too long a payback period to attract the private sector or those deemed too large or risky. Thus the government maintained or increased its role in irrigation, banking, railroads, communications, road building, and oil production. It also sought to eliminate economic bottlenecks by increasing the production of steel, chemicals, fertilizer, and railroad cars. The private sector, having seen how the government favored it during the war, welcomed such investment, especially in energy production. During Alemán's 1946–52 term, 52 percent of the federal budget was allocated to economic development, compared with 39 percent under Ávila Camacho and 38 percent under Cárdenas. The eleven largest corporations in the nation, which included those producing oil and electricity and providing rail and phone service, were government-owned.

The emphasis on economic growth affected the entire society, as spending for economic development became a higher priority than social spending. By the end of the 1950s, the government was spending only 1.4 percent of the national product on education, while Argentina was spending 2.5 percent and Brazil 2.6 percent.

Thanks to pent-up consumer demand, protection from imports, high public spending, and $372 million of export income accumulated during World War II, economic growth during Alemán's term averaged 5.8 percent a year. In a testimony to the success of import-substitution industrialization, by 1955, domestically manufactured products accounted for 90 percent of the sales in Sears stores.

Mexican businessmen poured their profits back into the economy. During Alemán's term, the government financed investment by relying on taxes, monetary expansion, and income from state-owned enterprises. During the 1940s, 99.1 percent of industrialization was domestically financed.

Amidst the euphoria surrounding this development, few paused to notice some not so welcome trends. To entice investors, the government ensured that profits remained high by keeping salaries low. Salaries remained low and even decreased as inflation remained high. Workers could survive on low salaries since the government deliberately kept food prices low. This allowed handsome industrial profits but ultimately stymied agricultural development. Industrial workers were all too aware that there was a widening gap between wages and profits, but thanks to PRI-controlled labor unions and the repression of movements not directly controlled by the PRI, they could do little about this disparity. Finally, consumers were saddled with expensive goods due to the non-competitive nature of the factories that arose behind tariff barriers. However, they had no means to reject existing policies, which were set by PRI functionaries.

The Boom Years, 1954–1970

> Mexican industry grew behind high tariff walls, companies were cosseted and subsidized (e.g., by cheap fuel), and favored workers won featherbedded security. But even if aggregate output was thereby depressed (and consumers were ripped off), the system embodied elements of stability, reciprocity, and manageability.
>
> (Alan Knight, 2007)

The 1953 armistice in Korea brought an end to the boom in commodity exports to the United States. In 1954 to snap Mexico out of the ensuing economic slump, the peso was devalued. For Mexican buyers who paid for imports in pesos, prices increased, thus stimulating the sale of Mexican-produced goods. To maintain the momentum of import substitution, in 1965, there was a 6 percent increase in tariffs. By 1970, import quotas had been placed on nearly 13,000 categories of goods.

Between 1955 and 1970, Mexico adopted an economic development strategy known as "stabilizing development." This policy was based on: 1) price stability; 2) maintaining a fixed exchange rate between the peso and the dollar; 3) providing energy and government services to industry at low prices; 4) heavy government investment in roads and irrigation works; and 5) the use of foreign credit and foreign investment to complement domestic savings.

In contrast to the nineteenth century when exports financed much of Porfirian industrialization, after the end of the Korean War-induced commodities boom, Mexican exports were unable to finance the imports needed to industrialize. To finance such imports, Mexico increasingly turned to foreign direct investment (FDI). By 1970, this investment, 79 percent of which came from the United States, totaled $2.8 billion. Even though foreign investment was increasing rapidly, in 1970, 65 percent of Mexican industrial production remained in Mexican hands, largely financed by reinvesting the high profits resulting from tariff protection and low-cost labor.

Between 1953 and 1970, the Mexican economy, frequently referred to as the "Mexican miracle," was the envy of the world. Annual economic growth averaged 6.8 percent. Mexicans felt that they had finally found the path to prosperity. In 1964, Antonio Ortiz Mena, who served as treasury secretary from 1958 to 1970, commented: "The foremost concern of the Chief of the Executive was to transmit the conviction to the people that economic development would be continued and abundance would be procured with monetary stability."

Table 12.1 *Annual increase in gross domestic product, 1941–1970*

	GDP	GDP per capita
Ávila Camacho, 1941–46	6.2	3.3
Alemán, 1947–52	5.8	2.9
Ruiz Cortines, 1952–58	6.8	3.7
López Mateos, 1959–64	6.7	3.4
Díaz Ordaz, 1965–70	6.8	3.4

Source: Miguel Ramírez, *Mexico's Economic Crisis* (New York: Praeger, 1969), p. 46, Table 3.1

Roads and Car

> If schools can liberate us from ignorance, then highways . . . can liberate us from misery.
>
> (President Manuel Ávila Camacho, 1946)

The extension of the road system formed a key ingredient of the Mexican economic miracle. A wide variety of interests favored building roads. Mexican manufacturers sought roads to get their products to market and to lower the cost of bringing food to their workers. The U.S. auto industry, Mexican auto dealers, and Mexican construction companies also favored road construction.

Highways allowed the rapid transport of goods between major cities and extended sales into areas not reached by rail. Road construction facilitated Mexico's superb bus service, which to this day is light years ahead of its U.S. counterpart. By 1970 Mexico had 26,007 miles of paved road travelled on by 1,233,824 cars.

The Oil Industry

After the 1938 oil nationalization, the Mexican petroleum industry, which had been almost entirely export orientated, became closely linked to increased domestic motor vehicle use. Mexican oil production began a steady increase. In 1940, oil production only totaled 44.0 million barrels. By 1970, production had reached 156.6 million barrels.

In 1938, the government established a public enterprise, Pemex, that held a monopoly on oil production, refining, and fuel distribution. After the oil nationalization, exports largely ceased while demand within Mexico was soaring. To meet this demand Pemex reoriented its distribution system, which previously had consisted of pipelines from wells to ports on the Gulf of Mexico. After 1938 it was necessary not only to expand refining capacity but also to deliver fuel to users throughout Mexico.

A 1952 *New York Times* article commented on how Pemex's director Antonio Bermúdez had expanded exploration, reserves, production, consumption, and its distribution network: "Senator Bermúdez' role in building up Pemex to the status of a modern, progressive industry is one of the few things about Pemex that no one disputes whether they are for or against the nationalized oil company."

From the 1940s through the 1960s, Pemex maintained low prices in an effort to stimulate economic development. President Ávila Camacho stated that since the oil industry was nationalized, it "could operate without worrying about the profit motive, only taking into account the general interest." The availability of cheap energy did spur industrial growth. However, the policy had several drawbacks. Its effect was regressive, since it disproportionately benefited the wealthiest areas of the country, where the most fuel was consumed. It also lowered the revenue Pemex generated, so little money was available for oil exploration. Pemex's low prices and excessive hiring, which inflated costs, led the company to rely on foreign loans, which financed the majority of the company's investment by 1958. Finally, its low prices encouraged the profligate use of energy, which, beginning in the 1960s, forced Mexico to import oil to meet demand.

Pemex achieved labor peace by tolerating widespread corruption. Union leaders were allowed to enrich themselves if they ensured that the industry did not face serious labor problems. Such leaders regularly received contracts to supply Pemex with goods and services and then farmed the work out to others for a percentage of the profits. They sold Pemex jobs for between $450 and $1,200. Employees engaged in widespread theft of gasoline. Dissident workers were greeted with job loss and violence. This corruption extended up to the very top of the corporation. When President López Mateos chided Pemex director Pascual Gutiérrez Roldán for distributing Pemex contracts to his friends and business partners, the director replied, "Do you expect me to give them to my enemies!"

Despite its being hobbled by corruption and its low-price policy, Pemex retained its status as a national icon—a symbol of victorious Mexican nationalism. As a 1967 *Wall Street Journal* article noted, Pemex's positive image caused foreign oil companies to worry that it might attract imitators:

> Private oil company executives are worried about the impact an increasingly efficient Pemex might have on private oil operations in the rest of Latin America and in the Mideast. "As a successful government venture, Pemex is the model for other countries wanting to nationalize their oil," says an apprehensive vice president of a U.S.-based international petroleum concern.[7]

Tourism

Several events set the stage for modern Mexican tourism. U.S. tourists eventually realized that Mexico was no longer under the sway of bandoleer-clad revolutionaries or Marxist presidents who expropriated U.S. property. World War II favored Mexican tourism, since the war closed Europe to those with travel lust, and Mexico provided Americans with an opportunity to escape ration books.

After World War II, the elimination of malaria, increased highway mileage, and U.S. affluence led large numbers of Americans to visit Mexico. After 1959, the Cuban Revolution caused many who would have otherwise visited Cuba to divert to Mexico. In the 1960s, improved communications and the availability of cheap airfares on jet aircraft led to the arrival of still more tourists.

Between 1950 and 1972, foreign tourism increased at an annual rate of 12 percent, roughly double that of the economy as a whole. In 1972, receipts from foreign tourism totaled $1.7 billion, more than total merchandise exports. That year Mexico received almost 2 million tourists, nearly half the Latin American total. In 1965, 208,000 were employed directly in providing services to foreign tourists and in addition an estimated 1 million families were at least partially employed in supplying handicrafts for sale to tourists.

Agriculture

> During the period of ISI [import-substitution industrialization], Mexican agriculture, rural environment, and peasantry provided the cheap food, abundant labor, raw materials, and capital crucial to the development of industry.
>
> (David A. Sonnenfeld, 1992)

In response to wartime needs, Ávila Camacho shifted the focus from land reform to agricultural production. Thanks to increased agricultural prices, more government credit, and government spending on highways and irrigation, agricultural production increased by 52 percent between 1940 and 1944. Wartime agriculture was tailored toward meeting Allied industrial needs, not feeding Mexico's population.

In response to wartime food shortages and the generally low yields throughout Mexican agriculture, the government invited the Rockefeller Foundation to establish an agricultural research program in Mexico. Rockefeller researchers accepted the offer and developed a package of new technology, often referred to as the Green Revolution. It combined agricultural mechanization, extensive irrigation, and the use of hybrid seeds, inorganic fertilizers, and pesticides. Production of wheat, the crop to benefit most from the Green Revolution, increased from nearly 400,000 tons in 1940 to 2.1 million tons in 1970. The Rockefeller effort was so successful at raising yields that one of its chief scientists, Norman Borlaug, received the Nobel Peace Prize in recognition of his plant breeding efforts.

Due to limitations imposed by climate, soil, and topography, few existing farms could profit from Green Revolution technology. This technology was most widely applied on newly irrigated land in northwestern Mexico. Between 1945 and 1955, agricultural production increased by 5.8 percent a year, and in the following decade it increased by 4 percent a year.

A commercial revolution accompanied the Green Revolution as increasing amounts of machinery and other inputs were required to maintain production. Fertilizer use rose from 1,800 metric tons in 1940 to 533,700 in 1970. By 1960, Mexico had 39,000 farm tractors, more than any other Latin American country, including Argentina, which had roughly twice as much agricultural land as Mexico.

During the immediate postwar period, Mexican agriculture fed a rapidly increasing and urbanizing population and provided exports that financed the import of industrial machinery.

The government established low corn prices so that industrial wages would not have to be raised to cover food costs.

Mexico's success at feeding its urban population and exporting agricultural products to finance industry came at the expense of the environment. Increased irrigation led to soil salinization as the salt carried in by irrigation water remained in the soil when the water evaporated. Eventually more than a million irrigated acres were lost due to such salinity. Insecticides killed not only pests but predators that preyed on them. As farmers increased the volume of insecticides applied and switched to more costly compounds, insecticide purchase and application became the largest single cost of cotton production. Farmers found themselves on what has been called the "pesticide treadmill," involving ever increasing pesticide costs. Finally, while yields rose, the Green Revolution led to a sharp decline in energy efficiency. Crops produced with the new technology required enormous amounts of energy to manufacture and power farm equipment and to produce pesticides and fertilizer.

Agricultural policies after the Cárdenas administration consistently favored large growers. Only two days after his inauguration, President Alemán expanded the maximum legal size of land holdings to 100 hectares (247 acres) of irrigated land or 200 hectares of seasonal rain-fed land. Between 1940 and 1950, the area of privately owned, irrigated land nearly doubled, while there was only a 23 percent increase in irrigated *ejido* land. To encourage mechanization, which only larger farms could afford, the government exempted agricultural equipment from import duties and provided ample financing to facilitate its purchase. Water supplied by government irrigation projects was so heavily subsidized that water payments failed to recover distribution costs, let alone the initial cost of the dams and canals.

Growers who benefited most from the Green Revolution were the ones who most closely resembled U.S. farmers. They owned large farms, were better educated, had access to credit, and sought out new technology on their own. The marketing of cotton, Mexico's leading export between 1949 and 1969, was controlled by the U.S. agribusiness giant Anderson Clayton, which provided more credit for cotton than did the National Ejido Bank for all *ejidatarios*. In 1969 these large farms produced the bulk of Mexico's main agricultural exports—cotton, tomatoes, sugar, and melons. By 1970, 2 percent of Mexican farmers produced half of the value of agricultural and forest products

Ejidatarios and small private farmers were unable to plunge into the lucrative agricultural export market, so they concentrated on producing crops such as corn and beans whose price was deliberately kept low as a favor to urban interests. Corn prices, adjusted for inflation, declined 33 percent between 1957 and 1973. The reduced farm size, isolation, poverty, and frequent illiteracy of the small farmer formed an insurmountable obstacle to Green Revolution technology.

Despite its post-1940 neglect by policymakers, the *ejido* remained an important element of Mexican agriculture. In 1960, 34 percent of agricultural production, as measured by value, came from the *ejido*.

In terms of output, Mexican agriculture after the Cárdenas administration was quite successful. By 1965, Mexico had become self-sufficient in basic foods. Between 1950 and 1966, agricultural exports almost tripled in value. In large part this success was due to high levels of government support for commercial agro-exporters. Thanks to government investment in irrigation, especially in northern Mexico, the area cultivated increased by 1.5 percent a year between 1940 and 1970.

The generally positive results from the Mexican agricultural sector masked a dual system of large highly capitalized private farms with high productivity per worker and small farms with limited capital and low productivity per worker. As a result, average agricultural productivity was well below that of workers in other sectors. In 1970, the 30 percent of the population working in agriculture produced only 11 percent of GDP. Productivity per worker on many small farms declined due to reduced government support and large families whose children inherited ever smaller, less efficient plots.

Mining

Foreign investment in mining declined after the Ruiz Cortines administration (1952–58) granted substantial tax advantages to small mining enterprises, making it difficult for large foreign-owned mines to compete. Early 1960s legislation forced foreign mining companies to sell 51 percent of their capital to Mexicans and stipulated that new mining concessions would only be granted to firms with at least 66 percent Mexican capital. These measures, as well as labor unrest, ore depletion, high taxes, low export prices, and poor transport discouraged new investment in mining.

By the end of the 1960s, Mexicans had successfully assumed control of the mining sector. However, the mining sector did not maintain its previous dynamism. From 1910 through 1960, mining volume remained roughly the same, while the rest of economy boomed. Between 1940 and 1970, mining declined from 3.7 percent to 1.0 percent of the GDP.

The Good Old Days?

Between 1940 and 1970, consumer goods declined from 25 to 15 percent of Mexico's imports. This was accompanied by an expansion of industry, job creation, an increased standard of living for broad sectors of the population, and transfer of technology into Mexico. Between 1940 and 1970, manufacturing increased from 16.6 to 23.3 percent of GDP.

Between 1940 and 1970, Mexican per capita gross domestic product increased more rapidly than that of the rest of Latin America, that of the United States, and that of the world. During this thirty-year period, Mexican per capita income rose from 16 percent of U.S. per capita income to 22 percent. Factors permitting this rapid growth included political stability resulting from Cárdenas's land reform and PRI political domination, as well as ample access to credit from both private and public sources.

The most obvious economic problem resulting from the postwar development model was a growing balance of payments deficit. Mexican-made consumer goods, such as cars and refrigerators, were generally produced with imported machinery and contained imported materials and components. Multinational corporations were reluctant to substitute Mexican-made parts for imports from their own plants abroad. As a result, when production increased, imports increased. In 1970 each new car contained well above $1,000 of imported parts and materials. Between 1960 and 1970 Mexico's annual trade deficit rose from $457 million to $1.038 billion. This mounting trade deficit was compounded by foreign corporations taking profits, royalties, and other payments out of Mexico. Between 1960 and 1971 such payments totaled $3.48 billion—more than the total value of foreign direct investment during that period.

In theory, Mexican exports could have paid for the imports used in manufacturing. However, there was limited foreign demand for Mexican manufactured goods since there was no outside competition to stimulate productivity, quality control, or the adoption of new technologies. Mexican-made goods were costly to produce due to small production runs. The entire Mexican production of cars was well below that of a single integrated auto plant in the United States. As various auto manufacturers each maintained small assembly plants, the cars produced cost roughly 50 percent more than they did in the country where they were designed. The high cost of manufactured items deterred exports. Between 1960 and 1970 foreign trade (exports + imports) declined from 25 percent of gross domestic product to 20 percent.

Several other factors impeded exports. Even though Mexican inflation was higher than U.S. inflation, a fixed exchange rate was maintained between the peso and the dollar between 1954 and 1976. This resulted in an overvalued peso that discouraged exports. Since exporters were forced to rely on expensive Mexican-made inputs, their costs were higher than those of their foreign competitors who could use the cheapest inputs available.

Import substitution led to other economic problems. The government kept wages low to encourage investment in industry. Economist Victor Urquidi commented on the resulting poor income distribution: "Unless income distribution is improved, consumer-goods industries will gradually saturate their limited, and at times luxury, urban markets . . ." As industry increasingly relied on capital-intensive machines designed in nations with high labor costs, job creation lagged. In 1970, 43.1 percent of the labor force was underemployed. Multinational corporations exacerbated employment problems. In 1969, they accounted for 27.7 percent of manufacturing production but only 13.6 percent of manufacturing employment.

Import substitution clearly failed to end dependence on foreigners. In the early 1970s, the Coca-Cola Company controlled 42 percent of the Mexican soft drink market. It supplied local bottlers with syrup, advertising copy, promotional materials, and technical assistance. A similar pattern existed in many industries. A 1975 U.S. Senate report commented, "Through their control over vital industries, leading firms, and a substantial share of the national market, MNCs [multinational corporations] exercise a great deal of influence in the Mexican economy, and their conduct is crucial to its performance." Ironically, ending dependence on foreigners had been one of the initial justifications for import substitution.

THE NEW PARTNERSHIP, 1941–1970

> The United States recognizes Mexico's need to disagree with U.S. policy on matters which are important but not essential for the U.S and which are essential for Mexico. In exchange Mexico supports the United States on matters which are essential or even important for the U.S., but not for Mexico.
>
> (Mario Ojeda, 1976)

The War Years, 1941–1945

> The second world war was favourable to Mexico in many ways, mainly because it brought a great and lasting improvement in relations with the United States.
>
> (Angus Maddison, 1985)

A rapprochement with the United States accompanied Mexico's early 1940s shift to the political right. World War II gave Mexico a certain leverage in dealings with its northern neighbor. Mexico's leaders took advantage of this leverage to modernize the Mexican army at U.S. expense, to settle ongoing bi-national disputes, and to reap economic benefits from wartime trade with the United States.

Conciliatory discourse replaced the strident diplomatic language of the late 1930s. In 1942, U.S. Ambassador George Messersmith declared, "President Ávila Camacho believes that we must live in the present and look forward into the future and forget, so far as is possible, the past." That same year Mexican Foreign Secretary Ezequiel Padilla declared that the border was "a line that unites us rather than divides us." In 1943 to emphasize the cordiality and importance of U.S.–Mexican relations President Roosevelt visited Monterrey, Nuevo León—the first time a U.S. president had ventured beyond the border. Ávila Camacho responded with a visit to Roosevelt in Corpus Christi, Texas.

Mexico's World War II experience shaped the nation for decades to come. In 1937–38, only 56 percent of Mexico's trade was with the United States. By 1940, as World War II closed European markets, the United States accounted for 90 percent of Mexico's foreign trade. This overwhelming U.S. dominance of Mexican foreign trade continued after the war. By 1946, some 350 new foreign companies, mostly American, had begun operations in Mexico. This was only the beginning of a decades-long increase in U.S. investment. Mexico's wartime ability to settle debt disputes opened the way for Mexico's postwar reintegration into international capital markets. The U.S. embassy, whose staff increased from 400 to a wartime peak of 800, remained as a major presence after the war.

The Cold War Years, 1945–1970

In February 1945, to lay the groundwork for postwar cooperation with Latin America, the United States sponsored a pan-American conference at Chapultepec Castle in Mexico City. For the Latin Americans who attended, the most pressing concern was postwar economic development. They felt that the United States had an obligation to repay Latin American wartime cooperation with aid. Mexican Foreign Secretary Padilla proclaimed that Latin Americans should "do more than produce raw materials and live in a state of semi-colonialism." Mexico joined other Latin American nations in advocating tariffs to protect still vulnerable new industries, controls on foreign (meaning U.S.) investment to ensure that it was in the "public interest," and the stabilization of commodity prices. As historian Frank Niess observed, "All in all, the Latins' objective at Chapultepec was nothing less than a more equitable distribution of the profits of the inter-American division of labour."

At the Chapultepec Conference, the United States presented a very different economic vision for postwar Latin America. U.S. planners favored the unimpeded flow of capital, the elimination of trade barriers within the hemisphere, and free access to each country's markets and raw materials. The American delegates advocated the use of private capital, not foreign aid, to finance Latin American development.

As it enunciated its economic preferences, the United States touted its own free-market development model as the only viable path of development and dismissed models that strayed too far from it. The U.S. version of its own economic history conveniently omitted any mention of how in the nineteenth century the United States was the most tariff-protected nation in the world and how various nineteenth-century U.S. administrations had promoted economic development.

A 1947 exchange of visits between Presidents Harry Truman and Miguel Alemán indicated the cordiality in relations between the two nations. Truman visited Mexico City—a first for a U.S. president. While there, Truman made the dramatic gesture of laying a wreath at the monument to the Mexican cadets, known as the Niños Héroes, who died during the Mexican–American War. Foreign Secretary Jaime Torres Bodet rose to the occasion and proclaimed that Truman "threw a bridge across the chasm of the past." Alemán responded to Truman's visit with another first—a visit to the U.S. capital by a Mexican president. Alemán devoted a chapter in his memoirs to the exchange. As an indication of the asymmetry of relations between the two nations, Truman's much longer memoirs contained only three lines concerning his Mexico City visit and failed to even mention Alemán.

Harmonious U.S.–Mexican relations continued into the early 1950s. A 1951 CIA report observed, "Mexico supports US views in major international issues, and relations with this country have been increasingly friendly and mutually cooperative."

With the exception of the regime change in Guatemala, by the early 1950s Latin America had ceased to be a major focus of U.S. attention. The 1949 U.S. Mutual Defense Act provided for the expenditure of $1.3 billion to bolster friendly militaries around the world. Not a cent went to Latin America. Between 1945 and 1952, Belgium and Luxembourg, with an area less than the Mexican state of Puebla, received more direct aid than all of Latin America. As with the rest of Latin America, Mexico drew little attention from its northern neighbor, and U.S.–Mexican relations entered into what historian Alan Knight has described as "their long period of somnolence."

The Mexican government under President López Mateos (1958–64) maintained a delicate balance. To have fully supported the Cuban Revolution would have alienated the Church, the United States, and Mexican business interests. To have supported U.S. actions relating to Cuba, and especially the U.S.-sponsored Bay of Pigs invasion, would have alienated the Cuban government, Mexican intellectuals, and the Mexican left, which might have become even more radical. In 1964, Mexico alone rejected U.S. demands at the OAS that Latin America break diplomatic and trade relations with Cuba.

While Mexico maintained a public stance of support for the Castro regime, it secretly yielded to U.S. pressure. Prior to each Cubana Airlines departure from Mexico City to Havana, Mexican authorities supplied the Mexico City CIA station with a passenger list so that names could be checked. Mexico's ambassadors to Havana regularly supplied U.S. intelligence services with information on Cuba's internal political, economic, and social developments.

The presidency of Lyndon B. Johnson, who served between 1963 and 1969, marked the end of a simpler era. Problems were often localized and relatively easy to solve. During his administration, Johnson met with Díaz Ordaz on seven separate occasions. As president, he devoted more attention to Mexico than to any other Latin American nation. Before a scheduled 1967 meeting between Johnson and Díaz Ordaz, a U.S. intelligence report stated, "Relations between the Mexican and US governments are extremely friendly, and President Johnson is personally popular in Mexico."

Shared interests paved the way for increasingly close ties with the United States. Once U.S. manufacturers began locating plants inside Mexico, U.S. opposition to trade barriers faded. By 1970, the United States accounted for 79 percent of the $2.8 billion of direct foreign investment in Mexico. The volume of Mexico's trade with the United States steadily increased. Historian Daniel Cosío Villegas commented on the inexorably increasing U.S. economic and cultural influence, noting that like "that of the Christian god, it is all powerful and omnipresent."

The Mexico City CIA station, with fifty employees and a $5.5 million annual budget, became the largest in the Western Hemisphere. Former CIA agent Philip Agee reported that Gustavo Díaz Ordaz, who was appointed interior secretary in 1958, worked "extremely closely" with the CIA. Its agents would pass their findings to Mexican government agents, who used the information to plan "raids, arrests and other repressive action." The importance of the CIA was such that when station chief William Scott married in Mexico, President López Mateos and Interior Secretary (and future president) Díaz Ordaz served as official witnesses.

Braceros, Wetbacks, and Immigrants

The U.S. government, facing a World War II-induced labor shortage, formally requested a program to bring Mexican labor into the United States. Under the program agreed to by the two nations, Mexican workers known as *braceros* (from the Spanish word *brazo*, meaning "arm") would be contracted to work in the United States for periods of up to six months. The U.S. Department of Agriculture administered the program—contracting workers at recruitment centers in central Mexico and placing them with private U.S. employers. *Braceros* were guaranteed a minimum wage (unlike American farm workers) as well as housing, health benefits, and the cost of transportation to the worksite.

In September 1942, the first *braceros* began work, harvesting California sugar beets. By July 1945, there were 58,000 *braceros* working in agriculture and another 62,000 maintaining U.S. railroads. During the war, more than 300,000 came north to work. The *bracero* program benefited the United States by providing low-cost labor and benefited growers by lowering U.S. agricultural wages. Mexico gained by exporting surplus labor and receiving remittances. Individual Mexicans, despite their housing, food, and wages often falling below agreed-upon standards, earned eight to ten times what they could have earned had they remained in Mexico.

After the war, lobbyists for U.S. agricultural interests declared that *braceros* would still be needed since U.S. citizens would not perform stoop labor. They failed to mention that California's crops had been harvested by U.S. citizens during the 1930s. In response to the lobbyists' pleading, Congress extended the *bracero* program, thus allowing growers to pay wages so low that jobs on their farms would not be attractive to U.S. workers.

The number of *braceros* continued to increase until 1959, when it reached a peak of 447,000. After that date, the use of *braceros* declined due to the mechanization of U.S. agriculture.

Figure 12.4 *Contract workers who came to the U.S., known as braceros, were initially welcomed. Later contracting, which ceased in 1964, became more controversial.*

Source: University of Texas at El Paso Library, Special Collections Department, Julian Strauss "The Bracero" (M.A. Thesis, UTEP, 44).

U.S. agribusiness, which sought to maintain its access to cheap labor, favored the program's extension. The other principal advocate of extending the program was the Mexican government. In 1964, Mexico's Ambassador to the United States Antonio Carrillo Flores accurately predicted that the absence of a *bracero* agreement "would not end the problem but rather would give rise to a de facto situation: the illegal introduction of Mexican workers into the United States, which would be extremely prejudicial to the illegal workers and, as experience has shown, would also unfavorably affect American workers, which is precisely what the legislators of the United States are trying to prevent."

After 1961, with a Democrat in the White House, opponents of the *bracero* program received a more sympathetic hearing. American liberals, in a time of postwar prosperity, associated Mexican farm laborers with the impoverishment of migratory U.S.-born farm workers and therefore opposed their presence. Given mounting criticism, the U.S. Congress voted not to extend the program beyond December 1964. During its twenty-two-year-long history, 4.5 million bracero contracts were signed. About 2 million individuals, many of whom signed on more than once, participated in the program.

Between 1942 and 1964, even though the *bracero* program provided legal access to the United States, many Mexicans came to the United States to work illegally. They chose to come illegally so that they could avoid passing through a recruitment center and perhaps having to bribe a Mexican official to be considered for hiring. Undocumented workers could also work outside agriculture and railroads, the areas of employment to which *braceros* were legally restricted.

As Ambassador Carrillo Flores had predicted, the expiration of a formal *bracero* treaty did not halt the flow of Mexican workers into the United States. It simply drove the flow into illegality.

Between 1961 and 1965, 222,827 undocumented Mexicans were apprehended and deported. Between 1966 and 1970, after the end of the *bracero* agreement, 794,964 were deported. During the following five-year period, deportations totaled 2,865,173. Even though the number of undocumented Mexican workers in the United States increased rapidly after the expiration of the *bracero* agreement, their presence received limited attention since most who came illegally were concentrated in the rural Southwest and only stayed a short while before returning to Mexico.

Braceros and those who entered the United States illegally formed the two main streams of Mexicans coming to work in the United States. Legal immigrants, who numbered 61,000 during the 1940s, formed a third group. During the 1950s, the number of legal immigrants swelled to 300,000. In that decade, Mexico became the third largest source of legal immigrants to the United States, after Canada and Germany. During the 1960s, legal immigrants from Mexico totaled 454,000. Between 1940 and 1970 the number of U.S. residents who were born in Mexico increased from 377,433 to 759,711. This number includes *braceros* and undocumented workers who had remained in the United States as well as legal immigrants.

Due to the variety of interests affected and the ups and downs of the economic cycle, the United States had difficulty formulating a coherent policy concerning labor migration from Mexico. Illustrating this cloud of confusion, Roy Rubottom, who occupied the Mexico desk of the State Department in 1950, declared:

> Legalization of **wetbacks** is the most practical method of extricating ourselves from this situation. This approach will make no difference in the Lower Valley [of Texas] . . . since the wetbacks are already there by the thousands and are still flooding in . . . INS has insufficient personnel to carry out its program of rounding up wetbacks.[8]

Many Mexican towns in north-central Mexico developed a dependence on remittances and established a deep cultural tradition of migration. Young people grew up with the expectation that they would go north as a rite of passage. Older returnees offered advice on how to make the trip, and often relatives in the United States would welcome newcomers. At the time, crossing the border involved little risk.

The communities in Mexico whose residents worked in the United States benefited from the earnings these workers sent home. In 1957, *bracero* remittances ranked third, after tourism and cotton, as a foreign exchange earner. Money sent home paid for fertilizer, tractors, plow rental, and family consumption. Returning workers brought new skills and values.

There were also negative aspects to labor migration, such as the tendency of workers with above average educational levels to leave. The loss of workers to the United States produced labor shortages. In 1944, the governor of Durango lamented that half the schools could not open since teachers had departed to work in the United States. By the 1950s, half the population of *ejidos* near Ciudad Juárez had crossed the border to work.

The impact Mexican workers had on U.S. communities where they worked was minimal since most of them stayed in the United States for less than a year and then returned to Mexico. Since most such workers were young and unmarried, they placed few demands for services on the communities in which they worked. Employers grew wealthy as they paid as little as $2.50 for a twelve-hour day in 1950. After factoring in inflation, there had been no increase in agricultural wages in a quarter century. As Julian Samora noted in *Los Mojados*, his ground-breaking study of undocumented workers, "It goes without saying that growers set the wages, managed the labor supply, encouraged an oversupply of labor, and, with the help of law-enforcement officers, suppressed any attempts at strikes."

DOCUMENT 12.1

[Striking students published the following in the Mexico City paper *El Día* on September 13, 1968:]

TO THE PEOPLE:

The National Strike Committee invites all workers, peasants, teachers, students and the general public to the

GREAT SILENT MARCH

In support of our six-point petition:

1. Freedom for all political prisoners.
2. Revocation of Article 145 of the Federal Penal Code.*
3. Disbandment of the corps of granaderos.**
4. Dismissal of police officials Luis Cueto, Raúl Mendiolea, and A. Frías.
5. Payment of indemnities to the families of all those killed and injured since the beginning of the conflict.
6. Determination of the responsibility of individual government officials implicated in the bloodshed.

We have called this march to press for the immediate and complete satisfaction of our demands by the Executive Power.

We repeat that our Movement has no connection with the Twentieth Olympic Games to be held in our country or with the national holidays commemorating our Independence, and that this Committee has no intention of interfering with them in any way. We insist, once again, that all negotiations aimed at resolving this conflict must be public . . .

* This article criminalized "social dissolution," a catchall term used to suppress dissidents.
** Granaderos were the Mexico City riot squad.

Source: Reproduced in Elena Poniatowska (1975) *Massacre in Mexico*. New York: Viking.

NOTES

1   Octavio Paz, *The Other Mexico* (New York: Grove, 1972), pp. 12–13.

2   Alma Guillermoprieto, *The Heart that Bleeds* (New York: Knopf, 1994), p. 59.

3   Lorenzo Meyer, "De la estabilidad al cambio," *Historia general de México: Versión 2000* (Mexico City: Colegio de México, 2000), p. 933.

4   Lorenzo Meyer, "La debilidad histórica de la democracia mexicana," in *México: El reclamo democratic*, ed. Rolando Cordera Campos, Raúl Trejo Delarbre and Juan Enrique Vega (Mexico City: Siglo XXI, 1988), p. 81.

5   Daniel Seligma, "The Maddening, Promising Mexican Market," *Fortune*, January (1956), p. 173.

6   *Historia general de México*, p. 1043.

7   James C. Tanner, "Nationalized Oil Agency in Mexico so Successful It Worries the Industry," *Wall Street Journal*, January 26 (1967), p. 1.

8   Lester Langley, *Mexico and the United States* (Boston: Twayne, 1991), p. 45.

FURTHER READING

Cosío Villegas, Daniel (2002) "Mexico's Crisis," in *The Mexico Reader*, ed. Gilbert M. Joseph and Timothy J. Henderson, pp. 470–81. Durham, N.C.: Duke University Press.
    The English translation of a 1947 article that was very critical of the course of the Mexican Revolution.

Fuentes, Carlos (1964) *The Death of Artemio Cruz*. New York: Farrar, Straus.
>   This 1962 novel, part of the Latin American literary boom, deals with a Mexican politician who betrayed the ideals of the Revolution.

González Casanova, Pablo (1970) *Democracy in Mexico*. New York: Oxford University Press.
>   A critique of Mexico's post-World War II development model which demonstrated that although there had been substantial economic growth, there was persistent dependency, underdevelopment, and inequality.

Lewis, Oscar (1961) *The Children of Sanchez*. New York: Random House.
>   An American anthropologist's description of life among poor, urban Mexicans.

McCaughan, Edward (2012) *Art and Social Movements: Cultural Politics in Mexico and Aztlan*. Durham, N.C.: Duke University Press.
>   A consideration of how visual art was used by the 1968 student movement, a Zapotec indigenous struggle in Oaxaca, and the Chicano movement in California.

Niblo, Stephen R. (1999) *Mexico in the 1940s*. Wilmington, N.C.: Scholarly Resources.
>   A discussion of 1940s politics, media, and corruption.

Padilla, Tanalís (2008*) Rural Resistance in the Land of Zapata.* Durham, N.C.: Duke University Press.
>   The story of a former Zapatista who attempted to keep the dream of land reform alive after 1940 and was murdered by the government for his efforts.

Paz, Octavio (1972) *The Other Mexico*. New York: Grove.
>   An evaluation of Mexican reality in light of the 1968 student movement. In this book Paz described two Mexicos, one modern and one underdeveloped.

Poniatowska, Elena (1971) *Massacre in Mexico*. New York: Viking.
>   Vignettes published in the aftermath of the 1968 student movement.

Rath, Thomas (2013) *Myths of Demilitarization in Postrevolutionary Mexico, 1920–1960*. Chapel Hill, N.C.: University of North Carolina Press.
>   A description of the political role of Mexico's post-revolutionary army, with emphasis on the period after the Cárdenas presidency.

Smith, Peter H. (1990) "Mexico since 1946," *Cambridge History of Latin America* (vol. 7), ed. Leslie Bethell, pp. 83–157.
>   A discussion of politics and social movements from 1946 to 1988.

GLOSSARY TERMS

bracero
wetback

Chapter 13

Politics in Times of Crisis, 1971–2000

TIMELINE—WORLD

1971	1972	1973	1975	1976
U.S. goes off gold standard	Nixon visits China	Democratically elected Chilean president Salvador Allende ousted in coup	Vietcong take Saigon, ending war in Vietnam	Soweto massacre in South Africa

1989	1990	1991	1998	2000
Tiananmen Square massacre of Chinese students	Iraq invades Kuwait, followed by U.S. intervention to oust Iraq	Collapse of Soviet Union	Hugo Chávez elected president of Venezuela	George W. Bush declared winner of U.S. presidential election

TIMELINE—MEXICO

1970	1976	1977	1982	1982
Echeverría inaugurated as president	López Portillo inaugurated as president	A political reform legalized the Communist Party and opened the way for the registration of new political parties.	López Portillo nationalized banks	De la Madrid inaugurated as president

1994	1994–95	1997		
Zedillo inaugurated as president	Peso devaluation and recession	PRI loses control of Chamber of Deputies		

1979	1979	1979	1982	1989
Sandinistas oust Nicaraguan dictator Somoza	Soviet invasion of Afghanistan	U.S. and China establish diplomatic relations	War between Argentina and Britain over the Falkland Islands/Islas Malvinas	Berlin Wall comes down

1985	1988	1988	1994	1994
Earthquake devastates Mexico City	split within the PRI leads to candidacy of Cuauhtémoc Cárdenas	Salinas inaugurated as president	EZLN uprising in Chiapas	PRI presidential candidate Colosio assassinated

THIS CHAPTER CONSIDERS MAJOR POLITICAL AND SOCIAL CHANGES that set the stage for Mexico's entry into the twenty-first century. Politically Mexico evolved from a one-party, PRI-dominated nation to one where multiple parties competed for office. The role of the state shifted away from guiding economic development and assuming the responsibility for social welfare. This chapter concludes by considering societal changes including increased education, increased income concentration, increased female participation in the labor force, and the population's more than doubling.

THE SWAN SONG OF THE ACTIVIST POST-REVOLUTIONARY STATE, 1970–1982

On October 21, 1969, a spokesman for the National Peasant Confederation (CNC) declared that the group supported forty-seven-year-old Interior Secretary Luis Echeverría for the PRI's presidential nomination, thus signaling that Díaz Ordaz had chosen his successor.

On the campaign trail, Echeverría, a previously taciturn lawyer who had been viewed as a hard-line conservative, metamorphosed into an extrovert who criticized the government that he had so loyally served. He repeatedly emphasized that poverty had become a national problem and stressed the need to change Mexico's economic development model.

As expected, Echeverría breezed through the election with 85 percent of the vote, only 4 percent less than Díaz Ordaz had received in 1964. PRI candidates for the Chamber of Deputies won every single-member district, indicating the party's continued dominance of the political scene.

Echeverría's economic policy, known as "shared development," involved massive state intervention to stimulate the economy. The economic emphasis shifted from increasing gross national product to job creation and the redistribution of income. Echeverría initially planned to finance his ambitious programs by increasing taxes on the wealthy. However, this effort failed due to stiff opposition from the private sector and from within the PRI. As this incident indicated, presidents were powerful but not omnipotent.

Rather than relying on increased taxes, Echeverría financed government spending, which almost quadrupled between 1971 and 1975, by printing money and borrowing from aboard. This borrowing resulted in Mexico's public foreign debt increasing from $4.7 billion in 1970 to $21.6 billion in 1976. Historian Enrique Krauze commented on Echeverría's profligate spending: "With the money (printed or borrowed) raining down from his hands, he would wash away the responsibility for 1968."

By the beginning of 1976, Echeverría had lost control over public expenditures. Inflation surged, resulting in an overvalued peso, which discouraged exports. Echeverría committed the same error his successors would repeat later in the century—he kept the peso stable relative to the dollar rather than devaluing to stimulate exports. The financial elite was already alienated by Echeverría's leftist rhetoric and high government spending. It responded by reducing investment and sending an estimated $4 billion out of Mexico in 1976. At the same time, increased government investment resulted in massive imports, which worsened Mexico's trade deficit. Between 1970 and 1975, this deficit increased from $1.0 billion to $3.7 billion.

Eventually, Echeverría was forced to face the obvious—the exchange rate could no longer be maintained. On August 31, 1976, for the first time since 1954, the peso was devalued. The government allowed the peso to float—"like a rock" as Mexicans wryly noted—and it declined from 12.5 to the dollar to 28.5 before the end of the year.

Unlike the 1954 devaluation, which was well timed, the 1976 devaluation was far too late in coming. This allowed speculators to drain financial reserves and ruined the incumbents' reputation for sound financial management. It also left the government financially prostrate, so that it was forced to turn to the U.S. Treasury Department and the International Monetary Fund (IMF) for a bailout, thus sacrificing the nationalistic principles that Echeverría had proclaimed.

In an attempt to win back disaffected young people, Echeverría lowered the voting age and offered an amnesty to activists convicted of crimes associated with the 1968 student movement. He expanded social security coverage (which included health care) from 12 million to 22 million and increased government spending for social programs to almost 24 percent of the budget. Under Echeverría, the economy, which grew at an average rate of 5.6 percent, continued to outpace population growth.

Echeverría was extremely unpopular when he left office, and his presidency was widely regarded as a failure. The 1976 devaluation shattered the illusion of progress associated with Mexico's "economic miracle." That year inflation hit 40 percent and economic growth slowed to 2 percent of gross national product—well below the rate of population increase. In the final tense months of his administration, rumors of a military coup circulated widely.

On September 22, 1975, Mexicans learned that Treasury Secretary López Portillo would be their next president. On December 1, 1976, López Portillo took office in the midst of uncertainty, capital flight, inflation, and political and economic crisis. In his inaugural address, he announced that Mexico had to unite, heal its wounds, and move on as one. Absent from the speech was Echeverría's reformist rhetoric. Rather López Portillo attempted to regain the support of the business community by announcing an "alliance for production" between the public and private sectors. The president of the American Chamber of Commerce in Mexico declared the inaugural address reflected "the kind of philosophy that businessmen can understand."

By mid-term, José López Portillo found himself free of the IMF-mandated belt-tightening that had characterized his first years in office. Early in his term, it became apparent that Mexico's oil reserves were among the largest in the world. Rather than waiting for increased oil sales to finance an expansion of production capacity, Mexico began to borrow abroad. As billions of dollars were borrowed, it appeared that at long last Mexico could have it all—rapid economic growth and generous social programs.

López Portillo used oil revenue (or money borrowed in anticipation of oil revenue) to build new refineries, pipelines, tanker facilities, and petrochemical plants. The government undertook an ambitious program to stimulate food production and extended superhighways and Mexico City's subway system. A nuclear power plant, power lines to rural areas, and rural health centers sprang up. Airports, tourist facilities, and the steel industry were expanded. As historian Enrique Krauze noted, "Everything was to be modernized by the end of the *sexenio* [presidential term]."

Between 1978 and 1981, economic growth averaged 8.4 percent a year. Massive government investment accelerated economic growth, which induced foreign and domestic corporations to invest. Increased employment, investment, and demand had a ripple effect throughout the economy. The whole nation was caught up in what can only be described as "oil fever." López Portillo declared that in the future Mexico's biggest economic problem would be the "management of abundance."

Beginning in mid-1981, world oil prices plummeted due to a combination of energy conservation in the developed world, OPEC members' cheating on production quotas, and a worldwide recession. In response to the fall in oil prices, foreign lending ceased. Unfortunately for Mexico, just as oil prices were plummeting, the United States raised interest rates to combat inflation at home. As individuals and businesses observed the plunge in oil prices and the increase in U.S. interest rates, they began moving their money out of Mexico in anticipation of an economic crisis. In 1981 and 1982, capital flight totaled $20 billion.

Even though orthodox economic doctrine would have indicated a devaluation of the peso, López Portillo viewed such a move as surrendering to his enemies. In a speech on February 5, 1982, he said he would "defend the peso like a dog." Thirteen days later the peso was devalued, and its value plunged. By the end of 1982, the Mexican currency was trading at 157 to the dollar, down from 26 at the beginning of the year.

In August, Mexico grabbed headlines around the world when it announced that it could not service its $80 billion foreign debt—the largest among the developing countries. Loans to Mexico by the nine largest U.S. banks equaled 44 percent of their capital. The U.S. government, loath to see U.S. banks and the Mexican economy go under, stepped in. Paul Volcker, chairman of the U.S. Federal Reserve, cobbled together a rescue package to avoid the damage to the international monetary system that an outright default by a major debtor nation would produce.

SALVADOR NAVA

During the 1950s Gonzalo Santos established a political fiefdom (*cacicazgo*) in the state of San Luis Potosí. In 1958, Salvador Nava a forty-four-year-old oculist challenged Santos's control by running for mayor of the city of San Luis Potosí (both city and state bear the same name). Nava's twenty-to-one victory over Santos's candidate was recognized since the national PRI organization sought to weaken Santos, a *cacique* not sufficiently under its control.

As mayor, Nava publicly accounted for all municipal spending—a highly unusual move. As Nava's popularity soared, his backers urged him to run for governor and definitively undermine Santos's power. Nava accepted the challenge and declared he would like to be the PRI gubernatorial candidate. This presented the national PRI organization with a dilemma. If it allowed Nava to run and undercut Santos's power, it would set the unwanted precedent of citizens announcing gubernatorial candidacies on their own. However, if the party denied Nava the governorship, it would allow Santos to remain in power. The PRI decided that democracy was a greater danger to the party than a *cacique* and denied Nava the PRI candidacy, even though he was clearly the most popular political figure in the state.

Nava was not easily daunted and in 1961 ran as the gubernatorial candidate of the Potosí Civic Alliance, a coalition with a variegated base ranging from PANistas to Communists. The election, which historian Enrique Krauze characterized as a "scandalous fraud," denied Nava the governorship. Protestors were met by gunfire, which claimed numerous victims. Nava was arrested, tortured, and taken to Military Camp Number One in Mexico City. He was later transferred to Lecumberri Prison, where he was held a month and released. Santos's candidate was allowed to serve as governor. The political establishment thought it had seen the last of Nava.

Nava, however, returned to politics in 1982 to challenge the control Carlos Jonguitud, a new *cacique*, exercised over San Luis Potosí municipal politics. (Santos had died in 1978.) Many viewed Nava's second mayoral candidacy as quixotic since Jonguitud derived political strength not only as governor of the state, but also as head of the powerful National Teachers Union.

Nava successfully wrested control of the city from the Jonguitud machine by building broad-based support, which included railroad workers, dissident PRI members, and owners of medium-sized businesses. The PAN supported his candidacy, as did some of the left. Nava also enjoyed good neighborhood organization. In December 1982, Nava won the mayoral race with 58,575 votes, compared with 20,249 for the PRI. As was the case with other opposition victories early in the de la Madrid administration, Nava's victory was quickly recognized.

Once Nava became mayor, municipal workers, controlled by Jonguitud, refused to perform services. Rather than confront them, Nava supporters, especially rail workers, mobilized labor and equipment to keep the city running. With such strong support, Nava successfully finished his term.

In 1991, Nava announced his second gubernatorial candidacy, thus joining millions of other Mexicans in the struggle for democracy. He declared that what was important was not the ideology of the various political parties, but ending the one-party system. His campaign organization, the

Potosí Democratic Coalition, included both the PAN and the PRD. Nava's campaign was financed by passing the hat at campaign rallies. His campaign called for democratic elections, freedom of the press, independent electoral institutions, and ending corruption.

Opposing Nava was PRI candidate Fausto Zapata, a former senator who had served as press chief for President Echeverría. Zapata's campaign relied on the financial support of the twenty wealthiest businessmen in the state. President Salinas, who visited the state to inaugurate public works shortly before the election, strongly endorsed Zapata.

The media, which overwhelmingly supported Zapata, attempted to link Nava to "subversion" and referred to him as "violent." Nava commented on his inability to get coverage in the local press, "Our newspaper will be the public plazas." The Nava campaign even established its own newspaper, *La Tribuna*, to circumvent the news blackout.

In August 1991, Zapata was declared the winner of the election. Nava supporters charged that the PRI had added 100,000 "phantom voters" to the voter rolls, while purging 80,000 Nava supporters. Nava poll watchers were turned away at half of the polling places. Many Nava supporters were unable to vote since their voter registration cards had not been delivered. When asked how the 1991 elections differed from the gubernatorial elections that had been stolen from him in 1961, Nava replied, "Then they stole votes at gun point, now they use a computer." In 1991, while the Federal Electoral Institute was organizing increasingly clean presidential and congressional elections, gubernatorial and municipal elections were still under the sway of old-line PRI "dinosaurs" whose commitment to democracy was at best minimal.

On September 26, Fausto Zapata (nicknamed by Nava supporters as Fausto La Rata) was sworn in as governor in a heavily guarded auditorium. At the same time, Nava was sworn in as the "legitimate" governor before a crowd of 30,000 in a public plaza. To keep the electoral issue alive, Nava deliberately avoided the legally mandated appeal process, realizing that it would lead to a dead end and an affirmation of the PRI victory.

Rather Nava announced that he would stage a 287-mile protest march from San Luis Potosí to Mexico City. He scheduled his arrival for November 1, the date of Salinas's state of the nation speech. Nava's march, which began on September 28, had a single demand—that Salinas remove the "usurper" as governor of San Luis Potosí. (Cynics said Nava was demanding that one usurper remove another.) Walking nine miles a day, the seventy-seven-year-old Nava received more food and drink from sympathizers than he and his entourage could consume. Prominent intellectuals and opposition politicians, such as Cuauhtémoc Cárdenas and Vicente Fox, accompanied Nava for short stretches. The diversity of Nava's supporters was indicated by their footwear, which ranged from new Nikes to worn *huaraches* (sandals made from used tires). As it was intended, the march, known as the "March for Dignity," generated a never-ending series of images and sound bites for national media.

An all-woman sit-in surrounding the San Luis Potosí state capital building placed further pressure on Zapata. During Zapata's first six days as governor, he was only able to push his way into his office once—an effort which produced a violent confrontation between PRI members and Nava supporters who were blocking the building's entrances.

On October 9, after having been called to Mexico City to confer with President Salinas, Zapata resigned as governor "to avoid strife." Nava's tactics were especially effective since the longer the protests lasted, the more they tarnished Salinas's image at a time he was beginning negotiations for the North American Free Trade Agreement. Nava relied on his occupying the political center, which allowed him to unite the opposition and at the same time prevent the PRI from attacking him as a dangerous radical or a reactionary conservative.

As soon as Zapata resigned, Nava suspended his march and returned home as a conquering hero. Upon his return home, Nava commented, "It is a triumph of the struggle of the people of San Luis Potosí, but it is still not a triumph of democracy." He urged his followers to organize for upcoming municipal elections and for the special election to replace the interim governor who replaced Zapata. Dr. Nava was not a candidate in the race to replace the interim governor, since he died of cancer in 1992.

In his September 1982 state of the nation address, López Portillo stunned the nation by announcing the nationalization of Mexico's private banks. The bank nationalization was a desperate attempt to deflect criticism from the economic crisis, neutralize Mexico's restless left, and reassert the PRI's revolutionary credentials. The nationalization greatly increased the economic role of government, which began to allocate credit and manage the numerous industrial and commercial firms that the banks had owned.

López Portillo's 1982 bank nationalization produced a qualitative change in relations between business and government. For the first time since the Revolution, owners of capital abandoned closed-door negotiations with the political elite and sought political power for themselves. Owners of small and medium-sized businesses, especially in the north, felt that the bank nationalization indicated the danger of a presidency whose powers were unchecked by the political system— constrained neither by opposition political parties nor by Congress.

Inflation reduced buying power; the lack of credit halted job creation, and the budget crisis lowered social spending, including subsidies for bread, corn, electricity, and gasoline. The PAN, the Catholic Church, and private media joined the business elite in attacking the bank nationalization. The López Portillo administration was the swan song of the activist post-revolutionary state—a final, gigantic effort that left it exhausted and from which it never recovered.

Further undermining the image of the government during López Portillo's term was an explosion of corruption, facilitated by billions of poorly audited petrodollars flowing through state coffers. *New York Times* correspondent Alan Riding noted, "Almost every purchase by Petróleos Mexicanos involved a kickback of 10 or 15 percent." According to some estimates, López Portillo himself accumulated more than $1 billion during his presidency.

THE EMERGENCE OF NEOLIBERALISM, 1982–2000

On September 25, 1981, labor leader Fidel Velázquez announced that the 1982 PRI presidential candidate would be López Portillo's friend and disciple Budget and Planning Minister Miguel de la Madrid.

De la Madrid, an uninspiring speaker lacking the faintest glimmer of charisma, set out on a conventional PRI-style campaign. On the campaign trail, he emphasized that his administration would eliminate public corruption and modernize, but offered few specific solutions to Mexico's pressing economic problems. His was the first Mexican presidential campaign to rely heavily on television—a medium that repeatedly broadcast his interviews.

Seven political parties fielded presidential candidates in 1982 thanks to a political reform making it easier to register new political parties. The reform, however, did little to redress the imbalance between the PRI and the political opposition. While the government distributed $20 million to finance opposition campaigns, the PRI spent an estimated $300 million on its own campaign.

The 1982 economic collapse tainted both de la Madrid and the political system. The PRI candidate received only 70 percent of the vote, the lowest the official party had received in its history. Despite this decline, the PRI remained firmly in control of the electoral scene. Its candidates for the Chamber of Deputes won 299 of the 300 directly elected seats.

Upon taking office, de la Madrid faced rampant inflation, a huge budget deficit, massive foreign debt, collapsing oil prices, a shrinking economy, and growing labor unrest. He had little leeway in dealing with these problems since at the time of the 1982 economic crash, the Mexican government, in exchange for its IMF loan, had agreed to raise taxes, lower subsidies, reduce the budget deficit, cap wage increases, and limit public-sector borrowing.

De la Madrid reduced public investment and lowered subsidies for a wide range of goods and services, including food, electricity, health care, and the Mexico City subway. Finally, in a measure supported by the government-dominated trade union federation, the Mexican Workers Federation

(CTM), 1983 wage "increases" were limited to 40 percent while inflation reached nearly 81 percent. This last measure was aimed not at deficit reduction but at regaining business support.

De la Madrid's recovery program notwithstanding, the overriding economic issue became paying interest on the huge foreign debt accumulated under López Portillo, even if that meant sacrificing domestic consumption. Exports provided the wherewithal to make annual interest payments of $13 billion. Reduction of debt principal was a financial impossibility.

The economy shrank by 4.7 percent in 1983. An estimated 1 million Mexicans lost their jobs, many businesses closed, and most construction was suspended. The optimism of the 1950s and 1960s was replaced by despair.

As if the economy were not enough to tax de la Madrid, his economic problems soon became political problems. Owners of small and medium-sized businesses began to defect to the PAN, and austerity undermined the PRI's traditional labor and peasant base. To make matters worse, Mexicans quit blaming problems on presidents who as individuals made mistakes and began to question a system that put such power in the hands of a single individual.

By the end of 1983, the PRI had lost mayoral races in the capitals of San Luis Potosí, Durango, Guanajuato, Sonora, and Chihuahua, as well the race in Ciudad Juárez, the sixth largest city in the country.

Under pressure from local PRI cadres and an embarrassing string of electoral defeats, de la Madrid returned to the PRI's roots—election fraud. Labor leader Fidel Velázquez supported this shift noting: "We revolutionaries got where we are by bullets. Anyone wanting to remove us can't do it with the ballot, they'll have to use bullets too."

Beginning with the September 1983 elections in Baja California through the November 1984 elections in Yucatán, systematic government-managed electoral fraud became standard operating procedure. In 1984, the PRI claimed victory in thirty-five of the thirty-eight municipalities in the northern border state of Coahuila.

These electoral "victories" came at a high cost for the PRI. PAN members refused to play by the traditional rules of the game, which called for them to verbally protest PRI electoral fraud and then meekly wait until the next election when their participation would once again validate the process. Rather, a new generation of aggressive, militant PANistas raised the political ante. PAN protestors in Coahuila rioted and burned city halls in two of the cities where they claimed election fraud. To maximize their coverage in both domestic and foreign media, PANistas would seize bridges across the Rio Grande to publicize their fraud charges.

By 1986, rather than legitimizing the PRI, elections delegitimized the party. This created a negative feedback loop since local elections increasingly attracted national and international attention, which increasingly exposed fraud, which increasingly delegitimized the PRI.

Several factors—in addition to massive debt payments—retarded economic growth during de la Madrid's term. Between 1982 and 1988, public investment declined by 50 percent while private investment declined by 15 percent. Decreased private investment reflected a lack of confidence in government and excess production capacity. Despite receiving favorable treatment from the government, between 1983 and 1985, the wary business elite sent $16 billion out of the country. A fall in oil prices from $27 a barrel in 1985 to $14 in 1986 further undermined recovery efforts.

In response to severe economic problems, de la Madrid shifted the fundamental economic assumptions concerning the Mexican economy. His administration abandoned the model of an economy oriented toward the internal market with the state stimulating production in a Keynesian fashion and protecting industry from foreign competition. Replacing the old model was the notion that Mexico should create an internationally competitive export-oriented economy. Foreign investment was to become the engine of growth. Such a model, often referred to as "neoliberal," foresaw the government's ceasing to direct energies and initiatives of society and instead simply regulating and overseeing growth. Allowing business to make most investment decisions represented a major shift in power from government to the private sector.

While economic problems were mounting, an informal group within the PRI, which became known as the Democratic Current, questioned de la Madrid's economic and social policies and raised the issue of democratic candidate selection. It also highlighted the uncomfortable fact that the PRI served to implement presidential decisions and promote presidentially selected candidates, not to discuss issues.

In July 1987, the Democratic Current offered Cuauhtémoc Cárdenas as a potential PRI presidential candidate. Cárdenas, a former governor of Michoacán, was best known as the son of President Lázaro Cárdenas.

On the morning of October 4, 1987, the PRI brought in a compliant crowd to support its presidential candidate, whose name they were not yet aware of. Just as they were expected to do, its members cheered when they were informed that Carlos Salinas de Gortari, de la Madrid's secretary of budget and planning, would be the PRI candidate.

On October 14, 1987, Cuauhtémoc Cárdenas accepted the nomination of the Authentic Party of the Mexican Revolution, a small political party that had previously backed PRI presidential candidates. Subsequently two other small parties also nominated Cárdenas. This joint campaign, which became known as the Democratic National Front (FDN), soon incorporated a variety of social movements that were not recognized as political parties.

Despite his lack of financial backing and organization, several factors favored Cárdenas. As the son of one of Mexico's most revered presidents, he inherited a deep well of popularity and good will. Though he lacked traditional political charisma, his somber style attracted many who were repelled by PRI demagogy. Cárdenas could appeal to broad sectors of the population that had suffered as a result of the economic crisis of the 1980s.

The FDN platform declared de la Madrid's economic policies were impoverishing the majority. It called for limiting foreign investment and proposed a return to populist redistribution of wealth, an end to the privatization of state enterprises, and a suspension of foreign debt payments.

LETTER TO CÁRDENAS

[During his 1988 presidential campaign Cuauhtémoc Cárdenas raised the hopes of many of Mexico's downtrodden. They wrote many letters such as the following expressing their hopes and lamenting their problems.]

Sir: You are the Hope of all of the Poor You must sit in the presidential chair so as to put a stop to all these diabolical functionaries who think only about how to raise the price of everything with you as president in 6 years you will be able to put everything in order you will visit all the poor neighborhoods and get to know the poor people you will hear all of the commentaries of the people who have been dragged along by the PRI in its cycle the people are very wrought up they no longer believe in it. You are the hope you must give all you have to the poor people you being president we are going to invite the people to sell all they can and give you all the money we collect so as to pay the debts sir. forgive the poor writing and lack of penmanship but go with all the heart of a Mexican citizen who desires with all his family and friends your triumph for the well being of the Mexican people thank you.

Tampico

Source: Gilbert Joseph and Timothy J. Henderson (eds.) (2002) *The Mexico Reader*. Durham, N.C.: Duke University Press, p. 591.

The dominant theme of Salinas's campaign, which cost an estimated $800 million, was "modernization." Such modernization included a continuation of de la Madrid's opening the Mexican market to imports, export promotion, continued debt service, and the welcoming of foreign capital.

The PRI proudly proclaimed election returns would be tabulated on a central government computer and made available to the public real time. However, on the evening of election day, July 6, 1988, just as the returns began coming in, the computer crashed. Early returns from urban boxes had favored Cárdenas, and the PRI was apparently afraid its traditional rural base would be incapable of overcoming Cárdenas's lead.

A week after the election, the official results declared Salinas a winner with 50.7 percent of the vote. The returns credited Cárdenas with 31.1 percent and Manuel Clouthier, the PAN candidate, with 16.8 percent. Two other small parties received the remainder of the vote. In the bellwether Federal District, the PRI claimed only 27.3 percent of the vote.

The official returns can be interpreted in three ways. First, they accurately reflected the vote. Second, Salinas won with only a plurality, and the official total was inflated to enhance his mandate. A Cárdenas victory is a third possibility.

An August 1989 *Los Angeles Times* poll found that only 24 percent of Mexicans believed that Salinas had won. Partially burned ballots marked for Cárdenas were found in many locations. Statistical anomalies abounded. In some precincts, by official count, Salinas received 100 percent of the vote, while in adjacent precincts with the same socioeconomic make-up, he only received 30 percent. Far more than 10 percent of the PRI ballot box totals ended in zero, indicating not random distribution but election officials adding a zero to the PRI vote total on the assumption that no one would notice a zero.

Cárdenas claimed that he had won the presidency, but fearing uncontrollable escalation, he did not call for his followers to engage in illegal acts, such as seizing buildings, to press his claim. He concluded he could not overturn the official results by creating disorder.

The 1988 elections were significant because for the first time they clearly indicated that opposition parties were strong enough to win, shattering the assumption that PRI victories were inevitable. The departure of Cuauhtémoc Cárdenas and the Democratic Current from the PRI left the party more conservative since it removed the political heirs of Lázaro Cárdenas from inside the party.

After his inauguration, Salinas quickly confounded his critics by making several bold moves. On January 10, 1989, he sent the army to arrest Joaquín Hernández Galicia who, as head of the oil workers, presided over Mexico's most powerful and corrupt labor union. The removal of Hernández Galicia repaid him for his support for Cárdenas in the 1988 elections. Soon after that, Salinas forced the retirement of Carlos Jonguitud Barrios, the long-entrenched leader of the national teachers union, who had proved unable to quell dissident teachers who favored union democracy. These moves established that, the dubious election notwithstanding, Salinas was very much the man in charge.

After the 1988 elections, the PAN and Cárdenas's FDN formed a de facto alliance to protest electoral fraud. Once in office, Salinas adroitly split this alliance, creating his own de facto alliance with the PAN leadership, while isolating the Cárdenas-led faction. This led the PAN president to announce that the Salinas administration could "legitimize itself through the exercising power well."

At the beginning of the Salinas administration, the debt question cast a pall over Mexico. Even though interest and amortization paid during the de la Madrid administration totaled $60 billion, the foreign debt increased from $92 billion in 1982 to $100 billion in 1988. In 1988 interest payments on the debt totaled 17.7 percent of GDP.

In October 1988, Cárdenas called for the replacement of the FDN—an unwieldy four-party alliance that was already disintegrating—with a new center-left party, the Party of the Democratic

Revolution (PRD). The PRD, which proclaimed to uphold the values of the Mexican Revolution, refused to cooperate with what it branded the "usurper" administration.

Salinas's effort to split the post-election alliance between Cárdenas and the PAN dovetailed with the PAN's own perception that it would gain stature and power by working with the PRI and refashioning its image as that of a party that could govern. This emerging PAN–PRI alliance saw Salinas recognizing some PAN electoral victories and the PAN's embracing flawed PRI political reforms that the PRI did not have enough votes to pass on its own in the Chamber of Deputies. Salinas felt comfortable working with the PAN since, after the PRI's switch to neoliberal policies, the PRI and the PAN were close ideologically.

Salinas's favoring the PAN became apparent when, after repeated protests charging stolen gubernatorial elections, a PAN victory was recognized in the 1989 gubernatorial election in Baja California.

Salinas undercut the three major pillars of the Revolution. He privatized numerous state enterprises, abandoned Mexico's traditionally independent foreign policy, and allowed the sale of *ejido* land. He welcomed the pope and privatized the Cananea copper mine—a revolutionary icon. The popularity of his moves was such that, at the time of his last state of the nation address, he was widely applauded for his accomplishments.

Salinas further refined the neoliberal economic model he had helped introduce during the de la Madrid administration. He renegotiated the foreign debt and negotiated a free trade agreement with the United States and Canada (NAFTA). He deregulated the economy to attract foreign investment and reestablished amicable relations with the business sector, which led to increased investment.

Given Salinas's popularity, it appeared that the 1994 transfer of power to Salinas's successor would be routine. On November 28, 1993, Salinas named Secretary of Social Development Luis Donaldo Colosio as the PRI's presidential candidate. Before joining Salinas's cabinet, Colosio had served as president of the PRI and as a senator.

The indigenous rebellion in Chiapas on New Year's Day 1994 upset the carefully laid plans for Colosio's campaign. The Mexican public's attention was so firmly riveted on Chiapas that the first two months of Colosio's ill-fated campaign passed almost unnoticed.

On March 23, as he was leaving a campaign rally in the border city of Tijuana, Colosio was gunned down. A twenty-three-year old factory worker, Mario Aburto, was arrested on the spot and charged with assassinating Colosio. The government declared that Aburto was a "lone nut" (à la Lee Harvey Oswald) and sentenced him to forty-two years in prison. Conspiracy theories to explain the assassination abounded. Blame was most commonly laid at the feet of hardliners at the national level of the PRI who feared reforms Colosio might carry out. None of the various explanations officially offered for the Colosio assassination have satisfied Mexican public opinion.

On March 29, six days after Colosio's assassination, Salinas assembled a group of state governors and PRI officials in the presidential residence and informed them that the replacement presidential candidate would be Ernesto Zedillo, who had served in his cabinet as secretary of budget and planning and as secretary of education.

The August 21, 1994 presidential election featured a number of innovations that were clearly an improvement over elections past. They were organized by an independent agency, the Federal Electoral Institute (IFE), headed by Jorge Carpizo, the widely respected former director of the National Human Rights Commission (CNDH).

The final vote totals only confirmed what polling data had indicated. Zedillo received 50.18 percent of the valid votes, PAN candidate Diego Fernández de Cevallos 26.69 percent, and Cárdenas, who was the PRD candidate, 17.08 percent. The PRI won 275 of the 300 single-member congressional districts. In an apparent validation of the democratic process, voter turn-out was a near record 77.7 percent.

Having a popular incumbent president favored the PRI, as did the party's having far more resources at its disposal than did other parties. A study by the IFE reported that the PRI accounted for 71.4 percent of campaign spending, leaving the other parties with 28.6 percent. As in elections past, media coverage favored the PRI.

At the end of his term in November 1994, Salinas enjoyed a 66 percent approval rating. By February of 1995, 77 percent of those queried felt that Salinas should be put on trial. Rarely in history has any president's popularity fallen so precipitously so soon after leaving office.

A few weeks after Salinas left office, Mexico suffered its worst economic downturn since the Depression. The peso had become seriously overvalued and, rather than devaluing it before he left office, Salinas left the devaluation for his successor. The blame he received for this was intensified by the widespread belief that his failure to devalue resulted from his aspiring to become executive director of the newly created World Trade Organization—a post he would be unlikely to receive if he were perceived as having bungled the economy.

On December 19, 1994, eighteen days after Zedillo's inauguration, Mexico's peso collapsed. The crisis resulted from the combination of:

- the increasing outflow of dollars resulting from debt payments and fear of political instability;
- the increasing overvaluation of the peso which led to the trade deficit's ballooning from $1 billion in 1990 to $18.5 billion in 1994;
- the increasing use of short-term, high-interest treasury bonds (*tesobonos*) to finance this outflow;
- the U.S. Federal Reserve's raising interest rates, which made investing in Mexico less attractive.

In response to the crisis, the government devalued the peso by 50 percent. Zedillo offered an austerity plan designed to restart the economy and restore investor confidence. It included further decreases in government expenditures, increases in the price of gasoline and electricity, and an increase in value-added tax (VAT) from 10 percent to 15 percent.

In January U.S. President Bill Clinton provided Mexico with $20 billion in loan guarantees from the Treasury Department's Exchange Stabilization Fund. This was accompanied by loans of $17.8 billion from the IMF and $10 billion from the Bank of International Settlements. Clinton and the international financiers felt it was necessary to intervene to: 1) protect U.S. investors who otherwise would have lost their capital; 2) restore calm in international financial markets; 3) support Zedillo and the PRI; 4) maintain confidence in NAFTA; 5) prevent a massive decline of U.S. exports to Mexico; and 6) avoid a possible refugee crisis.

The impact of lower government spending, higher government fees and taxes, and higher interest rates (to keep even more investors from fleeing Mexico) threw the economy into reverse. In 1995, the GDP fell by 6.6 percent. That year, as more than 1 million Mexicans reached working age, there were 750,000 layoffs. Per capita income fell below the 1980 level. The annual interest on loans, mortgages, and credit cards reached 100 percent, causing massive defaults among middle-class debtors. Banks, businesses, producers, and consumers all suffered as a result of the crisis.

In response to the crash of the peso and the Chiapas uprising, the Zedillo administration legislated another political reform in hopes of reversing a spate of PRI electoral defeats. This reform, the last of the twentieth century, had special significance since it set the ground rules for the 2000 presidential race.

The 1996 political reform granted Congress the power to select nine general council members who would head the Federal Electoral Institute (IFE). This provided the IFE with complete autonomy from political parties and the executive branch of government. Campaign financing was greatly increased and made more equitable.

In 1997, the IFE spent $264 million on organizing truly competitive congressional elections. Clear limits on campaign spending, more access to radio and TV for opposition parties, and more balanced coverage of the opposition on TV newscasts contributed to electoral fairness. For the first time, the distribution of public campaign financing roughly matched the proportion of the vote the major parties received.

The PRI received only 39.1 percent of the vote in the 1997 elections, which cost it its majority in the Chamber of Deputies. Several of those taking seats in the newly elected Congress were veterans of the 1968 student movement. Almost as remarkable as the PRI's losing its control over Congress was the broad range of opinion that characterized the elections as fair. Historian Enrique Krauze declared, "True democracy finally came to Mexico." By 1997, as a result of numerous political reforms, the political playing field in Mexico was as close to level as those in many established democracies.

Reinvigorating Mexico's economy forms a lasting part of Zedillo's legacy. Between 1996 and 2000, buoyed by high oil prices and exports to its booming NAFTA partner to the north, Mexico's GDP averaged 5.4 percent growth. By the end of Zedillo's term, inflation had declined to a single digit. In 2000, the Mexican economy was deemed so sound that, for the first time, Moody's Investment Service rated Mexico as investment grade.

Democratization, as well as economic recovery, enhanced Zedillo's legacy. His handling of the 2000 presidential election further bolstered his standing. The week before the election, *Wall Street Journal* writers Peter Fritsch and José de Córdoba commented, "The victor in Mexico's hotly contested presidential election this Sunday is clear: Ernesto Zedillo Ponce de León." Not surprisingly, at the end of his term, Zedillo enjoyed a 69 percent approval rating, up from 31 percent five years earlier.

THE MILITARY

As the military suppressed the urban and rural guerrilla groups that sprang up after the 1968 student movement, its influence in governing circles increased. During the Echeverría administration (1970–76), a new 900-acre military academy was built on the southern outskirts of Mexico City—its cost a military secret.

Military involvement with Chiapas increased after the indigenous rebellion there in 1994. After its initial ten-day counteroffensive, the military was assigned the role of cordoning off, but not crushing, the rebel force. Tens of thousands of troops were permanently stationed around rebel-occupied areas.

The military assumed a greatly increased role in fighting illegal drug production. By 2000, 36,000 troops were involved in drug eradication. In parts of Oaxaca, Sinaloa, Jalisco, and Guerrero, where the military concentrated its forces to fight drugs, the army became de facto the supreme authority. The military's role in drug enforcement inevitably opened the door to corruption. It also led to widespread human rights abuse. In 1990, Americas Watch reported that "torture and political killings are still institutionalized techniques in the military."

As Mexico opened its economy to the rest of the world, the Mexican military also opened itself to the outside world, which, given the reality of geopolitics, meant the United States. U.S. arms sales to Mexico, which had totaled only $32.3 million dollars between 1950 and 1979, soared to $508.4 million between 1980 and 1988. The number of Mexican military officers trained in the United States increased.

The military's new responsibilities were reflected in an increased share of the federal budget and in the number of troops. After World War II Mexican military spending was very low by world standards—typically between 2 and 3 percent of the federal budget. However, under President Zedillo with increased military participation in the war against drugs, unrest in Central America, and home-grown conflicts such as the rebellion in Chiapas, military spending rose to 5 percent of the federal budget. Army personnel increased from 92,659 in 1976 to 196,697 in 2000.

THE POLITICAL OPPOSITION

The Party of the Democratic Revolution (PRD)

The broad goals of the new party, the PRD, were democratization, social justice, an independent foreign policy, a role for the state in the economy, and defense of the revolutionary heritage, including Pemex. The party's positions echoed the nationalistic, populist rhetoric the PRI abandoned after the 1980s. Even though the PRI tarred the PRD as forming a part of the radical left, it would have been considered a moderate social democratic party if it had been in Europe.

The fortunes of the PRD improved after the 1994 elections. The party's improved fortunes were apparent in 1997, as Cuauhtémoc Cárdenas, the PRD candidate for mayor of Mexico City, won with 46 percent of the vote, the same percentage of the vote he received there in 1988. This impressive total was facilitated by Cárdenas's using the vastly increased financial resources provided by the 1996 political reform to produce sophisticated, clever TV commercials. Just before the 2000 presidential elections, 116 deputies and fourteen senators represented the party in Congress. PRD mayors and governors presided over a quarter of the population, and the party was either the first or second strongest political force in fourteen states.

The National Action Party (PAN)

> The forces leading the Mexican Revolution to victory came from the North. This same region is now home to forces that propose to bury the Revolution.
>
> (Abraham Nuncio, 1986)

José Ángel Conchello's 1972–75 term as PAN president marked a turning point in the history of the party. Conchello, a Nuevo León businessman, considered that Echeverría's fiscal policies were irresponsible and that the increasing economic role of the state was detrimental to the market and to private property. This emphasis on economic policy soon drew the wrath of traditionalists under the leadership of 1970 PAN presidential candidate Efraín González Morfín. Traditionalists argued that the political upstarts, led by Conchello, were threatening to undermine the party's identity and open the way into the party for political opportunists who had no interest in the party's doctrine. The heated debate over the direction the party should take went on almost unnoticed by the public. The lack of public interest in the PAN is indicated by the party's winning only nineteen mayoral elections between 1970 and 1976.

Three events moved the PAN from civic education to contending for power, especially in northern Mexico. The first was a massive land expropriation in northwest Mexico carried out in 1976 by President Echeverría. The second was the 1982 bank nationalization ordered by President López Portillo. The third was the economic crisis of the 1980s. These events convinced many, including large numbers of small- and medium-sized business owners, that the PRI could no longer be trusted with the reins of power and that the PAN was the logical alternative. Early in de la Madrid's 1982–88 term, these three events led to a wave of PAN electoral victories in northern Mexico.

As the old political and economic model was collapsing in the 1980s, the PAN successfully capitalized on discontent based on: 1) its long-term opposition to an overarching state; 2) opposition to an all-powerful presidency; 3) its advocacy of private enterprise; and 4) its promotion of municipal and states rights. The party de-emphasized its earlier adherence to Christian doctrine. Instead it became a vehicle for middle-class protest. Critiques of the incumbent government dominated its campaigns. The party increasingly emphasized individual merit and the notion that the state had very limited social responsibility. The PAN, which had been considered as an anachronism during the Mexican economic miracle of the 1960s, emerged as the standard-bearer

369

of modernity. By the 1980s, as the PAN rode a wave of democracy and free-market economics, the authoritarian PRI increasingly appeared to be the anachronism.

During the Salinas administration, dealing with a regime of dubious legitimacy presented the PAN with a dilemma. Luis H. Álvarez, who served as president of the party between 1987 and 1993, decided the best interests of the party would be served by positioning the PAN as an alternative governing party. Salinas needed the PAN to enhance his own democratic image. Álvarez used the threat of breaking off contact with Salinas to ensure the recognition of PAN electoral victories and to leverage political and economic reforms to his party's liking.

Regardless of whether they were compatible with traditional PAN doctrine, the policies adopted by the party during the Salinas administration were an enormous electoral success. The PAN's vote increased from 3.2 million in 1988 to 9.0 million in 1994.

The party's momentum continued into the Zedillo administration (1994–2000) since: 1) after the PAN won the governorship of Baja California, the PRI was seen as vulnerable; 2) the party was considered to be a peaceful path to change, as opposed (especially) to the indigenous rebels in Chiapas; 3) existing PAN governments were considered more efficient and honest than their PRI predecessors; 4) the PAN had developed the image as a stable, well-established party; and 5) the party made effective use of radio and TV. As of June 1999, there were six PAN governors and 215 mayors. The party held 24 percent of the seats in both the Chamber of Deputies and the Senate and administered 33.1 percent of the population at the state or municipal level.

At the end of the century, business-oriented PANistas held sway in the party. They brought the PAN much needed financial resources, leadership styles, organizational capabilities, and new advertising techniques drawn from their own private-sector experience. They often emphasized the link between leader and voter, ignoring the party and the government. They envisioned a sharp reduction in the state's role in Mexican society and were guided by an aggressive individualism and the notion that the best government was the least government.

HUMAN RIGHTS

The notion of human rights only entered Mexican political discourse in the relatively recent past. None of those protesting government suppression of the 1968 student movement invoked the notion of "human rights." Rather, condemnation of government action revolved around such notions as repression and violations of university autonomy.

Between 1970 and 1976, just as human rights issues were taking on increased significance throughout the Americas, Mexico went though a largely secret version of the same "Dirty War" that flared up in other Latin American countries. In Mexico, a part of the generation of 1968 organized guerilla groups which clashed with the government and the army. During this period, political arrests, torture, disappearances, and murder by security forces increased markedly. The government itself later identified more than 700 cases of enforced disappearances and more than a hundred extrajudicial executions during the Dirty War.

By 1994, Salinas's last year in office, there were no signs of his "modernization" when it came to human rights. An Amnesty International account of events that year reported:

> Scores of prisoners of conscience, mostly indigenous peasants, were detained. The widespread use of torture and ill-treatment by law enforcement agents continued to be reported. At least twenty people "disappeared" and the whereabouts of hundreds who "disappeared" in previous years remained unknown. Dozens of people were extrajudicially executed. Those responsible for human rights violations continued to benefit from impunity.[1]

In general, as long-time human rights activist Mariclaire Acosta observed, the human rights situation worsened under President Zedillo (1994–2000) as:

- rampant human rights violations occurred in Chiapas;
- the institutionalized presence of the military in many rural areas produced serious human rights abuses;
- those responsible for various massacres, especially in the state of Guerrero, remained unpunished.

MEXICAN SOCIETY

Trends

Several trends continued from mid-twentieth century through the end of the century. They include population increase, migration to the United States, and rural-to-urban migration.

This last trend, rural-to-urban migration, dates back to the nineteenth century. It has been driven by population increase, rural job loss, and higher wages and better employment opportunities in urban areas. Between 1970 and 2000, the rural population fell from 41.3 percent of Mexico's total population to 25.3 percent. However, during this period, due to increased population, the rural population actually rose from 19.9 million to 24.6 million.

Another long-term trend is an increase in the percentage of the workforce in the service sector, which includes commerce. In 1910, only 14.2 percent of the workforce was employed in the service sector. By 2000, this figure had increased to 56 percent.

Another trend is the massive expansion of the informal sector. The informal sector includes a wide variety of employment, such as ambulatory vendors, domestics, and street-corner services (shoe-shiners, for example). The defining characteristic of the informal sector is that it produces goods (such as tamales for sale on the street) or services (such as washing windshields at traffic lights) that are legal. However, it is distinct from what is often called the formal sector in that some or all regulations governing trade unions, the minimum wage, social security, taxes, and health and safety regulations are not observed.

Several factors drove millions into the informal sector. Well before the advent of NAFTA, the formal economy could not absorb the number of young people seeking a job for the first time. As wages declined in the 1980s, there was little monetary incentive to obtain a factory job rather than a job in the informal sector. The booming export sector was highly capital intensive. Between 1991 and 2001, exports increased by more than 300 percent, but formal employment in the export sector increased by less than 50 percent. High social security taxes deterred the hiring of low-skilled labor with formal contracts. Instead, such workers obtained informal employment. Finally, the cost and time required to obtain the legally required licenses to operate a business led many to bypass these requirements.

During the boom years, 1950 to 1980, the informal sector shrank from 37.4 percent to 35 percent of the workforce as formal job creation exceeded new entrants to the labor force. Between 1980 and 1994 this trend was reversed as only 3.7 million formal-sector jobs were created, but almost 1 million young people entered the labor force annually. Between 1989 and 2005, more than 70 percent of new job creation was in the informal sector.

The Social Impact of Neoliberal Development

Through the 1970s, the lot of the average Mexican continued to improve. The buying power of wages increased by 2.4 percent annually between 1971 and 1979. The government set guarantee prices for crops, subsidized agricultural credit, food for urban dwellers, and farm inputs such as fertilizer. Between 1970 and 1981 there was a 4.8 percent annual increase in job creation. The combination of rapid job growth, social programs, and government support for labor resulted in wealth becoming more evenly distributed during the 1970s. Those living in poverty declined from 75 percent of the population in 1960 to 48 percent in 1981.

As a result of the 1982 debt crisis and the decision to adopt neoliberal economic policies, per capita government social spending declined by 32.7 percent between 1982 and 1988. To reduce imports, the peso was devalued and as a result inflation soared. Since wage increases lagged far behind inflation, the buying power of wages declined by more than 7 percent annually between 1983 and 1988. Rather than intervening to distribute the costs of the crisis, the government welcomed the decline in wages, since that lowered the cost of labor and made Mexico more attractive to foreign investors, whom the government expected to finance Mexican development.

During the 1980s, 400,000 jobs disappeared, while at the same time the labor force increased by 8 million. Few jobs replaced those lost since both public and private investment declined. Those living on wages fared worse than those living on rents and property, thus worsening income distribution. Not only did income become less evenly distributed but there was also less to distribute as the per capita GDP declined by 10 percent between 1982 and 1987. The proportion of the Mexican population living in poverty increased from 68.5 percent in 1984 to 73.4 percent in 1989.

Between 1994 and 2003, non-*maquiladora* manufacturing wages declined, while productivity increased 24.7 percent. Many small- and medium-sized manufacturing firms closed their doors since they lacked access to credit which would have allowed them to modernize and compete in the global market. The owners of many mom-and-pop stores lost income as they were displaced by large-scale retail establishments such as Wal-Mart. The declining income of the rural poor, forced to compete with low-cost grain imports, also contributed to income concentration.

The rapid expansion of exports further concentrated wealth. Between 1993 and 1997, 300 firms, which produced 54.6 percent of Mexican exports, dominated the lucrative export sector. Technologically sophisticated plants producing goods for export required an increasingly skilled labor force. As a result, between 1984 and 1995, the buying power of skilled workers increased by 8 percent, while that of unskilled workers decreased by 22 percent.

The Elite

At the end of the century, Mexico's elite included top government officials, owners of large firms, managers of foreign corporations, and administrators of public-sector firms such as Pemex. The transfer of government-owned corporations to members of the elite greatly increased their wealth. In 1999, the wealthiest 10 percent of Mexicans received 55.3 percent of income.

In 1994, *Forbes* magazine found that the number of Mexican billionaires (as measured in U.S. dollars) had reached twenty-four, up from only one in 1990—a 2,400 percent increase. In the same four-year period, 1990 to 1994, per capita GDP increased by only 4 percent. At the time, the magazine commented, "Of the 358 people identified as billionaires in the latest *Forbes* world survey, 24 were Mexican—a percentage out of all proportion to Mexico's place in the world economy."

The Middle Class

Mexico's middle class expanded as a result of: 1) urbanization; 2) education; and 3) government jobs. Due to these factors, by the 1970s, the middle class encompassed roughly 30 percent of Mexico's population. This figure declined by a quarter after 1980 due to the economic crisis.

The early 1980s economic bust and bank nationalization turned the middle class against the system. Its members were especially hard hit, since they were highly reliant on salaried income, which declined by 36 percent between 1981 and 1985. Fewer middle-class jobs were created, and many were eliminated, especially in government.

By the 1990s, the cumulative effects of the 1968 student movement, repeated economic crises, poor handling of relief efforts after the 1985 Mexico City earthquake, and the fraudulent 1988 presidential elections had cost the PRI middle-class support. As Dennis Gilbert noted in his study of the middle class, "By the late 1990s, middle-class Mexicans had little faith in the dual myths of the revolution and the Mexican economic miracle." Not surprisingly, in the 2000 election, PAN presidential candidate Vicente Fox received 58 percent of the middle-class vote.

After the 1994–95 economic crisis, neoliberal economic policies favored the middle class as well as the elite. The number of families with monthly incomes in the $600 to $1,500 range rose from just over 5 million in 1992 to more than 9 million in 2004. As has been the case throughout Latin America, this newly emerging middle class is increasingly linked to the market, not the state. Gilbert noted that in 2000 the middle class was "bigger, better educated and more affluent than it was in the early 1980s."

Labor

Through the 1970s, labor remained a major part of the ruling PRI coalition. Roughly 16 percent of workers were members of PRI-affiliated unions. The government consulted union leadership concerning economic, labor, and electoral issues. Leaders of the CTM, the main labor federation, received lucrative government posts.

During the early 1980s, policymakers began to favor sharply decreased wages in an effort to make Mexico more attractive to foreign investors and to make the country more competitive in international markets. Inflation, which averaged 93 percent annually between 1983 and 1987, presented the government with the perfect opportunity to lower the value of wages. The government only had to ensure that the rate of wage increase fell behind the rate of inflation. The desired reduction in wages occurred, as workers' buying power declined by 61 percent between 1983 and 1988.

There are several explanations for the government's ability to impose such sharp wage reductions on a workforce with a long tradition of union struggle:

- Leaders of organized labor supported government policy. Based on long experience, they realized that their tenure in office was based on loyalty to the political elite, not to serving their membership.
- Labor unions were hurt by the shift of industry away from central Mexico, with a strong union tradition, to northern Mexico, where unions were traditionally weak or non-existent.
- The government, official unions, and management would resort to extralegal means to enforce acceptance of lowered wages. In 1992, human rights activists Mariclaire Acosta and Rocío Culebro observed, "Serious violations of individual, social, economic, and political rights of workers occur with impunity in Mexico today."
- One of the rights denied was the right to strike. In 1990, the human rights journal *Christus* commented: "The right to strike which previously was exercised with relative frequency, has been practically denied to unions. Declaring a strike illegal is the typical response of the labor boards and tribunals." Between 1983 and 1988, federal authorities accepted as legal only 1.8 percent of workers' petitions declaring their intention to strike.
- As foreign imports began to compete with locally produced goods, management could convincingly argue that wages had to decline to protect jobs.

At the turn of the century, the outlook for labor was discouraging. Union membership had declined to 9.8 percent of the labor force. In 1999, labor activist Berta Luján found that the greatest obstacles to union freedom were: 1) the proliferation of contracts signed between management and union leaders, without the knowledge or consent of the workers affected; 2) the declaration that strikes were illegal; 3) the government taking over firms to break strikes; and 3) the lack of a secret ballot in union certification elections.

Rural Mexico

> Perhaps peasant producers are not as efficient as rural entrepreneurs when measured by the standards of private business, but without a doubt they are infinitely more efficient if we consider social, cultural, and environmental impacts, categories where agribusiness clearly flunks the test of sustainability.
>
> (Armando Bartra, 2004)

Through the 1970s, rural poverty was at least mitigated by government intervention in the rural economy. The government-owned National Bank of Rural Credit (Banrural) supplied credit at subsidized prices. Specialized government agencies such as INMECAFE and TABAMEX purchased coffee and tobacco at guaranteed prices. There were also subsidies for agricultural inputs such as electricity, fuel, and fertilizer. The government grain agency, CONASUPO, became the third largest enterprise in Mexico. It bought and sold twelve different grains, operated a retail chain with more than 20,000 outlets, and maintained a network of grain silos and food-processing plants. Such efforts attempted to shield producers from the vagaries of the market and provide inexpensive food to the poor.

While such government support did transfer wealth to small producers, it also created problems. *Caciques* and government bureaucrats would often gain control of credit allocation and use this control to their personal advantage. Credit from the Banrural came with so many restrictions concerning the type of crop and production techniques that producers were left with little decision-making power. The government role in peasants' lives became so pervasive that cynics declared that peasants fought for "*tierra y libertad*" ("land and liberty") but instead received "*tierra y el estado*" ("land and the state").

Given the emphasis on servicing the national debt, under President de la Madrid (1982–88) there were sharp decreases in government intervention in the agricultural sector. This left small producers without crop insurance, credit, fertilizer subsidies, or marketing facilities. The government dismantled the guarantee prices of twelve food crops. Between 1981 and 1988, government investment in rural development declined from 2.4 percent of GDP to 0.2 percent.

Institutional changes continued to impact rural Mexico through the 1990s. Salinas amended Article 27 of the constitution to end the land reform. Then NAFTA allowed (after a grace period in some cases) the tariff-free importation of food from the United States. In 1999 the government ended its guarantee prices on corn and beans. This reflected its policy of letting Mexican food prices adjust to international levels, even if it forced some domestic producers out of business.

Public investment in rural development declined 74.2 percent between 1991–93 and 2000–02. The remaining federal support was directed to farms, such as those producing fresh fruit and vegetables, that were competitive in the export market. Smaller producers on rain-fed land were considered as a social welfare concern rather than as an economic policy matter.

Population increase, a multiplicity of very small farms, soil degradation, declining government support, and competition from imports mired rural Mexico in endemic poverty. Roughly a quarter of Mexico's population lived in rural areas, but only contributed 5 percent of GDP. Only 38 percent of rural households owned any land at all, and of those with land, more than two-thirds had less than five acres. Agricultural income was poorly distributed, as the 77 percent of farms relying on rainfall received only 44 percent of agricultural income. In 2004, 56.9 percent of the rural population was living in poverty.

NAFTA and neoliberal policies are frequently blamed for impoverishing Mexico's rural population. That charge is unjust in that there was endemic rural poverty before neoliberal policies were adopted in the 1980s. What neoliberal policies failed to do was to provide rural residents either with sufficient income or with urban jobs to which they could move and thus escape poverty.

Given rising population, declining farm income, and physical limitations (lack of access to water and good land), rural people increasingly turned to non-agricultural sources of income. As early as 1975 anthropologist Ralph Beals found that for rural Oaxacans "farming is neither their primary occupation nor is it the main source of income . . . Their ways of making a living hence are numerous and varied." During the 1990s, as the government reduced its role in the agricultural economy and population continued to increase, reliance on sales of one's crops continued to decline, and survival was based increasingly on consuming one's own crop production, day labor, government subsidies, and remittances from relatives in the United States.

One response to rural problems has been out-migration. As anthropologist Pierre Beaucage noted, "After twenty-five years of intense exposure to modernity, nobody wants to return to the old days, where you worked from dawn to dusk and were happy to have enough corn to eat and a few pesos to spend at the fiesta."

The Indigenous Population

Indigenous people in Mexico speak sixty-two different languages, which places the country second in linguistic diversity behind India, with its sixty-five languages. In 1970, 3.1 million Mexicans over age four spoke one of these indigenous languages. By 2000, that number had reached 6.0 million, a 94 percent increase. This was very close to Mexico's total population increase of 102 percent during these same years and far greater than the 24 percent increase in the rural population.

Mexico's indigenous population increase resulted from high birth rates and sharply declining death rates. The Indian population would have grown even more rapidly if out-migration and assimilation to outside society had not reduced its size.

Indigenous people have migrated from their communities due to a combination of environmental degradation (especially soil loss), poverty, and population increase. More than 1 million of these migrants settled in Mexico City, where they were among the poorest residents. Seasonal migrants harvested sugar cane in Morelos and commercial crops in northern Mexico. A politically active community of Mixtec agricultural workers formed in the San Quintín Valley of Baja California.

Between 1970 and 1976, to further its indigenista goals, the National Indigenous Institute (INI) expanded its network of coordination centers in Indian areas from twelve to sixty-four. The INI budget increased by more than 700 percent during this period. Another twenty-one centers were opened during the López Portillo (1976–82) administration. As part of this effort, schools and clinics were built and roads were extended into Indian areas.

During the 1970s and 1980s, indigenous leaders began to demand a much greater role in the design and implementation of policy affecting Indians. The number of Indian protests rose dramatically in the 1970s and was still higher during the 1980s. Beginning in the 1980s, Indian demands were two-pronged. Some concerned solutions to concrete problems such as the freeing of political prisoners, the removal of abusive municipal authorities, and an end of repression by *caciques*, landowners, and government officials. A second set of demands concerned modifying the institutional relations between the nation and its indigenous population.

During the 1980s and early 1990s, old assumptions concerning assimilation vanished as the government decided to accept ethnic differences rather than to suppress them. While the nature of government discourse shifted, Indians suffered the same hardship as other rural people when the government, in its effort to service its foreign debt, reduced programs in rural areas. Indians also suffered because there was a 51 percent reduction in spending by the INI.

The 1994 rebellion in Chiapas made it clear to the world that past policy had failed to meet the material needs of indigenous people or to guarantee them the rule of law. The rebellion led to unprecedented Indian activism and protests throughout Mexico. Finally, even though Indians had been discussing autonomy among themselves, the rebellion brought that notion to the forefront of discussion concerning Indian rights.

One of the reasons that autonomy received widespread support was that past experience indicated that policy made for Indians rather than by Indians yielded such unsatisfactory results.

Finally, Indians remained marginalized politically. At the close of the twentieth century, there were only fourteen indigenous members of the Chamber of Deputies, a fifth of what there would have been if Indians had been represented in proportion to their population.

The 1994 uprising in Chiapas by the Zapatista National Liberation Army (EZLN) highlighted the degraded condition of indigenous people throughout Mexico. (See Document 13.1.) Heavily indigenous Chiapas was the state with the highest number of illiterates, the highest number of those over fifteen who had not finished elementary school, and the highest percentage of population lacking electricity. In the 1980s the population of Chiapas increased by 52 percent, exacerbating social problems. Chiapas faced not only these chronic problems, but the neoliberal development model's offering little to rural southern Mexico and NAFTA's threatening to overwhelm farmers with tariff-free grain imports.

On New Year's Day 1994 residents and tourists awoke in San Cristóbal, the main city in highland Chiapas, to find ski-masked rebels huddled around bonfires. Rather than facing the overwhelming firepower of the Mexican army, the rebels withdrew from San Cristóbal and other cites they had occupied. The army responded swiftly, resulting in numerous allegations of human rights abuses. Between January 1 and January 11, roughly 132 were killed in combat. Most of the dead were rebel combatants and civilians.

On January 12, amid saturation media coverage, President Salinas offered a ceasefire which was accepted by the rebels. Since then the rebels have occupied a small area of eastern Chiapas where they have constructed their own government, schools, and healthcare system. They have refused all government aid and have declined to participate in state and national elections.

Even though the government has the military power to occupy the rebel-controlled area, just as Porfirio Díaz's army occupied the last stronghold of Maya rebels in Yucatán, it has not been

Figure 13.1 *The uprising by the largely indigenous Zapatista National Front (EZLN) in Chiapas was timed to coincide with NAFTA taking effect. It became the first major political movement to rely on the Internet to disseminate information.*

Credit: Benjamin Flores/*Proceso.*

ordered to do so. Rather, in the late 1990s the federal government lavished $3.5 billion on Chiapas's indigenous communities that did not support the rebels, improving schools and clinics, supporting agriculture, and providing food. The government also supported paramilitaries who waged low-intensity warfare against communities supporting the EZLN. Deaths attributed to the paramilitaries soon outnumbered those who died in formal combat in January 1994. In one single incident in 1997, paramilitaries attacked at Acteal, killing seven men, nineteen women, and nineteen children.

One of the great successes of the EZLN was stimulating Indian activism throughout Mexico. After he retired, Chiapas Bishop Samuel Ruiz commented: "Overall something which is irreversible is raising the level of Indian consciousness continent-wide. They are taking control of their own history."

Women

If in the first half of the twentieth century it was the mechanical tortilla mill that changed women's lives, in the second half it was increased access to education. Parents became increasingly willing to make sacrifices for their daughters' education since, with expanded employment opportunities for women, education increased their daughters' productive capacity in both rural and urban settings.

Between 1970 and 2000, the average educational level for women increased from 3.2 years to 7.3 years. For the entire age range between six and nineteen years, a higher percentage of females were enrolled as students than males. Women increasingly entered formerly male-dominated fields. For example, they constituted more than 50 percent of medical school enrolment. Education not only increased women's employment opportunities but was the factor most closely correlated with lower infant mortality and lower fecundity.

At centuries' end, the three main areas of female employment remained services, with 5.5 million workers, commerce with 3.2 million, and industry with 2.6 million. Women constituted some 40 percent of the 5.4 million professionals working in Mexico. Some 63 percent of teachers were women, as were 54.7 percent of sales workers. An increasing number of jobs opened for women in agriculture since emigration depleted the male labor force and the export of fruit, vegetables, and flowers increased employment opportunities. Such agricultural employment though was hardly liberating, since women occupied dead-end positions, received low wages, and worked long hours in poor conditions.

Paralleling women's increased entry into the formal labor force was an increased role in the formal political process, traditionally the domain of a small male elite. The number of women serving in the Chamber of Deputies reflected this. In 1952, its first woman member constituted 0.6 percent of that body. In 1997, 17 percent of the members of the Chamber of Deputies were women.

Table 13.1 *Mexican Population, 1970–2000*

	Population	Annual percentage increase during previous decade
1970	46,225,238	3.0
1980	66,846,833	2.9
1990	82,249,645	2.3
2000	97,014,867	1.8

Source: Philip L. Russell, *The History of Mexico: From Pre-Conquest to Present* (New York: Routledge, 2010), p. 522, Table 24.1

Population

> Here is the dilemma, either the developed Mexico will absorb and integrate the other, or
> the underdeveloped Mexico, by sheer dead weight of demographic increase, will end up
> strangling the developed Mexico.
>
> (Octavio Paz, 1972)

The 1970 census enumerated 48 million Mexicans. During the 1970s population increase averaged 2.9 percent a year. By the 1990s this rate had declined to 1.8 percent. Nonetheless, by 2000 Mexico's population totalled 97 million. Between 1970 and 2000, as the birth rate declined, those below age fifteen declined from 46 percent of the population to 34 percent.

Even though the rate of population increase declined, between 1970 and 2000 Mexican population increase exceeded the population increase that occurred between the arrival of the first human in Mexico and 1970. The number of births occurring annually only started to decline in 1995.

Some of the causes suggested for Mexico's decline in fertility include:

- an increased awareness of the economic advantages of small family size;
- increased access to and acceptance of contraceptives;
- the cost of raising children skyrocketing since providing them with at least an elementary education became accepted as a family responsibility;
- the mechanization and proletarianization of agriculture, which reduced the economic advantages of having children;
- women increasingly entered the labor force and obtaining better jobs, resulting in remaining at home to raise children becoming an increasingly costly option.

In 2000, Mexico City's population reached 18 million, up from 8.8 million in 1970. The city's rapid growth, based on industrial jobs, continued through the 1970s. During that decade the city's population increased by 4.2 million—it's fastest growth ever. The city's population only increased by 2.3 million during the 1980s. This reflected the Federal District's losing 108,600 industrial jobs between 1985 and 1988 as old industries closed and new ones opened closer to the U.S. market. As commerce and services replaced industry in the 1990s, the city's population increased by 2.7 million.

While Mexico City's share of national population remained static from 1970 to 2000, the northern border states' share increased from 16.3 to 17.1 percent of national population. The increase from 7.8 million to 16.6 million during these years reflected the increase in the number of assembly plants known as *maquiladoras*. In 1998, Francisco Gaytán, of the economic development agency of the state of Chihuahua, estimated that 95 percent of the economy of Ciudad Juárez was based on the *maquiladora*. He commented, "Everything revolves around the maquiladora, and we have given absolute priority to its development."

Education

Mexico made steady progress at raising literacy and the educational level of its population during the last decades of the twentieth century. In 1970, 74.2 percent of the population was literate, and the average educational level was 3.4 years. By 2000, 91 percent of the population was literate, and the average educational level was 8.2 years. While these statistics indicate substantial progress, the educational levels of other Latin American nations such as Chile, Argentina, and Colombia surpassed that of Mexico. Mexico remained even further behind the educational levels of economic rivals such as South Korea.

Elementary school enrollment increased from 9.2 million in 1970–71 to 15.4 million in 1983–84 and then began to decline, reaching 14.8 million in 1999–2000. The *decline* in primary school enrollment reflected two trends—fewer children being born and fewer children repeating grades.

The number of secondary school students (seventh to ninth grade) continued to increase since an increasing percentage of students remained in school after finishing primary. Secondary enrollment increased from 1.1 million in 1970 to 5.3 million in 1999–2000. Between 1970 and 2000, college undergraduate enrollment increased from 0.25 million to 1.847 million.

As a result of President Echeverría's educational effort, enrolment in public universities surged. This led to a glut of college-educated students for whom a bachelor's degree no longer provided access to the middle class. The cachet previous generations had attached to a public-university degree was lost. Increasingly the key to success became a degree from an expensive private university, such as the Universidad Iberoamericana, the alma mater of President Vicente Fox (2000–06).

In the aftermath of a bitter student strike over tuition increases that paralyzed the National University for a year (1999–2000), political scientist Denise Dresser commented on how higher education mirrored Mexican society:

> On the threshold of the millennium there are millions of Mexicans who don't have an entry ticket. They see a bright future for politicians, bilingual bankers, and intellectuals with international reputations. They see an elite that disparages the poor for being disheveled, longhaired, dark-skinned guerrillas who do not speak eloquently. They see an educated, elegant elite for whom the notion of social justice is interesting but irrelevant. The university rebellion reflects a badly divided country.[2]

THE INTELLECTUAL SCENE

The Intellectuals

During the Echeverría administration, the Mexican intelligentsia divided into two groups that would endure for the rest of the century. One was led by Octavio Paz who, after resigning his ambassadorship to India in 1968, remained aboard until 1971. That year he returned to Mexico and founded *Plural*, a cultural supplement to the paper *Excé Isior*. After the removal of that paper's editor in 1976, he resigned from *Plural* to protest the removal and founded the independent magazine *Vuelta*, where he was joined by historian Enrique Krauze. *Vuelta* became highly influential even though its circulation never rose above 18,000.

In 1978, as a counterpoint to *Vuelta*, a group of writers founded the magazine *Nexos*, modeled on the *New York Review of Books*. While democracy was the central goal of writers at *Vuelta*, the *Nexos* group saw democracy as one goal among many, including social justice. Its founders brought academic research to bear on public policy and took on topics the mainstream press considered too hot to touch.

The death of Octavio Paz in 1997 symbolically marked the end of the era of the intellectual in Mexico. Paz—who received the Nobel Prize for Literature in 1990—is remembered for his vast oeuvre, which includes almost thirty volumes of poetry and more than thirty volumes of essays, as well as his founding journals and contributing to public discourse. As critic Rafael Pérez Gay noted, Paz was "first and foremost a poet, and wanted to be remembered this way, his works combine contemplation and action, reflection and criticism, the local and the universal. His literary interests were as vast and diverse as his own work."

Religion

> The average Mexican ranks family, work, and religion most important to his life and considers it far more significant than politics.
>
> (Roderic Camp, 1997)

In 1979, the government facilitated Pope John Paul II's visit to Mexico to open the Latin American bishops' conference in Puebla. The outpouring of enthusiasm for the pope by perhaps 20 million Mexicans served as a reminder of Mexico's deep Catholic roots. The conference issued a statement strongly condemning poverty in Latin America. The pope urged the Church to become engaged in social issues so as not to become irrelevant. Yet at the same time he attempted to rein in proponents of liberation theology by declaring, "The concept of Christ as a political revolutionary, as a subversive, is not in keeping with the teachings of the Church."

During the Salinas administration (1988–94), several constitutional amendments largely eliminated anti-clericalism, which was so woven into the document that it was necessary to amend five different articles. Article 3 was modified to allow the Church to impart primary education, something that in fact was already occurring. A revised Article 24 allowed religious ceremonies to be staged outside of churches and private homes. Article 130 was changed to recognize the legal existence of religious associations such as the Catholic Church. In addition, priests and ministers were granted the right to vote. In 1992, Salinas followed up his reforms by establishing diplomatic relations with the Vatican for the first time since the end of the Maximilian government in 1867.

Since he was not a practicing Catholic, Salinas's reforms did not appear to be religiously motivated. His building bridges to the Catholic Church broadened his political base, since Mexico's largely Catholic population favored the constitutional reforms. In addition, the normalization of Church–state relations made Mexico a better suitor for the upcoming negotiations to establish NAFTA.

Between 1970 and 1990, the number of Protestants increased by 17.6 percent a year, and in southern Mexico, by 24 percent a year. By 2000 the more than 5 million Protestants made up 5 percent of the population. The Protestant churches with the largest following included the Mormons with 783,000 members and Jehovah's Witnesses with 518,000.

The evangelical churches have been especially successfully in obtaining converts in the poor, indigenous states of southern Mexico. In 2000, Protestants made up 14.5 percent of the population of Chiapas, while in traditionally Catholic Guanajuato, they comprised only 1.4 percent. Many Mexicans appear to convert to Protestantism in response to the anomie caused by modernization. For such converts, Protestantism is a mechanism for providing order and meaning in the lives of the dispossessed.

DOCUMENT 13.1: DECLARATION OF THE LACANDÓN RAIN FOREST

[The initial communiqué of the EZLN was entitled "Declaration of the Lacandón Rain Forest." Later EZLN communiqués shifted emphasis from changing power at the national level to securing autonomy for indigenous communities.]

Declaration of the Lacandón Rain Forest

Today we say, "Enough is enough!"

To the Mexican people:

To our Mexican brothers and sisters:

We are the product of 500 years of struggle. Our first struggle was against slavery. Then came the War of Independence from Spain, led by the insurgents. After that came the struggle to prevent our being absorbed by U.S. expansionism. Still later we promulgated our constitution and expelled the French imperialists from our soil. Then, after the Díaz dictatorship refused to enforce the laws of the Reform in a just manner, the people rebelled. Villa and Zapata, who were poor men like us, emerged as their leaders.

We have been denied the most elemental education, so they can use us as cannon fodder and pillage the wealth of the country. It does not matter to them that we are dying of hunger and curable diseases. We have nothing, absolutely nothing—not a decent home, no land, no job, no health care, no food, and no education. We don't even have the right to democratically elect our officials. We have neither independence from foreigners nor peace and justice for our children and ourselves.

Today we say, "Enough is enough!" We are the descendants of those who forged this nation. We, the dispossessed, number in the millions. We urge our brothers and sisters to heed this call. It is the only way to avoid dying of hunger, given the insatiable greed of the dictatorship. For more than 70 years, this dictatorship has been run by a clique of traitors who represent the most conservative groups which sell out the country. They are the same ones who opposed Hidalgo and Morelos and betrayed Vicente Guerrero. They are the same ones who sold more than half of our nation to the foreign invader. They are the same ones who brought a European prince to govern us. They are the same ones who created the dictatorship led by Díaz's *científicos*. They are the same ones who opposed nationalizing the oil industry. They are the same ones who massacred railroad workers in 1958 and students in 1968. They are the same ones who take everything, absolutely everything from us today.

To prevent all of this, and as our last hope, after having attempted to exercise the rights guaranteed by our Constitution, we invoke the authority granted by Article 39 of our Constitution, which states:

> National sovereignty resides essentially and originally in the people. The powers of government come from the people and are instituted to benefit them. The citizens have, at all times, the inalienable right to change or modify their form of government.

Thus, based on our constitutional rights, we direct this message to the Mexican army, the foundation of the dictatorship which we suffer under. This one-party dictatorship is led by the illegal head of the executive branch, Carlos Salinas de Gortari.

Based on this declaration of war, we ask that the judicial and legislative branches assume the responsibility of restoring legality and stability to Mexico by deposing the dictator.

We also request that the International Red Cross and other international agencies monitor combat involving our forces, thus protecting the civilian population. We declare that we are now and always will be subject to the provisions of the Geneva Convention. The EZLN is a true belligerent force engaged in a struggle of liberation. The Mexican people are on our side. We have our homeland, and the tricolor flag, which is loved and respected by insurgent combatants. We use the colors red and black in our uniforms, since they are the symbols of working people on strike. Our flag carries the letters EZLN, Zapatista Army of National Liberation. We will always carry it into combat.

We reject beforehand our enemies' attempt to discredit the justice of our cause by referring to us as drug traffickers, narco-guerrillas, bandits and other such terms. Our struggle is based on constitutional law and has as its goals justice and equality.

Based on this Declaration of War, we are ordering the military forces of the Zapatista Army of National Liberation to:

1) Advance on the national capital, defeating the federal army while protecting the civilian population and permitting those liberated to democratically elect their own authorities.

2) Respect the lives of prisoners and turn the wounded over to the International Red Cross so they can receive medical care.

3) Begin summary treason trials of federal army soldiers and the political police who have been advised, trained, and paid by foreigners, either inside Mexico or abroad. Those repressing or mistreating the civilian population or robbing or harming the national patrimony will also be charged with treason.

4) Form new military units made up of all Mexicans who are willing to join our just cause, including those enemy soldiers who gave up without fighting and promise to follow the orders of the General Command of the Zapatista Army of National Liberation.

5) Ask the unconditional surrender of enemy units before engaging in combat.

6) End the pillaging or our natural resources in areas controlled by the EZLN.

To the people of Mexico:

We, free men and women, are conscious that the war we have declared is our last resort. Nevertheless, it is a just action. For many years, the dictators have been waging an undeclared, genocidal war against our people,

Thus, we ask your active support of this declaration of the Mexican people, who are struggling for jobs, land, housing, food, healthcare, education, independence, liberty, democracy, justice and peace. We will fight until these basic demands of the Mexican people have been met by the formation of a free democratic government.

Join the insurgent forces of the Emiliano Zapata Army of National Liberation!

General Command of the EZLN, 1993.

NOTES

1   *Human Rights Violations in Mexico* (New York: Amnesty International), p. 210.

2   Denise Dresser, *Proceso*, February 13 (2000), p. 41.

FURTHER READING

Barry, Tom (1995) *Zapata's Revenge*. Boston: South End.
    A consideration of how neoliberal policies impacted rural Mexico.

Bruhn, Kathleen (1997) *Taking on Goliath*. University Park, PA: Pennsylvania State University Press.
    A detailed history of the PRD, beginning with the Democratic Current.

—— (1999) "The Resurrection of the Mexican Left in the 1997 Elections," in *Towards Mexico's Democratization*, ed. Jorge Domínguez and Alandro Poiré , pp. 114–36. New York: Routledge.
    Bruhn updated her 1997 work to include the 1997 elections.

Dawson, Alexander (2006) *First World Dreams*. London: Zed.
    A short, readable description of Mexico as it entered the new millennium.

Harvey, Neil (1998) *The Chiapas Rebellion*. Durham, N.C.: Duke University Press.
    A discussion of the 1994 indigenous rebellion in Chiapas with emphasis on the role of peasant organizations before 1994.

Hellman, Judith (1983) *Mexico in Crisis* (2nd ed). New York: Holmes & Meier.
    A critical look at the Mexican political system and society.

Poniatowska, Elena (2001) *Here's to You, Jesusa!* New York: Farrar, Straus, and Giroux.
    A novel based on the life of a washerwomen the author befriended. It introduces slum life to the reader.

Preston, Julia and Samuel Dillon (2004) *Opening Mexico*. New York: Farrar, Straus, and Giroux.
    Virtually a sequel to *Distant Neighbors* (see below) by two *New York Times* correspondents.

Riding, Alan (1985) *Distant Neighbors*. New York: Knopf.
    The best-selling description of 1980s Mexico by a *New York Times* correspondent.

Rodríguez, Victoria and Peter M. Ward (eds.) (1995) *Opposition Governments in Mexico*. Albuquerque, N.M.: University of New Mexico Press.
    Essays describing how PRD and PAN state and municipal governments functioned before 2000.

Chapter 14

Plunging Back into the International Market, 1971–2000

TIMELINE—WORLD

1971	1972	1973	1975	1976
U.S. goes off gold standard	Nixon visits China	Democratically elected Chilean president Salvador Allende ousted in coup	Vietcong take Saigon, ending war in Vietnam	Soweto massacre in South Africa

1989	1990	1991	1998	2000
Tiananmen Square massacre of Chinese students	Iraq invades Kuwait, followed by U.S. intervention to oust Iraq	Collapse of Soviet Union	Hugo Chávez elected president of Venezuela	George W. Bush declared winner of U.S. presidential election

TIMELINE—MEXICO

1968	1971	1973	1976	1976
Julio Scherer appointed editor of *Excélsior*	Publication of *La Noche de Tlatelolco*	Televisa TV network formed	Julio Scherer ousted as *Excélsior* editor	Newsmagazine *Proceso* founded

1994
NAFTA takes effect

1979	1979	1979	1982	1989
Sandinistas oust Nicaraguan dictator Somoza	Soviet invasion of Afghanistan	U.S. and China establish diplomatic relations	War between Argentina and Great Britain over the Falkland Islands/Islas Malvinas	Berlin Wall comes down

1976	1986	1986	1992	1993
Supergiant oil field Cantarell discovered	Mexico joins GATT	IRCA passed to reform U.S. immigration policy	NAFTA negotiations concluded	Newspaper *Reforma* founded

THIS CHAPTER CONSIDERS WHY, TOWARD THE END OF THE TWENTIETH CENTURY, the old import-substitution economic model was abandoned. In its place a new model, often known as neoliberal, emphasized international trade and foreign investment. In order to implement this model the North American Free Trade Agreement (NAFTA) was signed with Canada and the United States. This treaty required revisiting Mexico's traditional stand-off approach toward the United States. Replacing it was the notion that strengthening ties between Mexico and the United States would be beneficial for both nations. Finally, this chapter considers the two chronic problems of the U.S.–Mexico relationship—drugs and immigration.

THE OLD MODEL CRUMBLES

The import-substitution model of economic development that Mexico adopted after 1940 served the country for nearly half a century and produced the Mexican economic miracle—a source of envy throughout much of the developing world. Between 1940 and 1982, Mexico's per capita income increased by 440 percent, manufacturing by 1460 percent, and agriculture by 420 percent, while population only increased by 240 percent.

However, by the end of López Portillo's term (1976–82), the development model was showing signs of disfunction. These signs included: 1) 150 percent inflation in 1982; 2) depletion of foreign exchange reserves; 3) virtual collapse of non-oil exports; 4) high foreign indebtedness; and 5) capital flight.

In retrospect, it is clear the import-substitution model suffered from numerous flaws. These flaws include Mexico's market being too small to permit manufacturing economies of scale. As a result, goods manufactured in Mexico were roughly 50 percent more expensive and of lower quality than their foreign equivalents. Import substitution placed a constant drain on Mexico foreign currency reserves since factories established under its aegis constantly required foreign purchases of components, intermediate materials, and capital goods. In the early post-World War II period, agricultural exports financed such purchases. However, after the mid-1960s, agricultural exports declined. Also, just as opponents of massive foreign investment had predicted, foreign investors withdrew $5.3 billion more than they brought into Mexico between 1974 and 1984.

The old economic model exacerbated several existing problems. Most of Mexico's manufacturing was concentrated in the Valley of Mexico, Guadalajara, and Monterrey—leaving little benefit for the rest of the nation. Direct economic benefits were restricted to plant owners and the relatively small, organized industrial working class while the vast majority of the population waited for wealth to trickle down. As economist Manuel Gollás observed, "Industrialization was a very inefficient method of promoting economic justice."

By the mid-1980s, economic policymakers deemed these problems to be sufficient cause for adopting a new economic model. While the problems associated with the import substitution are undeniable, the question arises as to whether Mexico needed a sudden shift in economic model, as occurred, or whether it could have entered a globalizing economy in a slower, less damaging manner.[1]

THE NEW ECONOMIC MODEL

By 1985, it had become apparent that the government was unable to restore economic growth using traditional mechanisms. Then, after oil prices plunged from $24 a barrel in December 1985 to $9 a barrel in July 1986, Mexican planners undertook what economist James Cypher characterized as "the most profound shift in economic policymaking that had occurred in 50 years."

Economic policy emphasis shifted from the domestic market to exports. In 1986, Mexico joined the General Agreement on Tariffs and Trade (GATT), a group of nations pledging to reduce barriers to world commerce. Upon joining, Mexico agreed to a maximum tariff of 50 percent and other measures to promote international trade. Between 1971 and 1980, 74.1 percent of Mexico's imports required a license. By 1989, only 14.2 percent required one. Between 1981 and 1988, the average tariff declined from 18.3 percent to 6.1 percent. The divestiture of government-owned corporations formed another key aspect of de la Madrid's economic policy. In 1982, the government owned 1,155 corporations, while by 1988 only 446 remained public hands.

Other key elements of de la Madrid's new economic policy, often characterized as neoliberal, were a reduced level of government spending, an end to government social programs, the end of a state industrial policy, and the deregulation of goods, service, labor, and capital markets. This deregulation included lowering (or eliminating) tariffs and welcoming foreign investment. The underlying assumption of de la Madrid's policy was that the market could allocate capital more efficiently than the state, thus accelerating economic growth.

The advocates of **neoliberalism** proclaimed that no currently developed nation had developed without foreign trade as a major component of its economy. However, these advocates overlooked an equally important aspect of the currently developed nations—development did not occur simply by opening borders. During the later part of the twentieth century, in the rapidly developing East Asian nations, trade barriers were eventually removed, but only after new jobs were provided in export industries. Infant industries were targeted, protected, and subsidized by East Asian governments in multiple ways. Foreign multinationals were welcomed, but only if their investment involved transfer of technology. These nations worked actively to reduce poverty and the growth of inequality, believing that such policies were important for maintaining social cohesion—a precondition for investment and growth.

President Salinas (1988–94) continued de la Madrid's economic policies, which is not surprising. As secretary of budget and planning under his predecessor, Salinas was one of the main architects of the 1980s changes in economic policy.

Even though he had earlier declared that a free trade agreement with the United States was unwise, the changing world situation caused Salinas to reverse his position. The Mexican people learned of this reversal thanks to a March 27, 1990 *Wall Street Journal* article which reported that the previous month U.S. and Mexican officials had met and agreed to negotiate a free trade agreement.

In August 1992, after fourteen months of haggling, negotiations on a free trade agreement between Mexico, Canada, and the United States were concluded. The final product was a document more than 1,100 pages long. A conspicuous absence from the document was an allowance for cross-border movement of labor. The United States was very clear—inclusion of a provision allowing workers to freely move across borders, as happens with the European Union, would kill the treaty.

The North American Free Trade Agreement (NAFTA) provided that tariffs and import quotas between the three member nations would be eliminated over a fifteen-year period. Given special political and economic sensitivities, detailed provisions were spelled out for different products. For example, Mexico was allowed to exclude foreign investment from the oil industry.

Since trade was already nearly tariff-free, NAFTA had its greatest impact on investment rules and intellectual property rights. Mexican analyst (and later U.N. ambassador) Adolfo Aguilar Zínzer acknowledged this when he stated, "This is not a trade agreement, but rather an agreement about investments."

Zedillo's unwavering support for neoliberalism paid dividends. After the 1994 crisis, thanks to NAFTA exports, industrial production reached pre-crisis levels in just one year, compared with the nine years required after the 1982 crisis. The economy grew at an average rate of 4.4 percent from 1997 to 2000 and foreign direct investment (FDI) came in at the highest rate in Mexican history. These figures of course ignore the impact of the 1982 and 1994 economic crises. Between 1982 and 2000, per capita economic growth averaged an almost imperceptible 0.1 percent per year.

Revenue from privatizations, direct foreign investment, remittances from Mexicans working abroad, and oil sales allowed the Zedillo administration (1994–2000) to pay down Mexico's foreign debt from $101 billion in 1995 to $85 billion in 2000. As a result of lower interest rates and economic growth, debt service declined from 40.1 percent of export earnings to 20.8 percent during these same years. Nonetheless, service costs—$13.3 billion in 1999 alone—of the still massive foreign debt formed a persisting drag on the economy.

OIL

Between 1938 and 1973 Mexico nearly ceased exporting oil. Through the 1960s, Pemex relied on fields its private forebears had discovered in the Golden Lane—the string of fields along Mexico's east coast.

Two events caused Pemex to abandon its almost static post-Cárdenas operational mode. In 1970 Pemex registered its first overall petroleum trade deficit as Mexico's demand for oil exceeded production. In 1973 the initial OPEC-induced oil price increase caused Mexico's oil import bill to rise to $800 million a year.

As a result of these events, Echeverría launched a $1.4 billion program to locate new oil reserves and thus ensure oil self-sufficiency. This effort resulted in the discovery of the massive Reforma field on the border between Tabasco and Chiapas. The even larger Cantarell field was located in the Gulf of Campeche, a hundred miles off the Yucatán Peninsula.

Echeverría's oil exploration program was so successful that by 1974 Mexico was able to not only meet its domestic needs but to resume exporting oil. The following year Mexican oil production exceeded the record set by foreign firms in 1921.

President López Portillo (1976–82) undertook a massive expansion of oil production and export in response to the domestic economic crisis and high prices on the international oil market. He appointed as Pemex's director general Jorge Díaz Serrano, a firm believer in exploring for new fields and expanding Pemex at breakneck speed.

A few disquieting trends were almost lost in the chorus praising oil development. Given the amount of money invested, relatively few jobs were created in the highly capital-intensive oil industry. Much of the wealth was dissipated, since as oil-industry expert George Grayson noted, oil workers "demonstrated an unusual talent for enriching themselves and their organization from the national patrimony." As had been the case with Venezuela and Nigeria, which had also undergone rapid oil-induced growth, imports flooded in and income distribution worsened. Inflation associated with the boom, as well as government neglect, undermined other exports.

Well before the rest of Mexico awoke from its oil-induced stupor, Heberto Castillo, an engineer who had been jailed for his support of the 1968 student movement, emerged as Mexico's foremost critic of rapid oil development. He presciently warned of reserves becoming exhausted within decades. Castillo declared the decision to rapidly exploit and export oil was a capitulation to U.S. interests that resulted in Mexican natural resources being sold off cheaply for short-term benefit to the detriment of Mexico's long-term needs. Given his numerous books and articles in the newsweekly *Proceso*, his views were widely disseminated, though little heeded.

At the national level, Castillo's was almost a lone voice questioning the course of energy development. At the local level, his solo voice was accompanied by a chorus of aggrieved peasants and fishermen. Pemex drilled wells, built roads, laid pipelines, constructed petrochemical complexes, dredged rivers, and filled lagoons at breakneck speed with little consideration for the environment. Contamination from this activity found its way onto fields and into wells, rivers, and coastal fishing grounds. Thus unlike the United States, where having oil on one's land was a stroke of luck, for Tabasco peasants the presence of oil was a curse.

The oil workers' union typified the worst of Mexican trade unionism in that office holders became extremely wealthy and resorted to violence—including multiple murders—to maintain their positions. Rather than confront the power of the union, between 1981 and 1989 the government allowed the number of Pemex employees to increase from 122,000 to 172,900 even as exploration and production declined. In referring to oil-worker head Joaquín Hernández Galicia, Grayson declared, "The crude Machiavellian labour chief and his toadies gripped Pemex with a stranglehold that rivalled eastern Europe's domination by Communist party bosses."

By the end of the century, the once shining icon of Mexican nationalism had become tarnished. In 2000, Grayson observed that Pemex was burdened with "enclaves of corruption, a peso-hemorrhaging petrochemical division, an archaic tax regime, a tangle of red tape, and the huge expense of health, educational and recreational programs provided to its bloated work force."

THE AUTO INDUSTRY

During the de la Madrid administration (1982–88), the focus of the automobile industry shifted from the domestic market to the export market. This resulted from: 1) Mexicans by and large being unable to afford new cars after the 1982 economic crisis; 2) sharply increased government pressure to export in order to earn money to service the debt; and 3) U.S. auto makers facing increased foreign competition in their home market and turning to Mexico to lower labor costs.

As a result of this shift, the auto industry decentralized and moved north. Establishing plants in northern Mexico not only lowered the cost of shipping finished vehicles to the United States but also allowed plants to escape the combative unions found in central Mexico. Automakers typically selected plant locations in areas where they could hire workers without previous factory or union experience.

Auto exports boomed even before NAFTA came into effect. Between 1986 and 1993, the value of auto exports increased from $657 million to $4.25 billion. This increase in exports reflected both high worker productivity and high vehicle quality. These exports were highly profitable as a result of low wages, a well-trained, highly motivated workforce, tax exemptions, and government-funded infrastructure development. This profitability attracted more investment, which resulted in increased exports.

As a result of NAFTA, parts and new vehicles produced in any NAFTA nation could be shipped to another NAFTA nation without tariffs. Auto plants located in Mexico could specialize in the production of a limited number of models, most of which were exported. Producers in Mexico could offer Mexican buyers a complete line of their products, since they were free to import from Canada and the United States models not produced in Mexico.

New investment was attracted by economic stability, low interest rates, low wages, and the ability to sell in the booming U.S. auto market. By the late 1990s, the auto industry accounted for more than 22 percent of manufactured exports, and vehicles and auto parts formed the largest single component of NAFTA trade. In 2001, exports of autos and auto parts generated more foreign exchange than either tourism or oil exports.

THE *MAQUILADORA*

In the last third of the twentieth century, Mexican manufacturing plants known as *maquiladoras* become an integral part of the economy. *Maquila* originally meant the share of flour the mill owner retained for milling a farmer's grain. Unlike, say, the oil or auto industries, *maquiladoras* produce a wide variety of products including auto parts, computers, electronics, and apparel. Initially they were simple assembly operations—combining imported parts and exporting finished products.

The growth of the *maquiladora* was based on: 1) low wages in Mexico; 2) high-quality labor; 3) Mexican government subsidies to border areas; 4) low transport costs to the United States; 5) U.S. managers being able to live on the U.S. side of the border and work in Mexico; 6) proximity to the home office; 7) low political risk; and 8) lax enforcement of labor and environmental regulations.

After the 1994 peso devaluation, *maquiladora* employment soared as the dollar value of wages plummeted and a robust U.S. economy demanded ever more goods. Between 1994 and 2000, *maquiladora* employment rose from 465,261 to 1,338,970. Between 1980 and 2000, exports from *maquiladoras* increased from 15 percent of all Mexican exports to 50 percent.

As managers learned that Mexican workers could perform not only simple assembly but also sophisticated operations, they brought in more capital-intensive production of electronics, computers, and auto parts. During the 1990s, a new generation of *maquiladora* plants involved transforming components, rather than just assembling them, and required higher skill levels of their workers. A 1999 study found, "The electronics factories started to encompass high-technology investments, greater automation, quality circles, flexible production strategies, an increase in skill levels, a rise in the number of workers per plant, and a diversification of products manufactured."

Although the *maquiladora* provided jobs to hundreds of thousands, it also created serious problems. These problems largely flowed from the combination of low wages, corporations successfully demanding that they remain virtually tax-free, and the mushrooming population on the Mexican side of the border. Historian Richard Sinkin commented on the result: "In some border locations—like Tijuana and Ciudad Juárez—the growth of the maquilas has overwhelmed the ability to provide adequate water, sewage disposal, electricity, roads, adequate housing for workers, and in some cases even workers themselves."

Lax enforcement, or non-enforcement, of environmental regulations led to a variety of environmental problems. There were many documented cases of chemical discharges into waterways. In other cases, toxics were illegally deposited in the desert outside cities where *maquiladoras* were located. Finally, massive amounts of toxic materials were sometimes left at abandoned *maquiladora* sites. Greenpeace México reported that at the abandoned Metales y Derivados site on the Otay Mesa outside Tijuana there were 6,000 to 10,000 tons of lead, cyanide, nickel, cadmium, and zinc. Environmental problems in the border area, where most *maquiladoras* are located, continued to deteriorate after NAFTA went into effect in 1994.

The financial liberty of *maquiladora* operators contrasted sharply with tight restrictions on workers' freedom to form unions and choose leaders. Management had the support of the Mexican government in preventing the formation of independent unions. The usual union-busting tools were available to *maquiladora* managers, including government repression, strikebreakers, and the threat or the reality of relocation. When *maquiladoras* were established in new areas in central Mexico, they typically hired young women who had never held jobs before and thus were viewed as unlikely to press demands for effective union representation.

While *maquiladoras* provided jobs, they failed to become integrated with the rest of the Mexican economy. Only a small percentage of the materials used in production were of Mexican origin. One reason for the small percentage of Mexican inputs, especially compared with Asian inputs in similar Asian operations, was that much long-established Mexican industry was located near the Valley of Mexico and thus could not easily ship to *maquiladoras*. Those in charge of purchasing for *maquiladoras* often worked in the United States and so were unaware of what is available in Mexico. Finally, many Mexican producers were unable to meet delivery times and international price and quality standards.

TOURISM

In 1970 roughly 2 million tourists visited Mexico, spending $1.4 billion. Since then Mexican tourism has benefited from the vast expansion of jet travel and from increased world affluence. In this context, Mexico took advantage of its natural strengths, which include 6,000 miles of coastline, a fine climate, and the world's sixth greatest biodiversity. Its diverse indigenous heritage, which ranges from Zapotec communities in Oaxaca to the Purépecha in Michoacán, formed an additional attraction.

In contrast to the rest of the economy where the government largely bowed out, the government played a major role in promoting tourism. The most prominent example of this government role was Cancún, which in 1970 was an offshore jungle island along the remote coast of Quintana Roo.

The development of Cancún resulted from Banco de México officials deciding that in order to share in rapidly expanding international tourism by jet, Mexico would have to develop new tourist sites. Planners took an inventory of the Mexican coast and fed data on climate, water temperature, and beach conditions into a computer. The computer selected Cancún as the most desirable site. Government agencies then became in effect the governing power in Cancún. They dredged lagoons, expropriated and cleared land, and erected a complete city, with basic infrastructure, a golf course, and a central market.

In 1975, a year after the first hotel opened, 99,500 tourists visited Cancún. In 1986 Cancún drew more tourists than Acapulco, and in 1989 it surpassed Mexico City to become Mexico's most popular foreign tourist destination. In 2004 2.3 million tourists visited Cancún.

The government continued to play a strong role in tourist development. Once Cancún was developed, Banco de México officials facilitated the development of four other major tourist destinations, Los Cabos and Loreto on the Baja California peninsula, Bahías de Huatulco in Oaxaca, and Ixtapa on the Pacific Coast near Acapulco.

Even though it was once rather simplistically referred to as the "industry without chimneys," tourism had drawbacks, including what might be considered the original sin of Mexican tourism. In many locations such as Cancún and Huatulco, the government expropriated land from the local residents, provided at best meager compensation, and in subsequent development only offered them low-paid wage labor. Infrastructure was developed at government expense, and land was then turned over to large corporations, many of which were foreign.

Since sewage treatment was expensive and provided no quick return on investment, tourists and the workers who served them fouled the waters in many locations, especially those located on bay-enclosed beaches such as Huatuclo. In 2003, the Special Federal Prosecutor's Office for Environmental Protection released a report that listed twenty-six beaches and coastal areas that it described as highly contaminated. Included in this list were several well-known Pacific resorts such as Acapulco, Zihuatanejo, and Puerto Vallarta.

Relatively little tourist revenue found its way into the hands of ordinary resort residents. As a result of low wages and intermittent employment, many people had no other choice than to live in the shantytowns that have formed around major destinations such as Acapulco and Cancún. Most tourist dollars flow to airlines and multinational hotel chains, not local service providers. Package travel deals, which included meals, made it difficult for local food providers to tap into the tourist trade. As journalist Marc Cooper observed, "Finding a small family-run Mexican *taquería* or *panadería*—a taco stand or traditional bakery—is much easier in downtown Los Angeles or Chicago than it is in Cancún."

AGRICULTURE

As Mexican population and meat consumption increased, Mexico lost its food self-sufficiency. During the 1970s, grain imports became so massive that they created costly bottlenecks in the rail system. In 1980, Mexico imported 12 million tons of grain.

Under President de la Madrid (1982–88), food self-sufficiency was abandoned as a goal. Policymakers decided to rely on the notion of comparative advantage, producing and exporting fruits and vegetables and relying on imports to bridge gaps in food supply. Food henceforth was to be treated simply as another commodity.

Salinas successfully promoted amending Article 27 of the constitution to allow *ejidatarios* to sell, rent, and mortgage *ejido* land. After some 250 million acres had been distributed during the course of the land reform, his administration declared there would be no further distribution of land. As political scientist Nora Hamilton observed, "Not only was this a devastating blow to landless or land-poor peasants who still had hopes of benefiting from land distribution, but an assault on one of the basic principles of the revolution."

Proponents of legalizing the sale of *ejido* land felt that such sales would allow the creation of larger, more efficient farming units that would attract capital that the *ejido* was unable to attract. In addition, private owners would be more willing to invest in their own land since they would no longer face the threat of their land being expropriated for the land reform. Salinas stated, "The reforms to Article 27 returned to peasants decision-making power in the ejido and ended massive state intervention in its internal life."

TEQUILA

Tequila is an alcoholic beverage produced from the agave, or century plant, just as pulque is. It differs from pulque in that the juice of the agave is both fermented and distilled, yielding a beverage in the 80–110 proof range.

Tequila differs from mescal, another agave-based beverage, in that any beverage labeled tequila is legally required to be the product of the blue agave, a specific species (*agave tequilana* Weber) which derives its name from the blue tint of its leaves. The law also requires that any beverage labeled tequila be produced within a specific geographical area centered on the state of Jalisco, where 95 percent of tequila is produced. A final legal requirement is that at least 51 percent of the sugar used in the fermentation process be from the agave plant, rather than from cane sugar added in.

Travelers in Jalisco can see fields with rows of agave stretching into the distance, just as Midwesterners can see cornfields stretching into the distance. Skilled workers, known as *jimadores*, harvest plants from these fields by cutting off their roseate leaves, leaving the stem, which is called a *piña* (pineapple), since it resembles a large pineapple. *Piñas*, which often weigh more than 100 pounds, are trucked to the distillery where they are baked in a steam oven to convert the starch in the piña to fermentable sugar.

After the *piña* leaves the oven, it is pressed to extract its juice which is then fermented for four days. The fermented juice is usually distilled twice to produce the final product, which may be bottled on site or shipped in bulk to foreign markets—mainly the United States—where it is bottled. The entire production process, which formerly was artisanal, is now industrialized to accommodate high-volume production.

In 1825 Englishman Robert W. H. Hardy visited the village of Tequila, near Guadalajara, and reported that distillers there produced a "whiskey" from agave. Beverage production in Tequila had been thriving since colonial times.

As the railroad allowed shipment to distant markets, production increased. In 1870 a single producer was distilling 660,000 liters a year. Only in the early twentieth century did the distilled beverage produced in Tequila become known as tequila, thus distinguishing itself from the more humble mescal, which is produced from any of several different species of agave.

As late as 1970 tequila was still in its infancy, with production reaching 30 million liters a year, a sixth of which were exported. In 1972 tequila was being produced at 35 distilleries in Jalisco, only 19 of which were in Tequila.

Then, thanks to a highly successful PR effort, tequila drinking caught on in the United States and production soared. By 1995 annual production exceeded 100 million liters, and by 2005 it exceeded 200 million liters. Production eventually peaked in 2008 at 312 million liters. As tequila expert Lucinda Hutson noted, with mass marketing sales were "often based on more hype than heritage. Too often, the bottle outshines the tequila within." High volume attracted investors and the attention of *Fortune* magazine (March 31, 2008). Herradura distillery was sold in 2008 for $776 million. Most of the distilleries, despite their quaint names, are now owned by multinationals.

A commonly recognized type of tequila is known as *blanco* (white) or *plata* (silver) which is bottled immediately after it leaves the still. *Reposado* is a tequila which has been aged from two months to a year. *Añejo* refers to tequila which has been aged from one to three years, usually in oak casks which impart both flavor and a golden color. Tequila that is aged for more than three years is known as *extra añejo*. Tequila produced with added sugar is known as *mixto*, while that which is produced with agave sugar alone is labeled "100% *agave*."

Connoisseurs of the beverage note a wide variety of flavors in tequila even though it is all produced from the same species of agave. Flavor in part results from variables in the place where the agave is grown. Such variables include soil, climate, altitude, and cultivation practices. Different procedures in the distillery yield still more variety. Some distilleries have their own proprietary variety of yeast that they use in fermentation. The casks used to age tequila yield still more variety. Casks vary according to the type of wood and the previous use of the casks. Casks that have previously been used to age other alcoholic beverages are especially prized.

Once the tequila is poured out of the bottle it may be served in innumerable ways. Two of the better-known tequila-based drinks are the tequila sunrise which combines tequila and orange juice and most famously the margarita which combines tequila, lime juice, and Cointreau.

Additional information on this classic Mexican beverage may be found in Lucinda Hutson's beautifully illustrated *¡Viva Tequila!* (Austin: University of Texas Press, 2013).

Critics denounced these changes as counter-revolutionary and claimed they would further concentrate land in the hands of a few. In any case, the peasant movement and its intellectual allies were so weak that they were unable to effectively oppose the end of land reform.

Many saw Salinas's reforms as marking the end of the *ejido*, which at the time of the 1992 reform constituted 52 percent of Mexican territory. Most *ejidos*, however, continued intact, highlighting their positive aspects. Their biggest success was contributing to eight decades of rural stability. The *ejido* also proved to be as productive as private farms of the same size, while at the same time giving dignity to generations of participating peasants. The *ejido* was more energy efficient, fostered biodiversity, and used fewer chemical inputs. *Ejidos* and privately held small farms, since they relied more on manual labor and animal traction, had a positive energy output (as measured in kilocalories) while large farms relying on mechanization and manufactured inputs had negative energy balances.

A few thousand growers, roughly 5 percent of all producers exporting fruits, vegetables, and livestock, found considerable success under NAFTA. Most of these farms were relatively large and were associated with foreign firms. Between 1994 and 2005, Mexican agricultural exports tripled to $8.3 billion.

NAFTA also produced some not-so-welcome trends. Between 1982 and 2007, agricultural imports soared from $1.8 billion to $19.3 billion. Between 1993 and 2007, Mexican agricultural output only increased by 1.5 percent annually. The anticipated investment in agriculture never arrived. As investment was directed to manufacturing exports and oil development, agriculture declined from 12 percent of GDP in 1970 to 5.8 percent in 2000.

A major reason for this lack of investment and growth was that, as a result of NAFTA, Mexican agriculture must compete with U.S. agriculture, which enjoys fertile, well-watered soil, a temperate climate, and massive government subsidies. As commodity prices fell to international levels, Mexican farmers were saddled with expensive credit, machinery, and electricity, as well as high transportation costs resulting from poor highways.

A study by the Carnegie Endowment found that in the decade after NAFTA took effect some 1.3 million small farms had been displaced by the flood of farm imports. Thanks to NAFTA, Mexico became increasingly dependent on food imports from the United States.

Small corn growers, who produce a dietary mainstay that is regarded as a symbol of life itself, were especially hard hit by the imports permitted under NAFTA. Three million corn producers suffered when the price of corn in Mexico plunged from $5 a bushel in 1995 to $1.80 in 2000 due to the opening of the market to international competition.

PRINT MEDIA

The Old Order

> At the end of the 1970s, the government strictly controlled information. Daily newspapers, with some notable exceptions, reported what the regime wanted to hear.
>
> (José Aguilar Rivera, 2003)

The PRI's system of media control maintained a pliant press into the 1980s. In his 1985 classic *Distant Neighbors*, Alan Riding observed that "hundreds" of Mexico City and provincial newspapers received between 60 and 80 percent of their revenue by publishing government handouts as ads or disguised as news stories. This led to extensive coverage promoting the president and his administration.

The results of government largesse were visible in both the quality (favorable) and quantity (voluminous) of PRI political campaign coverage. Journalists covering PRI campaigns received free transportation, food, and rooms in the best hotels as well as envelopes full of cash. Government ties were key to financial success in newspaper publishing, while readership was largely incidental. In the mid-1990s, Mexico City's twenty-three daily newspapers had a combined circulation of fewer than 500,000. Government assistance allowed many of these papers to operate without serious regard to circulation or commercial advertising.

The New Order

The 1968 appointment of Julio Scherer García as the editor of *Excélsior* initiated a chain of events that changed Mexican journalism forever. He soon introduced investigative reporting on topics such as election fraud, government repression, and environmental damage. His goal was not to topple the government but to make visible the illegal activity of the ruling elite. Scherer García assumed that ending impunity began with informing the public of what was happening. *Excélsior*'s newly empowered reporters also investigated the corruption of union leaders and commented on misguided economic policy. The paper ceased to brand as communist-inspired any effort to promote social justice and no longer repeated as divine revelation everything declared by the PRI and the government. Independent academics such as Daniel Cosío Villegas and Rodolfo Stavenhagen were invited to write columns.

Excélsior's independence eventually exceeded President Echeverría's tolerance. He took advantage of *Excélsior*'s unique management structure to bring the paper back into Mexico's sycophantic journalistic chorus. In order to insulate it from outside pressure, the paper had been organized as a cooperative, which chose its editor. With Echeverría's backing, some conservative reporters and printers packed a meeting of the cooperative with goons and voted Scherer García out of the editorship. More than 200 writers, reporters, and photographers then walked out of the paper in protest.

After Scherer García's ouster, those who seized control of *Excélsior* scrambled to hire a new staff—a staff that included Eduardo Borrell, who had served as minister of education under Cuban dictator Fulgencio Batista. The formerly proud paper became a pro-government rag that began a slow descent into insolvency and irrelevance.

Rather than remaining silent, Scherer García soon founded a weekly news magazine, *Proceso*, which began to publish outspoken journalism of a quality that Mexico had not seen since the advent of PRI rule. It repeatedly denounced financial impropriety and published proof of its occurrence. Ironically, the coverage provided by *Proceso* on topics such as electoral fraud, repression, environmental damage, and biased media coverage was even more hard-hitting than that provided by *Excélsior* under Scherer García.

ELENA PONIATOWSKA

Writer Elena Poniatowska was born in Paris in 1932. Given her background, it would not have taken much imagination to think she would make her mark on the world. On her father's side she was descended from various illustrious figures, including Benjamin Franklin and the last king of Poland Stanislaus Augusto Poniatowski. In 1863 her maternal great-grandfather José María Amor y Escandón fled civil war in Mexico and settled in France, the homeland of his wife.

Had it not been for World War II Poniatowska would likely have made her mark in Europe. However, in 1942 Poniatowska, her mother, and her sister fled Nazi-occupied France and returned to her mother's ancestral homeland.

Poniatowska was enrolled in a private school in Mexico City and later attended high school at the Convent of the Sacred heart near Philadelphia. Her stint in the United States allowed her to master English, in addition to the French and Spanish she had already acquired. While in high school she began her literary career by winning an essay contest. Her essay "On Nothing" —written in English—was published in 1950 in the *Current Literary Coin*.

Then an unexpected event—the devaluation of the Mexican peso—changed the course of her life. Her family had planned to send her to college in the United States. However, after the devaluation, funds for higher education ran short, so she returned to Mexico where she faced the same dilemma faced by Sor Juana—what should a talented, intelligent young woman do in a male-dominated society.

Fortunately for her, times had changed—a little—since colonial days. Through a classmate's uncle who worked at the paper *Excélsior,* she was hired as a reporter. She was assigned to report for the social section, the only position open to women regardless of talent.

Poniatowska dutifully set about covering weddings, baptisms, first communions, and other rites of Mexico City's elite. In her first break with tradition, she insisted on actually attending events she reported on, rather than simply inquiring by phone, "What did the bride wear?"

Not long after she was hired, she met U.S. ambassador Francis White at a cocktail party and interviewed him. This interview, published in *Excélsior,* was the first of many and brought her to the attention of the Mexican literary establishment. For years she conducted interviews with a broad range of figures including filmmaker Luis Buñel, writer Octavio Paz, muralist Diego Rivera, and actresses Dolores del Rio and Grace Kelly. Another interview subject was Mexican astrophysicist Guillermo Haro, whom she later married. In the 1990s her interviews were collected in an eight-volume set entitled *Todo México.*

A co-worker at her paper remarked: "Fortunately she hadn't studied journalism. This allowed her to follow her own instinct." Poniatowska had a less charitable view of her journalism stint: "Misogyny always made me feel I'd been stabbed in the back. They never paid me as much as the men. They never gave me the same space or the same recognition."

Subsequently Poniatowska branched out and wrote more than forty books, including short stories, plays, chronicles, reportage, novels, essays, and biographies. In 1954 she published *Lilus Kirkus*, a semi-autobiographical collection of short stories about a curious, privileged girl. As was typical of the time, the book had a press run of 500.

Two years later she published a satirical play *Melés y Teléo*. In 1963 she published *Todo empezó el domingo*, an illustrated description of the life of street people. Six years later *Hasta no verte Jesús mío* (*Here's to You, Jesusa!*, 2001) was released. This novel, which depicts a slum dweller, was based on the life of Jesusa Palancares, a washerwoman whom Poniatowska befriended. The novel went through forty-five printings. These last two works indicate her turning her back on the elite and becoming a voice for those without a voice—a path she would continue through her career.

The 1968 student massacre transformed Poniatowska into a prominent literary figure. She collected first-person testimony, songs, posters, photos, and published them as a collage entitled *La Noche de Tlatelolco* (*Massacre in Mexico*, 1975). Initially, sales were spurred by the rumor that authorities would remove the book from the market for its telling the truth about what happened to the students. Eventually the book sold more than 600,000 copies. Its publication marked another milestone in Poniatowska's career—her unabashed association with the Mexican left.

Ever since her literary career has flourished. Following the 1985 Mexico City earthquake she published *Nada, nadie: las voces del temblor* (*Nothing, Nobody: The Voices of the Mexico City Earthquake*, 1995). The 1990s saw *Tinísima* (*Tinisma*, 1998), a novel based on the life of 1920s photographer and political activist Tina Modotti.

Poniatowska continued to produce a steady stream of works. In 2014 she declared she "would write faster because there's less time left." Her vast output has been translated into Polish, French, Danish, Dutch, English, German, Russian, Japanese, and Italian.

In addition to her literary activity, for decades Poniatowska has promoted progressive causes. She repeatedly visited Lecumberri Prison to interview political prisoners jailed there for their participation, among other things, in the 1968 student movement and the 1959 railroad strike. After expressing support for the EZLN, she was invited to Chiapas where she interviewed rebel leader Marcos. When Andrés Manuel López Obrador ran for president, she frequently appeared with him to support his candidacy.

Poniatowska has received several honorary doctorates and numerous awards, including in 2013 the Premio Cervantes, the highest award for Spanish literature. She commented that receiving the award was "the most important event of my literary life." In her acceptance speech she discussed Mexico's current problems and reaffirmed her interest in Mexico's common people. She declared them to be more interesting than the bourgeoisie appearing in the social section.

For decades *Proceso* remained as the most widely circulated, most influential political weekly in Mexico. However, after Scherer García retired in 1996, its circulation declined from 200,000 to 70,000, and it faced increasing competition from other newsmagazines such as *Este País*, *Milenio Semanal*, and *Voz y Voto*. It also faced increased competition from the increasingly independent electronic media.

Journalistic independence also increased with the 1993 founding of another Mexico City newspaper—*Reforma*. Since they received some of the highest salaries in the industry, $1,500 to $3,000 a month, *Reforma* reporters were not forced into seeking government funds in exchange for favorable coverage. By 2002, the paper had a circulation of 126,000, despite the PRI-dominated newspaper vendors' union refusing to sell it, and was considered the most influential paper in Mexico.

The success of *Reforma* and *Proceso* paved the way for more independent journalism throughout Mexico. Other papers, ranging from *El Diario de Yucatán* in Mérida to *Zeta* in Tijuana, plunged into critical journalism.

By 2000, Mexico's media had evolved from a closed, corrupt, establishment-oriented press to a reasonably vigorous Fourth Estate. There was regular coverage of official repression, corruption, lying, impunity, and electoral fraud. This independence did not emerge overnight, but was the product of more than two decades of learning and struggle.

TELEVISION

> It is difficult to overstate the potential influence of television on Mexican political life. Over two-thirds of Mexicans get their information about politics primarily from the small screen, and even among the most affluent and educated segments of the population, television remains the dominant medium.
>
> (Chappell Lawson, 2004)

In 1973, Mexico's two TV networks merged to form Televisa (which is short for Televisión via Satélite), thus creating what was for all intents and purposes a private television monopoly. The merger created the largest television network in Latin America. Televisa became a far-flung conglomerate, broadcasting Spanish-language television in the United States, exporting its soap operas to roughly ninety countries, producing film and print media, and staging sports and artistic events. Eventually Televisa became the world's largest producer of TV programming.

For more than two decades, Televisa and the PRI were deeply intertwined, with the network depending on the regime for broadcast licenses and infrastructure development, and successive PRI regimes depending on Televisa for political marketing. Emilio Azcárraga Milmo, who assumed control of the family broadcast empire after his father's death in 1972, made the network's pro-PRI slant explicit. In January 1988, he stated: "We're from the PRI, we're members of the PRI, we don't believe in any other party. And as members of our party, we will do everything possible to make sure our candidate wins."

In their 2001 biography of Azcárraga, authors Claudia Fernández and Andrew Paxman proclaimed him to have been "the most powerful businessman Mexico has ever seen." This power came from his enjoying a quasi-monopoly on television. In 1993, Televisa produced all of the twenty top-rated shows in Mexico. In 1994, *Forbes* placed his family's net worth at $5.4 billion. Azcárraga was a famously autocratic leader, a man of vast appetites, and extravagant gestures. His 243-feet long custom-built yacht *Eco* cost an estimated $45 million.

Change came more slowly to television than to print media, since Televisa's quasi-monopolistic nature shielded it from competitive pressure. Serious competition to Televisa only emerged in 1993 when the Salinas administration privatized a little-watched government TV network, selling it to Ricardo Salinas Pliego (no kin to the president) for $642 million dollars.

Electoral coverage on television reflected the changes in Mexican politics and society. By 1994, the airtime dedicated to major parties approximated their share of the national vote. The change was not only in volume, but in tone, in that the opposition was not routinely denigrated. In 2000, the two most watched news shows gave PAN candidate Fox 36 percent of their airtime, while PRI candidate Labastida received 33 percent. Rather than reflecting a new political bias, this imbalance likely resulted from the baritone-voiced Fox being a master at showmanship and the PRI candidate's being conspicuously bland.

UNSUSTAINABILITY

During the last forty years of the twentieth century, Mexico lost 30 percent of its forest and jungle and continued to lose between 600,000 and 800,000 hectares a year. Roughly 95 percent of this loss was due to the clearing of land for cattle raising or for poor peasants to farm.

Erosion resulting from deforestation caused the loss of millions of tons of soil annually. Denuded hillsides shed water much more quickly, and floodwaters rose higher as river channels silted up. In 1999, after a week of storms in southeastern Mexico, at least 373 were confirmed dead from flooding.

In 2000, the value of Mexico's standing forests was 6.5 times the value of timber harvested. The value of standing timber results from trees mitigating flooding and evening out water flow. Given Mexico's minimal commitment to preservation, as the economy expanded under NAFTA there was, not surprisingly, a significant increase in deforestation.

Even though Mexico had many sound environmental laws on the books, they were not vigorously enforced due to corruption, poor administration, or high short-term economic cost. In the decade after NAFTA went into effect, the number of plant-level inspections dropped precipitously, suggesting that Mexico had become less assiduous about enforcement. In 2005, economist Kevin Gallagher described the result of poor environmental infrastructure and lax law enforcement:

> Here in Mexico, just about every environmental measure has worsened since about 1985. If you look at levels of soil erosion, municipal solid waste, urban air pollution, urban water pollution, they've all grown faster than the economy itself and population growth in Mexico. According to the Mexican government's own estimates, that environmental degradation has cost the Mexican government about 10 percent of its GDP each year or about $45 billion each year in a country where half its hundred million people live in poverty, on less than two dollars a day.[2]

THE END OF NATIONALISM, 1971–2000

From Distant Neighbor to NAFTA Partner

For six Mexican presidential terms after World War II, the United States did not publicly meddle in Mexican affairs. Officials in Washington showed unusual flexibility concerning the notion of democracy. Stability was preferred over the more unpredictable consequences of political reform. U.S. policymakers viewed Mexican stability as essential for national security and protecting U.S. investment in Mexico. In 1972, a secret U.S. government document stated, "It is important to our security that there be in Mexico a friendly, cooperative, and politically stable government and that no hostile power have access to the territory of Mexico."

President Echeverría (1970–76) sought to diversify Mexico's international political and economic relations. His administration played a leading role in formulating the proposal for a new international economic order that was endorsed by the United Nations General Assembly. The Mexican president stridently proclaimed Mexico's "victimization" at the hands of the "colossus of the north."

During Echeverría's term, his rhetoric about sovereignty and independence notwithstanding, Mexican reliance on the United States, as measured by foreign investment, external debt, foreign trade, and the role of American banks, increased. Ironically, the United States, rather than Echeverría's Third World allies, bailed him out of his end-of-term financial crisis by providing a $600-million loan to support the peso.

During both Echeverría's term and that of his successor, Central America emerged as a thorn in the side of U.S.–Mexican relations. For U.S. policymakers, conflicts in Nicaragua and El Salvador were part of the Cold War fomented by Cuba and the Soviet Union. This led them to view each Central American nation as a potential domino that could spread revolution and endanger the United States.

Mexican policymakers viewed violence in Central America not as falling dominos but as an attempt to right social injustice and end political oppression. They felt conflicts there were a prelude to political modernization that the United States and local oligarchies sought to thwart.

Neither Echeverría's anti-imperialist rhetoric nor his Central American policy seriously undermined the two nations' well-established modus vivendi. In 1977 a CIA document stated, "Since most Mexican administrations have believed that Mexico's economic health is dependent upon maintaining good relations with the U.S., foreign policy toward the U.S. has been consciously pragmatic and non-ideological in content and non-contentious in style."

Despite López Portillo's attempt to set a more independent foreign policy, U.S. economic domination of Mexico increased during the years of the oil boom. Between 1977 and 1980, U.S.–Mexico trade increased by 42 percent a year. U.S. investment likewise increased. In 1981, as two-way trade between the two nations exceeded $26 billion, Mexico became the third largest U.S. trading partner.

U.S. influence over Mexico increased still further after the 1982 debt crisis, since the U.S. and the IMF (in which the United States exercised strong influence) conditioned their loans on certain financial behavior. At the time the United States became seriously concerned about the collapse of the Mexican economic and political system. During the mid-1980s, international investors, the U.S. media, the U.S. Congress, and U.S. officials began to express concern about the lack of democracy in Mexico, due not so much to deeply felt democratic convictions but to a sudden awareness of the danger a chaotic situation in Mexico augured for the United States.

Pro-democracy activist Sergio Aguayo commented on the U.S. failure to criticize undemocratic practices for so long, "I believe that the PRI's capacity to survive has been greatly enhanced by the support of the international community, and in particular the United States."

After a brief flirtation with the PAN in the mid-1980s, the U.S. embrace of Mexican incumbents resumed with the meeting of Carlos Salinas de Gortari and George H. W. Bush in Houston, when both were presidents-elect. This closeness resulted from U.S. awareness that, as the 1988 Mexican election showed, Salinas had a weak political base, which could easily result in instability. The renewed appreciation for PRI administrations also reflected leftist candidate Cuauhtémoc Cárdenas's emerging as the main challenger to the PRI. Another factor contributing to improved U.S.–Mexican relations was the 1980s crisis resulting in Mexico's adopting economic policies that won U.S. approval. As Lorenzo Meyer noted in 1989, "From the rabid right to the moderate left—not to mention the big banks and corporations—almost everyone agrees, for now, that the U.S. national interest requires real, open support for the Salinas government because there are few options, and all the others are worse."

The marked improvement in U.S.–Mexican relations provided tangible results for both nations. The Clinton administration invested considerable political capital to secure the passage of NAFTA and then went out on a limb to arrange a massive economic bailout early in 1995. The U.S.-sponsored Brady Plan reduced the amount of debt and the amount of payments due to the nearly 500 participating banks. Finally, the United States did not allow specific issues, such as drug trafficking or immigration, to cast a pall over U.S.–Mexican relations in general.

The United States gained as Mexico ceased its traditional gringo-baiting. As analyst (and later foreign minister) Jorge G. Castañeda noted, "It made no sense, on the one hand to put all of Mexico's eggs in one basket (namely the one that held foreign financing, business confidence, and U.S. support) and then proceed to kick and quarrel with the owner of the basket."

Presidents Zedillo (1994–2000) and Clinton met at least once a year and continued their predecessors' efforts to develop a cooperative bilateral relationship. Several indicators show the depth of the relations that had developed by the end of their terms. The U.S. embassy in Mexico City employed roughly 1,000 people, making it the largest U.S. embassy in the world. Some fifty different bilateral commissions addressed problems concerning agriculture, transportation, NAFTA rules of origin, health standards, customs cooperation, labor matters, and the environment. The number of NGOs, media outlets, and corporations linking the two nations soared. By the end of the 1990s, roughly 600,000 U.S. citizens lived in Mexico.

NAFTA not only led to increased trade and investment, but marked a shift in U.S.–Mexican relations. Mexicans ceased defining their national interest in terms of independence from the United States and protecting their economy from foreign competition. The new paradigm embraced closeness to and integration with the United States. Relations with the United States became increasingly dominated by economic considerations.

Drug Trafficking

In the 1950s and 1960s, opium poppies were cultivated in the north-central states of Sinaloa, Durango, and Chihuahua. During this period, Mexico supplied 10–15 percent of the heroin consumed in the United States and as much as 75 percent of the imported marijuana. Drugs were usually grown on small farms and then spirited into the United States by members of well-established smuggling families, some of which got their start running alcohol across the border during Prohibition. Such trafficking involved the bribing of local and regional officials, but did not lead to significant violence. The CIA knew Mexican officials were involved in drug trafficking, but Cold War priorities led them to keep this involvement quiet.

The modern era of drug trafficking between Mexico and the United States began on September 21, 1969 as the U.S. government launched Operation Intercept to pressure the Mexican government into more vigorously combating drug trafficking. Without even giving the Mexican government advance notice, some 2,000 U.S. customs officials began thoroughly searching all cars crossing into the United States from Mexico. Quite predictably enormous traffic jams ensued, and local economies on both sides of the border suffered. Operation Intercept responded to the huge increase in marijuana imports from Mexico and indicated President Nixon's desire to project a "tough-on-crime" image. It was successful in that it pressured the Mexican government to increase enforcement efforts.

During 1975 and 1976, Mexico spent $35 million to deploy 5,000 soldiers and 350 police to eradicate drugs in the states of Sinaloa, Durango, and Chihuahua. Troops in the field manually eradicated plants, and aircraft sprayed a highly toxic herbicide, paraquat, on fields. This mobilization—known as Operation Condor—was most effective against small producers. As production by small producers declined, there was a sharp decline in illegal drugs coming from Mexico. However, major producers survived these eradication efforts and increased in strength. Strikingly, even though hundreds of peasants were detained, tortured, and jailed, not a single major trafficker was arrested.

In the late 1970s and early 1980s, cocaine was flown across the Caribbean from Colombia to the United States. To close this smuggling route, Drug Enforcement Agency surveillance planes blanketed U.S. coastal waters. Rather than abandoning the U.S. market, Colombian traffickers diverted their cocaine flights to Mexico. Then the drugs would be spirited across some isolated border region or hidden in one of the hundreds of thousands of vehicles that cross the U.S.–Mexico border daily. Mexico's emergence as a transshipment point for northbound cocaine can easily be quantified. In 1982–83, only 300 kilograms of cocaine were seized in Mexico. By 1991, this figure had risen to more than fifty tons. As Colombian cartels split apart, Mexicans assumed the dominant position in supplying the U.S. market with South American cocaine.

U.S. actions to combat drug trafficking increased during the 1980s. During Reagan's tenure (1981–89), Washington consistently demonstrated its preference for preventing drugs from reaching the U.S. consumer over, as historian Oscar Martínez expressed it, "seriously facing up to the voracious consumption of drugs in U.S. society and coming up with effective means to reduce demand."

In response to increased enforcement efforts, marijuana growers retreated into inaccessible regions of the Sierra Madre Occidental. Increased interdictions forced traffickers into entrepreneurial organizations that were fewer in number, financially stronger, and more dangerous to society and government. Traffickers increasingly bribed and employed violence to protect themselves. At a 1987 U.S. Senate sub-committee hearing, U.S. Customs Commissioner William Von Raab stated: "The good news is that we are catching more drugs because we are getting better at doing our jobs. We have more resources. The bad news is that we are catching more because more is coming across."

During Salinas's term (1988–94) more than 102,000 were jailed for trafficking, and drug seizure and plant eradication reached record levels. Prisons were filled with small-time traffickers and those subject to dubious arrests, thus earning praise from U.S. officials as a sign of getting tough on drugs. At that time traffickers brought in more dollars than oil or tourism. Enforcement efforts notwithstanding, Salinas preferred to downplay drug trafficking as he burnished Mexico's image to ensure the passage of NAFTA.

Increased enforcement did little to stem the flow of drugs from Mexico. In 2000, an estimated 20–30 percent of heroin, 50–60 percent of cocaine, and up to 80 percent of marijuana imported by the United States came from Mexico. NAFTA greatly facilitated drug trafficking as smugglers inserted drugs into legal cargo loaded onto commercial trucks. They relied on the inability of customs to thoroughly inspect each shipment. Traffickers also used shipping containers and individuals known as "mules" who would walk drugs across the border.

Mexico's failure to suppress the drug trade is not surprising since for decades Mexico's highly centralized power structure actively protected drug trafficking. In exchange for an estimated $500 million in annual payoffs to local, state, and federal officials, traffickers went practically unchallenged and operated in relative harmony with each other. Under this protective umbrella, the cartels became extremely powerful.

Exodus

The end of the *bracero* program in 1965 essentially moved the same people, or their fellow villagers, from the category of *bracero* to unauthorized entrant. In 1964, 86,597 deportable aliens (the term used by the U.S. government) were located, while by 1970 that number had increased to 345,353. These increased numbers reflect the low number of jobs created in Mexico, as well as the enormous gap between U.S. and Mexican per capita income. In 1970, U.S. per capita income was more than $5,000, compared with about $700 in Mexico. The 1982 economic crisis led to increased immigration to the United States as wages and job creation declined in Mexico.

Before 1986, border enforcement to deter illegal crossings was largely a ritualized performance. All parties understood that after being repatriated would-be migrants would attempt to cross the border again and that on the next or subsequent attempt they would probably enter the United States successfully. In 1974, Commissioner of Immigration Leonard F. Chapman virtually decreed the border to be open when he declared that unauthorized workers apprehended outside the border area would no longer be detained or returned to their homelands.

Between 1965 and 1986, an estimated 28.0 million Mexicans entered the United States as unauthorized immigrants, compared with just 1.3 million legal immigrants and a mere 46,000 contract workers. Of the 28.0 million, 23.4 million worked for a short period and then voluntarily returned to Mexico.

To address the high volume of illegal immigration, Congress passed the Immigration Reform and Control Act of 1986 (IRCA). The main provisions of the bill were: 1) economic sanctions against U.S. employers who "knowingly employed" unauthorized workers; 2) permanent amnesty for unauthorized workers who could prove continuous unlawful residence in the United States

Figure 14.1 *The border fence is the site of frequent protests concerning immigration policy. This section of fence extends into the Pacific Ocean.*

Source: John Nelson/*San Diego Union-Tribune.*

since January 1, 1982; 3) an additional amnesty for agricultural workers who had worked at least ninety consecutive days between May 1, 1985 and May 1, 1986; and 4) sharply increased border enforcement.

IRCA granted amnesty to more than 3 million previously unauthorized workers, 75 percent of whom were estimated to be from Mexico. Once legalized, beneficiaries of IRCA legally brought in close relatives and offered a base to millions of friends and fellow villagers who immigrated illegally. Those who had arrived after 1982 remained as unauthorized workers.

For several years, IRCA did convince the U.S. public that it had regained control of its borders. It also decreased apprehensions for illegal entry from 1.77 million in 1986 to 0.95 million in 1989 as those who had been apprehended crossing illegally now crossed the border legally.

After 1989, this trend reversed, and undocumented immigration, as reflected in the number of apprehensions, began a steady increase. This resulted from job creation in Mexico languishing and immigrant networks providing jobs, housing, and economic support for the newly arrived. In addition the 1994 economic crash resulted in Mexican wages plummeting. This surge in undocumented immigration also reflected the almost total absence of the enforcement measures mandated by IRCA. In 1990, only fifteen firms were fined more than $5,000 for hiring unauthorized immigrants. The number of sanctioned firms subsequently declined, reaching zero in 2004, even as undocumented immigration surged.

President Clinton (1993–2001) was confronted with both push and pull forces of immigration. The U.S. economy was generating many low-wage (by U.S. standards), low-status jobs that the native-born were generally unwilling to fill. At the same time, Mexicans born in the 1970s and 1980s were coming of age and finding Mexico offered either no jobs or low-wage (even by Mexican standards) jobs. Mexicans, most of whom lacked legally required documents, responded by crossing the border to work. Between 1990 and 2000, the number of Mexicans in the United States rose from 4.3 million to 9.1 million.

The U.S. government responded to increased undocumented immigration with an escalation of enforcement activity. Between 1980 and 2000 the number of border patrol agents rose from 5,400 to 12,200. During this period, the amount budgeted for border enforcement increased by 1,200 percent—a figure that reflected increased man-hours, more extensive use of high-tech surveillance technology, and the constructing of border barriers.

Heightened enforcement had unanticipated effects. Rather than simply walking across the border on their own, those seeking unauthorized entry into the United States increasingly hired smugglers at a cost ranging from $1,200 to $1,500. Given isolation, rugged terrain, and temperature extremes in the areas where unauthorized entry was attempted, the number dying increased and has remained high ever since, averaging 413 a year between 2004 and 2006. Finally, given the increased cost and danger of crossing the border, unauthorized Mexican workers, once they arrived in the United States, remained. Before IRCA, 25 to 30 percent of unauthorized workers returned annually on a voluntary basis. However, after 1998 only 10 percent did. As sociologist Douglas Massey noted, "Paradoxically, the principal effect of border militarization has been to reduce the odds of going home, not of coming in the first place." Despite the deployment of increased manpower and equipment, the number of undocumented immigrants apprehended rose inexorably, reaching 1.81 million in 2000.

DOCUMENT 14.1: THE IMMIGRANT MOTHER

[The following is a poem about immigrant life in the United States.]

ELENA
by Pat Mora

My Spanish isn't enough
I'd remember how I'd smile
listening to my little ones,
understanding every word they'd say,
their jokes, their songs, their plots.
Vamos a pedirle dulces a mamá. Vamos.
But that was in Mexico.
Now my children go to American high schools.
They speak English. At night they sit around
The kitchen table, laugh with one another.
I stand by the stove and feel dumb, alone.
I bought a book to learn English.
My husband frowned, drank more beer.
My oldest said, "*Mamá,* he doesn't want you
to be smarter than he is." I'm forty,
embarrassed at mispronouncing words,
embarrassed at the laughter of my children,
the grocer, the mailman. Sometimes I take
my English books and lock myself in the bathroom,
say the thick words softly,
for if I stop trying, I will be deaf.
When my children need my help.

Source: Gilbert Joseph and Timothy J. Henderson (eds.) (2002) *The Mexico Reader.*
Durham, N.C.: Duke University Press, pp. 731–32.

NOTES

1   For commentary on the possibility of a less precipitous shift from import-substitution industrialization to an export-based economy see Louise Walker, *Waking from the Dream* (Stanford, CA: Stanford University Press, 2013), pp. 223–34, notes 66–68, and James Cypher and Raúl Delgado, *Mexico's Economic Dilemma* (Lanham, MD: 2010), pp. 40–42.

2   "Living on Earth," National Public Radio, July 8, 2005.

FURTHER READING

Andreas, Peter (1998) "The Political Economy of Narco-Corruption in Mexico," *Current History* 97 (April), pp. 160–65.
  Andreas discusses the interaction between government and drug traffickers.

Cypher, James (1990) *The State and Capital in Mexico.* Boulder, CO: Westview Press.
  An examination of how Mexico adopted import substitution in the 1940s and then shifted to neoliberal policies in the 1980s.

Davidow, Jeffrey (2004) *The U.S. and Mexico: The Bear and the Porcupine.* Princeton, NJ: Markus Weiner.
  A study of U.S.–Mexican relations by a former U.S. ambassador to Mexico.

Gentleman, Judith (1987) "Mexico after the Oil Boom," *Mexican Politics in Transition*, ed. Judith Gentleman, pp. 41–62. Boulder, CO: Westview.
  An examination of how Mexico responded to the 1980s economic crisis.

Grayson, George W. (1988) *Oil and Mexican Foreign Policy.* Pittsburgh, PA: University of Pittsburgh Press.
Grayson considers the Mexican oil industry and how oil shaped Mexican foreign policy.

Lustig, Nora (1992) *Mexico: The Remaking of an Economy.* Washington, D.C.: Brookings Institution.
An economist looks at the shift to neoliberal economic policies.

Marichal, Carlos (1997) "The Vicious Cycles of Mexican Debt," *NACLA Report on the Americas* (Nov.–Dec.), pp. 25–31.
A description of 1980s high finance.

Massing, Michael (2000) "The Narco State," *New York Review of Books* 47 (June 15), pp. 24–29.
A look at late twentieth-century drug trafficking.

Smith, Peter (1996) *Talons of the Eagle.* New York: Oxford University Press.
Smith considers twentieth-century U.S.–Latin American relations.

Weintraub, Sidney (1990) *A Marriage of Convenience.* New York: Oxford University Press.
Weintraub discusses the increased integration between the U.S. and Mexico.

GLOSSARY TERM

neoliberalism

The Twenty-first Century

Chapter 15

Twenty-first-century Mexico

TIMELINE—WORLD

2000	2000	2001	2001	2003
Atmospheric CO_2 levels measured at Mauna Loa Obersatory, Hawaii, average 370 parts per million	George W. Bush declared winner of U.S. presidential election	9/11 terrorist attacks in U.S.	U.S. invades Afghanistan	U.S. invades Iraq

2012	2013	2014	2014	
World population reaches 7 billion, 13 years after reaching 6 billion	Atmospheric CO_2 levels measured at Mauna Loa exceed 400 parts per million for first time	Russia annexes Crimea	ISIS emerges as major force in Syria and Iraq	

TIMELINE—MEXICO

2000	2004	2006	2007	2009
Vicente Fox elected president and Andrés Manuel López Obrador elected mayor of Mexico City	Some 250,000 demonstrate against violent crime in Mexico City	Felipe Calderón elected in disputed election	Carlos Slim declared to be world's richest man	Outbreak of swine flu

2003	2004	2008	2010	2011
India and Pakistan restore full diplomatic relations	Congress Party victory wins Indian general election	Barack Obama elected U.S. president	China becomes world's largest energy consumer	Osama bin Laden killed

2009	2012	2014	2014	2014
PRI continues comeback, winning 48 percent of seats in Chamber of Deputies	Peña Nieto election marks return of PRI to presidency	*Autodefensa* forces combat cartels in Michoacán	Joaquín "El Chapo" Guzmán arrested	43 normal school students from Ayotzinapa, Guerrero, kidnapped and presumably murdered

THIS CHAPTER CONSIDERS TWENTY-FIRST CENTURY MEXICO. It begins with a description of how formal democracy has functioned under the presidencies of Vicente Fox, Felipe Calderón, and Enrique Peña Nieto. It also describes how the major parties have evolved since the inauguration of Fox in 2000. The chapter then considers societal changes since 2000. Next is a description of how the Mexican economy has performed and what impact the North American Free Trade Agreement (NAFTA) has had after its being in force for twenty years. Finally, there is a description of how U.S.–Mexican relations have evolved during the administrations of George W. Bush and Barack Obama.

MULTI-PARTY MEXICO

The 2000 Election

As the year 2000 approached, the Revolutionary Institutional Party (PRI) faced a task that it had never before confronted—deciding how it would select its presidential candidate. Since President Zedillo refused to make the selection personally, the party decided to hold a primary election, which was won by Francisco Labastida, a former governor of Sinaloa who had served in three cabinet posts. PAN candidate Vicente Fox, the governor of Guanajuato and a former Coca-Cola executive, selected himself. Breaking with PAN tradition, three years before the election Fox announced he was seeking the nomination. He organized an independent group, the Friends of Fox, to promote his candidacy. Fox—a towering figure, over six foot six in his trademark cowboy boots—toured Mexico, taking the PAN by storm. He stressed the need for change and courted business by declaring, "The private sector will be completely integrated into the task of governing." By the fall of 1999, he had built up so much political momentum that no other candidate registered for the PAN presidential primary, leaving Fox as the PAN candidate by default.

As was the case with the PAN, PRD candidate selection was a product of self-selection. In April 1999, while still serving as Mexico City mayor, Cuauhtémoc Cárdenas announced he would seek the presidency for a third time. He faced no serious challengers from within the party.

At the end of November 1999, 43 percent of voters polled declared they would vote for Labastida, while Fox's support was 27 percent and Cárdenas's 8 percent, with 22 percent undecided. The three main presidential candidates agreed there was a pressing need for foreign investment and fiscal discipline. None of the three advocated turning away from the economic policies set in place by former president Carlos Salinas and his successor Ernesto Zedillo. This is not surprising since during the first nine months of 2000 Mexico's economy was growing at a brisk 7.5 percent.

More than ever before, the 2000 Mexican presidential campaign was media-driven, taking on the trappings of U.S. presidential campaigns. Fox summed up the crucial role of TV during the campaign: "Have charisma, and look good on TV, and you can become president." PRD leader Andrés Manuel López Obrador was less upbeat on the role of media, declaring, "Combine money, television, and the large number of Mexican voters who are nearly illiterate, and you could elect a cow as president."

As the date of the July election approached, most polls showed Labastida remained ahead of Fox, but the difference between the two candidates was less than the margin of error. What was clear was that in the five months before the election, there had been a 12 percent shift in voter preferences away from Labastida and toward Fox. It was the campaign itself that had caused this shift, not voters' political loyalties at the start of the 2000 campaign.

Figure 15.1 *Vicente Fox, who learned marketing as a Coca-Cola executive, excelled at marketing himself as a candidate.*

Source: Benjamin Flores/*Proceso.*

At 8 a.m., July 2, 2000, almost all of the 113,000 polling places around Mexico opened on time. At 11 p.m., José Woldenberg, president of the Federal Electoral Institute (IFE), announced on television that Fox had won. He declared, "We are a country in which a change of government can be accomplished peacefully by means of regulated competition, without recourse to force by the loser, without risk of retrogression." Immediately after Woldenberg spoke, Zedillo pre-empted any attempt by the PRI to challenge the results. He confirmed Fox's victory and declared, "For the good of our beloved Mexico, I sincerely hope for the success of the next government which will be led by Vicente Fox."

Rather than resorting to the standard litany of election losers, "We wuz robbed," the losing candidates accepted that Fox had won with 43 percent of the vote. The PRI had little choice but to accept the results of the election which credited its candidate with 37 percent of the vote since it had few of the levers of power that it had held in 1988.

Political scientist Lorenzo Meyer reflected the consensus when he stated, "In July 2000, Mexico underwent its first orderly and relatively peaceful change of political regime in its history as an independent country." Immediately after the elections, a majority of Mexicans, regardless of their party affiliation, considered that Mexico was a democracy.

Annalists scrutinizing the 2000 election pointed to several indicators of a functioning democracy. As a result of the elections, seventy-one years of one-party rule ended. Numerous voters split their ticket, selecting Fox and congress members from parties other than the PAN. Unlike previous presidential elections in which the outcome was foreordained, the campaign itself changed the outcome of the election. The principal criticism of the election was that it became a dispute between two parties that were so similar ideologically that they did not offer voters significant choice of policy, as opposed to personality.

411

Table 15.1 *Twenty-first-century presidential election results (%)*

	2000	2006	2012
PRI	36.89	22.11	38.21
PRD	17.00	35.15	31.59
PAN	43.43	35.71	24.41

Notes: totals do not equal 100% since minor parties were on the ballot and some ballots were nullified; totals in some cases reflect coalitions between a major party and minor parties

Sources: Philip Russell, *History of Mexico: From Pre-Conquest to Present* (New York: Routledge, 2010), pp. 585, 601 and *Reforma*, August 31, 2012, p. 4

Why Democracy Triumphed

Fox was able to get out his message, which emphasized "change," "booting the PRI out of Los Pinos (the presidential residence)," and taking on corrupt interests. However, he was never very specific on just what changes he sought.

The creation of a truly independent Federal Electoral Institute (IFE) was crucial for the emergence of electoral democracy. Once election administration was removed from the executive branch to the IFE, the PRI could not reverse this reform since it lacked sufficient seats in the Chamber of Deputies to change the law.

Much of the movement towards democracy in the 1990s occurred thanks to non-governmental organizations (NGOs) that brought together youthful reformers, environmentalists, old leftists, feminists, and other reform-minded people. These NGOs formed the non-partisan Civic Alliance (*Alianza Cívica*) which observed the 1994 elections. It continued to observe elections and press for further reform. Rather than mobilizing to support any one candidate, the Civic Alliance remained non-partisan and dedicated itself to ensuring electoral fairness.

Independent media was also crucial to the emergence of democracy. In the 2000 elections, the all-important TV coverage was generally balanced. Repeated press reports on scandals had undermined the establishment.

The PRI lost power because it implemented too many political reforms. Each reform was designed to placate the opposition while maintaining hegemony. After economic crises, it offered political reform, since it had nothing else to offer. Eventually these reforms created a relatively level playing field, forcing the PRI candidate to run on his own merits, which the voters found lacking.

The 2000 U.S. and Mexican Elections Compared

The progress Mexico made toward democratization during the last quarter of the twentieth century can be put into perspective by comparing Mexico's 2000 presidential election with the U.S. presidential election held the same year:

- In Mexico, each vote has equal weight. In the United States, as a result of the Electoral College, votes from states with low population count more. Thus it is possible, as occurred in the 2000 U.S. presidential elections, for the declared winner to receive fewer votes than his opponent.
- In Mexico, the non-partisan IFE organized the elections so that the administration of elections did not favor any one party. In the United States, elections were in the hands of partisan local officials, who may have, wittingly or unwittingly, made decisions favoring their own party.
- The candidates of all parties in the Mexican presidential elections were allowed into the first round of the televised debates. After the public had had a chance to hear their views, the three most popular candidates were selected, based on their polling numbers, to participate in the

second round. Opening the debate to all parties allowed the airing of ideas not widely voiced in the mainstream. For example, in the first debate, minor party candidate Gilberto Rincón Gallardo denounced intolerance against minority groups. He specifically mentioned the murder of homosexuals in Chiapas. In the U.S. election, only the Democratic and Republican candidates were allowed to debate.

- In Mexico, political parties and elections were publicly funded, and presidential campaigns had a $52 million spending limit. Corporate donations were prohibited. In 2000, the IFE distributed $300 million to the parties to maintain their organizations and to carry out campaigns. This sharply reduces the influence of moneyed interests in the electoral process. The IFE took these funding limitations seriously. The PAN and its coalition partner in the 2000 election were fined $48.8 million for failure to disclose donations of $8.1 million, for exceeding spending limits by $1.6 million, and for receiving $4 million from corporations. The PRI was fined $98 million for receiving $45 million that Pemex channeled through the oil workers' union to support the Labastida campaign.

- As a condition for receiving radio and TV licenses, Mexican broadcasters were required to allow candidates free access to the media. In Mexico, each party received 200 free TV hours and 250 hours of radio time and could use public funding to buy more airtime. This made candidates less beholden to moneyed groups than they were in the United States.

- A larger proportion of the electorate was involved in selecting Mexico's president in 2000. In Mexico, voter turnout was 64 percent. Only 51 percent voted in the U.S. elections. The difference in the percentage of adults voting is even wider than these figures would indicate since Mexico has a proactive voter registration program. Registrars go from house to house to register voters. In 2000, 93 percent of those over eighteen had been issued a voter ID. Only 63.9 percent of the U.S. population over eighteen was registered.

The Fox Administration, 2000–2006

When Vicente Fox took the oath of office in December 2000, he enjoyed an 80 percent approval rating. Even though many had predicted that replacing the experienced PRI with the novice PAN would plunge Mexico into chaos, the transition was impeccably smooth. The future seemed to bode socioeconomic change every bit as radical and far-reaching as the political change Fox's election victory represented.

Early in his presidency it became apparent that Fox was much better as a campaigner than as a president. In mid-2002, political scientist Lorenzo Meyer noted: "Fox is not the captain of the ship. We are just floating. I worry that the rest of his term is going to be characterized by just surviving." Congress, where Fox's PAN lacked a majority, handed him legislative defeats early in his administration. After that he was never able to regroup and seize the initiative. Fox found the media focused on his romance with his spokesperson Marta Sahagún, his marriage to her, her presidential aspirations, and the subsequent controversies involving the bride and groom's having their previous marriages annulled by the Catholic Church.

It became clear that Fox was not willing to confront the major interests created during decades of PRI rule. Among them were Pemex, Telmex, the Federal Electricity Company, the teachers' union, the oil workers' union, and the television duopoly. Fox's enormous legitimacy when he took office would have allowed him to successfully limit their power. Rather than clean house the Fox administration found it easier to establish alliances with corrupt, but powerful trade unions and with the PRI in hopes of getting its cooperation to pass legislation.

The mid-term elections in 2003 only compounded Fox's legislative problems. As a result of the elections, the PAN's delegation in the Chamber of Deputies shrank from 207 to 151, while that of the PRI increased from 211 to 224 and that of the PRD from 50 to 97.

During 2001 and 2002 economic growth averaged 0.42 percent. In 2003 voters punished the PAN for failing to deliver the 7 percent annual economic growth Fox had promised during his campaign. They slammed the PAN for Fox's failure to enact major fiscal reform. Also, as has happened throughout Latin America, the coming of democracy created high expectations that governments were not able to address immediately in terms of reduced poverty and economic inequality. Low turnout in 2003, as compared with 2000, reflected the large number of voters who voted to oust the PRI in 2000 but who saw no reason to vote again in 2003.

It was inevitable that Fox's presidency would lead to disappointment simply because problems resulting from seventy-one years of PRI rule were so systemic and because Fox had raised such high expectations. In addition, Fox was saddled with problems over which he had no control, including economic downturn in the United States, the impact of the 9/11 attacks, and an unscrupulous PRI opposition determined to make his administration fail.

The two main accomplishments for which Fox will be remembered are defeating the PRI and maintaining macroeconomic stability. Between 2000 and 2006, the Fox administration also reduced extreme poverty from 24.1 to 13.8 percent of the population—the result of wage increases, remittances sent from the United States, and his anti-poverty program *Oportunidades*. He instituted a very popular, voluntary health insurance program (*Seguro Popular*), which by 2006 served 3.7 million families, 95 percent of whom were in the bottom fifth of income earners. He also introduced a popular microcredit program that distributed $660 million. Finally, legislation established a transparency-in-government program analogous to that created by the U.S. Freedom of Information Act.

History will undoubtedly regard Fox as a transitional figure, much like Boris Yeltsin and Lech Walesa. As *Los Angeles Times* reporter Sam Enríquez noted just before the 2006 elections, "His accomplishments since booting out Mexico's long-ruling party six years ago have fallen short of his promises." Despite his failing to fulfill many of his promises, since people liked him as a person Fox left office with an approval rating of 61 percent.

The 2006 Election

The Candidates

> For the first time in a century, the right and the left are clearly defined as dominant political forces.
>
> (Sergio Aguayo, 2006)

The 2006 election cycle started out with a clear front-runner—Andrés Manuel López Obrador, widely referred to simply as AMLO. In 2000, López Obrador was elected mayor of Mexico City. PRD strength in Mexico City, plus López Obrador's natural gifts as a campaigner, enabled him to edge out two formable opponents—well-known lawyer and former PAN deputy Santiago Creel and former Mexican ambassador to the United States Jesús Silva-Herzog.

Rather than focusing on reform during the last half of his administration, Fox used the presidency to prevent AMLO from becoming president. His administration called for the removal of López Obrador's immunity from criminal prosecution. The Mexico City mayor, along with other top government officials, can only be indicted if Congress votes to strip of them of the immunity enjoyed by office holders. According to Mexican law, those who are under indictment cannot run for office.

The indictment the Fox administration sought resulted from López Obrador's supposedly having ignored a judge's order to halt construction on a road that crossed private property to provide access to a hospital. AMLO not only denied any wrongdoing but declared that removing his immunity was a desperate attempt to keep him off the 2006 ballot. On April 7, 2005, Congress voted 360 to 127 to strip AMLO of his criminal immunity, a process known as **desafuero**. In response, on April 24 more than 1 million staged a peaceful demonstration to protest the *desafuero*. Foreign media almost universally viewed the *desafuero* as being a politically motivated maneuver to keep a formidable rival off the ballot. Fox, afraid that the whole effort might lead to instability and spook investors, dismissed his attorney general, who was handing the matter, and did not raise the question of AMLO's supposed offense again. Rather than keeping AMLO off the ballot, the *desafuero* enhanced his popularity by casting him as an underdog standing up to the powerful.

While López Obrador gained national prominence as an outsider challenging the system, the PAN's 2006 presidential candidate began life as a political insider. His father was Luis Calderón Vega, an early PAN leader. The younger Calderón spent his childhood in a highly politicized environment, handing out leaflets and painting political signs on walls—the main form of political discourse before television—to promote PAN candidates.

In 1987, Calderón graduated from Mexico City's prestigious private Escuela Libre de Derecho with a law degree. He later received a master's in economics from the Autonomous Technological Institute of Mexico (ITAM) and another master's in public administration from the JFK School of Government at Harvard. From 2000 to 2003, Calderón served as the PAN coordinator in the Chamber of Deputies. He later served as Fox's secretary of energy.

For the 2006 presidential race, the PAN held a primary election to select its presidential candidate. Calderón won the PAN presidential primary with 51.79 percent of the vote. Calderón proved to be an effective campaigner, and his deep roots in the party appealed to party stalwarts who were less than enthusiastic about his main opponent, Santiago Creel, who only joined the party in 1999.

PRI candidate Roberto Madrazo first reached national prominence in 1994 when he was elected governor of Tabasco. AMLO, his opponent, charged that he had stolen the elections. That image had hardly faded before documents were leaked showing that he had spent $70 million dollars—many times the legal limit—during his gubernatorial campaign.

The Campaigns

Six major polls in January 2006 showed PRD candidate López Obrador with a 5 to 10 percent lead over his closest rival, Felipe Calderón. These same polls showed the PRI in a distant third place, where it would remain.

AMLO's campaign slogan was "First the Poor." His campaign style emphasized face-to-face contact at rallies held around the country. These rallies played to AMLO's great strength—his campaign charisma.

AMLO shared with all the candidates a commitment to address Mexico's chronic poverty, which he attributed to the neoliberal development model:

> The principal problem of the neoliberal model has been precisely the lack of economic growth. Between 1982 and 2003, the GDP has grown at an average annual rate of 2.2 percent. But if we consider population increase, *per capita* growth is barely 0.3 percent, that is, the economic policies of the last two decades measured merely quantitatively—without considering other factors such as income distribution—have been a failure and have not led to progress for Mexico.[1]

While AMLO attributed Mexico's problems to the neoliberal development model, Calderón embraced neoliberalism. Both AMLO and Calderón promised massive job creation. The PAN candidate differed from his main rival in declaring that during his administration job creation would be based on attracting foreign investment and that his administration would guarantee security.

In March the PAN began a blitz of negative TV spots that emphasized that AMLO was a "danger to Mexico." They were influenced by U.S. political consultant Dick Morris who advised the

Calderón campaign. Some ads juxtaposed AMLO and Venezuelan President Hugo Chávez. Another ad declared (with considerable exaggeration) that as mayor AMLO had bankrupted Mexico City with expensive public works projects. Other ads attempted to portray AMLO as an authoritarian, messianic, irresponsible populist who had ties to the revolutionary left and who was surrounded by corruption. As political scientist Denise Dresser noted in April, the PAN "feels that AMLO should be stopped and is using all the instruments at its disposal, including covering him with mud."

The barrage of attack ads had their intended effect. In mid-May, polls showed Calderón leading AMLO by about five percentage points. Then as the PRD also went negative with its ads and AMLO did well in the second presidential debate on June 6, this gap closed, with late June polls showing a dead heat. The burning question was whether AMLO was just shy of closing the gap or whether it had closed it.

After the Election

On election day July 2, 2006, the IFE did not receive a single report of anyone attempting to rig the vote. The election proceeded so smoothly that the next day the *New York Times* ran the following headline, "On a peaceful election day across Mexico, growing signs of a maturing democracy."

At 11 p.m. on election day, IFE President Luis Carlos Ugalde appeared on national television and announced that the election was too close to call. Finally, four days later the count ended with Calderón being credited with 0.58 percent more votes than López Obrador.

López Obrador, rather than conceding what appeared to be an extremely close election, charged election fraud and mobilized his supporters to defend the victory he claimed. On July 8, 500,000 AMLO supporters rallied in Mexico City's main plaza to protest "election fraud." On July 16, more than a million gathered in the plaza in one of the largest political demonstrations in Mexican history. On July 30, AMLO called for a massive sit-in in the plaza known as the Zócalo and along a major commercial avenue, the Paseo de la Reforma. The five-mile-long sit-in was the equivalent in length and impact to a prolonged sit-in blocking New York's Broadway from Houston Street to 92nd Street. This occupation lasted until September 15—a month and a half.

On September 5, the Federal Electoral Tribunal ruled that Calderón had won by 233,831 of the 41.6 million votes cast. According to Mexican law, decisions by the Federal Election Tribunal are final and cannot be appealed.

The PRD, which was credited with 35 percent of the vote, more than doubled the presidential vote it had won in 1994 and 2000. The party emerged as the second power in the Chamber of Deputies with 127 seats, a thirty-seat increase from 2003 to 2006, and twenty-six senate seats, an eleven-seat increase.

Calderón ran a well-organized, media-driven campaign. To a large extent, Calderón successfully transformed the election into a referendum on the Fox administration. Fox's success in lowering inflation and interest rates, increasing consumer credit, and maintaining anti-poverty programs attracted voters to the PAN.

The Calderon Administration, 2006–2012

Calderón was more successful at working with Congress to pass legislation than was Fox. In 2008 Congress passed a judicial reform. It introduced oral arguments into criminal trials and an adversarial system. In criminal trials there would be a presumption of innocence. Evidence beyond confessions—which in the past have often been the product of torture—would be required for conviction. The law instituting this reform provided for a phased implementation, so it will be years before its impact can be evaluated. It may well become Calderón's most positive legacy.

The first three years of the Calderón administration lacked any striking initiatives, as his government became increasingly bogged down in the war on drugs. Economic growth suffered due to recession in the United States. The 2009 congressional election served as a referendum on the first half of the Calderón presidency. His party, the PAN, lost sixty-three congressional seats. The election resulted in a significant weakening of Calderón's presidency. Columnist Lorenzo Meyer wrote that the president ran the "risk of becoming a political zombie."

If the latter part of the Fox administration was dominated by stopping AMLO, the latter part of the Calderón administration was dominated by the drug war. In 2010, Columnist Jorge Alcocer wrote, "The drug war which was declared against organized crime has not only consumed the energy of the President and his government, but has come to a dead end in which all that's left is the daily body count."

The 2008–09 recession sharply reduced foreign direct investment, remittances, exports, and tourism. On a per capita basis economic growth during Calderón's term was below 1 percent per year—one of the lowest rates in Latin America. Calderón clearly failed to deliver on his two major campaign promises—jobs and security.

The 2012 Election

> The PRI victory in 2012 was not due to its having a clear vision of the future. It was due to the ineptitude of the PAN when it was in power.
>
> (Lorenzo Meyer, 2013)

The PRD's 2012 presidential candidate, by mutual agreement of the two frontrunners, Andres Manuel López Obrador and Mexico City Mayor Marcelo Ebrard, was determined by a national poll that measured the popularity of the two. Each agreed not to run for president in 2012 if the other won the poll. AMLO out-polled Ebrard, thus becoming the PRD candidate.

For his campaign López Obrador stole the playbook from Peruvian president Ollanta Humala, who ran for president in 2006. In his 2006 campaign Humala's opposition successfully portrayed him as a virtual clone of Venezuelan president Hugo Chávez. Humala lost the election. In 2011, Humala ran again and won the presidency, making a point of embracing ex-Brazilian president Luis Ignácio Lula da Silva and distancing himself from Chávez. In 2012 López Obrador attempted the same strategy, positioning himself as a moderate. He ceased referring to Mexico's businessmen as a "mafia." In fact he became so conciliatory that pundits began referring to him as AMLOVE rather than AMLO.

Josefina Vázquez Mota became the PAN's presidential nominee by winning an internal primary election with 55 percent of the vote. She had worked for Fox's 2000 presidential campaign and served as his minister of social development. She resigned from that post to coordinate Felipe Calderón's 2006 political campaign and is widely regarded as having guided the campaign to victory.

Enrique Peña Nieto, the scion of a PRI-aligned political family in the state of Mexico, first achieved prominence as governor of the state of Mexico—Mexico's most populous state. As far back as September 2010, polls showed Peña Nieto far ahead of other potential presidential candidates. In that month, 43 percent of those polled said they preferred him to Santiago Creel (the top PAN contender) and AMLO (the top PRD contender).

In the first candidate debate Peña Nieto performed well above what was expected of him. Both Vázquez Mota and AMLO concentrated on attacking him, thus keeping the opposition more or less evenly divided.

A post-debate poll showed 49.6 percent of those declaring a preference opting for Peña Nieto, 24.8 percent for AMLO, and 23.1 percent for Vázquez Mota. Attention shifted to the two candidates jockeying for second place, since a Peña Nieto victory appeared foreordained. During

#YOSOY132

At a May 11, 2012 speaking appearance at the Universidad Iberoamericana presidential candidate Peña Nieto received a critical verbal reception which he had not expected from the school's elite students. Much of the criticism focused on a violently repressed protest in the small town of San Salvador Atenco, in the state of Mexico, when Peña Nieto was governor of that state. The Peña Nieto campaign charged that those challenging the PRI candidate were outside agitators brought in to discredit the campaign.

To prove Peña Nieto's reception was a reflection of student opinion, not of infiltrators, 131 Iberoamericana students produced an eleven-minute video showing each holding up their university

Figure 15.2 *Many Mexico City political demonstrations begin at the monument in the background known as the Angel of Independence. This protest by the #yosoy132 group criticized media bias.*

Source: Hugo Cruz/Procesofoto/DF.

ID. They posted the video on You Tube, where it was subsequently downloaded more than one million times. After viewing the video students from other universities, who began to use hashtag #YoSoy132, launched a protest movement along with Iberoamericana students.

Their first act was to a stage protest march from the Iberoamericana campus to Televisa studios. There they demanded balanced campaign coverage and charged that Peña Nieto was a candidate imposed and supported by Televisa.

During the final two months of the campaign, the protest movement spread to other states and brought in non-students. Activists staged well-attended protests at other Televisa installations where they repeated the charges made at the first march. As is common with social movements #YoSoy132 had an umbrella effect and drew in others advocating issues concerning women, gay rights, and the environment. Just as Alianza Cívica a generation earlier, #YoSoy132 did not endorse or even share organizing with any of the recognized political parties. Unlike traditional social movements, it remained very horizontal and did not have strong individual leaders.

Some individual actions of #YoSoy132 included:

- Setting up a website "wikifraude" which allowed people to present documents and testimony relating to election misconduct.
- Organizing a presidential candidate debate on June 19. Vázquez Mota, AMLO, and a minor party candidate attended. Peña Nieto was invited but declined to participate, charging the forum would be prejudiced against him.
- Issuing a post-election report that evaluated more than 2,700 pieces of evidence. The report concluded the presidential election was tainted by widespread vote buying, undue pressurizing of voters, spending above the legal limit, the illegal use of public resources, and the use of opinion polls designed not to measure public opinion but to promote Peña Nieto's candidacy. The report also noted there were 150 charges of election-related violence. Of these offenses, 97 percent were attributed to PRI.

Political scientist Augustín Basave concluded that the movement undermined the PRI sufficiently to deprive it of a majority in the Chamber of Deputies. This forced Peña Nieto to sign on to the 2012 Pact and to accede to the demands of other parties in drafting reform legislation.

#YoSoy132 clearly put democratization of the media on the national agenda. It also pressured Televisa to air a program *Sin Filtro* (Unfiltered) that aired a variety of student opinion.

#YoSoy132 was the first movement since the EZLN to elicit sympathy nationwide. If the EZLN was the first Mexican movement to show the power of the Internet, #YoSoy132 was the first to show the power of social media. Even though the movement has now faded away, as was the case with the 1968 student movement, many activists became politicized and continued organizing.

the campaign, AMLO (or AMLOVE) picked up 12 percentage points of preference, at the expense of both Peña Nieto and Vázquez.

From the debate until the July 1 election date, there was little change in the candidates' standing. On August 30 the Supreme Electoral Court declared Peña Nieto had won the election, which had been had been challenged by AMLO. Peña received 38.21 percent of the vote, compared to AMLO's 31.59 percent and Vázquez Mota's 24.41 percent. In congressional elections the same day, the PAN lost seats in both the Senate and the Chamber of Deputies, underlining voters' disapproval of twelve years of PAN administration, which had seen an increase in organized crime, lackluster economic growth, widespread allegations of corruption, and a lack of major reform.

Peña Nieto ran a well-organized, media-driven campaign. He promised profound reforms to snap Mexico out of twelve years of mediocre economic growth. He benefited from his being the candidate of the PRI—the only truly national party. His movie star-good looks also served him as 41 percent of women voted for him despite's Vázquez Mota's being the first major-party female presidential candidate.

AMLO filed a legal brief challenging the validity of the elections, listing a long list of campaign-rule violations. His allegations, which the Election Court dismissed, were summarized by Mexican legal scholar John Ackerman: "In 2012, extreme cases of media bias, vote-buying and overspending by the winning candidate went almost without notice by the authorities." A September 2013 poll indicated that only 38 percent of those polled felt the election was clean, while 59 percent did not.

The Peña Nieto Administration

Unlike his two immediate predecessors, Peña Nieto proved capable of forging a working relationship with Congress. One day after his December 1, 2012 inauguration he announced the Pact for Mexico—an agreement by the three major parties to work together in Congress to pass legislation advancing ninety-five enumerated problems, including the economy, employment, justice reform, and corruption. The PRI signed on because it was solidly united behind Peña Nieto. The PAN signed on because it wanted to erase the image of ineffectiveness generated by the two previous presidential terms. The PRD sought to use its congressional base to influence upcoming legislation, rather than simply being obtuse as it was during the Calderón administration. The PRD leadership felt this would extend the PRD base beyond AMLO loyalists. By virtue of the Pact, within the first year of his administration, Peña Nieto was able to break the twelve-year old congressional legislative logjam.

During Peña Nieto's first thirteen months in office, thanks to multiparty support, major reforms were passed involving education, telecommunications, banking, taxation, election rules, and energy.

The fiscal reform passed by congress increased taxes to enable the government to address its commitments in areas such as education, healthcare, and pensions and to end its over-reliance on Pemex to finance the federal budget. The agreed upon increase in taxes, including the value added tax (VAT), added roughly one percentage point of gross domestic product to government coffers. By virtue of its working within the Pact, the PRD was able to prevent food and medicine from being included in the list of items subject to the VAT.

The political reform eliminated the prohibition on re-election for mayors, state legislators, governors, and members of congress. The ban on presidential re-election was not removed. The reform replaced the Federal Electoral Institute (IFE) with a National Electoral Institute, which will not only organize presidential and congressional elections, but will exercise authority over elections for governor, mayors, and state legislations—jurisdiction denied to the IFE.

An educational reform implemented teacher evaluations and created an autonomous institute run by specialists to evaluate educational quality. The passage of the reform set off a wave of massive protest by unionized teachers who rejected it, claiming they had been left out of the loop in drafting it, that it placed excessive reliance on standardized tests, and that it attempted to implement nationwide standards, rather than allowing evaluation on a state-by-state basis. State-by-state evaluation could consider income levels and the number of indigenous students for whom Spanish is a second language. The vehemence of the protesters, who descended on Mexico City, set up prolonged encampments, and held sit-ins blocking traffic on major streets for hours, indicated that it's one thing to pass reform legislation and another thing to implement it.

The final reform—the reform that probably more than anything else will define Peña Nieto's legacy—involved energy. This reform removed the constitutional prohibition on private interests producing oil and generating and selling electricity. The reform was strongly opposed by AMLO and the PRD, which left the Pact to protest what they considered caving into financial interests to the detriment of Mexico's population.

While Peña Nieto moved forward on reforms at a pace not seen in a generation, security received less attention. The government estimated 15,000 homicides in 2014, down from 22,000 in 2012. In addition there was a wave of extortion and kidnappings. Peña Nieto's failure to control organized

Figure 15.3 *President Peña Nieto's standing rose early in his term, but then declined due to continued high levels of violence and the appearance of corruption.*

Source: Mario Armas/Procesofoto/Léon, Gto.

crime became glaringly obvious in Guerrrero where forty-three normal school students were kidnapped and presumably murdered. As security analyst Ana María Salazar noted in October 2013, "Insecurity and criminality remain the most difficult problem facing the country."

On the campaign trail Peña Nieto promised economic growth between 4 and 5 percent. In 2013 and 2014 economic growth averaged below 2 percent. Foreign demand remained lackluster in Mexico's export-oriented economy. The domestic economy failed to grow at promised rates as low-wage workers added little to demand and the newly installed government had yet to ramp up spending on projects such as public housing.

After two years in office, Peña Nieto's approval rating was only 39 percent, the lowest since the 1990s. Clearly poverty and insecurity weighed more heavily on those polled than reams of reform legislation, which as past experience has shown, often produced far less benefit than promised by reform supporters.

Political Parties

The PRI

The PRI, long accustomed to receiving orders from the incumbent president, faced two major challenges under Fox—determining who would be its leader and determining what the party stood for as an opposition party. The party did in fact drift rudderless and clueless for a period after Fox's inauguration. Finally Roberto Madrazo, the former governor of Tabasco, was selected PRI president, giving the party direction. Madrazo's leadership, the party's still formidable grass-roots machine, and its loyal base who almost instinctively voted for the PRI enabled the party to rebound.

The 2000 loss of the presidency was such a shock to the PRI that many considered the party might disappear. However the party's grass-roots structure served it well, so that between 2001 and 2004 the PRI won 49 percent of the 2,046 municipal elections. In 2003 it won 53 percent of the single member congressional districts, twice the PAN total. The party became a state-level party, with PRI governors sharing influence with the party's newly empowered National Executive Committee. Just as it had in the twentieth century, the party tried to be all things to all people. Political scientist Joy Langston characterized the post-2000 PRI as "amorphous and vague."

Thanks to the leadership of savvy president Beatriz Paredes, former governor of Tlaxcala, as well as the PAN's lackluster performance in terms of economic growth and security, the PRI further rebounded under Calderón. In 2008 PRI governors presided over 57 percent of Mexico's population at the state level. The big winner in 2009 mid-term elections was the PRI, which gained 131 seats and came in first or second in more than 90 percent of congressional districts. The successful PRI campaign adopted the slogan, "Today's PRI. Proven Experience. New attitude." In addition to its catchy slogan the PRI victory combined: 1) attractive candidates; 2) television; 3) money; 4) a nationwide political machine; and 5) party unity.

The PRI did well in 2009 since it occupied a vaguely defined political center, while the leadership of both the PRD and the PAN had become more polarized than the electorate. Lorenzo Meyer described the PRI as "searching for power for power's sake." Luis Rubio, the head of a Mexico City think tank, paraphrased the position of the PRI as, "We might be corrupt, but we're more efficient than the other guys."

Early in the Peña Nieto administration the PRI did not fare well. Economic growth and continued activity by drug cartels undermined the credibility of the incumbent president. Also the fact both Peña Nieto and his treasury secretary were found to own houses financed by a construction company that had won major government contracts undercut Peña Nieto's claim the party had turned over a new leaf.

The PAN

The PAN under Fox faced three challenges: 1) forging a working relationship between the PAN congressional delegation and the president; 2) forging a working relationship between the PAN congressional delegation (which remained a minority) and the delegations of other parties so that legislation could be passed; and 3) projecting a clear message of what the party stood for once the PRI had been removed from the presidency. The first task was made more difficult by Fox's having bypassed the party to win the PAN nomination and the presidential election, by his failure to appoint sufficient PAN members to his cabinet, and by PAN old-timers considering him an outsider who came late to the party after having had a career in business. The party's poor showing in the 2003 elections made the second task even more difficult. The party never rose to the third task facing it—clearly stating that it had something to offer beyond economic orthodoxy and a continuation of PRI social policies.

In 2006 the party benefited from increased economic growth between 2003 and 2006. Even though this growth was based largely on higher oil prices and U.S. imports, credit accrued to the PAN in the presidential election. However, once the election was over, a combination of forces led to a decline in the party's credibility. The 2008–09 recession put into question the economic management of the PAN administration. The mounting body count in the drug war during the Calderón administration further undermined the party. Finally, the party neglected its former strong suits—nationalism and social justice. These factors underlay the PAN's inability to retain the presidency in 2012.

The PRD

The PRD also faced an identity crisis, since it, like the PAN, had been founded to challenge the PRI for power. As with the left throughout Latin America, it had to articulate what it meant to be on the left in an increasingly globalized world. The party's message was further blurred by its becoming a haven for former members of the PRI, many of whom left the PRI when they failed to receive a desired nomination. As of early 2007, two-thirds of the party presidents had come from the PRI, as well as four of the seven governors who had been elected on the PRD ticket. The party's lack of a clear message is reflected in its receiving fewer votes than the PRI or the PAN in the 2003 congressional elections.

From the time of its formation up until 2000, the PRD was under the influence of Cuauhtémoc Cárdenas. After Cárdenas's third defeat as presidential candidate, Andrés Manuel López Obrador, mayor of Mexico City, became the dominant personality within the party.

The PRD's fortunes under Calderón were the direct opposite of the PRI's. López Obrador's prolonged demonstrations protesting the 2006 presidential election and his refusal to recognize Calderón as president played well to the PRD's radical wing, but cost substantial support among other voters.

The biggest loser in the 2009 election was the PRD, which in the 2006 congressional elections had received 29 percent of the vote—a record for the party. The party's vote share declined to 12 percent in 2009, reflecting disapproval of AMLO's post-election protests, the negative impact of the PRD's ongoing, very public internal struggles and its failure to articulate a clear position regarding the economic crisis.

The twenty-first century left, which has traditionally favored a stronger government role in economic affairs and has prioritized social justice over economic development, faces an uphill battle. The PRD's only strong leaders, Cárdenas born in 1934 and AMLO born in 1953, had difficulty connecting with younger voters. Before the 2012 elections, AMLO created MORENA, an independent support organization analogous to Fox's Friends of Fox. In September 2012, he announced that he would convert MORENA into a new political party that would focus on opposing the use of private capital to develop the oil industry—a measure he described as a counter-reform. AMLO's leaving the PRD complicates the left's political task. The minority of voters leaning to the left will be divided between the PRD and MORENA.

The forty-three students who were kidnapped also reflected negatively on the PRD. Both the mayor of Iguala, where they were kidnapped, and the governor of the state, Guerrero, were elected on the PRD ticket. In the aftermath of the kidnapping, founding member Cuauhtémoc Cárdenas resigned from the party, accusing it of "shortsightedness, opportunism, and self-compliancy."

The Military

In the twenty-first century, as was the case in the twentieth, the Mexican military confronts internal threats, not external foes. When Calderón initiated his aggressive campaign against drug trafficking, he assigned a major role to the military due the corruption and lack of professionalization in Mexico's police forces. As the military became more deeply involved in the war on drugs, the security budget increased from $4.5 billion in 2004 to $8 billion in 2008.

Rather than increasing civilian control over the military, as has occurred elsewhere in Latin America, Mexico has seen remilitarization in terms of troop levels, budgets, and the military's policing role and its political leverage. Even though Congress passes the military budget and on occasion calls the secretaries of navy and defense to testify, the military continues to operate with a high degree of autonomy.

In addition to resulting in many casualties, the increased military role in the war on drugs has produced a dramatic increase in the number of alleged human rights abuses attributed to soldiers.

Corruption has become so extensive that certain units are passed over for high-profile operations. Reliance on navy personal, who are viewed as more reliable, has increased even in strictly land operations. Thus navy personal carried out operations which resulted in the 2009 death of Arturo Beltrán Leyva in Cuernavaca and the 2014 arrest of Joaquín "El Chapo" Guzmán in Mazatlán. Despite, or perhaps because of, the military's role in the war on drugs, in 2011 the army enjoyed a 77 percent public approval rating—the highest of any government institution.

Cartels

After 2000, Mexican cartels, also known as drug-trafficking organizations, no longer enjoyed carte blanche and became involved in bitter struggles to control access to the U.S. market. Thanks to these cartels, in 2006, an estimated 70 to 90 percent of the drugs illegally imported into the United States came from Mexico. That year authorities discovered a McDonnell Douglas DC-9 in Campeche with 5.6 tons of cocaine aboard. A 2007 raid in the upscale Lomas de Chapultepec neighborhood in Mexico City indicated the financial power of the traffickers. Police searched a safe house there and found 205 million U.S. dollars in cash, thought to be the product of smuggling methamphetamines into the United States.

In order to keep the drugs flowing north, traffickers altered their modus operandi. The most significant change was a relentless increase in violence as enforcement fragmented long-established distribution systems and more young bucks attempted to enter the business. The end of PRI rule shattered the cozy relationship that had existed between politicians and traffickers. The rapid increase in domestic drug consumption also led to increased violence as traffickers fought to control neighborhoods where they sold drugs. Violence was directed at members of rival cartels, government officials whose efforts at drug enforcement were seen as an obstacle to trafficking, and journalists who brought unwelcome attention. Traffickers turned to increasingly lethal arms including machine guns, bazookas, and hand grenades. During Fox's 2000–06 term, the death toll from the drug-related violence was 9,000.

In response to escalating drug-related violence, ten days after his inauguration, President Calderón sent the army into six states to combat the cartels. By 2010 more than 45,000 troops were deployed in the war against drugs. By the end of his term there was no indication that this deployment had halted the northward flow of drugs or the reverse flow of arms. Cartels not only continued to smuggle drugs, but branched out into kidnapping, extortion, human trafficking, and money laundering. During Calderón's term some 70,000 were killed in cartel-related violence, and thousands more had disappeared or been displaced from their homes. Many of those displaced were entrepreneurs who took their wealth and families to the United States, enriching Mexico's northern neighbor at Mexico's expense. Despite the widespread involvement of the military, as Michael Collins of the Drug Policy Alliance observed, during the Calderón administration the flow of drugs continued unabated and drug-related violence, human rights violations, and corruption increased.

In addition to inflicting an appalling death toll, the traffickers' billions corrupt officials at all levels of government. A notebook recovered from trafficker Juan García Ábrego at the time of his arrest included a list of payoffs, ranging from $1 million to the commander of the Federal Judicial Police down to $100,000 paid to the federal police commander in the border city of Matamoros. Such payments purchase an essential service monopolized by government officials—the non-enforcement of the law. Those in charge of enforcement must be bribed because they cannot be entirely bullied or bypassed. In a 2009 poll 63 percent of Mexicans stated that corruption was the primary cause of drug-related problems, while only 26 percent declared U.S. demand to be the cause.

The cartels' power spills into virtually every aspect of Mexican society. They employ an estimated 450,000 people. Threats from cartels lead candidates to withdraw from races. If threats fail, candidates are murdered. In 2010 the virtually certain winner of the gubernatorial race was gunned down in Tamaulipas. According to an estimate by BBVA Bancomer, Mexico's largest bank, drug violence costs Mexico 1 percent of annual economic growth. Drug trafficking inculcates a culture of crime and corruption which, as the Sicilian example indicates, is extremely difficult to eradicate once instilled.

The one clear result in the war on drugs has been to drive cocaine smuggling into Central America where weaker governmental institutions facilitate trafficking. In 2000 Central American cocaine seizures were below those in Mexico. In 2011 Central American seizures were twelve times those in Mexico. As the *Economist* observed, "as long as drugs that people want to consume are prohibited, and therefore provided by criminals, driving the trade out of one bloodstained area will only push it into some other godforsaken place."

Human Rights

In 2000 Vicente Fox's new administration seemed to bode well for human rights. As he had promised during his campaign, he named a special prosecutor for crimes committed during the Dirty War. He also appointed human rights activist Mariclaire Acosta as under-secretary of foreign affairs for human rights and democracy. His foreign secretary declared that international human rights monitors would be welcome in Mexico.

By 2006, those who had pinned their hopes on Fox were sorely disappointed. As Amnesty International reported in 2007, "President Vicente Fox completed his mandate without fulfilling the administration's commitment to end human rights violations and impunity, which remained widespread."

Human rights reports published during the Calderón administration made it clear that rather than bringing an improvement in human rights, having a PAN president in Los Pinos simply meant violations as usual. The 2009 U.S. State Department report on human rights highlighted unlawful killings by security forces, kidnappings, arbitrary arrests and detentions, and a lack of transparency in the judicial system.

The return to PRI administration did little to engender respect for human rights. A Human Rights Watch report commented on the first year of the Peña Nieto administration: "The government has made little progress in prosecuting widespread killings, enforced disappearances, and torture committed by soldiers and police in the course of efforts to combat organized crime, including during Peña Nieto's tenure. Members of the military accused of human rights violations continue to be prosecuted within the biased military justice system, ensuring impunity."

While there has been little progress at addressing traditional human rights concerns, there has been progress concerning gay rights. In 1997 the first openly lesbian member began serving in the federal congress. In 2013 Benjamín Medrano Félix was elected mayor of Fresnillo, Zacatecas, thus becoming Mexico's first openly gay elected mayor. In 2003 Mexico became the second Latin American country to enact anti-discrimination laws that protect people based on sexual orientation. In a 2013 decision balancing free speech and non-discrimination, Mexico's Supreme Court ruled that Mexicans do not have a free speech-protected right to use classic epithets directed at homosexuals. In 2014 the Court ruled that widows and widowers of same-sex marriages have the same social security rights as heterosexuals. Several states legalize same-sex unions. Since 1979 gay pride marches in Mexico City have drawn as many as 200,000.

Despite such progress, homophobic hate crimes and murder of homosexuals remain a fact of modern Mexican life. The National Committee on Hate Crimes estimated that in a ten-year period more than 900 homosexuals had been murdered. Such crimes are almost never prosecuted. As author Alexander Dawson observed, "Gays, lesbians, bisexuals, and transvestites live in fear of brutality, knowing full well that few Mexicans sympathize with their plight."

Society

The gap between the rich and the poor is wider in Mexico than in any other nation in the OECD, the club of rich nations. Clearly whatever the social impact of the Mexican Revolution was, it is now long gone. That said, for the decade following 1996 there was a trend toward more equalitarian income distribution as anti-poverty programs targeted more individuals and workers' wages increased along with their educational level. However, this trend only had a modest impact on income disparity. In 2010 the poorest 20 percent of Mexicans received 5 percent of income, while the top 20 percent received 53 percent.

As was the case in the late twentieth century, informal or "off the books" employment accounted for roughly half of all jobs. In 2013, as in previous years, the 1.2 million new job seekers far exceeded the 463,000 formal jobs created. Productivity among informal workers is typically low since they are poorly educated, receive little training, and are provided with little equipment. Informal workers are often linked to organized crime by selling stolen, counterfeit, pirated, and smuggled products.

According to official figures, the poor, which included most informal and part-time workers, and the unemployed, declined from 52.4 percent of the population in 1994 to 42.7 percent in 2008. Then thanks to the 2008–09 recession, 3.2 million plunged back into poverty. Despite ample government social spending, the number of poor Mexicans now exceeds Mexico's entire 1960 population, indicating how demography and poverty are linked. Poverty levels would be even higher if millions had not emigrated to the United States.

The lack of progress in combating poverty indicates the importance of establishing coherence between poverty alleviation programs and economic reform. No poverty program can substitute for development policies that effectively incorporate the poor into growth-oriented sectors of the economy. Nor can poverty programs compensate for the loss of productive employment, the drastic reduction in wages, and lack of investment in productive and human assets.

Thanks to increased income and government spending, Mexicans do enjoy substantially better access to healthcare and nutrition than they did a generation ago. This is indicated by the average life expectancy rising from sixty-one years in 1970 to seventy-five years in 2013. In 1970 life expectancy in the United States was ten years more than in Mexico. This gap has now narrowed to 3.5 years.

The Elite

PAN presidential candidate Vicente Fox received substantial support from business interests. Not surprisingly, once Fox took office, the influence of the business elite increased, along with that of the Church, to the detriment of the middle class, labor, and the peasants. Historian Enrique Semo commented on the Business Coordinating Council's massive illegal media buys that attempted to influence the 2006 election, "Never before has the Mexican business elite intervened as flagrantly and directly in a political campaign."

While the government institutes anti-poverty programs such as Oportunidades, many of its other policies serve to concentrate wealth. It has tolerated monopolies and duopolies, especially in telecommunications, which benefit a handful of owners. Its massive electric rate subsidy disproportionally benefits affluent owners of appliances and air conditioners. In 2002, the government spent five times as much on its electricity subsidy as it did on poverty eradication programs. Similarly subsidies for gasoline and higher education mainly benefit the already affluent. As part of the FOBAPROA bank bailout Banamex received $3 billion. In 2001, its owner, Roberto Hernández, sold the bank for $12.5 billion to Citigroup. Hernández was not required to return the $3 billion.

Mexico never regained the share of the world's billionaires that it enjoyed in 1994. Between 1994 and 2014, Mexico's share of billionaires declined from 7 percent to 0.7 percent, not due to

Mexico becoming more egalitarian but due to the rest of the world generating wealth more rapidly than Mexico. In 2014, of the world's 1,645 billionaires, twelve were Mexican.

The Middle Class

"Middle class" is a notoriously difficult term to define since the definition can be based on education, occupation, or income. Basing the concept on income is tricky since there are no clear upper and lower limits to those considered middle class. In any case in 2010 the official government statistical agency declared that 39.2 percent of the population formed the middle class, leaving 1.7 percent in the upper class, and 59.1 percent as the lower class.

During the Fox administration (2000–06), members of the middle class enjoyed increased access to consumer credit. This enabled them to purchase such middle-class trappings as refrigerators and washing machines. Lower interest rates resulted in a housing boom as mortgage rates tumbled and twenty-five-year mortgages became available. Previously lenders offered only ten-year mortgages. In the first five years of the Fox administration, 2,355,000 housing loans were issued, more than twice the number issued under Zedillo.

The middle class, which had already turned away from the PRI, turned out for Fox in 2000. In 2006, they remained largely with the PAN and gave Calderón his victory margin. As a political block this group is up for grabs and is not tightly linked to any one party.

Labor

Rather than bringing sweeping change to the traditional union structure, President Fox left the same labor leaders in place. Mexico's long-entrenched labor leaders received backing from Fox due to his fear that radicals would dominate labor if there was a leadership change and due to the feeling that incumbents could be used to ensure the passage of legislation waiving rights that had long been guaranteed to labor, at least on paper. In 2005, CTM head Leonardo Rodríguez Alcaine died in office at age eighty-six, once again indicating the sclerosis of official Mexican labor.

Both Fox and Calderón relied on union weakness to ensure pro-business labor policies. They maintained the same approach that was introduced with neoliberalism in the 1980s—low wages, compliant unions, few strikes, and strong employer control over industrial relations. Given this approach, the average income of salaried workers only rose by 4.5 percent between 1994 and 2009.

Virtually every trend indicated declining union power. The percentage of the labor force represented by a union of any kind remained well below the level of representation during the Mexican economic miracle. The number of strikes declined for decades. Between 2007 and 2009 they averaged only twenty-three a year—a fifth the number twenty years earlier. The number of seats in the Chamber of Deputies held by labor representatives declined from ninety-six in 1982 to thirty-six in 2009. Workers in the informal sector remained beyond the reach of traditional unions.

Given their immunity from retaliation by rank-and-file, many union leaders became grotesquely corrupt. Teachers' union leader Elba Ester Gordillo, arrested after she opposed Peña Nieto's educational reforms, owned an estimated sixty properties, including eight homes in the United States. She had various bank accounts and during the three years prior to her arrest she spent an average of $64,000 a month at Nieman Marcus. Paulina Romero, daughter of Carlos Romero Deschamps, the oil union leader, created quite a stir after posting Facebook pictures of her flying to Europe in a private jet. She commented she preferred private jets to commercial flights because she could take her dogs along.

The unions that retained strength and the ability to defend their membership's interests past the end of PRI rule were unions in the public sector, especially the teachers' union, which by definition could not relocate, the mine workers' union, which similarly did not face companies relocating, and the rare private-sector union, such as the Volkswagen workers' union, which relied on its being prohibitively costly for VW to relocate its sprawling Puebla facility.

Rural Society

As in Mexican society as a whole, rural wealth is highly concentrated. The top 15,000 agricultural producers generate half of agricultural income and often specialize in exporting fruits and vegetables. The remaining 4.5 million farms have trouble breaking into the export market. Between 2000 and 2009, employment in agriculture, forestry, and fishing declined from 6.7 million to 5.6 million as large producers dominated production and imports flooded in.

Indigenous Mexico

For a fleeting moment, the twenty-first century seemed to offer the promise of autonomy for indigenous peoples and a peaceful settlement to the standoff in Chiapas, where Zapatista rebels have remained since the 1994 uprising. On the day he took office, December 1, 2000, President Fox ordered a troop withdrawal from more than fifty positions the military held around the rebel-controlled area. On December 5, he sent to Congress the agreements concerning autonomy for Indian areas that had been negotiated with the rebels during the Zedillo administration.

In response to Fox's overtures, the Zapatista rebels made a dramatic 3,000-mile march to Mexico City in 2001 to present their case to the Mexican nation. The march, nicknamed the Zapatour, traveled through twelve states and arrived in Mexico City where more than 100,000 provided a tumultuous welcome. Zapatista Comandante Ester, a small, frail indigenous woman, presented the Zapatistas' case to Congress in broken Spanish, in full view of the national media.

Once the Zapatistas went home and the issue was no longer on the front pages, momentum on the proposed law was lost. Even though Fox presented the proposed autonomy law to Congress, members of Fox's own party felt the agreement ceded too much federal power and watered it down. When finally passed, the reform lacked several key provisions that Indians had hoped for. Autonomy for indigenous people was defined at the municipal level, not the regional level. Soil, subsoil, and water rights remained vested in private interests, upon which autonomous indigenous communities would have little leverage. Individual states, whose commitment to indigenous autonomy was often questionable, were charged with interpreting and implementing much of the legislation. The revised legislation, which was passed by Congress and incorporated into the constitution, did recognize Indian communities had the right to form autonomous municipal governments.

The 1994 Chiapas uprising failed to pave the way for the type of autonomy many Indians and their supporters sought. However, it did pave the way for changing non-Indians' outlook on Indians as political actors. During the five centuries following the Spanish conquest, non-Indians formulated detailed plans on how to save Indians from heathenism, poverty, malnutrition, and exploitation. However, it was only as the twentieth century wound down that Mexican society accepted Indians as intellectual actors who could, on their own initiative, address these problems.

Mexico remained as the nation in the Americas with the largest number of indigenous, even though some smaller nations such as Guatemala and Bolivia have a higher percentage of indigenous people. Between 2000 and 2010, the number of individuals age five and older who speak an indigenous language increased from 6.0 million to 6.7 million. This 11.7 percent increase is below the 15.8 percent increase in overall population during this period. In 2012, 72 percent of the indigenous population was classified as poor, while 43 percent of the non-indigenous population was.

Women

A combination of societal change and explicit quotas has allowed women to increase their representation in the Chamber of Deputies from 16.8 percent in the 2000–03 session to 37.4 percent in the 2012–15 session. In 2012 for the first time a major political party, the PAN, nominated a woman as its presidential candidate. As of 2012 only five women had ever been elected as governor, and none were serving early in the Peña Nieto administrating. Progress is also meager at the municipal level as only 6.8 percent of mayors were women in 2014.

Reflecting both the influence of the Catholic Church and traditional pro-natal views, abortion was outlawed through the twentieth century. The first major shift in abortion policy came in 2007, when the PRD-dominated Legislative Assembly of the Federal District voted to legalize abortion during the first three months of pregnancy, a measure that affected only the Federal District. Pope Benedict XVI publicly condemned the bill, as did Felipe Aguirre Franco, archbishop of Acapulco, who declared lawmakers who voted for the bill would be automatically excommunicated. Demonstrators marched in the streets to express their views, pro and con. A marcher opposed to legalization carried a placard with an image of the Virgin of Guadalupe and the slogan: "You killed one of my children! Are you going to kill more?" A supporter of the bill countered with a sign declaring, "Keep your rosaries off my ovaries."

Rather than signaling a trend toward legalizing abortion, the Federal District legislation created a backlash. By 2010, seventeen states had passed constitutional amendments declaring that the fertilized human egg is a person and therefore is protected by the constitution.

Population

The 2010 census indicated Mexico's population had reached 112.3 million and that between 2005 and 2010 it was increasing by 1.8 percent per year. In 2010, the average age was twenty-six years, up from twenty-two in 2000. Mexico's rural population rose from 24.6 million in 2000 to 34.5 million in 2010, as a result of a birth rate that was higher than the national average,

Education

> If our educational system doesn't improve, we won't resolve the immense, painful problem of poverty.
>
> (Jorge Castañeda, 2004)

Problems of low quality are pervasive throughout the public educational system. This decline in quality began in the 1970s as emphasis was placed on increasing the number of students, not maintaining educational quality. Standards further declined in the 1980s as educational budgets were slashed. Teachers' salaries lost 70 percent of their buying power between 1981 and 1989. Even as educational budgets increased in the 1990s, teaching remained one of the poorest paid professions and, as a result, it had difficulty attracting highly qualified individuals. In 2009 Mexico was placed last among members of the OECD in an exam administered internationally.

Numerous reasons have been suggested for the continued poor quality of Mexican education. Blame is often attributed to the one-million-member teachers' union protecting teachers' perks. Examples of pernicious practices include the union's allowing the inheriting or selling of teacher positions, rather than seeking out the most qualified teachers. Political scientist Lorenzo Meyer described Mexico's teachers as "a poorly paid, poorly prepared army." Insufficient educational spending does not appear to be the cause of poor quality, since the educational budget amounts to 6 percent of gross domestic product—a figure in line with international standards.

Primary schools now enroll 97.9 percent of children between 6 and 12. After that there is a sharp drop in attendance. Of every 100 children who started elementary school in 1999, only

429

36 percent finished high school (*preparatoria*) in 2010. Only about 10 percent of young people continue to obtain a college degree.

As has occurred throughout Latin America, the poor quality of public education has led to the proliferation of private schools, which reinforces the economic gap between those who can pay for a good education and those who cannot. Many members of elite families now attend private schools from kindergarten through college. At the other extreme, public universities annually reject 300,000 applicants—most of whom cannot afford private universities—since there is no space for them.

Media

While the delinking of Televisa from the PRI and the founding of another network, TV Azteca, were initially considered as opening the way for critical reporting, it soon became apparent that a narrow range of vested interested interests set policy for both networks. This became apparent as they used their media power to influence elections, regulatory bodies, and legislation concerning telecommunications. As Antonio Menéndez Alarcón noted in his study of Dominican TV, "Even if television network owners and sponsors compete at the economic level, their basic ideas and philosophy uphold the same model of social organization." Televisa went from being a servant of the PRI to the government becoming a servant of Televisa.

Print media—books, magazines, and newspapers—continues to offer the widest range of views. However due to its cost and sometimes its intellectual language, it remains an elite media. Its reach is far overshadowed by broadcast television.

Since 2000 a wide variety of actors, such as drug traffickers, other organized criminal groups, and the henchmen of crooked politicians, have attempted to silence those whose messages are unwelcome. Between 2000 and 2014, eighty-eight journalists were killed and eighteen others disappeared. Due to these attacks, in 2014 Reporters without Borders ranked Mexico 152 out of 180 nations in terms of press freedom. The death toll would undoubtedly have been higher had media not resorted to self-censorship in matters concerning organized crime.

Religion

In 2011, 76 percent of Mexicans expressed confidence in the Church. However, they are increasingly making up their own minds on matters of individual behavior. Even among peasant women, traditionally viewed as more conservative, more than 53 percent practice birth control and one in five has had an abortion. Similarly few Mexicans followed Church counsel concerning the film *The Crime of Father Amaro*, which depicts a priest who has an affair with a parishioner and portrays the Church as being in league with drug traffickers. The Church declared the film blasphemous and announced its support for anyone protesting it. Thanks in large part to the Church's publicizing it extensively, the film was a huge box-office success. After the Federal District legalized abortion in 2007, an initial sampling of the women choosing a legal abortion found that 81.4 percent were Catholic.

Mexican society has continued to grow more intellectually independent and secular. Between 2000 and 2010, the percentage of the population identifying themselves as Catholics declined from 92.0 percent to 89.3 percent. Indicators of this independence are the 2007 legalization of abortion in the Federal District as well as the approval of same-sex unions that year in the District and in the northern state of Coahuila. As journalist Patrick Corcoran commented:

> The recent series of events are simply an affirmation of what has long been true: the Church now, more than ever, is not Mexico's pre-eminent moral guide. It is simply a guide, followed by some, ignored by others. Just as in the United States, the Church in Mexico has been damaged by a series of sex scandals.[2]

TWENTY-FIRST-CENTURY NEOLIBERALISM

The first three twenty-first-century presidents adhered to the neoliberal economic model. Fox saw no reason to question assumptions behind an apparently healthy economy in 2000. In his effort to undermine AMLO, Calderón campaigned on maintaining the macroeconomic stability achieved during the Fox administration. Peña Nieto's campaign stressed the necessity of sweeping reforms to allow the neoliberal model to reach its full potential.

Agriculture

Between 1993 and 2008, Mexican corn production increased from 18 million tons to a record 24 million tons. However, as there were increases in both population and meat consumption, the dependency on grain imports to feed both people and livestock increased. In addition, as almost 20 percent of the U.S. corn crop was devoted to producing ethanol, U.S. corn prices doubled within a year. Since Mexico imports so much U.S. corn, the increase in U.S. corn prices resulted in Mexican tortilla prices rising by more than 60 percent in some places. Speculators added to the price increase. Rather than the free market neoliberal planners had envisioned, at each stage of the food supply chain there is a very high degree of concentration that makes food prices ripe for speculation. Grupo Maseca, for example, controls 85 percent of the market for corn flour.

This spike in tortilla prices threatened social stability since it is the dietary staple of Mexico's poor. To keep tortillas affordable, the government allowed the import of an additional 650,000 tons of corn above the 8 million tons imported in 2006. As ecologist Lester Brown commented, "In this world of high oil prices, supermarkets and service stations will compete in commodity markets for basic food commodities such as wheat, corn, soybeans, and sugarcane."

In 2013 Mexican farmers took advantage of their country's long growing season and inexpensive labor to produce and export $7.3 billion worth of fruits and vegetables, mainly to the United States. Farmers in the U.S. Midwest grew and exported to Mexico $3.7 billion worth of grain. On a purely economic level this is an example of NAFTA performing as planned. This arrangement, however, leaves Mexico vulnerable to price spikes and shortages of grain in the world market. It also has a high social cost since much of the seasonal labor that produces food for export is paid very low wages. The large Mexican farms producing export crops are more pesticide- and water-intensive than small farms. Finally, the heavy reliance on imported corn has undermined small rural producers creating social problems and threatening the rich biodiversity in corn that only small farmers maintain.

Autos

Mexican auto production benefited from manufacturers' having located much of their capacity to manufacture compacts in Mexico—cars that were suddenly in high demand as U.S. fuel prices increased. In addition, Ford, GM, and Chrysler shifted production to Mexico to reduce labor costs. Increased investment in the auto sector by Japanese and European producers responded to Mexico's proximity to the U.S. market, low wages, and a stable peso.

The auto sector plays a crucial role in the Mexican economy, directly employing 600,000 people. In 1994 Mexico accounted for 6 percent of North American auto production. In 2014, that figure was 19 percent. In 2014 a record 3.2 million vehicles, most of which were exported, were produced. The $70.6 billion in auto exports is more valuable than oil exports or remittances.

Auto plants in each of the NAFTA nations specialize and achieve economies of scale. Engines and transmissions are often produced in one nation and incorporated into vehicles assembled elsewhere. Ford pickups, for example, were assembled in Cuautitlán, just north of Mexico City, with engines coming from Windsor, Ontario, and transmissions from Livonia, Michigan. Thanks

431

to NAFTA rules of origin for parts, many European and Asian parts manufacturers have relocated to Mexico. In Puebla, seventy parts manufacturers have clustered around the sprawling Volkswagen factory.

Despite having productivity as high as or even higher than workers doing the same work in the U.S., Mexican labor costs remain far below those of the United States. This limits the amount of stimulus to the domestic market that autoworkers' wages can provide.

Energy

During the Fox administration, oil production increased—a result of budgeting between $10 and $12 billion annually for oil and gas exploration and production. These investments paid off as production rose to a record 3.4 million barrels a day in 2004.

After having reached record production levels during the Fox administration, production began to decline as Mexican fields became exhausted. By 2014, production had dropped to 2.3 million barrels a day. As domestic demand continues to rise and production declines, exports get squeezed.

For many Pemex continues to be a symbol of Mexican nationalism. Thus the controversy concerning the 2013 reform ending Pemex's constitutionally protected monopoly on oil and gas production. Those calling for reform cite the high costs of Pemex-produced oil, the result of poor administration and corruption under both PRI and PAN administrations. Critics declare that Peña Nieto's "counter-reform" will allow large domestic and foreign firms to appropriate a large part of the oil wealth that previously belonged to the public. Regardless of whether private producers find the terms allowing them to enter production attractive, there will be no sizable production increases during Peña Nieto's term. The end of his term in 2018 does not allow time for contracts to be signed and exploration to be concluded.

Maquiladoras

During the early Fox administration, *maquiladora* employment fell to 1.07 million as China began to flood the U.S. market with exports, the U.S. economy lost dynamism, and more than 600 *maquiladora* plants relocated to China. From a 2002 low, *maquiladora* employment rebounded in the latter part of the Fox administration. By 2006, as the U.S. economy expanded, *maquiladora* plants earned Mexico $16 billion in foreign currency, created 17 percent of industrial jobs, and accounted for more than 65 percent of industrial exports. *Maquiladora* production plunged again in 2008 and 2009 due to recession, but rebounded once again as exports to the United States increased and as rising wages in China caused the gap between Chinese and Mexican wages to virtually disappear.

China

At the beginning of the twenty-first century, China exercised a strong influence on Mexico. The world's most populous nation attracted investment that might otherwise have gone to Mexico by guaranteeing manufacturers the absence of militant unions and providing workers who worked for wages that were only a quarter of Mexican wages. A large, fast-growing market and well-developed infrastructure (roads, ports, etc.) also attracted investment.

China impacted the Mexican economy since it competed with Mexico for foreign investment. Between 2001 and 2003, Mexico lost an estimated 400,000 jobs to China. China also competed with Mexico in the U.S. market. In 1990, China exported only $3.08 billion to United States, while Mexico exported $6.09 billion. In 2008, U.S. imports from China totaled $356 billion, while U.S. imports from Mexico totaled only $218 billion. Finally, China's highly efficient, low-wage industries successfully competed for Mexico's domestic market. China exported to Mexico a wide range of clothing, toys, and house wares, not to mention Mexican flags and porcelain figurines of the Virgin of Guadalupe.

As Chinese wages rose to roughly the same level as Mexican wages, Mexico has been able to halt the steep decline in U.S. market share. In 2008 Mexican exports to the United States equaled 59 percent of Chinese exports to the United States. In 2014 the comparable figure was 63 percent. Mexico's trade deficit with China increased from $8.4 billion in 2003 to $60 billion in 2014.

Unsustainability

In 2014, INEGI, the government statistical agency estimated that environmental damage lowers Mexico's gross domestic product by 6.3 percent. This estimate considered the impact of air, water, and soil pollution. The agency estimated that air pollution alone cost Mexico $40 billion a year. Deforestation and aquifer depletion were other factors contributing to this total.

Roughly 66 percent of Mexico's land area shows some signs of degradation and 36 percent is classified as desertified—the most degraded. In addition, 35 percent of irrigated land has been abandoned due to erosion or its being hopelessly contaminated. The amount of arable land in the Mixtec region of Oaxaca has been reduced by 70 percent due to erosion. The result is massive job loss and out-migration of the area's indigenous population.

MARTHA ISABEL "PATI" RUIZ CORZO

Martha Isabel "Pati" Ruiz Corzo's parents took her out into the countryside frequently as she was growing up. There she learned to appreciate nature. However, it took some time for this love of nature to blossom.

For the first quarter century of her life Pati, as she is universally called, lived a very conventional life. By the time she was thirty she had married and had settled into middle-class life in Mexico City. She taught school while her husband worked as an accountant.

However, she began to have a nagging feeling that putting on makeup and high heels every day to teach school was not the course she wanted her life to follow. Then she and one of her sons began to have health problems which she attributed to Mexico City's toxic atmosphere.

Her family then made a momentous decision—leave Mexico City and establish themselves in the Sierra Gorda, a mountainous area 100 miles north of Mexico City. Ruiz Corzo plunged into schooling her sons and community organizing around environmental issues. She began to give classes in local schools, playing the accordion to establish rapport with local people. Meanwhile her husband began planting trees on many of the deforested hillsides of the Sierra Gorda.

To broaden participation in their efforts, she and her husband and a few family members founded the Sierra Gorda Ecological Group in 1987. Through the persistence of this group in 1998 the Sierra Gorda was declared to be a biosphere preserve. (Biosphere preserves are U.N.-recognized natural areas, analogous to U.S. national parks, but with the provision that those living in the area are allowed to remain.)

The Sierra Gorda Biosphere preserve covers some one million acres—the eastern third of the state of Querétaro—and includes 639 communities. It is located astride the Sierra Madre Oriental, which catches moisture coming off the Gulf of Mexico. On its eastern fringe it is decidedly moist and tropical. At higher elevations there are pines, junipers, oaks, maples, walnuts, and areas of cloud forest. To the west in the rain shadow of the Sierra, the biosphere is a cactus-studded desert. Within the biosphere there are some 2,000 plant varieties, 650 different butterflies, and 200 bird species, including the magnificent military macaw.

Pati started from the premise that nature was more important to the peasants living in the Sierra Gorda than to the professionals usually associated with conservation groups. Since the overwhelming majority of the population was poor, it was obvious that making a living had to be a key element in environmental restoration. Thus she has raised funds to pay local farmers to maintain some of the six million trees planted by the organization. Income-generating activities encouraged by the group include embroidery and raising vegetables and medicinal plants. Farmers have diversified by planting fruit trees, coffee, and cacao. Some softwood trees are planted to be cut as an income source. Such trees are not as damaging to soil as plow agriculture. Since much deforestation results from cutting trees for fuel, the group has played a key role in providing energy-efficient stoves, thus lowering the need to cut wood. The group also builds and sells odorless latrines, thus addressing a long-standing problem in the Sierra—water pollution.

A key element of the group's work has been to partner with 150 primary and secondary schools in the region. Teams go out from the group's headquarters daily to make environmental presentations in area schools. Students, having witnessed the presentations, are then asked to pitch in. Many of the area's 115 recycling centers are associated with these schools. A long-term effect of the group's school presentations is now visible—some of the students who witnessed school presentations decades ago are now mayors of the communities in which they live. Pati's most innovate work has been to focus on placing a price on the environmental services provided by a healthy environment. She notes that recharged aquifers and clean flowing streams are more valuable than gains on the stock exchange, but that society rarely places a monetary value on these services. She also notes that the price in carbon markets for carbon emissions is $15 a ton. Then she estimated that there are 124,000,000 tons of carbon sequestered in Sierra Gorda trees—a value of $1.86 billon—more than the land or the wood itself are priced at. Following this line of reasoning, the group has obtained funds to pay hundreds of families to manage their land to maximize carbon sequestration rather than clear cutting and planting an annual crop.

As if problems such as deforestation and poverty weren't enough, global warming has presented a new set of challenges. Rather than being an abstract issue producing policy discussion, global climate change is a very evident problem. Many pines are succumbing to pests which were not able to establish themselves before the climate began to change.

Pati has received a long list of honors for her work in the Sierra Gorda. After receiving the National Geographic Prize in 2012, Mexican writer Elena Poniatowska declared: "Her work in the Sierra Gorda is admirable. She says the prize is not for her, but for the people of the Sierra who have struggled and continue to struggle to save the forests." In 2013, Pati was declared to be an "Earth Champion"—the U.N.'s highest environmental award.

Now in her sixties Pati continues to devote her unbounded energy to the Sierra Gorda, as do her husband and two sons. She has no plans for slowing down any time soon, noting, "Restoring mountains is a gigantic task."

Mexicans rely on aquifers to supply water for irrigation and domestic use. Some 41 percent of this water is pumped from aquifers that are being depleted faster than they are being recharged. Each year water withdrawals consume 79.5 billion cubic meters of water. Irrigation consumes 80 percent of this water, which is often supplied by the government at highly subsidized prices, so there is little incentive to conserve. As water supply declined and population rose, Mexico's water supply per capita declined from 18,000 cubic meters in 1950 to 4,000 in 2010.

Deforestation exacerbates flooding. In 2007, massive flooding in Tabasco cost an estimated $3.1 billion. In addition to exacerbating flooding, deforestation results in lost biodiversity and huge releases of carbon dioxide. Each year 40,000 hectares of Mexico's 32 million hectares of temperate forest are deforested. Cleared land is mainly used for agriculture and cattle rising.

Mexico is not blameless in global warming, since hydrocarbons meet 80 percent of its energy needs. Even though it lags far behind the U.S. rate of 19.0 tons of annual carbon-dioxide emissions per capita, its rate of 3.97 tons per capita is increasing rapidly. This demand increase has been driven by heavy fuel subsidies and by massive road construction projects. In addition, by international standards, Mexico uses energy inefficiently.

The government has set aside large areas for preservation. However, given the lack of strong government protection, these natural preserves fall victim to squatters, illegal loggers, traffickers in plants and animals, and drug dealers who plant marijuana and opium poppies. Just to cite one example, the preserve set aside in Michoacán to protect the monarch butterfly lost 20 percent of its forest cover in twenty-five years due to illegal logging.

NAFTA AT TWENTY

> Mexico's experience with NAFTA provides a cautionary tale. The goal of economic integration should be to raise living standards, but it is clear that trade liberalization by itself is not sufficient to achieve this. There is no doubt that trade and development are vitally important for economic growth but the real challenge is to pursue liberalization in a manner which promotes sustainable development, in which those at the bottom and middle see incomes rising.
>
> (Joseph Stiglitz and Andrew Charlton, 2005)

Wal-Mart, which opened its first Mexican store in 1991, is emblematic of economic change in Mexico. In 2002, the company became the largest private employer in Mexico, and in 2004 it became the largest private corporation in Mexico as measured by sales. In 2014, the company had 2,500 retail outlets in Mexico.

Figure 15.4 *Maquiladoras and later NAFTA traffic overloaded existing border infrastructure. Pictured here is the bridge connecting Nuevo Laredo with Laredo, Texas.*

Source: J. Michael Short.

As with many other new investments, Wal-Mart displaces existing businesses. Since retailing until recently has largely been in the hands of small shops and street vendors, its impact has been even greater than the impact Wal-Mart had in small U.S. towns. For example, prior to its 2005 arrival in Juchitán, Oaxaca, population 86,000, there were 4,100 merchants, 98 percent of whom were considered small. At the same time that it displaces small retailers, Wal-Mart raises the standard of living of millions who take advantage of its everyday low prices to stretch their incomes further.

In 2014 there was a flurry of studies published to coincide with the twentieth anniversary of NAFTA taking effect. Some aspects of the treaty are clear. It was definitely oversold both north and south of the border. Also, free-trade agreements of themselves cannot guarantee sound development, as the more comprehensive treaty of the European Union demonstrates. Finally, decades after the passage of NAFTA, other factors such as the rise of China as an economic superpower and Mexico's signing trade treaties with many other nations make it difficult to isolate the impact of NAFTA.

Those favoring NAFTA share the views laid out in Thomas L. Friedman's book *The Earth is Flat*. They see Mexico's successfully plunging into the global marketplace and benefiting from the opportunity to develop specialized niches and to achieve economies of scale in manufacturing. Advocates of NAFTA and globalization cite a wealth of data to support their position:

- During the eight-year period before NAFTA went into effect, foreign direct investment averaged only $3.47 billion a year, while during the following eight-year period it exceeded $13 billion a year. The 2013 total was $32.5 billion.
- Between 2000 and 2013 Mexico's exports increased from $117.5 billion to $349.4 billion, providing jobs paying higher than average wages.
- Mexican consumers now have access to a much wider range of goods, ranging from imported luxury cars to inexpensive goods supplied by retail chains.
- For the last nineteen years Mexico has had a positive trade balance with its NAFTA partners.

Critics of NAFTA such as James Cypher and Raúl Delgado Wise laid out their case in *Mexico's Economic Dilemma*. They saw NAFTA as leading to a dead end of low-wage assembly jobs, without bringing the rest of the economy along. These are some of the NAFTA shortcomings critics cite:

- The promised convergence between Mexican manufacturing wages and U.S. manufacturing wages has been excruciatingly slow. Between 1994 and 2011 they only rose from 13 percent of the U.S. level to 17 percent. Between 2000 and 2009, 81 percent of the jobs created in Mexico paid less than $5,976 per year.
- NAFTA has led to the deindustrialization of Mexico since imported components going into products assembled in Mexico have replaced Mexican-made components. Between 1997 and 2013 manufacturing declined from 22.6 percent of gross domestic product to 18 percent. Between 2000 and 2013 industrial employment decreased from 27 percent to 26 percent of the workforce.
- NAFTA has exacerbated existing regional disparities since most foreign investment goes to the wealthier states. Mexico's five poorest states received only 0.34 percent of direct foreign investment during NAFTA's first nine years and much of that went to already developed tourist spots such as Acapulco.
- Rather than creating new jobs, much foreign investment has simply bought out existing enterprises, such as banks and supermarket chains. In 2013 for example, the $32.2 billion in direct foreign investment included $13.2 billion for the purchase by Belgian interests of beer maker Grupo Modelo.
- One hundred firms account for half of all exports, contributing to income concentration.

- The rate of economic growth under NAFTA is not only less than promised but has been steadily declining. Under Zedillo (1994–2000) it averaged 3.3 percent, under Fox (2000–06) 2.2 percent, and Calderón (2006–12) 2.1 percent.
- Between 1993 and 2013, employment only increased by 20 percent, while the population increased by 30 percent.
- Productivity per worker between 1981 and 2005 declined by 0.7 percent a year, while between 1940 and 1981 it increased by 3.1 percent annually.

U.S.–MEXICAN RELATIONS

The twenty-first century has seen no sharp changes in relations between the United States and Mexico. The two nations share a 1,933 mile-long border—the world's longest between a wealthy and a developing state. Given the failure of NAFTA to close the wealth gap between the two nations, U.S. economic power continues to be far greater than that of Mexico. Disputes arising over two chronic issues—drugs and undocumented immigration— have not derailed continued cooperation between the two nations.

In February 2001, President George W. Bush emphasized both the cordiality and importance of U.S.–Mexican relations by making his first foreign presidential trip to President Vicente Fox's ranch. On the occasion of Fox's September 5, 2001 state visit to Washington, Bush declared, "The United States has no more important relationship in the world than our relationship with Mexico." Even the most critical press in Mexico was forced to acknowledge that never before had a Mexican president been received as well in the U.S. capital.

The terrorist attacks of September 11, 2001 interrupted the cordiality of U.S.–Mexico relations. In the wake of the attacks, some officials in the Bush administration felt the Mexican government failed to sufficiently manifest public support for the United States. U.S. concerns shifted from relations with Mexico to securing its borders against terrorists. Relations were further chilled when Mexico, which at the time occupied a non-permanent seat on the U.N. Security Council, refused to endorse the U.S. invasion of Iraq.

During the Calderón administration (2006–12) relations warmed again and co-operation on drug interdiction expanded. In 2007, the two nations signed a multi-year agreement known as the Mérida Initiative. It called for the United States to provide Mexico and Central America with $1.6 billion in training and equipment to interdict drug smuggling. This initiative included Black Hawk helicopters and high-tech border inspection gear as well as training for thousands of police officers, judges, and prison guards. While the Mérida Initiative represented a sharp increase in U.S. funding, it represented less than 10 percent of Mexico's annual spending on the drug war. As with previous efforts in the war on drugs, the Mérida Initiative stressed choking off the supply of drugs reaching the United States, rather than lowering demand within the United States.

The Obama administration, which overlapped both Calderón's and Peña Nieto's presidencies, changed the rhetorical tone concerning trafficking in illegal drugs by admitting co-responsibility in illegal drug trafficking. In March 2009, Secretary of State Hillary Clinton declared, "Our insatiable demand for illegal drugs fuels the drug trade . . . Our inability to prevent weapons from being illegally smuggled across the border to arm these criminals causes the deaths of police officers, soldiers and civilians."

Cooperation on the drug war extended well beyond the Mérida Initiative. The U.S. government supplied information, some of which was obtained by drones flying deep into Mexico, which allowed Mexicans to bust *capos*. Numerous governmental agencies, including defense departments, established closer links with their counterparts on the other side of the border.

Increased interdependence in the war against drugs was mirrored by increased economic interdependence. Mexico is the third largest U.S. trading partner and America's second largest export market. An estimated 800,000 U.S. jobs depend directly on trade with Mexico.

The U.S.–Mexico border is the world's busiest, with more than $1 billion worth of goods and almost a million people crossing daily. Prosperity on one side of the border increases prosperity on the other, just as economic decline on one side inexorably leads to lost jobs in the export sector of the other partner.

The links are also demographic, environmental, musical, and gastronomic, to name just a few areas. Hollywood movies and pop music inundate Mexico, while hundreds of Spanish-language newspapers, magazines, and radio and TV stations flourish in the United States. Despite cultural influence running in both directions, there is clearly asymmetry even in cultural matters. This was illustrated in early 2014 when *Time* put Peña Nieto on its cover and Alfonso Cuarón received an Oscar for his directing *Gravity*. Each of these events produced days of commentary in Mexican media. It is hard to imagine any award granted to an American in Mexico or any American on a Mexican magazine cover even reaching the awareness of American commentators, much less producing extended comment.

While trade has settled into a mutually agreed upon framework, agreement on immigration has been much more elusive. Soon after his 2000 election, Vicente Fox and his foreign minister Jorge Castañeda made immigration reform the leading issue on the bilateral agenda. The Mexicans' proposal, which became known as the "whole enchilada," included: 1) an amnesty for Mexicans already in the United States; 2) a temporary work program to address U.S. labor market demands and the needs of potential Mexican migrants; 3) more visas for family reunification; 4) heightened border security; and 5) regional development plans for areas in Mexico from which many traditionally emigrated.

The year 2001 was not propitious for immigration reform. Had the 9/11 terrorist attacks not occurred, it is far from clear that the "whole enchilada" would have been enacted by the Republican-dominated Congress, which was inclined less favorably toward reform than was President Bush. After the September 11 attacks, the U.S. government shifted its attention to security matters.

Even though Presidents Bush and Obama both favored major immigration reform, no legislation was forthcoming. Members of Bush's own party balked at passing legislative reforms he sought. During the first two years of Obama's presidency, when Democrats controlled Congress, other legislative priorities pushed immigration reform aside. After that Republicans in the House of Representatives blocked passage.

Given Obama's inability to come to agreement with Congress on immigration legislation, he took two executive actions to remove the threat of deportation from an estimated 4.4 million individuals. In 2012 Deferred Action for Childhood Arrivals (DACA) allowed most persons who entered the United States without proper documentation to receive temporary residency permits if 1) they arrived before age sixteen and 2) had lived in the United States since 2007. In 2014 Deferred Action for Parents of Americans and Lawful Permanent Residents (DAPA) extended temporary legal residency to most parents of U.S. citizens or lawful permanent residents who had been in the United States since 2010.

During the late twentieth century, the Mexican economy was unable to generate sufficient jobs. As political scientist Wayne Cornelius noted, Mexico's neoliberal capital-intensive development model "has much less capacity to create employment than the old import-substituting industrial model that it replaced. Indeed, the new model's goals of efficiency and global competitiveness are inversely related to job creation."

At the beginning of the twenty-first century Mexico was the world's major source of emigrants. Their number exceeded the number leaving China—a nation with ten times Mexico's population. As former U.S. ambassador to Mexico Jeffrey Davidow observed, "At base the emigration phenomenon is largely the product of a massive increase in national population during the second half of the twentieth century." Even though millions of jobs were created in Mexico between 1950 and 2000, the job market was overwhelmed by a population increase of 72 million during this period. Many chose to move north across the border in response to the U.S. economy's creating many low-wage jobs shunned by native-born Americans, the persistent difference in wage levels between the two countries, security concerns in Mexico, and to join family members already in the United States. In 2010 there were an estimated 11.9 million Mexicans in the United States.

To the surprise of many, economic and demographic forces halted what legislation and enforcement could not. Beginning in roughly 2007, a distinct decline in immigration from Mexico began. For the next four years the number of Mexican immigrants steadily plunged. In 2011 immigration expert Douglas Massey observed, "No one wants to hear it, but the flow has already stopped. For the first time in 60 years, the net traffic has gone to zero and is probably a little bit negative."

While not all observers agree that net immigration from Mexico had reached zero, there was consensus that the number of immigrants was well below turn-of-the-century levels. Suggested causes include expanded economic and educational opportunities in Mexico, rising border crime, a narrowing in the gap between U.S. and Mexican wages, and increased border enforcement. Another contributing factor was the impact of the 2008–09 recession on the United States, which hit immigrant-heavy sectors such as construction especially hard.

This dramatic decline in immigration from Mexico has not been reflected in U.S. policy. The number of border patrol agents increased from 5,900 in 1996 to 25,500 in 2010. In 2006 President Bush signed the Secure Fence Act which mandated the construction of 350 miles of double-layer fence costing roughly $6.5 million per mile. In 2008, Bush's last year in office, deportations rose to 383,000. Rather than reconsidering Bush's deportation policies, the Obama administration continued massive deportations. From 2009 through 2014 annual deportations averaged 379,000.

There is no consensus on why Obama increased deportation. Suggested reasons include simply enforcing immigration laws, removing criminals from the United States, and attempting to convince Republican legislators that he is tough enough on immigration to enforce reform legislation. Regardless of the reasoning behind it, Obama's deportation policy became one of the most contentious domestic issues of his administration—issues which he in part responded to with DACA and DAPA.

Even though the net flow of immigrants has sharply declined, Mexican immigrants in the United States continue to impact Mexico. They send back more than $20 billion a year in remittances, which benefit millions of Mexican households. In addition to maintaining families, remittances finance a variety of projects in immigrants' hometowns. At the same time the population of many towns has been hollowed out due to mass out-migration. Between 2000 and 2005, more than half of Mexico's municipalities lost population.

It remains to be seen if massive emigration from Mexico will resume in response to economic growth in the United States or if reforms in Mexico will stimulate the economy, further reducing the desire to emigrate. Journalist Jorge Ramos commented on the end of massive immigration to the United States:

> This is an enormous change for Mexicans, with profound consequences. Mexico no longer will have an escape valve which has prevented social disturbances for decades. But it will retain the energy, creativity, and vision of millions of young people who until recently felt going to the U.S. was their only way of getting ahead."[3]

AFTERWORD

> It is difficult to make predictions, especially about the future.

In keeping with the epigraph above, sometimes attributed to Yogi Berra, this afterward will not include any predictions. However, it will note some of the crucial factors that will shape Mexico's future.

Corruption

Non-profit organization Transparency International measures the perception of corruption worldwide. It notes that there is a strong correlation between poverty and corruption, although it is difficult to separate cause and effect. According to that organization's Corruption Perception Index, Mexico's level of corruption has been worsening. In 2001 Mexico was more corrupt than fifty other nations. By 2014, it was more corrupt than 101 nations. The causes of corruption are complex. Clearly corruption is not some deterministic legacy of Spanish colonialism. In the 2014 index seven Spanish American nations were viewed as less corrupt than Mexico.

Justice

The rule of law in both civil and criminal matters is frequently lacking in Mexico. This makes investors reluctant to invest. In 2014, when asked what reforms Mexico still needed former President Zedillo commented, "Three things are lacking: the rule of law, the rule of law, and the rule of law." Similarly Mexican columnist Macario Schettino observed, "When property rights are guaranteed and contracts fulfilled, Mexico will be truly transformed."

Education

As noted earlier in the text, Mexican students fare poorly compared with students from other nations, many of which compete with Mexico in global markets. Only time will tell what the impact of educational reforms passed in 2013 will be. In 2014 the state government of Oaxaca and the state's teachers rejected federally mandated reforms and decided to create their own education model. Teachers' resistance will make any reform difficult to implement. Also in 2014 the secretary of education decided to quit applying a standardized exam known by its acronym ENLACE. The absence of this exam, which has been given year after year, will make measuring progress in educational reform difficult.

Peña Nieto's Reforms

The impact of Peña Nieto's reforms will only be felt as they take effect over a number of years. In 2014 the OECD estimated that the lack of competition in telecommunications cost Mexico 1.8 percent of gross domestic product. The impact of energy reforms could be even larger

Global Economic Future

Since Mexico is now so enmeshed in the globalized economy its economic wellbeing to a large extent depends on the global economy. Since 78.8 percent of its exports go to the United States, it is especially sensitive to shifts in the U.S. economy.

Economic Model

Mexico's three twenty-first-century presidents have been committed to a neoliberal, export-driven model. Learjet fuselages are now built in Querétaro and shipped to Wichita for final assembly. Mexico is the world's largest recipient of aerospace investment. It is the sixth largest auto exporter and the world's largest producer of smartphones. Such cutting-edge industrialization could spread, pulling Mexico up, much as the U.S. south industrialized and came to rival the industrialized U.S. north.

However, some observers view Mexico's current development path as dooming the country to a limited future of low-wage assembly. They cite the example of East Asian nations, especially China, which had a definite industrial policy. Rather than letting the market determine where production occurred and under what conditions, these nations consciously chose which investments to accept and how technology was to be shared. Economists James Cypher and Raúl Delgado Wise (see Further Reading) noted that in east Asia: "Only investors willing to put capital into projects that fit with the overall lSI [Import-Substitution Industrialization] strategy were welcomed. And some sort of technology sharing or reverse engineering was seen as a requisite by-product of accepting any foreign participation in the development schema." Of course as Nobel Prize-winning economist A. Michel Spence noted, the model the Asian Tigers adopted might not work today since it relied on a nearly insatiable demand for imports by the United States.

Climate Change

Climate change models foresee an especially severe impact on Mexico. Temperatures in the already arid north and northwest will increase and rainfall will decline. Rising sea levels and more severe hurricanes will impact the Gulf Coast. As if this were not enough, Mexico faces what could be considered the evil twin of globalization. Thus the impact of climate changes elsewhere could, via its impact on the world grain market, impact Mexico. The possible magnitude of this problem is indicated by 320 million people in India and China relying on food watered from over-pumped aquifers. Should climate change further deplete these aquifers, the global scramble for grain could lead to shortages in Mexico.

Social Cohesion

In many parts of the world as manufacturing requires fewer jobs, more women join the workforce, and population increases, there are simply not enough jobs. This has been the case in Mexico where social cohesion has been severely strained. A 2008 Pentagon report warned that Mexico "bears consideration for a rapid and sudden collapse." Strains on social cohesion could be lessened by sound political leadership. However, given the past track record and the low esteem the political elite are held in, this is not a given. Perhaps change could come from social movements outside the political establishment, much as it did in 2014 in Ukraine. Mexico has seen a plethora of social movements in recent years. Mass movement-driven social change, however, faces the twin obstacles of lacking consensus on just what change is desired and by the current elite's tenaciously clinging to their privileged position.

Political Disenchantment

Just before the 2015 mid-term elections 91 percent of those polled considered the existing political parties to be corrupt. In the midterms, voting reflected this alienation. Compared to 2012, the PRI lost three percentage points, the PAN five, and the PRD eight. Voters awarded AMLO's new, untested party MORENA eight percent of the vote.

DOCUMENT 15.1: DECLARATION OF THE AQUILA SELF-DEFENSE GROUP

[In 2014 the state of Michoacán made headlines nationally and internationally. A cartel known as the Knights Templar, which was involved in drug trafficking, extortion, and kidnapping, was beyond the reach of the law. Neither the police nor the army appeared able or willing to take on these outlaws, so local citizens began organizing self-defense groups (*autodefensas*) to combat the cartel. On January 18, 2014 the Self-Defense Group of Aquila, Michoacán, issued this statement:]

Today the residents of the municipal seat of Aquila, tired of the extortions, rapes, killings, kidnappings and all sorts of criminal acts by the Knights Templar and given the complete abandonment of the citizenry by the municipal and state governments which for 12 years did not provide the security needed for our people to have a peaceful and dignified life, have decided to organize our self-defense group in order to expel organized crime from our town. We invite the rest of the people of the municipality to rise up against crime, so they never again feel fear or pay protection fees.

The self-defense phenomenon in Michoacán has great momentum. Every day there are more people who decide to expel the criminals from their regions, which has caused the Templars to migrate to neighboring regions, in particular into our area, increasing the wave of violence in Aquila. So we are faced with the panorama of violence which we are returning to live in again, with the complicity of our state and municipal governments and the apathy of our federal government. It is for these reasons that the residents of the municipal seat of Michoacán opened our eyes and decided to organize as a self-defense group in order to expel all criminals from the area. Our social struggle will not end just when Federico González, alias "El Loco," the boss of the Knights Templar cartel in the Aquila-Coahuayana region falls, but when all his partners and gunmen do so.

Our self-defense movement organized by the residents and people in general of the Aquila area is inclusive. Because of this we gave a vote of confidence to municipal president Juan Hernández Ramírez and invited him to join the struggle against crime. But the mayor once again showed his Templar leanings and decided to leave the area. As such, our self-defense group and the people who support it condemn the criminal and indifferent attitude of Juan Hernández Ramírez. Let it be clear that our self-defense movement was born of social necessity, against organized crime. It seeks to re-establish peace and order for our people. We invite other towns, villages and communities in the municipality of Aquila to join our struggle, as we seek only well-being and social peace.

Sincerely,

The Self-Defense Council of Aguila, Michoacán

Source: Oaxaca Solidarity Alert List (trans. Scott Campbell)

NOTES

1   Andrés Manuel Obrador, *Un proyecto alternativo de nación* (Mexico City: Grijalbo), p. 43.

2   Patrick Corcoran, *El Heraldo*, April 20, 2007.

3   Jorge Ramos, "Mejor que quedamos," *Reforma*, October 9, 2011, p. 12.

FURTHER READING

Camp, Roderic Ai (ed.) (2012) *The Oxford Handbook of Mexican Politics*. New York: Oxford University Press.
  A massive (824 pages) compendium of thirty-one articles on different facets of contemporary Mexico.

Camp, Roderic Ai (2010) *Politics in Mexico* (6th ed.). Oxford: Oxford University Press.
  A description of Mexican politics, attitudes, institutions, and historical influences after 12 years of PAN administration.

Cypher, James M. and Raúl Delgado Wise (2011) *Mexico's Economic Dilemma*. Lanham, MD: Rowman & Littlefield.
An analysis of the Mexican economy that makes the case for adopting an economic model more in line with that adopted by East Asian nations.

Guillermoprieto, Alma (2015) "Mexico: The Murder of the Young," *New York Review of Books* 62 (January 8), pp. 56–60.
Reporting from Iguala, where forty-three normal school students were kidnapped and presumably murdered.

Meyer, Lorenzo (2013) *Nuestra Tragedia Persistente*. Mexico City: Random House Mondadori.
A less optimistic (cf. O'Neal below) examination of Mexican politics, drug wars, social movements, and U.S.–Mexican relations.

North American Congress on Latin America (2014) "Mexico: the State Against the Working Class," *NACLA Report on the Americas* 47 (Spring).
An issue devoted to Mexico with articles on the economy, labor, criminality, poverty, and energy.

O'Neal, Shannon K. (2013) *Two Nations Indivisible: Mexico, the United States, and the Road Ahead*. New York: Oxford University Press.
An upbeat (cf. Meyer above) examination of twenty-first century Mexico and its relations with the United States.

Sierra Club (2014) *NAFTA: 20 Years of Costs to Communities and the Environment*. San Francisco: Sierra Club.
A detailed examination of the environmental impact of NAFTA

Starr, Pamela K. (2014) "Mexico's Problematic Reforms," *Current History* (February), pp. 51–56.
A consideration of Peña Nieto's first year and his strategy for passing reform legislation.

GLOSSARY TERM

desafuero

Glossary

agave: a genus of succulent plants that includes henequen and the century plant (maguey), different varieties of which produce pulque, mescal, and tequila

agiotista: a private individual who lent money to the government at usurious rates

alcabala: a tax paid on the sale of goods and on moving goods from one tax zone into another

altepetl: the smallest political-religious subdivision of the Aztec empire, comprising a ceremonial center and outlying communities

Anglo: in the U.S. Southwest, a non-Hispanic of European ancestry

audiencia: a judicial body serving as a court of appeals and a consultative body

bracero: a contract laborer from Mexico working legally in the U.S.

casta: a person of mixed race

caudillo: an individual who commanded private armies and held regional and even national power

chia: a plant cultivated by the Aztecs. Its seeds were used to make a refreshing beverage

chinampa: an intensively cultivated artificial island

científico: one of President Díaz's elite political and economic advisors

cofradía: a term often translated as brotherhood. *Cofradías* organized religious observances for such entities as indigenous villages and guilds. They maintained their own finances independent of the state and at times engaged in social welfare functions

composición: the legalization of land titles by paying a fee

congregación: the forced resettlement of Indians into compact villages

Constitutionalist: a member of the forces led by Venustiano Carranza or a supporter of his faction

corregidor: the person in charge of an administrative area known as a *corregimiento*

creole: a person of European ancestry born in the New World

curandero: a practitioner of folk medicine

desafuero: Congressional action which strips high-office holders of their immunity from criminal prosecution

ejido: land, usually divided into plots for individuals to farm, which has been transferred as part of the land reform

ejidatario: a person who has received *ejido* land through the land reform

empresario: the holder of a grant to bring foreign settlers to settle in Texas

encomendero: the holder of an *encomienda* grant

encomienda: a grant entitling its holder to collect tribute from the Indians in a certain area in exchange for Christianizing them.

fuero: special legal status granted to clergy and the military which allowed them to be tried in separate court systems run by priests and military officers, respectively

hacendado: the owner of a large estate known as a hacienda

henequen: a fiber obtained from an agave plant of the same name, which was grown in Yucatán and which served to make twine

hunter-gatherer: a person whose main food sources are hunting and gathering wild plants

insurgents: the name given to members of the irregular forces supporting independence from Spain

land reform: a sweeping government-mandated change in land ownership to meet some official goal, such as raising production or lowering poverty

maguey: the agave that produces pulque

Manifest Destiny: the nineteenth-century belief that the United States was destined, even divinely ordained, to spread across North America

Maximato: the period during which Calles functioned as the power behind the throne

Mesoamerica: the area in Mexico and Central America where civilizations arose based on raising corn

mestizo: a person of mixed indigenous and European ancestry

Moors: the Muslim people of mixed Arab and Berber descent who invaded Spain in the eighth century

neoliberalism: an economic policy that assigns a reduced role to the state. In Mexico this policy was implemented by reducing tariffs, privatizing government-owned corporations, reducing the scope of government social programs, ending government industrial policy, and deregulating goods, service, labor, and capital markets.

Northern Division (División del Norte): a member of the highly mobile military force led by Pancho Villa

Nueces River: the river in president-day south Texas which during the Spanish colonial period served as the southern border of Texas

Nueva Galicia: the Spanish colonial subdivision comprising present-day Jalisco and adjacent areas

plan: a call to revolt which typically lists justifications for revolt and then describes what rebels plan to do after taking power

Porfiriato: the period 1877–1911 during which Porfirio Díaz was president of Mexico

pulque: the alcoholic beverage produced by fermenting agave juice

Quetzalcoatl: a pre-Columbian deity depicted as a plumed serpent

Reconquest: the prolonged process by which Christian forces expelled Moors from the Iberian Peninsula, concluding in 1492 with the fall of Granada

repartimiento: a labor draft that obligated Indians to work for non-Indians

requerimiento: a charge read to indigenous people directing them to accept Spanish rule and Christianity

royalists: the name given to those supporting continued Spanish rule

rural (pl. *rurales*): a member of the national police force that served during the Porfiriato

stela (pl. *stelae*): a carved stone commemorative monument

tribute: goods provided to dominant groups as a form of taxation in pre-monetary societies

viceroy: an administrative official in charge of a large area (a viceroyalty) as a representative of the king

Virgin of Guadalupe: a 1531 appearance of the Virgin Mary at Tepeyac Hill north of Mexico City. The appearance is also referred to as the Virgin of Tepeyac

wetback: an undocumented Mexican entrant into the U.S. The "wet" refers to the entrant's having swum the Rio Grande. The term was widely used in the 1950s by the U.S. government, journalists, Hispanic and Anglo academics, and by illegal entrants themselves

Zapatista: a member of the guerrilla forces led by Emiliano Zapata who fought for immediate land reform in Morelos and adjacent states

Index